Research Methods

Research Methods

A Process of Inquiry

SIXTH EDITION

Anthony M. Graziano

State University of New York at Buffalo

Michael L. Raulin

State University of New York at Buffalo

PEARSON

Boston • New York • San Francisco
Mexico City • Montreal • Toronto • London • Madrid • Munich • Paris
Hong Kong • Singapore • Tokyo • Cape Town • Sydney

Editor in Chief: *Susan Hartman*
Series Editorial Assistant: *Therese Felser*
Marketing Manager: *Karen Natale*
Production Supervisor: *Karen Mason*
Project Management and Electronic Composition: *Pre-Press Company, Inc.*
Composition Buyer: *Linda Cox*
Manufacturing Buyer: *JoAnne Sweeney*
Cover Administrator: *Linda Knowles*

For related titles and support materials, visit our online catalog at www.ablongman.com

Between the time website information is gathered and then published, it is not unusual for some sites to have closed. Also, the transcription of URLs can result in typographical errors. The publisher would appreciate notification where these errors occur so that they may be corrected in subsequent editions.

Library of Congress Cataloging-in-Publication Data

Graziano, Anthony M., 1932–
    Research methods : a process of inquiry / Anthony M. Graziano, Michael L. Raulin. –
6th ed.
        p. cm.
    Includes bibliographical references and indexes.
    ISBN 0-205-48475-1
        1. Research—Methodology. I. Raulin, Michael L. II. Title.

Q180.55.M4G7 2007
001.4'2—dc22   2006042756

Printed in the United States of America

10   9   8   7   6   5   4   3   2   1 [RRD-OH] 11   10   09   08   07   06

Contents

3 *The Starting Point: Asking Questions*   **55**

4 *Data and the Nature of Measurement*   **75**

14 *Final Preparations Before Data Collection*   *331*

Preface

The sixth edition of *Research Methods: A Process of Inquiry* is another significant step in the evolution of a curriculum that now includes the most extensive and best-integrated website in its field. The authors have refined the concepts and tools in this curriculum over years of teaching research methods, supervising student research, conducting and reporting on our own research, writing other textbooks, and continuously revising earlier editions of this one. The textbook is the anchor for this package. It provides all the necessary content for a research methods course, with supportive elements to aid students' learning. The full curriculum accompanying this sixth edition includes a thoroughly integrated Student Resource Website and an optional statistical analysis CD (SPSS for Windows). Both will be described later in this preface.

Pedagogical Considerations: Teaching the Concepts of Research

The pedagogical needs of undergraduates have guided every phase of the development of all six editions, culminating in this textbook and its integrated website. Every change made to this edition has been designed to enhance content, function, readability, and interest level. Research concepts, rather than cookbook-like strategies, are emphasized in order to help students to develop an understanding of scientific research as both an integrated process of thinking and an exciting enterprise. We want students to appreciate that science involves the continuous interplay of rationalism and empiricism, a combination that makes stringent demands on the evidence gathered and the research methods used. The first two chapters provide a basic foundation of scientific concepts to support the subsequent presentation of research methods. The remaining chapters build on this foundation.

Programmatic Nature of the Textbook

We believe that difficult or unfamiliar concepts are best taught programmatically. Thus, complex concepts such as validity, operational definitions, and statistical inference are introduced and defined early in the textbook, but only to the degree needed for those introductory discussions. Concepts are then systematically reexamined throughout the textbook, where new facets are added and related ideas are brought together into a coherent model, progressively building more complete and sophisticated conceptualizations. This programmatic development of concepts

- provides students with a systematic, progressive mastery of ideas, beginning with basic levels and building to more complex and more complete concepts;
- results in sequential rather than independent chapters, with each chapter building on earlier material;
- requires repetition, discussing the same concepts several times, but at progressively higher levels of sophistication; and
- requires a coherent theoretical model of research.

The programmatic approach makes complex material more accessible and understandable to students. A complete glossary and a detailed index are also included to help students quickly locate specific material and discussions.

Features of the Textbook

Consistent with our pedagogical focus, this sixth edition provides numerous features that are designed to enhance student learning. These features include boxed topical readings designed to organize material into clearly defined lessons for students. These new features include

- *Historical Lessons,* which use historical examples from psychology or science to illustrate important principles of research;
- *The Cost of Neglect,* which provide vivid examples of how badly research can turn out if one does not pay attention to details during the design process;
- *Extending the Concept,* which is an embedded feature that explicitly ties new information to concepts that students have learned previously; and
- *Putting It into Practice,* which is an embedded feature just before each chapter summary, which challenges students to take what they have learned in the chapter and apply it to everyday situations. It is designed to make the content of the chapter more understandable and expand the critical thinking skills of students.

This texbook incorporates several traditional pedagogical features proven to enhance student learning, including

- chapter outlines that preview the content of the chapter;
- quick-check review questions at the end of each major section, which challenge students to see if they learned the key material in that section;
- chapter summaries that organize the key points of the chapter;
- exercises at the end of each chapter to encourage students to integrate the information in the chapter;
- a list of key terms at the end of each chapter; and
- a glossary with over five hundred entries that provides detailed definitions of the technical terms of the discipline.

The textbook also includes some less traditional pedagogical features that optimize usability and provide an organizational structure for using the principles of research design. These features include

- **decision-tree flowcharts** that teach students how to select appropriate statistical analyses; and
- a **pre-data checklist** of items that should be completed before data collection (similar to the preflight checklists used by pilots).

Pedagogical strategies employed by the textbook authors include

- programmatic development of concepts;
- presentation of a coherent model of research;
- extensive use of examples, several of which are repeated to provide continuity to the presentation; and
- expanded treatment of the history of science and the history of psychology that sets modern research into a historical context.

Appendices

In addition to the features already described, the textbook includes several key appendices, many of which are expanded on the Student Resource Website (www.ablongman.com/graziano6e), including

- *Using the Student Resource Website,*
- *Writing a Research Report in APA Style,*
- *Conducting Library Research,*
- *Table of Random Numbers,* and
- *Answers to Quick-Check Review Questions.*

The Student Resource Website for the textbook is by far the most extensive in its market. It provides students with a comprehensive list of resources to enhance their learning of the material. Many of these features are interactive and others walk students through procedures with animations to explain what they will be doing. Chapter-relevant resources that are found on the Student Resource Website are listed at the beginning of each chapter and are identified with icons within the chapter. The Student Resource Website is described in more detail later in this preface.

A Coherent Model of the Research Enterprise

This textbook organizes the research process around a coherent descriptive model. This model integrates inductive and deductive reasoning, empirical observation, concepts of validity, and the phases of research (the basic steps through which each research project progresses).

The model also introduces the concept of *levels of constraint*, which refers to the degree of control that the researcher exercises over the research process. Valuable research can be carried out at any level of constraint, a point on which we differ from some other textbook authors. Experimental research (Chapters 8 to 12) is the most rigorous and allows us to answer questions of causality. However, other research questions are also important, such as questions about the strength and direction of the relationships among variables, about differences between existing groups, and about individuals and their response to manipulations. Furthermore, low-constraint scientific observations can lead to the formation of causal hypotheses that can be tested with higher constraint research. We want the students to learn that appropriate scientific research design depends on the nature of the questions asked and that research at all levels of constraint, whether naturalistic, case-study, correlation, differential, quasi-experimental, or experimental, is appropriate and useful.

The textbook builds a conceptual foundation leading to experimental research by developing each level of constraint, thereby providing students with a full spectrum of research knowledge and skills. We have also devoted three chapters (6, 7, and 13) to nonexperimental research procedures, because we believe that nonexperimental designs are valuable tools for psychologists.

Research Ethics

Ethical considerations are an integral part of the research design process. Because of the importance of ethical issues, this topic is covered extensively early in the text (Chapter 3) and, consistent with the textbook's general organization, is revisited repeatedly for more detailed discussions. Research ethics are addressed in every chapter of the textbook, either as a substantial section or as a sentence or two. In either case, our intent is to remind students of the importance of ethical concerns in research. We want to keep the issue visible throughout the text. Our aim is to foster student sensitivity to ethical issues in human and animal research and to teach the basic skills needed for dealing with these ethical issues.

Treatment of Statistics

This is a research design textbook, not a statistics treatise. However, because research design and statistics are so closely connected, an appropriate discussion of statistics must be included. Decisions regarding statistical analyses are an integral part of the design process and are not to be added after data collection. Basic statistical concepts are introduced early in the textbook (Chapters 4 and 5), and their integration into the design process is maintained throughout. Statistical procedures are presented conceptually, with an emphasis on understanding what they can do.

Choosing an appropriate statistical procedure is often confusing for students. We teach that the choice of appropriate statistical analyses follows systematically from the design characteristics of the study. Chapter 14 enhances the textual presentation with flowcharts that lead the student step by step through the characteristics of a basic research design so they can choose appropriate statistical analysis procedures. The flowcharts are also programmed into the Student Resource Website, helping students to identify the appropriate statistical procedure and linking them to detailed descriptions of how to carry out the procedure, either manually or using SPSS for Windows. (An optional *SPSS for Windows*

CD can be bundled with the textbook at the instructor's discretion for a small additional charge. Contact your local Allyn & Bacon sales representative for details.)

The bulk of the statistical coverage in the textbook is conceptual, whereas the Student Resource Website includes computational procedures and other statistical resources such as statistical tables. The Student Resource Website also includes considerable theoretical background on statistics for those instructors who want to integrate statistics and research methods in a single course. This organization gives instructors maximum flexibility, allowing them to cover as much or as little statistical material as they wish.

New in the Sixth Edition

The previous editions of this textbook have been highly successful and were adopted at hundreds of colleges and universities. The approach outlined previously has been continued in this sixth edition. In addition, we have made the following improvements:

- greatly expanded the content of the Student Resource Website. This online resource center provides learning materials that are superior to those available with any other research methods textbook;
- an updated final chapter on new directions in research methodology;
- provided new coverage of statistical theory and concepts on the Student Resource Website;
- added additional material and expanded informational essays on the Student Resource Website;
- replaced the existing boxed material with new thematic feature boxes (*Historical Lessons* and *The Cost of Neglect*);
- added two new embedded features (*Expanding the Concept* and *Putting It into Practice*);
- rewrote and reorganized content for improved clarity;
- made more than 150 content changes within the textbook, including adding new exercises at the end of each chapter, updating examples, references, the test bank, and PowerPoint slides, expanding treatment of research ethics, and making extensive edits to the glossary.

The Student Resource Website

This sixth edition includes an extensive and integrated Student Resource Website, which provides a variety of resources for students. The website address is *www.ablongman. com/graziano6e*. Recognizing that most, but not all, students have access to computing resources, we have been careful not to sacrifice anything in the textbook for the Student Resource Website. The textbook covers all essential topics, so no student is *required* to access the Student Resource Website for coverage of core material (unless assigned by the instructor). However, for those instructors and students who want to use the Student Resource

Website, there is a wealth of information, pedagogical aids, and other useful resources. *Our goal is to provide nothing less than the most comprehensive set of student learning resources of any research methods textbook package on the market.*

Rather than being simply a supplement to the textbook, the Student Resource Website is an electronic extension of the textbook. Access is provided free with each textbook purchase. The Student Resource Website is designed to

- be used interactively with the textbook;
- clarify conceptual material presented in the textbook;
- present examples of research concepts, procedures, and findings;
- expand concepts at a more detailed level for those students and instructors who wish to enhance their classroom assignments with additional readings; and
- introduce new material that is not ordinarily presented in methods textbooks.

The Student Resource Website provides dozens of specific resources. Instructors and students can select the elements that are most helpful from the following resources:

- an **interactive study guide/lab manual**, with chapter summaries; key terms linked to the glossary; fill-in-the-blank, true-false, and multiple-choice questions with immediate feedback; essay questions; laboratory exercises; and suggested readings;
- a **library research tutorial,** with examples of library searches that use Flash animations and exercises to improve library skills;
- an **APA style tutorial and reference manual** so students can learn both the basics of APA style and have access to more advanced features, without the necessity of purchasing the APA Style Manual;
- a **glossary** linked to other resources on the Student Resource Website;
- a **random number generator program**, with instructions for its use in sampling and assigning participants to groups;
- **research examples,** organized by both chapter and topic, drawn from both classic and current research;
- coverage of **statistical theory** for those faculty who want to integrate statistical concepts into the research methods course;
- **statistical computation instructions** for those faculty who want students to do manual computation of statistical procedures;
- a **tutorial on using SPSS for Windows** (Flash animation-based) for use in courses that require students to do computerized statistical analyses; and
- **supplementary resources,** such as background information on topics covered in the textbook, more extensive coverage of topics only introduced in the textbook, examples to help students understand difficult concepts, and an expanded discussion of the history of science and psychology.

Although the textbook's usability is in no way dependent on the Student Resource Website, using the website will greatly enhance students' learning experiences. If you take a few minutes to explore the Student Resource Website, we think you will be pleasantly surprised by what you find.

Optional SPSS for Windows Application

The student version of SPSS for Windows can be bundled with the textbook for a modest additional cost. This application is one of the most comprehensive and easy-to-use data analysis programs available. It is a powerful and intuitive application that should meet the needs of your students in this course and beyond. This special edition of SPSS for Windows will run for 13 months after installation. If you would like to know more about this option, contact your Allyn & Bacon sales representative or consult the publisher's website for details (*www.ablongman.com*). The publisher's website also has a locator function to help you to identify your local sales representative.

Additional Supplements

In addition to the Student Resource Website and the optional SPSS for Windows program, the adoption package includes an Instructor's Manual, a computerized test bank, a program to construct exams, and basic PowerPoint lectures. All of these resources can be downloaded from the instructor's website. Authorization to access that website can be obtained from your local sales representative.

The instructor's manual provides the following for each chapter:

- a list of resources available to the instructor in the Chapter-at-a-Glance table
- a list of learning objects
- a chapter summary
- a detailed outline of the chapter
- a list of lecture launcher points and/or classroom discussion ideas
- a list of key terms
- a bibliography

In addition to the instructor's manual, there is a computerized test bank that can be accessed by the TestGen-EQ Program. This program allows instructors to select from over 2,500 multiple-choice items, modify or write new items, and construct examinations. This program is available in both Windows and Macintosh versions.

Finally, a complete set of PowerPoint lectures is available for download from the instructor's website. These lectures include both basic coverage and supplemental slides that instructors can use if they desire.

Acknowledgments

A project of this scope would not be possible without the valuable assistance of many people. We wish to acknowledge the feedback and suggestions of our many reviewers. The sixth edition was reviewed by:

Jackie Adamson, *South Dakota School of Mines and Technology*
Keith Busby, *University of Ottawa*
Dennis Cogan, *Texas Tech University*
Susan Franzbleau, *Fayetteville State University*
Robert Harvey, *Virginia Tech University*
Steve Hoover, *St. Cloud University*
Edythe Kirk, *Lamar University*
Robert Matchock, *Pennsylvania State University–Altoona*
Sal Meyers, *Simpson College*
Blaine Peden, *University of Wisconsin–Eau Claire*
Celinda Reese, *Oklahoma State University*
Matthew Reysen, *University of Mississippi*
Margaret Ruddy, *The College of New Jersey*
Richard Siegel, *University of Massachusetts–Lowell*
David A. Stevens, *Clark University*

We would also like to thank the previous edition reviewers:

Vincent J. Adesso, *University of Wisconsin, Milwaukee*
Patricia L. Alexander, *Long Beach City College*
Jeffrey S. Anastasi, *Francis Marion University*
Joanne C. Basta, *Niagara University*
Burt R. Brown, *Rutgers—The State University of New Jersey*
Susan Franzblau, *Fayetteville State University*
Robert Harvey, *Virginia Tech University*
Steven L. Cohen, *Bloomsburg University*
Donald A. Czech, *Marquette University*
Wendy Domjan, *University of Texas at Austin*
Stephen E. Edgell, *University of Louisville*
Jeffrey S. Feddon, *Florida State University*
Mary Beth Gilboy, *Immaculata College*
Gregory T. Golden, *Immaculata College*
Timothy E. Goldsmith, *The University of New Mexico*
Lawrence R. Gordon, *University of Vermont*
Robert Grissom, *San Francisco State University*
Richard Hagen, *Florida State University*
Charles G. Halcomb, *Texas Tech University*
Madeline Heilman, *New York University*
John P. Hostetler, *Albion College*
Sherri L. Jackson, *Jacksonville University*
Linda James, *Georgian Court College*
Cindy J. Lahar, *University of Calgary*
Daniel W. Leger, *University of Nebraska*
Margaret F. Lynch, *San Francisco State University*
Richard G. Marriott, *Lamar University*
Karen M. McCollam, *University of Virginia*

Linda Mealey, *College of St. Benedict/St. John's University*
Daniel D. Moriarty, Jr. *University of San Diego*
Robert M. Murphey, *University of California, Davis*
James L. Pate, *Georgia State University*
Samuel L. Seaman, *Baylor University*
Jerry I. Shaw, *California State University Northridge*
Jobie Skaggs, *Bradley University*
Patrick D. Slattery, *Auburn University at Montgomery*
Robert M. Stern, *The Pennsylvania State University*
Lois E. Tetrick, *Wayne State University*
Peter Urcuioli, *Purdue University*
Frank W. Weathers, *Auburn University*

In addition, several faculty colleagues provided valuable consultation in this and/or earlier editions of the textbook, including Irving Biederman, B. Richard Bugelski, Jennifer Crocker, Jeremy Finn, Edwin Hollander, Elaine Hull, Mark Kristal, Murray Levine, Kenneth Levy, Brenda Major, John Meacham, Dean Pruitt, Mark Ring, James Sawusch, and C. James Smith.

Authors' Statement

We hope that this textbook, the Student Resource Website, the resources available to instructors on the instructor's website, and the optional SPSS for Windows application will meet your teaching needs. We understand that this is a challenging course to teach, and we have tried hard to provide superior resources for your use. Feel free to send us your comments and evaluations of this text using the evaluation form that is available at our website. You can also contact us directly through e-mail (*amgraz@earthlink.net; Raulin@MikeRaulin.org*).

Anthony M. Graziano
Michael L. Raulin

Curiosity, Creativity, and Commitment

Among scientists are collectors, classifiers, and compulsive tidiers-up; many are detectives by temperament, and many are explorers; some are artists, and others artisans. There are poet-scientists, philosopher scientists, and even a few mystics.

—Peter Bryan Medawar, 1967, *The Art of the Soluble*

Web Resource Material

For us, research activity is the most intensely fascinating, engaging, challenging, and rewarding part of psychology. It is possible, we suppose, that our own enthusiasm might not yet be shared by many students, some of whom may view a course on research methods with some trepidation. These students should consider this: As you go through each day, you frequently conduct informal psychological research. However imprecise it may be, it is nevertheless research. Each time you observe people and try to figure out what they are thinking and what they are going to do next, you are conducting psychological research. Whenever you try a new strategy to lose weight, improve your study habits, or make a better impression on someone, you are conducting a psychological experiment. In this course, you will learn about these and more formalized research strategies that psychologists use to answer questions about behavior. The questions are endless. For example, Darley and Latané (1968) wanted to know when people are most likely to come to the aid of someone in need of help. Ainsworth (1985) asked how parents could build a secure and trusting relationship with their children. Barlow (2002) wanted to know who is most likely to develop a panic disorder. Provine (2004) wondered what tickling and laughing might have to do with the evolution of speech, and Wixted (2005) wondered why we forgot things that we once knew well. These are only a few of the thousands of issues studied by psychologists.

Psychology is a discipline devoted to the scientific study of behavior, and this textbook covers the research strategies used in modern psychology. To understand the science of psychology, you must first understand science. Therefore, this chapter provides background on the history and philosophy of science and research.

Using the Resources of This Text

This sixth edition of *Research Methods* is supplemented by two special teaching aids to help you to learn how to conceptualize and design research: a Student Resource Website and an optional *SPSS for Windows* CD.

Exploring the Student Resource Website

On the website you will find a wealth of information to help you to study and to understand the course material, including a student study guide with exercises and test questions, a lab manual, and tutorials on APA writing style, library usage, and statistical computations. Those are critical skills in a research methods course, but normally there is no room in a textbook for more than a brief overview.

The best way to learn anything is through *active learning*, in which one manipulates and plays with the concepts one is trying to learn. We want you to do that right now with the Student Resource Website. The website's address is *www.ablongman.com/graziano6e.* This website is available only to users of this textbook, so you will need to log on by following the instructions found in the Access Kit shrinkwrapped with this text. Once you log in, the welcome screen shown in Figure 1.1 will appear. Take a few minutes to skim this screen and read about what is available on the website. Next, click on any section in the table of contents, which can be found on the left side of the screen.

Spend some time now exploring the website. Access several sections and look through them. You need not study them now; you will do that later. For now, just practice moving around in the website, navigating from the table of contents to other sections. Try this: in the table of contents select *Exploring the Website.* There you will find brief instructions on how to use the Student Resource Website. Now, just for your information, take a look at the section called *About the Authors.* You will even find our pictures there. OK, so we're not movie stars. Now click on *Chapter Resources.* We have organized much of the material on the website by chapter. At the beginning of each chapter in the text, there is a list of the website resources for that chapter. In the left margins of the text, icons will alert you that specific resources on the website are relevant to the particular discussion. These icons, each with its own code number, appear throughout the text, telling you where additional information is located on the Student Resource Website. The numbers *before* the colon in each code number indicate the chapter, and the numbers *after* the colon indicate the resource number for that chapter. Click on *Chapter Resources* in the table of contents, select the chapter, and then select the resource by number. Next, look through the textbook, find other icons, and locate them on the website.

FIGURE 1.1
Welcome Screen for the Companion Website The opening screen of the Student Resource Website lists resources and includes a table of contents (on the left side of the screen) that will allow you to quickly locate each resource.

Continue to browse through the website and you will see that it includes many resources. Click on the Study Guide/Lab Manual, select a chapter, and take a close look at it. Several sections of the Study Guide are interactive, giving you immediate feedback and sometimes even giving you hints when you are stuck. It is like having a personal tutor. Select *Library Research* in the table of contents and browse through it. Note that there are detailed animations that walk you through how you would search for specific information using a computerized database. Animations are also used to show you how to set up computer analyses using SPSS for Windows, how to conduct library searches, and how to use various web browser programs.

Using SPSS for Windows

SPSS stands for Statistical Package for the Social Sciences.[1] The *SPSS for Windows* CD is a student version of this sophisticated but easy to use statistical analysis package for analyzing the data from dozens of different research designs used in psychology. In addition to the tutorials on the *SPSS for Windows* CD, there are also extensive tutorials on the Student Resource Website about how to use the program. Note that if you purchase the special student version, it will expire 13 months after installation.

Quick-Check Review 1.1: Using the Resources of this Text	1. What are some of the resources available on the Student Resource Website? 2. What does the SPSS program do?

Science

The cornerstone of this textbook is science. **Science,** one of several ways of learning about the world, employs systematic observation and rational processes to create new knowledge. This section covers how scientists think about the world, how they ask questions, and how science and art actually share much in common.

Science Is a Way of Thinking

In science, knowing how to ask questions is as crucial as knowing how to answer them, and scientists seek knowledge through highly refined questioning skills. **Scientific research** is a

---

[1]The *SPSS for Windows* CD will be available to you if your instructor has chosen to use it. The publisher of this textbook has contracted with the SPSS Corporation to provide a version of this program with selected textbooks at a discounted price. If your instructor has elected not to include this software with the text, you can order it yourself through a bookstore or through the publisher's website (*www.ablongman.com*). However, the cost may differ from the package price.

process of formulating specific questions and then finding answers that help us to understand nature. Science is a **process of inquiry**—a particular way of thinking about questions.

This process of inquiry generates many useful tools and products, such as laboratory equipment, statistical procedures, computers, space flight, medicines, and consumer goods. Too often the tools and products of science are mistaken for its essence, but the essence of science is the scientist's way of thinking—the logic used in systematically asking and answering questions. A scientist can operate scientifically while sitting under a tree in the woods, thinking through a problem, and using apparatus no more technical than paper and pencil. It is not the bubbling liquids and laboratory equipment that make the discipline of chemistry "scientific." Likewise, knowing how to use an electron microscope or run a computer program does not make one a scientist. The television image of the white-coated laboratory worker surrounded by complex machines is a common visual metaphor, but it does not portray the essence of science any more than a skyscraper really scrapes the sky. *The essence of science is its way of thinking and the disciplined way in which questions are posed and answered. Logical processes and demands for evidence, not technologies, lie at the center of science. It is an intellectual process, and its ultimate goal is to understand the natural universe.*

Asking Questions

Asking questions is not new. Socrates and his students asked sophisticated questions over two thousand years ago. A question is one side of an idea; on the other side is an unknown quantity—a potential answer. Every question points to the existence of an unknown, to some area of human ignorance or uncertainty. Socrates knew, apparently to his delight, that posing sharp questions about religion, politics, and morality could reveal the ignorance and uncertainties of even the most dignified citizens. Unfortunately for Socrates, the good citizens were made so uncomfortable that they executed him as a subversive and corrupter of youth. It was thus established early in history that asking questions can be hazardous to one's health. Nevertheless, risk taking is part of science. Those who raise questions and expose ignorance create social and political strains, and often these people suffer reprisals. Leonardo da Vinci and Galileo challenged church dogma concerning the nature of the solar system. Their challenges went far beyond the heliocentric controversy and challenged many ideas about the nature of the solar system.

Charles Darwin, Alfred Russel Wallace, and a number of 19th-century geologists implicitly challenged the biblical account of creation by suggesting that the earth was millions of years old and that the creatures populating the earth evolved from other creatures. However, such conflicts did not occur only in the distant past. Consider the trial of John T. Scopes in 1925 (the so-called "monkey trial"). Scopes, a public school science teacher, was convicted of violating a Tennessee law that prohibited teaching Darwinian evolution in public schools. This verdict was later voided on a technicality, but the underlying law remained on the books until 1965. Even today, many school boards have tried to suppress the teaching of evolution in high school biology texts (Goodstein, 2005; Johnson, 2006), and many teachers de-emphasize evolution in their biology courses in order to avoid controversy ("Afraid to discuss evolution," 2005). Recently, in an extremely important decision, a federal judge ruled it unconstitutional for a school district to teach intelligent design as an alternative to evolution in high school biology classes (Goodstein, 2005).

Governments often try to suppress scientific knowledge, because information is valuable. For example, U.S. agents canceled 100 scheduled papers at an engineering convention in 1982 because the Department of Defense was concerned that some of the information might be of military value to Russia, whose scientists would be in attendance. A few years later, Alaska's attorney general ordered state scientists not to publish or publicly discuss information that might have helped in the cleanup following the Exxon Valdez oil spill, fearing that such information might be of use to the Exxon Corporation in legal actions (Busch, 1991). In 2003, the U. S. Department of the Treasury ruled that American researchers could no longer edit scientific papers written by scientists from Iran (Bhattacharjee, 2003); the government later softened this stance (Bhattacharjee, 2004). Even more recently, some states, caught up in political controversy, are now proposing to outlaw some types of stem cell research (Belluck, 2005).

Although some may be threatened by the information that science might produce, scientists thrive on new knowledge. Scientists are pervasive **skeptics,** challenging accepted wisdom in their search for more complete answers. They are willing to tolerate uncertainty, and they find intellectual excitement in raising questions and seeking answers about nature (Sternberg & Lubart, 1992). Asking a question is a creative endeavor that provides scientists with the personal satisfaction of exercising their curiosity. *What, how,* and *why* are critical words in the scientist's vocabulary. Curiosity may have killed the cat, but it sustains the scientist. J. Robert Oppenheimer (1956), whose research team created the atomic bomb, said that scientific research is "responsive to a primitive, permanent, and pervasive human curiosity" (p. 128). According to Linus Pauling (1981), who was awarded two Nobel prizes, satisfying one's curiosity is one of life's greatest sources of happiness. B. F. Skinner (1956), who was an enormously influential psychologist, agreed, arguing that "when you run into something interesting, [you should] drop everything else and study it" (p. 223).

A scientist's pursuit of curiosity follows unknown paths, sometimes resulting in dramatic and unanticipated discoveries that can appear to be accidental. However, when scientists drop everything to indulge their curiosity, they do so with a *prepared mind*: a disciplined curiosity that makes them sharply alert to the possibility of unanticipated discoveries. As the scientist Albert Szent-Gyorgyi noted, a discovery is "an accident meeting a prepared mind" (quoted in Bachrach, 1981, p. 3). Louis Pasteur, while a guest of honor at a reception, was asked, "Isn't it extraordinary these days how many scientific achievements are arrived at by accident?" Pasteur replied, "It really is remarkable when you think of it and, furthermore, did you ever observe to whom the accidents happen?" (Nelson, 1970, p. 263). The curiosity of a scientist is not idle, but active. It leads to discoveries, not through blind luck, but because it is embedded within a prepared mind and nurtured by long hours of research. It is a disciplined curiosity, sharpened by labor and frustrations, as well as by successes. *Historical Lesson 1.1,* The Three Princes of Serendip, illustrates the importance of a prepared mind.

The disciplined approach that scientists use to address questions tends to produce predictable results. An idiosyncratic result, not easily explained by current wisdom, will lead scientists to ask what is happening and why it is happening. As often happens in science, important discoveries may be made independently by different researchers working from similar theoretical perspectives. *Historical Lesson 1.2,* Charles Darwin and Alfred Russel Wallace, illustrates one of the most famous examples of this phenomenon.

Science and Art

Certain characteristics are almost universal in scientists, such as curiosity, creativity, skepticism, tolerance for ambiguity, commitment to hard work, and systematic thinking. However, these same characteristics are also well developed in poets, sculptors, painters, composers, philosophers, writers, and others. All engage in a mix of artistic and intellectual

HISTORICAL LESSON 1.1:   *The Three Princes of Serendip*

The term **serendipity** comes from the tale *The Three Princes of Serendip* (Serendip is the former name of Sri Lanka). According to the English novelist Horace Walpole, these princes were constantly stumbling on lucky finds. In science, serendipity has come to mean unanticipated discoveries. Some might call them "lucky." Such finds do not come from systematic applications of existing theory or research, but rather were discovered while the scientist was looking for something else.

These serendipitous findings are usually not the "happy accidents" that they appear to be. They could easily have been missed had the scientist not been alert to the implication of his or her observation. Such alertness requires both a prepared mind and a real sense of curiosity.

There are numerous examples in science of serendipitous findings (Roberts, 1989). For example, James Olds and Peter Milner (1954) discovered the brain's reward center when the electrode they had intended to implant in the reticular formation of one of their rats missed its target. Surgically implanting a tiny electrode in an area that is smaller than a grain of rice was difficult, and not every implanted electrode found its mark. Usually, when the electrode missed its mark, nothing much happened. However, Olds and Milner were intrigued by the behavior of one of their rats. The rat kept returning to the place where it had previously received the electrical stimulation, almost as if it wanted more. Alert to the fact that they were observing something new and very exciting, these investigators began a series of studies of how the brain shapes behavior through reward (Olds, 1958).

Another example comes from the Princeton laboratory of Charles Gross. Gross and his colleagues were studying visual processing in the monkey brain, measuring the response of individual neurons to a standard set of visual stimuli (dots, lines, and colored squares). After hours of fruitless testing with one neuron, the researchers finally gave up. As they were about to shut down the apparatus, Gross waved good night to his monkey, and the neuron they were studying immediately responded. Puzzled but intrigued, Gross began a series of systematic studies into this chance finding. He and his colleagues had discovered that individual neurons can be sensitive to complex stimuli, such as hands, faces, and even images of food. This discovery stimulated highly significant research into responses of this brain area and helped to create what has become the modern field of cognitive neuroscience.

Another example occurred in the same laboratory about 20 years later. Michael Graziano and Gross (1993, 1998) set out to study visual processing in a small, little-understood brain area called the *claustrum*. They implanted electrodes to measure the activity of individual neurons to visual stimuli, but they discovered that these neurons not only responded to the sight of objects, but also to the feel of objects touching the body. The researchers soon realized that they were not studying the claustrum at all, but had accidentally implanted the electrodes into a nearby area, the *putamen*. They discovered neurons that allow the monkey to judge the locations of nearby objects using data from multiple senses. This information guides movements either toward or away from these objects. Again, an accidental discovery led to development of an important area of neuroscience research.

What do these examples have in common? Scientists' curiosity is not idle, but rather is active and always questioning. These were not lucky discoveries. Each of these scientists knew that they had discovered something interesting, although initially they were uncertain about what it was. They each had prepared minds that had been nurtured by long hours of research. Without such prepared minds, they would have never realized the importance of their puzzling results and would have dismissed them as meaningless. It is this kind of disciplined curiosity that characterizes good scientists.

HISTORICAL LESSON 1.2:   Charles Darwin and Alfred Russel Wallace

Charles Darwin (1809–1882) was one of the most important scientists in history. His work *On the Origin of Species* (1859) has had profound effects on science, philosophy, religion, and politics. After completing his famous journeys, Darwin spent the next 21 years refining his ideas for publication. In June 1858, when his book was still far from completion, Darwin received a manuscript in the mail that made the same evolutionary argument that Darwin had been developing.

Darwin had been preempted by another naturalist, Alfred Russel Wallace (1823–1913). Wallace had traveled in the Amazon and the South Pacific, like Darwin had done many years before (Keith, 1954). Wallace was impressed by the diversity of life he found there, and he followed, completely independently, the same line of reasoning as Darwin in making sense of his observations. The result was Wallace's manuscript on the biological operation of natural selection in the origins of new species. Wallace mailed his discovery to Darwin for comment.

Who was to be the first to present this momentous discovery to the world? Darwin's associates arranged to have the two men's work presented simultaneously at a meeting of the Linnean Society in London on July 1, 1858. The Greeks had developed a concept of evolution over 2000 years earlier. However, it was Wallace and Darwin who gathered the mass of data and recognized that the driving force of evolution was natural selection. During the following year, Darwin completed *On the Origin of Species* and soon became the acknowledged originator of the idea of natural selection and the model that derived from it. Wallace, apparently content with this, made no great effort to share in the subsequent acclaim, and the two men remained lifelong friends. Wallace made important contributions to science and is recognized as an eminent naturalist. However, it is Darwin who is remembered for a great biological discovery.

endeavors, indulge their own curiosity, and explore their worlds with skeptical questioning and sharp observations. They attempt to answer their own questions and to represent parts of nature through their own particular medium, whether it is color, shape, sound, or language. Their representations of ideas become part of the public domain, where they may be viewed, discussed, criticized, accepted, rejected, or worse, ignored. They are compelled by a combination of curiosity and creativity, and they delight in their discoveries of relationships in nature and in their representations of nature.

Their statements are *tentative*. Symphonies, paintings, and research investigations are presented, not as fixed or complete truths, but as tentative statements of their originators' understanding at a given point in time. This is not to argue that science and art are the same, because they are not. Yet each employs a variation of the same theme—human curiosity combined with a disciplined process of inquiry—and both produce representations of ideas. Although artists and scientists comprise only a small part of the world's population, they have created an enduring array of ideas and products that have significantly affected the world.

There is a common belief that art and science are so different that artists and scientists are alienated from each other. People often will describe a poet, musician, or actor as the "artistic type," implying that the person has no aptitude for science or math. Alternatively, they may assume that a scientist or mathematician cannot appreciate art and literature. These assumptions are false. Consider the 40 national winners of the annual high school-level Intel Science Talent Search. Many of these young people, who have demonstrated high achievement in science, mathematics, and technology, are also talented in other creative activities, such as music, writing, and the visual arts. This should not be surprising. As you will see, art, science, and technology were all generated from the same pool of human skills early in civilization. *Historical Lesson 1.3* shows how well science and art can complement one another, as illustrated by the incredible work of Leonardo da Vinci.

HISTORICAL LESSON 1.3:   *Leonardo da Vinci*

The European Renaissance was a time of transition from medieval to modern life. It saw upheaval and change and a loosening of the old values of the Middle Ages. Humanism flourished, and the understanding, improvement, and celebration of life was pursued through momentous developments in art, science, literature, architecture, technology, commerce, politics, and virtually all aspects of human creativity. It was in this setting that Leonardo da Vinci (1452–1519) blended science and art in remarkable ways, demonstrating clearly the natural affinity of these disciplines. His education was ordinary, but he did manage to get solid training in the natural sciences, mechanics (physics), and music. He even invented a new musical instrument. He apprenticed with a famous painter, Verocchio, and within 10 years was a recognized master himself.

Leonardo studied anatomy to enhance his art, but eventually he became absorbed in the study of anatomy for its own sake. Going far beyond the artistic study of the human body, he developed detailed knowledge and drawings of the major anatomical systems: skeletal, muscular, cardiovascular, respiratory, genitourinary, and embryological. These studies reflect the meticulously detailed observation that is common to the artist and scientist alike. He also studied comparative anatomy, dissecting animal bodies and making detailed examinations and drawings. In effect, he was the first great medical illustrator (Gross, 1997). In his studies of bird wings, we see the artist making observations and recording them in detailed drawings. We also see the scientist and engineer trying to understand the mechanics of the articulation of the bird's wing—which muscles control which actions and what happens to the particular limbs, joints, and feathers in the action of flying. From his study of bird wings, he sketched plans for a flying machine nearly 500 years before the dawn of modern aviation.

Leonardo possessed great skills in science, technology, and art, and his creativity was far ranging. As a military engineer, he helped develop military fortifications and designed tank-like war machines, an apparatus for troops to breathe under water, a submarine, and a crop irrigation system. Yet he still found time for other pursuits. For example, he sculpted a huge model for an equestrian monument, which was never completed because bronze was needed to make cannons. He drew plans for buildings and monuments, pursued studies of mathematics and anatomy, and made detailed observations of fossils, river movements, and rock strata. The latter led him to brilliant conclusions that modern paleontologists would not develop for another 300 years (Gould, 1997). As if this were not enough, this monumental scientist also created magnificent works of art, including *The Last Supper* and the *Mona Lisa*.

Leonardo's work wove together science and art using mathematics, anatomy, mechanics, painting, and sculpture. His artistic labor alternated continuously with his scientific inquiry and, although much of his work has been lost, more than 5000 pages of drawings and notes survive (Gross, 1997). He exemplified the affinity of art and science in the pursuit of understanding nature. There were no arbitrary divisions between science and art in this Renaissance genius.

Quick-Check Review 1.2: Science	1. What is the essence of science?
	2. How can a scientist practice science while sitting under a tree?
	3. What is meant by *a prepared mind* in science?
	4. What are some of the major characteristics of scientists?
	5. What do art and science have in common?

Acquiring Knowledge

To learn about nature, scientists employ systematic thinking, which places heavy demands on the adequacy of information and on the processes applied to that information. However, science is only one of many ways of acquiring knowledge. Other ways are tenacity, intuition, authority, rationalism, and empiricism (Helmstadter, 1970). These methods differ in the demands made on the adequacy of the information and on the nature of the processing of the information. Science, which uses both rationalism and empiricism, is the most demanding, whereas tenacity, intuition, and authority make few demands on information and require minimal processing. These ways of acquiring knowledge are summarized in Table 1.1.

Tenacity

Tenacity is a willingness to maintain ideas as valid knowledge despite a lack of supporting evidence or even despite contrary evidence. Ideas that have been accepted for a long time or have been constantly repeated may acquire an aura of unquestioned truth. An example from the history of psychology is the powerful belief, held by early 20th-century male psychologists, that women were not as intelligent as men (Shields, 1982). Perhaps due in part to this belief, women were excluded from many university programs and professional positions well into the 1930s. Those male psychologists did not question their tenacious beliefs, and they actively ignored and rejected contrary evidence. Tenacity also operates in modern political campaigns when incorrect or distorted ideas are repeated so incessantly that voters begin to accept them as true. Advertisers likewise use this method, repeating messages in the hope that consumers will accept them as truth. When tenacity operates, there is no demand to check the accuracy of ideas, no serious consideration of alternative ideas, and no subjecting of the ideas to skeptical, critical, and objective review.

In a wonderfully provocative book on how people influence others, Robert Cialdini offers insight into the mechanism behind tenacity (Cialdini, 1993). He suggests that peo-

TABLE 1.1   *Ways of Knowing*

Ways of Knowing	*Definition*
Tenacity	Accepting ideas as valid because they have been accepted for so long or repeated so often that they seem true
Intuition	Accepting ideas as valid because they "feel" intuitively true
Authority	Accepting ideas as valid because some respected authority asserts that the ideas are true
Rationalism	Developing valid ideas using existing ideas and principles of logic
Empiricism	Gaining knowledge through observation
Science	A process that combines the principles of rationalism with the process of empiricism, using rationalism to develop theories and empiricism to test the theories

ple generally strive to be consistent in their behavior. Inconsistency is often viewed as a negative trait, because it suggests that the person has not thought through the issues at hand. Hence, once people act, they often have a strong need to continue to act in the same way, even if the initial action was ill advised or the situation has changed so that the action is no longer appropriate. For many people, it is better to have a strongly held, but incorrect, position than to be seen as being inconsistent.

Intuition

Intuition is the supposed direct acquisition of knowledge without intellectual effort or sensory processing. Examples of such supposedly direct-access knowledge include extrasensory perception (a contradiction in terms), which self-styled psychics claim to possess, and knowledge received directly from God, claimed by persons who have powerful religious experiences. Mysticism, spiritualism, and even drug-induced altered states of consciousness can lead people to the absolute conviction that they have found truth and knowledge.

Intuition is common in everyday life. For example, we often instantly like or dislike another person we have just met. We seldom examine our response rationally; we just "feel" it. People commonly have hunches or gut feelings. These serve us well in many situations, but they also lead to errors. Such intuitive responses are rapid assessments based on unexamined experiences, attitudes, and feelings (Myers, 2002). What makes these experiences intuitive is that people accept this knowledge quickly, without rational thought or examination of facts. Scientists also employ hunches, making conceptual leaps without examining the facts. These hunches, on careful testing, sometimes prove to have been very productive in advancing research. However, when they are wrong, the process of science will identify that fact and weed them out.

Authority

Authority is the acceptance of an idea as valid knowledge because some respected source, such as the Bible, the Koran, Aristotle, the Supreme Court, or the president claims that it is valid.

Tenacity, intuition, and authority make few demands on information and the processes to evaluate that information. Indeed, one thing these methods share is an uncritical acceptance of information. They assert that an idea is true because (1) it has always been accepted as true, (2) it feels true, or (3) an authority says it is true.

People use these methods every day and are perfectly willing to make many decisions based on them. Such methods have value in smoothing personal lives. You might, for example, accept religious teachings intuitively or on authority and experience personal satisfaction in your beliefs. You might act upon an urge to have pasta for dinner, without any need for further evaluation. But would you also uncritically agree to saunter across a six-lane highway with your eyes closed, because a psychic says he knows you will be perfectly safe, despite the 360 cars per minute hurtling by from both directions at 75 mph? Clearly, for some decisions, the information and the process employed to gather and test it need to be more adequate. Both rationalism and empiricism provide a stronger basis for accepting information as knowledge.

Rationalism

Rationalism is a way of acquiring knowledge through reasoning. In the rationalistic approach, existing information is carefully stated and logical rules are followed to arrive at acceptable conclusions. Consider this classic deductive syllogism:

> All crows are black (major premise).
> This is a crow (minor premise).
> Therefore, this crow is black (conclusion).

The conclusion is logically derived from the major and minor premises. The same logical processes would lead to the rejection of the following conclusion:

> All crows are black.
> This is black.
> Therefore, this is a crow.

01:01

In the rationalistic approach, the conclusion is reached through **logic**—systematic rules that allow us to draw accurate conclusions from a basic set of facts or statements. Logic is a more reliable way to acquire knowledge than tenacity, intuition, or authority. However, rationalism has its limitations. Consider this syllogism:

> All four-year-old children develop fears of the dark.
> Lisa is a four-year-old child.
> Therefore, Lisa has developed fears of the dark.

The logic is clear and the conclusion is correct, unless of course Lisa has not developed fears of the dark. What is the limitation? Suppose that it is not true that all four-year-old children develop fears of the dark, or suppose that Lisa is actually seven and not four, or suppose that "Lisa" is the name of a yacht and not a child. The major limitation of rationalism is that the premises must be true, as determined by some other evidence, to arrive at the correct conclusions. Accurate conclusions depend on both the reasoning process and the accuracy of the premises. There is no provision for assessing their accuracy in the purely rationalistic approach.

Empiricism

Empiricism involves gaining knowledge through observation—that is, knowing something by experiencing it through our senses. It is a method as old as civilization. For the empiricist, it is not enough to know through reason (or tenacity or intuition or authority) alone. It is necessary to experience the world—to see, hear, touch, taste, and smell it. "I won't believe it unless I see it!" is the empiricist's motto. We are good empiricists when we notice a dark sky and a distant rumbling of thunder and decide to take an umbrella. Our senses are telling us something. Thales, Hippocrates, Galen, Copernicus, Galileo, and Darwin all based their important conclusions about nature largely on their observations. They rejected the more widely held conceptions provided by mythology, religion, appeal to authority, and rationalism.

However, empiricism also has limitations. There are two types of empiricism: **naive empiricism** and **sophisticated empiricism.** The statement "I won't believe it unless I see it!" is an example of naive empiricism. If you have never seen Hong Kong, Manchester, Prague, Nyack, or Chippewa Falls, does this mean that these places do not exist? Because you have never seen gravity or the measles virus, should you conclude that you will never fall down or get the measles? If your empirical observations lead you to assert "I have never been run down while walking along the middle of a highway," does that mean you can continue walking down highways with impunity? And how about when you see something clearly that turns out to be an illusion, as in Figure 1.2?

Sophisticated empiricism goes further. People cannot see gravity or heat or, with unaided eyesight, the measles virus. But they can measure the increase in temperature as they turn up a heat source, note how rapidly an object falls to the ground, and view a virus through an electron microscope. Empirical observations in science are not limited to direct observations; we can also observe phenomena *indirectly* through the observation of their impact on other objects. An example of this is observing the impact of gravity by dropping something on the floor.

Empirical observations are critical in science, but if scientists did nothing but collect facts, they would achieve only long lists of facts. They would know nothing about how the facts go together or what the facts mean. Facts are most useful when people can think about them, organize them, draw meaning from them, and use them to make predictions. In other words, empiricism needs to be integrated with rational thinking so that the two bolster each other. This is exactly what science does.

Science

Science brings together elements of both rationalism and empiricism, employing rational logic and checking each step with empirical observation. Scientists constantly shuttle between empirical observation, rational thought about general principles, and further empirical observation of specific facts. This repeated return to empirical observation in an otherwise rationalistic process characterized the 16th century's apparently sudden surge into science. Much of the progress in science since then has been based on strengthening the empirical component by developing more precise methods of observation.

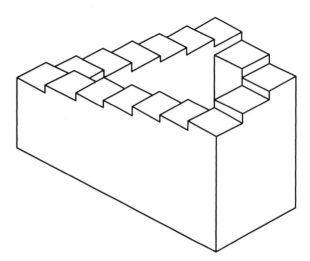

FIGURE 1.2 *Reality or Illusion?* You cannot always trust what you see.

Source: Reprinted with permission of The M.C. Escher Company B.V.

Science is a way of thinking that involves a continuous and systematic interplay of rational thought and empirical observation. Observed events, such as the movements of planets or the behavior of children, are the facts of science. But the simple empirical observation of events and the resulting identification or listing of facts is not sufficient in modern science. Scientists must go beyond observable facts to construct general principles and to make new predictions about nature based on those principles.

Quick-Check Review 1.3: Acquiring Knowledge	1. What are the common methods of acquiring knowledge? 2. Which two methods are combined in science? 3. What is meant by *naïve empiricism*? By *sophisticated empiricism*? 4. What are the limitations of rationalism? Of empiricism?

Emergence of Science

01:02

The rapid development of science in the 15th and 16th centuries suggests that science was suddenly created and that there was no science before Copernicus, Galileo, or Newton. Actually, science has been one of Western civilization's alternative methods of acquiring knowledge since the ancient Greeks of 2400 years ago, and its antecedents date back 8000 years. Not until the Renaissance in the 17th century did science become independent enough to begin its ascent into the powerful social movement that it is today. There is an extended discussion of the history of science on the textbook's website.

Early Civilization

Civilization developed from primitive hunter-gatherers, through organized nomadic hunting, to settled societies. Over millennia, humans developed a broad array of skills until, in the relatively short period from about 6000 to 4000 B.C., the accumulation of skills enabled a remarkable surge of progress from the late Neolithic period (when humans used polished stone tools) to the age of metals. Urban settlements grew, technological, social, and intellectual tools accumulated, and societies spread around the eastern Mediterranean. The magnificent civilizations of the Babylonians and Egyptians flourished. The skills on which those civilizations depended included architecture, agriculture, animal husbandry, food preparation, mining, smelting, and tool manufacturing. Commercial enterprises depended on long-distance land and sea navigation, on weighing and numerical calculations, on written records, and on tracking the seasons with accurate calendars. By 4000 B.C., books on astronomy, medicine, surgery, and mathematics had been written. All these advances coexisted with mystical beliefs about a universe filled with gods, demons, and spirits.

By 1000 B.C., there was a rich legacy of skills, with emphasis on practical information about agriculture, manufacturing, and commerce. The concrete manipulation of the environment led to practical skills and knowledge and, from that, more abstract ideas about nature were gradually developed (Farrington, 1949a, b).

Agriculture and metallurgy are good examples. Using their practical skills, early farmers observed weather phenomena, moon phases, sun positions, and other changes in the sky for clues to help in farming. These observations led to the development of accurate calendars. Farmers also learned about fertilizers and plant growth and developed practical mathematics to measure plots and set boundaries. Artisans learned to recognize types of ores and how to mine them. They knew that heat transformed solids into liquids, they could measure by weighing, and they understood proportionality, allowing them to reproduce the particular mixtures needed for various alloys.

These skills required an abstract understanding of nature gathered and refined through generations of empirical observations and concrete manipulations. The young apprentices of the day did not study abstract astronomy or mathematics, but embedded in their crafts were early elements of these disciplines. Thus, in these early Mediterranean civilizations, the components of modern science were present in the arts and crafts. Science, art, and technology were inseparable in practice.

Science rests on the **orderliness belief** (Whitehead, 1925), which is the implicit belief that the universe operates in an orderly, lawful manner. If the universe were not orderly and predictable, it would not stay the same long enough to be studied. To apply their skills in a reliable manner, early artisans had to expect orderliness. How else could they depend on *this* type of rock, when heated, to release *that* kind of metal, which will always have *these* properties, regardless of the different pieces of the rock used?

Greek Science

The roots of empirical science date to the pre-Socratic Greek period (about 600–400 B.C.). Thales (ca. 625–547 B.C.) was the first Greek philosopher to combine empirical and rational views of the universe. He lived in Ionia, a Greek colony whose citizens developed impressive commercial skills. The Ionians were pragmatic realists, primarily artisans, farmers, and tradespeople. Empirical knowledge was basic in their culture, and when some, like Thales, turned to philosophy, they developed an empirical view of nature. Thales' philosophy stressed the observation of natural events in a natural universe and rejected mysticism. He speculated about a natural cosmology in which water was the basic substance from which all else developed and to which all will ultimately return. He studied Babylonian astronomy and predicted the solar eclipse that occurred on May 25 in 585 B.C. He was known for his careful and painstaking observations (Whitehead, 1925). Thales founded abstract geometry and Ionian philosophy and is considered to be the father of science.

Thales's naturalistic speculations were continued by others. Anaximander's (610–547 B.C.) observation that sharks had mammalian characteristics led him to propose that higher-order creatures, including humans, developed from fishes. Xenophanes (ca. 560–ca. 478 B.C.) observed rock imprints of fish and seaweed on mountains and in stone quarries and proposed a theory of geological change over time. Hippocrates (c. 460–c. 377 B.C.) suggested radical ideas for treating illness. At the time, most people believed that illness was caused by demons invading the body and could be cured by prayers and exorcisms. Hippocrates attributed illness to natural events. He taught that demons and gods played no part in disease, and prayers and exorcisms would not heal a sick person. The Hippocratic physician relied on careful observations of patients and on rational thought in trying to understand illness.

From Thales through Hippocrates, Ionian science emphasized observation of naturally occurring events. The Ionians were careful observers and systematic thinkers, but not systematic manipulators of events. A later Ionian, Strato (d. ca. 270 B.C.), developed the next important step—making the scientist an active observer who manipulates and controls the conditions of observations. Strato, a successor to Aristotle, accepted the Ionian emphasis on natural events, its basic belief in an orderly and knowable universe, and its rejection of mysticism. He believed that the best method of acquiring knowledge was empirical manipulation and observation—that is, **experimentation.** He performed experiments on air and water, demonstrating many of their properties, and from these experiments he developed some general explanatory principles about nature.

However, by Strato's time, Ionian empirical science was already in decline. Strato's scientific view stood as an alternative to the mystical views propounded by religious authorities and by such philosophers as Plato and Socrates. Then, as now, these views conflicted, leading to the near total suppression of one by the other. The result was that this early empirical science was virtually lost for almost 1900 years.

After Socrates, the highest ideals were religion, politics, and rationalistic, mystical philosophy. The pursuit of practical goals was necessary, but was left to slaves, laborers, artisans, farmers, and tradespeople, whereas upper-class scholars pursued pure reason and abstract ideas. As a result, theology and abstract philosophy were carefully taught and preserved in writing. In contrast, empirical skills, not admitted into the realm of scholarship, remained in the oral tradition and were not as fully recorded or preserved. Social stratification was not the only factor contributing to the suppression of empiricism. Religion was gaining social power, and religious leaders attacked the natural philosophy of the Ionians as atheistic, factually wrong, and subversive.

The genius of the early Greeks created an empirical science that described an orderly universe operating according to a few basic principles. Greek philosophy was one of humanity's major intellectual achievements. The movement away from this empiricism after 400 B.C. was led by Plato and Socrates, who focused on the pursuit of pure reason. As Farrington (1949a) noted, "When Plato died (about 347 B.C.), he left behind him a mystical view of the universe set forth in his dialogues in a unique combination of logic and drama. Its weakness was not that it lacked supports in argument, but that it was not open to correction from experience." After 400 B.C., Greek philosophy became increasingly mystical. This growing mysticism changed the way people viewed discoveries. For example, the regularity of number relationships and the orderliness observed in astronomy were taken as evidence that nature was controlled by divine intelligence. This led to a shift in the goals of philosophy and science. Earlier investigators were interested in understanding and controlling nature, but later philosophers sought to illustrate divine intelligence through their study of nature. Science was beginning to be used in the service of religion, a role that continued for 2000 years.

Medieval Science

By the end of the fourth century, Christianity had become the Roman Empire's sole state religion, and it remained a major social institution and political power in Western Europe for the next thousand years. Greek reliance on intuition and reason was continued by medieval Christian scholars, who believed that divine intelligence controlled the universe and the scriptures were the ultimate source of truth. **Theology,** the study of God and God's relationship to the universe, dominated; revelation, rationalism, and authority were its major methods of acquiring knowledge. All other methods of study, including empiricism, were secondary to theology. Christian scholars continued empirical studies in astronomy, optics, and zoology, but always secondary to, and in the service of, religion (Nagel, 1948).

By the 13th century, such theological scholars as Thomas Aquinas and Roger Bacon, influenced by the rediscovery of early classical scholarship, elevated the value of empiricism. Bacon repeated optical experiments performed earlier by Islamic scientists. A Dominican cleric, Dietrich of Frieberg (ca. 1300) used water-filled glass balls to experiment with the visible spectrum, discovering that colors are refracted on the inside of spherical water drops. At about the same time, Jordanus DeNemore experimented with various types of levers and the equilibrium of weights on inclined planes. In 1269, Peter the Stranger of Maricourt published sophisticated experiments with magnets (Clagett, 1948, p. 119). Reflecting this increased emphasis on empiricism, Dietrich of Frieberg noted that "one ought never to renounce what had been made manifest by the senses" (cited in Clagett, 1948, p. 119).

The 12th and 13th centuries saw great changes in politics, art, commerce, and exploration. People focused more on the world around them, and a revival of the ancient Greek, Greco-Roman, and Islamic scholarship occurred. Western Europeans expanded their trade around the Mediterranean. They encountered works of Islamic scholars, who had been part of the Moorish high civilization in Spain. These scholars had brought with them Arabic versions of classical works, which they translated into Latin. By the end of the 12th century, medieval scholars knew Hippocratic and Galenic writings in medicine, Euclid's mathematics, Ptolemy's astronomy, Archimedes' physics, and Hindu mathematics. Medical schools, largely based on these traditions, were established across Europe, and the empirically based study of medicine, mathematics, and physics was revived. This rebirth of empirical science remained within the bounds of theology, where, for a while, there was room for it to grow. However, science challenged theology and, by the 17th century, began to escape from its constraints.

Two constraints on empirical science were established by the Greeks and later strengthened by Christian theologians. The first was that empirical science was not allowed to contradict theological dogma. If a dispute arose between knowledge gained through the senses and knowledge arrived at by revelation or through church authority, the resolution was simple: truth lay with theology, and any contradictory ideas were false. The second constraint was that empiricism was to be used only in the service of religion. But scientists challenged both constraints. For example, scholars argued that science could be used for the betterment of humanity, such as to combat sickness. The church tolerated this application of science to humanity as long as it did not challenge church dogma. Eventually, however, such challenges did occur.

The Scientific Revolution

By the 13th century, science was firmly established in the new medical centers, and scholars recognized the value of science in the service of humanity. Service to humanity was to become a major theme in science, one that Francis Bacon would stress in the 16th century. However, science remained under the control of religious and political authorities well into the 14th century. Its growth to independent status occurred during a seething 400 years of social change.

During the 13th through 16th centuries, science increasingly conflicted with religious dogma. For example, both Catholics and Protestants condemned René Descartes (1596–1650) for his views. A philosopher and mathematician, Descartes questioned the theological concepts of the soul, arguing for more objective observation and study of consciousness. Two of his ideas became critical in the later development of psychology: his concepts of mind-body dualism and his doctrine of ideas (which posits that ideas arise both innately from processes within the mind and through experience in the external world). Galileo (1564–1642), an astronomer, physicist, philosopher, and mathematician, also challenged church dogma. In 1633, he was forced by the inquisition to recant his support of the Copernican concept that the earth orbits the sun. However, by then the scientific revolution, fueled by Copernicus, Bacon, Galileo, Kepler, Newton, and others, had already begun. Established institutions fought what they perceived to be the scientists' attack on religion. However, by the beginning of the 19th century, science had been reestablished and, for the first time since about 400 B.C., had achieved independent status. By the 18th and 19th centuries, scientific centers existed in universities, social resources were available to support science, and scientists were sought after by industries, universities, and governments. By the 20th century, science had become a major social movement.

Science developed rapidly in the latter part of the 20th century and continues in the twenty-first. For example, developments in high-energy physics have provided insights into the building blocks of matter. In biology, the ability to read and manipulate DNA structure has led to new variations of life forms. Neuroscience integrated psychology, biology, neurology, and molecular genetics and has led to such new technologies as magnetic resonance imaging (MRI). The development of high-temperature superconducting materials and faster computer chips has enormous potential for future applications.

Modern science depends on a heavily endowed social structure that includes research centers, universities, industries, and private agencies. Networks of scientific societies exist, with annual meetings in which scientists communicate their findings and lobby for greater public resources. Scientists also communicate with the general public through newspapers, magazines, radio, television, books, and electronic media. Scientists and laboratories are supported by the general public, as well as by special groups, such as industries or foundations.

Scientists have investigated many phenomena and have created specialized disciplines, each with its own content and procedures. The phenomena studied differ from one discipline to another, with methodological procedures differing according to what phenomena are being studied, the kinds of questions asked, and the technologies associated with each discipline. Whatever their specialization, all scientists share a strong curiosity about nature and a commitment to the combined use of empiricism and rationalism as a way to understand nature.

Science is not new, but the public often views science as a recent development. One reason for this view may be the close association of science and technology. Technology is always changing, so current technology is always new. In fact, the pace of technological development has been astounding. Consider the development of aircraft. In 1903, after years of research, Orville Wright flew for 12 seconds in the world's first powered and piloted heavier-than-air flight. By the time Orville Wright died in 1948, Chuck Yeager had already broken the sound barrier in a jet plane, and the first manned flight into space was only 13 years away. Could Orville have imagined at the turn of the century, when he and Wilbur were experimenting with their wind machines and wing surfaces, that such dramatic developments would occur in such a short time?

Ethical Concerns

The development of modern science during the 18th and 19th centuries was paralleled by the growth of humanitarianism and the expression of human rights, all of which were indebted to the Protestant Reformation and the Enlightenment. Mary Shelley's masterpiece *Frankenstein*, written in 1816, was a metaphor for the potential dangers in the misuse of the power of science and a warning that science could grow out-of-control. By the mid-20th century, modern science had become a powerful factor in the world. It was fully recognized that science exists within the context of culture, and it must cooperatively interact with, and not dominate, other aspects of culture. Suddenly, people were thinking about the moral implications of science. Over the past six decades in particular, those moral concerns have shaped continued discussion and the development of ethical guidelines for scientific research. Every student must learn these ethical guidelines and must realize that the ethics of science and scientific research are immensely important in this modern world.

Quick-Check Review 1.4: Emergence of Science	1. How did the early practical skills of artisans contribute to modern science? 2. What contribution did Thales make to science? 3. What was the relationship of science and theology during the Middle Ages? 4. Distinguish between modern technology and modern science. 5. What is the orderliness belief, and what does it have to do with science? 6. What novel highlighted the growing concern over the ethics of scientific research?

Psychology

01:03

Psychology, which has been an independent science for fewer than 150 years, was originally part of philosophy, a discipline that has been recognized for more than 2000 years. Several texts provide detailed treatment of psychology's history (Benjafield, 1996; Benjamin, 1997; Fancher, 2000, Goodwin, 1999; Hergenhahn, 1997; Schultz & Schultz, 2000). We provide only a brief overview here. An expanded treatment of the history of psychology is presented on the Student Resource Website.

The History of Psychology

The context for the emerging discipline of psychology was in place by the mid-19th century. This context included 19th-century physiology and the philosophies of romanticism, rationalism, and empiricism. Romanticism fueled the 19th-century humanitarian reform movements, while rationalism and empiricism were the major supports of modern science. The earliest psychological research focused on neurophysiology, including studies of reflex action and localization of brain function.

Scientific psychology was profoundly influenced by evolutionary theory. The concept of evolution suggested the continuity of structure and function between humans and other animals, called **phylogenetic continuity,** an idea that ran counter to religious and previous philosophical thought. That idea suggested that studying animal functioning could help scientists to understand human functioning. Furthermore, the evolutionists' emphasis on adaptation of organisms to their environments highlighted the importance of studying function as well as structure. Darwin's use of data from many sources—geology, paleontology, archeology,

01:04

biology, and observation of nature—legitimized the use of diverse data sources and methodologies. The concept of natural selection emphasized individual differences, which helped set the stage for later psychological work on personality, intelligence, and psychological testing. The influence of evolutionary theory on modern psychological science has been enormous.

Prescientific psychology dates to Aristotle, but the scientific study of psychology did not begin until the mid-19th century. Psychology evolved from earlier studies in philosophy, biology, mathematics, physiology, physics, and even astronomy. Ernst Weber (1795–1878) and Gustav Fechner (1801–1887) were among the first researchers to study perceptual processes objectively. They presented carefully measured stimuli to people under controlled conditions and recorded the participants' responses, an approach known as **psychophysics.**

The early history of psychology was dominated by a series of *schools* or movements. Each school of psychology was defined by a central focus, a set of underlying assumptions, accepted research methodologies, and a general philosophy about human functioning and the best ways to study it.

Structuralism.   Wilhelm Wundt (1832–1920) established the world's first psychological laboratory in 1879 in Leipzig, Germany. Wundt's influence in psychology was extensive, because many of his students eventually set up psychological laboratories in other countries. Wundt studied the structure of consciousness using introspection. That is, he tried to infer the basic elements of conscious experience from participants' verbal reports of their mental experiences. Since Wundt was interested in the structure of consciousness, his work was known as **structuralism,** and it dominated psychology during the late 19th and early 20th centuries. Wundt argued that experimentation could not be used to study higher mental processes. However, Hermann Ebbinghaus (1850–1909) showed that rigorous experimental procedures could be applied to higher mental processes. His work profoundly influenced the development of psychology as a science.

Functionalism.   By the turn of the 20th century, American psychologists shifted the focus from structuralism to how the mind operates, and this new approach was called **functionalism.** Functional psychologists, such as G. Stanley Hall (1844–1924), William James (1842–1910), John Dewey (1859–952), J. McKeen Cattell (1860–1944), and E. L. Witmer (1867–1956), were interested in practical questions of education, training, treatment, and child rearing. Witmer, for example, worked with children with mental retardation and emotional disorders. He created the first psychological clinic and is credited with founding and naming the field of clinical psychology. This new functionalism was shaped by the cultural differences between the United States and Germany. It was heavily influenced by Darwin and by Darwin's cousin, Francis Galton (1822–1911), and it relied heavily on the study of animal behavior as a way to understand human behavior.

Both structuralism and functionalism have disappeared, but the spirit of functionalism continues today in the general orientation of Western psychology toward practical applications and understanding functional processes.

Psychodynamics.   **Psychodynamic theory** argued that behavior was a function of complex and often contradictory internal influences, many of which were outside of a person's conscious awareness. Sigmund Freud (1856–1939) is credited with developing psychodynamic theory, and his ideas were built on the work of others going back to the early 1800s. Freud was profoundly influenced by Darwin's evolutionary theory, including his work on unconscious processes, the importance of dreams, the child–to–adulthood continuity of emotional behavior, and sex as a basic human biological drive (Schultz & Schultz, 2000; Sulloway, 1979; Ritvo, 1990). While other psychologists were studying human consciousness, Freud focused on unconscious processes. He and his followers carried out studies in clinical settings, rather than in laboratories. In fact, virtually all of his work took place outside of mainstream academia.

Freud was accepted by only a few American psychologists, such as G. Stanley Hall, who arranged for Freud's only visit to the United States. In 1909, Freud presented five lectures in German at Clark University in Worcester, Massachusetts. Despite his support and public acclaim in Europe, Freud was initially ignored and later vigorously criticized by most American academic psychologists for his lack of scientific rigor. Despite such criticisms, Freud grew in popularity, and the public eventually came to view psychodynamic theory and the treatment that grew out of it, called **psychoanalysis,** as mainstream psychology (Fancher, 2000). By the time of his death in 1939, Freud had become world famous.

At the same time that Freud was achieving popular acclaim, American psychologists began to subject his ideas to empirical testing. In the 1940s and 1950s, hundreds of articles on psychodynamic concepts and procedures were published, both supportive and critical (Fancher, 2000). Psychoanalysis became a major clinical model of psychotherapy, reaching its peak in the1940s and influencing psychology, psychiatry, social work, sociology, literature, and history. Although it is no longer a dominant model, psychoanalysis continues to be used clinically by a few groups of adherents.

Gestalt Psychology. Two important developments emerged around 1912, and both were critical of structuralism. One of those, **Gestalt psychology,** originated in Germany. Its founders were Max Wertheimer (1880–1943), Kurt Koffka (1886–1941), and Wolfgang Kohler (1887–1967), who argued that the structuralists' efforts to divide consciousness into separate parts lost sight of the whole experience. Gestalt psychologists argued that, especially with perception, the whole is greater than the sum of its parts. The perceptual system may detect lines, edges, and movements, but when the brain puts these together, humans see meaningful objects.

Behaviorism. Another development around 1912, **behaviorism,** emerged in the United States. It criticized psychology as too **mentalistic** (that is, based only on one's subjective experience). John B. Watson (1878–1958) argued that one should reject such mentalistic concepts as mind, conscious-ness, and the id. He maintained that such concepts were meaningless carryovers from prescientific philosophy. The psychology of consciousness, according to Watson, needed to be replaced by an objective psychology of observed behavior.

Animal psychology was a major factor in modern behavioral psychology. Behaviorists such as Ivan Pavlov (1849–1936), E. L. Thorndike (1874–1949), E. C. Tolman (1886–1959), E. R. Guthrie (1896–951), C. L. Hull (1884–1952), and B. F. Skinner (1904–1990) believed that studying animal behavior provided clues about such complex processes as learning. It had previously been thought that animal behavior was instinctual. However, animal psychologists found that it was flexible, varied, and systematically modifiable. Even lower animals could learn new and complex behavior.

An applied result of animal behaviorists' research is **behavior modification.** If animal behavior could be modified using behavioral techniques, then similar procedures might modify human behavior, enhancing education and psychological treatment. Behavioral principles could also be used to help to teach people cognitive and behavioral skills. First studied in the 1920s, behavior modification had become a major component of education and treatment by the 1960s.

Humanistic Psychology.   Emerging in the middle of the 20th century and having roots in the early 19th-century Romantic movement, humanistic psychology was briefly influential, but never developed into a school or movement (Schultz & Schultz, 2000). **Humanistic psychology,** as developed by Abraham Maslow (1908–1970) and Carl Rogers (1902–1987), focused on human conscious experience, creativity, and personal growth and assumed that there was a natural tendency toward self-actualization—the full expression of one's human potential. Most of its research was on therapeutic interventions. Its ideas were consistent with an egalitarian American democracy and have been integrated into much of mainstream psychological thought.

Cognitive Psychology.   **Cognitive psychology** is the study of perception, memory, and learning. It grew out of both the early work on human perceptual processes and efforts to study verbal learning in humans. Once almost exclusively an academic discipline, cognitive psychology now routinely addresses applied questions. The design of high-performance aircraft and modern computer software, to name two examples, relies heavily on cognitive psychology research. Cognitive psychologists employ sophisticated experimental methods and logic to infer cognitive processes. However, this approach has had its critics. Skinner (1990) argued from a behaviorist's perspective that cognitive psychologists were speculating too much about what was going on inside a person's head, rather than focusing on the person's observable behavior. Modern cognitive psychology often crosses over into the broader discipline known as *cognitive science*. **Cognitive science** bridges once-separate disciplines, like psychology, **behavioral neuroscience,** computer science, neurophysiology, and linguistics, providing an integrated perspective on brain-behavior relationships.

Women and Minorities in Psychology

The late 19th century and the first years of the 20th century were exciting years for the emerging discipline of psychology. However, like virtually all modern professions at the time, psychology, was a white-male–dominated field. Women and ethnic minorities, notably African Americans, were traditionally excluded. In the European tradition, women were not allowed to enroll in colleges. It was not until nearly 1835 that a few colleges admitted a handful of women, but only as undergraduates. The few women who did earn degrees in the early 20th century and who attained important academic and other positions did so against great prejudice.

For example, Christine Ladd Franklin (1847–1930) was refused a doctorate in mathematics by Johns Hopkins University because she was a woman, despite the fact that she had completed all degree requirements (Shultz & Shultz, 2000). The university finally awarded her the degree 45 years later.

Mary Whiton Calkins (1863–1930) completed all requirements at Harvard for the doctorate, but Harvard refused to award it to her. Years later, because of Calkins's outstanding contributions to psychology, Columbia University awarded her an honorary doctorate. She was also elected the first woman President of the American Psychological Association.

Edward B. Tichener, one of the most influential of America's early psychologists, steadfastly barred women from his weekly research meetings at Cornell. Nevertheless, he was an advocate for women's rights to study at universities and to earn degrees. He just did not want them at his cigar-smoking, male-only research meetings. Margaret Floy Washburn (1871–1939) was Tichener's first doctoral student and the first woman to earn a doctorate in psychology. She went on to contribute important work in comparative psychology, becoming president of the American Psychological Association and the first female psychologist elected to the National Academy of Science. But despite Tichener's support of her work, he never allowed her into those research meetings.

Helen Thompson Woolley (1874–1947) studied sex differences for her 1903 doctoral dissertation, in which she found that males and females did not differ on intelligence or emotional functioning, and, in fact, women were slightly higher than men in memory and sensory perception. Woolley was strongly criticized for her alleged bias in failing to find the expected superiority of men.

Leta Stetter Hollingworth (1886–1939), a Phi Beta Kappa graduate of the University of Nebraska, was forced to resign from high school teaching when she married. The administrators believed that if a married woman was allowed to work outside the home, her husband and children would suffer (Schultz & Schultz, 2000). Eight years later, Hollingworth earned a Ph.D. at Columbia University and went on to contribute significant research in emotional behavior, childhood education, and the needs of gifted children.

Largely barred from academic positions, women with doctorates in psychology obtained jobs in applied areas, such as schools, clinics, and hospitals, where they succeeded, making dozens of important contributions to applied psychology. Currently most doctoral-level psychologists are men; however, this is rapidly changing, because most undergraduate and graduate psychology students are now women.

While women were the largest group that was discriminated against in the early years of modern psychology, other minorities (e.g., Jews and persons of color) were also targets of prejudice. At the turn of the century some prestigious universities excluded Jewish men and women from faculty positions and well into the 1960s there remained quotas for Jewish applicants to many graduate schools (Schultz & Schultz, 2000).

For African Americans the prejudice was even more severe. From 1920 to 1966, only 8 of more than 3,700 doctorates awarded by the 10 most prestigious psychology departments went to Black scholars (Russo & Denmark,1987; Schultz & Schultz, 2000).

Francis Cecil Sumner (1895–1954) was the first African American to be awarded the Ph.D. in psychology. He had studied at Clark University under G. Stanley Hall, a leading academic psychologist, who was among the few to encourage women and minorities to apply to graduate schools. Sumner went on to become chairperson of the psychology department at Howard University.

Kenneth Clark (1914–2005), whose application for graduate admission had been rejected at Clark University "on the basis of race" (Clark, 1978), eventually earned the Ph.D. at Columbia University. Clark's wife, Mamie Phipps Clark (1917–1983), also a Ph.D. psychologist, faced similar discrimination and was barred from university positions. In the early 1940s, the Clarks carried out research with Black children on racial identity and self-concept. Their research was an important part of the 1954 U.S. Supreme Court decision ending racial segregation in public schools. In 1971, Kenneth Clark became the first African American president of the American Psychological Association.

Modern Psychology

World War II catapulted psychology from an academic discipline to an academic and applied discipline. Although some psychologists carried out testing and counseling, the applied mental health field was dominated by psychiatry prior to World War II, and the major psychotherapeutic model was psychoanalysis. World War II brought academic psychologists into the armed forces to deal with issues of selection, training, rehabilitation, and treatment of military personnel. Many of these psychologists brought with them their objective, laboratory-based procedures and their behavioral orientations. The success of psychology during World War II challenged the dominance of psychiatry and psychoanalysis. Following World War II, the federal government became a major supporter of training programs in clinical psychology.

The clashes between schools of thought that were common in the early history of psychology have given way in the last 50 years to efforts to integrate ideas from different schools. For example, *social analysts* such as Karen Horney (1885–1952) and Harry Stack Sullivan (1892–1949) applied sociological theory to psychoanalysis. E. C. Tolman integrated concepts from Gestalt psychology, early cognitive psychology, and behaviorism in his theory of learning. Kurt Lewin (1890–1947) integrated Gestalt concepts with social psychology and child development, and Dollard and Miller (1950) modernized psychoanalysis by integrating it with Hull's (1943) learning theory.

Over the last 30 years, **behavioral medicine** and **health psychology** have brought together behavior modification, medicine, nutrition, and health. Since the 1970s, cognitively oriented clinical psychologists have integrated behavioral learning theory and cognitive psychology, essentially bringing consciousness back into behaviorism. The past 25 years have seen the development of integrated disciplines, such as **behavioral neuroscience,** which incorporates such diverse disciplines as cognitive and physiological psychology, neurology, and language development.

Psychology continues to build on earlier work and to create new research technologies. For example, there is a growing collaboration between cognitive science and neuroscience, as scientists learn to monitor the brain in action using advanced technology. Psychologists are now able to integrate psychological experiences with biological mechanisms, producing a sophisticated understanding of psychological concepts that only a few years ago seemed too complex to unravel (e.g., Sutton & Davidson, 1997).

In more applied areas, such as clinical and counseling psychology, this growth in the understanding of psychological and biological mechanisms has led to impressive improvements in the treatment of psychological disorders (Barlow, 2001). In the past, a single psychotherapeutic approach would be applied to virtually every problem. Today, effective individualized treatments exist for dozens of specific conditions (Chambless & Ollendick, 2001). There has also been a surge of interest by social psychologists in personality development and psychopathology, topics that bring together aspects of social and clinical psychology.

Today's psychologists are unlikely to be strong adherents of any particular school. Rather, most represent **mainstream psychology,** which is integrative in nature, drawing from many psychological theories and many areas of research.

Throughout its history, psychology has increased the understanding of factors that influence behavior. Among the processes studied by psychologists are learning, motivation, memory, personality, physiology, sensation, perception, intelligence, language, problem solving, emotion, development, psychopathology, and social influences on behavior. Today, psychology is an independent scientific discipline that overlaps several other disciplines. For example, biopsychology combines biology and psychology; cognitive psychology overlaps with computer science, linguistics, and neurology; and the psychological study of the sensory processes of vision and hearing involves knowledge of the physics of light and sound and the physiology of the brain.

Psychology is a large discipline. More than 150,000 psychologists are members of the American Psychological Association, and another 5100 psychologists are members of the Canadian Psychological Association (American Psychological Association, 2005; Canadian Psychological Association, 2004). Many psychologists are members of other associations, such as the Association for Psychological Science, the Association for Behavioral and Cognitive Therapies, the Psychonomic Society, the Society for Neuroscience, and the Society for Research in Child Development.

01:05

Psychology, like most sciences, is divided into several subdisciplines, each with its own focus. The diversity in psychology is reflected by the fact that there are over fifty divisions within the APA, each devoted to a specific area of interest. Although all psychologists receive scientific education, many work professionally in such applied settings as hospitals, clinics, schools, industry, and government service, where their research training helps them solve practical problems for their clients.

Psychology is often considered to be a social science, but its roots are clearly in the natural sciences. There are many research areas within psychology, each with its own particular content and methods. However, all areas of psychology use the scientific model to study behavior. The focus of this book is on the use of scientific research methods in psychological inquiry.

The Science of Psychology

Why is science so critical in psychology? People observe the world, themselves, their actions, and the behavior of others, and try to make sense of it all. Most people are amateur psychologists. But psychology is a field in which amateurs often perform poorly. For example, people think that "seeing is believing," but the science of psychology demonstrates that human perceptual systems are limited, biased, and subject to all kinds of distortions. People believe that they remember past experiences, but the science of psychology demonstrates that their memories are fragile at best, almost always biased, and capable of changing a remembered event into something entirely different. People know how their experiences have changed them, shaping their current personalities, but the science of psychology shows that such events seem to have little impact on later behavior and that genes play a powerful role in shaping people. People believe that the more individuals nearby, the more likely that someone will help them when they need it. The science of psychology shows that just the opposite is true: the more people available to help, the less likely that one will get help from anyone. In other words, what most people "know" to be true about the psychological world is often false. The scientific study of psychological phenomena often uncovers surprises.

Even more critical, the science of psychology protects us from the pseudoscience of psychology. Most scientific disciplines have some related pseudoscience. Astrologers use the language of astronomers in their claims to foretell the future. Alchemists use the language of chemistry to explain how they turn lead into gold. Likewise, psychology is burdened with a plethora of pseudoscience, almost all of it promulgated by people who are not psychologists. People who would never offer a thought about nuclear physics are perfectly willing to offer theories about personality, psychopathology, social behavior, and child development. Some of these theories are reasonable; others are silly and simplistic. But they are often reported in the popular press as if they were established facts (Lilienfeld, 1998; Lynn et al., 2003). Much of this pseudo-psychology is benign and does little harm, but some of it is far from benign. Often the people behind these theories are well-meaning individuals who are scientifically naïve. The major problem occurs when they put such ideas and theories into action and thus cause harm to unsuspecting persons. As the philosopher Goethe (1749–1832) noted, "Nothing is [more] terrible than ignorance in action."

One example involves the theory of recovered memories of childhood sexual abuse (Bass & Davis, 1988, 1994; Loftus & Ketcham, 1994; Loftus & Polage, 1999). Research suggests that childhood sexual abuse is more common than most people think and is a major social problem. But some therapists have claimed to see evidence of sexual abuse, and even "satanic" or ritualistic abuse, in a surprising number of their clients. Parents, grandparents, teachers, and family friends have been accused of such abuse after the patients, with the help of a therapist, have "recovered" their memories of the abuse.

Few people doubted that the therapists involved were well meaning and caring, but scientific research shows that the methods that these therapists used to help their clients almost certainly created memories of events that may never have occurred. Not long ago, these therapists were telling other people how naïve they were to not realize the extent of sexual abuse. Today, they are more likely telling juries why they should not be found guilty of malpractice for not knowing the most basic scientific facts about human memory—facts that would certainly have discouraged them from using their techniques (Danitz, 1997).

Another example is the application of a procedure called *facilitated communication* in the education and treatment of nonverbal persons with autism. The method has the person with autism use a keyboard with the assistance of a facilitator, such as a teacher or therapist. People with autism, who for all of their lives had been uncommunicative and considered mentally retarded, suddenly began to communicate avidly, typing complex messages with the aid of a facilitator. Professional excitement soared as some 2000 speech therapists and special education teachers rushed to learn this new technique. The whole concept of autism was overturned; hundreds of autistic persons were put into facilitated communication programs; and parents of autistic children were profoundly affected, because their children were apparently communicating with them, revealing their love and thoughts. However, controlled experimentation revealed that the communication had not been produced by the autistic persons at all but, rather, by the facilitators, who were subtly, and unknowingly, guiding the autistic persons' responses (reviewed by Jacobson, Mulick, & Schwartz, 1995).

Why were so many parents and professionals so gullible? Because they fervently wanted to believe that their children, clients, and students really did have clear and complex thoughts. The critical point is that they had failed to be skeptical. They had failed to recognize one of the most elementary ideas in scientific research: that any phenomenon can have more than one explanation, and, as you will learn in later chapters, only controlled research can eliminate alternative explanations. In this case, there were two explanations: (1) the child with autism is communicating and (2) the facilitator is communicating. Because they wanted to believe, they chose explanation (1) and failed to apply the most basic critical evaluation. (Their problem, perhaps, was that they had not taken a good course in research methods.)

Most pseudoscience in psychology is not meant to be malicious, but it can easily end up that way, tearing people's lives apart. Being muddleheaded can be every bit as dangerous as being malicious when you are playing with people's lives. The science of psychology has taught us that people's experiences and impressions are not always correct. It has provided real solutions to critical problems, including better teaching methods, more effective treatment for psychological problems, better ways to solve social problems, and ways to help people to deal with the world around them. The pseudoscientific nonsense that masquerades as psychology presents simplistic explanations for complex phenomena, often giving people confidence in ideas and actions that they should view with skepticism. However, pseudoscience has never provided real solutions to real psychological problems. In contrast, the hardheaded scientific research of dedicated psychologists has led to hundreds of improvements in everyday lives. This is why psychological research is so important and this is the reason for this course and this textbook. This issue is discussed in *The Cost of Neglect 1.1* box.

THE COST OF NEGLECT 1.1:   *Science and Pseudoscience*

Pseudoscience uses unscientific methods, theories, assumptions, and conclusions that pretend to be scientific. The ideas are wrapped in distorted, erroneous science, but with enough of the trappings of science to be convincing. The intent of pseudoscience is to be convincing, not to be true. Being convinced by such claims can lead people to engage in behavior and activities that are, at best, ineffective in helping people to reach their goals and, at worst, could be harmful.

Among the most common practitioners of pseudoscience are television advertisers. Their attempts to cloak the supposed benefits of their products with the trappings of science are often blatantly obvious. The scene is a physician's office or a science laboratory, with perhaps a nurse or a lab assistant working in the background. The actor is everybody's idea of the mature and dependable scientist or physician—a well-groomed, professional man (seldom a woman), wearing a white lab coat and possibly with a stethoscope hanging from the pocket. Some colorful, but probably meaningless, charts are on the wall. He holds up a package of the product and in a smooth, professional voice tells us how effective it is. Even if the words science and research are never spoken, the entire staged set is meant to convey the scientific backing of the product. Unfortunately, many people fall for it.

Pseudoscience can appear convincing, so how do you recognize it? To identify pseudoscience, ask yourself three questions: (1) What is the nature of the evidence for the claims that are made? (2) In what forms is the evidence reported and made public? (3) What are the affiliations of the supposed scientists?

The evidence for pseudoscience is typically a presentation of personal testimonials, use of authority figures (like the fake physician in the TV commercial), and reports of medical or scientific cases. All this is anecdotal evidence, presented in a convincing manner and uncritically accepted by the public. Personal testimony, case reports, and other anecdotal evidence can be starting points for legitimate research, but in pseudoscience they are almost always the primary or only evidence. The major problem with anecdotal evidence is that it is not gathered under controlled conditions. It is highly selective evidence, carefully chosen from many possibilities. In pseudoscience, to prove that a product or idea really works, you need only to put forth some cases in which it did seem to work and ignore cases in which it clearly did not.

Pseudoscience almost never presents its data in mainstream science journals, in which there is quality control through peer review by other scientists. Rather, it is reported in popular magazines, in newspaper articles, on the Internet, on television, and in radio broadcasts. Unlike scientific journals, these outlets do not provide the details needed to evaluate the validity of the claims and procedures.

Pseudoscientists rarely practice their science in academic or industrial settings. Many are freelance individuals, or private businesses with impressive-sounding titles, or obscure institutes or colleges. They typically are not affiliated with mainstream universities, colleges, or laboratories, where their work would be subjected to review by other professionals.

Be alert to pseudoscience; be careful about uncritically accepting anecdotal evidence. Practice some healthy skepticism! A good reference is *Voodoo Science: The Road from Foolishness to Fraud* (Park, 1999).

<table>
<tr><td>Quick-Check
Review 1.5:
Psychology</td><td>1. What were some of the more influential schools of psychology?
2. What is the nature of modern mainstream psychology?
3. Why is it critical that psychology be scientific and objective?
4. Is psychology a social, physical, or biological science?</td></tr>
</table>

<table>
<tr><td>*PUTTING IT
INTO PRACTICE*</td><td>Nothing helps you to learn material better than to create an organizational system in your head before you study the material. Each chapter in this text begins with an outline, which will give you the organizational system for that chapter. However, it would be a very good idea to create your own organizational system for the course. Take 30 minutes and page through the text. Your goal is just to see what topics are covered and when, not to learn all the material in the book. This half-hour preview of the text will make it easier to learn and organize material throughout the course.

Take another 30 minutes to explore the resources on the textbook website (*www.ablongman.com/graziano6e*). You will find that the website has several tutorials, extended discussion of topics, and useful study resources, such as the online study guide and practice quizzes.</td></tr>
</table>

Chapter Summary

Science is a systematic way of asking and answering questions—a disciplined curiosity. There are many ways to gain knowledge, including tenacity, intuition, authority, rationalism, empiricism, and science. Science combines rationalism and empiricism. Scientists organize their thinking rationally and seek facts through empirical observations. Empiricism enables scientists to test their rationally derived theories.

The combination of rationalism and empiricism was first developed in ancient Greece, but was later weakened by a shift to more rational and abstract approaches to knowing the world, particularly as influenced by Plato. Medieval Christian scholars used science, but considered it secondary to theology. Scientific thought increased through the Renaissance and emerged by the 17th century as largely independent of religion. By the 20th century, science had developed into a widely accepted way of thinking about the universe. As the power of science increased, concern about its implications also increased, leading to the development of ethical guidelines that continue to evolve, even to this day.

Psychology is a relatively new scientific discipline that studies behavior. It has grown from a small discipline to a vast enterprise studying hundreds of basic and applied issues. Psychology's research methods are drawn primarily from the natural sciences.

Using the sophistication of science in studies of human behavior is critical, because observations and impressions are often deceiving. What people think is true about human behavior often turns out to be false when studied with scientific rigor. Furthermore, many of the simplistic theories that have been offered by people not well grounded in the science of psychology have proved to be less than useless, often causing considerable harm. Psychology cannot tolerate pseudoscience, because psychological applications affect the lives of people in significant ways.

In psychology, as in all science, there has been continued debate and refinement of ethical guidelines for research. Every student must be familiar with these guidelines and must recognize their importance in this modern world.

Chapter Exercises

1. Define the following key terms. Be sure that you understand them. They are discussed in the chapter and defined in the glossary.

psychology
science
scientific research
process of inquiry
skeptic
serendipity
tenacity
intuition
authority
rationalism
logic
empiricism
naive empiricism
sophisticated empiricism
orderliness belief
experimentation
theology
phylogenetic continuity

psychophysics
structuralism
functionalism
psychodynamic theory
psychoanalysis
Gestalt psychology
behaviorism
mentalistic
behavior modification
humanistic psychology
cognitive psychology
cognitive science
behavioral medicine
health psychology
behavioral neuroscience
mainstream psychology
pseudoscience

2. Explain this statement: For some types of decisions, most of the common ways of knowing are insufficient, and we need the precision of science.

3. Your friend asserts that scientists "can't make up their minds—they argue with each other constantly, and they even change their views from one time to another. So how can they claim they know what they are talking about when they can't even stick to their views or agree with each other?" How would you answer this?

4. Review the criteria for pseudoscience. How can you recognize it? Identify several examples of pseudoscience that are currently in the popular culture.

5. Suppose you are in a discussion or a debate and the topic is "hard" sciences versus "soft" sciences. Someone argues that psychology is not a true science at all. How would you defend the proposition that psychology is a true science?

6. Think about the problems that women and minorities had entering universities and professions in the first part of the 20th century. Consider those problems in the light of today's society. Are there comparable barriers today to groups of people?

7. A common belief is that scientists and artists are fundamentally different types of people with little in common. A scientific person supposedly cannot appreciate art, and the artistic person cannot understand science and math. If you were talking with someone who asserted this, how would you respond?

2

Research Is a Process of Inquiry

> *Science is built up with facts, as a house is with stones. But a collection of facts is no more a science than a heap of stones is a house.*
>
> —Jules Henri Poincaré 1854–1912

Web Resource Material

Research is a systematic search for information—a process of inquiry. It can be carried out in libraries, laboratories, schoolrooms, hospitals, factories, in the pages of the Bible, on street corners, or in the wild studying a herd of elephants. Research can be carried out anywhere, on any phenomena in nature, and by anyone. Scientists, rabbis, and head chefs can all carry out systematic inquiry in their own domains. Although all research is a systematic process of inquiry, not all research is scientific. A religious scholar might study religious writings. The scholar's research is a serious, systematic process of inquiry, but it is not, and it is not meant to be, scientific. What distinguishes scientific research from other research is the emphasis in science on using integrated empirical and rational processes. This chapter introduces the concepts on which science is built, the assumptions of science, and the most powerful tool in science—theories. The chapter closes with a description of a model that provides the organization for this text.

The Scientific Process

In Chapter 1 you learned that science is a way of thinking. In this section, you will learn what that means. The section starts with the basic assumptions on which all science rests. It then describes the two fundamental processes of science, observation and inference, which represent the empirical and rational elements of science, respectively. It then introduces conceptual models before discussing the use of both inductive and deductive thinking.

Basic Assumptions of Science

Every discipline, including science, is built on **assumptions**—ideas that are tentatively accepted as being true without further examination. Science makes few assumptions, preferring to subject most ideas to the rigorous demands of rational and empirical challenges. Nevertheless, the assumptions underlying science provide a strong platform for understanding nature. Whatever their particular discipline, scientists share the following basic assumptions about nature:

1. A true, physical universe exists.
2. Although there may be randomness and thus unpredictability in the universe, it is primarily an orderly system.
3. The principles of this orderly universe can be discovered, particularly through scientific research.
4. Knowledge of the universe is always incomplete. New knowledge can, and should, alter current ideas and theories. Therefore, all knowledge and theories are tentative.

The assumption that theories and knowledge are tentative is as much an admonition to scientists as an assumption. Although in principle scientists can discover how the world works, no one has the wisdom to create the perfect theory. So, in time, the flaws and limitations of every theory will be exposed.

Note what is not in this list of scientific assumptions. Scientists do not assume that the entire universe is visible. In fact, scientists would argue that some of the most interesting aspects of the universe may not be detectable through human senses. Scientists routinely hypothesize about such invisible, but presumably real, forces such as gravity. However, even concepts about unseen factors like gravity must conform to the twin constraints of rationalism and empiricism. Scientists are confident in using concepts about unseen events because they constantly challenge the accuracy of these concepts. Only concepts that have survived repeated empirical challenges reach the level of "generally accepted scientific theory." Even then, scientists will challenge an accepted theory by (1) exposing its flaws with well-designed research, and/or (2) proposing a better theory, one that explains current research information and predicts and explains new phenomena that have yet to be studied.

Observation and Inference: Facts and Constructs

At a minimum, scientific research involves the following:

1. Posing a question
2. Developing procedures to answer the question
3. Planning for, and then making, appropriate empirical observations
4. Rationally interpreting the empirical observations
5. Using those interpretations to predict other events

Scientists carefully observe events, reason about why those events occurred, and then make predictions based on the ideas developed during this reasoning process. The elements of empirical observation and rational abstraction are interlaced in a dynamic process to create a coherent understanding of the phenomena. Scientists refer to empirical observations as collecting **data,** which are the facts of research. **Facts** are those events that can be directly, empirically, and repeatedly observed, and each scientific discipline has its particular kinds of facts. In psychology, observed facts include the physiological structures of participants, the physical conditions around them, the behavior of other organisms (including the researcher), and, of course, the participants' own behavior. Most facts observed in psychology are **behaviors:** verbal behavior, nonverbal communication, physiological activity, social behavior, and so on. Scientists can observe the behavior of children at play, shoppers in stores, participants in research laboratories, clients talking about their feelings, workers at machines, or senators in debate. They can also study animal behaviors in the laboratory and in the natural environment. All these behaviors can be observed and recorded. **Observation** is the empirical process of using one's senses to recognize and record factual events.

In addition to studying behavioral facts, psychologists also study memory, emotion, intelligence, attitudes, values, creativity, thinking, perception, humor, and so on. These are not directly observable behavioral events. In other words, they are not facts. We cannot directly observe intelligence or thinking or perception, but we can observe behavior that we believe to be related to these unobservable concepts. For example, in some early work with children with autism (Graziano, 1974), we observed that the children frequently exhibited highly disruptive behavior in which they injured themselves and others and caused upheaval in their therapy program. Their behavior was a fact; it was repeatedly observed, measured, and recorded. Treatment reduced both the intensity and duration of the disruptive behavior, but not its frequency. That is, the children were "blowing up" just as often as before treatment, but the episodes were shorter and less intense. We had made progress, but still wanted to reduce the frequency of these outbursts. Continued careful observation revealed a subtle, but observable, change in the child's behavior just prior to the outbursts. All activity stopped, the child's facial expression became contorted, their limbs stiffened, and then the severe behavior exploded. We could find no external cause for these facial and body changes that reliably preceded the outbursts. Therefore, we inferred that, just prior to their outbursts, the children were feeling some intense internal arousal which may have cued the outbursts. Thus, we reasoned, to reduce the frequency of the outbursts, we would have to control the internal arousal. But how were we to accomplish this? From the behavior therapy research literature, we selected an approach called systematic desensitization (Wolpe, 1958, 1990), which employs relaxation training as a first step. Although used with adults, it had not, to our knowledge, ever been applied to children. Given our inference that the children's aroused state triggered their outbursts, it seemed a reasonable approach to try. We trained the children in relaxation, and soon the frequency of their outbursts decreased to zero.

This example illustrates the distinction between our observations of behavior (the outbursts and the facial expressions that preceded the outbursts) and our inferences of an internal condition (the arousal). The internal condition is not observable; it is inferred from the observations of behavior. An **inference** is an intellectual process in which conclusions are derived from observed facts or from other ideas.

Scientists draw inferences from observations of events, and most psychological research deals with inferences. When psychologists study anxiety, intelligence, or memory, they are working with inferences. Because inferences are largely drawn from empirical observations (the facts), it is critical that the observations be precise. Otherwise, little confidence can be placed in any inference that one draws. We need to use precisely defined empirical methods in research in order to develop a solid observational base for drawing inferences about events that cannot be directly observed. Inferences can also be drawn from other inferences, but in science an important starting point for making inferences is careful observation. In general, the better the observational base, and the more ways in which inferences are tied to that base, the more confidence scientists have in those inferences. When making inferences, we should stay close to the data. As Detective Sergeant Joe Friday used to say to witnesses in the old *Dragnet* television series, "Just give us the facts, ma'am." He might have added, "We'll draw our own inferences."

When a researcher draws an inference about a research participant, the inference resides in the researcher and not in the participant. The process involves the researcher's rational activity of accepting the sensory data (the observations) as true and then drawing from those observations an idea (inference) about events that were not observed. With the autism example, the inference was that a state of arousal existed. The inferred state of arousal was not a fact; it was an idea. In other words, the inference of an internal arousal was not in the child; it was an idea created by the researchers, who had no direct observation of what was really going on in the child. The hypothesis of an internal arousal, although plausible, should not be confused with reality. It is an explanatory idea. It helped to explain the observed behavior, and it helped to generate a possible course of action that proved to be effective. This is an important point. Inferred events, such as gravity, electricity, intelligence, memory, anxiety, perception, id, and ego, are all rational ideas that have been constructed by researchers. Ideas constructed in this way by the researcher are called **constructs.** Constructs are used analogically; that is, *as if* they exist in fact and *as if* they really have a relationship with observable events. In the example, the researchers never observed the children's internal states of arousal. They operated *as if* the inferred state actually existed and would be reduced if the children were trained to relax. Furthermore, they predicted that if the inferred state were reduced, then the frequency of the disruptive behavior would decrease.

The analogical nature of constructs must never be forgotten. A construct may be used so frequently that people begin to think of it as a fact, and they lose sight of its very tentative, analogical nature. For example, some people may believe there really is an id, an ego, or a superego inside each of us. These constructs take on a reality that they were never meant to have. Confusing a construct for a fact is a logical error known as reification of a construct. **Reification of a construct** is just one of several errors that scientists avoid by using logic in their work. Some of the more common errors are described in Table 2.1.

Scientists use both observations and constructs in their day-to-day work. Note the relationship between the construct of internal arousal and the observed facts in the example of the children with autism. First, the construct was inferred from observed behavior. Then the construct was used as a basis for predicting new behavior that could be observed—specifically, that reducing the internal arousal would reduce the disruptive behavior. Thus, the construct is related to observed facts in two ways: it was derived from the observations, and it served as a basis for predicting future observations. You learned in Chapter 1 that science involves the continual, interactive movement between empirical observation and rational abstractions. Now you can see that this interactive movement is between observations and constructs. The scientist moves from one to the other and back again, at each step refining constructs from observations and predicting new observations from constructs. This process provides a description or explanation of relationships among facts and constructs. With the children, the relationship between the observations and the constructs provided a potential explanation of the observed phenomenon of disruptive behavior. We then used the construct as if it adequately represented what was really happening, although we could not observe all the parts.

Inductive and Deductive Thinking

Sherlock Holmes buffs will probably argue that the great detective never said it, but the statement attributed to Holmes, perhaps first voiced in a movie version, has entertained and misled people for years. You know the scene: at the site of the crime Holmes inspects the room, his keen eyes darting and his nose alert to lingering tobacco smoke. Suddenly, with an explosive "Aha!" he pounces on a partially burnt matchstick cracked in the middle with a small flake of tobacco stuck to its tip. Holmes examines it closely and then announces, "Our culprit, Watson, is 44 years old, 5 feet 8½ inches tall, and 173 pounds. He is right-handed, a veteran of the India conflicts, and still carries a lead bullet in his right calf. He is a gentleman, Watson, and had no intention of committing a crime when he entered this room. He left hurriedly by way of that window when he heard us at the door, and, if I am not mistaken, he will return here to confess his crime and will knock on that door precisely . . . now!"

A tentative knocking is heard at the door. Watson opens it revealing the gentleman so precisely described by Holmes.

"Egads, Holmes!" says Watson, wide-eyed. "How did you ever know that?"

"Deduction, my dear Watson," says Holmes. "A simple process of deduction."

Actually, it was not deduction alone. What Holmes should have said was "Induction–deduction, my dear Watson. . . . A simple process of induction–deduction."

TABLE 2.1   *Logical Interpretation Errors*

Reification of a construct is one of many problems that scientists are trained to recognize and avoid. Listed here are others. You may have used some of these in your everyday thinking. Everyone does. But in science, fuzzy thinking interferes with the challenging work of understanding nature.

Errors	Description
Nominal Fallacy	People commit this error when they mistake the naming of phenomena for an explanation of the phenomena. For example, if you recognize that some people consistently behave aggressively, you might appropriately label them as aggressive. But you may also be tempted to explain their aggressive behavior by noting that they are aggressive people. The label, based on their behavior, later becomes the explanation for their behavior—an entirely circular argument.
The All-or-None Bias	This is a tendency to see a statement as either true or false, when in most cases in science the statement is probabilistic. Most good theories explain many things, but they almost never explain everything under every condition. Therefore, they are technically false, although scientists tend to view them as true because they are often, although not always, true. It is best to remember that no theory is completely true; rather, it provides accurate explanations for a certain percentage of situations or events.
Similarity-Uniqueness Paradox	This is the tendency to view two things as either similar to one another or different from one another, when in reality they are probably both. For example, two people may be similar in their backgrounds but different in their aspirations. People have a tendency to simplify such comparisons, which can often blind them to important elements.
Barnum Statement	This effect is named after P. T. Barnum of the Barnum and Bailey Circus, who is alleged to have said "there is a sucker born every minute." Barnum statements appear to be insightful comments about an issue, when in fact they are nothing more than statements that are true for almost all issues, situations, or people. For example, telling someone that she "tries to do what is right but sometimes finds that temptation is strong" will probably be readily accepted by most people as an insightful comment on their personality. But it is not insightful at all. You can say the same thing to 100 different people at random, and almost all of them will be impressed by your insight.
Evaluative Biases of Language	Science should be nonjudgmental, but the truth is that language often inserts subtle judgments into the descriptions of objective behaviors. For example, if a person cuts off a telemarketer in the first few seconds of a call by saying, "I do not take unsolicited sales calls," is the person being assertive or aggressive? Labeling the behavior as assertive gives a very different impression than labeling it as aggressive.

Assuming that the great Holmes could in fact have drawn such complete conclusions from such limited evidence, his process was one familiar to everyone. He observed some specific clues and inferred (the *induction*) something he could not directly observe—specifically, the type of person who would have committed the crime and left those clues. Holmes then made the prediction (the *deduction*) that the man would return.

When we reason from the particular to the general, we are using **inductive reasoning;** when we use the more abstract and general ideas to return to specifics, that is, to make predictions about future observations, we are using **deductive reasoning** (Copi &

02:01

Cohen, 2002).[1] The rational processes of induction and deduction are used constantly by scientists. A researcher who begins with empirical observations and then infers constructs is engaged in inductive reasoning. Using constructs as the basis of making predictions about new, specific observations is deductive reasoning. A scientist must use both processes to build and validate conceptual models.

Inductive–deductive reasoning is not unique to science; these processes are used constantly in everyday life. When I return from work on a cold winter day and find the front door left partly open and a single muddy sneaker on the hall rug, I inductively infer "the kids are home from school." Knowing a good deal about these kids, I can also deductively predict that right now my daughter Lisa is upstairs talking on the telephone with one of her friends. I can then go upstairs to make observations and check the accuracy of my predictions. From the specific observation to the general idea, from the general idea back to the more specific observation, these are the processes of induction and deduction.

People have been thinking inductively and deductively all their lives, although probably not with the precision of the scientist. This last point is important. Although scientists use the same kind of reasoning processes used in everyday life, they must use these processes with a precision rarely seen in everyday life. Indeed, the entire scientific research enterprise can be seen as the development of a framework within which scientists can carry out inductive and deductive reasoning under the most precise conditions.

Building on a point made in Chapter 1, the essence of science is its process of thinking, a process that entails systematic inductive–deductive logic. Science, more than any other way of gaining knowledge, bases its inductive reasoning on carefully observed facts. Making the observations or getting the facts is one of the critical components of scientific research. Thus, the enterprise of scientific research uses facts to fuel the inductive-deductive process and obtains the facts with the greatest precision possible.

Quick-Check Review 2.1: The Scientific Process	1. What are the data in psychology?
	2. How do facts and constructs differ?
	3. What is reification of a construct?
	4. Explain the two ways in which constructs are related to facts.
	5. What are the basic assumptions that all scientists accept about the universe?
	6. What is the difference between inductive and deductive reasoning?

Models and Theories in Science

Scientists study many phenomena. Their research helps to solve such practical problems as building bridges and curing disease, and also leads to basic discoveries about nature. However, regardless of the phenomena studied or the goals of the research, scientists develop

[1]Psychologists tend to use the concepts of induction and deduction as discussed here. However, philosophy students will recognize that this distinction is incomplete, distinguishing only one kind of induction from one kind of deduction (Reese, 1996).

and use theories. It has been said that a major goal of science is to develop good theories because, in science, there is nothing more useful and practical than a good theory. This section begins by defining theories and discussing how they are developed and used by scientists. Then four types of theories are defined. The section ends with a discussion of the importance of judging theories on both their usefulness and their accuracy.

A **theory** is a formalized set of concepts that summarizes and organizes observations and inferences, provides tentative explanations for phenomena, and provides the bases for making predictions. To be scientific, a theory must be testable; that is, it must make specific predictions that can be tested empirically. Furthermore, a theory is scientific only if the predictions can be contradicted by empirical evidence. In other words, a theory that predicts everything can never be contradicted. Such a theory is useless, because it says that anything at all could happen. Scientific theories must be able to stand the test of *disconfirmation* or *falsifiability* (Popper, 1959).

A good theory demands a solid empirical base and a set of carefully developed constructs, neither of which can be created easily. Scientific theories are not mere guesses and hunches, nor are they flimsy and ephemeral flights of fancy. They are carefully constructed from empirical observations, constructs, and inductive and deductive logic. In building theories, the scientist brings together and integrates what has been learned about the phenomena under study. Developing adequate theories that organize, predict, and explain natural phenomena is a major goal of scientists.

It is often difficult for a beginning student to appreciate the importance of theory to science. Theory is not required in order to use most of the procedures described in this text to discover new facts, but the facts will be much less useful without the organizing framework of theory. Theory provides a blueprint that organizes facts into ideas and ideas into an understanding of the world. Scientists want their theories to be functional and strong. A functional theory works; it explains how variables are related to one another. A strong theory makes specific predictions that can be confirmed by empirical observation. The strongest theories make unique predictions, that is, predictions that other theories do not make, and these predictions are consistent with subsequent observations. Scientists prefer **parsimony** (literally, the thrifty or economical); a simple, straightforward, thrifty theory is preferred over a complex theory if the theories provide equivalent predictive ability. A single theory that explains several different phenomena is preferred over several theories that collectively explain the same phenomenon. The principle of parsimony, however, never supersedes the concept that the theory must possess **validity;** that is, it must make specific testable predictions that are confirmed by observation.

Theories are the glue that holds science together, and they are the mechanism that allows scientists to build on the work of other scientists. Even the most brilliant scientists would never be able to make significant breakthroughs if they had to reinvent each finding and concept before moving on to more challenging questions. Science builds on existing science, moving our understanding of nature to the next level. This basic principle is nicely illustrated in *Historical Lesson 2.1,* which discusses the real story behind the first successful powered flight of the Wright brothers.

02:02

All scientific theories involve both induction and deduction, but they often differ in the degree to which they emphasize one or the other. Theories that emphasize induction, called **inductive theories,** stay very close to the empirical data. Inductive theorists follow the data wherever they may lead. Skinner (1972, 1990) epitomized this inductive method of

HISTORICAL LESSON 2.1:   The Wright Brothers as Scientists

It is often said that the Wright brothers invented the airplane in a burst of Yankee ingenuity. They have been portrayed as mechanical tinkerers in their bicycle shop, whose achievement had little to do with systematic scholarship and research. But in a 1906 interview, the Wrights complained about the way in which they were described in newspapers, noting, "Nearly every writer has characterized us as mechanics, and taken it for granted that our invention has come from mechanical skill. We object to this as neither true nor fair. We are not mechanics; we are scientists" (Oppel, 1987, p. 18). The Wright brothers were referring to their years of study of theoretical principles of flight, their knowledge of the many possible forms of aircraft, and their awareness of the attempts at and successes of lighter- and heavier-than-air flight by their predecessors. The Wrights used careful development, experimentation, and testing in their Ohio workshop and on the windy sand dunes near Kitty Hawk, North Carolina.

The brothers built on the previous work of scientists and engineers. More than a hundred years earlier, George Cayley had developed mathematical principles of mechanical flight. He built and flew models and full-sized gliders and established the fixed-wing concept for aircraft, a major departure from the earlier (and later) flapping-wing contraptions. His book, *On Aerial Navigation*, provided descriptions of a future flying machine, including its lift surfaces, stabilizer, engine, and propellers. In 1889, Otto Lilienthal, a German engineer, published *Bird Flight as the Basis of Aviation*. Lilienthal became the first person to make controlled, heavier-than-air flights, making more than 2000 successful glides in his biplanes and monoplanes. In 1896, with relatively light gasoline-powered engines available, Lilienthal was working on a design for a powered airplane. Unfortunately, he was killed in the crash of one of his gliders before he could develop a powered airplane. Octave Chanute, a civil engineer, followed Lilienthal's work and developed a number of gliders, publishing *Progress in Flying Machines* in 1894. In 1901, he gave the Wrights both his expertise and enthusiastic support.

On hearing of Lilienthal's death, the Wrights increased their efforts. Building on the work of Chanute, Lilienthal, Langley, and others, the Wrights perfected their gliders and raced to achieve powered flight. They learned that Samuel Langley, a physicist at the Smithsonian Institution, was also close to success. Langley had successfully flown a small-scale model of a steam-driven airplane in 1896 and a larger gasoline-powered model in 1902, which were the first unpiloted flights of powered airplanes. All was set in December 1903 for Langley to test his human-piloted, gas-powered airplane. However, his attempt failed, and the press concluded that heavier-than-air flight would not be developed for hundreds of years. Just nine days later the Wright Flyer I, propelled by a 12-horsepower engine and piloted by Orville, flew successfully at Kill Devil Hill.

A long process of scientific and technological advances led to the work of Lilienthal, Chanute, Langley, and the Wrights. This history included the early work of Leonardo da Vinci in the 1500s, the successful balloon flights from France to England in the late 1700s, the improvement of propeller designs by Jean-Pierre Blanchard in 1797, several books on the mathematics and physics of mechanical flight published from 1780 to the 1890s, and the development of the gasoline engine. The Wright brothers developed powered flight within the context of this vast array of scientific and technical development. Building on the work of many others, they added the final developments that made powered flight possible. Their experimentation was neither mere tinkering nor their own solitary invention, but was based on knowledge of all the preceding work. Their achievement is a good example of how science builds on previous discoveries to expand the scientific knowledge base and to create new technologies.

---

theory construction. He built his theories on extensive observational data, being careful not to extend the theory beyond the data. In an eloquent presentation only days before his death, Skinner (1990) continued to argue that there are serious risks associated with postulating theories that go well beyond the data and that involve processes not directly observable.

The more traditional formalized theory, the **deductive theory,** emphasizes deductions from constructs. The deductions are stated as hypotheses and are then empirically tested through research. An example is Meehl's (1990) theorizing about the underlying cause(s) of schizophrenia. Meehl postulated a strong theory that made specific deductive predictions. The theory is tested every time a prediction is investigated and is weakened when a prediction is not confirmed. Unlike Skinner's more inductive theories, Meehl's deductive theories go well beyond the data, challenging scientists to make new observations. It is worth noting that Skinner and Meehl were colleagues during their early careers at the University of Minnesota. Their discussions on the role of theory in science must have been intense and dynamic.

Most psychological theories are **functional theories** that place fairly equal emphasis on induction and deduction. All three types of theories have the same characteristic functions: organizing knowledge, predicting new observations, and explaining relationships among events.

A fourth type of theory is the **model.** Any phenomenon can be represented by a model. The word *model* derives from the Latin *modulus*, meaning a small measure of something. In science, it has come to mean a miniature representation of reality. A model is a description or analogy that helps scientists to understand something usually unseen and/or more complex. A model is somewhat less developed than a formal theory. Consequently, models are sometimes referred to as "mini-theories." A model airplane is a good example. It clearly is not equivalent to a real airplane. It has the general form and many of the characteristics of a real airplane, such as wings, rudder, propellers, and/or jet engines. Although these characteristics may correspond faithfully to those of a real airplane, the model is not an exact replica of the real airplane. It is smaller, does not have all the working parts, and is constructed of balsa wood or plastic instead of metal alloys or carbon fibers.

A model represents reality; it does not duplicate it. Models are useful, because constructing and examining a model helps scientists to organize knowledge and hypotheses about the reality represented by the model. They can examine a model, observe relationships among its parts, and observe how it operates. They can generate new ideas from the model about how the real world is constructed and how it operates. For example, a model airplane in a wind tunnel can give researchers ideas about how a real airplane might behave and lead them to new ideas or hypotheses about the design and operation of real airplanes. The original stealth fighter, the F-117A Nighthawk, started out as a model. The model demonstrated that a plane could be built that was virtually undetectable by radar (Ball, 2003). Likewise, our model of the relationship of internal arousal and disruptive behavior in children with autism led us to new applications of behavior therapy.

Models can be constructed to represent any aspect of the universe. We can build models of airplanes or the solar system, of an atom or a bacterium, of wave motions, neurons, memory, thinking processes, or genetic structure. Our knowledge of any phenomenon can be organized into models to represent reality. Furthermore, the models need not be physical in their construction, such as a balsa wood airplane. They can be abstract or conceptual models, constructed of ideas and expressed in verbal and/or mathematical language. The classical model of human memory is a good example of an abstract model. It assumes multiple levels of memory, with each level having its own characteristics. The sensory store is assumed to hold extensive information for a very short period of time (about one second). The short-term memory holds information longer (about 15 seconds), but has a restricted capacity. The long-term memory provides the long-term, high-capacity storage that people usually think of when they think about memory. Few cognitive psychologists believe such structures exist or that their model is the way information is stored and processed. But a model does not have to be real or true to be useful. It need only make accurate predictions about relationships between observable events. The classical model of memory is a strong one, because it is based on hundreds of independent observations. In other words, the model is closely tied to the observational base on which it was first developed. Furthermore, the model proved useful by correctly predicting new observations that were confirmed by careful scientific study. It is not a perfect model of memory and will be replaced by better models as research identifies relationships that the model cannot predict or explain. In fact, this model of memory has already been seriously challenged. Nevertheless, it is convenient and useful and has contributed enormously to our understanding of how individuals remember things.

Models can also be purely mathematical. For example, there are mathematical models in the field of artificial intelligence (AI) that describe how learning agents can modify their behavior in response to reinforcement signals and thereby increase the reward they receive (Sutton & Barto, 1998). Built on the mathematics of linear algebra and dynamic programming, these models use a system of simultaneous equations to describe the interaction between a learning agent (i.e., a person, laboratory animal, or robot) and its environment. As the agent gradually modifies its behavior to increase the number of rewards, these modifications directly correspond to successively better approximations of the equations' solutions, thereby increasing the rate of reinforcement. These mathematical models help us to understand the role of reinforcement in learning.

All models share the following characteristics:

1. Models are simplified representations of phenomena and have point-to-point correspondence with some of the characteristics of the phenomena.
2. Models provide convenient, manageable, and compact representations of the larger, complex, and mostly unknown reality.
3. Models are incomplete, tentative, and analogical.
4. Manipulating models helps organize information, illustrate relationships among parts, create new ideas and predict new observations.

You should not think of models and theories only in terms of whether they are right or wrong (that is, in terms of their validity). Scientists also judge models and theories by how useful they are in organizing information, explaining phenomena, and generating accurate predictions. For example, the theory of Newtonian mechanics is clearly wrong, at least at high speeds. When objects move at a velocity approaching the speed of light, they do not behave the way Newtonian mechanics predict. Einstein's general theory of relativity describes the movement of objects accurately regardless of how fast the object is traveling. But Newtonian mechanics survives and is taught extensively in high school and college. Why? The reason is simple. Everyday objects hardly ever travel at speeds approaching the speed of light. Therefore, the theories developed by Newton accurately describe the motion of most ordinary objects. The theory survives, because it is useful and accurate in a wide range of situations.

Science and Art
Although many people think of science and art as very different enterprises, they actually have much in common.

"This is Gronski's new model of the synaptic transmission mechanism. Nobody understands it, but it won third prize in the campus art competition."

Quick-Check Review 2.2: Models and Theories in Science

1. What is a *theory* and how is it useful in science?
2. What is the difference between inductive and deductive theories?
3. What is a *model,* and how is it used in science?
4. Distinguish between observation and inference.
5. Why should theories be judged on both their usefulness and their accuracy?
6. What is meant by falsifiability in science?

A Model of the Research Process

We can study almost any phenomenon scientifically and develop a model to represent it. One purpose of a model is to help organize the activities of the person using the model. This section presents a model of psychological research methods to serve as an outline for the text. The model of research presented here is a variation of a model presented by Hyman (1964). Like any model, this one is not a complete representation of reality. It simplifies the complexity of psychological research in order to organize some important aspects of the research process. The model of research presented here has two dimensions: phases of research and levels of constraint.

Phases of Research

Psychological research usually proceeds in an orderly manner through successive phases. This sequencing of phases can vary, but the most general sequence is described in Table 2.2. The concept of **phases of research** provides one dimension of the conceptual model on which this text is based. Research begins with ideas and flows through the successive, overlapping phases of the research process. Each phase has its own characteristics. Different work is accomplished in each phase in preparation for the next phase. This aggregate flow of activity constitutes the process of research.

02:03

Idea-Generating Phase.   All research begins with an idea. For example, a researcher may have an interest in children's reasoning processes, but no particular idea for a research project. The interest, however, is enough to point the researcher to an area within which more defined ideas can be developed. Being interested in the area to be studied is critical in helping to sustain the work to follow. This repeats the point made in Chapter 1 that the scientist's curiosity is critical in research, both in helping to generate ideas and in sustaining the researcher's efforts.

The idea phase can begin with vague thoughts, and initial ideas can emerge in very unscientific ways. Archimedes is supposed to have had a flash of creative thought while sitting in a bath. Ideas can be generated while conversing, reading novels, watching television, walking in the woods, buying a hamburger, crossing the street, or even while dreaming. However, getting research ideas is not usually so unsystematic, and most research ideas are generated in a systematic fashion from other research results. Research ideas vary from unsystematic hunches to highly systematic and precise steps in logical thinking. The former are most characteristic of **exploratory research,** which occurs in the early history of a research area; the latter are characteristic of research at more advanced levels of the research area.

We should not be too quick to criticize initial ideas, because premature criticism might destroy an emerging good idea. Early ideas ought to be taken seriously and nourished. Curiosity, interest, hunches, and enthusiasm are important ingredients in science.

TABLE 2.2   *The Phases of a Research Study*

Research Phase	Activity
Idea-generating phase	Identify a topic of interest to study.
Problem-definition phase	Refine the vague and general idea(s) generated in the previous step into a precise question to be studied.
Procedures-design phase	Decide on the specific procedures to be used in the gathering and statistical analysis of the data.
Observation phase	Use the procedures devised in the previous step to collect your observations.
Data-analysis phase	Analyze the data collected, using appropriate statistical procedures.
Interpretation phase	Compare your results with the results predicted on the basis of your theory. Do your results support the theory?
Communication phase	Prepare a written or oral report of your study for publication or presentation to colleagues. Your report should include a description of all the preceding steps.

Once an area of interest is identified, it is useful to dive right in by reading articles and books and talking with people who work in the area.

Little is known about the processes involved in the creative idea-generating phase of research, although this is beginning to change (McGuire, 1997). Indeed, here is a good area for research: How are creative ideas generated? What seems clear is that productive scientists have many ideas. When asked in a television interview where scientists find their good ideas, the Nobel Prize winner Linus Pauling replied, "Well, you have lots of ideas, and you throw out the bad ones."

Problem-Definition Phase.   The research process begins by identifying an area of interest and generating ideas for study. Vague ideas, however, are not sufficient. They must be clarified and refined. In this part of the process, the scientist examines the research literature and learns how other researchers have conceptualized, measured, and tested these and related ideas. This careful examination of the literature, usually called library research, is an important part of science. Appendix C provides a brief overview of this process, and the Student Resource Website has a much more extensive tutorial on library research. The published research literature provides the detailed information that is critical in understanding the complexity of a research problem. The scientist continues working on the ideas, clarifying, defining, specifying, and refining them based on what he or she has learned from the research literature. The goal is to produce one or more clearly posed questions based on (1) well-developed knowledge of previous research and theory, and (2) the scientist's own ideas and speculations.

02:04

Carefully conceptualizing and phrasing the research question is critical, because everything the researcher does in the remainder of the research process will be aimed at answering this question. The question might involve a highly specific and precise hypothesis or it might be phrased in a much more general manner, which is more typical of exploratory research. The research questions will largely control the way the rest of the process is carried out. The activities of the problem-definition phase are rational, abstract processes that manipulate and develop ideas toward the goal of refining those ideas into researchable questions. This rational process is used to prepare for the next phase, in which the procedures to make the observations are designed.

Procedures-Design Phase.   The design phase is active, systematic, and complex. Much of the content of research methods courses focuses specifically on this phase. Before any data are collected, the researcher must determine which observations to make and under what conditions, how to record the observations, what statistical methods to use to analyze the data, and so on. The researcher also makes decisions in this phase about what participants to test. Since decisions are being made about using living organisms in research, ethical issues must be considered. The ethics of scientific research includes guidelines for humane treatment of participants. Before the researcher contacts a single participant, the research plan must survive ethical evaluation and must be modified whenever ethical guidelines are not met.[2] Only when the plan can stand up to ethical challenge does the investigator proceed with the next phase—making observations.

---

[2]The ethics of psychological research is a major area that every researcher must know, understand, and be able to apply.

Observation Phase.   Making observations (getting data) is the most familiar phase to beginning students, who often see this as actually "doing the research." This is the empirical phase in which the researcher carries out the procedures that were designed in the previous phase and makes observations of the participants' behavior under the conditions specified. The observation phase is central in all science. Note that the earlier phases serve as preparation for making the empirical observations, and the remaining phases focus on using those observations by processing, interpreting, and communicating them. All scientific research revolves around this most central aspect of the process—making empirical observations.

Data-Analysis Phase.   In the data-analysis phase, the researcher processes and makes sense out of the data. Recall that the data-analysis procedures are selected in the design phase, before the data are gathered. As you will see later in this text, many design decisions, such as sample size, will follow from the choice of data-analysis procedures. In almost all psychological research, the data will be in the form of a numerical record representing the observations made and the numerical data must be organized and analyzed. Statistical procedures are used to describe and evaluate numerical data and to help to determine the significance of the observations. The statistical procedures might be as simple as counting responses and drawing graphs to show response changes over time, or they may be as complex as a two-way analysis of variance (described in Chapter 12). Whatever the statistical procedures, the important point is that the researcher must choose procedures that are appropriate to the question being asked and to the observational procedures being used. As you will see in Chapter 14, the choice of statistical procedure is determined by the nature of the question and the observational procedures.

Interpretation Phase.   Having statistically analyzed the data, the researcher interprets the statistical results in terms of (1) how they help to answer the research question and (2) how this answer contributes to the knowledge in the field. The interpretation relates the findings, not only to the original questions, but also to other concepts and findings in the field. This stage represents the flip side of the problem-definition phase. When defining the research problem, scientists use theories to suggest important questions. Here the scientists use the answers to their questions to determine how accurately their theories predict new observations. The problem-definition phase uses deductive reasoning, working from the general theory to the specific prediction. The interpretation phase uses inductive reasoning, working from the specific results of the study back to the generality of the theory. The results of a study may suggest ways to expand or modify the theory to increase its usefulness and validity.

Communication Phase.   Science is a public enterprise, a critical component of which is the communication of research findings. Scientific communication occurs through presentations at scientific meetings and through publication in journals and books. Scientists communicate not only the results, but also the procedures used and the rationales behind them. Specific guidelines are used to organize concisely all the information needed in a research report. Such guidelines are provided by the *APA Publication Manual* (2001). Writing a research report in APA style is covered in Appendix

02:05
02:06

B. In addition, there is an extensive tutorial on writing in APA Style on the textbook website, as well as a reference source for APA style.

Scientific publications should describe procedures in detail, not only so that other scientists can understand the research, but also to allow them to replicate it. **Replication** means repeating a study to see if the same results are obtained. If a research finding cannot be replicated, then considerable doubt is cast on the genuineness of that finding. By presenting full accounts of research rationale, procedures, findings, and interpretation, the researcher is making the work available for others to evaluate. The writing of a research report should be clear and concise, and not like Calvin's book report in the *Calvin and Hobbes* cartoon reproduced here.

In the research process, each project can serve as the basis for further questions and further empirical research. That follow-up research may be conducted by either the initial researcher or by other researchers. Now we have come full circle, back to the beginning phase of generating ideas. In a developing field of research, the ideas for asking new questions and making new observations are mainly ideas that have been generated by previous research. Scientists are stimulated by the work of their colleagues and derive research questions from them. In turn, their own work stimulates others. Figure 2.1 illustrates the circular nature of this process.

Scientists use two major avenues for communicating their work. The most formal is written communication in books and scientific journals. These reports become a permanent record, part of the archives of a scientific discipline. They are preserved and can be retrieved and studied by colleagues soon after publication or many years later. A minor disadvantage of written reports is that the publication process is lengthy. It usually takes a year or more for written reports of completed research to become available in journals and books.

More immediate and more interactive are the researcher's oral and graphic presentations made at scientific meetings, as well as informal communication among colleagues.

Calvin and Hobbes

by Bill Watterson

Scientific Writing This is not how one should write research reports.

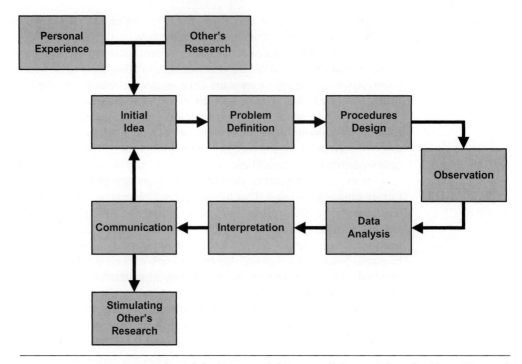

FIGURE 2.1 *A Representation of the Process of Conceptualizing and Carrying Out a Research Project* Each research project goes through several phases, from initial idea to final communication of findings. Ideas for research are generated both from sources outside the specific research project and from ideas generated within the research process. Research findings also stimulate new ideas in other researchers.

Scientists visit each other's laboratories, talk on the telephone or during poker games, exchange letters and e-mail, and so on. This informal, highly interactive network of communication has been called the "invisible college," and it serves the important function of keeping scientists in communication with each other. Indeed, some believe it is the most critical means of communication among scientists. It is important for the young researcher, if seriously interested in a research career, to become involved actively in this invisible-college network of communications (Osberg & Raulin, 1989).

The nature of this exchange of research findings has been changing rapidly in the information age. Journals are still the major source for disseminating research findings. An increasing number of these journals are online (e.g., Winerman, 2004). However, even online journals are unable to get new information out to other researchers rapidly enough. Many researchers routinely post prepublication versions of their articles online before they appear in journals. Research organizations often announce recently accepted articles by their members in their newsletters and on their websites. Scientists are also testing methods of publication that would provide free access to research articles through the Internet instead of forcing libraries or researchers to purchase expensive journals (Harper, 2004). Often an e-mail is all that is needed to get a copy of an article months before it appears in press.

The move toward putting more and more information online for instant access is accelerating. For example, Google is now planning on making entire libraries available online (Rupley, 2004). It is getting easier and cheaper for scientists to communicate what they have learned, and the result is that science is better able to build on the available knowledge, extending our understanding.

The research process just described is common to all sciences. Particular observations may vary from one discipline to another, because each discipline is interested in observing and understanding different phenomena. But the basic processes and the systematic way of studying problems are common elements of science, regardless of each discipline's subject matter. The process, and not the content, distinguishes science from other ways of knowing. Content—the particular phenomena and facts of interest—distinguishes one scientific discipline from another.

Although it is generally true that research proceeds in the sequence described here, the sequence of phases is not rigid. New ideas might occur while the researcher is involved in the data-analysis phase, and he or she might design and run another study before interpreting and communicating the results of the first. It is also common for some of the phases, such as data-analysis and interpretation, to overlap while the researcher moves back and forth among them.

The empirical observation phase is the center of the research process. Researchers first generate and refine ideas, sharpening them into answerable questions. They then decide on the procedures to use to answer the questions. All this work is in preparation for the central activity of making empirical observations. The remaining phases focus on analyzing these empirical observations and determining and communicating their importance. This central activity, making empirical observations within a systematic rational process, is what characterizes science as a process that is different from other ways of seeking knowledge. Note that in this process, the scientist moves through a systematic, consistent cycle: rational thinking, followed by empirical observations, followed by more rational thinking. All research revolves around the empirical component. The more systematically and carefully we make the observations, the more solid will be the database on which we build an understanding of psychological phenomena.

Levels of Constraint

Chapter 1 discussed the various ways in which people have pursued knowledge: tenacity, intuition, authority, rationalism, empiricism, and science. In the order listed these approaches range from making low to high demands on the adequacy of the information used and on how that information is processed.

Of these approaches, science is the most demanding. Within science itself, already at the high-demand end of this continuum, there are many approaches to gaining knowledge. Some scientific approaches place fewer demands on the adequacy of the information and the nature of processing it; others place more demands. Thus, within scientific research, some methods are more demanding than others, but they all have their useful place in the scientific research scheme. We call this continuum of demands on the adequacy of the information **levels of constraint.**

Within each level of constraint, the researcher must make decisions about how to develop the research plan. The plan may be general, leaving the ideas, questions, and procedures relatively unrefined. This is common in exploratory research undertaken early in the investigation of a phenomenon. On the other hand, the plan might be detailed and refined, with precise hypotheses, procedures, and statistical analyses. In each of these two extremes, the researcher moves through all the phases, but each is obviously at a different level of refinement. Exploratory research is lower constraint and makes relatively few demands for structure or precision on the procedures in each phase. In contrast, highly refined research projects are higher constraint and make many demands on the procedures.

For example, suppose that a psychologist is operating a special training program for exceptional children and has just admitted some children diagnosed with moderate mental retardation. To plan adequately, the psychologist might want to know whether these children behave aggressively. Answering this question would not be difficult; the psychologist could ask the parents or could go into a room with several of the children and watch them for a few hours. These observations might generate some tentative ideas about the aggressive behavior of children with moderate retardation. Continuing the research process, these observations and tentative conclusions might then be reported to colleagues in the program, perhaps in a staff meeting. As simple as this procedure seems, it is a complete process of empirical research from original idea to communication of results. It is not highly detailed or structured, but it is research.

Note that, because of the noncomplex nature of the question and the observational procedures, there was little demand that the question or procedures be precise, complex, or highly structured. If something interesting and unexpected is noticed, the observation procedure can easily be modified to follow up on this observation. Here, the activities in each phase are flexible. As the research questions become more complex and precise, the activities in each phase of research must become correspondingly more precise and controlled. Increased control is most readily seen in the observation phase of the process. As control over the conditions and methods of observation is increased, more constraints on the researcher's freedom to be flexible are imposed.

In essence, in the search for precision, we give up flexibility. In almost all research decisions, scientists are required to make trade-offs, and every design decision has a price associated with it. Beginning students often believe that the best way to conduct research is always to be precise and controlled. But precision and control may not always be the ideal, because sometimes the loss of flexibility is too great a price to pay.

The idea of constraint provides a second dimension for our model of the research enterprise. The two dimensions are:

1. **The phases of research.** Each complete research project proceeds along this dimension from original ideas to communication of new ideas.
2. **The levels of constraint.** This dimension is one of precision, structure, and control. Projects of the highest precision demand the greatest constraint on activities in each phase; constraint is most clearly seen in the controls imposed in the observation phase. *Levels of constraint* refer to the degree to which the researcher imposes limits or controls on any part of the research process.

These concepts form a two-dimensional descriptive model of research, which is outlined in Table 2.3. Note that the table gives names to the successive levels of constraint, ranging from the lowest constraint (naturalistic observation) to the highest constraint (ex-

TABLE 2.3   *A Two-Dimensional Model of Scientific Research*

This model of the research process includes a range of five levels of constraint; each is defined by the precision and/or flexibility of the observational procedures and/or settings. Regardless of the level of constraint, each research project goes through the same phases, from initial idea to final communication.

	Phase of Research						
	(1) *Idea-Generating*	*(2)* *Problem Definition*	*(3)* *Procedures Design*	*(4)* *Obser-vation*	*(5)* *Data Analysis*	*(6)* *Interpre-tation*	*(7)* *Commu-nication*
Levels of Constraint							
Naturalistic observation							
Case-study method							
Correlational research							
Differential research							
Experimental research							

perimental research). With the exception of differential research, these are all commonly used labels. The term *differential research* represents a broad class of research often overlooked in research methods texts (Hyman, 1964). All the constraint levels represent scientific research and combine observation and rational inference.

Some researchers hold the view that only high-constraint methods can properly be considered scientific. In our model, all these methods are scientific and can be effective when used properly. The use of a particular constraint level is determined by the nature of the question being asked, the precision of the existing knowledge, and practical and ethical constraints. For example, when Jane Goodall (Goodall, 1986, 1988; Goodall & Marks, 2003) was interested in learning about the social behavior of chimpanzees, naturalistic observation was the most appropriate method. Her research produced new knowledge about these animals. Her questions were general and flexible, so the level of research had to be equally general and flexible. High-constraint research would not have been appropriate and could not have given the information sought. The general nature of Goodall's questions was not a flaw in her work. Any scientist breaking new ground might very well start with just such low-constraint questions. Although all the levels of research in our model are scientific, scientists try to refine their questions so they can be answered using the highest constraint level possible, given both current knowledge and the practical and ethical constraints on the researcher.

Note that Table 2.3 is blank except for the labels of the phases of research and the levels of constraint. This table is essentially the outline for the remainder of the text. Later chapters will provide the information that defines each of the implied cells in this two-dimensional model.

Like the phases of research, constraint levels are overlapping rather than sharply categorical. This constraint dimension should be understood as forming a continuum and the labels (naturalistic, case study, and so on) as indicating bands or portions of the continuum. The number of levels identified for this model of research is not critical in understanding the research activity that the model seeks to represent. The important concept is that constraint ranges from low to high, and that these five labels are adequate for describing most psychological research. Later chapters will discuss the levels of constraint in more detail. Here each is briefly defined, with Table 2.4 summarizing these definitions.

Naturalistic Observation.   **Naturalistic observation** requires the researcher to observe the behavior of participants in their natural environment and to make no attempt to change or limit the environment or the behavior of the participants. The only constraints that do exist are those that researchers impose on their observational methods. However, researchers usually are not bound by strong hypotheses that demand a particular set of observational procedures. Therefore, they are free to shift their attention to any behaviors that seem interesting. This flexible approach is common in the early stages of research on a given topic and is useful in generating hypotheses that can later be tested in higher-constraint research. Such flexible techniques are replaced by higher-constraint procedures as researchers develop familiarity with an area. It is important to make the distinction between naturalistic observation, as defined here, and higher-constraint research in naturalistic settings. As you will see in Chapters 6 and 13, research in naturalistic settings need not be low constraint; in fact, it often involves detailed and precise procedures.

Case-Study Research.   In **case-study research,** the researcher may intervene in the participant's functioning, such as asking questions of a participant. Even though slightly more constrained than naturalistic observation, case studies still allow the researcher flexibility to shift attention to whatever behaviors seem interesting and relevant. Case-study research is not limited to research on psychopathology or psychotherapy. Rather, these methods can be applied to many issues.

Correlational Research.   **Correlational research** requires greater constraint on the procedures used to measure behavior. The setting can range from a naturalistic one to the highly constrained setting of a scientific laboratory. However, because researchers are

TABLE 2.4   *The Levels of Constraint of Scientific Research*

Level of Constraint	*Description*
Naturalistic observation	Observing participants in their natural environment. The researcher should do nothing to limit or change the environment or the behavior of the participants.
Case-study research	Studying the participants in a moderately limiting environment, intervening to a slight degree, and observing the participant's responses.
Correlational research	Quantifying the strength of the relationship between two variables. The measurement procedures must be carefully defined and precisely followed.
Differential research	Comparing two or more preexisting groups of participants. The setting is usually highly constrained, and the measurement procedures must be carefully defined and precisely followed.
Experimental research	Similar to differential research, except that the participants are randomly assigned to groups or conditions in the study.

interested in quantifying the relationship between two or more variables when they use the correlational method, they must use precise and consistent procedures for measuring each variable. As you will see, knowing the relationship between two variables allows researchers to predict the value of one variable from the value of the other.

Differential Research. **Differential research** involves comparing two or more groups of participants. To make the comparison meaningful, the variables must be measured in exactly the same way in each group. That is, the settings and observational procedures must be constrained across groups. When done properly, the only thing that is not identical across groups is the variable that defines the groups. In differential research, the variable that defines the groups is a **preexisting variable** that is not under the researcher's control. Such preexisting variables can include clinical diagnoses, age, IQ, gender, and so on. For example, research comparing adults born and raised in Canada with adults born and raised in England is differential research that utilizes preexisting groups.

Experimental Research. In **experimental research,** comparisons are made among participants under different conditions. A major difference between differential and experimental research is the way that participants are assigned to the groups or conditions. In experimental research, participants are assigned to conditions randomly. In contrast, differential research assigns participants based on a preexisting variable that is not within the researcher's control.

The concept of level of constraint does not represent a single dimension. Some levels differ on the basis of the constraint applied to the setting in which the observations take place, some differ on the basis of the constraint placed on the measurement procedures, and others differ on the basis of the constraint placed on the participant selection and assignment. But as the researcher moves from low-constraint methods to high-constraint methods, more constraint is placed on more aspects of the research. In pure naturalistic observation, the constraint is placed only on the observer. In pure experimental methods, every aspect of the study is planned in advance, and explicit procedures must be followed throughout the study.

Once the constraint level of the question has been determined, then the remainder of the research process must be carried out at this same level of constraint. For example, it would be a mistake to draw high-constraint conclusions from low-constraint data. Also, suppose that we are trying to conduct a field experiment in a school setting. It would be a political mistake to try and force high-constraint laboratory methods upon the classroom. We would not be allowed to randomly remove some children from the classroom and assign others to different experimental conditions. We would not be allowed to alter the seating arrangements in the room or to change the duration of class periods. We would not be allowed to stop all traffic in the hall outside the room to control noise, and so on. It would not work; the principal would probably throw us out for disrupting the school. You will understand more about levels of constraint as you proceed through this text. For now, just remember that when we mix constraint levels, we run the serious risk of distorting information.

A major function of low-constraint research is the generation of ideas for higher-constraint research. Conclusions drawn from well-executed, low-constraint research can serve as the starting points for high-constraint questions and research methods. For example, when a clinical psychologist observes a consistent pattern of reported childhood trauma in clients with depression, she might ask, "Now that I have observed these consistencies in my clinical sample, do the same consistencies hold in the general population of depressed persons?" This question could lead to research utilizing careful sampling procedures to select participants who adequately represent the general population of depressed people. In this example, it would be unwarranted to conclude that childhood trauma is associated with depression based only on a single clinical sample from a single therapist. The clients of this psychologist might be unusual in some way, thus creating the impression that childhood trauma is typical of clients with depression. Concluding that all depressed individuals have childhood trauma, based only on this one clinical sample, would be a large leap from her low-constraint data to higher-constraint conclusions. By asking the question as posed above, she could have moved from low- to higher-constraint research.

As we move from low- to high-constraint research, the procedures and findings become more precise. However, we also run the risk that the procedures will become more artificial and more removed from the real world, and therefore less relevant. To help to reduce this **precision-versus-relevance-problem,** researchers should carry out their research at the highest constraint levels possible and then test their findings in natural settings. For example, there is a growing concern about the possible dangers of using a cell phone while driving. Research has shown that driving is not significantly impaired by listening to a radio or tape. However, manipulating equipment, such as dialing a cell phone or adjusting the radio, does interfere with driving (Briem & Hedman, 2001). But what are the effects of actually holding a conversation on the phone while driving? A high-constraint laboratory experiment can be set up using a driving simulator and participants presented with a standard set of road challenges, such as a child suddenly darting in front of the vehicle. The reactions of the participant drivers would be electronically recorded and scored. Participants could be assigned to conditions, such as having a cell-phone conversation while driving and having no cell-phone use while driving, and their driving performance compared.

Strayer and Johnston (2000) carried out this type of high-constraint laboratory experiments to simulate cell-phone use while driving. The participants manipulated a joystick to track a constantly moving pattern on a video screen. At unpredicted times a red or green light flashed. At the red light the participant was to press a "brake button" on the joystick. Participants were randomly assigned to three groups: radio control, hands-free cell phone, and hand-held cell phone. The researchers found that response to the red light was not disrupted by listening to the radio, but was negatively affected by having cell-phone conversations in both the hands-free and hand-held cell phone conditions. They concluded that the driving disruption was mediated through interference with attention to driving, regardless of whether the driver's hands were actually on the cell phone. They followed up this study with additional research to pin down exactly what was happening. They found that it was neither holding the phone nor even speaking, but rather carrying on a conversation on the phone, which distracted the driver (Stayer & Johnston, 2001). Stayer et al. (2003) studied the problem further by using sophisticated eye-movement monitoring of participants driving in a simulator and carrying on a conversation with another party on a hands-free cell phone. They found that the conversations disrupted normal scanning, and thus negatively affected driving performance. In a newspaper interview, Stayer emphasized that conversations on hands-free and hand-held phones are equally dangerous (Hafner & George, 2005). Laws that allow hands-free use, he said, are sending the wrong message, because they suggest that hands-free use is safe, when it actually is not.

This high constraint research provides precise answers to this question: Does cell-phone use disrupt simulated driving and increase the chance of driver error? It can serve as a good basis for making public policy about cell-phone use in automobiles. However, as compelling as the research is, we cannot be sure that the laboratory findings would hold in the natural environment. Therefore, it would be useful to design laboratory settings that more closely resemble real driving and to follow up the laboratory findings with research on cell phone use in actual driving conditions. However, if you think about this research, you will realize that there are both practical and ethical reasons that restrict researchers' choices in situations in which there might be danger to the participants. These and other ethical concerns will be covered in Chapter 3. The rationale for verifying laboratory results in natural settings—that is, seeking **ecological validity**—will be discussed in Chapter 8.

Quick-Check Review 2.3: A Model of the Research Process	1. What are the two main dimensions of the model of research presented in this section?
	2. Name the phases of research.
	3. Define levels of constraint.
	4. What is the major difference between differential and experimental research?
	5. What is *ecological validity?*

Putting It Into Practice	To appreciate the process of research, you might consider doing a little research project of your own. Look around and find something interesting. For example, you might notice people studying in the library who are making faces as they read. You might ask yourself whether this is common, and observe other people. You could ask whether there is a gender difference in this phenomenon, or whether the type of material that the person is studying makes a difference. Use the phases of research described in this chapter to guide your informal research. Find something that really interests you to make this exercise fun, and let your curiosity run wild.

Chapter Summary

Scientists use empirical observations and rational thinking to study natural phenomena. Based on specific empirical observations, the researcher employs a rational intellectual process of inductive inference to develop more general constructs that represent events that cannot (yet) be observed. Using these more general constructs, the researcher then makes deductive inferences or predictions, which can be tested with observations. The inductive-deductive process (specific to general to specific process) is highly interac-

tive, and it ties together the empiricism and rationalism basic to scientific thinking.

Research is a process of inquiry in which the researcher poses a question and proceeds systematically to gather, analyze, interpret, and communicate the information necessary to answer the question. The central part of this research process is making empirical observations. All activities that take place prior to the observations are preparation for the actual gathering of data. All activities following the observations focus on analyzing, interpreting, and communicating these observations.

A two-dimensional model of the research enterprise provides the framework for this text. The two dimensions are (1) the phases through which each research project progresses and (2) the levels of constraint at which the research is carried out.

Chapter Exercises

1. Define the following key terms. Be sure that you understand them. They are discussed in the chapter and defined in the glossary.

assumptions of science	model
data	phases of research
facts	idea-generating phase
behavior	exploratory research
observation	problem-definition phase
inference	procedures-design phase
constructs	observation phase
reification of a construct	data-analysis phase
nominal fallacy	interpretation phase
all-or-none bias	communication phase
similarity-uniqueness	replication
paradox	levels of constraint
Barnum statement	naturalistic observation
evaluative biases of	case-study research
language	correlational research
inductive reasoning	differential research
deductive reasoning	preexisting variable
theory	experimental research
parsimony	precision-versus-
validity	relevance-problem
inductive theory	ecological validity
deductive theory	
functional theories	

2. Think of some issue in your life and try to generate as many general research ideas as you can. You might begin some of your questions with "I wonder what would happen if . . . ?" or "I wonder why . . . ?" For example: "I wonder why I wake up every morning just a moment or two before my alarm rings?"

3. For these brief descriptions of research, identify the level of constraint.

   a. A therapy researcher has several clients with similar problems. He compares their statements in therapy to see what might be common among all of the cases.

   b. A researcher compares participants' reaction times to visual stimuli in a laboratory setting.

   c. Two groups of rats are compared for their accuracy in running a maze. One group is fed just before the comparison, and the other is fed four hours earlier.

   d. Third-grade and sixth-grade classes are compared based on their taste preferences.

   e. A researcher observes prairie dog colonies to learn more about their behavior.

   f. A researcher evaluates the relationship between the number of calories consumed and weight.

4. Here's a challenge to your creativity! Create a reasonable conceptual model that might explain each of the following phenomena.

   a. Huge centuries-old drawings have been found on the ground in Central America. They are so large that they can be seen only from hundreds of feet in the air. However, there were no aircraft in existence at that time.

   b. People who are usually rational and controlled can nevertheless become highly emotional and irrational when in a crowd.

   c. Despite the fact that adolescents and young adults know the danger of certain behaviors, such as smoking, many nevertheless continue those behaviors.

   d. Many people overeat to the point of becoming obese.

   e. Siblings can look, think, and act very differently from one another, even though they have the same parents and have been raised in the same family.

5. A radio talk-show host argues "Let's face it folks, evolution is only a theory; it's not a fact!" As a scientist, how would you answer that?

3

The Starting Point: Asking Questions

It appears to me that . . . philosophical . . . difficulties and disagreements . . . are mainly due to a very simple cause: namely to the attempt to answer questions without first discovering precisely what *question it is which you desire to answer.*

—George Edward Moore, *Principia Ethica,* 1903

Web Resource Material

Research methods are used to answer specific research questions, and formulating the right question is one of the most critical elements of good research. This chapter begins by covering the process of formulating and refining questions for research. It then introduces some of the language that is critical in understanding research questions and describing them to other professionals. This includes defining the various types of variables used in research. The concept of *validity*, perhaps the most central concept in all research, is also introduced in this chapter. Finally, the chapter ends with a discussion of research ethics.

Asking and Refining Questions

Scientists begin research by asking questions. A question is a problem or statement in need of a solution or answer. What are the causes of child abuse? Why are some things so hard to remember? How can we get drunk drivers off the road? Why do some people become depressed? Questions are everywhere; all you have to do is observe and be curious. This section describes several common sources of research questions. It also discusses refining a research question in preparation for a study.

Pursuing Your Personal Interests

Your own interests and observations can lead to personally relevant research. For example, you might be interested in emotions, memory, creativity, or social interactions, or you might wonder about some aspect of yourself or your family members. You may be puzzled by something you observe and ask yourself, "Why did that happen?" Any of these interests or observations can serve as a starting point for research.

Following Up on the Work of Others

Research often raises more questions than it answers, and these new questions can serve as starting points for more research. Examples of theories and research that have generated considerable study are Freud's (1938a, 1938b) psychoanalytic theory, Skinner's (1938, 1972) research on learning, Miller's (1971) work on physiological influences on motivation, Bandura's (1969) research on modeling, Festinger's (1957) theory of cognitive dissonance, Lovaas's (1973) research with autistic children, Seligman's studies of learned helplessness and depression (Abramson, Seligman, & Teasdale, 1978; Seligman, 1974), Gleick's (1987) discussion of chaos theory, and the controversy surrounding repressed memory (Bass & Davis, 1988, 1994; Loftus & Ketcham, 1994; Loftus & Polage, 1999). You can derive ideas from existing research by studying published research on a topic. The more you know about a research area, the stronger will be the base for generating new research ideas. For beginning students, it is difficult to read journals and recognize the new questions that are explicitly and implicitly being posed. Secondary sources, such as textbooks or review chapters, are often more useful. For example, the *Annual Review of Psychology* publishes review chapters on as many as 24 research areas in psychology each year. It is an excellent source of cutting-edge information for both students and professionals. Textbooks typically provide more background information on a given topic, making it easier to understand an area, but textbooks tend to be less comprehensive and less cutting edge than review articles or review chapters. These sources, designed to teach about particular areas, devote considerable space to explaining ideas. In contrast, research journals have severe space restrictions, and most articles are condensed and difficult to understand unless you already have a good background in the area under study. As you gain sophistication in research and in particular areas of research, journal articles become the major source of information.

Libraries have well-organized systems for identifying relevant research by topic and/or authors. These systems allow students and scientists alike to quickly locate relevant research. Most of these systems are now computerized, making the task of finding relevant research easier than ever before. In psychology, the *Psychological Abstracts* are the primary source of such data. Its online version, *PsycINFO,* provides abstracts of literature from 1887 to the present and includes more than one million records. Other important abstracts include *Index Medicus* (the online version is *Medline*) and the *Social Sciences Citation Index.* Reference librarians are very helpful to students seeking to learn how to search abstract systems. Appendix C covers the basics of library research. A more detailed tutorial on library research is included on the Student Resource Website.

03:01

Theories and prior research raise questions for further research in two ways: heuristically and systematically. **Heuristic influence** occurs when a proposed theory or a set of research findings generates interest, including disbelief or outright antagonism, and in this process suggests further research questions. The works of Darwin and Freud are good examples of theories that have had heuristic influence. **Systematic influence** occurs when theories or research provide explicit, testable propositions for further research. Research on conditioning, for example, has systematically generated considerable new research. Both types of influence are important to the continued development of science.

Applied and Basic Research

Research is often categorized as either *applied* or *basic*. Much of psychology is **applied psychology**—psychology focused on solving real-world problems. Consequently, much of the research in psychology is **applied research,** in which the goal is to find solutions to practical problems. Applied research questions in psychology are fairly easy for the beginning student to generate. Table 3.1 lists some examples. Try generating some of your own.

TABLE 3.1 *Examples of Applied Research Questions*

1. How can we train people to be better drivers?
2. What can department stores do to reduce shoplifting?
3. How can a teacher or parent help an underachieving child to improve academically?
4. What placement of dials and levers on a machine will best reduce worker fatigue and errors?
5. What is an effective approach to calming children before and after surgery?
6. How can nuclear-power-plant control rooms be designed to minimize operator error?
7. How can psychologists change human behavior on a large scale so as to reduce the incidence of such diseases as lung cancer and AIDS?
8. How can society promote better parenting to reduce child abuse?
9. What can be done to reduce violence in society?
10. What is the most effective treatment for depression?

Basic research, also known as **fundamental research** or **pure research,** is designed to increase scientific understanding of phenomena without any particular practical goals. Basic research findings often become incorporated into applied research. For example, basic research on language development in children might be used to develop training methods for persons with language deficiencies, emotional problems, or developmental disabilities.

Unfortunately, it is often more difficult for basic researchers to obtain financial support than it is for applied researchers, perhaps because those who allocate funds do not realize the importance of basic research as a necessary background for most applied research. Think of it this way: solving practical problems requires a background of knowledge, and much of that information comes from basic research. It is difficult for even the most creative of individuals to imagine the applications an area of research might have until some basic understanding of the area is achieved.

In many cases, research does not break down neatly into either applied or basic research. Instead, the findings of a study contribute both to applications and a basic understanding of a problem. Table 3.2 lists some recent examples of basic research.

Refining Questions for Research

Research begins with a question. The question is gradually refined until it becomes specific enough to give the researcher a clear direction for answering it. Developing the initial question is critical, because it determines how the research should be conducted. Beginning students may wonder what level of constraint to use, what observational methods are best, or how to select the right statistical tests. Answers to these and similar issues lie partly in the nature of the question asked. Once the initial question is refined, then these other decisions follow.

Suppose that a team of psychologists is studying the parenting behavior of elephants in the wild. They want to know how long baby elephants are dependent on their parents or other adults, whether and to what degree male and female elephants engage in parenting,

---

TABLE 3.2 *Recent Examples of Basic Research*

1. Studying the nature of the sleep-wake cycle and the factors that regulate it (Easton et al., 2004)

2. Studying bimodal neuron functioning in the parietal lobe (Graziano, Cooke, & Taylor, 2000)

3. Studying the process of associative learning in animals (Pearce & Bouton, 2001)

4. Identifying the factors that influence the development of visual attention in infants (Colombo, 2001)

5. Studying the neural basis of hearing in everyday situations (Feng & Ratnam, 2000)

6. Identifying the mechanisms by which the body regulates food intake (Duva et al., 2005)

7. Studying how cross-cultural language differences can influence the perception of color (Davidoff, 2004)

8. Studying the influence of testosterone level on the accuracy of special memory (Okkelova et al., 2003)

9. Studying ethnic and educational differences that affect the impact of cortisol on awakening (Bennett et al., 2004)

10. Studying differences in retina sensitivity to threat-related stimulation (Calvo & Castillo, 2005).

and whether a baby elephant's care is shared by other adult elephants. These questions can be further refined as follows:

1. In their natural habitat, which adult elephants assist in the birth and early care of infant elephants and in the primary care of the growing young?
2. At what age do young elephants raised in their natural habitat become independent from parents and/or caretakers?

Note two important points about the initial questions. First, the questions specify the behavior to be observed: parenting behavior of the adults and independent behavior of the young. Second, the conditions under which the observations are to be made (the elephants' natural habitat) have also been identified in the question. These specific elements are referred to as **variables.**

A variable is any set of events that may have different values. Height is a variable because organisms and inanimate objects exist at different heights. Gender is a variable because there are two genders. Behavior is a variable, because a great number of actions can be performed. Any specific behavior, such as aggression, can be a variable, because it can occur in different forms and degrees. Some variables can be easily manipulated, such as the amount of food eaten. Manipulating food intake might change other variables, such as the eater's weight; at least that's the hope of dieters.

In the study of elephants' behavior, two variables are of interest: (1) the setting in which the elephants are observed and (2) the behavior of the elephants. Elephants can be observed in many different settings, including zoos, circuses, and natural habitats. This study will focus on the natural habitat of elephants, where the elephants' natural behavior is likely to be so variable and complex that the researchers will want to simplify it by establishing broad categories into which behavior can be classified.

Note that the initial questions have also begun to narrow the choices of just how this research will be designed and conducted. By specifying the natural habitat, the researchers are committed to low-constraint observations in natural settings. Because the questions are about the normal flow of behavior under natural conditions, the researchers will use naturalistic observations of the animals without manipulating the animals' behavior in any way.

In formulating initial questions, researchers proceed through a lengthy process of thinking about their area of interest, posing loosely defined questions, studying the research literature, and gradually refining their ideas into research questions. This process might take researchers far from their starting point, and their refined questions might be very different from the original questions. They are guided in this process of refining ideas into researchable questions by the theories and research of other investigators. Theories are particularly important in this enterprise, because good theories organize and structure vast amounts of information into a few general concepts. Theories often act like maps of research areas, revealing which areas are well understood and which areas could benefit from additional research.

Once refined, the initial question implicitly helps to identify the major variables of interest and to structure the design and conduct of the research. The level of constraint of a research project, and therefore the degree and types of controls, the kinds of observations, and even the kinds of statistical analyses to be used, depend largely on the nature of the question.

In general, researchers try to develop the initial question to the highest level of refinement possible given the state of knowledge about the particular area of interest. The more they know about an area, the more refined the question will be and the more likely that high-constraint research methods will be used to answer it. In areas in which little is known about a phenomenon, the initial question will be correspondingly unrefined and less specific, and the procedures will therefore be carried out at lower constraint levels. In the example of elephants' parenting behavior, the question was general, rather than detailed and specific, because little was known about such behavior in elephants. It was impossible to define critical behaviors because the researchers were not sure what behaviors might be included in the broad category of parenting. They did not want to constrain the observations by trying to be overly specific about what behaviors to observe and how and when to observe them. Doing so might have caused them to miss something important that had not been expected. In this case, the researchers wanted to maintain maximum flexibility, so no constraints were placed on the behavior of the elephants and few constraints were imposed on the researchers, other than to avoid interfering with the elephants. Had more been known about elephants before beginning the research, the questions would have been more specific and the researchers' behavior would have been more constrained by a specific focus.

Quick-Check Review 3.1: Asking and Refining Questions	1. What are the main sources of research questions? 2. How do you distinguish between applied and basic research? 3. What is a *variable*? 4. How can basic research be valuable in solving practical problems?

Types of Variables in Research

All research involves studying the relationship among variables. There are several important ways of classifying psychological variables, which are summarized in Table 3.3. Variables can be classified either on the basis of their nature or on how they are used in research.

Classifying Variables Based on Their Nature

Three types of variables are defined by their nature: behavioral variables, stimulus variables, and organismic variables.

Behavioral Variables.   Any observable response of an organism is a **behavioral variable.** This includes a rat running a maze, a chimpanzee opening a puzzle box, a child playing with a toy, an adult pressing computer keys, a person playing the piano, or people talking to each other. Behavioral variables can range from relatively simple behavior, such as a single keystroke, to complex responses, such as social and verbal behavior. Because psychology is defined as the study of behavior, behavioral variables are of particular importance and are the type of variable most often observed in psychological research.

TABLE 3.3   *Classes of Research Variables*

Variables Defined by Their Nature	
Behavioral variable	Any observable response of an organism
Stimulus variable	Specific factors that have actual or potential effects on an organism's responses
Organismic variable (or subject variable)	A characteristic of an organism that can be used to classify the organism **(or subject** for research purposes
Variables Defined by Their Use in Research	
Independent variable	A variable that is actively manipulated by the researcher to see what its impact will be on other variables
Dependent variable	A variable that is hypothesized to be affected by the independent-variable manipulation
Extraneous variable	Any variable (other than the independent variable) that might affect the dependent measure in a study
A constant	Any variable that is prevented from varying

Stimulus Variables.   Behavior always occurs in a context that consists of the total situation surrounding the behaving organism and all the factors that make up that situation. Those factors that have actual or potential effects on the organism's response are **stimulus variables.** Stimulus variables may be specific and easily measurable or controllable, such as a flashing light as a signal for the participant to respond. They also may be more general, such as the total situation surrounding the participant. Examples of complex stimulus variables are the habitat in which elephants are observed or the condition of a classroom in which a child is observed. Stimulus variables range from simple, such as a light signal, to complex, such as long-term social situations. In psychological research, the researcher typically controls stimulus variables and observes behavioral variables. As research moves from lower to higher levels of constraint, the researcher increases the level of control over stimulus variables.

Some stimulus variables, such as mood, are internal to the participant. Although some procedures may affect such internal stimuli, these variables are difficult to manipulate and are generally not under the direct control of the experimenter. Nevertheless, they are still a part of the participant's environment and can affect behavior.

Organismic Variables.   **Organismic variables,** sometimes called **subject variables,** are characteristics of the participants, such as age, gender, racial attitudes, musical ability, psychiatric diagnosis, and so on. Some of the participants' characteristics, such as gender, can be directly observed and are referred to as **observed organismic variables.** Other participant characteristics, such as racial attitudes, cannot be directly observed, but are inferred from the participant's behavior. These are called **response-inferred organismic variables.** Response-inferred organismic variables are constructs, which were discussed in Chapter 2. Organismic variables can be used to classify participants. For example, researchers might measure the anxiety level of participants and then divide the participants into three groups: high, moderate, and low anxiety.

Some variables can be classified under more than one of the preceding categories, depending on how they fit into the research situation. For example, education level would normally be thought of as an organismic variable because it is a characteristic of participants. However, education level could also be a stimulus variable if the researcher provided an educational experience for participants as part of a study. It might also be a behavioral variable if the researcher is interested in the behavior of obtaining more education and what factors might influence this behavior. Thus, it is not just the characteristics of the variable that define it as behavioral, stimulus, or organismic, but also how the variable fits into the research project. It can be confusing at times, but do not despair; in a few weeks, these distinctions will be second nature to you.

Classifying Variables Based on Their Use in Research

In addition to classifying variables on the basis of their characteristics, researchers also classify variables based on how they are used in research. This section will define independent variables, dependent variables, extraneous variables, and constants.

Independent and Dependent Variables.   **Independent variables** are manipulated by the experimenter. **Dependent variables** are the participant's responses. For example, suppose that a researcher hypothesizes that verbal criticism and aggression escalate as frustration increases. Participants are randomly assigned to simulated workgroups of three persons. They are given a series of work-related problems to be solved as a group. The variables in this study are frustration and verbal criticism/aggression. The researcher manipulates the independent variable, which in this case is frustration. Some groups are given all the information needed to solve the problems readily (the no-frustration condition). Other groups have some of the information withheld so that the problem is still solvable, but with difficulty (the moderate-frustration condition). Enough information is withheld from still other groups so that the problem appears solvable but, in reality, cannot be solved (the high-frustration condition). Each group's verbal interactions are recorded and all instances of the dependent variable of verbal criticism/aggression are counted. In other words, the independent variable of frustration is manipulated, and changes in the dependent variable of criticism/aggression are observed and measured. The hypothesis is that the dependent variable will be affected by the independent-variable manipulation.

There are two kinds of independent variables: (1) manipulated independent variables and (2) nonmanipulated independent variables.[1] **Manipulated independent variables** are those that the experimenter actively controls, such as the frustration level in the preceding study. With **nonmanipulated independent variables,** also called **classification variables,** participants are assigned to groups on the basis of preexisting characteristics. The largest category of nonmanipulated independent variables in psychology are organismic vari-

---

[1]Some would disagree with using the term *nonmanipulated independent variable*, arguing that an independent variable by definition is manipulated. In general usage, however, the term *independent variable* is used more broadly to include organismic variables as possible independent variables. We have made the distinction between manipulated and nonmanipulated independent variables explicit to minimize confusion for students, while acknowledging the broad and somewhat inaccurate general usage of the term.

ables—those variables that are preexisting characteristics of the participants, such as IQ, religious affiliation, age, and political affiliation. The researcher does not actively manipulate such variables but, rather, assigns participants to groups based on them. For example, suppose that a researcher wanted to test the hypothesis that moral problem-solving skills are related to age in children. Children would be assigned to groups based on their age. They would then take a moral problem-solving test, and the test scores of the various age groups would be compared to determine whether there were significant group differences.

Researchers often hypothesize a causal relationship between the independent and dependent variables. A **causal relationship** between two variables exists when changes in one variable result in a predictable change in the other. However, as you will see in later chapters, it is difficult to draw causal conclusions without the control provided by actively manipulating the independent variable. Thus, conclusions about causal relationships in a study with nonmanipulated independent variables must be tentative.

These issues will be discussed more in later chapters. For now, it is important that you be able to make two distinctions: (1) between the independent and the dependent variable and (2) between manipulated and nonmanipulated independent variables.

Extraneous Variables.   **Extraneous variables** are unplanned and uncontrolled factors that can arise in an experiment and affect the outcome. Consequently, extraneous variables must be controlled to avoid their potential effects. For example, suppose that a researcher was studying academic learning and the dependent variable was course grade, which was based on three examinations. Cheating on the examinations would be a potential extraneous variable that might distort the measure of how much was learned (i.e., the test). Therefore, the researcher would take steps to discourage cheating. Distractions during the examinations might also constitute extraneous variables. Therefore, it would be wise to give the examinations in a quiet room to remove this potential extraneous variable.

Variables as Constants.   A **constant** is a variable that is prevented from varying. For example, suppose that a researcher is using animals in a study of the effects of hormones on learning. Earlier research has suggested that the response to specific hormones varies depending on the age and sex of the animals. The researcher decides to hold these two variables constant and uses only four-month-old male rats. Thus, sex and age are constants in this study. By holding these variables constant, they do not affect the outcome of the research. If they were not held constant or were not otherwise controlled, the results of the experiment might be due to uncontrolled variables and not to the variable(s) being manipulated.

Quick-Check Review 3.2: Types of Variables in Research

1. Define independent and dependent variables. How are they used in research?
2. Define *manipulated* and *nonmanipulated independent variables.*
3. What does it mean to hold a variable constant in research?

Validity and the Control of Extraneous Variables

Validity is one of the most important concepts in research and a central theme throughout this text. It refers to how well a study, a procedure, or a measure does what it is supposed to do. Validity is a complex idea, and there are many types of validity. Some common questions about validity are:

Does this study really answer the question it posed?
Does this test measure what it is supposed to measure?
What does this laboratory study reveal about the real world?

One fundamental task of research is to insure the validity of its procedures by including appropriate controls. This section provides a conceptual introduction to validity. However, the concept of validity will be revisited repeatedly throughout this textbook, because it is at the core of the entire research enterprise.

Recall that empirical observation can be thought of as the midpoint in the scientific research process. Observations in psychological research are usually observations of behavior, which may be influenced by many factors, some known and others unknown to the researcher. Some factors may be of theoretical interest to the researcher, whereas others may be extraneous, distorting the results and making it impossible for the researcher to draw meaningful conclusions. In other words, extraneous variables reduce the validity of the research. Thus, it is important to reduce the influence of extraneous variables on the behavior being observed.

Controls in research are the procedures used to reduce extraneous influences in research. Thus, the concept of control in research refers to the *systematic methods employed by the researcher to reduce threats to the validity of the study posed by extraneous influences on the behavior of both the participants and the observer.* Although such controls are most important in higher-constraint research, they are part of the procedures at all levels. For example, in a case-study research project, we might want to observe problem solving in children by testing each child individually. What controls might we apply in such a setting? The researcher could find a quiet place to do the testing so that the child is not interrupted by other children, who might make distracting noises or volunteer their own solutions. Even in this low-constraint research, controlling the observational setting reduces the effects of extraneous variables.

The control of extraneous variables is the heart of the research enterprise. Without control, we cannot be confident of the research findings. Virtually this entire textbook is devoted to this topic. You will learn that there are several ways to achieve control. The most powerful is to use research designs that have effective controls built into them. However, some control procedures can be added to any research study regardless of the level of constraint. For now, you need to remember two things. The first is that uncontrolled extraneous variables threaten the validity of research. The second is that effective controls exist and that it is the responsibility of the researcher to select the necessary controls and include them in the study in order to enhance validity. In later chapters, you will learn what these controls are, how to select them, and how to implement them.

Quick-Check Review 3.3: Validity and the Control of Extraneous Variables	1. What are extraneous variables? 2. Why do extraneous variables have to be controlled in research? 3. What is meant by *validity*? 4. What do controls have to do with validity?

Research Ethics

The researcher makes a series of decisions before observing even a single participant. One of the most important involves research ethics. Researchers make decisions about how they will use living organisms for research purposes. Ethical concerns must be included in the decision process. This section will focus on research ethics, but it is important to note that ethical concerns also apply to other activities of psychology, such as testing, psychotherapy, and teaching.

Ethical Principles for Human Research

Concern about ethical issues in research was first raised by the revelations following World War II of the incredibly inhumane treatment of people forced to be a part of research studies by German scientists. Such organizations as the American Psychological Association and the American Medical Association began to examine their own research practices. Although no inhumanities were found to approximate those of the Germans, concern developed that even in the United States some research participants might be treated inappropriately. For example, in the 1950s and 1960s, there were growing criticisms of biomedical research that placed human participants at risk without informing them of the risks. In some instances, live disease organisms were injected into participants or new surgical techniques were practiced on patients who were undergoing surgery not related to the new techniques. Researchers were careful to provide the best-known medical safeguards; nevertheless, these procedures were carried out without participants' knowledge and consent. To tell participants only that they were to be given a test of biological resistance, while withholding the information that the substance injected into them contained live cancer cells, is at best a serious deception.

Many professionals maintained that research participants must be protected against deception, dangerous procedures, and invasion of privacy. Participants, they said, have a right to know what is going to be done to them and to be given enough clear information that they can freely decide for themselves whether to participate. These issues continue to be debated (Reynolds et al. 2001; Rosenthal, 1994; Yassour-Borochowitz, 2004), and these debates have led to more rigorous safeguards for participants.

Psychological research with human participants is rarely physically intrusive, and the risks to participants are not as great as in some biomedical research. Nevertheless, issues of deception, invasion of privacy, and participants' right to be informed so as to be able to make a free choice still apply to psychological research. Potential **invasions of privacy** occur when researchers examine highly personal and sensitive areas of psychological adjustment, such as sexual behavior, private thoughts and fears, or the relationship of a couple. Social scientists often access confidential records of patients in hospitals or of children in schools for research purposes.

Deception involves deliberately misleading participants. Deception is frequently employed in some types of psychological research (Pittenger, 2002). Its use rose from 16% of empirical studies reported in a leading psychology journal in 1961 to 47% by 1992 (Bower, 1998). Although deception in psychological research has increased, it is generally more innocuous than in the past (Korn, 1997). However, the use of *any* deception places the participant at risk. Therefore, if deception is used, safeguards must be employed. The most common safeguards are (1) the researcher's judgment that the deception poses no serious or long-term risks and (2) explaining the true nature of the deception in a **debriefing** of the participant following the study. In this debriefing, the participant is informed about the procedures and why they were used. This should counter any lingering misconceptions, possible discomfort, or risk that may have been generated by the deception.

Finally, participants have the right to make their own decisions, but they can make reasonable decisions only if they have all the relevant information on which to base their decisions. This principle is referred to as **informed consent.**

At the center of these issues lies a genuine conflict of interests and a moral problem. On the one hand, society demands scientific solutions to a large array of problems. On the other hand, searching for such solutions may at times violate individuals' rights to privacy and to proper treatment. To meet society's demands for new knowledge and treatments for such physical illnesses as AIDS and cancer, to solve such social problems as poverty or aggression, or to improve teaching, scientists must be able to carry out scientific research, and this requires the cooperation of participants. It is in the long-term interest of society for individuals to contribute to scientific efforts. One way is by serving as participants in research. Responsible people will consider donating their time, effort, and information as participants to promote scientific knowledge for its potential benefits to society, even when they do not personally benefit.

Of course, the decision is up to each individual. A moral dilemma arises because research sometimes exposes participants to potential risks. In attempting to solve this dilemma, most research agencies, universities, and professional organizations have adopted the following ideas:

1. Scientific research offers potential benefits to society.
2. It is reasonable to expect that people will behave in a socially responsible manner and contribute to knowledge by participating in research.
3. Participants have basic rights when they elect to participate in a research study, including rights to privacy and to protection from physical and psychological harm. They must also be given clear and sufficient information on which to base their decisions about participating in any research project.
4. It is the responsibility of researchers to conduct research in such manner as to respect participants' rights and to protect participants from possible harm.

03:02
03:03

The American Psychological Association (APA) was one of the first professional organizations to develop ethical guidelines for research, recognizing both the need for research and the rights of participants. The APA acknowledged that research may use deception, may make participants uncomfortable, or may ask for personal information. These and other aspects of research place participants at risk, which means that the potential exists for the participants to suffer harm as a result of the study. The ethical principles are guides for minimizing risks to participants. Federal policy regarding human participants in research is detailed in several reports (e.g., National Institutes of Health, 1995, 1998) and it is constantly being updated. Federal funding agencies, such as the National Institutes of Health (NIH), publish current regulations on their websites. The APA (Sales & Folkman, 2000) has recently updated its ethical code for human research. The Student Resource Website reviews these ethical guidelines. But ethical principles are constantly evolving, pushed largely by the discussion of these principles by psychological researchers. For example, the Science Directorate of the APA, which supports the scientific activity of psychologists, recently published its own ethical recommendations for academic researchers, which supplement the APA Ethical Guidelines (Smith, 2003).

The most important safeguard built into the APA guidelines is the idea that it is the *participant* who decides to participate in research. A participant has the right to refuse to participate or to discontinue participating in the study at any time, even after having agreed to participate. The ethical researcher is bound to honor this right and can neither coerce participants nor prevent them from withdrawing. Data collection cannot start until participants give their unequivocal consent. Informed consent is an important safeguard. It means that researchers must provide participants with enough information about the research to enable them to make informed decisions about their participation.

Another important safeguard concerns the responsibility of the researcher to maintain strict **confidentiality** of the information gathered about participants. This is particularly important when the research deals with sensitive personal information or information derived from normally confidential records, such as hospital or school records. To protect participants' confidentiality, researchers commonly use code numbers, rather than names, on records that contain sensitive information.

When participants are children or have mental or emotional disorders, they may have difficulty in understanding the information or in giving consent. Under those conditions, greater responsibility is placed on both the researcher and the designated person, such as a parent, school administrator, or other institutional official, who acts on behalf of the participants to ensure that participants' rights and well-being are protected.

Institutional Review Boards.   **Institutional Review Boards (IRBs)** consist of researchers' peers and members of the community at large. Universities, research institutes, hospitals, and school systems establish IRBs to review research proposals to see if they meet ethical guidelines. Every institution that receives federal funding is required to submit all human-participant research proposals to this board. Members of the board are usually appointed by the institution's president or another administrator of the institution. It is the responsibility of researchers to be sure that their proposals are submitted to, and approved by, the appropriate IRB before gathering data.

When it functions well, an IRB is a helpful advisory group that expedites research, advises researchers, and suggests improvements. The IRB provides an additional safeguard, assisting researchers in clarifying and solving potential ethical issues. Even well-meaning researchers might make self-serving decisions in their research, blinding them to potential ethical problems. The IRB provides an external viewpoint to reduce this problem. However, it does not reduce the researcher's ethical responsibility to design acceptable research. *The final ethical responsibility always rests with the researcher.*

Researchers must judge their research in terms of its value to science, the risk it poses to participants, whether potential benefits outweigh risks, and whether adequate safeguards have been included to minimize the risks. Should risks to participants outweigh potential benefits, the ethical researcher must redesign or discontinue the project. Thus, if the research is badly designed or carried out so that its results are of little or no scientific value, then (1) the potential informational value will be minimal and (2) participants will have wasted their time and perhaps been exposed to risks in a largely valueless endeavor. The researcher therefore has an ethical responsibility to develop well-designed projects and execute them with care.

Ethical Checks.   Assume that you are designing a research project with human participants. You have identified an area of interest and refined the initial question. You have also identified and defined the major variables and determined the nature of the participants, how they will be selected, and how you propose to observe them. The next step is to perform the **ethical checks** listed in Table 3.4. These ethical checks will help you

---

TABLE 3.4   *Ethical Checks Before Beginning the Study*

---

1. Is the proposed research sufficiently well designed to be of informational value?

2. Does the research pose risk of physical or psychological harm to participants by using deception; obtaining sensitive information; or using minors or others who cannot readily give consent?

3. If risks exist, does the research adequately control these risks by including such procedures as debriefing, removing or reducing risks of physical harm, or guaranteeing that all information will be obtained anonymously? If that is not possible, will it guarantee that it will remain confidential, and provide special safeguards for minors and participants who may have impairments?

4. Is there a provision for obtaining informed consent from every participant or, if participants cannot give it, from responsible people acting for the benefit of the participant? Will sufficient information be provided to potential participants so that they will be able to give their informed consent? Is there a clear agreement in writing (the *informed consent form*) between the researcher and potential participants? The informed consent should also make it clear that the participant is free to withdraw from the experiment at any time.

5. Will participants receive adequate feedback at the completion of the study, including a debriefing if deception is used?

6. Do I accept *my full responsibility* for the ethical and safe treatment of all participants by myself and *all research assistants*?

7. Has the proposal been reviewed and approved by the appropriate Institutional Review Board?

---

identify and correct most ethical problems. Ethical checks are a necessary final test before a proposal is submitted to the Institutional Review Board.

Ethical principles in research continue to evolve as psychologists debate larger issues involving social values and scientific research (Kendler, 1993; Prilleltensky, 1994). The American Psychological Association (Sales & Folkman, 2000) appointed a task force to update ethical principles in research with human participants. *The Cost of Neglect 3.1* illustrates how the evolution of scientific technology requires a parallel evolution of ethical principles.

Inevitably, researchers have started to study IRBs. For example, Ferraro, Szigeti, Dawes, and Pan (1999) surveyed over three hundred university faculty and graduate students about their experiences with IRBs. A major recommendation of this study is that more needs to be known about the IRB members' qualifications, attitudes, and methods of evaluation. Researchers' concerns about IRB operations and the credentials of IRB members are appropriate. Researchers who are naïve about IRB operations may come to view

---

THE COST OF NEGLECT 3.1: *Never Let Technology Outrun Ethics*

Moral or ethical questions cannot be answered by empirical studies alone. Consider two questions that arise from the application of research on the human genome (Murray, 1996) and fetal development (Graziano, 2001).

1. Should fetuses be aborted when prenatal examination shows the presence of serious chromosomal abnormalities?
2. Should children or animals be conceived specifically for the purpose of providing fetal tissues, organs, or bone marrow to people with illness?

Let's examine one of these questions. The technology exists to conceive and then to abort the fetus at certain optimal points, and harvest the needed tissues to treat ill persons. But should the technology be used just because it exists? Science and technology determine if the procedures can be carried out and if they can be successful in medical treatment. But science cannot determine if they *should* be carried out.

One example is a case in which one reason for conceiving a child was to provide a bone marrow transplant for a 16-year-old girl who was suffering from myelogenous leukemia (Tomlinson, 1990). Because of conflicting blood types, no suitable donors were available, and the girl would live only a few more years if a donor was not found. The parents decided to conceive another child, based on odds of one in four that the child would be a suitable match. A girl was born, the match was successful, and the older daughter received the bone marrow transplant from her infant sister. At this point, both girls are doing well and are enjoying a loving family life. Although this case had a happy ending, should such procedures be done? Are some procedures ethically acceptable and others not? Think about it. How would you answer such questions?

If we do not consider potential ethical issues now, before the technology is developed that raises those issues, technology is likely to outpace ethics. There are dozens of technologies available now, or in development, that raise enormous ethical issues, including the Human Genome Project (Goodey, 2003), cloning (Jaenisch, 2004), and automatic facial-recognition computer programs that could someday be used to track the movements of everyone (Shenon, 2003). Psychologists are studying ways to look into the brain to track emotional responses that might normally be hidden by people (Ochsner & Gross, 2004); risk factors for psychological disorders (e.g., Goodwin et al., 2004); and brain features that predict violence (Raine, 2002). These technologies offer tremendous benefits, but they also have the potential for great harm. The time to think about their implications is now.

these boards as adversaries and as impediments to conducting their research. Informed researchers, however, understand the important oversight functions of IRBs. They also recognize that by maintaining these oversight functions the IRB helps to bolster public confidence about research. Such confidence is necessary if people are to continue to volunteer to participate in studies.

Ethics and Diversity Issues in Research

A research issue that is related both to good research design and to ethical concerns is that of the diversity of participants. **Diversity** refers to how well various ethnic, cultural, age, and gender groups are represented in the research sample. In psychological and medical research, women, children, and many ethnic groups have traditionally been underrepresented. Consequently, information gained from such research may not apply to all members of our increasingly heterogeneous society. For example, the efficacy of some medical treatments was initially tested primarily, or even exclusively, on adult Caucasian males. These treatments were then applied to others on the assumption that they are generally effective, but this assumption might be false. Treatments that are effective for Caucasian men might not be effective for women, children, or ethnic minorities, thus placing these people at a medical disadvantage.

Psychological research has often failed to represent population diversity, thus limiting its value. For example, we never know until the research has been completed whether the same psychological findings apply to different ethnic groups. For this reason, funding agencies such as the National Institutes of Health now require that researchers actively recruit participants to reflect the diversity of the population, unless it is scientifically justified not to include them (National Institutes of Health, 2005). This means that men, women, children, and members of minority groups must be included. If they are not included, a scientifically valid rationale for their exclusion must be presented. Of course, it makes no sense to include children in studies of Alzheimer's disease or men in studies of postpartum depression. However, practical difficulties in recruiting a broad sample of participants are not valid reasons for not having such groups represented in the study.

Ethical Principles for Animal Research

Concern for the ethical and humane treatment of animals in research is just as important as concern for human participants. Animal research is conducted in many biomedical disciplines, and large numbers of animals are studied each year. There are thousands of psychologists who use animals in research (Akins et al., 2005).

The major ethical concerns in animal research involve two issues. First, animals are captive participants and, of course, are not capable of providing informed consent. Second, research carried out on animals is generally more invasive than that carried out on humans, and animal participants often incur more serious risks than human participants. Therefore, the researcher bears more responsibility for ensuring that animals are treated humanely.

For years, professional and governmental organizations have followed ethical guidelines in the use of animal participants. The APA, for example, has had ongoing professional committees since 1925 to address issues of animal research. This early concern has evolved into a set of standards for animal research that are periodically reviewed. Most scientific societies or government agencies whose members use animals in research have their own policy statements (e.g., American College of Surgeons, 1991; American Psychological Association, 1996, 2002; Canadian Council on Animal Care, 1993; National Institutes of Health, 1994, 1996; Society for Neuroscience, 1991, 1995). Anyone who publishes in APA journals and who uses animals as research participants must attest that their research was conducted in accordance with APA guidelines (American Psychological Association, 2002). All researchers who submit studies to the *Journal of Neuroscience* or to neuroscience meetings must attest that they have complied with animal-use standards and policy as set out by the National Institutes of Health (1994, 1996) and the Society for Neuroscience (1991, 1995). The guidelines cover areas such as appropriate selection of animals, adequate and humane housing, preoperative and postoperative care, concern about inflicting as little pain and discomfort as possible, and the need to have as much confidence as possible that the proposed research is both necessary and well designed.

In addition to the policies demanded by various professional groups, animal research is also constrained by other regulations. Every animal laboratory in the United States, Canada, and Mexico must abide by applicable federal, state, and local laws governing the use and care of animals. In the United States, all laboratories that receive federal funds must have a **Laboratory Animal Care Committee,** which serves the same function as the IRB does for human research. These committees include veterinarians and nonprofessional community representatives, as well as the researcher's professional colleagues. They review and must approve all proposed animal care and use procedures, focusing not only on the specifics of humane care for the animals, but also on the relevance of the proposed research to human and animal health, to the advancement of knowledge, and to society.

Animal researchers must proceed in much the same way as those using human participants. They must thoroughly review the ethical animal-use issues raised by their planned research, must assume full responsibility for the ethical conduct of the research, and must submit the research plan to their local Laboratory Care Committee for evaluation and approval.

An estimated 22 million animals each year are used in research in the United States, representing a slight decline over the past two decades. Animal use in research has remained constant in Canada over the same time frame. It has declined in the United Kingdom and some European countries (Mukerjee, 1997), but the decline in Europe has slowed in recent years (European Science Foundation, 2001).

Efforts are being made to reduce the number of live animals used both in experimentation and in training researchers and practitioners. Some institutions involved in this effort are the Johns Hopkins Center for Alternatives to Animal Testing; the Center for Animal Alternatives, University of California at Davis; the American Veterinary Society; and Psychologists for the Ethical Treatment of Animals. Reductions are being accomplished by sharpening the design of experiments so that fewer animals are needed, substituting computer simulation for live animals, using cells cultured in laboratories rather than live animals, and substituting realistic models of animals for live specimens. However, it is difficult to develop alternatives for behavioral studies, because functioning animals are needed to observe behavior and the factors affecting behavior.

Some writers have argued that animal research is unnecessary and contributes little meaningful information. Botting and Morrison (1997) have responded that animal research has been critically important in medicine. It has facilitated the development of vaccinations against many severe infectious diseases, treatments such as kidney dialysis, organ transplants, open-heart surgery, heart-valve replacement, and drug treatments for hypertension and diabetes (Morrison, 2001).

Neal Miller (1985) pointed out that animal research has also led to the development of successful medical and psychological treatments for such disorders as enuresis, encopresis, scoliosis (a severe curvature of the spine), anorexia, life-threatening vomiting in infants, and retraining use of limbs following accidents or surgery. Miller and others have noted that animal research has not only contributed greater understanding of disease processes, improved services, and reduced risks for humans, but has also led to more effective and humane care for animals and solutions to problems that animals face in natural environments. For example, behavioral research on taste aversion has led to humane alternatives to shooting or poisoning animals that destroy crops or attack livestock. Behavioral and biological research has led to improved habitat preservation for wildlife, to successful reintroductions of Atlantic salmon and other fish to areas where they had been killed off, and to successful treatment for, and vaccination against, many diseases of pets, livestock, and zoo animals.

Concern for humane and ethical treatment of animals in research is legitimate, and few researchers deny its importance. The *Journal of Applied Animal Welfare Science* presents issues and developments in the humane care of animals in research, training, and society in general. Discussions of animal research are frequent in psychological journals. For example, the *American Psychologist* published a series of five articles in 1997 addressing important issues in animal research. Influential books have been written on the ethics of animal research (e.g., Akins et al., 2005). Even animal researchers have challenged past and current practices. Ulrich (1991), for example, argued that misuse and overuse of animals has occurred in research and that scientists, like everyone else, have been thoughtlessly guilty of our culture's propensity to consume anything, without regard to ecological issues. Ulrich, an animal researcher for many years, writes thoughtfully about scientists' responsibilities to other life forms and the necessity to consider seriously the ethical issues involved in animal research.

Research with animals has made enormous contributions to the scientific understanding of nature. As with all research, the costs in terms of risks to the participants must be balanced by the potential benefits to society (Carroll & Overmier, 2001). A summary of the APA Ethical Guidelines for the use of animals in research are included on the Student Resource Website.

03:04

Quick-Check Review 3.4: Research Ethics	1. What is the moral dilemma in research concerning individuals and society? 2. What is informed consent? How is it obtained, and why is it important? 3. What are Institutional Review Boards? What do they do? 4. What are the major ethical principles applicable to research with animals? 5. What is meant by diversity issues in research?

<table>
<tr>
<td>

***PUTTING IT
INTO PRACTICE***

</td>
<td>

Can research questions really be found anywhere? They can if you look for them and are open to them. Take a few minutes each day and look around. Perhaps you are sitting in the library studying. Find things of interest to you, and then speculate about why they are the way they are. For example, some people study at open tables while others study in enclosed study carrels. Is one better than the other for studying? Do individual differences determine which type of study environment is optimal for each person? What are the best ways to study?

With a little practice, you will discover that important and interesting questions really are all around us. Once you have learned to see these questions, start to look at them the way a scientist would. Identify the variables you might wish to study, and begin to speculate how those variables are related to one another. If you put a little energy into this assignment, you will find it eye opening and enjoyable. You will rekindle some of the enthusiastic curiosity that you had as a child, and you will begin to realize what it is that drives scientists.

</td>
</tr>
</table>

Chapter Summary

We start research by finding an area of interest and generating questions. Research questions can be readily developed from personal experiences and interests, from the published theoretical and empirical work of others, and from attempts to solve practical problems. New research can be generated from current research both heuristically (by stimulating interest or opposition) and systematically (by making precise predictions about the logical next step in the research process).

Psychological research can be categorized as (1) basic research, in which scientists develop new information without specific practical goals; and (2) applied research, in which scientists address questions to help to solve practical problems.

Vague research ideas must be refined and sharpened until they are as precise as possible. How the question is refined is of considerable importance, because it influences how the research will proceed. Refining the initial question implicitly identifies the major variables, and structures the ways in which the research will be carried out. The observational procedures, methods of measurement, controls, and statistical analyses used all depend to a great extent on the nature of the question.

It is necessary to identify not only variables of interest, but also variables in which the researcher has

no interest, but which might nevertheless affect the outcome of research. These extraneous variables must be controlled to avoid threatening the study's validity.

One category of pre-observational decisions concerns ethics. The rights of participants must always be balanced against society's need for scientific information. The APA has developed ethical guidelines for psychological research with human participants, which focus on insuring that participants are not coerced, that they have sufficient information to make an informed decision about participation, that the research is meaningful, and that it poses no undue hazards to participants. It is the responsibility of individual researchers to see that risks to participants are minimized and to have each project reviewed by an appropriate Institutional Review Board.

Ethical concerns in the use of animal participants are equally important. The guidelines for animal research focus on adequacy of housing, general care of laboratory animals, minimizing pain and discomfort, and the need for and value of the proposed research. Animal researchers must submit their research plans to their local Laboratory Animal Care Committee for review and approval.

Chapter Exercises

1. Define the following key terms. Be sure that you understand them. They are discussed in the chapter and defined in the glossary.

heuristic influence
systematic influence
applied psychology
applied research
basic research
fundamental research
pure research
variable
behavioral variable
stimulus variables
organismic variables
subject variables
observed organismic variables
response-inferred organismic variables
independent variables
dependent variables
manipulated independent variables

nonmanipulated independent variables
classification variable
causal relationship
extraneous variables
constant
control in research
invasion of privacy
deception
debriefing
informed consent
confidentiality
Institutional Review Board (IRB)
ethical checks
diversity
Laboratory Animal Care Committee

2. Create five research questions. For each one identify the major variables involved, the type of variable each is (that is, stimulus, behavioral, organismic, independent, etc.), and whether the research question represents basic or applied research.

3. Identify ethical issues that must be addressed in the research questions you developed in the previous question.

4. Think of several examples of variables that could be independent variables in one study and dependent variables in another.

5. Create several research situations in which you would use deception. For each one, (a) explain why the deception is needed and (b) how you would deal with the ethical issues raised by the deception.

6. Suppose your Institutional Review Board rejects your research proposal as "ethically unacceptable" because the design is so flawed that the information from the study would be meaningless. Why is this criticism an ethical issue and not just a design problem?

7. Some research situations follow. What are the potential ethical problems in each? Indicate what safeguards you would use.

   a. A researcher is going to test third- and fourth-graders to compare boys' and girls' interest in math problems.

   b. A study of small-group interactions is being conducted with adults as participants. The participants, observed in groups of five people, do not know that three of the five members of their group are actually assistants of the researcher and that their behavior during the small-group meeting has been planned ahead of time.

   c. A researcher wants to examine the files on hospitalized patients with serious depression to obtain basic information about their families.

4

Data and the Nature of Measurement

Since the measuring device has been constructed by the observer . . . we have to remember that what we observe is not nature in itself but nature exposed to our method of questioning.

—Werner Karl Heisenberg, *Physics and Philosophy,* 1958

Web Resource Material

Chapter 2 introduced the idea that observation is the pivotal phase in the research process. You learned in Chapter 3 that every research project measures and/or manipulates one or more variables. The quality of the research depends on how well every variable is measured or manipulated. This chapter takes these ideas a step further by discussing the measurement process. The chapter begins with a description of what measurement is and then introduces the concept of scales of measurement. The chapter also covers the process of measurement, the best ways to develop measures, and how measures are evaluated.

Measurement

Every research project, whatever its level of constraint, includes one or more sets of variables that the researcher manipulates and/or measures. As you learned in Chapter 3, a variable is any characteristic that can take more than one form or value. Because scientific research can study any natural phenomena, any varying event can become a research variable. Variables such as intelligence and memory are complex events that vary from one participant to another or from one condition to another. If the events of interest are static, with no variation, they cannot serve as research variables. Simply put, *a variable must vary.* The major task in measurement is to represent the research variables numerically.

To measure a variable is to assign numbers that represent values of the variable. The measurements for each participant constitute the data, which are later analyzed and interpreted. The statistical analyses depend on how the dependent variables are measured. Beginning students are often puzzled about what statistical procedures to use. As you will see in this chapter and again in Chapter 14, choosing appropriate statistical procedures is relatively simple once the observational procedures have been designed and the procedures to measure the dependent variable have been determined.

In assigning numbers to a variable, the researcher works with two sets of information. The first set is the abstract number system, with all its characteristics. The second set is the variable to be measured, with all of *its* characteristics. The task for the researcher is to bring the two systems together, applying one to the other so that the numbers accurately represent the variable. The task may become complicated, because the two systems do not necessarily function according to the same rules. The abstract number system has specific and well-defined rules. However, variables in psychology are not usually so well defined, and they do not necessarily function according to the same clear rules as the abstract number system. Thus, the two systems cannot always be easily matched. It is necessary for the researcher to determine how the characteristics of a measure might fail to match those of the abstract number system so that the appropriate statistical methods can be selected.

The characteristics or **properties of the abstract number system** are identity, magnitude, equal intervals, and a true zero. **Identity** means that each number has a particular meaning. **Magnitude** means that numbers have an inherent order from smaller to larger. We have **equal intervals** when the difference between units is the same anywhere on the scale. For example, the difference between 2 and 3 is the same as the difference between 99 and 100. The zero on the abstract number scale is a **true zero,** which means that zero represents a zero level of the variable being measured.

Because of these properties, numbers can be added, subtracted, multiplied, and divided. However, if the abstract number system is applied to a psychological variable, such as intelligence, the number system and the variable of intelligence do not match exactly. The number system has a true zero point, but the psychological variable of intelligence does not. Zero on an intelligence test is an arbitrary number. There is no living person with zero intelligence. That is, in the unlikely event that a score of zero was obtained, it would not indicate zero intelligence. In this situation, the number system and the psychological variable do not match exactly. In the abstract number system, 100 is twice as much as 50, but because the psychological variable of intelligence has no zero point, we cannot say that an intelligence test score of 100 shows twice the intelligence as a score of 50.

Suppose that you were doing a study of taste preferences. You give your participants samples of solutions to taste, and you ask them to rank the drinks according to which one they liked the most, which one second best, which one third, and so on. You assign numbers (1, 2, 3, etc.) to the ranked preferences with number 1 as the most preferred, number 2 second, and so on. Would the difference in preference between 1 and 2 be the same as between 2 and 3? In other words, would this scale have equal intervals?

Suppose, for example, that you asked your participants to rank Coke, Pepsi, and vinegar from most to least preferred. Now, unless they have strange tastes, their rankings would probably be either 1-2-3 or 2-1-3 for Coke, Pepsi, and vinegar, respectively. Clearly, the difference in preference between Coke and Pepsi is much smaller than that between either of those drinks and vinegar, even though the difference in rank orderings is the same. Therefore, the differences between rank orderings will not necessarily be equal at all points on the scale. Similarly, it makes no sense to say that the drink ranked 1 is three times as preferred as the drink ranked 3.

In these two examples, the characteristics of the variables as they are measured do not match the characteristics of the number system, and so one is limited in the type of mathematical operations that can be performed on the data. In some cases, however, the variable and the number system can be matched. For example, suppose that an educational psychologist wanted to study how many questions children ask of their teacher. Each question asked by a child was recorded, and the total number of questions asked by each child in each school day was computed. Table 4.1 shows sample data for five days of observation for 10 children.

TABLE 4.1 *Example of Measurement*

Listed here are the numbers of questions asked by 10 students in class over five days.

Student ID	Days					Total
	Mon	Tues	Wed	Thurs	Fri	
01	1	2	1	1	1	6
02	0	0	1	0	1	2
03	4	2	3	3	3	15
04	6	4	5	3	4	22
05	1	3	1	0	2	7
06	2	0	2	1	0	5
07	2	3	1	2	2	10
08	2	0	1	1	0	4
09	1	1	0	2	1	5
10	4	3	5	3	3	18
Totals	23	18	20	16	17	94

THE COST OF NEGLECT 4.1:   Missing Mars

It did not really miss Mars. Indeed, NASA's Mars Climate Orbiter most definitely hit the red planet, or at least its atmosphere, with enough force and heat to destroy itself and cost taxpayers more than $125 million. Its mission was to orbit Mars and serve as a radio relay system for a second rocket, the Mars Polar Lander, which was scheduled to touch down three months later to explore the Martian surface.

What had gone wrong? After all, this was "rocket science," where technological precision is routine. It appears that an elementary mistake had been made in measurement. The two teams working on this Mars mission, the Jet Propulsion Laboratory in Pasadena and Lockheed Martin Astronautics in Denver, *had used two different units of measurement.* The Denver group based its calculations for the propulsion system on pounds of force, while the Pasadena group based its calculations on the metric system. The result was that information based on two different measurement systems conflicted, causing navigational errors and sending the orbiter out of control into the Martian atmosphere, where it burned up.

A most elementary error had been committed. The engineers had failed to convert one measurement system to the other and to use consistent measurements for feeding data into the navigational systems. There is a moral to this sad tale: *Make sure you have your measurements in order before "launching" your research!*

Because of the nature of the data, all mathematical operations are applicable. We can add the number of daily questions for each child and arrive at each child's total number of questions for the week. If you look across each row in Table 4.1 at the totals for each child, you will see that child 02 asked only 2 questions, whereas child 04 asked 22. This large difference suggests that the children are very different from one another with regard to their willingness to ask questions in class. We can subtract the totals or divide one by the other and report that, in this particular week, participant 04 asked 20 more questions or 11 times as many questions as participant 02. We can also divide the total for the week by the number of children and report the average number of questions per child for the week. In summary, this number-of-questions variable shows a magnitude in the same direction as the number system, so 22 responses is more than 20 responses. It also has equal intervals, so the difference in response between 4 and 6 is the same as the difference between 10 and 12. Finally, it has a true zero point, which means that a child with a score of zero asked no questions during the observation period. Because of the match of the characteristics of the dependent variable with those of the number system, all mathematical operations on the data are legitimate: addition, subtraction, multiplication, and division. This allows researchers to use powerful statistical tests that cannot properly be used with dependent variables that are not as well matched with the real number system.

Accurate measurement is critical in science and technology. Even an elementary mistake can invalidate an entire project, as illustrated in the infamous case discussed in *The Cost of Neglect 4.1.*

Misconduct in Science

Before we leave this general discussion of measurement accuracy, we must comment on a rare, but serious, event—the deliberate falsification of data. This kind of error does not occur because of inadvertent mistakes, but rather because of ethical violations by the researcher.

Such cases in science are rare, but each is an attack on the entire scientific enterprise. Society seems to have a high tolerance for the deliberate distortion of facts and ideas; certainly advertisers and politicians do this freely, and often quite creatively, and they are rarely challenged. Most people probably engage in "harmless exaggeration." If we are honest about it, we would probably have to admit that we have all occasionally pushed some argument beyond complete honesty and accuracy in order to make a point. However, such distortion is intolerable in science. The willful distortion of data is one of the most egregious ethical offenses that a scientist can commit. Those who do so are ultimately found out through the rigorous peer review processes, and they suffer serious reprisals, such as loss of their jobs, their professions, and their very honor and reputation. In our view, they deserve no less. The integrity of scientific disciplines depends upon each scientist's honesty in the use and reporting of data.

It is a distressing fact that scientific information is sometimes deliberately distorted in one way or another to serve goals that are not in the least scientific. Who perpetrates these distortions, why they do it, how they do it, and what effects these distortions have, present a complex and disturbing picture of this ultimate ethical transgression. Whatever specific form the violations might take, they all include the deliberate falsification of data, procedures, and conclusions in order to mislead someone else, such as a promotion committee, a funding agency, members of Congress, or the general public. The goal in such cases is not scientific knowledge, but selfish aggrandizement or profit. To the best of our knowledge, only a small proportion of scientific research involves such misconduct. However, when it does occur, it threatens the whole scientific enterprise.

While most of the scientific misconduct cases reported in the media involve individual researchers (e.g., Kintisch, 2005), a particularly ominous form is the distortion carried out by large, powerful segments of society. When an industry suppresses, distorts, or manufactures scientific data in order to protect its profits or a government does so for political reasons (Rensberger, 2005), then a serious breach has occurred, with potentially destructive impact on the public. We hope students will be alert to all forms of scientific misconduct.

Quick-Check Review 4.1: Measurement	1. What is measurement?
	2. Why is accurate measurement so critical?
	3. What are the important properties of the abstract number system?
	4. What makes misconduct in science so dangerous?

Scales of Measurement

Some variables used in psychological research closely match the number system, whereas others do not. To help to identify the closeness of match, Stevens (1946, 1957) classified variables into four levels or **scales of measurement**.[1] The scales, arranged from least

---

[1]Some people disagree with Stevens, challenging his distinction between scales of measurement on mathematical grounds (Gaito, 1980; Michell, 1986). Although we are sympathetic to these arguments, we believe that Stevens' approach is still a useful teaching and organizational tool for a textbook at this level.

04:01

to most matched with the number system, are nominal, ordinal, interval, and ratio scales. For more complete discussions, see Coombs, Raiffa, and Thrall (1954) and Roberts (1979).

Nominal Scales

Nominal scales are at the lowest level of measurement; they are the scales that least match the number system. Nominal scales are naming scales, and their only property is identity. Such dependent variables as place of birth (Chicago, Toronto, Tokyo, Nyack), brand name choice (Ford, Honda, Volvo), political affiliation (Democrat, Republican, Green Party, Independent), diagnostic category (panic disorder, schizophrenia, bipolar disorder), and sex of the participant are all nominal scales of measurement. The differences between the categories of nominal scales are qualitative and not quantitative. We can assign numbers to represent different categories. For example, we could label Chicago as 1, Toronto as 2, Tokyo as 3, and Nyack as 4, but the numbers are only arbitrary labels for the categories. Except for identity, these numbers have none of the properties of the number system and, therefore, we cannot meaningfully add, subtract, multiply, or divide them. Is Chicago, with its assigned number of 1, to be understood as only one-fourth of Nyack, with its assigned number of 4? Nominal scales have no zero point, cannot be ordered low to high, and make no assumption about equal units of measurement. In other words, they are not numbers at all, at least not in the sense that we usually think of numbers. Nominal scales classify or categorize participants, and researchers work with the frequency of participants who fall into each category. The data from nominal scales are called **nominal data** or **categorical data.** Chi square is the most commonly used statistical tests for nominal data. Although we describe in this section the appropriate statistical procedures to use with each scale of measurement, we do not cover all of these procedures in this text. However, basic computational procedures are included on the textbook website.

04:02

Ordinal Scales

Ordinal scales measure a variable in order of magnitude. Thus, ordinal scales have the property of magnitude as well as identity. In ordinal scales, numbers represent an ordering, with some numbers representing more of the variable than others. How much more is unclear in an ordinal scale. For example, using socioeconomic class as a variable, we could categorize participants as belonging to the lower, middle, or upper socioeconomic class. There is a clear underlying concept here of order of magnitude, from low to high. Other examples of ordinal scales are measurements by rankings, such as a student's academic standing in class, or measurements by ranked categories, such as grades of A, B, C, D, or F. Data measured on ordinal scales are called **ordered data.**

Ordinal scales give the relative order of magnitude, but they do not provide information about the differences between categories or ranks. If students are ranked, we can determine from the data which student is first, second, and so on, but we cannot determine how much higher the top-ranked student is than the second. That is, the numbers provide information about relative position, but not about the intervals between ranks. The difference in academic achievement between students ranked 1 and 2 might be very small (or large) compared with the difference between students ranked 12 and 13.

As illustrated in the example of ranking preferred taste for Coke, Pepsi, and vinegar, the intervals in ordinal scaling are not necessarily equal. In fact, it is usually assumed that they are unequal. Therefore, it is inappropriate to analyze ordered data with statistical procedures that implicitly require equal intervals of measurement. The most commonly used statistical tests with ordered data are nonparametric tests, such as the Mann-Whitney *U*-test or the Wilcoxon matched-pairs signed-rank test.

Interval Scales

When the measurements convey information about both the order and the distance between values, then we have interval scaling. **Interval scales** have the properties of ordinal scales in addition to equal intervals between consecutive values on the scale. Thus, interval scales come close to matching the number system, but still do not have a true zero point.

The most commonly used example of an interval scale is the measurement of temperature on either the Fahrenheit or Celsius scale. The units of the thermometer are at equal intervals representing equal volumes of mercury. Therefore, 90° is hotter than 45°, and the difference in temperature between 60° and 70° is the same as the difference between 30° and 40°. However, the zero points on these scales are arbitrary and not true zero points. A temperature of zero degrees does not indicate a total absence of heat.

Most variables in psychology are measured on interval scales or near-interval scales, including IQ test scores, neuroticism scores, and attitude measures. With an IQ test, for example, we can report that the measured IQ difference between two people with IQs of 60 and 120 is 60 IQ points. However, because there is no true zero point on the IQ scale, it cannot be said that the second person is twice as smart as the other. Most test scores are not true interval scales, but by convention they are treated as interval scales, because they are closer to being interval scales than ordinal scales. The scales of measurement, much like the levels of constraint, are overlapping rather than discrete. Data measured on interval or ratio scales are referred to as **score data.**

Ratio Scales

Ratio scales have all the properties of the preceding scales (identity, magnitude, and equal intervals) as well as a true zero point. Ratio scales provide the best match to the number system, which means that all mathematical operations are possible on such scales. Such physical dimensions as weight, distance, length, volume, number of responses, and time duration are measured on ratio scales. These scales are called ratio scales because dividing a point on the scale by another point on the scale (taking a ratio of values) gives a legitimate and meaningful value. For example, a person who runs 10 miles is running twice as far as a person who runs 5 miles and five times as far as someone who runs 2 miles. The true zero point and equal intervals give the ratio scale this property. Data measured on a ratio scale are called score data. A variety of statistical techniques are typically used for score data, including *t*-tests, analysis of variance (ANOVA), and product-moment correlations. Although many variables in psychology can be measured on ratio scales, some can be measured only on ordinal or interval scales of measurement.

The characteristics of the various scales of measurement, along with examples and the statistical procedures most commonly used, are summarized in Table 4.2.

TABLE 4.2 *Some Aspects of Scales of Measurement*

	Levels of Measurement			
	Nominal	*Ordinal*	*Interval*	*Ratio*
Examples	Diagnostic categories; brand names; political or religious affiliation	Socioeconomic class; ranks	Test scores; personality and attitude scales	Weight; length; reaction time; number of responses
Properties	Identity	Identity; magnitude	Identity; magnitude; equal intervals	Identity; magnitude; equal intervals; true zero point
Mathematical Operations	None	Rank order	Add; subtract	Add; subtract; multiply; divide
Type of Data	Nominal	Ordered	Score	Score
Statistics Used	Chi square	Mann-Whitney *U*-test	*t*-test; ANOVA	*t*-test; ANOVA

Note: Many more examples of each scale and additional appropriate statistical procedures could be given.

Quick-Check Review 4.2: Scales of Measurement	1. List and define the four scales of measurement. 2. What type of data does each scale produce? 3. What are the properties of each scale of measurement? 4. What is the concept of true zero? What is its importance in measurement?

Measuring and Controlling Variables

Now that you have learned about the different types of variables, scales of measurement, and types of data, you can learn how to measure and manipulate variables. A simple example involving the effects of food intake on weight will illustrate several aspects of measurement. Food intake is the independent variable (the variable to be manipulated in the study). The question is this: What effect does manipulation of food intake have on participants' weight? Therefore, *weight* is the dependent variable. The hypothesis is that weight fluctuations will be dependent on manipulations of food intake. This example will help to illustrate the concepts of measurement error and operational definitions.

Measurement Error

Consider the problem of measuring weight. Suppose that you have the participant stand on a standard scale. If the participant leans against the wall, the measurement of weight is distorted. If the participant were weighed at one time wearing a heavy coat and boots and the next time in bare feet and no coat, the two weights would not be comparable. Such factors are sources of **measurement error.** Measurement error distorts the scores so that the observations do not accurately reflect reality. Measurement error can also attenuate (reduce) the observed strength of a relationship between variables, giving the impression that two variables are less related than they actually are.

Other sources of measurement error are **response-set biases.** A powerful response-set bias is social desirability. **Social desirability** is the tendency to respond in what participants believe to be the most socially acceptable manner. For example, suppose that you were studying the relationship between level of food intake and weight in a weight-loss program. Have you ever cheated when you were on a diet? If you did, would you always be willing to admit it? There is a good chance that you would not admit it, because you would find it embarrassing. In this case, some participants might underreport their food intake, because they do not want to admit to the socially undesirable behavior of cheating on a diet. This social desirability response set would affect the validity of the measurement and create measurement error.

Minimizing measurement error is critical. This is best accomplished by developing a well-thought-out operational definition of the measurement procedure and by diligently using the operational definition in the research. This is the next topic.

Operational Definitions

Most people measure their weight periodically by standing on a scale. Measuring your weight is easy, because the scales are already developed and readily available. Consider the process of weighing yourself. What you are doing is operationally defining the concept of weight. Think of it this way: concepts like weight, gravity, intelligence, or aggression are *ideas*—abstract, theoretical statements that exist on an intellectual level. To carry out empirical research on such concepts, the researcher must translate them from the abstract level to a concrete level so that they can be manipulated or measured. The process of translating a concept from the abstract level to the concrete level is achieved by developing operational definitions. An **operational definition** is a definition of a variable in terms of the actual procedures used by the researcher to measure and/or manipulate it (Kerlinger, 1992). In this example, the abstract concept of weight is turned into an empirical event by creating an operational definition: specifically, by standing on a scale that records pounds or kilograms.

This is the very core of an operational definition; it brings theoretical abstractions to an empirical level, thus describing exactly how the theoretical abstraction will be measured. An operational definition is like a recipe that specifies exactly how to measure and/or manipulate the variables in a study. This is necessary to carry out the study and to communicate the procedures to other researchers. All research requires operational definitions. Whatever the theoretical concepts under study, if you are to study them empirically, you must define them operationally. Even for simple measures like weight, every step of the measurement procedure should be carefully planned to avoid confusion and sloppiness in running the study.

04:03

Measuring a variable like food intake requires a scale different from the weight scale. Scientists know from past research that food intake is measured in terms of calories and that foods differ in their levels of calories. If you know the caloric value of each type of food and how much of each type of food was consumed, you can compute the total calorie intake. This process of measuring food intake is based on considerable research and theory. We can be reasonably sure that this approach to measuring food intake is effective, because it has worked well for researchers in the past, a fact that can be confirmed by reading earlier research.

Researchers often want to create a particular response in participants, such as increasing their motivation, anxiety, or alertness. These factors are within the participants and are therefore difficult to observe. However, such variables can be studied by operationally defining the set of procedures for manipulating them. In a study discussed earlier, the relaxation level of autistic children was manipulated to see whether it would reduce disruptive behavior. The manipulation was defined in terms of the following set of procedures:

> A corner of the room was selected for relaxation training, which was labeled the "quiet spot" and used for no other activity. Lights were dimmed and the children were invited to lie down on a soft blanket. The therapist said in a soft, calm voice, "Close your eyes, just like when you're in bed, nice and comfortable. That's it. Breathe slow and easy, that's it, good job, nice and easy, real relaxed." She continued her soothing, quiet instruction and paired the gentle manipulation of arms, legs, and necks with verbal instructions to relax. Any approximations of relaxed behavior were given immediate verbal reinforcement until the children learned to relax on verbal instructions alone (paraphrased from Graziano, 1974, p. 170).

The first training session was about one minute in duration and session length was increased daily until a criterion of five consecutive minutes of relaxation had been reached for 12 consecutive training sessions. Relaxation involved the child's being quiet, without talking or squirming and with no perceptible rigidity or muscle tension.

The preceding operational definition gives a clear description of the relaxation procedures. Although wordy, this operational definition served the purpose of giving researchers a clear set of instructions to define the independent variable. Once this independent variable is operationally defined, it is referred to simply as "relaxation training," with the understanding that it refers to the entire set of procedures. A good operational definition defines procedures so precisely that another researcher could replicate them by simply following the description.

In the study of disruptive behavior in autistic children, the dependent variable of disruptive behavior was operationally defined as follows:

> Disruptive behavior is any observed, sudden change in a child's behavior from calm, quiet, cooperative, and appropriate behavior to explosive tantrums, including sudden attacks on people, smashing and throwing objects, throwing oneself into walls or on the floor, self-abuse such as head-banging, biting, scratching, picking sores, and so on, all carried out in a rapid, near "frenzied" manner. Each disruptive behavior incident will be considered to have ended when the child has returned to the previous level of calm, appropriate behavior for at least three consecutive minutes.

> **Frequency:** Each occurrence of disruptive behavior is recorded as a single event. The frequency score per child is the total number of disruptive behaviors.

> **Duration:** Each disruptive event is timed by stopwatch from the observed beginning to its end.

> **Intensity:** Each disruptive event is rated by the observers on a three-point scale of intensity: low, moderate, high. The rating is made immediately after the event is over and is made for the perceived peak of intensity for the incident (paraphrased from Graziano, 1974).

Developing an operational definition involves drawing on past research, as well as making some arbitrary decisions. The arbitrary decisions are based on an analysis of how best to measure a variable from both a theoretical and a practical sense. For example, the decision to set the relaxation criterion at five consecutive minutes for 12 consecutive sessions is somewhat arbitrary. Instructions to use a "soft, gentle, calm, voice" leave room for interpretation by other researchers who may want to replicate the study.

Operational definitions used in research vary in constraint. Under some conditions, it is difficult to create precise operational definitions for the variables. Under other conditions, we can operationally define variables very precisely. In any study, the researcher should operationally define the independent and dependent variables as clearly and precisely as possible. The completeness and detail of an operational definition depends on the nature of the issues being investigated, the participants used, and the settings in which the observations are made.

Most concepts can be operationally defined in several ways (see Table 4.3). Each definition can lead to different procedures and thus different research projects. For example, suppose that a researcher is studying how hunger affects mood. Participants are randomly assigned to three groups (high hunger, moderate hunger, low hunger), and their moods are measured. Here there are two variables to be operationally defined: the independent variable, *hunger*, and the dependent variable, *mood*. Each can be operationally defined in several ways. Hunger can be defined as the number of hours since the previous meal, the number of

---

TABLE 4.3 *Examples of Operational Definitions*

Independent and dependent variables should be defined in terms of how they are to be measured and/or manipulated. A variable can be operationally defined in different ways, and different operational definitions of the same concept lead to different procedures and thus to different studies. Several examples follow.

Variable	*Operational Definition*
Anxiety	1. A physiological measure, such as heart rate
	2. A self-report of anxiety level
	3. Behavioral observation of avoidance behavior
Aggression in children	1. Ratings of aggressive behavior made by a child's teacher
	2. Direct observation during play periods of the number of times a child hits, pushes, or forcibly takes toys from other children
	3. A child's rate of hitting a punching doll in an experimental situation
	4. The number of acts of aggression in stories created by participants in response to pictures
Obesity	1. The *pinch test*, a measure of fat folds at waist
	2. The volume of water displaced by a submerged participant
	3. Comparison of a participant's height-weight ratio against standard charts
Intelligence	1. Score on a standardized IQ test
	2. Judgment by others of person's ability to solve problems
	3. Grades in school

calories consumed when food is made available, physiological measures associated with hunger, or a score on a questionnaire about how hungry the participant feels. Likewise, mood needs to be operationally defined. (Think about how you might measure mood.)

Over time, many different operational definitions of such concepts as hunger and mood have been developed, and these are available in the research literature. That there is a multiplicity of operational definitions for each concept has several advantages. First, by defining the concept in different ways (e.g., physiologically, behaviorally, or cognitively), different aspects of a complex phenomenon can be studied. Second, when many studies using different operational definitions tend to point to common findings, we have **convergent validity:** multiple lines of evidence converging on the same conclusion. Finally, by knowing the literature, any researcher can select and use operational definitions that have been useful in prior research.

Sometimes when we measure things in divergent ways, we do not find the convergent validity that we expect, but what we do find often gives us a greater appreciation for the complexity of a psychological construct. Take anxiety, for example. We all have a pretty good idea of what anxiety is and could probably name several ways in which we could measure it. For example, anxiety is a feeling that we could report, it is characterized by such physiological changes as an increased heart rate or sweaty palms, and it drives certain behavior, such as withdrawing from the anxiety-provoking situation. Peter Lang (1985) has shown that these three approaches to measuring anxiety actually tap different aspects of anxiety. People can show the physiological arousal of anxiety without being aware of it, or they can be very aware of their anxiety and still not withdraw from the anxiety-provoking situation. Understanding that anxiety is not a simple concept that could be measured equally well by each of these possible measures (self-report, physiological, or behavioral) has improved the understanding of anxiety and anxiety disorders, which has led to improvements in the treatment of anxiety problems (Barlow, 2002).

Developing operational definitions is one of the careful step-by-step processes that make up the overall process of a research project. It takes a broad concept and narrows that concept into a detailed and precise statement of exactly how a variable is to be measured and/or manipulated. These are critical steps in research, and they require knowledge of the literature and experience with the process of specifying operations.

Quick-Check Review 4.3: Measuring and Controlling Variables	1. What is the best way to reduce measurement error in research? 2. How do operational definitions transform theoretical concepts into concrete events? 3. What is social desirability bias in research? How might it affect research? 4. Explain the concept of convergent validity. What is its importance?

Evaluating Measures

Developing measures by operationally defining variables is a critical first step, but researchers are also responsible for evaluating the quality of the measures. Such evaluations should be a routine part of any study that uses new operational definitions of variables. Evaluating the quality of measures and publishing these findings provides other re-

04:04

searchers with the information necessary to guide their selection of the best available measures for their research projects. This section will discuss three factors that are relevant to such evaluations: reliability, effective range, and validity.

Reliability

Good measures give consistent results, regardless of who does the measuring. This is referred to as the **reliability** of the measure. In measuring weight, for example, a scale is said to be reliable if it always gives the same reading when measuring the same object, assuming that the object remains constant in weight. There are three types of reliability: interrater reliability, test-retest reliability, and internal consistency reliability.

Interrater Reliability.   If a measure involves behavior ratings made by observers, there should be at least two independent observers to rate the same sample of behavior. To rate independently, both raters must be **blind** to the ratings of the other observer—that is, they must be unaware of the other observer's ratings. This type of reliability is referred to as **interrater reliability.** It should be used whenever the measure is a rating or judgment. A measure is not wholly reliable or unreliable, but varies in its degree of reliability. If two raters always agree with one another, then the interrater reliability would be perfect. If their ratings are unrelated to one another, then the interrater reliability is zero. However, the actual level of reliability is likely to be somewhere in between. The concept of interrater reliability is illustrated in Figure 4.1. A correlation coefficient (discussed in Chapter 5) can be used to quantify the degree of reliability, although more sophisticated indices are also available (see Nunnally & Bernstein, 1993).

Test-Retest Reliability.   Variables that should remain stable over time should produce similar scores if participants are tested twice with a period of time between testings. This type of reliability is known as **test-retest reliability.** Like interrater reliability, test-retest reliability is not an all-or-nothing phenomenon and is usually quantified with a correlation coefficient. If you change the labels in Figure 4.1 of "rater 1" and "rater 2" to "time 1" and "time 2," you will have a graphical representation of test-retest reliability. In specifying test-retest reliability, it is customary to include both the observed correlation and the

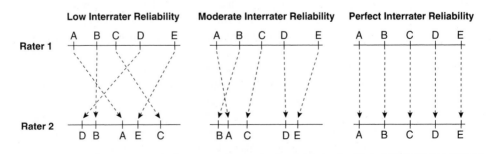

FIGURE 4.1   *Interrater Reliability*   This illustration has two raters (1 and 2) and five participants (A, B, C, D, and E). Each horizontal line represents the scale on which the participants were rated. The more disagreement shown in the ratings, the lower the interrater reliability.

length of time between testings. For example, you might report, "The test-retest reliability over ten weeks was .74."

Internal Consistency Reliability.   Another type of reliability is referred to as **internal consistency reliability,** which is relevant when several observations are made to obtain a score for each participant. This might be the case if participants complete a test with several items or if their behavior is observed several times. Internal consistency reliability is high if each item or behavioral observation correlates with the other observations—that is, if all the items are measuring the same thing. A scale that is internally consistent measures one construct with several independent observations.

Discussing all the ramifications of internal consistency reliability is beyond the scope of this book, but one principle should be mentioned. Generally, *the more observations that are made to obtain a score for a participant, the greater will be the internal consistency re-liability of the score.* Take, for example, the typical tests that are used in courses to determine students' grades. The test could be considered an operational definition of the level of knowledge of students in the course. A test with many questions covering all the different topics in the course should give a consistent indication of how much students know. Asking only one or two questions will not provide the same level of consistency, because it is possible that students may misinterpret any given question and answer it incorrectly even though they know the material. This same principle holds for behavioral observations. It is better to have several observations of behavior on which to base the measurement of a construct than to rely on only one or two.

The reason that the concept of reliability of measures is critical in research is that, if the measures are not reliable, the study cannot produce useful information. The factors that contribute to reliability include (1) the precision and clarity of the operational definition of the construct, (2) the care with which the researcher follows the operational definition, and (3) the number of independent observations on which the score is based (Anastasi & Urbina, 1997).

Effective Range

Another factor to consider in measuring variables is the **effective range** of the scale. If we are interested in weight changes in people, a normal bathroom scale will usually have sufficient range, because it typically can weigh objects between 0 and 300 pounds. However, weighing very large or very small objects, such as elephants or mice, would require different scales that are capable of accurately measuring weight in whatever range necessary. Although the concept of weight is the same for both mice and elephants, it is unlikely that a scale constructed to measure one can also measure the other. The heavy-duty construction required of a scale to measure an elephant would make the scale insensitive to the relatively light weight of a little mouse.

Effective range issues are relevant to most psychological measures. For example, a test of mathematical skill sensitive enough to detect differences among college math majors would be too difficult to detect differences among third graders. A measure of social skills designed for use with children would probably not be appropriate for use with adults. A measure of memory ability challenging enough to detect differences among college students would be too difficult to detect memory differences among brain-injured adults. Procedures such as inducing anxiety or relaxation designed to affect one group of participants might not be appropriate for other participants.

The procedures might lack the range to work with any and all participants. When designing or selecting measures for research, we must keep in mind who the participants will be. This information will guide the selection of measures that have an appropriate effective range for that group.

A problem related to the effective range of a measure is **scale attenuation effects.** In this context, *attenuation* refers to restricting the range of a scale. Using a measure with a restricted range—not ranging high enough or low enough or both—can result in data that shows participants bunched near the top or bottom of the scale. For example, suppose that we are conducting a study on changing college students' attitudes toward tobacco use. For obvious health reasons, we hope to bring about more negative attitudes. We administer our pretest of attitudes, and we find that virtually all participants are already highly negative toward tobacco use. Suppose that we then apply the attitude change intervention and take post-intervention measures of attitudes. The posttest results cannot possibly show much change toward greater negative attitudes, even if the intervention is effective. The participants are already at the top of the scale before the intervention, and therefore they have no room to show change toward still higher scores. This direction of scale attenuation is called a **ceiling effect.**

A scale can also be attenuated by having a restricted lower range, thus creating a possible **floor effect.** In this situation, participants would tend to score near the bottom of the scale only because the scale does not allow a sufficiently low range. A floor effect would occur if an instructor gave an examination that was too difficult for the class and almost all students scored low. If the scale had a greater lower range, the students' scores might be more spread out, rather than bunched at the bottom of the scale.

Ceiling and floor effects are illustrated in Figure 4.2. The true weights of each of 10 people are illustrated in the first panel by the height of a bar. The second and third panels

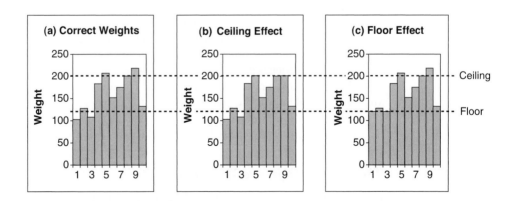

FIGURE 4.2 *Floor and Ceiling Effects* Floor and ceiling effects distort the data by not measuring the full range of a variable. Panel (b) shows the impact of a ceiling effect, in which weights above 200 pounds are read as 200. Similarly, panel (c) shows the impact of a floor effect, in which weight below 120 pounds are read as 120.

illustrate what would happen if there were a ceiling or floor effect, respectively. A ceiling effect might occur if the scale read weights up to only 200 pounds. A floor effect might occur if the needle stuck so that it never read below 120 pounds. Note that the scores are compressed by both floor and ceiling effects and that the scores for people outside the effective range are not accurate.

Scale attenuation effects restrict the range of possible scores for participants' responses; that is, they reduce the potential variability of the data. As we will discuss at some length in Chapter 10, restricting variability results in serious errors. Having sufficient variability is essential in research.

Validity

The third factor that must be considered is the validity of the measure. To say that a scale to measure weight is valid means that the scale measures what it is supposed to measure—weight. Validity is *not* the same as reliability, which refers to how consistently the weight is measured. A scale for measuring weight, for example, might not be properly adjusted, thereby giving a reading 10 pounds lighter than the object really is. The scale is reliable if it consistently gives that same weight, but it would not be valid, because that weight is not the true weight. A *measure cannot be valid unless it is reliable, but a measure can be reliable without being a valid measure of the variable of interest.* Validity, like reliability, is not an all-or-nothing concept. Degrees of potential validity range from none to perfect. Once again, a correlation coefficient is typically used to quantify the degree of validity.

We evaluate the validity of a measure by quantifying the ability of the measure to predict other variables. For example, a researcher might want to know if SAT scores predict performance in college. The variable that we want to predict is called the **criterion;** the measure used to predict the criterion is called the **predictor.**

When this concept of validity is used, we must always specify the criterion measure. It makes no sense to say that the SAT test is valid without saying what it is valid for. For example, the SAT score may be a valid predictor of freshman college grades. It probably is a less valid predictor of whether a student will complete college, because many factors besides ability determine this criterion. Finally, the SAT is probably not a valid predictor of the number of friends a student has or how happy the student is.

Validity is a central concept in research. Therefore, we will revisit the concept after you have learned more of the basics of research.

Figure 4.3 illustrates levels of validity. Note the similarity between Figure 4.1, which illustrates reliability, and Figure 4.3, which illustrates validity.

The Need for Objective Measurement

Every science stresses the need for objectivity, or **objective measures**, but often scientists do not make clear why objectivity is so important. Vague references to how objectivity is somehow more accurate than subjectivity are common, but *why* is it more accurate? One reason is that subjective measures are person specific; they represent the judgment of only one person. If other people in the same situation make different judgments, the findings will not be reproducible.

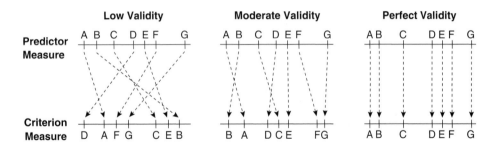

FIGURE 4.3 *Validity* This illustration has two measures (the predictor and the criterion) and seven participants (A, B, C, D, E, F, and G). The top horizontal line represents the predictor measure, and the bottom line represents the criterion measure. The more disagreement shown in the rank ordering of participants on the predictor and criterion measures, the lower the validity.

A hallmark of science is that the laws of nature should hold no matter who tests them. There may be many reasons why two people disagree on their subjective impressions of a phenomenon. For example, Ellie might judge a room to be hotter than Jenny does, because Ellie is accustomed to cooler temperatures and so, by comparison, the room seems hot. Another reason for Ellie and Jenny's disagreement about room temperature might be a differential sensitivity to features other than heat, such as humidity. Yet another reason might be a physiological deficiency in the ability of one or both to sense temperature. Even with something as simple as temperature, subjective impressions pose many problems. If an objective measure of temperature, such as the thermometer, had not been developed, most of the physical laws relating temperature to other phenomena would have remained undiscovered. The thermometer measures temperature independently of such other variables as humidity. It can measure temperature reliably and across a much greater range than can be accomplished without such an instrument. Finally, the thermometer provides at least an interval scale of measurement of temperature. Although this concept may be difficult to grasp on the basis of this brief discussion, it is important to note that an interval scale greatly simplifies the mathematical description of the relationship of temperature to other phenomena.

If so many problems can emerge with subjective measures of something as simple as temperature, imagine the problems that might arise when trying to measure a complicated construct like self-esteem. Many psychological phenomena are events that involve human emotions, which can distort perceptions of the phenomena. For example, people who are easily upset by anger might be more sensitive to the presence of anger in an individual who is being frustrated as part of a study on frustration and aggression. Therefore, they might rate the anger as stronger than would people who are less sensitive to anger. Good research, therefore, demands objective measures that can be performed by anyone properly trained to use them and that give the same results regardless of who does the measuring.

Statistical procedures are central to modern research because they provide objective ways of evaluating patterns of events. Insisting on the use of statistical analyses for drawing conclusions is an extension of the argument that objectivity is critical in science. This is the reason that psychology relies so heavily on statistical analyses to evaluate research data.

Quick-Check Review 4.4: Evaluating Measures	1. Define reliability and list the types of reliability.
	2. Can a measure be reliable but not valid? Can it be valid but not reliable?
	3. Why must the effective range of a measure be appropriate for the study's sample?
	4. What are floor and ceiling effects?
	5. How is validity different from reliability?

PUTTING IT INTO PRACTICE	Psychologists have developed and refined hundreds of measures of psychological phenomena, and these high-quality measures are available to researchers. However, each had to be conceptualized and operationally defined before it could be used as a measure.
	Take a few minutes each day for the next week to look around and identify psychological variables in the environment. For example, if you see two people arguing, the psychological variables that might be of interest are the degree of anger each feels, how frustrating the actions of one party are to the other party, and how public the argument is. Think about each variable and how you might measure it, and try to think of as many ways of measuring it as possible. For example, you can always ask people how angry they are, but are there other ways that you might measure anger that does not involve the self-report of the person?

Chapter Summary

Researchers study relationships among variables. Assessing variables means quantifying them. The quantification process, called *measurement*, involves applying the number system to the variable.

The number system has four properties: identity, magnitude, equal intervals, and absolute zero, but the characteristics of variables seldom match all the properties of the number system. Consequently, in applying the number system to variables, we will find that some variables match the number system well, whereas others do not.

Four levels of measurement have been described: nominal, ordinal, interval, and ratio measurements. The selection of an appropriate statistical test depends in part on the level of measurement.

An operational definition details the procedures needed to measure a variable. The specifications should be as precise as possible. This will increase the measurement's reliability and validity and make replication easier.

Reliability is an index of the measure's consistency; validity is its effectiveness in reflecting the characteristic measured. A measure cannot be valid unless it is reliable, but a measure can be reliable without being valid.

Objectivity is essential in scientific research. Well-conceived operational definitions improve objectivity. Statistical procedures provide objectivity in the analysis of data. Objectivity improves reliability and makes it more likely that researchers will discover valid relationships among variables.

Chapter Exercises

1. Define the following key terms. Be sure that you understand them. They are discussed in the chapter and defined in the glossary.

   properties of the abstract
      number system
   identity
   magnitude
   equal intervals
   true zero
   scales of measurement
   nominal scales
   nominal data
   categorical data
   ordinal scales
   ordered data
   interval scales
   score data
   ratio scales
   measurement error
   response-set biases

   social desirability
   operational definition
   convergent validity
   reliability
   blind
   interrater reliability
   test-retest reliability
   internal consistency
      reliability
   effective range
   scale attenuation effects
   ceiling effect
   floor effect
   criterion
   predictor
   objective measures

2. Write two operational definitions for each of the following variables, one that produces ordinal data, and one that produces score data.

   a. potential little league player's baseball skill

   b. the strength of one's social support network

   c. a lab rat's level of hunger

   d. the level of conflict in a business environment

3. Following are brief descriptions of research projects. For each one identify (i) which is the independent variable and what type of independent variable it is, (ii) which is/are the dependent variable(s), and (iii) the level of measurement and type of data for each dependent variable.

   a. In a study on the effects of television violence on aggressive behavior, schoolchildren are assigned to two conditions. In one condition, the participants watch a typical half-hour of television in which eight violent acts are portrayed (aggressive TV condition); in the other condition, the participants watch a half-hour of television in which no violent acts are portrayed (non-aggressive TV condition). Following the TV viewing, participants are observed in a playroom for aggressive behavior. The hypotheses are that the group exposed to aggressive TV (i) will perform a greater number of aggressive acts and (ii) will perform acts rated as more highly aggressive than the participants in the non-aggressive TV condition. The rating will be done using a five-point rating scale in which the units are not equal intervals.

   b. College students are timed on how quickly they solve a series of puzzles. One-third of the participants are told they will be paid more if they solve the problems quickly; one-third are told they will be paid a fixed amount; and one-third are not told anything about being paid.

4. Identify at least ten situations in which one might experience problems with a dependent measure because the measure has a restriction of range problem.

5. Following is a list of possible dependent variables. For each, identify its level of measurement and the type of data it generates.

   a. Number of disruptive outbursts

   b. Time needed (number of seconds) for a response to occur

   c. Place or position of each runner at the end of a race

   d. Speed of each runner during the race

   e. Annual income of participants

   f. Car preference of each participant

6. For each of the following variables, write an operational definition for a subjective measure of the variable, write a second operational definition for an objective measure of the same variable, and identify potential problems with the subjective measure that might distort the data if it were to be used in an actual study. The variables are:

   a. the participant's ambivalence regarding their career goals

   b. the degree of frustration experienced while engaging in a laboratory task

   c. competitiveness

5

Statistical Analysis of Data

The union of the mathematician with the poet, fervor with measure, passion with correctness, this surely is the ideal.

—William James (1842–1910), *Collected Essays,* 1920

Web Resource Material

Once one decides how to measure the research variables, the next step is to determine how to analyze the data statistically. **Statistics** are powerful tools for organizing and understanding data. They provide ways to represent and describe groups, summarize results, and evaluate data. Without the use of statistics, little could be learned from most studies.

Statistical procedures and research design are interrelated. The decisions concerning which statistical procedures to use are made in the procedures-design phase as an integral part of the research design. They are not just something tacked on after data collection. Although this chapter cannot replace a course in statistics, it will provide an overview of some basic statistical concepts. It begins with a discussion of the reason for statistical procedures. Strategies for organizing and describing data are then introduced. There is a brief introduction to the logic of statistical decision making, followed by a discussion of inferential statistics.

05:01
05:02
05:03
05:15

More detailed coverage of statistical concepts and procedures is included in later chapters and on the Student Resource Website, which provides resources, tutorials, theory, and practice exercises. The website also presents a hands-on tutorial on how to use SPSS for Windows for data analysis.

Individual Differences

Statistical procedures depend on variability or differences in responses among participants. No two participants or groups will respond in exactly the same manner. Suppose, for example, that a researcher predicts that participants who are given special memory training will perform better on a memory task than those who are not trained. In this study, participants are assigned to one of two conditions: (1) memory training or (2) no training. The dependent measure is a memory test that yields scores from 0 to 100.

Hypothetical data are shown in Table 5.1. Note that the groups differ in their mean (average) scores, but there is also considerable variability of scores within each group. The scores in Group A range from 66 to 98, and those in Group B range from 56 to 94. The variation within each group illustrates that there are **individual differences** in memory

TABLE 5.1   *Examples of Descriptive Statistics*

These hypothetical data are from 22 participants in a memory study, half of whom received memory training, and the other half of whom did not.

	Group A (trained)	Group B (nontrained)
	98	94
	93	88
	90	82
	89	77
	87	75
	87	74
	84	72
	81	72
	78	67
	71	61
	66	56
Median	87	74
Mode	87	72
Mean	84	74.36

skills. Some people, with or without training, remember well; others remember very little; most people fall somewhere in between. All organismic variables studied in psychology show individual differences. Therefore, in the memory study, we cannot be sure whether memory training is the reason for the observed group differences; participants in the training group may have had better memory to begin with and would have performed better regardless of the training.

Most of the variables manipulated in psychology describe only small differences in how people perform, compared with the individual differences that already exist among people. Statistics help researchers to decide whether group differences on dependent measures are due to research manipulations or are the result of existing individual differences.

Research studies generate many measures or scores. They typically vary from participant to participant. With so many measurements and so much variability, a way is needed to organize and simplify the numbers.

Descriptive statistics summarize, simplify, and describe a large number of measurements. **Inferential statistics** help researchers to interpret what the data mean. For example, in the study on memory training, the *means* (a descriptive statistic) of the two groups are different.

As predicted, the trained group shows a higher mean score than the nontrained group. However, the researcher wants to know whether the mean difference is large enough to conclude that it is due to more than chance variation among participants. That is, is the difference found between the groups so large that the difference probably did not occur by chance? Inferential statistics help to answer such questions.

These two groups of statistics complement each other. Both descriptive and inferential procedures are applied to the data in virtually every research study.

Quick-Check *Review 5.1:* *Individual* *Differences*	1. What is another term for *the differences among people*? 2. Define descriptive statistics and inferential statistics.

Organizing Data

This section will introduce two important groups of descriptive procedures: (1) frequency distributions and (2) graphical representations of data. These procedures are illustrated with the hypothetical data in Table 5.2, which represent responses from 24 participants, aged 18 and above, selected at random from the population of a moderate-sized city. The researchers are interested in variables that may relate to voting patterns. The information gathered from each participant includes (1) age, (2) income, (3) number of times voted in the last 5 years, (4) sex, and (5) political affiliation (coded as Democrat, Republican, or Other).

What type of data does each of these variables generate? The participant's age, income, and the number of times he or she voted are measured on a ratio scale (score data). Each of these measures has the property of magnitude; for example, 34 is older than 25, $35,000 is more than $28,000, and so on. All three measures have the property of equal intervals; for example, the difference in age between 25 and 20 is the same as the difference between 38 and 33. The variables are measured on ratio scales because they not only have the property of equal intervals, but they each have a true zero point. A person who is zero years old is just being born; a person whose income is zero doesn't earn anything; a person who has voted zero times in the last five years has not voted in that time. The other two variables, sex of the participant and political affiliation, are measured on nominal scales. These data are nominal or categorical, and there is no logical way of ordering the categories.

Frequency Distributions

Nominal and Ordinal Data. For most nominal and ordinal data, statistical simplification involves computing **frequencies:** the number of participants who fall into each category. The frequencies are organized into **frequency distributions,** which show the frequency in each category. Table 5.3 shows the frequency distribution of sex for the data from Table 5.2. In any frequency distribution, when we sum across all categories, the total should equal the total number of participants. It is helpful to convert frequencies to percentages by dividing the frequency in each cell by the total number of participants and multiplying each of these proportions by 100, as was done in Table 5.3.

TABLE 5.2   Sample Data from 24 Participants

Person	Age	Income	Number of Times Voted in Last 5 Years	Sex	Political Affiliation
1	28	$32,000	6	M	R
2	46	50,000	4	M	D
3	33	44,000	0	F	D
4	40	45,000	5	M	R
5	21	30,000	1	M	R
6	26	35,000	0	F	O
7	39	42,000	6	M	O
8	23	34,000	0	F	D
9	20	27,000	1	M	O
10	26	31,000	2	M	R
11	29	39,000	6	F	R
12	24	34,000	2	M	D
13	34	44,000	2	M	O
14	35	45,000	3	M	O
15	52	46,000	8	M	O
16	31	39,000	4	F	D
17	30	43,000	6	M	R
18	45	47,000	7	F	D
19	18	28,000	0	M	O
20	29	44,000	7	M	R
21	26	38,000	6	F	D
22	23	37,000	3	M	O
23	47	48,000	7	M	D
24	53	51,000	8	M	D

TABLE 5.3   Frequency of Males and Females in Our Sample

	Males	Females	Total
Frequency	17	7	24
Percentage	71	29	100

Sometimes it is useful to categorize participants on the basis of more than one variable at the same time. This is called **cross-tabulation.** For example, participants can be categorized on the basis of each participant's sex and political affiliation. Cross-tabulation can help the researcher to see relationships between nominal measures. In this example, there are two levels of the variable *sex* (male and female) and three levels of the variable *political affiliation* (Democrat, Republican, and Other), giving a total of six (2 × 3) possible joint categories.

The data are arranged in a 2 × 3 matrix in Table 5.4, in which the numbers in the matrix are the frequency of people in each of the joint categories. For example, the first cell represents the number of male Democrats. Note that the sum of all the frequencies in the six cells equals the total number of participants. Also note that the row and column totals represent the **univariate** (one-variable) frequency distribution for the political affiliation and sex variables, respectively. For example, the column totals in Table 5.4 of 17 males and 7 females represent the frequency distribution for the single variable of sex and, not surprisingly, are the same numbers that appear in Table 5.3.

Score Data.   Different statistical procedures are used with score data. The simplest way to organize a set of score data is to create a frequency distribution. It is difficult to organize all 24 scores at a glance for the variable "number of times a participant voted in the last five years," which is shown in Table 5.2. Some of the participants have not voted at all during that time, and two participants voted eight times, but where do the rest of the participants tend to fall? A frequency distribution organizes the data to answer a question like this at a glance. There may be no participants for some of the scores, in which case the frequency would be zero. Table 5.5 shows the frequency distribution for this variable.

If there are many possible scores (25 or more) between the lowest and the highest scores, then the frequency distribution will be long and almost as difficult to read as the original data. In this situation, a **grouped frequency distribution** should be used. This shortens the table to a more manageable size by grouping the scores into 10 to 20 intervals. A grouped frequency distribution is required with a **continuous variable,** in which there are theoretically an infinite number of possible scores between the lowest and the highest score. Table 5.6 shows a grouped frequency distribution for the continuous variable *income*, which ranges from $27,000 to $51,000. Grouping salary into $2000 intervals yields 13 intervals.

TABLE 5.4   *Cross-Tabulation by Sex and Political Affiliation*

	Males	*Females*	*Total*
Democrats	4	5	9
Republicans	6	1	7
Other	7	1	8
Totals	17	7	24

TABLE 5.5   *Frequency of Voting in Last 5 Years*

Number of Times Voted	Frequency
8	2
7	3
6	5
5	1
4	2
3	2
2	3
1	2
0	4

TABLE 5.6   *Grouped Frequency Distribution for Income*

Annual Income	Frequency
$50,000–51,999	2
$48,000–49,999	1
$46,000–47,999	2
$44,000–45,999	5
$42,000–43,999	2
$40,000–41,999	0
$38,000–39,999	3
$36,000–37,999	1
$34,000–35,999	3
$32,000–33,999	1
$30,000–31,999	2
$28,000–29,999	1
$26,000–27,999	1

Graphical Representation of Data

A Chinese proverb states "one picture is worth a thousand words" (Bartlett, 1980), and this is especially true when dealing with statistical information. **Graphs** often clarify a data set by presenting the data visually. Most people find graphic representations easier to understand than other statistical procedures. Graphs and tables are excellent supplements to other statistical procedures.

Frequency or grouped frequency distributions can be represented graphically by using either a **histogram** or a **frequency polygon.** Figure 5.1 shows both a histogram and a frequency polygon representing the voting data summarized in Table 5.5. They were generated in just a few seconds using the SPSS for Windows data analysis program. These figures are the actual output of the program as it would be seen on the computer screen. Both the histogram and the frequency polygon represent data on a two-dimensional graph, in which the horizontal axis (**x-axis** or **abscissa**) represents the range of scores for the variable and the vertical axis (**y-axis** or **ordinate**) represents the frequency of the scores. In a histogram, the frequency of a score is represented by the height of a bar above that score, as shown in Figure 5.1(a). In the frequency polygon, the frequency is indicated by the height of a point above each score on the abscissa. Connecting the adjacent points, as

(a)

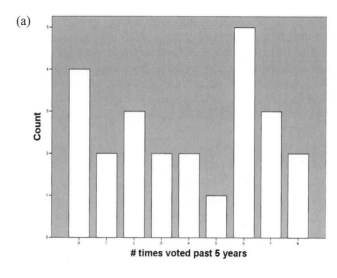

(b)

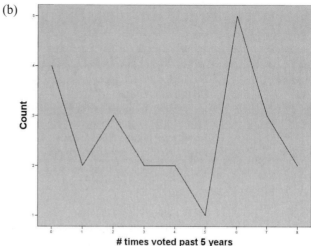

FIGURE 5.1 *Histograms and Frequency Polygons* Graphing the distribution of scores with either a histogram or a frequency polygon helps the researcher to visualize the data.

shown in Figure 5.1(b), completes the frequency polygon. To aid in the interpretation of histograms and frequency polygons, it is important to label both axes carefully.

Two or more frequency distributions can be displayed on the same graph. So that one can compare the distributions, each is graphed independently with different colors or different types of lines to distinguish one distribution from the other. Figure 5.2 shows the distribution for the variable "number of times voted in the last five years," graphed separately for males and females.

When group size is small, a frequency polygon is usually jagged. There is an overall shape to the distribution, but the lines connecting the points go up and down from one interval to another. The distributions graphed in Figures 5.1 and 5.2 have this jagged appearance. As group size increases, the frequency polygon tends to look more like a smooth curve. Data are often described by drawing smooth curves, even though such curves are seen only when the group sizes are extremely large.

Figure 5.3 represents several smooth-curve drawings illustrating various distribution shapes. Figure 5.3(a) shows a common shape for a **symmetric distribution:** a bell-shaped curve. In symmetric distributions, the right side is the mirror image of the left side. In a bell-shaped curve, most of the participants are near the middle of the distribution. Distributions with this shape are referred to as normal curves or **normal distributions.** The normal curve is actually defined by a mathematical equation, but many variables in psychology form distributions similar in shape to a true normal curve. For example, measures of most human characteristics, such as height, weight, and intelligence, are distributed normally. Figures 5.3(b) and 5.3(c) represent **skewed distributions.** In skewed distributions, the scores pile up on one end of the distribution. The direction of the skew is indicated by the tail of the curve. In Figure 5.3(b), the curve is **positively skewed,** with most of the scores piled up near the bottom (the tail points toward the high or positive end of the scale). Figure 5.3(c) is **skewed negatively.** Such distributions might be seen on an easy classroom test, on which almost everyone does well

FIGURE 5.2 *Comparing Two Distributions* Graphing frequency data from two or more groups on the same histogram or frequency polygon gives a visual representation of how the groups compare. In this example, we are comparing men (cross-hatched bars) and women (white bars) on the number of times that they have voted in the past five years.

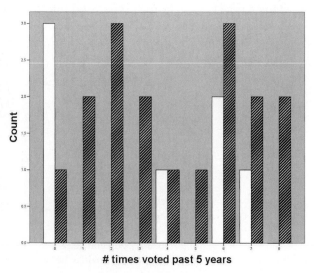

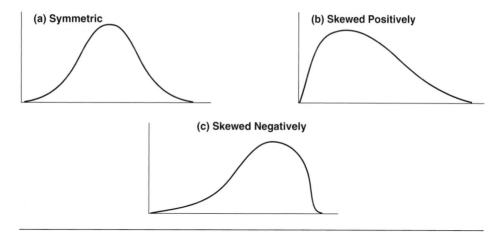

FIGURE 5.3 *Symmetric and Skewed Distributions* Many measures yield the classic bell-shaped distribution. When scores bunch up at either the top or the bottom of the distribution, the distributions are skewed.

and only a few people do poorly. These are the distribution shapes most often seen in psychology. In addition to the shape of the curve, distributions can also be described in terms of the location of the middle of the distribution on the *x*-axis, which is called the **central tendency** of the distribution. We can also quantify the horizontal spread of the distribution, which is called the **variability** of the distribution. An excellent book on graphical presentation of data is Tufte (1997).

Quick-Check Review 5.2: Organizing Data	1. What are frequency distributions? With what kind of data can we use frequency distributions?
	2. Define cross-tabulation.
	3. What is the difference between frequency and grouped frequency distributions?
	4. What type of variable requires a grouped frequency distribution?
	5. What are the basic shapes of distributions found in psychology?

Descriptive Statistics

Descriptive statistics serve two purposes. The first is to describe data with just one or two numbers, which makes it easier to compare groups. The second is to provide a basis for later analyses using inferential statistics. This section covers measures of central tendency, variability, and relationship and introduces you to standard scores.

Measures of Central Tendency

Measures of central tendency describe the typical or average score. They are so named because they provide an indication of the center of the distribution, where most of the scores tend to cluster. The three measures of central tendency—mode, median, and mean—are summarized in Table 5.7.

The **mode** is the most frequently occurring score in the distribution. In the example shown in Table 5.1, 87 is the mode for Group A and 72 in the mode for Group B. If a frequency distribution like the one in Table 5.5 has been prepared, the mode can be computed by finding the largest number in the frequency column and noting the score with that frequency. In Table 5.5, the mode is 6. The mode has the advantage of being easily computed, but it has the disadvantage of being unstable, which means that it can be affected by a change in only a few scores. The mode can be appropriately used with all scales of measurement.

A distribution may have more than one mode. If there are two, then the distribution is **bimodal;** if there are three, it is **trimodal.**

A second measure of central tendency is the **median.** This is the middle score in a distribution in which the scores have been ordered from lowest to highest. The median is also the 50th percentile, which means that half the scores fall below the median. The median can be easily computed if there are few scores and they have been ordered from lowest to highest. With an odd number of scores, the median is the $(N + 1)/2$ score, in which N is the number of scores. In Table 5.1, there are 11 scores. Therefore, the sixth score $[(11 + 1)/2]$ will be the median. The sixth score in a group of 11 scores will be exactly in the middle, with 5 scores above it and 5 scores below it. In Table 5.1, the median for Group A is 87; in Group B, it is 74. When there is an even number of scores, there will be two middle scores; the median is the average of the two middle scores. The median can be appropriately used with ordered and score data, but not with nominal data. (Why is the median not appropriate for *nominal data*?)

The most commonly used measure of central tendency is the **mean,** the arithmetic average of all of the scores. The mean is computed by summing the scores and dividing by the number of scores as follows:

$$Mean = \overline{X} = \frac{\sum X}{N} \tag{5.1}$$

The term $\overline{X}$ (read "X bar") is the notation for the mean. The term $\sum X$ (read "sigma X") is summation notation and simply means to add all the scores. Table 5.8 shows a sample computation of a mean. The mean is appropriately used only with score data. (Why is this so?)

TABLE 5.7 *Measures of Central Tendency*

Mode	Most frequently occurring score in a distribution
Median	Middle score in a distribution; the score at the 50th percentile
Mean	Arithmetic average of the scores in a distribution; computed by summing the scores and dividing by the number of scores

TABLE 5.8 *Sample Computation of a Mean*

Compute the mean for the following 10 scores: 12, 7, 8, 5, 10, 8, 9, 13, 9, 6

1. Start by listing the scores in no particular order in a column.
2. Sum the column.
3. Use the following computational formula to compute the mean.

$$
\begin{array}{c}
X \\
\hline
12 \\
7 \\
8 \\
5 \\
10 \\
8 \\
9 \\
13 \\
9 \\
6 \\
\hline
\sum X = 87
\end{array}
$$

Computing the mean $\overline{X} = \dfrac{\sum X}{N} = \dfrac{87}{10} = 8.7$

The mean and the median are frequently used to describe the average score. The median gives a better indication of what the typical score is if there are a few deviant scores in the distribution (e.g., unusually high or low scores), as discussed in *The Cost of Neglect 5.1*. The mean, on the other hand, is more useful in other statistical procedures, such as inferential statistics.

THE COST OF NEGLECT 5.1:   *Lies, Damn Lies, and Statistics: A Matter of Ethics*

The old joke that there are lies, damn lies, and statistics strikes a responsive cord for many people. However, there is nothing about statistics that is inherently deceptive. If you do not understand statistics, however, it is easy for someone to deceive you by selecting those statistics that make their case and ignoring the ones that contradict it. Let's play with some numbers to show how easy this is.

Imagine a five-person company in which everyone makes an annual salary of $40,000. The mean, median, and mode are all $40,000. Now suppose that business picks up dramatically and profits soar. The owner of the company decides to take all the additional profit, giving none of it to the employees. So now four people make $40,000, and the owner makes $340,000. These results are illustrated in Table 5.9.

(continued)

Because of all this new business, the owner wants to hire new people to continue the growth. To entice new people, the owner offers a starting salary of $30,000, but tells prospective employees that there is plenty of room for advancement, noting that the mean salary is $100,000 and that the average percentage increase in salary in the past year was 150%. Those statistics are all accurate, but do they lie? The answer is actually no. The owner may be lying by presenting a misleading selection of statistics, but the statistics themselves are true.

Statistics don't lie to people who (1) have all the relevant statistics and (2) know how to interpret them. If you apply for a job and are told the mean income for the company, you should ask what the median income is. Almost every company has a few critical people who get paid more than most of the rest of the company's employees, so the median will give you a better idea than the mean what the typical salary is. If you are told that the mean salary increase last year was 150%, you might want to ask if that was across the board (meaning everyone got a 150% increase). If not, you might ask what the median increase was. For this hypothetical company, the median increase was 0%. If you insist on having all the statistics, you cannot be lied to unless the statistics were deliberately falsified. In that case, it is not the statistics that are lying, but rather the statistician who falsified the statistics.

Scientists have an ethical obligation to present their findings and the statistics that summarize those findings in a manner that accurately reflects the data. Selecting data or using statistical procedures that deliberately emphasize some aspects while de-emphasizing other aspects is dishonest. That puts quite a burden on scientists, because scientists are people, too. They are subject to the same expectations and biases that characterize all human beings. (We will discuss those biases in later chapters.) Scientists are expected to use

their training to identify sources of such biases and use procedures that reduce or eliminate them. In analyzing data, the intellectually honest scientist who respects ethical obligations will be objective about how well data support his or her own theory and/or the theories offered by other researchers.

TABLE 5.9   *Mean versus Median*

This table shows the computations for our hypothetical company's income figures.

First Year	*Second Year*	*Change*
$40,000	$ 40,000	0%
40,000	40,000	0%
40,000	40,000	0%
40,000	40,000	0%
40,000	340,000	750%

In the first year, the mean, median, and mode are all $40,000, but in the second year, the owner's salary jumps dramatically and the four employees get no increase in salary. What happens to the measures of central tendency then? The mode (most frequent salary) is still $40,000, and the median (the middle salary) is still $40,000. However, the mean is now $100,000 ($500,000/5).

The third column reflects the percentage change in the salary for each employee. Both the mode and the median for these salary increases was 0%, but the owner got 750%. If you compute the mean salary increase, you get 150%, although that hardly reflects the typical situation in this company.

Measures of Variability

In addition to measures of central tendency, it is also important to determine the variability of scores. The concept of variability is illustrated in Figure 5.4, which shows two distributions with identical means. However, curve A is narrower; that is, the scores are bunched closer together. They are less variable than the scores of Curve B. For example, if you compared the ages of people who attend county fairs with the ages of those who at-

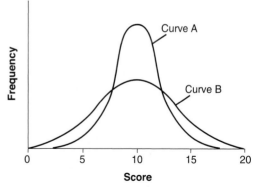

FIGURE 5.4 *Two Distributions with the Same Mean but Different Variances* Even though both of these distributions have the same mean, they clearly differ on another characteristic: thier variablility.

tend pop music concerts, you would probably find that those attending county fairs range from infants to people over 90, whereas pop concert attendees are mostly in their teens and early twenties, with few preteens and few people over thirty. Clearly, there is far more variability in the age of attendees at a county fair than at a typical pop concert.

Variability is one of the most important concepts in research. It is also a fact of life. Individuals differ from one another on many factors, and these differences affect their responses to stimuli. This natural variability among participants often masks the effects of the variables under study. Most research designs and statistical procedures were developed to control or minimize the effects of the natural variability of scores.

As important as the concept of variability is, it is an easy concept to understand. Participants differ from one another, and these differences are reflected in differences in scores for a variable. For some variables, there are large differences among participants; for other variables, the differences are small. There may be many reasons why scores vary among participants, but you need not worry about the reasons at this point. The important ideas to remember are that scores vary and that the degree of variability can be quantified.

The measures of variability are summarized in Table 5.10. The simplest measure of variability is the **range,** the distance from the lowest to the highest score. Although the

TABLE 5.10 *Measures of Variability*

Range	Distance from the lowest to the highest score in a distribution; may be specified by either giving both the lowest and highest scores or by subtracting the lowest from the highest score and reporting this value
Average deviation	Arithmetic average of the distance that each score is from the mean
Variance	Essentially the average squared distance from the mean; the variance is computed by summing the squared distances from the mean and dividing by the degrees of freedom (equal to the number of scores minus 1)
Standard deviation	Square root of the variance

range is easy to compute, it is unstable, because it depends on only two scores (the highest and lowest). A single deviant score can dramatically affect the range. For example, the scores for curve A in Figure 5.4 range from 4 to 16 (a range of 12), and the scores for curve B range from 1 to 19 (a range of 18). However, if one more score were added to curve A (a score of 22), the ranges for curves A and B would be equal. Note that even with the addition of this one deviant score, the scores are more tightly clustered (less variable) in curve A than in curve B.

A better measure of variability is the **variance.** The variance utilizes all of the scores, instead of just the lowest and highest scores. Furthermore, it has statistical properties that make it useful in inferential statistics. To begin our discussion of variance, suppose that you have a set of scores, and you have calculated the mean of this set. Now suppose that you ask a reasonable question about variability: On average, how much do the scores in this set differ from the mean of the set? It is a simple matter to find this value; just subtract the mean from each score (called the deviation), add up these deviations (ignoring the + and − signs), and find their average by dividing the sum of the deviations by the number of scores. This computation is shown in the example in Table 5.11.

When you divide this sum by the number of scores, you get the **average deviation.** The scores in Table 5.11 differ from the mean by an average of 1.9 units.

The plus or minus sign is ignored when adding the deviations because, if the sign is not ignored, the average deviation from the mean will always be zero, no matter how variable the scores.

The average deviation is included here only to help to explain the concept of deviation. It is never used in statistical analyses, because it lacks the statistical qualities that would make it useful. Instead, the variance and standard deviation are used, both of which are based on the same concept of variability of scores from the mean.

The variance is calculated by squaring the deviations of the scores from the mean to make them all positive. Therefore, the variance is essentially the average squared deviation of each score from the mean. The notation s^2 refers to variance. The formula for variance is

$$s^2 = \frac{SS(Sum\ of\ Squares)}{df(Degrees\ of\ Freedom)} = \frac{\sum(X - \overline{X})^2}{N - 1} \tag{5.2}$$

05:04

That is, the variance equals the sum of the squared differences of each score from the mean (called the **sum of squares**) divided by the number of scores (N) minus 1 (called the degrees of freedom). The **degrees of freedom** is an important concept in statistics, referring to the number of scores that are free to vary. This concept is explained in more detail on the Student Resource Website. To use Formula 5.2, the mean is first computed. The mean is then subtracted from each score and the difference is squared. The squared differences are summed to calculate the sum of squares. The sum of squares is short for "the sum of squared deviations from the mean" and is often abbreviated in formulas as SS. The sum of squares is divided by $N - 1$, the degrees of freedom, to obtain the variance. In Table 5.11, the variance is computed for the data presented in Table 5.8. The reason why a squared quantity (the variance) is so useful statistically is also explained on the Student Resource Website.

TABLE 5.11 *Computing Measures of Variability*

Compute the average deviation, the variance, and the standard deviation for the data from Table 5.8.

Steps in computing the average deviation

1. List the scores (in no particular order) in a column labeled X.
2. Compute the mean as was done in Table 5.8.
3. Label another column $|X - \overline{X}|$.
4. Compute the values of $|X - \overline{X}|$, then add up the numbers in the column. This total is the numerator of the average deviation formula.
5. Divide by the number of scores to get the average deviation.

Steps in computing the variance and standard deviation

1. Start by listing the scores in no particular order in a column labeled X.
2. Compute the mean as was done in Table 5.8.
3. Label another column $(X - \overline{X})^2$.
4. Compute the values of $(X - \overline{X})^2$; then add up the numbers in the column. This total is the numerator for the variance formula.
5. Use Formula 5.2 to compute the variance and Formula 5.3 to compute the standard deviation.

X	$|X - \overline{X}|$	$(X - \overline{X})^2$
12	3.3	10.89
7	1.7	2.89
8	.7	.49
5	3.7	13.69
10	1.3	1.69
8	.7	.49
9	.3	.09
13	4.3	18.49
9	.3	.09
6	2.7	7.29
$\sum X = 87$	$\sum|X - \overline{X}| = 19.0$	$\sum(X - \overline{X})^2 = 56.10$

$$\overline{X} = \frac{\sum X}{N} = \frac{87}{10} = 8.7$$

$$Average\ Deviation = \frac{\sum|X - \overline{X}|}{N} = \frac{19.0}{10} = 1.9$$

$$s^2 = \frac{\sum(X - \overline{X})^2}{N - 1} = \frac{56.10}{10 - 1} = \frac{56.10}{9} = 6.23$$

$$s = \sqrt{s^2} = \sqrt{6.23} = 2.50$$

05:05

The variance is an excellent measure of variability and is used in many inferential statistics. Note that the variance is expressed in squared units, whereas the mean is expressed in the original units of the variable. A measure called the standard deviation can be computed to transform the variance back into the same units as the original scores. The **standard deviation** (written s) is equal to the square root of the variance. The variance and standard deviation are appropriately used only with score data.

$$s = \sqrt{s^2} = \sqrt{Variance} \tag{5.3}$$

Measures of Relationship

At times we want to quantify the strength of the **relationship** between two or more variables, which indicates the degree to which the two scores tend to vary together. This relationship between variables is best indexed with a **correlation coefficient,** also referred to as a **correlation.** A correlation is a descriptive statistic in that it describes some aspect of the data. However, it is different from other descriptive statistics because it always involves at least two variables. There are different correlation coefficients for different types of data. With score data, the Pearson product-moment correlation should be used; with ordered data, the Spearman rank-order correlation should be used.

05:06

Pearson Product-Moment Correlation.   The **Pearson product-moment correlation** is the most widely used correlation index. Its computational procedures are detailed on the Student Resource Website. The Pearson product-moment correlation can range from -1.00 to $+1.00$. A correlation of $+1.00$ means that the two variables are perfectly related in a positive direction: as one variable increases, the other variable also increases by a predictable amount. A correlation of -1.00 represents a perfect negative relationship: as one variable increases, the other decreases by a predictable amount. A correlation of zero means that there is no relationship between the variables.

The strength of the relationship is indicated by the absolute value of the correlation coefficient. For example, a correlation of .55 indicates a stronger relationship than a correlation of .25, and a correlation of $-.85$ indicates an even stronger relationship. Remember, the sign of the correlation indicates only the direction of the relationship and not its strength.

The standard notation for correlation is r. Thus, the correlations above would be noted as $r = 1.00$, $r = -1.00$, $r = .55$, $r = .25$, and $r = -.85$.

The Pearson product-moment correlation is an index of the degree of **linear relationship** between two variables. What this means is best illustrated by examining a **scatter plot,** which is a graphic technique used to represent the relationship between two variables. To construct one, standard x- and y-axes are labeled with the names of the two variables. Each axis is divided into a sufficient number of equal intervals to handle the range for the variable represented by the axis. A scatter plot for the relationship between age and income using data from Table 5.2 is graphed in Figure 5.5. As indicated in the figure, participant 1 is 28 years old and earns $32,000 a year. The point representing participant 1 is

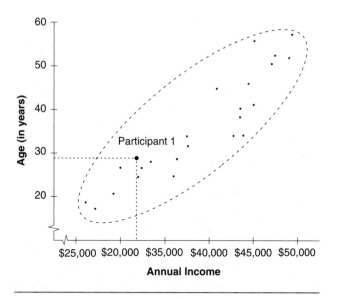

FIGURE 5.5 *Scatter Plot for Age and Salary* A scatter plot is constructed by graphing each person's data point. The data point is determined by the two scores for the person.

directly above $32,000 on the *x*-axis and directly across from 28 on the *y*-axis. To complete the scatter plot, each person's set of scores is plotted in the same way.

The pattern of scores in the scatter plot is informative. For example, in Figure 5.5 the people with the highest incomes are all older; younger people tend to have lower incomes. We could draw a straight line through the middle of the dots from the lower left to upper right of the graph, with most of the dots falling close to that line.

This is a good example of a linear relationship because the points in this scatter plot cluster around a straight line. It is a **positive correlation,** because incomes are higher for older participants. It is not a perfect correlation. In a **perfect correlation** ($r = 1.00$), all the dots form a straight line, as seen in Figure 5.6(a).

The scatter plots in Figure 5.6 also illustrate other types of relationships. Figure 5.6(b) illustrates a strong **negative correlation** ($r = -.92$). Note that the points cluster close to a straight line.

Figure 5.6(c) illustrates a zero correlation ($r = .00$).

Figure 5.6(d) illustrates a **nonlinear relationship,** in which the product-moment correlation coefficient does not represent the data well. In fact, in this case the correlation ($r = -.03$) is misleading. The near-zero correlation suggests there is no relationship between the variables, but the scatter plot indicates there is a relationship; it is just not a linear relationship. This is one reason why it is advisable to create a scatter plot to see how the scores cluster, instead of relying on a single number (the correlation coefficient) to summarize the relationship between variables. With modern computer packages, it takes just a few seconds to create a scatter plot.

Spearman Rank-Order Correlation.   If either or both variables are ordinal and neither variable is nominal, the appropriate coefficient is the **Spearman rank-order correlation.** The Student Resource Website shows the relevant computational procedures.

The Spearman rank-order correlation is interpreted like the product-moment correlation: a correlation of -1.00 is a perfect negative relationship; a correlation of $+1.00$ is a perfect positive relationship; a correlation of zero means that no linear relationship exists. Scatter plots can be drawn using the rank of each participant for each variable.

Correlation coefficients quantify the degree and direction of relationship between variables. Finding such relationships is a major goal of science. Another goal is to make predictions about events. The correlation coefficient is an important part of this, because a strong relationship between two variables provides information that will help to predict one variable by knowing the values of the other. For example, if a correlation is found between test scores and later job performance, then we have information that may help us to predict future job performance.

Regression.   The prediction of the value of one variable from the value of another is called **regression.** We typically assume a linear or straight-line relationship. Nonlinear

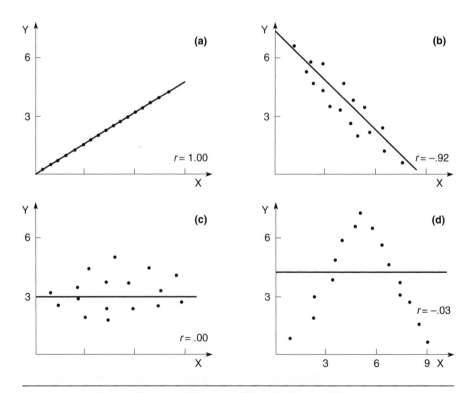

FIGURE 5.6   *Scatter Plots and Regression Lines* You cannot always tell what the relationship between two variables is like from the correlation. A scatter plot allows you to see the relationship, including such complex relationships as the one shown in panel (d).

regression is possible, but the applicable procedures are well beyond the level of this text. If you are interested in learning more about nonlinear regression, we recommend Cohen and Cohen (1983) or Myers and Well (2003).

You may have noticed that a line was drawn in each of the scatter plots in Figure 5.6. This line is the linear regression line for predicting the variable Y from the variable X. In Figures 5.6(a) and (b) the points cluster close to the line, suggesting a strong linear relationship. Where the correlation is zero, as in Figure 5.6(c), the line is horizontal. Where the correlation between X and Y is zero, the best prediction for Y will always be the mean of Y, regardless of the value of X.

05:08

In Figure 5.6(d) the regression line, like the correlation, is misleading in that it does not reflect the data well. The computational procedures for linear regression are included on the Student Resource Website.

Statistical analysis packages can compute a regression line easily for any data set. However, you should always request a scatter plot so that you can see how well the data fit a straight-line function.

Reliability Indices.   The concept of reliability was introduced in Chapter 4. Correlation coefficients are used to quantify many types of reliability, including test-retest and interrater reliability. Typically, a product-moment correlation is computed between two test scores. Since these reliability indices are correlations, they behave like any other correlation. They range from a -1.00 to a $+1.00$. Negative correlations are unlikely unless something is seriously amiss, such as raters using different rating scales. A correlation of $+1.00$ indicates perfect reliability, and a correlation of 0.00 indicates no reliability.

05:09

The internal consistency reliability index, called **coefficient alpha,** is also a correlation coefficient, although a much more complicated one than those covered in this chapter. Coefficient alpha is an index of how intercorrelated the items in a measure are. The more highly correlated the items are with one another, the higher the coefficient alpha. The Student Resource Website gives a more detailed description of these reliability indices and computational formulas.

Standard Scores

The **standard score** (written Z; also called the **Z-score**) is a transformation frequently used in research. The standard score is computed by subtracting the mean from the score and dividing the difference by the standard deviation, as shown in Formula 5.4. This is referred to as a **relative score** because it tells how the participant scored *relative* to the rest of the participants. If the participant scores above the mean, the standard score is positive; if the participant scores below the mean, the standard score is negative. The size of the standard score indicates how far from the mean the participant scored.

Many tests convert the standard score to avoid negative numbers and decimals. For example, the standard score on an IQ test is converted into an IQ by multiplying the standard score by 15 and adding 100, producing an IQ distribution with a mean of 100 and a standard deviation of 15. The subtests of the SAT have similarly been converted from standard scores to a distribution with a mean of 500 and a standard deviation of 100.

$$Z = \frac{(X - \overline{X})}{s} \tag{5.4}$$

The standard score is useful in many situations. Converting several measures to standard scores before summing them will give each measure the same weight in the total. Instructors often use this principle in computing grades: they sum the standard scores for each exam, rather than the raw scores. Many statistical procedures use an implicit conversion to standard scores, including most advanced regression procedures.

Finally, if the distribution is approximately normal, the standard score can be easily converted into a percentile rank. A person's **percentile rank** tells what percent of the group scored below the person. The details of this transformation are included on the Student Resource Website.

05:10

Quick-Check Review 5.3: Descriptive Statistics	1. What are the three measures of central tendency?
	2. What are the chief measures of variability?
	3. Define *correlation* and *regression*. How are these used?
	4. What is a *standard score*, and how is it computed?
	5. Why is the variance a better measure of variability than the range?
	6. Why is the mean a better measure of central tendency than the mode?
	7. How does a correlation differ from other descriptive statistics?

Statistical Inference

Using statistics to describe data is only the first step in analyzing the results of a research study. The rest of the analysis is concerned not so much with the specific participants tested, but with what these participants indicate about a larger group of people. This section will cover the logic of this process, and the next section will cover the actual statistical procedures.

This section starts by discussing the differences between samples and populations and the processes of drawing inferences about populations based on samples. It then introduces the concepts of the null hypothesis and statistical decision making. It closes with a discussion of the limits of statistical decision making; specifically, judging the error rates in the decision process.

Populations and Samples

It is seldom possible to observe whole populations. Therefore, samples are drawn from populations and observed. In human research, a **population** is the larger group to which all the people of interest belong. The **sample** is a subset of the population. For example, a researcher might select a sample of high school students from the population of all high school students in the county. A sample is used as if that sample adequately represented the population. We want to draw conclusions about a population on the basis of a sample from that population, but no two samples drawn from the same population will be exactly alike. For example, one sample of participants from the general population may have a mean IQ of 102.2, whereas another sample from the same population might have a mean IQ of 100. Most samples are reasonably representative of the population from which they are drawn, but sometimes samples are unrepresentative of the population, even though the sampling procedure may have been carried out flawlessly. The variation among different samples drawn from the same population is referred to as **sampling error.** This term is misleading in that it does not represent a mistake. Rather, sampling error refers to variability among samples due to chance. Because samples are not perfectly representative of the population from which they are drawn, we cannot be sure that conclusions drawn from samples will apply to the entire population. In fact, we can never be sure that inferences drawn from a sample are valid for the population; the best we can do is to calculate **probabilities** about potential inferences. Probability provides a numerical indication of how likely it is that a given event will occur. It is a critical concept in inferential statistics.

Suppose that a researcher is interested in sex differences in reaction time and compares men and women. The variable, reaction time, is measured by recording how quickly participants press a button in response to an auditory signal. The samples of men and women would be drawn from the population of men and women. Suppose that it is found that mean reaction time from the samples was 0.278 seconds for the men and 0.254 seconds for the women. Clearly, the sample means are different, but not very different. However, the researcher is actually interested in the population of men and the population of women. That is, the researcher wants to draw conclusions about characteristics of the populations from the results of the samples. Would the observed difference in mean reaction time in the samples lead us to believe that a similar difference exists between the populations, or could the observed difference simply be a result of sampling error? This question, comparing population means, is the type most often raised in such research. Suppose for the moment that the reaction time means for the populations were not different. In this case, samples drawn from the populations should have approximately equal mean reaction times. Are the mean reaction times of 0.278 and 0.254 approximately equal? Are they close enough to infer that the population means, which are unknown, are also approximately equal? This process is referred to as testing the null hypothesis.

The Null Hypothesis

The **null hypothesis** states that there is no statistical difference between the population means. Null is from the Latin *nullus*, meaning "not any." If the observed sample means were very different, we would reject the null hypothesis and conclude that the population means are not equal. But how different is "very different"? Inferential statistics give a probabilistic answer to this question.

Before proceeding, you need to understand the difference between a population parameter and a sample statistic. If a characteristic of the population, such as the mean, is computed by testing everyone in the population, it is called a **population parameter.** If the same characteristic is computed for a sample drawn from that population, it is called a **sample statistic.** The task in inferential statistics is to draw conclusions about population parameters on the basis of sample statistics.

Statistical Decisions and Alpha Levels

Inferential statistics are used to compute the probability of obtaining the observed data *if* the null hypothesis is true. If this probability is small, the null hypothesis is probably false. In such a case, the researcher would say that the results are **statistically significant.**

A somewhat arbitrary cutoff point called the **alpha level** (written α) is used for making this decision.[1] Traditionally, researchers set alpha to a small value, such as 0.05 or 0.01. Referring back to the example will help to clarify these difficult but important concepts.

1. The researcher is interested in the reaction time of men and women.
2. The null hypothesis is that the mean reaction times are the same in these two populations.
3. The inferential statistical procedure evaluates the size of the observed mean difference between the samples.
4. If the sample means are so different that it is unlikely that the samples could have come from populations with equal means, then we reject the null hypothesis and conclude that the populations must be different.

Type I and Type II Errors

The alpha level guides decisions about the null hypothesis. When the probability is greater than the alpha level, the null hypothesis is retained; when the probability is equal to or less than the alpha level, the null hypothesis is rejected. Of course, there is always the chance that a researcher's decision will be wrong. For example, a researcher might reject the null hypothesis and conclude that the population means are not equal when they are actually equal. In this case, the researcher has made a **Type I error.** The probability of this error is equal to the alpha level that was set by the researcher. If an alpha of .05 is used, Type I errors will occur 5% of the time. If the alpha is .01, Type I errors will occur 1% of the time. In other words, the alpha level is the proportion of Type I errors that we can expect a researcher to make if he or she repeats their study many times.

If alpha is the level of Type I error and the researcher decides what alpha to use, why not set alpha to zero to avoid all Type I errors? The reason is that there is another possible error, known as a Type II error. A **Type II error** occurs when we fail to reject the null hypothesis when it is false.

The term **beta** (β) refers to the probability of making a Type II error. Researchers want to avoid both errors, but because we can never be sure of the real state of nature, there is always the chance for error in the decision. Decreasing the Type I error rate, without doing anything else, will automatically increase the Type II error rate. Therefore, these two errors have to be balanced against one another. Table 5.12 summarizes the definitions of Type I and Type II errors.

---

[1]*Alpha*, as used here, is entirely different from the reliability index concept of *coefficient alpha*. It is a historical accident that the first letter of the Greek alphabet was used for these two statistical concepts.

TABLE 5.12   *Type I and Type II Errors*

True State of Nature	Researcher's Decision	
	Reject the Null Hypothesis	*Retain the Null Hypothesis*[a]
Null hypothesis is true	Type I error	Correct decision
Null hypothesis is false	Correct decision	Type II error

[a]Technically, we never actually accept the null hypothesis. Instead, we retain or fail to reject the null hypothesis. The interested student should consult an introductory statistics textbook for the reasoning behind this subtle distinction.

Quick-Check Review 5.4: Statistical Inference	1. Distinguish populations from samples. 2. What is sampling error? 3. Define population parameter and sample statistic. 4. Define alpha level, Type I error, and Type II error.

Inferential Statistics

This section introduces the most common inferential statistics: the *t*-test and the analysis of variance. It also briefly covers several related topics, including statistical power, statistical versus practical significance, effect size, and meta-analysis.

Testing for Mean Differences

Inferential statistics are used most frequently to evaluate mean differences between groups. Such statistical techniques are valuable because we can often specify research hypotheses in terms of mean differences. This section covers several tests for evaluating mean differences between groups.

t*-Test for Independent Groups.**   The **t-test for independent groups** is used with score data from two **independent samples.** Samples are *independent* if different individuals appear in each sample and if the participants in the two samples are not matched in any way. The null hypothesis is that there is no difference between the two population means; put another way, the observed difference between the sample means is due only to sampling error. The test statistic is called *t*. The general procedure in this, and most other inferential statistics, is to compute the test statistic and the probability (p*-value**) of obtaining this value of the test statistic if the null hypothesis is true. If the *p*-value is less than alpha, we reject the null hypothesis and conclude that the population means are different. Computational procedures for *t* can be found on the Student Resource Website, which also shows how to use SPSS for Windows to conduct a *t*-test.

05:11

Correlated* t-*Test.   Some research designs do not use independent samples. One such design is called a **within-subjects design,** in which the same participants appear in each group. In this design, the groups represent different conditions under which the participants are tested. Another design is the **matched-subjects design** in which all participants are matched in pairs and then randomly assigned so that one member of each pair goes into one group and the other member goes into the other group. These designs will be discussed in Chapter 11.

05:12

In either case, a **correlated *t*-test** is the appropriate statistic to use to analyze the results of the study. Computational procedures and instructions on how to use statistical software to do the computations for the correlated *t*-test are included on the Student Resource Website.

Analysis of Variance.   When testing for mean differences among more than two groups, an **analysis of variance (ANOVA)** is the appropriate test. The term *analysis of variance* is confusing because the test actually compares the group means, but it compares these means by computing and comparing different population variance estimates. (Explaining how this is accomplished is beyond the scope of this book.) This section will focus on the conceptual basis of ANOVA. Standard terminology and interpretation will be discussed in Chapters 10 through 12. Computational procedures and statistical software instructions are included on the Student Resource Website.

05:13

Analysis of variance is a flexible tool for analyzing the results of research. It can analyze the results of studies that use one independent variable or studies that use two or more independent variables. When there is more than one independent variable, the independent variables are referred to as **factors,** and the research design is said to be **factorial.** The analysis of a study with only one independent variable is referred to as a **one-way ANOVA;** one with two independent variables is referred to as a **two-way ANOVA;** and so forth. ANOVAs can also be used to analyze data from studies in which different participants appear in each condition (called a **between-subjects design**) or studies in which the same participants appear in all conditions (a **within-subjects design**). An ANOVA used to analyze data from a within-subjects design is referred to as a **repeated measures ANOVA.**

All these concepts will be discussed in more detail in later chapters.

The Power of a Statistical Test

The term **power** or **statistical power** refers to the sensitivity of a statistical procedure to the hypothesized mean differences. In other words, power is the capability of correctly rejecting the null hypothesis when it is false. It is equal to $1 - \beta$, where β is the probability of a Type II error. Power is not a function of the statistical procedure alone, but also depends on the precision of the research design. The traditional way to increase power is to increase sample size. The sample size needed to achieve a specified level of power can be computed on the basis of pilot data as part of the procedures-design phase, a process called **power analysis** (Cohen, 1988, 1992).

Increasing sample size is not the only way to increase power. Any improvement in a research design that increases sensitivity will increase power, including sampling more precisely, using more precise measures, using better standardization of procedures, or controlling individual differences through the choice of a research design (see Chapter 10).

Effect Size

In recent years it has become commonplace to go a step beyond significance testing by computing the **effect size** of an experimental manipulation. This is a measure of the difference between the group means (a difference supposedly brought about by the experimental manipulation of the independent variable). This difference is expressed in standard deviation units and is independent of the size of the sample. Cohen (1992) proposed a scale for the size of the effect (small, moderate, or large) to help to guide researchers in interpreting the calculated effect, and this scale has become widely used. Effect size and power are related: as effect size increases, power increases. The reason for the increase in power is that it is easier to detect large differences in population means than small differences.

05:14

Effect size is covered more fully on the Student Resource Website.

Statistical versus Practical Significance

Researchers are usually pleased when they find a statistically significant result, especially if it is in the predicted direction. However, a statistically significant finding may not have practical significance. For example, suppose that a researcher compares two groups of seriously obese adults. The experimental group attends a weight-reduction program and the control group is put on a waiting list. After six months, the treated group has lost a mean of 3.4 pounds, whereas the control group has gained a mean of 0.2 pounds. This difference between the groups is statistically significant. Despite this statistical significance, one might ask, "Is the loss of just over three pounds after six months of expensive dieting, exercise, and group meetings of any personal significance to those obese people who wanted to lose weight?" Most of the dieters would probably say "No!" Thus, when evaluating the effectiveness of the weight-reduction program in practical terms, we should not let the statistically significant findings blind us to the possibility that the program might not have been practically or personally successful for these people.

Meta-analysis

A relatively recent and very important innovation is meta-analysis. **Meta-analysis** is a procedure that allows statistical averaging of results from independent studies of the same phenomenon, in effect creating the statistical equivalent of a "super study" (Cooper & Lindsay, 1998). Meta-analyses have become more common in recent years because they provide a more objective way of integrating the findings from several studies on the same general question. Meta-analysis is discussed more extensively in Chapter 15.

<table>
<tr>
<td>

Quick-Check Review 5.5: Inferential Statistics
</td>
<td>

1. What statistical tests are used to test for mean differences? Under what conditions should each of these statistics be used?

2. What is *power analysis* and why is it important?

3. What is the difference between statistical and practical significance?

4. What is a *meta-analysis*?
</td>
</tr>
</table>

<table>
<tr>
<td>

PUTTING IT INTO PRACTICE
</td>
<td>

Data everywhere show that individual differences exist. All you need to do is open a newspaper. Look at the batting averages of baseball players on the sports page, at home prices in the paper's housing section, or at the stock charts in the financial section, which show annual percentage changes in price. Pick one of these and prepare a frequency distribution and a graph of the distribution. If you have access to a data analysis program, such as SPSS for Windows, input the data and compute descriptive statistics. Based on your computations, look back at individual ballplayers, houses, or stocks and see how they compare. For example, what is a typical batting average and what batting average is truly exceptional? What is the median housing price in your community? What is the typical one-year gain in the price of a stock? Taking time to do this exercise will give you a feel for how descriptive statistics can help you visualize what would otherwise be an overwhelming amount of data.
</td>
</tr>
</table>

Chapter Summary

Statistics are tools that help researchers to interpret the results of studies. Some statistical procedures (descriptive statistics) describe data from a study. These include measures of central tendency, measures of variability, and correlations. Others (inferential statistics) are designed to help to interpret the data. The most commonly used inferential statistics are the *t*-test and the analysis of variance.

The appropriate statistic(s) will depend on the nature of the data and on the nature of the questions. Inferential statistics help researchers to make deci-

sions about populations on the basis of samples drawn from those populations, but these procedures are not perfect and decision errors are possible.

This chapter discusses the most commonly used statistics. The Student Resource Website outlines procedures for computing statistics manually and with a popular statistical analysis package, SPSS for Windows. (Chapter 14 presents a flowchart for selecting the appropriate statistical technique based on the research design.)

Chapter Exercises

1. Define the following key terms. Be sure that you understand them. They are discussed in the chapter and defined in the glossary.

statistics
individual differences
descriptive statistics
inferential statistics
frequencies
frequency distribution
cross-tabulation
univariate
grouped frequency
  distribution
continuous variable
graphs
histogram
frequency polygon
x-axis, or abscissa
y-axis, or ordinate
symmetric
  distribution
normal distribution
skewed distribution
positively skewed
negatively skewed
central tendency
variability
measures of central
  tendency
mode
bimodal
trimodal
median
mean
range
average deviation
variance
sum of squares
degrees of freedom

standard deviation
relationship
correlation coefficient,
  or correlation
Pearson product-moment
  correlation
linear relationship
scatter plot
positive correlation
perfect correlation
negative correlation
nonlinear relationship
Spearman rank-order
  correlation
regression
coefficient alpha
standard score, or *Z*-score
relative score
percentile rank
population
sample
sampling error
probability
null hypothesis
population parameter
sample statistic
statistically significant
alpha level
Type I error
Type II error
beta
t-test for independent
  groups
independent samples
p-value
within-subjects design

matched-subjects design
correlated *t*-test
analysis of variance
  (ANOVA)
factors
factorial
one-way ANOVA
two-way ANOVA
between-subjects design
repeated-measures
  ANOVA

power (statistical power)
power analysis
effect size
meta-analysis
statistical symbols: Σ
(sigma);
  $\overline{X}$; N; s; s^2; SS; α
(alpha);
  β (beta); t

2. For each of the following data sets, graph the data, compute the measures of central tendency, and compute the measures of variability.

   a. 20 exam scores: 8; 6; 4; 3; 9; 5; 7; 8; 6; 7; 9; 5; 9; 8; 9; 7; 4; 8; 7; 9

   b. 15 IQ scores: 104; 121; 94; 107; 81; 96; 100; 96; 102; 115; 87; 101; 91; 114; 111

3. Draw each of the following: a positively skewed curve, a negatively skewed curve, and a symmetrical curve.

4. Draw approximate scatter plots for correlations of .22, .50, −.73, .02, −.02, 1.00.

5. What kind of statistical test would answer each of the following research questions?

   a. Is the weight of sixth-grade boys related to their aggressiveness?

   b. Are girls better than boys at fine motor coordination?

   c. Will laboratory animals' behavior change as each participant is tested under conditions of increasing noise?

   d. Do fourth-, fifth-, and sixth-grade children differ in their animal welfare concerns?

6

Field Research: Naturalistic and Case-Study Research

(Scientists) must acquire an extensive portfolio of methods . . . and must apply their skills aided by an immense base of shared knowledge about the domain and the profession.

—David Klahr and Herbert Simon, 2001

*Web Resource Material*_____

06:01 Applied Research Strategies

06:02 For What Is a Scientist Remembered? (Sociology of Science)

06:03 Making ObservationsTutorial

06:04 Student Study Guide/Laboratory Manual

06:05 Related Internet Sites

The term **field research** applies to a variety of research methods, ranging from low to high constraint. They share a focus on observing naturally occurring behavior under largely natural conditions—that is, observing behavior "in the field." Table 6.1 describes six types of field research. Field research will be covered in two chapters. The lower-constraint field-research methods of naturalistic observation, archival research, and case studies will be discussed in this chapter. After you have learned about higher-constraint research, Chapter 13 will provide a second look at field research, covering the higher-constraint field-research methods of program evaluation, surveys, and field experiments.

Naturalistic and case-study methods are flexible approaches that allow the researcher to take advantage of unexpected occurrences and new ideas developed during the observations. These methods focus on the natural flow of behavior without controls or manipulations by the researcher. Naturalistic research is carried out in the participant's natural environment, such as an animal's habitat, a schoolroom, or a workplace. Case-study research is slightly higher in constraint: the researcher intervenes to some degree to create situations likely to produce interesting information.

This chapter begins by discussing the challenge and the value of low-constraint research, primarily using classic examples of naturalistic and case-study research. The chapter then discusses how such research should be carried out and analyzed, and ends with a discussion of the limitations of these methods.

The Challenge of Low-Constraint Research

You might think that, because researchers impose few controls and make observations in a flexible manner, low-constraint methods are easy to carry out. As in all research, however, care and effort are required. Indeed, the very lack of high-constraint procedures adds a

TABLE 6.1 *Categories of Field Research*

Naturalistic observation	Observation of events as they occur in natural settings
Archival research	Studying information from existing records made in natural settings
Surveys	Asking direct questions of persons in natural settings
Case studies	Making extensive observations of a single group or a person
Program evaluation	Conducting evaluations of applied procedures in natural settings
Field experiments	Conducting experiments in natural settings in order to understand causal relationships among variables

Note: Surveys, program evaluation, and field experiments will be covered in Chapter 13.

06:01

considerable burden, because researchers cannot depend on the supports found in laboratory settings. The Student Resource Website discusses several applied research strategies.

Examples of Naturalistic Observation

The defining characteristic of naturalistic observation is that the researcher observes and
systematically records naturally occurring events and later develops hypotheses about why
they occurred. This section illustrates these characteristics with examples drawn from the
fields of biology, ethology, sociology, and psychology.

Biology.   Naturalistic observation has a long history in science, predating modern science and the emergence of psychology. One body of classic naturalistic research is Darwin's observations of animals and plants, generally considered to be the most important
research in all of biology (Trefil & Hazan, 2001). Darwin's work was introduced in
Chapter 1. He recorded detailed observations of hundreds of species of plants and animals
and then devoted years to trying to understand the processes that might account for the
patterns that he observed. From his observations, Darwin developed his concepts of natural selection. Darwin also contributed a pioneering study of child development, recording detailed naturalistic observations of his son's infancy and childhood (Darwin, 1877).
Darwin's work illustrates how powerful naturalistic observation can be in the hands of
gifted scientists, as discussed in *Historical Lesson 6.1*. The Student Resource Website also
has additional information about Darwin.

06:02

Ethology.   **Ethology** is the study of organisms in their natural environments. Ethologists
have used research methods to study hundreds of species of animals. Jane Goodall (1986,
1988), for example, studied chimpanzees in Tanzania, persisting for two difficult years in
the forest before she was able to make any substantial observations. However, her persis-
tence paid off, because her naturalistic research presents a remarkable picture of chimpanzees as highly social creatures. She is now applying her knowledge to the conservation
of these endangered animals (Stephens, 2003).

Observations by Goodall and others illustrate the range of adaptive behavior in
chimpanzees. For example, Boesch and Boesch-Acherman (1991) observed chimpanzees
using stones to crack open nuts. The stones were selected according to the type and size of
nuts to be opened and were used with great skill. This was the first observation of the ham-
mer-and-anvil principle being used by non-human primates.

Goodall (1978) observed that chimps hunt, kill, and eat monkeys, antelopes, and
wild pigs. Boesch and Boesch-Acherman (1991) observed chimps hunting cooperatively—a behavior considered by many to be a major step in social evolution. McGrew
(1992) identified 19 different kinds of tools used by chimpanzees. Whiten and Boesch
(2001) collated naturalistic observations from several research groups in Africa, describing distinct cultural differences between groups of chimpanzees. These are behaviors that
are unique to one group of chimpanzees and are passed on to the next generation through
instruction by the older animals. In other words, these chimps create and pass on cultural
traditions much as human cultures do.

Sociology.   Adeline Levine's (1982) sociological study of the Love Canal disaster is a
now-classic example of naturalistic research with human participants. In 1950, the city of

HISTORICAL LESSON 6.1:   Naturalistic Research and Evolution

Naturalistic observation may be the lowest-constraint scientific research, but it is still a valuable and powerful tool in the hands of gifted scientists. Charles Darwin and his scientific contemporary, Alfred Russel Wallace, both made extensive observations of plants and animals on their extended journeys, carefully recording their observations with descriptions and drawings. These studies took place long before the development of photographic equipment and recording devices. Nevertheless, they both recorded sufficient detail that each was independently able to recognize what looked like clear patterns in their data.

Both Darwin and Wallace found that species were not random. Instead, they fell into discernible groups that shared a remarkable number of features. Both Darwin and Wallace asked themselves the critical question of how such a pattern might have occurred. Remember our discussion of inductive and deductive reasoning in Chapter 2, using Sherlock Holmes to illustrate these processes. Darwin and Wallace used inductive reasoning to ask what kind of process would have created this kind of pattern of species characteristics and distributions. Both came to the same conclusion: species that become geographically separated from one another will gradually diverge as the members in each isolated group that are most adapted to the specific demands of the local environment are more successful at survival and mating. In time, each isolated group from this single species will experience so much genetic drift that the two groups will diverge into separate, but obviously related, species. Darwin delayed the publication of his theory of evolution through natural selection for years, while he tried to anticipate

and counter every conceivable argument against the theory (Larson, 2004). He was well aware of the social upheaval that his theory might cause—upheaval that continues to this day (e.g., Afraid to discuss evolution, 2005). But, as you learned in Chapter 2, Wallace's manuscript, which he sent to Darwin for comments before publication, spurred Darwin to finally publish what is perhaps the most celebrated book in all of science: *On the Origin of Species* (Darwin, 1859).

As groundbreaking as the theory of evolution was, it would have been little more than a footnote in history if it were not for the deductive reasoning of tens of thousands of scientists over nearly 150 years of research. These scientists took the theory and derived specific predictions, which they evaluated in specific research studies. The vast majority of those predictions were upheld by the data (Larson, 2004). In those instances when the prediction failed, the information pointed scientists toward refinement of the theory of evolution (Trefil & Hazan, 2001). There is perhaps no theory in the history of science that has been tested so thoroughly.

Although there is currently no doubt that evolutionary processes occur, there are still questions that are unanswered as scientists struggle to pin down the details of the process (Trefil & Hazan, 2001). The tens of thousands of independent research studies in more than a dozen different scientific disciplines have established evolutionary theory as probably the best-validated theory in all of science, but it was the low-constraint naturalistic observation of Darwin and Wallace, coupled with their brilliant insights, that created the theory that changed biological science (Wynn & Wiggins, 1997).

Niagara Falls, New York built a grammar school right on top of a toxic dumpsite, and the surrounding land became a housing development. Unknown to the residents, thousands of toxin-filled metal drums were quietly corroding underground, releasing their poisons into the soil. Over the next two decades, the chemicals spread underground, bubbling to the surface and into residents' cellars. Small explosions occurred, "brown ooze" clung to the legs of schoolchildren, and odors were so foul after heavy rains that the school playground had to be closed. Pets died and several children were burned by the chemicals. Cancers, miscarriages, and intestinal and respiratory diseases were common in the neighborhood. By 1978, more than twenty-five years after the toxic dump had been covered up, the residents knew that their neighborhood was contaminated with dangerous toxins, and hundreds of families had to abandon their homes.

Levine (1982) wanted to understand how such a catastrophe could have happened, how it affected residents, how community leaders responded, and how everyone coped with it. These questions cannot be addressed in a laboratory. Instead, Levine and her students reviewed historical records, met with residents and officials, attended public meetings, and monitored newspaper reports and news broadcasts. They documented the events and the psychological, social, and financial impact. Levine's findings have important implications for government policy, and her research could not have been carried out in any way other than through the use of naturalistic research methods.

Another example from sociology is Phillip Davis's research on corporal punishment of children (Davis & Kii, 1997). Some forms of corporal punishment, such as hitting, spanking, whipping, and shaking, are routinely used by more than 80% of American parents and may be an important factor in children's development (Graziano, 1992). Most studies of corporal punishment use surveys asking parents and children for their retrospective reports, but with a sensitive topic such as this, there are obvious problems in simply asking parents, "How often and how severely do you hit your kids?"

Davis wanted to know what actually happens to children when they get hit, and he examined the patterns of behavior of the parents, children, and bystanders. He used naturalistic observations of parents and children in such public places as shopping malls. His method was classic naturalistic observation. He walked through the malls, watching for adults hitting children, and then unobtrusively observed for a few moments. The following is an example of one of the 250 hitting incidents.

> Two men, a woman, and a boy (about six) shop in a department store, one man trying out a treadmill. When the boy gets on (another) treadmill the man snaps "(If) you don't get down, I'm gonna whip you in two seconds!" The boy gets astride a bicycle on display and the man on the treadmill tells the others to do something. The other man pulls the boy from the bike, but the bike nearly topples and the man gives the boy a swat on the bottom. He directs a few hushed words at the boy [then] sees the boy making a face at him. He grabs furiously at the boy's jacketed shoulder with a muffled thud and clutches a handful of collar. Twisting the jacket hard in his fist and jerking the boy forward, he leans into the boy's face and angrily snarls something under his breath. Then he spins the boy around, holds him steady, and hits his bottom hard. As the group is about to leave, the man . . . on the treadmill snaps at the boy "One more time and you're OUT!" They stroll away, but the boy gets on a stair-step machine. The treadmill man tries to take the boy's arm and the boy pulls back slightly. As though offended by the little show of resistance, the man spanks the boy's bottom five times. He says a few angry words and casually walks away. Frozen and mute at first, the boy breaks into a soft cry before bustling after the group. (Davis & Kii, 1997, p. 7)

Psychology.   Rosenhan (1973) investigated the use of psychiatric diagnoses and the experiences of mental patients in hospitals. He wanted to understand how psychiatrists handled an ambiguous diagnostic decision in a real-world hospital setting and how they responded later to contradictory information once a diagnosis had been made. He had eight pseudopatients (his research assistants) admit themselves to various mental hospitals with feigned complaints of hearing voices saying "thud, hollow, and empty." The pseudopatients were instructed to display no other signs of mental disorder during their hospital stay. In fact, once admitted, the pseudopatients behaved normally and gave no indication of their supposed hallucinations. Hearing voices is usually a symptom of psychosis, but without additional symptoms, the person would not qualify for any specific diagnosis. Furthermore, the voices that Rosenhan had the pseudopatients report were not typical for patients with psychotic disorders. This should have raised some questions or doubt in the psychiatrists. The eight researchers were admitted to 12 different hospitals, and apparently none of the hospitals' staff discerned that they were not real patients, although some of the other patients apparently did realize it. Most of the pseudopatients were diagnosed with schizophrenia. They observed hospital conditions and the behavior of staff and patients, much like an anthropologist might. They were more than neutral observers in that they were an active part of the hospitals' environments. As in the Levine study, naturalistic methods were not only appropriate, but were the best way to investigate the issue.

Scientists use naturalistic methods to study a variety of human behaviors in public places, such as smoking, eating, and drinking in restaurants and bars; drivers' behavior at intersections; children on school grounds or in classrooms, and shoppers in stores. Additional examples of naturalistic studies are given in Table 6.2.

Examples of Case-Study Research

Case-study research imposes mild constraints on the procedures. For example, case studies are not typically carried out in natural environments, but in settings selected by the researcher. In addition, the researcher selects the behavior to be studied, rather than focusing on the total context and natural flow of behavior. By imposing constraints, case studies narrow the focus, but retain the essential interest in participants' natural behavior. This section briefly describes the classic case-study research of Freud, Witmer, and Piaget, and some contemporary case studies of two puzzling clinical phenomena.

Sigmund Freud.   In the 19th century, Freud interviewed patients within the mild constraints of his office. As the patients talked of their early lives, dreams, fears, and fantasies, Freud noted patterns, drew inferences about their subjective functioning, and gradually developed psychoanalytic theories and treatment protocols. He believed that case studies, rather than laboratory research, were the best way to understand his clients and their problems. Focusing on the psychology of unconscious processes, he popularized an alternative to the then-dominant laboratory-based psychology of consciousness.

E. L. Witmer.   At the turn of the 20th century, E. L. Witmer treated children with learning and behavioral problems and created the first psychological clinic at the University of Pennsylvania (Brotemarkle, 1966). Witmer used medical and psychological examinations of each child to determine whether the child's problems were due to brain pathology or to inadequate teaching and learning. Relying on careful measurements, he tried to determine what treatments would actually work. Witmer developed a case-study based, treatment-educational approach to children that he called "psychoeducation." He also coined the term "clinical psychology" and is widely viewed as the father of clinical psychology.

Jean Piaget.   Whereas Freud and Witmer used case-study methods to treat persons with psychological problems, Piaget studied normal cognitive development. He studied a small number of children over several years of development. Presenting specific questions and tasks, he observed how each child solved practical problems, and he drew inferences about their developing thought processes. His case-study approach allowed him to alter methods

TABLE 6.2   *Examples of Naturalistic Observation Studies*

1. **Naturalistic observation of athletic drug use patterns in body-builders.** Participant observation was used to gather data on the use of performance-enhancing drugs by bodybuilders. The data revealed a far greater use of drugs and more extensive communication and support among the athletes than was formerly believed (Auge, Wayne, & Auge, 1999).

2. **Young children doing mathematics: Observations of everyday activities.** The authors observed children in free play and recorded instances in which the children engaged in a variety of mathematical explorations and applications. Many of these instances were advanced well beyond what educators consider to be the children's developmental levels. The authors conclude that these observations can serve as bases for higher-level education in mathematics for young children (Ginsburg, Inoue, & Seo, 1999).

3. **Aggression among young adults in bars.** Naturalistic observation was used to observe incidents of aggression in bars. The observations, carried out between midnight and 2:30 A.M., revealed that most aggressive incidents had no clear beginning or ending, the participants' roles often shifted during the incident, and most involved five or more persons. Almost 75% of the incidents involved only males (Graham & Wells, 2001).

4. **Reactivity effects during naturalistic observation of distressed and non-distressed families.** Audiotaping was used to record families' verbal interactions during dinner times in order to answer the question of whether this type of naturalistic observation is reactive. The data showed that there was no significant reactivity of either the distressed or the non-distressed families to the recording procedure (Jacob, Tennenbaum, Seilhamer, & Bargrel, 1994).

5. **Childhood depression and family interaction.** Naturalistic observation was used to compare family interactions of third- to fifth-grade children diagnosed with depression and a non-depressed control group of children. The study found that (1) the family environments of the depressed children were less rewarding, more aversive, and more disengaged than those of controls and (2) the depressed children and their parents mutually affected each others' behaviors (Messer & Gross, 1995).

6. **Naturalistic observation of adolescent tobacco use.** This naturalistic study was carried out to determine the ecological validity of earlier laboratory findings, and most of its data did validate the earlier reports. However, these data unexpectedly revealed that direct peer pressure to smoke is not as frequent, or apparently as important, as was previously thought. More subtle social control, perhaps through advertising, might be more important (Sussman et al., 1993).

7. **Naturalistic observation of children with autism.** Children with autism were observed for their spontaneous verbalizations during social conflict situations and positive social interactions. The data suggested that social conflict might actually be a significant vehicle for the development of social competence, a hypothesis that can be tested in higher-constraint research (Toomey & Adams, 1995).

and take advantage of ideas or observations that occurred during his studies. His hypotheses about cognitive development showed considerable insight and have held up well under examination by later, higher-constraint research.

Contemporary Case Studies.   A recent series of case studies describes two puzzling and rare clinical phenomena, *body dysmorphic disorder* and *apotemnophilia*. Both disorders are characterized by severely distorted perceptions of one's physical body. Katherine Phillips (1996, 2004) studied people who suffer from body dysmorphic disorder. These clients believe that they are ugly and disfigured despite clearly contradictory evidence. Their powerful beliefs cause severe disruptions of their lives. Other clinical researchers have studied individuals with apotemnophilia, which is a desire to have one or more body parts amputated because the person finds amputation sexually arousing (e.g., Bensler &

Paauw, 2003; Money & Jobaris, 1977). Michael First (2004) describes his interviews with 52 people with the disorder, 9 of whom had actually had the amputations performed. One man had both legs surgically amputated. By presenting descriptive, clinical case studies, these researchers are laying groundwork for understanding these phenomena and developing hypotheses that can be followed up with higher-constraint research. This is an area in which research is just beginning, and using such low-constraint case studies is an appropriate way to proceed toward greater understanding and successful treatment.

Quick-Check Review 6.1: The Challenge of Low-Constraint Research	1. What made the research of Darwin and Goodall naturalistic research? 2. Why is the work of Freud, Witmer, Piaget, and Phillips classified as case studies? 3. Differentiate case-study research and naturalistic research.

The Value of Low-Constraint Methods

The previous examples illustrate the value of low-constraint research. This section provides a more detailed discussion of its value, when to use these techniques, and what can be learned from them.

Conditions for Using Low-Constraint Research

Low-constraint research is most appropriate when the question concerns the natural flow of behavior in natural settings. For example, if researchers are interested in studying passenger behavior at airports, seating patterns in theaters, or the first behavioral responses of infants to mothers, then the best research methods will involve direct observations of these events as they occur in their natural settings.

Perhaps the most productive use of low-constraint methods is at the early stages of a research area; that is, in **exploratory research.** For example, adults can organize their behavior with reference to time, but can children do so? A researcher might begin studying this question at a low-constraint level by observing young children at a nursery school. The researcher is seeking evidence in the child's behavior that indicates an awareness of time. Perhaps it will be a child fighting for a toy with the argument "I saw it first!" This suggests that the child has a concept of sequencing of events and thus some idea of time, although the child may only be echoing an argument that he or she saw was successful for another child. Such observations stimulate ideas or hypotheses that can then be tested at higher constraint levels.

It would be a mistake for anyone to think that low-constraint research, in its function as an exploratory phase, is *only* exploratory or only a prelude to the "real" research. Low-constraint research can be the creative and significant starting point for new areas of exploration, facilitating leaps to the next levels of discovery on the very edges of new knowledge.

Low-constraint methods are not only useful but necessary in contemporary science. Klahr and Simon (2001) argue this point in a thought-provoking article in which they discuss the importance of low-constraint methods in scientific problem solving. In their model, scientists employ strong methods that are highly constrained in their application.

These high-constraint methods, such as experimentation, allow the valid testing of causal hypotheses. Klahr and Simon argue that the so-called "weak" methods are also critically important to science. These weak methods include thinking by analogy, recognition of patterns, and making conceptual leaps based on our fund of knowledge. In our terminology, these are low-constraint methods that allow an unfettered, wide-ranging search for contingencies. This level of methodology makes important contributions in exploratory research. The best scientists routinely employ both high- and low-constraint methodologies as they pursue their studies (e.g., Dunbar, 1994; Thagard, 1998).

Naturalistic observation can also familiarize researchers with participants or settings that are new to them. Suppose that a researcher has little experience in studying young children, but wants to extend some part of Piaget's work on conservation in children. *Conservation* refers to the understanding that the properties of an object or substance do not change when its appearance is superficially changed, such as when a fixed volume of liquid is poured into containers of different shapes. It would be useful for the researcher to spend a few hours observing young children in a nursery school. Such direct experience with children would supplement the scientific information in the research literature.

Low-constraint procedures can also be used to demonstrate a new research or treatment technique. Here the question is whether a technique is feasible. The researcher is not attempting to test a prediction or develop new hypotheses, but only to see whether some method can be carried out. For example, the researcher who wanted to study conservation will want to be certain that children are likely to find the tasks interesting enough that they will cooperate.

Case-study and naturalistic research can also enhance the generalizability of research findings, especially in areas in which virtually all the research has been conducted in laboratory settings. In this context, **generalizability** refers to how well laboratory findings predict events in a real-world setting. The advantages of laboratory research are enormous, but we cannot be sure that the behavior observed in the laboratory is representative of behavior in the natural environment. Naturalistic research methods, and to some degree case-study research, can be used to test the generalizability of the theories developed or refined on the basis of laboratory studies. The most useful laws of behavior are those that predict behavior in the real world. Naturalistic research allows us to generalize how findings relate to real-world settings.

Case-study research is particularly valuable for studying specific individuals. Under such conditions, there is no concern for developing inferences and concepts that can be generalized to a population. This concept is especially relevant for clinical psychologists, who want to understand individual clients and the causes of each client's problems. This issue is discussed in *Historical Lesson 6.2.*

Information Gained from Low-Constraint Research

Low-constraint observations provide descriptive information. For example, Goodall's (1978) observation that a group of chimpanzees in the wild attacked and killed another group was the first observation of chimpanzee behavior that resembled warfare. These observations could not explain the event or determine what caused it. However, her observations did establish a new fact that had never before been observed and, in the process, raised some very interesting questions. For example, what triggers the chimpanzees to cooperate with allies and display aggression toward opponents, behavior that is characteristic of warfare, and what cognitive abilities are necessary to engage in such activities?

HISTORICAL LESSON 6.2:   *The Therapist as Scientist*

Case studies can be used in settings other than research. For example, a therapist must gather information and generate hypotheses about the reasons for a client's behavior. The effective use of research methods, especially methods of inference, can greatly improve the therapist's effectiveness. The phases of research presented in Chapter 2 are applicable to the therapy session. The therapist generates ideas about the client's problems, how they developed, and how they might be corrected. The initial information might be vague, suggesting several ideas. The clinician then translates these ideas into specific hypotheses and develops plans for testing them. The observation phase may involve asking the client specific questions or closely observing how the client responds to specific situations. The analysis phase relies less on statistics and more on rational inferences, and the analysis and interpretation phases are difficult to separate. Therapists record their observations in progress notes so that the information will be available to them or to other clinicians who might work with the client in the future. The important point is that clinicians, in gathering the information necessary for treatment planning, are operating like research scientists. It is no accident that the most widely accepted model for the training of a clinical psychologist is the **scientist-practitioner model**, which argues that therapist training requires extensive training in the scientific method and the thought processes that are part of that method. Understanding the way scientists gather information and draw conclusions sharpens clinicians' skills in information gathering and treatment planning.

One of the most valuable functions of low-constraint research is that it can negate a general proposition. For example, suppose that prior to Goodall's observation a naturalist had stated the general proposition that "chimpanzees do not engage in group aggression resembling warfare." Goodall's observations of chimpanzees engaging in warlike behavior show that this general proposition is incorrect.

Another example of negating a general proposition involves the statement "Man's superiority over other creatures is due to the fact that man is the only tool-making and tool-using animal." Again, the naturalistic observations of Goodall refute this general proposition. She observed chimpanzees selecting twigs, stripping off the leaves to fashion a flexible rod, inserting the twigs into the narrow tunnels of a termite nest, waiting a moment, and then withdrawing the twig and licking off the termites clinging to it. This was purposeful and sophisticated behavior. The chimpanzees selected and then modified a natural object, preparing it for use as a food-gathering tool.

A final example involves some early research with autistic children. Psychologists who had pioneered the use of relaxation in behavior therapy believed that neither children nor psychotic adults could learn relaxation (Wolpe, 1958). Graziano and Kean (1968) succeeded in training four autistic children in relaxation skills, procedures that have since been repeated many times with other children (e.g., Mullins & Christian, 2001; Reese et al., 1998). This case study successfully negated the general proposition that children cannot be taught relaxation skills.

Low-constraint research can negate a general proposition, but it cannot establish one. We cannot conclude from Goodall's observations that all chimps engage in warfare or from the Graziano and Kean study that all children can be taught relaxation skills. We never know if the low-constraint observations are representative of the larger population. This limitation is related to issues of *sampling,* which will be discussed in more detail later in this chapter and again in Chapter 9.

Low-constraint studies seek to identify and understand relationships among variables. The type of relationship that is studied varies from one level of constraint to another. Experimental research identifies causal relationships among variables. In low-constraint research such causal inferences cannot be made, but other useful information about relationships among variables can be obtained. For example, the ethologist Niko Tinbergen (1951, 1963) observed that the parent herring gull provides food for its chick when the young bird pecks a red spot on the adult's bill. When the spot appears, the chick pecks at it; when the chick pecks at the spot, the parent provides food (i.e., when X occurs, then Y will probably occur). Note that this does not state that X causes Y, but only that there is a high probability of one event occurring when the other event is present. This describes a probabilistic relationship between two variables. When the young bird pecks on the parent's bill, there is a high probability that the parent will provide food. This kind of probabilistic relationship is referred to as a **contingency.** Low-constraint research can identify contingent relationships among variables, and these contingencies can stimulate higher-constraint research. This is exactly what Tinbergen did once he noticed the contingent relationship between the chick's pecking and the adult's feeding behavior: he followed up this observation by conducting systematic experiments. Contingent relationships observed in low-constraint research can be an important source for hypotheses to be tested with higher-constraint research.

Note that flexibility is an advantage of both naturalistic and case-study research. Unlike the formal, high-constraint experiment, the researcher in low-constraint studies is free to vary procedures during the study by changing the focus on the basis of the obtained data or the changing interests of the researcher. Table 6.3 summarizes the value of low-constraint research.

TABLE 6.3   *The Value of Low-Constraint Research*

Naturalistic and Case-Study Research is Useful

1. As exploratory research at the beginning of a new research area in which little information is available
2. When the researcher wishes to gain familiarity with typical characteristics of settings or participants before planning high-constraint research
3. When the questions specifically focus on the natural flow of behavior and/or on behavior in natural settings
4. When the study is of a single individual, group, or set of events, and the questions are specific to these people, settings, or events
5. For demonstrations or illustrations, such as demonstrating a new procedure
6. As a way of discovering contingencies that can then be used as a basis for higher-constraint questions and research
7. As a way of evaluating the generalizability of findings from laboratory research to natural environments

Furthermore, Naturalistic and Case-Study Research Can

1. Describe events, including events never before observed
2. Identify contingent relationships among variables
3. Suggest hypotheses to be tested with higher-constraint research
4. Negate general propositions, although these methods cannot establish general propositions or causal inferences

Quick-Check Review 6.2: The Value of Low-Constraint Methods	1. When should naturalistic research be used? Case study research?
	2. What are contingencies, and how are they used in later research?
	3. Why does naturalistic research generalize more easily than laboratory research?
	4. Explain how naturalistic research can negate, but not establish, a general proposition.

Using Low-Constraint Methods

In higher-constraint research, we can rely on formalized procedures to provide many of the controls that increase the validity of the research. In lower-constraint research, validity depends more on the researcher's clarity of thought. The low-constraint research methods used in ethology have been extended in recent years to such disciplines as education, sociology, management, nursing, communications, and psychology (see Table 6.2). Known collectively as **qualitative research methods,** their major goal is to describe and analyze functioning in everyday settings, ranging from informal conversations among friends to courtroom proceedings. The research methods include, for example, naturalistic and participant observation, the use of questionnaires, and analyzing conversations and social networks.

This section presents the basics of conducting low-constraint research, including formulating problem statements and research hypotheses, making observations, and selecting samples. Size constraints on this textbook make it impossible to cover all these low-constraint methods. The interested student should consult Maxwell (2005), Berg (2004), and Ritchie and Lewis (2003).

Problem Statements and Research Hypotheses

We noted in Chapter 3 the importance of developing a statement of the problem for each research project. Problem statements and research hypotheses are most highly formalized at the experimental level of constraint, but they are important at all levels of constraint. Problem statements help to organize the researcher's thinking. The inferences that can confidently be drawn differ depending on the constraint level. At the experimental level, the focus is on questions of causality. In differential studies, the focus is on determining differences between groups; at the correlational level, the focus is on the direction and strength of relationships among variables; and at the naturalistic and case-study levels, the focus is on contingencies. Causal inferences can be drawn safely only at the experimental level, where the most complete controls are applied.

Problem statements in low-constraint research are often general, because there might be no basis for generating more specific questions. Problem statements also change readily in low-constraint research as the researcher begins to grasp the issues through observation and starts to focus attention on specific behavior. Suppose, for example, that an industrial-organizational psychologist is called in to evaluate a communication problem in a company. The psychologist knows about the dynamics of business organizations and the strategies that might be applied to specific problems, but does not know what this particular company's so-called "communication problem" is.

The initial problem statement in this case might be "I wonder what is wrong." Interviewing several key people will likely provide the psychologist with some insight into the problem, but there will be different opinions. Careful observation of interactions among members of the company might suggest an underlying defensiveness. The psychologist might narrow the problem statement to focus more on this if he or she suspects that it may be a key to understanding the problem. On the other hand, further observation and discussion with employees and managers may suggest that this inferred defensiveness is more likely an effect than a cause of problems in the company. The psychologist might then begin to work with two or three narrower problem statements, which are based in part on his or her knowledge of what types of situations could create the scenario observed. Each of these might be independently evaluated through continued observation, fact gathering, and interviewing. All this might occur in just the first day of the psychologist's visit, or it might take several days or weeks to get this far.

This example illustrates how low-constraint research can move flexibly from one area to another depending on what is found. Of course, eventually the psychologist will need to focus on key elements, gather relevant data, and make specific suggestions. However, an early narrow focus might blind the psychologist to critical issues and lead to poor recommendations.

This example also illustrates how problem statements tend to start out in a more general form and become more focused as the researcher learns more about the issues. Problem statements gradually evolve into specific hypotheses, which guide the researcher in gathering specific information relevant to the hypotheses. However, there is an inherent limitation in this process. Low-constraint research can provide only so much information. If we want to know with confidence what is causing what, then the hypotheses must be translated into higher-constraint research questions. It is often tempting to try to draw causal inferences from low-constraint research, but it would be a serious mistake to do so.

Making Observations

The central phase of any research project is the observation or data-gathering phase. In higher-constraint research, detailed plans of how to gather and analyze the data are prepared before any observations are made. In lower-constraint research, planning is less formal and more fluid. The researcher is free to change hypotheses and modify procedures in the middle of the observations. It is not unusual for an observer conducting naturalistic and case-study research to design a whole new study based on initial observations. While naturalistic and case-study procedures constitute low-constraint research, the observational methods used might nevertheless employ highly sophisticated instrumentation. The research is still low constraint; the technological equipment does not define the level of constraint.

The balance of this section discusses how to make observations, including how to use measures that have minimal impact on a person's natural behavior.

How to Observe.   There are two ways to gather data in naturalistic observation: as an unobtrusive observer or as a participant observer. As an **unobtrusive observer,** the researcher tries to avoid responding to, or influencing, the participant, such as in the example of Davis's studies on spanking children. In fact, the unobtrusive observer tries to blend into the surroundings so as not to be noticed.

As a **participant observer,** the researcher becomes a part of the situation and may even contribute to it. This may include making the normal contributions almost anyone would make in the situation, or it might consist of carefully planned and executed changes in the researcher's behavior that tentatively test specific hypotheses. Levine's study of the Love Canal crisis utilized participant observation for some aspects of the study.

It should be noted that when the observer becomes a participant, the procedure is no longer naturalistic observation but, rather, becomes a case study. One advantage of participant observation is that by manipulating one's behavior as an observer, the researcher is able to test hypotheses by creating situations that are unlikely to occur naturally. Case studies often use participant observation. For example, Piaget did not passively observe children. Instead, he asked questions, created test situations, interacted with the children, and observed their responses.

Whether we use unobtrusive observation or participant observation, the goal is to avoid influencing the natural behavior of the participants. The term **measurement reactivity** refers to the phenomenon of participants behaving differently than they might normally behave, because they know that they are being observed. Some measures, called **reactive measures,** are particularly prone to such distortions, whereas others, called **nonreactive measures,** are not.

Measurement reactivity is a function of what participants believe is the appropriate behavior in the situation. People have a tendency to behave in ways that they think are appropriate when they know that they are being observed. For example, how much more likely is it that you will use a fork and knife to eat your chicken if you are dining in a nice restaurant than if you are at home alone?

Unobtrusive Measures.   **Unobtrusive measures** are measures of behavior that are not obvious to the person being observed and, consequently, are less likely to influence the person's behavior. Webb, Campbell, Schwartz, and Sechrest (1966, 2000) described a number of clever unobtrusive measures. For example, suppose that you want to measure interest level for a museum exhibit. You first need an operational definition of level of interest. One operational definition might be the average of people's interest ratings. You ask each of the first 200 people who visit an exhibit to rate how interesting it is on a 10-point scale. This measure is not unobtrusive, because participants are aware that their interest level is being measured, which might make the measure reactive. An alternative operational definition of the level of interest is the number of people who view the exhibit. You could measure this unobtrusively by having an observer count the number of people who approach the exhibit. One advantage of this approach is that the observer can code other information, such as how long people observe the exhibit.

However, simpler measures could also provide the information you desire. One procedure suggested by Webb et al. (1966, 2000) is to note the degree of wear on the tiles of the floor surrounding the exhibit. Tiles around popular exhibits often need to be replaced every few weeks, whereas the tiles around other exhibits last for years. Another method is the nose-print approach, in which the exhibit is put in a glass display and arranged so that people can get the best view by putting their faces right up to the glass. The glass is cleaned at the start of each day. At day's end, the glass is dusted with fingerprint powder, and the number of nose prints is counted. Of course, not everyone will leave a nose print, and some people will press their nose to the glass in several places, so this method will not give an accurate count of how many people viewed the display. However, this type of accuracy isn't necessary. Remember, you wanted to measure how interesting the exhibit was. The number of people who viewed the exhibit is an operational definition of interest. The number of nose prints is also a reasonable operational definition of interest level and may, in some ways, be superior to the head-count method.

The preceding examples were presented to help you to think more creatively when you develop your own measures. Practice exercises and additional examples are provided on the Student Resource Website. There is nothing wrong with asking people to rate the interest level of museum exhibits, but it is valuable to seek some independent data to substantiate the ratings.

06:03

Ethics of Unobtrusive Measures.   Using unobtrusive measures raises ethical issues. Normally, participants should be made aware of the procedures so they can make an informed decision. However, this principle is not absolute. If it were, unobtrusive measures could never be used. To justify using unobtrusive measures, the researcher must show that non-deceptive measures would not work and that there is no significant risk of harm from use of the measure. These judgments, often difficult to make, are one reason for having a formal review process for all studies using human participants.

Archival Measures.   Some existing records provide information about events that have already occurred. These **archival records** may include school records, marriage and divorce records, driving records, census data, military, business, or industrial records. Archival records are usually in the form of printed text or numerals, but can also be pictorial, such as photographs, drawings, videotapes, or audiotapes. A wealth of archival data is stored all over the world, just waiting for some enterprising young researcher to come and mine that wealth. Governments gather archival data routinely to identify nationwide problems quickly. Statistics computed from such archival data as the *Index of Leading Economic Indicators* can be accurate predictors of future events. Data gathered from hospitals about diseases under treatment allow officials to identify new diseases and even narrow the range of possible causes of the diseases. Effective use of archival data depends on the quality of the data that are stored, their relevance to the question being asked, and careful planning by the researcher.

There are some difficulties in using data from archival records, most stemming from the fact that the researcher has had no part in defining, gathering, or storing the data. The records already exist, and the researcher has not defined the variables recorded nor imposed any research constraints on the procedures. Therefore, research with archival records is descriptive in nature. We can use existing records to identify variables, observe contingencies, calculate correlations, and make predictions about future events based on those correlations, but we cannot establish causality.

There may be problems of gaining access to some archives, and the data might be poorly organized, incomplete, or so all-inclusive as to be overwhelming. To make good use of archival data, researchers must have a clear idea of what they are looking for, clear definitions of variables, and hypotheses about expected relationships.

A set of procedures that are particularly useful in archival research is known as content analysis, in which the researcher examines records and tries to identify categories of events. For example one might analyze political speeches for the occurrence of "patriotic-emotion" phrases. One can analyze verbal interactions in psychotherapy or in mock jury deliberations, or analyze the language used in social psychology studies of leadership in small groups, and so on. Such content analyses must be carried out carefully and within the structure of a well–thought-out research plan with defined variables and objective, specified procedures.

It might appear that using archival records is a sloppy way to measure a phenomenon, but this is not always the case. Several sophisticated studies of genetic influences in psychopathology used archival records (e.g., Baker, 1989; Kety et al., 1968; Simonsen & Parnas, 1993; Wender et al., 1986). These investigators used records from many sources to track the rates of psychopathology in both the adoptive and biological families of severely disturbed adults who were adopted as infants. The majority of these studies were carried out in Denmark, where archival records are unusually accurate and complete.

Sampling of Participants

Deciding on the best way to observe participants is critical, but an equally important task is determining which participants to observe. The term **sampling** refers to the selection of participants. In low-constraint research, we need to pay particular attention to the sampling of participants. The more representative the sample, the more confidence we can have in the generalizability of the findings. Although sampling is covered in detail in Chapters 9 and 13, we want to introduce here the concept of **representativeness** and its relationship to generalizability. Representativeness refers to how closely a sample resembles the population to be studied.

In naturalistic and case-study research, sampling may be out of the researcher's control. For example, for psychotherapy researchers, the clients who come for treatment constitute the sample. In a study of the impact of a natural disaster, the people unfortunate enough to be present when the disaster occurs constitute the sample. With these naturally occurring samples, the question must be addressed of how well a sample represents the larger population. For example, people who go to a therapist for help might be different from people in general. They probably have more psychological problems and are more concerned with these problems than is the typical person. They may be wealthier than the typical person, since they can afford the cost of psychotherapy, or have insurance that will cover the cost.

To the extent that there are differences between the sample and the general population, the sample is said to be unrepresentative of the population. Whenever a sample is not representative of the general population, one must take care in generalizing the findings. If you generalize a finding, you are saying that what was observed in the sample of participants would also be observed in any other group of participants from the population. (Remember that you cannot generalize your findings unless your sample is representative of the population to which you want to make the generalization.)

Researchers seldom have the opportunity to select their own samples in naturalistic and case-study research. Therefore, they must judge how well the sample represents the population to which they want to generalize the results. The more representative the sample, the more confident their generalizations can be. However, with low-constraint research, caution is always needed in making generalizations. Such generalizations should be considered tentative hypotheses that must be tested with higher-constraint research methods. As you will see later, when researchers control the sampling procedures, they can almost guarantee the representativeness of the sample.

Sampling of Situations

EXTENDING THE CONCEPT OF REACTIVE MEASURES

The sampling of situations also affects generalizability. Suppose, for example, that you are studying the attentional focus of pilots. As part of the study, television cameras are installed in several aircraft cockpits to monitor pilot behavior.

From the previous section's discussion, you should recognize that the presence of the camera is likely to be reactive: the participants may behave differently because they know that they are being watched. However, this same problem can be viewed from another perspective, that of sampling. The sample of behaviors in this example comes from a situation that differs from the situations to which the researcher wants to generalize. Because closed circuit TV is not used to monitor pilots in most cockpits, this situation is not representative of the population of settings to which the researcher wants to generalize the results. Therefore, the researcher cannot generalize the findings with confidence.

The sample of situations can be distorted in numerous ways. Some variables are beyond the researcher's control, and others can be controlled only at great cost or inconvenience. Suppose that animals in the wild are to be the focus of study. Many animals behave differently during different seasons of the year. They are active during some seasons and inactive during others. Most animals also show diurnal fluctuations in activity. If observations of the animals were made only during morning hours and only during spring and summer, a distorted picture of animal behavior might emerge. An even worse violation of this principle would be studying animals in zoos, because they are close and easy to find. The situation in even the best zoos is dramatically different from the natural environment to which the findings are to be generalized. Therefore, a good rule of thumb in early studies of any population is to sample situations as widely as possible. The broader the sample of situations and the broader the sample of participants, the more confidence one can have in the generalizability of the findings.

Sampling of Behaviors

Another issue is the importance of adequately sampling behaviors. In any situation, organisms may behave in many different ways. Therefore, a single observation of behavior in a particular situation may lead to an incorrect conclusion about how the organism behaves in this setting. However, by sampling behaviors repeatedly in each situation, it is possible to identify whatever behavioral variability exists.

Evaluating and Interpreting Data

Once observations are made and data are gathered, the next step is to evaluate and interpret the results of the study. This usually involves statistical analyses. In many low-constraint studies, however, statistical analyses are not possible until the data are coded.

Low-constraint studies often involve observing and recording everything that happens. For example, in a study of labor contract negotiations, the data set might be the transcripts of all negotiation sessions. In analyzing the data, the interactions can be coded in terms of categories, such as hostile comments, requests for information, and suggested solutions. Dean Pruitt and his colleagues (e.g., Pruitt, Parker, & Mikolic, 1997; Rubin, Pruitt, & Kim, 1994) have used similar categories in a series of studies of negotiation and conflict resolution.

For lower-constraint studies, the statistical procedures may be no more complicated than descriptive statistics. Some natural comparisons may need to be made, such as between different groups of participants or among the same participants under more than one condition. In the preceding example, the researcher might want to compare the verbal statements of the labor negotiators with those of the management negotiators or compare the negotiation sessions that were fruitful with those that were not. If such comparisons are done, inferential statistics can be used. (Procedures for selecting the appropriate statistical test are reviewed in Chapter 14.)

Caution is needed when interpreting data from low-constraint research studies. By its very nature, low-constraint research employs few controls. Controls help to eliminate alternative explanations for results, making it easier to draw a strong conclusion. Because such controls are largely absent from this level of constraint, we seldom are able to draw strong conclusions. Furthermore, these limitations cannot be corrected by applying sophisticated statistical analyses. *No statistical analysis will create controls that were not part of the original study.*

Quick-Check Review 6.3: Using Low-Constraint Methods	1. What are problem statements like in low-constraint research?
	2. What are the two types of observers in research?
	3. What are unobtrusive measures, and what are their advantages?
	4. What are archival records, and how are they used in research?
	5. What is the researcher's goal in sampling participants?
	6. Why is it important to sample situations broadly in low-constraint research?
	7. Explain the concept of measurement reactivity.

Limitations of Low-Constraint Methods

So far, this chapter has focused on the value and procedures of low-constraint research. This section discusses the limitations of these techniques, beginning with a discussion of representativeness, which is almost always a problem in low-constraint research. We then discuss the dangers of trying to draw causal conclusions from low-constraint research. The section ends with a discussion of the limitations of observers and the all-too-common tendency to go beyond the data.

Poor Representativeness

A major weakness in low-constraint research is poor representativeness. Low-constraint research typically studies particular groups of respondents, and there is little basis for generalizing from the studied group to other groups. For example, a clinical psychologist cannot confidently generalize observations of her clients to all other clients. Why not? Her clients might be from a particular socioeconomic class that does not represent all clients, or they may have particular psychological problems that are not found in other client groups. Any clinical sample is biased, because participants select themselves for therapy and not every person in the population is equally likely to seek therapy. Likewise, if a researcher studies a particular group of chimpanzees, the findings cannot confidently be generalized to all groups of chimpanzees. If we want to generalize the findings from our particular sample to the larger population, then we must take care to select a sample that accurately represents the larger population. Such careful selection of a representative sample is a higher-constraint procedure and is not typically found in low-constraint research, particularly low-constraint research carried out in natural environments where laboratory controls are not readily available.

Poor Replicability

Another limitation of low-constraint research is related to the very characteristic that gives it its greatest strength—flexibility. Because observations of naturally occurring behavior are made in settings in which the observer has imposed few constraints on participant behavior, it is often difficult to replicate (i.e., repeat) such research. Different investigators studying the same phenomenon through low-constraint methods may make different observations and therefore draw different inferences. Replication is possible only if researchers clearly state the details of their procedures. In low-constraint research, observational methods can shift during a study. These changes are not necessarily planned at the start of the study. Thus, it can be difficult to document exactly what procedures were followed and why. This makes it difficult for other researchers to replicate what was done.

Causal Inference and Low-Constraint Research

Drawing causal inferences from low-constraint research is risky. **Causal inferences** are conclusions that imply that one or more variables brought about the observed state of another variable. For example, let us suppose that a researcher observes that a teacher appears to be angry. Also, suppose that the researcher subsequently learns that a child had been misbehaving, although the researcher did not observe the behavior. The researcher might be tempted to draw a causal inference that the teacher was angry because the child had misbehaved. This is an example of *ex-post-facto* (after the fact) reasoning.

Ex-post-facto conclusions are potential problems in low-constraint research. The fact that two variables are related is not sufficient to infer that variable A causes variable B. In the school example just presented, the child's misbehavior might have had nothing to do with the teacher's anger. It is possible that the teacher's anger had more to do with an argument with a colleague than with the child's behavior. Without more information, we cannot rule out this possibility. It is also possible that the teacher's demeanor stimulated the child's misbehavior. It is tempting to conclude that one event has caused the other, but low-constraint research almost never provides enough information to reasonably draw such causal inferences.

The identification of contingencies and other relationships among variables is useful in suggesting possible causal relationships. However, it does not provide the controls needed to rule out the possibility that other factors may have been involved. Clinical case studies, for example, are by their nature ex-post-facto approaches. They lack control over independent variables and are unable to rule out possible effects of other variables. For this reason, we cannot have confidence in any causal inference we might be tempted to draw. Such inferences must be treated as speculative hypotheses for further research. For this purpose, case-study methods can be very useful.

An **ex-post-facto fallacy** occurs when we draw unwarranted causal conclusions from the observation of a contingent relationship. It is a common and serious error in low-constraint research. It can mislead investigators into severe misinterpretations of the data. Table 6.4 lists several examples of ex-post-facto fallacies. A logical fallacy is obvious in some of the statements, whereas other parallel statements seem reasonable. Some of the assertions in the list may be ones that you have heard many times and may have accepted without giving them much thought.

The causal statements in Table 6.4 are not supported adequately by the ex-post-facto data being used. However, they are perfectly reasonable hypotheses. They should be treated as tentative statements to be tested, rather than as established conclusions.

When low-constraint results are interpreted as if they were equivalent to high-constraint research results, the conclusions drawn are suspect. These suspect conclusions can then damage the credibility of other research, even well-designed high-constraint research. For example, drinking beer and wine might not lead to alcoholism, but years of research suggest that a combination of heavy drinking and a genetic predisposition to alcoholism increases the risk of alcoholism. If teenagers dismiss the risk of alcoholism because well-meaning people have presented the simplistic and easily refutable arguments in

---

TABLE 6.4 *Examples of Possible Ex-Post-Facto Fallacies*

The relationships listed below might have validity, but this validity can never be established through ex-post-facto reasoning.

1. Hard-drug users all smoked marijuana before turning to hard drugs; therefore, marijuana use leads to hard-drug addiction.
2. Alcoholics started with beer and wine; therefore, drinking beer and wine lead to alcoholism.
3. Child-abusing parents were abused themselves as children; therefore, being abused as a child leads to becoming an abusive parent.
4. Most inmates in U.S. urban jails are black; therefore, being black leads to crime.
5. Many NHL hockey players are Canadian; therefore, being Canadian leads to playing professional hockey.
6. Aggressive children watch a great deal of television; therefore, watching a great deal of television leads to aggressive behavior in children.

Table 6.4 to dissuade teenage drinking, teenagers might ignore other research, believing that there is no risk associated with heavy drinking.

Limitations of the Observer

Another issue in low-constraint research concerns the limitations of the observer. When clients talk with their therapists, are they giving spontaneous verbalizations or are they saying what they think their therapists want to hear? Do the therapists influence their verbalizing? When anthropologists engage in participant observation, do they influence the behavior of the people that they observe? Likewise, when ethologists observe groups of chimps, does their presence alter the animals' normal behavior? The issue is one of experimenter reactivity or experimenter bias (Rosenthal, 1976).

Experimenter reactivity is any action by researchers that tends to influence the response of participants. For example, if therapists show more interest in their client's statements about feeling angry than in their statements about feeling happy, clients are likely to talk more about anger than happiness during sessions.

Experimenter bias is any impact that the researcher's expectations might have on the observations or recording of those observations. Whereas experimenter reactivity affects participants, experimenter bias affects researchers. For example, if a researcher expects males to be angrier than females, the researcher is likely to interpret ambiguous behavior, such as sarcastic comments, as anger in men, but as humor in women.

Both experimenter reactivity and experimenter bias distort the measurement process. To obtain natural behavior, the observer must be uninvolved. In case studies, it is difficult for observers to control their own reactivity and biases. However, controls that are available in higher-constraint research can minimize the observer's reactivity and bias.

Going Beyond the Data

Recall Rosenhan's (1973) naturalistic study of mental hospitals. It created quite a stir. Few of Rosenhan's critics argued with his data; instead, they criticized his interpretation of the data. Other interpretations are possible, and some of these alternatives are more reasonable given other available data. For example, Rosenhan argued that it is unreasonable to make a diagnosis of schizophrenia on the basis of the single symptom of hearing voices (11 out of 12 admissions received this diagnosis). Weiner (1975) notes, however, that by Rosenhan's own admission (1973, pp. 365–366), the pseudopatients showed "concomitant nervousness" and were apparently in serious distress because they had gone to a psychiatric hospital and requested admission. This pattern, plus the fact that the pseudopatients would likely have denied other symptoms and experiences that might have indicated alternative explanations for the hallucinations (Spitzer, 1975), makes schizophrenia the most likely diagnosis. Furthermore, Rosenhan interpreted the discharge diagnoses as indicating that the doctors never detected that the pseudopatients were not psychotic. However, Rosenhan reported that all the patients were diagnosed as "in remission" at discharge (Spitzer, 1975). The qualification "in remission" is almost never used in clinical practice and, therefore, Rosenhan's own data clearly indicate that the pseudo-patients were seen by the professional staff to be symptom free at discharge.

Rosenhan's research is still widely quoted. His was a powerful study with interesting findings, but there are some who argue that his interpretation of the findings was scientifically unjustified. Rosenhan drew strong conclusions from low-constraint research, conclusions that seem unreasonable when you compare his results with other research data, such as typical discharge diagnoses. His study illustrates both the strengths (the advantages inherent in studying a natural phenomenon in its natural setting) and the weaknesses (the hazards implicit in interpreting naturalistic data) of low-constraint naturalistic research.

Quick-Check Review 6.4: Limitations of Low-Constraint Methods	1. Why is poor representativeness often a problem in low-constraint research? 2. What aspect of low-constraint research complicates the process of replication? 3. What is an ex-post-facto fallacy? 4. What is the difference between *experimenter reactivity* and *experimenter bias*?

PUTTING IT INTO PRACTICE	The nice thing about naturalistic and case-study research is that you can carry it out almost anywhere. The next time you are riding on a bus, sitting in the student union, or waiting for a class to start, conduct a little naturalistic research of your own. Watch the people around you, observe their patterns of interaction, and try to understand what is influencing these behaviors. Can you tell the difference between two people who are in a committed relationship or married and two people who are flirting with one another? If so, what differences do you seem to see? If you have children or friends with children, you might want to play with the children as Piaget did, carefully observing their actions and thought processes. See if you can probe those thought processes a little with some well-selected questions or activities. You may find that this kind of informal research on human behavior is addictive. It is hard not to be curious about what makes people tick, and indulging that curiosity will make this course a lot more enjoyable and comprehensible.

Chapter Summary

This chapter covered field research, focusing on the low-constraint methods of naturalistic observation and case studies. These approaches place little constraint on the behavior of participants, although the behavior of the observer may be tightly constrained by the observational techniques employed. A major advantage of lower-constraint research methods is the flexibility that they allow the researcher.

The most common problem with low-constraint research is the tendency to overinterpret the results, either generalizing the results to a broader population than actually sampled or drawing a causal inference from the data. Even though we cannot easily generalize to other populations or draw causal inferences, low-constraint methods can provide useful information. They can describe events not previously observed, identify contingencies, and negate a general proposition if an appropriate counter-example is observed. Some questions about naturally occurring behavior in natural settings can be answered only with naturalistic research methods.

One major function served by low-constraint research is that of exploratory research. The key issue in low-constraint research is the observation of behavior.

Whether the observation is made with only unaided senses or with highly sophisticated equipment, the same general principles apply. Researchers should make observations in ways that will allow generalization to the population of interest. Researchers need to be aware of processes such as experimenter reactivity and experimenter bias that can cause misinterpretation of results.

Chapter Exercises _____

1. Define the following key terms. Be sure that you understand them. They are discussed in the chapter and defined in the glossary.

field research	measurement reactivity
ethology	reactive measures
exploratory research	nonreactive measures
generalizability	unobtrusive measure
scientist-practitioner	archival records
model	sampling
contingency	representativeness
qualitative research	causal inference
methods	ex-post-facto fallacy
unobtrusive observer	experimenter reactivity
participant observer	experimenter bias

2. Imagine doing groundbreaking research in the areas listed below. Because there is no prior research to draw on, you will need to utilize the flexible naturalistic and case-study approaches. Develop an initial research plan to accomplish these goals.

   a. Some people are concerned about the possible effects of televised wrestling on viewers and on society in general. How would you begin to study such an issue?

   b. Studies have shown that seat belts dramatically reduce the risk of injury or death. Nevertheless, many people still do not use seat belts. The issue of concern to you is how one might increase seat belt use.

   c. Naturalists worry about the welfare of animals in the natural environment, but most people are unconcerned with the impact of hunting, habitat destruction, environmental pollution, and so on. Your research seeks to develop ways to sensitize people so they will have greater concern for wildlife and make greater efforts to reduce human incursions. What research would you develop toward these goals?

   d. Shoplifting costs retail businesses and consumers billions of dollars annually. You have been hired by a national retail consortium to study shoplifting and recommend ways to control this problem. How would you begin such a study?

7

Correlational and Differential Methods of Research

You must be familiar with the very groundwork of science before you try to climb its heights.

—Ivan Pavlov, 1936

Web Resource Material

This chapter focuses on measuring relationships among variables (correlational research) and assessing the differences among groups defined by preexisting variables (differential research). As you will see, correlational and differential methods, although operationally different, are conceptually similar. The chapter begins with a conceptual discussion of each approach, followed by a comparison of the two. Then, the actual methods are discussed, as well as their limitations.

Correlational Research Methods

Correlational research assesses the strength of relationships between variables. For example, the researcher might want to see if adolescents' self-esteem is related to their earlier experiences of having been punished by their parents. She administers a test that measures self-esteem and a questionnaire about the amount of past punishment to participants. A correlation quantifies the strength and direction of the relationship between the two measures. As in naturalistic observation, variables in correlational research are not manipulated. However, there are important differences between correlational and naturalistic research. Correlational research always measures at least two variables, and plans for measuring variables are formalized prior to measurement.

Although a correlation does not imply causality, it does serve two useful functions. The first is that any consistent relationship can be used to predict future events. Prediction is possible, even if we have no idea why the relationship exists. For example, as early as A.D. 140, Ptolemy developed a complicated system to predict the movements of the planets. Although his predictions were remarkably accurate, he had little understanding of how the planets actually moved. In fact, his model of planetary movement, which posited that all celestial bodies revolve about the Earth, was incorrect. However, the inaccuracy of his assumptions did not diminish the accuracy of the predictions that could be made using his system.

A second valuable function of correlational research is to provide data that are either consistent or inconsistent with scientific theories. A correlational study cannot prove a theory correct, although it can negate a theory. One validates theories by deriving predictions from them that can be tested empirically.

For example, the question of what intelligence is and how it should be measured had been debated for over a century. British psychologist Charles Spearman (1904) hypothesized a general intellectual trait (the *g* (general) factor), which he said governed performance in all areas of cognitive functioning. One prediction from the Spearman *g* theory is that there should be a strong correlation between different cognitive abilities, because each ability is affected by the *g* factor.

Suppose that a randomly selected sample of participants is tested on both math and vocabulary skills, and the two are highly correlated—that is, people who score high on math skills also tend to score high on vocabulary. Do these data *prove* Spearman's theory? No, but they do provide support for it. The data show that one relationship out of thousands of possible predicted relationships exists. To prove the theory, we would have to test every possible prediction from it, which is often an impossible task because theories typically make many predictions. This is why scientists are so reluctant to use the word "prove." However, the data are consistent with the theory and thus increase confidence in the theory.

Suppose that the researcher also tests reading ability, abstract reasoning, short- and long-term memory, and the ability to solve riddles and finds that all possible correlations among the measures are large and positive. Does this prove the theory correct? The answer is still no, because there remain other predicted relationships that have yet to be tested. However, there would be considerably more confidence in the theory, because all the predictions of the theory that have been tested so far have been confirmed.

Now suppose that the researcher finds that memory and math ability are virtually uncorrelated. What do these data mean? If the procedures were done correctly, we would have to conclude that Spearman's *g* factor theory is incorrect. In other words, just as in naturalistic and case-study research, *correlational research cannot prove a theory, but it can negate one.*

Quick-Check Review 7.1: Correlational Research Methods	1. What is the main purpose of correlational research?
	2. What information can be obtained from correlational research?
	3. Can correlational research determine causality?
	4. How can correlational research help to validate or invalidate a theory?

Differential Research Methods

Differential research compares two or more groups that are differentiated on the basis of some preexisting variable. Groups can be determined by either a qualitative dimension, such as sex, political party, or psychiatric diagnosis, or by some quantitative dimension, such as the participant's age or number of years of education. Whether defined qualitatively or quantitatively, the group differences *existed before the study was conducted.* The researcher measures these differences and assigns participants to groups based on them. This classification variable is the independent variable, and the behaviors measured in the different groups are the dependent variables. Independent variables in differential research are nonmanipulated independent variables (see Chapter 3).

Because differential research involves only measuring, and not manipulating, variables, it involves studying relationships between variables. Thus, differential research is conceptually similar to correlational research. This conceptual similarity means that the same general principles will be used in interpreting the results from each of these approaches.

Drawing causal conclusions from either differential or correlational research studies should be avoided. There is a structural similarity in differential research and experimental research: both utilize different groups defined by an independent variable, and a dependent measure is taken on all participants in each group. This similarity means that the same statistical procedures are used to evaluate the data from these two approaches (see Table 7.1). Thus, differential research is similar to both correlational and experimental research.

TABLE 7.1   *Experimental versus Differential Designs*

A. An Experimental Design

Group 1 *Short Time Interval*	Group 2 *Moderate Time Interval*	Group 3 *Long Time Interval*
Participants	*Participants*	*Participants*
1	1	1
2	2	2
•	•	•
•	•	•
•	•	•
N	N	N

B. A Differential Design

Group 1 *Caucasian*	Group 2 *Black*	Group 3 *Asian*
Participants	*Participants*	*Participants*
1	1	1
2	2	2
•	•	•
•	•	•
•	•	•
N	N	N

Experimental and differential designs can look the same, but there are critical differences. In the experimental design, participants are randomly assigned to conditions, and the experimenter manipulates the conditions. In the differential design, the participants are included in conditions based on their preexisting characteristics. Because of this, causality cannot be inferred from the differential design.

Cross-Sectional versus Longitudinal Research

Differential research is used extensively by developmental psychologists in studying developmental processes. In a **cross-sectional design,** the developmental researcher compares groups of participants of different ages on some set of variables. For example, cognitive development might be explored by giving groups of 3-, 5-, and 7-year-olds a set of problems or puzzles. Differences between the younger and older children in performance on the task provide insight into cognitive development. This is a differential research design, because participants are assigned to groups on the basis of the preexisting characteristic of age.

As with all differential research, caution is needed in drawing conclusions from cross-sectional studies. Suppose that a researcher studies people in their 50s, 60s, 70s, and 80s to understand the aging process better. The researcher must be careful in interpreting the results from such a study, because some of the observed differences may be due to other variables besides age. For example, participants in their 80s will have lived through the Great Depression, whereas participants in their 50s would have grown up during relatively prosperous years. If the older subjects were more cautious about going into debt, it would be unwise to assume that this represented a developmental process, because it could just as easily be explained by differences in life experiences between the groups. The concept that the shared life experiences of people of a given age in a given culture may lead them to behave similarly throughout their lives, but differently from people of other ages, is known as a **cohort effect.** Those who grew up during the Great Depression shared an experience powerful enough that it likely shaped much of their thinking, their expectations, and even their emotional responses.

As you will see later, developmental psychologists have other research designs at their disposal, such as longitudinal designs and time-series designs. **Longitudinal designs** follow the same people over time to observe developmental changes, thus controlling for cohort effects. However, longitudinal designs have the disadvantage of taking a long time to complete. The aging study described earlier would take 40 years to complete with a longitudinal design. **Time-series designs** are variations of longitudinal designs that involve multiple measurements taken before and after a manipulation. They can be used with individual or groups of participants and are discussed in Chapter 11.

Artifacts and Confounding

Studying more than one group of individuals forces the researcher to add constraint by standardizing the observational methods. In naturalistic research, procedures can easily be changed in order to study any phenomenon that captured the researcher's interest. In differential research, however, observations in one group are compared with observations in other groups. Observations from two or more groups can be properly compared only if the observations are made in the same way in each group.

Variables are **confounded** if both vary at the same time. For example, if different observational methods are used in different groups, then any difference observed between the groups may be real or may merely be a function of the different observational methods. There would be no way of knowing which of these possibilities is correct. In other words, the two variables are confounded. In this example, as the group variable changes, the method of observation variable also changes. Because the two variables change together, it is unclear which of them is responsible for observed differences in the dependent variable.

The only way to avoid confounding variables is to make sure that they vary independently of one another. The simplest way to ensure this is to hold one of the variables constant. *The variable of least interest to the researcher should be held constant, and the variable of interest should be allowed to vary.*

In most differential research, the researcher is less interested in the effects of different observational procedures than in how the groups differ from one another. Therefore, the observational method is held constant and the group variable is allowed to vary. To do this, the researcher defines in advance the variables that will be measured and how they are to be measured. Once the study starts, the procedures are constrained by these design decisions, and the same measurement procedures must be used throughout.

Higher-constraint differential research methods are more effective in answering research questions than are lower-constraint naturalistic and case-study observation methods.

The increased effectiveness comes from the ability to compare groups of participants who differ on important variables. However, a price is paid for this additional effectiveness—a loss of flexibility. When there is only one group, the procedures can be modified easily. When there is more than one group, the same observational and measurement procedures must be used in each group in order to make valid comparisons between groups.

Failure to constrain procedures can lead to artifacts. An **artifact** is any apparent effect of an independent variable that is actually the result of some other variable that was not properly controlled. *An artifact is a result of confounding.* Therefore, if different measurement procedures had been used in the two groups, any observed difference between the groups might actually have been an artifact of changes in the measurement procedure, rather than evidence of real group differences.

EXTENDING THE CONCEPT OF CONSTRAINT

Higher-constraint research requires precise and consistent observational procedures and detailed planning. How can a researcher make such detailed plans before a study even begins? If the study is the first being conducted on a topic, the researcher usually cannot do so. Detailed planning is usually carried out when the phenomenon under study is already reasonably well understood. High-constraint research is thus seldom used in the early stages of studying a problem. Instead, flexible low-constraint methods, which allow the researcher to explore the phenomenon and to gain a sense of what to expect, are used. Such an understanding is necessary if we want to state explicit hypotheses and design appropriate procedures for testing those hypotheses. Research on a particular topic often begins with low-constraint methods and proceeds to higher-constraint research only after a basic understanding of the phenomenon is achieved.

Scientists usually study topics that other people have already studied extensively and so may not need to start with low-constraint research. However, most researchers often do at least some low-constraint research to gain familiarity with a phenomenon that would be difficult to understand solely from reading the published accounts of other investigators.

Quick-Check Review 7.2: Differential Research Methods	1. What is the main purpose of differential research?
	2. What type of independent variable is used in differential research?
	3. What are artifacts? How do they affect differential research?
	4. How is differential research structurally similar to experimental research?
	5. How is differential research conceptually similar to correlational research?

Understanding Correlational and Differential Methods

To understand correlational and differential research methods, it is necessary to understand how they are conceptually similar, what makes one higher constraint than the other, and when to use each method.

Comparing These Methods

Relationships among variables are measured in both correlational and differential research. However, we have listed differential research as being higher-constraint. One reason is that differential research is structurally similar to experimental research, in which comparisons of two or more groups are made on a dependent measure. However, other issues define the level of constraint for differential research.

The researcher conducting differential research is often interested in causal questions, which are ideally addressed with experimental research. However, ethical or practical constraints often prevent this. For example, it is impossible to randomly assign participants to groups of (1) people with schizophrenia and (2) people without schizophrenia. Randomly assigning participants to groups or conditions tends to equate the groups on potential confounding variables. The only consistent difference between the groups is the level of the independent variable. Therefore, it is relatively safe to conclude that any observed difference in the dependent variable is the result of the manipulation of the independent variable.

With differential research, participants are assigned to groups on the basis of a pre-existing variable. The groups typically differ on several other variables. For example, people with chronic schizophrenia tend to be from lower social classes, have fewer relationships in adolescence and early adulthood, and spend more time in hospitals than a randomly selected group of people from the general population. These differences are predictable and are well established by past research. Suppose that differences are found between a group of chronic patients with schizophrenia and a general control group on some dependent measure, such as eye movement abnormalities. There is no way of knowing whether these differences are due to schizophrenia, to social class differences, to social experiences during adolescence, or to effects of hospitalization or medication. In other words, these group differences are potential confounding variables. **Confounding variables** are uncontrolled variables that might affect the outcome of a study.

Researchers using differential methods are rarely content with this state of affairs. Stronger controls allow researchers to draw stronger conclusions. Therefore, instead of selecting a general control group, a researcher should select one or more specific control groups using selection criteria that assure that a given control group is comparable to the experimental group on some potential confounding variable. For example, a researcher suspecting that social class might affect the scores on the dependent variable might select a control group that is, on average, of the same social class as the patient group (see Raulin & Lilienfeld, 1999). This would ensure that social class could not confound the findings. Active control over sampling by the researcher is a form of constraint that minimizes confounding and therefore strengthens the conclusions drawn from the study. No comparable control is used in correlational research. Hence, differential research has more control procedures available and is higher constraint than correlational research.

When to Use These Methods

Differential research designs are used most often in situations in which the manipulation of an independent variable is impractical, impossible, or inappropriate. For example, a psychologist might want to compare the effectiveness of two theories of education in creating an effective learning environment. The psychologist could set up two separate schools, institute a different curriculum for each school, randomly assign students, and then evaluate the amount that the students learn. However, the expense of setting up such a research program would make the study impractical. An alternative would be to use two existing schools that already have the kinds of curricula that the researcher is interested in evaluating. This would be a differential research design, because these groups are naturally occurring instead of experimentally manipulated.

Differential designs are also used when an experimental manipulation is impossible to carry out, such as when studying the social development of individuals with superior intelligence. A newborn's intelligence cannot be experimentally raised or lowered, so random assignment to normal and superior intelligence groups is impossible. However, children of average and high intelligence could be selected, and their social development followed.

Finally, some experimental manipulations are technically possible, but unethical to carry out. For example, one might hypothesize that prolonged separation from parents during the first two years of life would lead to permanently retarded social development. It is unethical to select infants randomly and separate them from their parents to test the hypothesis experimentally. However, some children are separated from their parents for reasons that are beyond the researcher's control. Such naturally occurring groups might be suitable populations to study to explore this hypothesis.

Another field that uses correlational and differential research designs extensively, because of ethical considerations, is clinical neuropsychology. A neuropsychologist uses measures of behavior to infer the structural and functional condition of the brain. The neuropsychologist administers tests to people to determine what they can and cannot do. The patterns of such abilities and disabilities can suggest specific neurological problems. Neuropsychologists draw on a wealth of data when they evaluate a person. If a particular pattern of abilities and disabilities is consistently found in people later diagnosed with a specific type of brain problem, then it is reasonable to predict that another person with that pattern might well be suffering from the same neurological dysfunction. The data gathering in this case is correlational, because the researcher is seeking to identify relationships between behavior and brain dysfunction. Some of the relationships observed in neuropsychology are not easily quantifiable in terms of a simple correlation coefficient, but they are relationships nonetheless. By mapping these relationships, an accurate prediction of brain dysfunction can be made on the basis of a person's behavior. Remember, prediction is an important goal of correlational research.

Quick-Check Review 7.3: Understanding Correlational and Differential Methods	1. What do correlational and differential methods have in common? 2. Why is differential research considered higher constraint than correlational research? 3. What might prevent a researcher from using an experimental research design?

Conducting Correlational Research

07:01

Correlational research seeks to quantify the direction and strength of a relationship among two or more variables. Several examples of correlational research are included on the Student Resource Website.

The discussion here focuses on the relationships among two variables only. **Multivariate correlational designs,** which employ more than two variables, are described briefly later in this section.

Problem Statements

Unlike the flexible problem statements of naturalistic observation and case studies, the problem statements for correlational research are much more specific. They typically take the following form: "What is the strength and direction of the relationship between variable X and variable Y?" It is also common to also ask, "What is the best equation for predicting variable Y from variable X?" This is called the **regression equation.**

Detecting Demographic, Gender, or Cultural Effects

The most frequent use of correlational research is secondary statistical analyses. It is commonly done in higher-constraint research to help explain findings or describe the samples under study. For example, a researcher might conduct a differential research project comparing urban and suburban groups on their fear of being victimized by crime. A good researcher routinely collects data on **demographic variables,** which are characteristics of the sample, such as age, education, social class, and cultural distribution. It is common to compare groups to see if they are similar on these variables, because any of these variables could produce artifacts if the groups differ on them. It is also common to compute the correlation of each of these variables with the dependent measure(s) in the study. These correlations can give considerable insight into the data and are often highlighted in the research article. The problem statement would likely be this: What is the correlation of each of the demographic variables with the dependent variable(s)? Traditionally, these correlations are computed separately within each group, because the relationship might be different in the groups. Thus, if the researcher studying fear of crime victimization found that suburban groups are less fearful of crime than urban groups, he or she would want to see if there are any other differences between these groups that could account for that finding. For example, he or she might find that the suburban sample is younger and better educated than the urban sample. If either of these variables is correlated with fear of crime victimization, they might shed some light on the group finding.

Measuring the Variables

Developing effective operational definitions of the variables is critical in correlational research. Measurement depends on the adequacy of operational definitions. The operational definition of a variable involves more than just selecting a measure to administer. Researchers must consider every aspect of the measurement process, including how the measurement will be taken. As in any other research, the researcher needs to avoid the possibility of unintentionally influencing participants. This can be accomplished by (1) never allowing the same person to collect both measures on the participant or (2) never allowing the researcher to know participants' scores on the first measure until after the second measure has been taken.

Two effects need to be controlled: (1) **experimenter expectancy,** the tendency of investigators to see what they expect to see (Chapman & Chapman, 1969), and (2) *experimenter reactivity*, the tendency of investigators to influence the behavior of participants, which we covered in Chapter 6. Experimenter expectancy is minimized by using objective measures whenever possible, so that little subjective interpretation is necessary. The problem of experimenter reactivity may require the use of two independent researchers. A researcher is most likely to influence participants who are asked to give voluntary responses with the researcher present.

Experimenter effects on participants are discussed in more detail in Chapters 8 and 9.

EXTENDING THE CONCEPT OF MEASUREMENT REACTIVITY

Another potential problem in correlational research is the participant's own influence on measures. Participants like to be consistent, especially when they believe that they are being observed and evaluated. This is a variation on the measurement reactivity problem discussed in Chapter 6. It can give the impression of a strong relationship between variables when no relationship exists in reality.

There are several ways of reducing this effect. One is to disguise self-report measures by including filler items so that participants are unsure of what the investigator is studying. **Filler items** are not meant to measure anything, but rather to draw the participant's attention away from the real purpose of the measure. A second method of controlling the participant's influence on the data is to rely on one or more unobtrusive measures. In this way, participants are unaware that they are being observed and are thus less likely to modify their normal behavior. A third method is to separate the measures from one another, which can be done by taking measurements at different times or by having different researchers take the measurements. Probably the best way to deal with the problem of measurement reactivity is to use measures beyond the control of the participant. For example, anxiety might be assessed with psychophysiological measures rather than self-reports or behavioral observations. Most participants have less control over their physiological responses than over what they say or do.

Sampling

One major concern in most research is obtaining a sample that adequately represents the population to which generalizations are to be made. Another sampling issue, which is peculiar to correlational research, is whether the relationship between a given pair of variables is the same in all segments of the population. If such differences are suspected, samples might be drawn from separate subpopulations. For example, if one suspects that males and females demonstrate a different relationship between two variables, either in direction or strength, then separate samples of males and females should be selected and separate correlations computed for each group. In this example, sex is a **moderator variable**—a variable that seems to modify the relationship between other variables. In addition to sex, culture and ethnicity are common moderator variables. People raised in one culture may very well react differently to a situation than people raised in a different culture. It is now common in psychology to explore phenomena that have been studied extensively in Western cultures in other cultures to see how readily the findings generalize across cultures, a procedure called **cross-cultural research.** These are usually differential research studies comparing cultures. Early psychological research often ignored possible cultural influences, but there is now a realization that culture can significantly influence many psychological variables (Sorrentino et al., 2005).

If different subpopulations show different relationships between two variables, the relationships can be obscured if the variable that defines the subpopulations is not included as a moderator variable. For example, if the variables of dependency and hostility are positively correlated in males, but negatively correlated in females, the correlation in a mixed group of males and females will probably be close to zero, suggesting no relationship. The opposite relationships in the two groups cancel each other. In this example, sex is a moderator variable because it modifies the relationship between the variables of dependency and hostility. Recognizing potential moderator variables requires a thorough knowledge of the area under study. When in doubt, it is always better to compute correlations for different subgroups. If the same relationship is found in all the groups, you can be more confident that the relationship will hold for the entire population sampled.

Analyzing the Data

Data analysis in correlational research involves computing an index of the degree of relationship between variables. Which correlation coefficient should be used depends on the level of measurement of both variables. If both variables are measured on at least an interval scale, then a Pearson product-moment correlation coefficient should be computed. If one variable is measured on an ordinal scale and the other variable is at least ordinal, then the appropriate coefficient is a Spearman rank-order correlation.

Both correlation coefficients indicate the degree of linear relationship between two variables, and both range from -1.00 to $+1.00$. A -1.00 means a perfect negative relationship exists (as one variable increases, the other decreases in a perfectly predictable fashion). A $+1.00$ means a perfect positive relationship exists. A correlation of 0.00 means there is no linear relationship between the two variables. (See Figures 5.5 and 5.6 for examples of correlation scatter plots.) The computational procedures for these correlation coefficients are presented on the Student Resource Website.

07:02

The Pearson and Spearman correlations quantify the relationship between two variables. However, some research situations demand more complicated correlational analyses, such as correlating one variable with an entire set of variables **(multiple correlation)** or one set of variables with another set of variables **(canonical correlation).** It is also possible to correlate one variable with another after statistically removing the effects of a third variable **(partial correlation).** Analytical procedures, such as **path analysis,** can test the strength of evidence for a specific causal model using correlational data (Raulin & Graziano, 1995). Detailed discussion of these more sophisticated analytic procedures is beyond the scope of this book (see Loehlin, 2004; Myers & Well, 2003 or Nunnally & Bernstein, 1993), although some background information on these procedures is included on the Student Resource Website.

07:03

Interpreting the Correlation

The first step in interpreting a correlation is to note its direction and size. Is the correlation positive or negative? Is the relationship small (close to 0.00) or large (close to +1.00 or −1.00)?

The next step is to test for the statistical significance of the correlation—whether the observed correlation is large enough to convince the researcher that there is a nonzero correlation between the variables in the population from which the sample was drawn. To state it another way, the researcher is testing the null hypothesis that the variables are uncorrelated in the population.

Computer programs are available that compute the *p*-value for each correlation. This *p*-value is the probability of achieving a correlation this large or larger if the correlation in the population were actually zero. If this probability is low, it means that there is little chance that the population correlation is zero. In that case, we would say that the correlation is statistically significant. Traditionally the probability must be quite low (usually .05 or even .01) before researchers declare their findings to be statistically significant. For example, if the correlation between two variables is .67 with a *p*-value of .035, we would conclude that a significant relationship exists, because the *p*-value is less than the traditional alpha of .05.

See Chapter 5 for a more detailed explanation of this terminology.

When using correlation coefficients, we should also calculate the **coefficient of determination,** rather than just rely on the statistical significance of the correlation (Nunnally & Bernstein, 1993). The coefficient of determination is the square of the correlation. If the correlation is .50, then $r^2 = .25$. You can convert .25 to a percent by multiplying by 100 ($100 \times .25 = 25\%$). A correlation of .50 indicates that 25% of the variability in the first variable can be accounted for, or predicted, by knowing the scores on the second variable. This statement is usually shortened by referring to r^2 as the "proportion of variance accounted for." This procedure allows researchers to estimate how useful the relationship might be in prediction. However, it is appropriate to take r^2 seriously only if there is a good-sized sample (a minimum of thirty participants). Smaller samples do not provide stable estimates of population correlations.

Quick-Check Review 7.4: *Conducting Correlational Research*	1. What is the difference between experimenter expectancy and experimenter reactivity?
	2. What are moderator variables?
	3. What are the two most commonly used measures of correlation? Under what conditions is each measure used?
	4. What is the coefficient of determination? What does it indicate?

Conducting Differential Research

07:04

Differential research is used to compare existing groups on theoretically relevant variables. It is used when experimental procedures are impossible or unethical but the researcher is still interested in learning as much as possible about the differences between groups. This section covers the formulation of problem statements, measurement, selecting control groups, sampling, and analyzing and interpreting the data.

Problem Statements

Problem statements for differential research are among the most challenging in all of research. At one level they are simple. The problem statement is in this format: "Does Group *A* differ from Group *B* on the dependent variable(s)?"

We could create an infinite number of such problem statements by taking every possible group and comparing it with every other possible group. For example, why not ask, "Do balding college professors differ from laboratory rats in their preference for music?" One reason for not asking is that it is a pretty stupid question. Although you can compare any group with any other group, it makes little sense to do so unless the comparison tells us something meaningful. In other words, you want to make comparisons that have theoretical significance. Unfortunately, research is done and published using differential designs and making comparisons that make about as much theoretical sense as the balding professor–lab rat example. Picking two groups and comparing them on something is easy; picking the right groups and the right dependent variable in order to advance scientific understanding is much harder, but should always be the goal in differential research.

What makes a comparison in differential research theoretically significant? A useful study will tell the researcher something about factors that affect the dependent variable, rather than just revealing differences between two groups. No one would be surprised to find a difference in music preference between balding college professors and lab rats. In fact, we would expect to find differences on many variables, such as weight, eye color, diurnal cycle, night vision, and social skills. Suppose that differences on all these variables, as well as on music preference, were found. What would it mean? Who knows, or cares for that matter?

The problem with this comparison is that the two groups differ on so many variables that there is no way of knowing which are relevant. The first rule of thumb, therefore, is *develop problem statements that focus on comparing groups that differ on only one variable.* If you are interested in sex differences, do not compare balding professors (presumably male) with a group of fifth-grade girls. These groups differ not only on sex, but also on age, education, social class, and the types and range of experiences that they have had. If you found a difference, you would have no idea what caused it. A better comparison might be fifth-grade girls and fifth-grade boys. However, you still should be cautious in drawing conclusions about the role of sex based on this one comparison.

This leads us to the second rule of thumb: *Use several comparisons when trying to draw a conclusion about the role of a factor from differential research studies.* If you find similar results in comparisons of fifth-grade girls and boys, college males and females, male and female businesspeople, male and female college professors, and male and female truck drivers, you can be more confident in your hypothesis that sex differences account for all these findings. Even with this whole series of findings based on comparing groups that appear to differ only on sex, you have to be careful in drawing a causal conclusion.

Finally, good problem statements focus on group differences in theoretically relevant dependent measures. If you were interested in studying self-esteem, you would focus on variables like success, social support, childhood experiences, and internal cognitions. These variables are likely to affect, or be affected by, self-esteem. Variables like hat size, finger-tapping speed, visual acuity, and make and model of car are less likely to be theoretically relevant.

In summary, good problem statements for differential research compare two or more theoretically relevant groups on a theoretically relevant dependent measure, in which the groups ideally differ on only a single dimension. Because the ideal of groups differing on only a single dimension is rarely achieved, multiple comparisons are used in drawing conclusions about the influence of group differences on the dependent measure.

Measuring the Variables

In differential research, researchers distinguish between the independent variable and the dependent variable. The dependent variable is usually a continuous measure, but it might also be a discrete (categorical) measure. The independent variable is typically a discrete variable. For example, it might be an educational category with two values, such as high school graduate and high school dropout. The independent variable in differential research is measured, rather than manipulated. In the example of educational level, the researcher needs a procedure to measure the education of participants. This seems simple enough, but it can quickly become complicated. For example, in what category would you put someone who obtained a GED (general education diploma), which is a high school equivalency degree? Where do you get the information? Do you ask the person or check with the school that granted the diploma? You need to decide on all these issues before you begin the study. This set of procedures would be the operational definition of education level. (Note that the issues that apply to creating operational definitions for the independent variable are the same that apply in measuring the dependent variable.)

Although the nonmanipulated independent variable in differential research is usually a discrete variable, it is always possible to take a continuous variable, such as education level, and break it into discrete intervals, such as high school dropout, high school graduate, college graduate, and so on. This process converts a correlational research design into a differential research design.

Selecting Appropriate Control Groups

The researcher must decide which groups to include in a differential study. In some cases, the decision is simple. If, for example, the study were about sex differences, sex would be the independent variable, and there would be only two possibilities. Because the minimum number of groups required in differential research is two, the researcher would use both a male and a female group.

However, such is not the case with other independent variables. If the study is about psychopathology, there are dozens of psychiatric disorders. Choosing which of these disorders to compare must be done within a theoretical framework that guides the researcher in selecting the appropriate comparison groups. The term **control group** is used to refer to any group selected in differential research as a basis of comparison with the primary or **experimental group.**[1]

In some cases, the experimental-control group distinction is irrelevant. With the previous example of exploring sex differences, it makes little sense to say that one sex represents the experimental group and the other sex represents the control group. In other situations, the control group is arbitrarily defined as the group that has none of the characteristic that define the independent variable. For example, if the independent vari-

---

[1]Although the term *experimental group* is commonly used, it can be misleading in discussions of differential research. In spite of the common use of the term, differential research is *not* experimental.

able is college education and you have three groups (no college, some college, college graduate), it would be customary to refer to the no-college group as the control group.

Recall that control groups are designed to reduce the effects of potential confounding variables. A variable can have a confounding effect in a differential study only if (1) it affects the scores on the dependent variable(s) and (2) there is a difference between the experimental and control groups on the potential confounding variable. For example, suppose that you want to study sex differences in the ability to perceive details in visual scenes. You know that visual acuity affects performance on the task. Therefore, visual acuity is a potential confounding variable. However, if males and females do not differ on visual acuity, then it cannot differentially affect performance in the two groups and, therefore, cannot be a confounding variable in this study.

The control group should be selected with care if it is to be an effective control. *The ideal control group is identical to the experimental group on all variables except the independent variable that defines the groups.* For example, if a researcher was studying the effects of exposure to toxic chemicals on cognitive performance, the experimental group might consist of people who work in industries in which they are exposed to such toxins. An ideal control group would include workers of about the same age, social class, and education level, who do similar kinds of work, but work in an industry that does not expose them to these toxins. A group of office workers from the same company as the plant workers in the experimental group might be a convenient control group, but *not* a very good one. The office workers would probably differ from the plant workers on a number of important variables, such as education level, age, and the ratio of males to females. Any of these differences could affect cognitive performance and thus constitute potential confounding variables.

Consider another example of selecting a control group. Suppose that the research is a study of schizophrenia. The experimental group consists of people with schizophrenia. What is a good control group to compare with this experimental group? The choice will depend on the dependent measure and the confounding variables that might affect it. As noted earlier, a variable can have a confounding effect in a differential study only if (1) it affects the scores on the dependent variable(s) and (2) there is a difference between the experimental and control groups on the potential confounding variable.

To select an appropriate control group, therefore, factors that will affect the dependent measures must first be identified. These represent *potential* confounding factors, but they will not actually confound the results unless the experimental and control groups differ on these factors. Therefore, it is essential to select a control group that is comparable to the experimental group on these potential confounding factors.

EXTENDING THE CONCEPT OF CONTROL

If you are interested in, for example, measuring thought processes in people with schizophrenia, you should identify variables known to affect performance on such measures. You can usually find answers to this question by looking at the literature. Past research using the same or similar dependent measures often reports correlations with potential confounding variables. You may remember that we mentioned that most correlational research was included in higher-constraint studies as a routine part of the analyses. The reason for this routine inclusion is that it tests for possible confounding variables and it provides information to other researchers regarding variables to be concerned about in planning a research study.

Once the potential confounding variables are identified, you can identify a control group that is unlikely to differ from the experimental group on these variables. Potential confounding variables might include amount of education, age, and total amount of psychiatric hospitalization. To reduce the threat of these potential confounding variables, you should select a control group that is similar to the patients on these variables, or at least as many of these variables as possible. If you can accomplish this, the variables will not confound the results.

It is rare to find an ideal control group. Instead, researchers usually try to obtain a control group that controls some of the most important and most powerful confounding variables. A confounding variable is powerful if it is likely to have a large effect on the dependent measure. In the hypothetical study of the thought processes of persons with schizophrenia, a powerful confounding variable might be education. The researcher can identify education as a confounding variable, because the research literature shows that education is highly correlated with measures of cognitive performance.

Another way to deal with the problem of finding an ideal control group is to use multiple control groups. Each control group typically controls for one or more of the major confounding variables, but no group controls for all potential confounding variables. If each of the comparisons of experimental group and control group gives essentially the same results and leads to the same conclusion, then the researcher can be reasonably confident that the independent variable, and not one of the confounding variables, is responsible for the observed effect. Most of the research in medicine and the social sciences relies on such multiple comparisons. Because it is not always feasible to include all possible comparison groups in one study, research often involves multiple studies by different researchers in different laboratories, each using slightly different procedures and control groups. If the phenomenon under study is stronger than the potential confounding variables, each researcher will come to the same conclusion.

In some research, multiple comparison groups are selected for strong theoretical reasons. For example, anhedonia, which is the inability to experience pleasure, has been recognized as a central characteristic of schizophrenia for nearly one hundred years (Bleuler, 1911/1950). Of course, not experiencing pleasure is also a hallmark of other psychiatric disorders, such as depression. Therefore, it makes theoretical sense to ask if there are differences in the anhedonia experienced by people with schizophrenia and that found in people with severe depression. Blanchard, Horan, and Brown (2001) did just that. Their primary dependent measure was a scale to measure social anhedonia, or the failure to experience pleasure from social interactions (Chapman, Chapman, & Raulin, 1976; Eckblad, Chapman, Chapman, & Mishlove, 1982). They speculated that the difference between the anhedonia in schizophrenia and the anhedonia in depression is that the pleasure deficit comes and goes in depression, but remains constant in schizophrenia.

To test this hypothesis, they sampled three groups: people with schizophrenia, people with severe depression, and people with no psychiatric disorder. The group of people with no psychiatric disorder provided a baseline—a measure of normal levels of social anhedonia. These researchers minimized possible confounding by selecting the groups so that they would be approximately the same age, education, and ratio of males to females. They also tried to match as closely as possible on ethnic and marital status, although they found it more difficult matching on these variables. They then tested their participants, waited a year, and retested them.

Depression tends to come and go, so many of the people with severe depression were much less depressed at the retest. The findings, shown in Figure 7.1, were consistent with their hypothesis. Anhedonia remains high in people with schizophrenia and is not affected by the level of the schizophrenic symptoms. In contrast, anhedonia varies in people with depression, and the level of depression affects the level of anhedonia. Interestingly, the level of depression did not affect the level of anhedonia in people with schizophrenia. People with schizophrenia, like other people, are depressed at times and not depressed at other times. These findings suggest that failure to experience pleasure in social relationships may be a different phenomenon in different psychiatric disorders, although determining the exact nature of the difference will require more research.

We suspect that some students will find this discussion discouraging, because it can be so difficult to find ideal comparison groups. This is one of the reasons why it is so important to do multiple research studies.

Chapter 10 will discuss experimental research designs, in which groups are not defined on the basis of preexisting variables; instead, participants are randomly assigned to the groups. Such random assignment controls most of the problems described in this section. Our advice to students interested in studying areas in which experimentation is unethical or impossible is to realize that drawing strong conclusions is difficult at best.

Sampling

Regardless of the type of research, the same issues of sampling always apply. To be able to generalize to a larger population, researchers must sample randomly from the population.

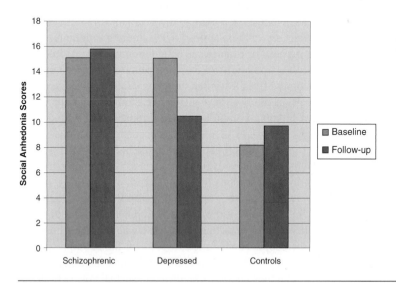

FIGURE 7.1 *Anhedonia in Schizophrenia and Depression* Blanchard et al. (2001) found that social anhedonia was a consistent characteristic in people with schizophrenia, but was present in people with depression only during the depressive episode.

Source: Adapted from Blanchard et al. (2001).

Random sampling is a procedure for selecting participants from a population in which each participant has an equal chance of being selected. To study people with schizophrenia, researchers should ideally utilize a procedure that samples randomly from all people with this disorder. This ideal is impossible to attain in practice. It would be much too expensive, for example, to obtain a sample of 30 people with schizophrenia from many different states and hospitals, because the cost of travel alone would be prohibitive. Usually, a sample is selected from all the participants available to the researcher. Unless there is reason to believe that participants from one part of the country are different from participants from another part, the sample need not be from the whole country to be able to generalize to the whole country.

A serious threat to generalizability is the subtle bias that can occur when a researcher has access only to certain groups. For example, if the researcher who is studying people with schizophrenia obtains all participants from one hospital, the sample might well be unrepresentative of schizophrenia, because most psychiatric hospitals specialize in the kinds of patients that they treat. Some hospitals handle chronic cases that require long-term hospitalization. A sample from such a hospital would under-represent those who recover quickly. Private hospitals serve more patients from higher socioeconomic levels than state-funded hospitals. In fact, choosing participants from hospitals might result in a biased sample. Many people with schizophrenia who could be cared for at home are in hospitals, because they have no family or home to go to. A hospital sample of people with schizophrenia might overrepresent those individuals from unstable homes.

Researchers studying other populations must also be sensitive to these subtle sampling biases. For example, a particular school might not have a representative sample of children. Depending on the location of the school, the children might come from higher or lower socioeconomic backgrounds than children in general. The sample might overrepresent or underrepresent certain ethnic groups. Its students might be of higher or lower intelligence than the average child. Any of these variables can affect the results of a study.

Even when researchers appear to be sampling randomly, it is important to be sensitive to subtle biases. For example, is a random sample of people in a shopping center representative of the population? A shopping center on the west side of town may have very different customers from a similar shopping center on the east side of town. A shopping center in the city is likely to have different customers than one in the suburbs. To obtain a representative sample, it might be best to sample people from several locations. The time of day or day of the week also could affect sample composition. A sample taken on a weekday afternoon would probably overrepresent homemakers, people who work evenings or weekends, the unemployed, kids playing hooky, or people on vacation. People who do not like shopping will also be underrepresented.

Finally, researchers may make subtle discriminations that produce a biased sample. Because no one likes to be turned away, researchers might choose to approach people who seem more likely to cooperate and avoid those who seem in a hurry. That apparently is what happened to the people conducting exit polls for the 2004 presidential election. It appears that Republican voters were consistently underrepresented in those polls. This distorted the results enough that they no longer predicted the actual vote (Morin, 2004). Whether Republican voters were less willing to talk, were too rushed to talk, or looked uninterested in talking is hotly debated, but what is not debated is that the exit-poll sample was biased.

The point is that it is easy to obtain an unrepresentative sample that might threaten the generalizability of a study. This is a problem with any research and is particularly rele-

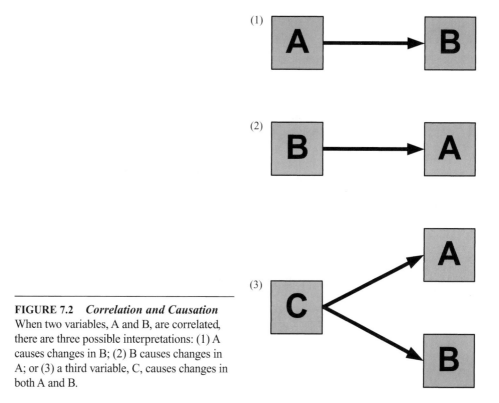

FIGURE 7.2 *Correlation and Causation*
When two variables, A and B, are correlated,
there are three possible interpretations: (1) A
causes changes in B; (2) B causes changes in
A; or (3) a third variable, C, causes changes in
both A and B.

metic. This is a plausible causal chain that could explain how better reading skills can lead to better arithmetic skills.

Another explanation for a strong correlation between arithmetic and reading abilities should be considered. What does it mean when there is a strong relationship between reading ability and arithmetic ability? We are not asking you to interpret this relationship but, rather, to define what it means in operational terms: how was this relationship quantified? In this case, a sample of people was asked to take tests of reading ability and arithmetic ability. What do the scores on the tests really mean? Suppose that the arithmetic test includes the following question:

> *John goes to the market and buys five tomatoes. If tomatoes sell for $6 per dozen, how much change should John receive if he gives the clerk a $5 bill?*

Clearly, this question measures the ability to multiply, divide, and subtract. If tomatoes are $6.00 per dozen, they are $0.50 each, and therefore five tomatoes would cost $2.50. The change that John should receive (assuming no sales tax) is $2.50. It seems simple enough. But what other abilities would this question measure? Consider the following example:

> *Jean va au marché et il acheté cinq tomates. Si les tomates se vendent á $6 la douzaine, combien de monnaie Jean doit-il recevoir s'il donne á la vendeuse un billet de $5?*

Unless you read French, you probably found this question considerably harder to answer, yet it is the same arithmetic question. The example illustrates how important reading ability is in tests, regardless of the material being tested. Therefore, a correlation between reading ability and arithmetic ability may actually be an artifact of the phenomenon that reading ability is required to perform well on either test.

Another point is often overlooked when interpreting a correlation. When we say that both *A* and *B* may be caused by some third variable *C,* we are not specifying what the third variable might be. In fact, variable *C* might be anything, so we do not have three interpretations to choose from, but rather hundreds. Suppose that you believe that you can eliminate the possibility that arithmetic skills caused reading skills and the possibility that reading skills caused arithmetic skills. Could you then conclude that the third factor (Spearman's *g* factor) is responsible for both? No, you cannot. Spearman's general intelligence factor is only one of many possible third-factor variables that could account for the observed correlation. General test-taking ability might be a relevant factor. Anxiety level during the testing might be a relevant factor. For example, have you ever taken an exam during which you panicked? The amount of distraction during the testing session might be important, or the level of motivation of participants, or the general quality of their education, or any one of a dozen other variables. Most likely, each of these variables contributes to the observed correlation. Yet it is tempting to conclude that the causal factor being hypothesized is the one that led to the observed relationship.

Now that we have stated that correlations do not imply causality, we want to acknowledge that some theorists disagree with this statement. There are sophisticated correlational designs, well beyond the scope of this textbook, that are sometimes used in disciplines in which direct experimentation may be unethical, such as in medicine or clinical psychology. Some researchers argue that the right combination of correlational studies can so effectively exclude other interpretations of a complex data set that a causal interpretation is reasonable. Even though this may be true, the research literature is littered with hundreds of examples of top scientists drawing incorrect causal interpretations from complex correlational data. Therefore, we believe that the best rule to follow is *do not draw causal inferences from correlational data!*

Confounding Variables

As noted earlier, another limitation of differential and correlational research methods is that it is often difficult or impossible to avoid confounding variables. Two variables are said to be confounded when they tend to vary together. Because they vary together, any observed relationships with other variables might be caused by either of the variables or both of them. In differential research in particular, confounding is more the rule than the exception. Some potential confounding variables may be controlled with a carefully selected control group, but rarely will the researcher be able to completely eliminate confounding. Such problems will always make interpretation difficult, although some researchers choose to think of them as simply making the task more challenging.

Quick-Check Review 7.6: Limitations of Correlational and Differential Research	1. What is the major limitation in interpreting correlational and differential research? 2. What are the reasons for this major limitation? 3. What are confounding variables? Define and explain the concept.

PUTTING IT INTO PRACTICE	By this point in the course, you are probably designing your own research studies, and many of the principles in this chapter will be helpful. However, these principles are valuable in other ways as well, such as helping you to interpret published research findings or improving your critical thinking skills. Here are two exercises that you might make a routine part of your life. When you read research articles, which you will do a lot in psychology, use the critical thinking skills covered in this text to identify potential sources of confounding. The more you practice these skills, the better you will get. You will find critical thinking extremely helpful to your education. The second exercise is to listen carefully to the arguments and the data on which those arguments are based when you watch the news. If you ask yourself whether the data support the argument being made and *only* that argument, you may be surprised. Many political and business pundits are willing to make strong statements with only the weakest of data to support them. The ability to see through such weak arguments will do much more than earn you good grades; it will give you an advantage in your professional and personal life.

Chapter Summary

Correlational and differential methods of research were covered together, because they share the common characteristic that they measure, but do not manipulate, variables. By not manipulating variables, the researcher surrenders considerable control and thus must be cautious in interpreting the data. It is difficult or impossible to draw causal conclusions from data derived from correlational or differential research.

Correlational and differential research designs are appropriate when the researcher is interested in relationships among variables. Sometimes researchers are interested in a causal relationship, but are unable to

conduct experiments due to practical or ethical concerns. In such cases, a differential design is appropriate. Experimental research is generally easier to interpret, and causal conclusions can be drawn more safely from experimental research. However, many questions of interest in psychology and medicine cannot use experimental methods. The effective use of correlational and differential research methods, coupled with a thorough knowledge of past research, good theory, and a sophisticated use of logic, can often answer some of these difficult yet critically important questions.

Chapter Exercises

1. Define the following key terms. Be sure that you understand them. They are discussed in the chapter and defined in the glossary.

   cross-sectional design
   cohort effect
   longitudinal designs
   time-series designs
   confounded
   artifact
   confounding variable
   multivariate correlational designs
   regression equation
   demographic variables
   experimenter expectancy

   filler items
   moderator variable
   cross-cultural research
   multiple correlation
   canonical correlation
   partial correlation
   path analysis
   coefficient of determination
   control group
   experimental group

2. Interpret each of the following correlations for statistical significance, proportion of variance accounted for, and conceptual interpretation.

   a. A correlation of .41 ($p = .007$) between age and height in grade school girls.

   b. A correlation of .32 ($p = .074$) between rank on a depression scale and rank order of activity level on the ward in a group of hospitalized psychiatric patients.

   c. A correlation of .20 ($p = .04$) between two different measures of assertiveness.

8

Hypothesis Testing, Validity, and Threats to Validity

Nothing is more dangerous than an idea when it is the only one we have.

—Emile Auguste Chartier, 1868-1951; *Libre propos*

Web Resource Material

The main goal of this chapter is to integrate concepts covered earlier in this text and to introduce several new concepts. Some of the material will be a review, and several concepts will be expanded. The chapter systematically lays out issues that must be addressed in designing experimental research, which is the focus of Chapters 8 through 13.

Hypothesis Testing

A crucial part of experimentation is developing and testing *research hypotheses.* Developing good research hypotheses involves several steps. First, the researcher refines an initial idea into a *statement of the problem,* drawing on initial observations of the phenomenon and a thorough review of previous research. The statement of the problem is converted into a research hypothesis when the *theoretical concepts* in the problem statement are converted into specific procedures for measurement or manipulation—that is, into *operational definitions* of the concept. This entire process is illustrated in Figure 8.1. Each of these ideas will be discussed at length in this section.

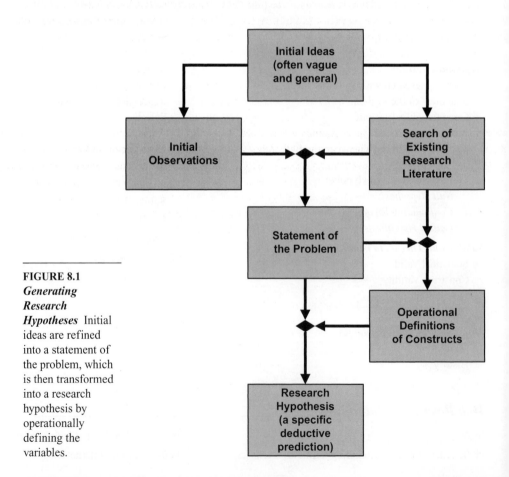

FIGURE 8.1
Generating Research Hypotheses Initial ideas are refined into a statement of the problem, which is then transformed into a research hypothesis by operationally defining the variables.

A research hypothesis is a specific prediction about the effects of a specific, operationally defined independent variable on a specific, operationally defined dependent variable.

Problem statements, operational definitions, and research hypotheses are important at all levels of research. Research hypotheses take different forms depending on the level of constraint. For example, you have learned that a research hypothesis at the correlational level of constraint takes this general form: There is a significant (positive or negative) relationship between variables *A* and *B*. At the differential level, the general form of the hypothesis is this: There is a significant difference between the groups on the dependent variable. At the experimental level, the research hypothesis might be this: Variable *A* will significantly affect variable *B*.

Note that the hypothesis might be directional (e.g., an increase or decrease in variable *B*) or it might be non-directional. Hypotheses are tested at all levels of research, but it is at the experimental level that one can draw causal inferences with the most confidence.

Starting Research with an Initial Idea

A research study begins with an initial idea that is refined and developed into one or more specific questions and predictions. The researcher designs the procedures to be used to test the predictions, and only then proceeds with the observations. Each step is planned carefully, addressing many conceptual and procedural questions. The initial idea can come from reading the research literature, from one's own personal interests and observation, or from the general need for a solution to a practical problem. Initial ideas focus one's research on specific variables. Some examples of initial ideas are listed in Table 8.1. Try to pick out the variables identified in each question in this table.

Having developed an initial idea, the researcher searches the literature to find research dealing with similar ideas and questions. It is common to find that one's "new idea" has already been studied. Published research often will provide considerable information, such as how other researchers defined their variables and what procedures they used. Initial ideas are modified, discarded, or retained based on this examination of the literature. The literature search is the first of many tests of a research idea. It will tell you what is known and what has yet to be studied, and it also will point you in the direction of promising areas

TABLE 8.1 *Initial Research Ideas*

Here are some examples of initial research ideas that may later be translated into specific research studies.

1. Will children do better in school if they are given immediate feedback of examination results?
2. Does cocaine affect learning?
3. Does nutrition affect performance on schoolwork?
4. Is productivity better when employees own stock in their company?
5. Is it true that older people have poorer memory than younger ones?
6. Do men and women have different brain organization?
7. What are the neural bases for locating objects in visual space?

08:01

for future study. The Student Resource Website provides an extensive tutorial on how to conduct such library research. A brief version of this tutorial is included in Appendix C.

Statement of the Problem

Initial ideas that survive the literature search are refined into a statement of the problem, which guides the researcher through the remainder of the research. In experimentation, the problem statement makes a causal prediction: Does variable *A* cause a specific change in variable *B*? For example, the initial idea "I wonder if nutrition affects schoolwork?" could become the problem statement "Will good breakfasts improve academic achievement?" The specific focus of the problem statement is often shaped by the information that the researcher learned in his or her literature search. Table 8.2 lists several examples of problem statements.

Problem statements are expressed in the form of questions, which at the experimental level concern causality. Where possible, the direction of the expected effect is stated. For example, immediate feedback is expected to improve arithmetic skill, cocaine administration is expected to reduce learning, and so on. Most experimental questions are directional, but sometimes a direction cannot be specified. For example, a researcher might suspect that a manipulation will bring about a change in racial attitudes, but cannot predict if it will make the attitudes more positive or more negative. Therefore, the experiment will test whether attitudes change in either direction.

The statement of the problem at the experimental level includes (1) a statement about an expected causal effect, (2) identification of at least two variables, and (3) when possible, an indication of the direction of the expected causal effects. Formulating a clear statement of the problem points the researcher toward an effective design.

Developing a clear statement of the problem requires skill and creativity. Consider bystander apathy, sometimes called the "Bad Samaritan" effect. This deadly social problem does not occur often but, when it does, leaves people bewildered, shaking their heads, and asking, "How can anyone behave like that? How can all of those people just stand there and watch and not do anything to help?"

TABLE 8.2 *Problem Statements*

Here are some examples of problem statements for experimental studies. Each of these problem statements addresses a question of causality.

1. Does the presence of male hormones increase aggressive behavior in rats?
2. Does the presence of a mediator increase the likelihood of reaching a compromise in a negotiation setting?
3. Are easily visualized words more readily learned than words that cannot be easily visualized?
4. Does the presence of a stranger in the room increase an infant's crying?
5. Do stimulants help hyperactive children control their behavior?
6. Does contingent reinforcement improve the accuracy of maze running in mice?
7. Are people more aggressive when they are frustrated?
8. Will sensory deprivation grossly distort thinking and emotional responsivity?
9. Will mandatory arrest and jail time reduce spousal abuse?

A particularly shocking example occurred on a Detroit bridge late in 1995 (Meredith, 1996). Traffic was stopped and drivers were irritated. It is not clear how it started, but a man began attacking another driver, a young woman. She screamed and ran; he pursued her, beat her, knocked her to the ground, and ripped off her clothes. He laughed and invited other men who were watching to join in. Forty or fifty people, sitting in their cars or standing outside to see better, watched as she screamed and pleaded for help. No one helped. After what seemed a long time, the beaten, near-naked woman ran frantically from the still-pursuing attacker, jumped onto the railing, and fell, or perhaps was thrown, into the water to her death. In all that time, although many had been within a few feet, not a single person had stirred to help the terrified young woman.

Such road rage is shocking to witnesses (Gryta, 1998). More shocking is the fact that no one helped her. Yet this was not the first such incident. In 1964, a young woman named Catherine (Kitty) Genovese was stabbed repeatedly for half an hour, while 38 of her neighbors watched from their apartments. No one came to her aid. No one even called the police until after she was dead. Incidents like these raise questions like "How could this happen?" or "Why didn't anyone help her?"

These questions are important, but they are too vague to be tested scientifically. Darley and Latane (1968) refined the questions into something more manageable. How did they do that? They studied reports of the Genovese attack and what the witnesses said about it. They looked for similar occurrences in police files and in the research literature. In the end, they focused their attention on only one or two factors, which allowed them to create a workable statement of the problem.

A major issue in the Genovese case was that none of the 38 people who witnessed the attack came to her aid. Common sense might lead you to believe that the more people that are present, the more likely it is that someone will help. This incident suggests that, contrary to common sense, as the number of people present increases, the likelihood that someone will help decreases. This idea suggests that one variable (the number of people present) might affect another variable (the likelihood of someone offering aid). You might develop the idea into the following problem statement: Will bystanders be less likely to help a victim when there are many people present than when there are only a few people present?

The statement of the problem can lead to specific research studies. When Darley and Latane (1968) studied the problem, they found that people were indeed less likely to help if other people were present. In fact, they were much less likely to help. People apparently assume that, when others are around, someone else will take responsibility.

Thus, composing a statement of the problem is an important early phase in designing research. Kerlinger (1992) lists the following characteristics of a good problem statement.

1. The problem should state the expected relationships between variables (in experimentation, this is a causal relationship).
2. The problem should be stated in the form of a question.
3. The statement of the problem must at least imply the possibility of an empirical test of the question.

In the next few pages we will pull together the major concepts that we have been discussing, using for our example the autism research that was discussed in earlier chapters (Graziano, 1974). Although completed many years ago, it still provides a good example for understanding these concepts. In that research, the major question was this: Can relaxation reduce disruption in children with autism? The independent variable was relaxation and the dependent variable was disruption. The expected effect was a decrease in disruption brought about by relaxation training.

With the statement of the problem clearly defined, the next step in the development of the research hypothesis is to define operationally the variables suggested by the problem statement.

Operational Definitions

Before the dependent variable can be measured or the independent variable manipulated, they must be defined. At all levels of research, variables are defined both conceptually and operationally. The independent variable in this study was relaxation. The concept of relaxation refers to an internal state, a condition in which people function without stress or anxiety. It cannot be directly observed, but it can be inferred. Therefore, relaxation is not an observed fact but an inferred construct. The conceptual definition of relaxation provides an idea of what to manipulate. But how can one manipulate something that is internal to the participant, and thus not directly observable or accessible? In other words, how was the manipulation of relaxation to be operationally defined?

You learned in Chapter 4 that the children were relaxed by having them lie down while the researcher encouraged them to relax with a soothing voice and muscle massage. The definition was spelled out by describing how the researcher should set up the room, as well as what should be said and done to relax the participants. Once the definition was created, the term *relaxation training* was understood to mean all these procedures. Because the definition provided detailed instructions, other researchers could replicate the procedure.

The dependent variable, disruption, was operationally defined as explosive tantrums that included a number of specific behaviors. Examples of specific disruptive behaviors clarified the concept and simplified the task of recognizing which behaviors were disruptive. Disruptive behavior was measured in terms of its frequency, duration, and intensity (see Chapter 4). This example shows how operational definitions can help a researcher move a step closer to formulating a research hypothesis.

Research Hypothesis

To evaluate the effects of relaxation on the disruptive behavior of children with autism, the researcher developed the problem statement into a specific, testable prediction, which became the research hypothesis. Note that the problem statement had already suggested one basic way to test it: measure disruptive behavior before and after relaxation training and see whether the predicted difference exists.

This approach is called a *pretest–posttest design* (see Figure 8.2). As you will see in later chapters, a pretest–posttest design has several weaknesses, and better designs are available to test the hypothesis. However, this simple design helps to illustrate the use of operational definitions.

Having operationally defined both the dependent variable (disruptive behavior) and the independent variable (relaxation training), we can now combine the operational definitions and the statement of the problem into a specific prediction, which is the research

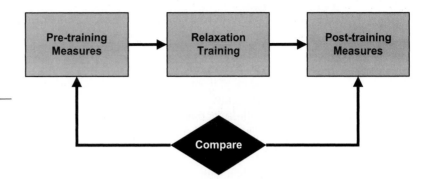

FIGURE 8.2 *A Single-Group, Pretest–Posttest Design* This design follows a single group of participants, testing them both before and after a manipulation.

hypothesis. In the example, the research hypothesis was this: Following relaxation training, the frequency, duration, and intensity of disruptive behavior will be significantly less than at the pretraining baseline.

A research hypothesis makes a declarative statement about the expected relationship among variables. Even though it is in this form, remember that it is only a tentative statement to be tested. The characteristics of a good research hypothesis are summarized in Table 8.3.

The Contribution of Theory to the Research Hypothesis

Theory plays a critical role in developing the research hypothesis. Even in a research area that has never been studied before, researchers usually have implicit theories about how things might relate. Most research involves studying constructs that have been studied extensively, and in such situations, explicit theories guide decisions about the research. Often several theories will guide design decisions. Some of these theories will be mature,

---

TABLE 8.3 *Characteristics of a Research Hypothesis*

The following are characteristics of a good research hypothesis:

1. It is a declarative sentence.
2. It is brief and clearly stated.
3. It identifies at least two variables.
4. It states a predicted relationship between at least one variable and at least one other variable.
5. It states the nature of the relationship. [Example: The amount of physical punishment that parents experienced as children will be positively correlated with parents' current use of physical punishment on their own children (a correlational hypothesis).]
6. It states the direction of the relationship. [Example: Participants in Group A will score significantly higher than participants in Group B (a directional prediction).]
7. It implies that the predicted relationship can be tested empirically.

with hundreds of research studies providing empirical confirmation of the theory's predictions. Some will be new, with only limited validation. On rare occasions, a theory is brand new, and will be tested for the first time in your study. Theories are usually interconnected, and a typical study will provide evidence concerning the validity of more than one theory. This network of theories and established empirical relationships provides a foundation for a proposed study.

To illustrate this, let's look more closely at the study of relaxation in children with autism. The following are only the most critical of the many theoretical ideas that contributed to the study.

1. Children with autism have severe functional impairments in emotional development, language, personal relationships, and general learning.
2. Most researchers accept a biological-causation model. That is, the primary condition is a currently unknown brain defect or defects caused by genetic factors.
3. Environmental factors are secondary, but still influence functioning.
4. The children's facial grimacing just before each outburst, and the nature of the outbursts, suggested the presence of strong autonomic arousal.
5. Arousal is a complex construct that relates to many different theories—some physiological, some psychological, and some involving both systems.
6. Several theories imply that arousal and relaxation are mutually exclusive.
7. Thus, inducing relaxation might well reduce the inferred state of autonomic arousal in these children with autism.

This brief review only scratches the surface of the role of theory in this relatively simple study. It is unlikely that all the theories that the researchers drew on in developing this one study were perfectly valid (i.e., that they described accurately all predicted relationships). However, the study provided an answer to the specific question that was posed and the information from the study also helped the researchers evaluate the adequacy of some of the ideas that guided the formulation of the question.

One idea affected by this study was the notion that autistic psychopathology prevents people with autism from learning new skills. Since these children were able to learn relaxation skills, the validity of this idea was seriously weakened, and subsequent research confirmed that children with autism were able to learn many skills (e.g., Koegel & Koegel, 1995; Lovaas, 1996; Pierce & Schriebman, 1997).

Testing the Research Hypothesis

The research hypothesis is a complex statement, which actually encompasses three hypotheses: the null or statistical hypothesis, the confounding variable hypothesis, and the causal hypothesis. Each will be described in this section.

Suppose that we carry out the study of children with autism as follows. First, we measure the frequency, intensity, and duration of the children's disruptive behavior during a four-week pretraining baseline period. Next, we then train the children for two months in relaxation to the criteria specified. Finally, after the training, we again measure the frequency, intensity, and duration of their disruptive behavior for a four-week post-training period. This is an example of a simple pretest–posttest design. Now suppose that, as predicted, there is less disruption after relaxation training.

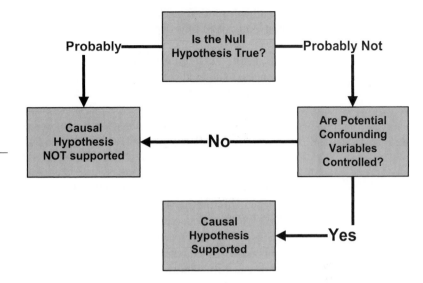

FIGURE 8.3   *Evaluating a Research Study's Results* The causal hypothesis that the independent variable affected the dependent variable cannot be accepted until both the null and confounding variable hypotheses have been rejected.

Can we conclude that the independent variable, relaxation training, reduced the children's disruptive behavior? Not yet, because to answer the research question we must rule out the two other hypotheses: the null or statistical hypothesis and the confounding variable hypothesis. Figure 8.3 illustrates the steps in this process. (Note that in Figure 8.3 the left and right paths are labeled "Probably" and "Probably not," instead of "yes" and "no." Why do you think this was done?)

Null Hypothesis.   Before we can conclude that relaxation reduces disruptive behavior, we must determine that the post-training measures of disruption are *significantly* smaller than the pretraining measures of disruption; that is, that the differences observed are not merely due to chance variation.

The first of the three hypotheses that we must test is the **statistical hypothesis.** The statistical hypothesis is tested with an appropriate inferential statistic (see Chapter 5). The *t*- or *F*-tests for correlated groups are appropriate here for two reasons. The first is that the dependent measure yields score data. The second is that the measures are correlated, because the same participants were measured both before and after treatment. The rationale for selecting the statistical test might be confusing, but for now take our word for it. Chapter 14 will present a flowchart system for determining the appropriate statistical procedures in this and most other research.

As you learned in Chapter 5, the null hypothesis states that there is no difference between the two conditions beyond chance differences. If a statistically significant difference is found, the null hypothesis is rejected. However, if the differences are within chance limits, the null hypothesis is not rejected. Suppose that a *t*- or *F*-test discloses that the post-training measures are significantly smaller than the pretraining measures, meaning that the differences are not due only to chance. The differences are large enough to permit us to reject the null hypothesis. Can we then accept the hypothesis that relaxation training is responsible for the observed reduction in disruptive behavior? Not yet; there is still one other hypothesis to consider.

Confounding Variable Hypothesis.   Although we have found statistically significant differences in the predicted direction in our example, we still cannot be sure that the observed differences are due to the independent variable of relaxation. They might be due to confounding variables. Rejecting the null hypothesis, while necessary, *is not sufficient to draw a causal inference*. We must also rule out the possibility that factors other than the independent variable might have had an effect on the dependent variable. The task here is to rule out confounding variables as explanations of the results. It is best to rule out confounding variables during the design phase, when you anticipate them and design controls to eliminate their effects. (This task will be the focus of the next several chapters.)

The **confounding variable hypothesis** suggests that the observed differences *might* be due to extraneous factors that affected the dependent measures. We accept the finding that there is a statistically significant difference, but being systematic scientists, we are not yet convinced that the difference is due to the independent variable. Rather, we consider the possibility that it might be due to the effects of confounding factors. For example, the relaxation training required two months, a long time in the life of a growing child. The children could have matured over these two months. The observed improvement might have been due to maturational factors and not to the independent variable of relaxation training. The independent variable is confounded with maturation. Therefore, it is unreasonable to conclude that relaxation training is the variable that brought about the improvement.

The confounding variable hypothesis recognizes that relaxation training is only one of several possible explanations for the improvement in disruptive behavior. To have confidence in the conclusions, we must carefully rule out *all* alternative explanations.

Unlike the statistical hypothesis, the confounding variable hypothesis is not directly tested. Rather, each confounding variable hypothesis is ruled out by first anticipating potential confounding variables, and then reducing their likelihood by using appropriate research design and controls. Careful inspection shows where the design is weak and where it is strong. The researcher must judge whether the design is strong enough to rule out the most likely confounding variables.

As you will see in later chapters, some designs are so powerful that they can rule out most confounding variables. Other designs are less effective in ruling out confounding variables, although careful measurement of possible confounding variables might be sufficient to rule them out.

As you learned in Chapter 7, a variable can confound results only if (1) it affects the scores on the dependent variable and (2) the groups or conditions being compared differ on the variable. If you can show that a potential confounding variable is either not correlated with the dependent measure or that the groups or conditions being compared do not differ on this potential confounding variable, you have effectively ruled it out as a source of confounding.

Ruling out alternative explanations is critical in science. Research is conducted not only to find evidence to support research hypotheses, but also to rule out alternative explanations, which are also known as *rival hypotheses*. Every uncontrolled confounding variable is a threat to the validity of a study. Experimental designs typically rule out most confounding variables.

Causal Hypothesis.   The **causal hypothesis** states that the independent variable had the predicted effect on the dependent variable. Suppose that you tested and rejected the null hypothesis and carefully ruled out confounding variables. (We will discuss how to control or rule out confounding variables in Chapter 9.)

You are now ready to return to the research hypothesis: Following relaxation training, the frequency, duration, and intensity of disruptive behavior will be significantly less than at the pretraining baseline. Remember that when this research hypothesis was first stated it was a tentative statement to be tested. If you find significantly less disruption after training than before training and can rule out alternative hypotheses, then only one viable hypothesis remains: that the independent variable affected the dependent variable as predicted. Note, however, that the assertion is not absolute, but rather it is a statement of probability. The first hypothesis was the statistical hypothesis, which was tested in terms of probability. Even though the data were sufficiently persuasive to convince us to reject the null hypothesis of no difference, there was always the possibility of a Type I error (see Chapter 5). It is wise to remember that there are so many complicated steps from initial conceptualization to running the study to interpreting the results that you must always be cautious in your interpretations. You can have confidence, but not certainty, in the results of a well-run study. Every finding in science is considered to be tentative and is subject to change as a result of new observations.

Another important point about developing research hypotheses is that most problem statements can be developed into several different research hypotheses, each of which can then be tested. Again, recall that the problem statement in the research on children with autism was "Can relaxation reduce the disruptive behavior of children with autism?" The essential question posed was whether there is a causal relationship between a child's relaxation and the degree of disruption. Relaxation was defined operationally in terms of procedures used to train the child to slow down, and disruption was operationally defined as the frequency, duration, and intensity of each disruptive behavior. These definitions led to this specific research hypothesis: Following relaxation training, the frequency, duration, and intensity of disruptive behavior will be significantly less than at the pretraining baseline.

Now suppose that you study another aspect of the relaxation-disruption hypothesis and operationally define relaxation in terms of the pharmacological effects of a particular drug. Each child is given a drug that is known to relax individuals. The research hypothesis is similar to the original hypothesis, but a different research hypothesis is being tested, because relaxation is operationally defined in a different way. This second study uses the same pretest–posttest design, but now drugs, instead of relaxation training, are used to induce relaxation. You are still evaluating the same statement of the problem, but with a different interpretation, expressed as a different research hypothesis.

You can make other changes in the way that you translate the statement of the problem into a research hypothesis. For example, a different research design could be used. Instead of using the pretest–posttest design, you could randomly assign each child with autism to one of two groups. One group is relaxed with the drug, whereas the other is not given the drug. The disruptive behavior of all participants is then measured, and the mean level of disruption in the two groups is compared. This design is called a *two-group posttest-only design*. It is illustrated in Figure 8.4.

The research hypothesis is stated differently from that of the previous example, because the independent variable and the research design have been changed. Here is the

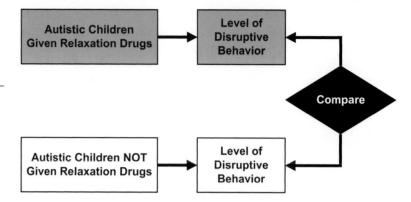

FIGURE 8.4   *A Two-Group, Posttest–Only Design* This design used two groups, only one of which received the relaxation drugs. The level of disruptive behavior is then measured in each group and these levels compared.

new research hypothesis: Children with autism who are given drugs that relax them will show less disruptive behavior than children with autism who do not receive such drugs. Thus, the same problem statement can be combined with different operational definitions of the independent and dependent variables and different research designs. This results in the generation of several different research hypotheses and, consequently, several different studies. In essence, the researcher is able to investigate the same basic problem in different ways by testing different facets of the same issue.

To summarize: In an experiment, initial ideas are refined into the problem statement, which identifies variables, implies causality, and indicates the direction of the expected causal effect. The variables are operationally defined, and a research hypothesis is constructed by combining these operational definitions with the problem statement. The research hypothesis states a specific testable prediction about the relationship between specific variables. Testing the research hypothesis involves several hypotheses: the null or statistical hypothesis, the confounding variable hypothesis, which is often a set of hypotheses, and the causal hypothesis. The causal hypothesis is accepted only after the null and confounding variable hypotheses are rejected. Testing the null hypothesis evaluates the likelihood that the findings were due to chance.

Statistical tests show only whether there is a significant difference between groups, but not whether the difference is due to the independent variable. To draw that conclusion, competing interpretations must be identified and ruled out.

Finally, one problem statement can be developed into several research hypotheses that lead to several different studies, thus examining different facets of the problem.

Quick-Check Review 8.1: Hypothesis Testing

1. Describe the process of refining initial ideas into a problem statement.
2. What concepts are combined to produce the research hypothesis?
3. What is the function of the research hypothesis?
4. What three hypotheses make up the research hypothesis?
5. Why is ruling out potential confounding variables so important?
6. Describe how one problem statement can be developed into several research hypotheses.

Validity and Threats to Validity

A major concern in research is the validity of the procedures and conclusions. The term *validity* has several meanings, the most basic of which refers to methodological soundness or appropriateness. That is, a valid test measures what it is supposed to measure; a valid research design tests what it is supposed to test.

Validity is relevant at any level of constraint, but it is especially important in experimental research, which addresses specific questions about causality. There are many potential threats to the validity of an experiment, and the researcher must (1) anticipate them and (2) create procedures to eliminate or reduce them. This section outlines the broad concept of validity. It follows closely the classic organization of Campbell and Stanley (1966) and Cook and Campbell (1979), who distinguished among four types of validity: statistical validity, construct validity, external validity, and internal validity (summarized in Table 8.4).

Statistical Validity

When statistical procedures are used to test the null hypothesis, the researcher is asking whether the results are due to some systematic factor (ideally, the independent variable) or merely to chance variations. Rejecting the null hypothesis is a necessary first step in testing the effects of the independent variable. **Statistical validity** addresses the question of whether these statistical conclusions are reasonable.

Several possible threats to a study's statistical validity must be controlled. One threat is the possibility that the measures used to assess the dependent variable are unreliable. Another threat to statistical validity is the violation of the assumptions that underlie the statistical tests. Each statistical procedure makes assumptions about the nature of the data. Statistics textbooks normally list the assumptions of each statistic. Violating these statistical assumptions distorts the p-value for the statistical test, and therefore the statistical decision is undependable.

Statistical validity addresses the question of whether the basis for a statistical decision is reasonable and dependable. It does not address whether the statistical decision

TABLE 8.4 *Types of Validity*

Type of Validity	Description
Statistical	The accuracy of the p-value on which a statistical decision is based
Construct	The degree to which the theory or theories behind the research study provide(s) the best explanation for the results observed
External	The extent to which the results of a particular study generalize to other people, places, or conditions
Internal	The extent to which we can be confident that the observed changes in the dependent variable were due to the effects of the independent variable, and not to the effects of extraneous variables

accurately reflects reality. Remember, a statistical decision is based on probability. If alpha is set at .05, it means that you will reject the null hypothesis if there is less than a 5% chance of it being correct. This still means that you will be rejecting the null hypothesis incorrectly 5% of the time. This is not a problem of statistical validity unless the probabilities are in error due to violations of statistical assumptions.

Construct Validity

Every hypothesis tested in research is constructed in a theoretical context of ideas. **Construct validity** refers to how well the study's results support the theory or constructs behind the research and whether the theory supported by the findings provides the best available explanation of the results. To help to reduce threats to construct validity, a researcher should use clearly stated definitions and carefully build hypotheses on solid, well-validated constructs. The theoretical bases must be clear and well supported, with rival theories carefully ruled out.

An example of a construct validity question is the continuing debate in psychology over the nature-nurture issue (Ridley, 2003). This question has been raised in many different research areas, from questions about the causes of schizophrenia (Erlenmeyer-Kimling et al., 2004) to investigations of why males usually score higher than females on math skill measures (Casey, 1996). On the latter, researchers debate how much of the difference is innate and how much is the result of environmental effects (Lubinski & Benbow, 1992). Environmental variables alone could shape the differences if males receive more training than females in math or are more likely than females to be told that learning math is important to success. The issue is whether the data on this question support the idea that an innate, genetically determined characteristic is responsible for the observed sex differences (nature) or whether the environment shaped the sex differences (nurture).

We are often tempted to interpret data as being consistent with our own preconceptions and ignore other explanations for the data. For example, the finding that men tend to take more math courses than women would seem to be consistent with the nurture hypothesis that males are better at math because they get more training in it. However, we could interpret this finding to mean that men take more math courses, because they tend to be good at math and choose courses in which they know they can excel. Therefore, the data are consistent with both a nature and a nurture hypothesis, and the construct validity of any one interpretation would be in doubt.

External Validity

In its strictest sense, the results of an experiment are limited to those participants and conditions used in the particular experiment. However, when researchers test college students' memory ability, for example, are they really interested in how well these particular 20 freshmen in Dr. Behling's introductory psychology class did on October 21? Not really. They are interested in memory functions in general. They want to generalize the results beyond the specific conditions and participants to other, similar participants and conditions. **External validity** refers to the degree to which researchers are able to generalize the results of a study to other participants, conditions, times, and places.

EXTENDING THE CONCEPT OF REPRESENTATIVE SAMPLES

To make statements about the overall population based on the findings of a particular sample, the sample must be selected in such a manner that it adequately represents the population. The process of inferring something about a population on the basis of findings from a sample drawn from the population is referred to as **generalization.** Problems of generalization from a sample to a population are best controlled by random selection of participants from the population, as you will learn in Chapter 9.

In similar fashion, the researcher must be careful about generalizing across times, places, and conditions; to do so, the researcher *must* sample across those times, places, or conditions. The term **ecological validity** is often used to refer to the appropriate generalization from the laboratory to real-life situations (Neisser, 1976). Questions of how laboratory-derived information will generalize to the real world and how much it can help scientists understand real-world issues will depend on how realistically the research captures the critical elements of the real-world scenario. This issue was raised in Chapter 6, when we talked about how naturalistic research can be used to see whether laboratory findings apply to real-world settings. Now you can see that such an evaluation is really checking for the ecological validity of the findings.

External validity is always an issue in research, because ethics require that we use only participants who have given informed consent. That means that no sample will ever be completely random unless everyone who is selected agrees to participate, which rarely happens. However, it is far better to accept that there will always be some limitations on external validity than to compromise ethical principles of research.

Internal Validity

Internal validity is of major concern to researchers because it involves the very heart of experimentation: the demonstration of causality. It concerns this question: Was the independent variable, and not some extraneous variable, responsible for the changes in the dependent variable? An experiment is internally valid when this question can be answered affirmatively. Any factor that weakens confidence that it was the independent variable that accounted for the results is a threat to the internal validity of the study.

In the next section, we will describe several confounding variables, but before we do that, let's look at some examples. Suppose that you are interested in the ability of patients with schizophrenia to identify briefly presented images. You predict that their identification accuracy will be significantly disrupted by intrusive auditory stimulation. You test patients under two conditions: (1) a high-stimulation condition, in which loud rhythmic music is played during testing, and (2) a low-stimulation condition, in which the testing room is kept quiet. Because of scheduling problems in the hospital, patients are available to you only on Monday and Thursday mornings, when the locked-ward and the open-ward patients, respectively, can be tested. You test the Monday patients under the high-stimulation condition and the Thursday patients under the low-stimulation condition. The research hypothesis is that patients with schizophrenia tested under high-stimulation conditions will make significantly more errors than those tested under low-stimulation conditions. You find that, indeed, significantly more errors are made under the high-stimulation condition, and therefore you conclude that external auditory stimulation is a significant factor that affects visual processing by patients with schizophrenia.

The major confounding variable in this study should be obvious: The participants in the two conditions differ not only in terms of the independent variable (high- versus low-auditory stimulation), but also in terms of setting, because one group consists of patients from a locked ward whereas the other group consists of patients from an open ward. Those on locked wards are typically more disturbed than those on open wards. It is not surprising that they perform more poorly on the perceptual processing task. Therefore, it would be unreasonable to attribute the difference between the two groups to the high- and low-stimulation conditions that were manipulated. The fact that the results may be due to severity of illness, rather than amount of auditory stimulation, provides an alternative explanation. In other words, your *selection* procedure created groups that are likely to be different before the study was ever run.

Consider also the hypothesis concerning the effects of relaxation training on the disruptive behavior of children with autism and the research procedures used to test it. Can we conclude with confidence that the independent variable of relaxation training is responsible for the observed reduction in disruptive behavior? In other words, can we be confident about the internal validity of this study? Consider the basic design of the first study, which tested this research hypothesis: Following relaxation training, the frequency, duration, and intensity of disruptive behavior will be significantly less than at the pretraining baseline. To test the hypothesis, we measured the disruptive behavior of the children with autism, then provided relaxation training, and finally measured disruption again. It required two months for all the children in the study to reach the criterion of successful relaxation. After relaxation training, the disruptive behavior was measurably less and the decrease was statistically significant.

It is tempting to conclude that relaxation training was responsible for the decrease in disruptive behavior, but what alternative explanations might there be for the results? That is, what confounding variables might have been operating to produce the results? As suggested earlier, the children might simply have improved over the two-month period through natural maturational processes, with relaxation having little to do with the observed improvement. Therefore, *maturation* is one potential confounding variable.

Another alternative explanation for the observed improvement is that some systematic factor in the program itself, other than relaxation, might have been responsible. The children were in a full-day, five-day-a-week therapy program that included many components. Could some other factor that was consistently applied to the children during the two months of relaxation training be responsible for the improvement? This is an example of the confounding variable of *history;* that is, other things that occurred during the course of the research might have produced the findings.

A phenomenon called *regression to the mean* might also have been operating. Behaviors naturally fluctuate in frequency and intensity, going through ups and downs of severity. Perhaps this research was started at the peak of severity; perhaps it was even begun because the severity was so great. As time passed, the behaviors returned to severity levels that were closer to the mean. It was then that the post-training measures were taken. If regression to the mean was operating, then the relaxation manipulation might have had little to do with the observed improvement in behavior.

Still another possible confounding variable should be considered. In the course of the research, the staff who observed the children's disruptive behavior might have changed the ways in which they observed and measured the behavior. They might have gradually become more accustomed to the children's severe behavior and, in time, tended to record it as less severe. Therefore, their criteria for observation—not the behavior of the children—might have changed during the course of the study. This process is called *instrumentation.*

There are many possible confounding variables in research, and there might be several in any given study. Their effects might all be in the same direction, thus compounding the errors, or in opposite directions, thus countering one another. If researchers wish to draw valid conclusions about the effects of one variable on another, they must anticipate and control potential confounding variables to eliminate rival hypotheses, leaving the causal hypothesis as the most likely explanation for the results. In the next section, you will learn about the wide range of confounding variables.

Quick-Check Review 8.2: Validity and Threats to Validity	1. What is validity?
	2. Define the various types of validity.
	3. Which type of validity is concerned about the accuracy of conclusions about the effects of the independent variable on the dependent variable?

Major Confounding Variables

08:02

Cook and Campbell (1979) identified several confounding variables, summarized in Table 8.5, which we will discuss here. The Student Resource Website includes exercises designed to help you to spot confounding variables in research.

Maturation

In longitudinal research, especially with children, participants grow older between the pre-treatment and post-treatment measures. As they age, they may also become more sophisticated, experienced, bigger, or stronger.

Natural **maturational** changes can also occur in participants other than children. Adults placed in a new environment tend to make predictable adjustments over time. Diseases tend to have predictable courses. Several types of observed changes may be due to maturational factors, rather than to effects of an independent variable. Of course, researchers must be particularly alert to maturation when studying children, because change and growth are virtual certainties in children.

History

During the course of a study, events that are independent of the study may occur that can affect the outcome. In general, threats to internal validity due to **history** increase with

TABLE 8.5 *Major Confounding Variables*

Confounding Variable	Description
Maturation	Changes in the dependent variable that are due to the normal maturation of the participant
History	Changes in the dependent variable that are due to historical events that occur during the study, but that are unrelated to the study
Testing	Any change in a participant's score on the dependent variable that is a function of having been tested previously
Instrumentation	Any change in the calibration of the measuring instrument over the course of the study that affects the scores on the dependent variable
Regression to the mean	The tendency for participants who are selected because they have extreme scores on a variable to be less extreme in a follow-up testing
Selection	Any factor that creates groups that are not equivalent at the beginning of the study
Attrition	The loss of participants during a study; differential loss is problematic because the participants who drop out are likely to be different from those who continue
Diffusion of treatment	Change in the response of participants in a particular condition because of information that the participants gained about other research conditions from participants in those other conditions
Sequence effects	Effects on a participant's performance in later conditions that result from the experience that the participant had in the previous conditions of the study

longer times between pretest and posttest measurements. Historical factors are most likely when you are measuring dependent variables that are responsive to environmental events. For example, weight, in contrast to height, is more affected by food intake. Weight also shows more natural fluctuation than height. Therefore, historical factors are more likely to be a confounding variable for weight than for height. Most weight-control procedures would be lucky to hold their own if they were evaluated during holidays, when people are constantly exposed to tempting high-calorie foods.

Testing

The repeated **testing** of participants can threaten internal validity, because participants gain proficiency through practice on the measuring instruments. Testing effects are most pronounced on measures in which the participant is asked to perform some skill-related task, such as tests of memory, IQ, or manual dexterity. Most people do better on the second administration of such a test because the first administration gave them practice.

Instrumentation

Apparent pre-post changes may be due to changes in the measuring instrument, rather than to independent variable manipulation. This confounding variable, known as

"OF COURSE I'VE BECOME MORE MATURE SINCE YOU STARTED
TREATING ME. YOU'VE BEEN AT IT SINCE I WAS 14 YEARS OLD."

Any process that takes time, including research studies, can be affected by maturational and historical factors. The improvement in this client might well be due to one or both of these confounding variables, rather than to the efforts of the therapist.

Reprinted by permission of S. Harris.

instrumentation, is particularly pronounced when the measuring instrument is a human observer. This is because an observer might become more proficient at making observations, or change his or her criteria for judgment over time.

Regression to the Mean

The concept of **regression to the mean** suggests that whenever participants are selected *because* their scores on a measure are extreme (either very high or very low), they will tend to be less extreme on a second testing. In other words, their scores will regress toward the mean. For example, consider the top 10% of students based on their first exam. How should these top students perform on the second exam? One would expect them to do well, but would they all do as well as they did on the first exam? It's not likely. The reason is that some of the students did well on the first exam because they studied unusually hard. On the second test, however, some of these students might not be as diligent. If you took the top 10% of students on the first test and computed their mean score on both the first and second tests, you would probably find that they scored, on average, closer to the mean on the second test. Similarly, if you took the bottom 10% of students on the first test and computed their mean score on both the first and second tests, you would find that they scored, on average, closer to the mean on the second test.

How much regression occurs will depend on how much of the test performance is due to variable factors, such as amount of study, and how much is due to consistent factors, such as skill and study habits. The more impact that variable factors have on the score, the more regression you can expect to see.

Selection

Confounding due to **selection** occurs when the groups being compared are not equivalent before the manipulations begin. Under ideal conditions, participants are randomly selected and then randomly assigned to different groups. When random selection and assignment are not possible, as in most naturalistic, case-study, and differential research, then the possibility of confounding due to selection exists.

Attrition

Sometimes participants drop out of a study; they might go on vacation in the middle of the study, forget their appointments, decide that they are no longer interested, or become ill, for example. If there are no biasing factors, such dropouts will probably be evenly distributed across groups, and they will not differentially affect one group more than others.

Confounding due to **attrition** occurs when participants are lost differentially, such as when there are more dropouts from one group than from another, or when participants with certain characteristics are more likely to drop out. Researchers must be careful not to create situations or use procedures that will bias some participants against completing the study, thus differentially affecting the outcome. For example, suppose that a researcher realized too late that nearly all the high school seniors failed to return for the second half of a study because it coincided with school parties, excitement, and general preparation for graduation. Their attrition left primarily underclass participants in the second half of the study, thus biasing the results.

Sometimes procedures can cause participants with certain characteristics to drop out, leaving a biased sample. For example, in an unpublished study by one of the authors, many sixth-grade boys dropped out because, it was learned later, they thought the procedures were "too girlish." Perhaps, in today's more egalitarian society, this might be less likely. In any event, care must be taken to avoid confounding studies by allowing attrition of participants to have a differential effect on the outcome.

Diffusion of Treatment

When participants in different experimental conditions are in close proximity and are able to communicate with each other, earlier participants might "give away" the procedures to those scheduled later. In addition, experimental participants who receive a treatment may communicate with control participants who do not receive that treatment or who may not have known that they were in a control group. Such information exchanges, called **diffusion of treatment,** can erode the planned experimental differences between groups, making the groups more similar because of the information exchange.

Diffusion of treatment can affect studies in many ways. For example, many psychologists use undergraduate participants. Students often hear about studies from other students, and many even select the study on the basis of what they hear. When they participate, the knowledge of what their friends experienced might affect how they respond. To compensate for this problem, many researchers try to make their study look the same to participants in all conditions.

Sequence Effects

Much of the research in psychology is designed so that each participant is exposed to more than one experimental condition. These are called within-subjects designs. Although they offer important advantages over other designs, they also introduce another confounding factor, **sequence effects,** in which experiences with earlier conditions of the study affect responses to later conditions. If, in a study with three conditions, the order of presentation of conditions is always condition *A* followed by condition *B* followed by condition *C*, then systematic confounding can occur. For example, performance in conditions *B* and *C* might reflect both the effect of the conditions and the effect of having already experienced condition *A*. Sequence effects are controlled by using more than one order of conditions. Sequence effects and some methods to handle them are discussed in more detail in Chapter 11.

Quick-Check Review 8.3: Major Confounding Variables	1. What is the difference between the confounding variables of history and maturation?
	2. If your hometown team wins this year's World Series, what prediction would you make for next year based on the concept of regression to the mean?
	3. Suppose that you are interested in sex differences in second graders, but your procedure is upsetting to girls raised in a single-parent home, and so several such girls drop out of your study before the end. What confounding variable would be operating and what effect might it have?
	4. What design has to contend with the confounding variable of sequence effects?

Subject and Experimenter Effects

There is a large category of threats to the validity of a study due to subject and experimenter effects. The expectations and biases of the researcher and the participants can systematically affect the results of a study in subtle ways, thus reducing the study's validity. This section describes subject and experimenter effects, and Chapter 9 discusses controls for these effects.

Subject Effects

Every psychological experiment is a social situation in which both participants and researchers participate in a common undertaking (Orne, 1962). Each behaves according to his or her understanding of how a participant or a researcher should behave. When participants enter an experiment, they are not entirely naive. They have ideas, understandings, and perhaps misunderstandings about what to expect in the study.

People participate for different reasons. Some do so because it is a course requirement. Others participate because of curiosity or because they will be paid for their participation. Some volunteer because they hope to learn something, perhaps about themselves. Participants enter and carry out their roles with a variety of motivations, understandings, expectations, and biases, all of which can affect their behavior in the research setting. Furthermore, an experiment is an artificial, contrived situation, far removed from participants' natural environments. When people know they are being observed, they may behave differently than they normally would. This can lead to **subject effects,** which refer to any changes in the behavior of participants that are attributable to being in the study, rather than to the variables under study.

Most participants do their best to be good subjects. This might lead some participants to try to discern the research hypothesis so that they will know how they are "supposed to behave." Participants are often particularly sensitive to cues from the researcher. Furthermore, researchers, with their own expectations and biases, might inadvertently give such cues. Cues given to participants on how they are expected to behave are called **demand characteristics.** Demand characteristics usually occur unintentionally. They include not only characteristics of the setting and procedures, but also information and even rumors about the researcher and the nature of the research.

A related phenomenon, the **placebo effect,** can occur when participants expect a specific effect of an experimental manipulation. For example, some participants in a drug study of pain control might enter the study with the clear expectation that the procedures will help, and actually report feeling better and even show physiological changes, all because of the suggestion that the procedure will work. Participants often report improvement when given a placebo treatment, such as a pill that looks and tastes like the true drug being tested but lacks the drug's active ingredient.

Experimenter Effects

Experimenter effects are any biasing effects in a study that are due to the actions of the researcher. The researcher attempts to carry out the research plan as objectively and as accurately as possible. However, researchers are human and carry their own expectations and motivations into the study. **Experimenter expectancies** are the expectations a researcher holds about the outcome of a study. These expectancies might lead researchers to bias results in several ways. These include influencing the participant's behavior toward support of the hypothesis, selecting data that best support the hypothesis, using statistical techniques that best show the particular effects but not other effects, and interpreting results in a biased manner. The latter occurs, for example, when conclusions are drawn that accept improbable explanations consistent with the research hypothesis, while ignoring more parsimonious explanations that do not support the hypothesis.

Common to all of these ways of introducing bias is the idea that the researcher will tend to make decisions and choices that favor the hypothesis being tested. This is not to say that researchers deliberately and knowingly falsify data. Rather, they behave in ways that tend to support their own expectations and do so without being aware of it.

For example, suppose that a researcher has two groups of participants. The participants have been randomly assigned to the groups to avoid confounding due to selection. Participants in each group are to be tested on a series of arithmetic problems and timed by the researcher. The prediction is that, because of the difference in instructions to the two groups, the experimental group will take significantly longer than the control group to complete the problems.

In this situation, there are several ways that researchers can influence participants. If the researcher knows to which group each participant is assigned and knows the research hypothesis, then it is possible that the researcher might tend to time the experimental participants in a way that would extend their times. The researcher also could influence the results by reading the same set of instructions in a slightly different tone to the two groups, emphasizing speed for the control participants. In either case, the researcher would probably be unaware of this systematic bias and would deny it. However, the bias, accumulated over all the participants in the group, could affect the outcome toward support of the hypothesis.

Much of the scientific understanding of experimenter expectancy effects is due to the research of Rosenthal and his colleagues. Rosenthal and Fode (1963a, b) suggested several ways in which an experimenter might affect a participant's responses and thus bias the results to favor the hypothesis. For example, a researcher might unintentionally present cues by variations in tone of voice or by changes in posture or facial expressions, verbally reinforce some responses and not others, or incorrectly record participants' responses.

Although such experimenter expectancy effects may occur, it has been difficult to demonstrate clearly that they do occur. Consequently, some question how big a problem this is (e.g., Barber & Silver, 1968). Nevertheless, in any research in which experimenter expectancy effects might occur, they provide an alternative explanation for the obtained results.

For example, suppose that a journal editor reads a research manuscript that has been submitted for possible publication and determines that such expectancy effects might have occurred. Just raising this possibility is sufficient to cast doubt on the validity of the experiment and lead to the rejection of the manuscript for publication. The editor need not provide data to support the alternative hypothesis that the obtained results were due to experimenter expectancy effects. If the rival hypothesis *could* be true, then we cannot accept the researcher's conclusions about the effects of the independent variable. The researcher would have to repeat the experiment, adding controls to eliminate the rival hypothesis.

Barber and Silver (1968) may be correct in doubting that such effects are as frequent as Rosenthal and Fode suggested. However, the existence of rival hypotheses in a study is sufficient to cast doubt on a researcher's findings, and it is therefore important for the researcher to control for potential experimenter expectancy effects.

<table>
<tr><td>Quick-Check
Review 8.4:
Subject and
Experimenter
Effects</td><td>1. What are subject effects?
2. How can demand characteristics lead to subject effects?
3. How can experimenter expectancies lead to experimenter effects?</td></tr>
</table>

PUTTING IT *INTO PRACTICE*	In the next few chapters, you will learn how researchers control confounding variables. For now, you need to recognize when such variables might be present. Spend some time looking around you and observing people's behavior. Formulate a hypothesis about why a given behavior might have occurred, then think of as many alternative hypotheses as you can, which essentially are confounding variables that may have been responsible for the behavior. For example, if you observe someone snapping at another person for something they said, your hypothesis might be that they were upset by what was said. What other explanations might you generate for the observed behavior? Another exercise is this: the next time someone asserts "I know why (such and such) happened" and then proceeds to give his or her explanation, listen respectfully, and give a few alternative explanations for the same event. Some pretty lively discussions can be generated this way. To avoid conflict, you may choose to not share your alternative explanations. Generate them nonetheless. By the way, ask yourself this question before you begin your observations. Are there any ethical issues involved in this exercise? If so, what might they be, and how do you propose to address them?

Chapter Summary

This chapter focused on how to develop and test research hypotheses. Constructing the research hypothesis is a critical step in all research, but it is most formalized and most fully developed at the experimental level of constraint. Testing the research hypothesis actually involves three hypotheses: the null hypothesis, the confounding variable hypothesis, and the causal hypothesis.

Validity and threats to validity should be considered in any research study. The researcher is concerned with four types of validity: statistical, construct, external, and internal. Each type can be threatened in several ways, and the researcher must anticipate the threats and design appropriate controls. The largest threat to internal validity comes from confounding variables. Researchers need to be alert to these confounding variables so that most can be eliminated in the design stage by adding proper controls. The specific controls vary according to the type of validity being threatened and the nature of the threats. Subject and experimenter effects can also threaten validity, and these should be routinely controlled in any study.

Chapter Exercises

1. Define the following key terms. Be sure that you understand them. They are discussed in the chapter and defined in the glossary.

statistical hypothesis
confounding variable
   hypothesis
causal hypothesis
statistical validity
construct validity
external validity
generalization
ecological validity
internal validity
maturation
history

testing
instrumentation
regression to the mean
selection
attrition
diffusion of treatment
sequence effects
subject effects
demand characteristics
placebo effect
experimenter effects
experimenter expectancies

2. For each of the following independent variables, indicate the number of levels of the independent variable and identify each:

   a. Studying the effects of high- and low-audio stimulation on performance.

   b. Using six levels of room temperature in a working-conditions study.

   c. A researcher compares rats' running times. One group is fed one hour prior to running, another two hours prior to running, and a third three hours prior to running.

   d. Four different arithmetic workbooks are tested in an elementary school.

3. Think of five or six experimental research ideas. Create them or obtain them from published reports of studies. For each of these research ideas, (1) develop a clear statement of a problem, (2) identify and operationally define the variables, and (3) combine the problem statement with the operational definitions into a specific research hypothesis.

4. Take the problem statements you developed in the preceding exercise, develop different operational definitions, and use them to develop new research hypotheses. Why is it important to be able to do this in research?

5. Explain how varying the operational definitions when developing research hypotheses from problem statements can replicate research findings. Give examples.

6. Develop a research project that might need to control experimenter and subject effects.

9

Controls to Reduce Threats to Validity

In the fields of observation, chance favors only the mind that is prepared.

—Louis Pasteur, 1822–1895

Web Resource Material

Control procedures counteract threats to validity, thus increasing confidence in the conclusions drawn from a study. Threats to validity and control procedures represent two sides of the same conceptual coin. Chapter 8 discussed the possible threats to validity. This chapter considers the major methods for controlling these threats to validity.

Control is any procedure used by the researcher to counteract potential threats to the validity of the research. Many procedures are available to control threats to validity, but not every threat to validity is likely to occur in every study. Thus, not every control procedure is needed in every study. Some control procedures are of general value and therefore should be used routinely. Other controls are relevant only in specific situations and should be carefully chosen to meet specific threats to validity. Controls are valuable at all levels of research but are most fully developed at the experimental level.

Four types of control are available to the researcher:

1. General control procedures
2. Control over subject and experimenter effects
3. Control through participant selection and assignment
4. Control through specific experimental design

This chapter covers the first three categories. The fourth category, specific experimental design, is introduced here, but covered in Chapters 10 through 13.

General Control Procedures

General control procedures include (1) preparation of the setting, (2) response measurement, and (3) replication.

Preparation of the Setting

The researcher should structure the setting in which the research is conducted in order to eliminate competing variables, simplify the situation, and increase control over independent variables. These steps will increase confidence in the results, because they reduce threats to internal validity. Many studies are conducted in the laboratory to optimize control. The advantage of the laboratory is that many extraneous variables can be eliminated, such as interfering stimuli (including the influence of other people).

Although laboratory settings have many advantages, they also have potential disadvantages. For example, a laboratory setting might reduce external validity if the setting becomes so artificial that it is unlike the natural situation. However, external validity need not be compromised if an effort is made to create a natural environment in the laboratory. For example, in a children's fear-reduction study, the laboratory was designed as a living room setting in which children were trained in fear-control skills that they would use at home (Graziano & Mooney, 1982). This setting was designed to enhance generalization. With modern computer simulation, realistic settings can be created almost anywhere. For example, Bornas, Tortella-Felio, Llabres, and Fullana (2001) used a realistic computer simulation of flying to help train people to control their fear of flying. Such technology makes realistic exposure possible in the laboratory, making it more likely that treatment will generalize to the real world. Thus, careful preparation of settings in laboratories can enhance both external and internal validity.

Response Measurement

Another general control procedure is the selection and preparation of the instruments used to measure the variables. Using measuring instruments of known reliability and validity improves both statistical and construct validity. We can use measures that have been developed by others or create new measures.

Creating a new measure is not a trivial task (Aiken, 1998). It is the researcher's responsibility to establish the reliability and validity of any new measures that are developed for a study. The quality of measuring instruments can have powerful effects on validity. Unfortunately, in their concern for operationalizing and manipulating the independent variable, researchers sometimes pay less attention to the dependent measures and thereby compromise the validity of the study. Of course, the opposite situation can also occur, in which a researcher becomes so involved in creating dependent measures (that's good) that details of the independent variables might be shortchanged (that's not good).

Replication

Although not everyone considers replication to be a control procedure, we believe it is. By specifying the laboratory setting, conditions, procedures, and measuring instruments, we make it easier for others to replicate the research. Successful replication provides important information. If phenomena observed in one study can be reliably demonstrated a second or third time, confidence in the original observations increases; if the study cannot be replicated, confidence is shaken.

Research in ESP (extrasensory perception) is an example. Some researchers have reported statistically significant ESP phenomena that fail to replicate in later research, thus leaving the earlier reports open to serious question (Milton & Wiseman, 1999). If a finding cannot be replicated, then it might be only a chance event and not an indication of a genuine phenomenon. In statistical terms, the researcher might have made a Type I error. This seems to be borne out by ESP research results, because only a handful of studies support ESP, while most fail to support it. If ESP cannot be reliably replicated, then we must ask if it exists at all.

There are three types of replication: exact replication, systematic replication, and conceptual replication. **Exact replication,** which repeats the experiment as nearly as possible in the way it was carried out originally, is rarely done in psychology. Journals seldom publish exact replication studies, and there are no career benefits to be gained by repeating other people's research.

Although exact replication is rare, researchers often replicate earlier findings by testing some theoretical or procedural modification of the original work, which is known as **systematic replication.** If, for example, a researcher finds an interesting phenomenon in the alcohol research laboratory, a colleague might reason that a particular systematic modification will bring about a specific result. The second researcher uses the initial work, making a systematic modification that, if the initial work was correct, should result in the predicted outcome.

A third type of replication is called **conceptual replication.** Recall that most problem statements can be developed into several different research hypotheses by combining the problem statement with various operational definitions of the research variables or by using different research designs (see Chapter 8). Thus, many different studies can be generated from the same problem statement. In essence, the researcher is replicating the concept of the problem statement with each study.

Although replication increases confidence in the validity of findings, it does not guarantee validity. For example, suppose that the results of a study were due to confounding factors. Then, if the procedures are replicated exactly, without recognizing and controlling the confounding factors, the replication might well produce the same invalid results as in the initial study.

Quick-Check Review 9.1: General Control Procedures	1. How can preparation of the research setting improve internal validity? What must be done to the research setting to maximize external validity?
	2. What characteristics should a research measure possess?
	3. What is the difference between exact replication and systematic replication?

Control over Subject and Experimenter Effects

The behavior of both the participants and the researcher may be influenced by factors other than the independent variable, thus threatening the validity of an experimental study. Factors such as motivation, knowledge, expectations, and information or misinformation about the study can influence behavior. Such factors can significantly bias participants and researchers, affecting not only the experimental procedure, but also the analysis and interpretation of data. Uncontrolled experimenter and/or subject effects are sufficient to cast doubt on research conclusions, because they provide alternative hypotheses.

Among the available controls for subject and experimenter effects are (1) *single-blind* and *double-blind procedures,* (2) *automation,* (3) use of *objective measures,* (4) multiple observers, and (5) use of deception.

Single- and Double-Blind Procedures

Experimenter effects arise from the experimenter's knowledge of (1) the hypothesis being tested, (2) the nature of the experimental and control conditions, and (3) the condition to which each participant is assigned. Such knowledge can subtly affect how the researcher interacts with participants. Experimenter effects are controlled by reducing the researcher's contact with, and/or knowledge about, the participants. A researcher might employ an assistant to run the study who does not know the condition to which each participant is assigned. In such a case, the assistant is said to be **blind** to the assignment of participants to conditions. This is a **single-blind procedure.**

A more powerful control is a **double-blind procedure,** in which both the researcher and participants are blind to the assignment of each participant to the conditions. The experiment is designed so that experimental and control procedures are indistinguishable.

Double-blind techniques are often used in drug studies. The experimental group typically receives the drug in the form of a capsule, whereas the control group receives a capsule, called a **placebo,** which is identical in appearance, but lacks the actual drug. Neither the participants nor the researchers know who is receiving the drug and who is receiving the placebo. This is achieved by having a research assistant, who is not involved in collecting the data, randomly assign participants to conditions and then prepare the capsules for participants. After the data are gathered, the information about each participant's experimental condition, which had been kept from the researchers, is used to analyze the results.

Using placebo control groups in psychological research is more difficult than in drug studies. For example, suppose that a clinical researcher wants to study the effectiveness of exposure therapy for treating adult fears. Participants are randomly assigned to an experimental and a control group. The experimental group is given the exposure therapy, and the control group is presented with a placebo treatment. The placebo treatment must be believable so that participants do not know that they are controls.

Creating experimentally adequate, ethically acceptable, and believable placebo manipulations is often a difficult task. In addition to design problems arising from the use of placebos, ethical issues must be considered. For ethical reasons, participants should be told that they might receive a placebo treatment. But, even with such notice, is it ethical to deny treatment to some participants? For both design and ethical reasons, the use of true placebos in medical and psychological research is not recommended when an effective treatment is available. Instead of comparing a new treatment with a placebo, researchers usually compare the new treatment with the best available treatment.

This is taking the principle that it is best to be as blind as possible to avoid expectancy effects just a bit too far.

Reprinted by permission of S. Harris.

"It was more of a 'triple-blind' test. The patients didn't know which ones were getting the real drug, the doctors didn't know, and, I'm afraid, nobody knew."

Researchers should be blind to the group or condition that each participant is in during data collection. They should also remain blind during the scoring of data, especially when the scoring involves judgments, because knowledge of the hypotheses and of the conditions under which each participant is tested might affect judgments made during scoring. In some cases, however, it is impossible for researchers to be blind during certain aspects of the study. For example, in a study of sex differences in aggression, the researcher testing participants will know which participants are male and which are female. In these situations, the researcher should attempt to be blind in as many ways as possible, even if it is impossible to be blind at every stage. If, for example, the measure of aggression is verbal behavior, someone otherwise not connected with the study should transcribe the tapes of participants' verbal responses so that auditory cues to a participant's sex are not available when the data are scored. Likewise, someone other than the person who tested the participants should do the scoring. In this study, the researchers who test participants should ideally be blind to the hypothesis, even if they cannot be blind to group membership. A general rule of thumb is to *test participants, and score data, as blindly as possible to avoid experimenter biases.*

Automation

Reducing experimenter-participant contact often reduces potential biases. One way to accomplish this is to **automate** procedures and mechanisms, such as those used to deliver instructions to participants and to obtain and record participants' responses. For example, instructions to participants can be recorded, and the timing of instructions and recording of participants' responses can be automated with electronic equipment. The use of computers to present stimuli in experiments has become standard procedure in many laboratories.

Using Objective Measures

Using **objective measures** of dependent variables is critical. A measure is objective when it is based on empirically observable and clearly specified events about which two or more people can easily agree. By contrast, a **subjective measure** involves the impressions of observers, which are often based on poorly specified and/or unobserved events. An example of a subjective measure is an observer's feeling that a person is anxious in a public-speaking situation. It is subjective because the observer does not specify what events were observed. Thus, it would be difficult for another observer to make the same observations and come to the same conclusions about the anxiety level of the speaker.

Good objective measures precisely define the behaviors to be observed and require minimal judgments on the part of the observer. Consequently, objective measures are less prone to experimenter biases. Such measures usually produce impressive levels of interrater agreement and make replication by other researchers easier. For example, public-speaking anxiety can be operationally defined in terms of observable behavior, such as sweating, stammering, rapid speech, and shaky hands (Harb et al., 2003). With objective measures, researchers know what a score means; with subjective measures, they are never sure.

Multiple Observers

In any research, especially when there might be questions about objectivity in making observations, a common control is to employ several observers to record participants' behavior. Data obtained by multiple observers are compared for agreement using interrater reliability coefficients or an index of **percent agreement.** Suppose, for example, that two raters are simultaneously observing a videotape of a group of chimpanzees. At random intervals, the observers are signaled to rate the behavior occurring at that moment as either aggressive or not aggressive. The observers are separated, but watch the same video. Thus, the observers are independently rating exactly the same behaviors. Ten signals are given, and each observer rates 10 instances of behavior as aggressive or not aggressive. The two observers' ratings can then be compared, as shown in Table 9.1, and a percent agreement computed.

A more sophisticated index of agreement is **Kappa,** which takes into account the **base rate**—the relative frequency of the behavior being rated. For example, if 5% of the behavior being rated is aggressive, the base rate for aggression is 5%. It is generally easier to get high percent agreement between raters when one behavior occurs almost all the time.

In our example of aggressive behavior, if we did not even bother to look at the behavior and instead just said that all behavior was not aggressive, we would be right 95% of the time. Kappa takes this statistical effect of the base rate into account. Using Kappa is beyond the scope of this textbook, but the interested student should consult Cohen (1960) or Raulin and Lilienfeld (1999). Computational procedures for Kappa are included on the Student Resource Website.

09:01

TABLE 9.1   *Computing Percent Agreement*

This hypothetical example illustrates the computation of percent agreement, or the percentage of times two raters agree on an observation.

Interval	Rater 1	Rater 2	Agree?
1	Aggressive	Aggressive	Yes
2	Aggressive	Aggressive	Yes
3	Not Aggressive	Aggressive	No
4	Not Aggressive	Not Aggressive	Yes
5	Not Aggressive	Not Aggressive	Yes
6	Not Aggressive	Not Aggressive	Yes
7	Aggressive	Aggressive	Yes
8	Aggressive	Not Aggressive	No
9	Not Aggressive	Not Aggressive	Yes
10	Aggressive	Aggressive	Yes

$$\text{Percent Agreement} = \frac{\# \text{ of agreements}}{\# \text{ of observations}} \times 100 = \frac{8}{10} \times 100 = 80\%$$

Having multiple observers also serves a second function. People, including research assistants, tend to be more careful about their work if they know that the work will be checked. A practical example of this phenomenon is people who chronically drive over the speed limit but who slow to the speed limit when driving on a highway known as a speed trap. The *Historical Lesson 9.1* box describes some classic research that illustrates how important this principle is to quality research. This study suggests that there should always be an interrater reliability check and that raters should have no idea which of their ratings will be checked. This gives raters incentive to do the best they can on all of the ratings they make.

HISTORICAL LESSON 9.1:   *Reliable Reliability*

Students often think of interrater reliability as an evaluation of the dependent measure, but when ratings are involved, the dependent measure is determined not by the scoring manual alone, but it is also affected by the degree of care that individual raters use in applying that scoring manual. Two raters who are conscientious and well trained may produce impressive levels of interrater reliability, while other less conscientious raters may produce poor interrater reliability. John Reid discovered that even well trained and motivated raters need the pressure of knowing that their work will be checked to produce consistently high quality work.

Reid (1970) trained several undergraduate research assistants to use a complex scoring system to rate videotapes of children. During the training, expert raters checked every tape, providing feedback and further instruction until the undergraduate assistants could use the scoring system reliably. Reid then had these assistants rate videotapes independently, although 20% of their tapes were checked by another rater to assess interrater reliability. The raters knew in advance which of their tapes would be checked, but the raters did not know that in actuality all of their tapes were being checked. Therefore, Dr. Reid had measures of reliability from when the raters thought their work was being checked and from when they thought their work would not be checked. He found large differences in interrater reliability in those two conditions. When the assistants knew that their work was being checked, they followed the manual faithfully and produced excellent interrater reliability. However, when they thought that no one would be looking over their shoulders, they were much less consistent in their ratings.

This clever study shows that actual interrater reliability is a function of (1) the quality of the scoring manual and the training provided to the raters and (2) the motivation of the raters. Dr. Reid's assistants were bright and highly motivated undergraduates, virtually all of whom were destined to go onto graduate school. Yet even these highly motivated people produced work that varied dramatically in quality depending on whether they thought they would be observed by someone else. This concept might sound familiar, because we talked about it earlier with respect to research participants. There we called it *measurement reactivity*—the tendency for people to behave differently than they might normally because they know they are being observed (see Chapter 6). Individuals who conduct research are no different from individuals who serve as research participants. They all behave differently when they know they are being watched.

There is a simple way to encourage research assistants to maintain high interrater reliability. Instead of telling them which 20% of their work will be checked, you tell them that 20% will be selected randomly and checked and they will never know what work will be checked. That is now the routine procedure for studies using behavioral ratings. It achieves two things. First, it provides an accurate indication of the level of interrater reliability. If Dr. Reid had been evaluating reliability only when he told his assistants that their reliability was being checked, he would have reported an interrater reliability that was much higher than his raters were actually producing. Second, such random checking of reliability maintains the motivation of raters to do their best work all the time, thus improving interrater reliability simultaneously with measuring it.

Using Deception

The most common control for subject effects is to obscure the true hypothesis of the study. The researcher can deliberately misinform participants about the study or withhold information that might reveal the hypothesis. This control, called **deception,** is usually minor, but deception can become quite elaborate. You learned in Chapter 3 that the ethical standards for research assume that the use of deception places the participants at risk. Therefore, plans to include deception must be justified, and the researcher must provide a complete debriefing at the end of the study. You will learn in this section that sometimes deception is the only reasonable way to test some hypotheses.

A procedure known as the **balanced placebo design** uses deception to study the effects of alcohol on behavior. Participants are asked to drink a beverage that contains either tonic or vodka and tonic (Marlatt, Demming, & Reid, 1973; Rohsenow & Marlatt, 1981). However, what participants drink and what they are told they are drinking are not necessarily the same thing. Suppose that the study included 100 participants; 50 participants are given vodka and tonic, and 50 are given tonic. Of the 50 participants who drink tonic, half (25) are told that they are drinking tonic, and the other half (25) are told that they are drinking vodka and tonic. Similarly, half (25) of the 50 participants who drink vodka and tonic are led to believe that they are drinking tonic, and the remaining participants (25) are told that they are drinking vodka and tonic. These conditions are illustrated in Table 9.2.

Because vodka is tasteless, it is almost impossible to distinguish it by taste alone, as long as the drink is not too strong. To reinforce the deception that participants are drinking a vodka-tonic mixture instead of only tonic, the drinks are mixed in front of participants. Vodka (actually water in the no-alcohol condition) is carefully measured from what appears to be a new, unopened vodka bottle, with tonic added from a separate, labeled bottle. This design is interesting in many respects. First, several ethical issues are raised by the deception and, therefore, appropriate safeguards must be included in the study. Second, it is equally desirable to have the experimenter blind to participant condition. To accomplish this, a cleverly hidden coding system is used on the bottles. The experimenter knows which bottle(s) to pour the drinks from, but does not know what each bottle contains.

TABLE 9.2   *Balanced Placebo Design*

This table illustrates the four cells of the balanced placebo design. This design separates the pharmacological effects of alcohol from the expectancy effects.

	People Led to Believe	
Actual Situation	Drinking Alcohol	Not Drinking Alcohol
Drinking Alcohol		
Not DrinkingAlcohol		

EXTENDING THE CONCEPT OF EXPECTANCY EFFECTS

The balanced placebo design has been used to separate the pharmacological effects of alcohol from the expectations of the drinker. In several studies (e.g., Lang & Sibrel, 1989), the behavior of the participants was affected more strongly by whether they thought they were drinking alcohol than whether they actually were drinking alcohol. In other words, the expectancy effects were more potent than the pharmacological effects of alcohol. This is an interesting psychological phenomenon. Normally, we think of the expectations of participants as a source of confounding, and in many situations it is. However, a balanced placebo design carefully controls expectations and measures their effects, because in this area of research the expectations *are* the psychological construct of interest. The results of several studies of alcohol consumption using the balanced placebo design illustrate just how powerful expectations can be, often overwhelming the actual pharmacological effect of the alcohol.

It is no wonder that researchers are so concerned about controlling unwanted expectancy effects in psychological studies. What makes the balanced placebo design work is that the participants *can* be deceived. As long as the drinks are not too strong or the participants do not drink too much alcohol, the taste and physiological cues are not strong enough to be detected.

Identifying the parameters that make a deception like this work requires careful pilot testing. In some cases, a balance placebo or similar deception is possible with some participants but not with others. For example, 10-year-old children with attention-deficit/hyperactivity disorder (ADHD) apparently cannot tell whether they are taking stimulant medication or a placebo, despite the dramatic effects that the medication has on their behavior. In contrast, 15-year-old children with ADHD can easily discriminate placebo from stimulant medication (Pelham, 1994: Pelham et al., 1992). In this case, a placebo deception is possible for the 10-year-olds, but not for the 15-year-olds.

Quick-Check Review 9.2: Control over Subject and Experimenter Effects	1. Describe the five types of controls for subject and experimenter effects. 2. How do single- and double-blind procedures differ? 3. How is deception used for control? What ethical issues does deception raise?

Control Through Participant Selection and Assignment

The manner in which participants are selected and assigned to groups can affect both the external and internal validity of a study.

Participant Selection

Participant selection refers to the identification of people asked to participate in a study. The term *sampling* is synonymous with participant selection. Appropriate participant selection enhances external validity, allowing researchers to generalize their results. In nearly all psychological research, the investigator's interest is not limited to specific participants, but rather is focused on the larger, more general group (i.e., the population).

For example, suppose that a poll is taken on Americans' attitudes toward (1) the animal rights movement, (2) hunting and trapping, and (3) gun ownership. The results of this hypothetical poll indicate that Americans are heavily opposed to animal rights (74%), highly supportive of hunting and trapping (98%), and strong opponents of gun control legislation (97%). A closer examination reveals that the poll was administered to licensed hunters in rural Montana. Obviously, there is a major problem of sampling and of external validity. From this sample of active hunters living in a Western state, it is unreasonable to draw conclusions about Americans in general. Because the sample was not selected to represent all Americans, the findings of the study cannot be generalized to all Americans, although it might tell us something about licensed hunters in Montana.

EXTENDING THE CONCEPT OF PARTICIPANT SELECTION

To understand participant selection, you must distinguish among (1) populations and samples; (2) general populations, target populations, and accessible populations; and (3) representative samples, random samples, stratified random samples, and ad hoc samples.

A *population* is the larger group of all events of interest (people, laboratory animals, and so on) from which a sample is selected. A *sample* is a smaller number of events selected from the population and used in a study as if the sample adequately represented the population.

These concepts were first introduced in Chapter 5 when we described the logic of inferential statistics. In this section, we will be looking at the sampling process from the standpoint of how it affects external validity, and we will be looking at it in more detail.

The **general population** is the group of all persons, events, and so on. The **target population** is the subset in which the researcher is ultimately interested. It is usually a naturally occurring subpopulation, such as all grammar-school children, all adult females, all registered voters, and so on. Target populations are typically not easily available. For example, suppose that you are interested in the level of understanding of basic science concepts in college freshmen. You cannot readily sample from all the college freshmen in the world. You do, however, have access to the 400 freshmen in two local colleges. The 400 freshmen become the **accessible population** from which you will select the sample. Generalizations from your study can be made confidently to the accessible population, but you must be cautious about generalizing to the target population. Because nearly all psychological research is carried out by sampling accessible populations, such as introductory psychology students at a particular university, *we must always be cautious about generalizations made to the target population*. Replication can strengthen confidence in broader generalizations, because each replication is likely to be carried out on different accessible populations. If the results replicate in each accessible population, your confidence in the generalizability of the findings will increase.

Researchers almost never study populations directly. Instead, they select a sample from an accessible population. They must be careful to select a **representative sample**—a sample that adequately reflects population characteristics—if they want to generalize their findings.

The basic idea of representativeness is simple. If the sample is representative, then the characteristics found in the population, such as sex distribution, age, intelligence, socioeconomic class, ethnicity, attitudes, political affiliations, and religious beliefs, will be found in the sample in the same proportions as in the target population. Although the concept is simple, actually obtaining a representative sample can be challenging. Furthermore, small samples often do not adequately represent populations. In general, large samples are more likely to adequately represent the population, because large samples tend to reduce the effects of sampling error. This issue is discussed in more detail on the Student Resource Website.

09:02

Another issue is that most psychological research is conducted with samples drawn from accessible populations that are not necessarily representative of the target population. The relationship among a general population, a target population, an accessible population, and a sample is illustrated in Figure 9.1.

Sampling of participants is a critical issue in social science research. Many methods have been developed to solve the problems of obtaining representative samples. Although some of the methods are beyond the scope of this text, we will consider three solutions to the problem of selecting a representative sample: (1) *random sampling,* (2) *stratified random sampling,* and (3) *ad hoc samples.*

Random Sampling. **Random sampling** from a population means drawing the sample so that (1) every member of the population has an equal chance of being selected for the sample and (2) the selections do not affect each other but instead are independent. With random sampling, no systematic biases lead some members of the population to have a greater chance than others of being selected. If the selection of participants is truly random, then characteristics of the population, such as age, ethnicity, and intelligence, will likely be distributed in the sample in roughly the same proportion as in the general population.

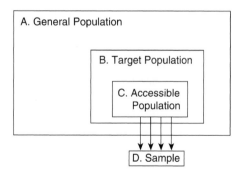

General population: All events, persons, animals, etc. (e.g., all children).
Target population: All events, persons, etc., of a particular class of interest to the researcher. This is the population to which we want to generalize our findings (e.g., all elementary school children).
Accessible population: The subset of a target population that is available to the research (e.g., elementary school children in the local school district).
Sample: The subset of an accessible population on which measures are taken. Note that a sample is rarely drawn directly from a target population.

FIGURE 9.1 *Populations and Samples*

09:03

The best way to draw an unbiased sample from a population is to draw a random sample. This is rather like picking numbers out of a hat. In actual practice, numbers are usually drawn, not from a hat, but from a **table of random numbers** (see Appendix D) or a **random-number generator** (a computer program for generating random numbers). The Student Resource Website includes a random number generator program.

Both random-number tables and random-number generators meet two criteria: (1) each number has the same chance of being selected and (2) each number is independent of the others. Suppose that you want to draw a sample of 60 participants from the accessible population of 400 freshmen in local colleges. You would list all 400 freshmen and assign each a number from 1 to 400. You would then use the table of random numbers or a random-number generator to get random numbers from 1 to 400 until you have a total of 60 unduplicated numbers.

Random numbers are useful for making any decision based on the principle of randomness. For example, later in this chapter you will learn about using random numbers for assigning participants to experimental conditions.

Stratified Random Sampling.   In **stratified random sampling,** separate random samples are drawn from each of several subpopulations. The subpopulations are defined in advance on the basis of one or more critical organismic variables that are likely to influence scores on the dependent measures. Small variations in the distribution of these variables in a sample can have a large effect on the results. For example, you might suspect that age is strongly correlated with the dependent measure of political preference. Therefore, the sample should closely approximate the distribution of age in the population studied. Rather than rely on random sampling, you divide the population into subpopulations on the basis of age. You then create a total sample by selecting the appropriate proportion of participants from each subpopulation. If 16% of the population is between the ages of 20 and 25, you select randomly, from that subpopulation, the number of participants it would take to make up 16% of the total sample. If the sample is 200 participants, 32 participants would be selected from the 20 to 25 age range. Stratified random samples are used extensively in sophisticated political polling operations. With this technique, samples as small as one thousand people can so closely represent the population that the outcome of elections involving several million voters can be accurately predicted. Any variable can be stratified, including, for example, socioeconomic level, education, sex, and ethnic identification.

Although random sampling is a major control for threats to external validity, psychological research rarely employs random sampling from a target population. Target populations are often difficult to access. For any large population, target or accessible, listing and numbering every individual to prepare for random selection are sizable tasks. Random and stratified random samplings from a target population are important in some research, such as in political surveys, but most psychological research does not employ random selection. Rather, participants are obtained from an accessible population, such as introductory psychology students or children from local schools. Furthermore, participants are almost always volunteers. Those who do not volunteer are not included, so any resulting sample may be biased. The ethical demand that participants be volunteers makes it difficult for researchers to obtain entirely random samples of any population.

Ad Hoc Samples. How can results be generalized from samples that are not randomly selected from a target population? The answer is twofold: first, you should generalize cautiously and conservatively; second, you should generalize only to other people (or to laboratory animals or events or places) having characteristics similar to those of the sample. That is, *researchers must be careful not to generalize beyond the limits of the sample.* In the examples given earlier, researchers can generalize their results only to people who are like those in their studies. In other words, the population to which you can safely generalize is defined by the characteristics of the sample. This type of sample, called an **ad hoc sample,** is used in most psychological research. For example, a great deal of psychological research is carried out with introductory psychology students as participants.

To generalize beyond ad hoc samples and yet maintain external validity, we must know the characteristics of the participants and keep the generalizations within the limits of these characteristics. Thus, when using ad hoc sampling, researchers need to obtain such descriptive data as participants' age, physical and psychological characteristics, and family socioeconomic data. The more completely the sample is described, the more secure we can be in establishing the limits of generalization and the more confidence we can have in making generalizations. When possible, it is valuable to obtain descriptive information on participants who are invited, but decline to participate, and participants who drop out before the study is completed. Comparing these participants with those who complete the study helps to pinpoint potential biases in participant selection and attrition that would limit generalization.

Accordingly, in your research you should draw a random sample whenever it is feasible. In most instances, it will not be feasible, and you will instead use an ad hoc sample. When you do this you should obtain sufficient descriptive information about the participants to establish the limits for generalization. The process of sampling research participants is illustrated in examples on the Student Resource Website.

09:04

Participant Assignment

After selecting participants, the researcher must assign them to experimental conditions. Unbiased **participant assignment** is critical. For example, suppose that you want to test the effectiveness of a new computerized program for teaching statistics to college students. In the experimental condition, students will have statistics lessons and assignments presented on the computer. In the control condition, students will have statistics lessons and assignments presented by a human instructor, using classroom lectures and demonstrations. There are two levels of the independent variable: computer presentation and teacher presentation. Suppose that 120 students have been selected as participants and that you want to assign 60 to each condition. You will want to avoid assigning all female participants to one condition and all male participants to the other, or assigning the best math students to the same condition. Random assignment will make it likely that the groups are comparable on these variables.

Take another example: In a study of office working conditions, six groups of typists are compared on their typing speed (number of words per minute) and accuracy (number of errors) under six different room temperatures: 55°, 60°, 65°, 70°, 75°, and 80°. A sample of 48 typists is selected and eight participants are randomly assigned to each of six groups. Random assignment makes it unlikely that all the best typists would be in one group. Therefore, it satisfies a very important basic principle, the **principle of initial equivalence,** which holds that all groups in an experiment must be equivalent at the start of the experiment. Random sampling automatically meets this requirement. Of course, the groups are never *exactly* equivalent. Rather, group differences are no more than would be expected from sampling error. Remember from Chapter 5 that *sampling error* refers to the small differences among groups that are randomly sampled from the same population.

The ideal experiment would include (1) random selection of participants from a known population and (2) random assignment of participants to conditions. The ideal, however, is seldom achieved. As noted earlier, random selection is rare in psychological research. Therefore, caution is needed when generalizing results. *Of far greater importance in an experiment is random assignment of participants to conditions.* Random assignment is a powerful control procedure that helps to reduce both known and unknown threats to internal validity. There are two ways to achieve random assignment: free random assignment and matched random assignment.

Free Random Assignment.   **Free random assignment** involves assigning participants to conditions in a random manner, so that the assignment of any one participant does not affect the assignment of the other participants. This is achieved by using a table of random numbers or a random-number generator as follows. In the experiment on typing speed and working conditions, the 48 participants can be randomly assigned to six conditions, 8 participants per condition. The researcher numbers the participants from 01 to 48, consults the table of random numbers or a random-number generator, and assigns the first participant number encountered to the first condition, the next participant number to the second condition, and so on. The seventh participant is assigned to the first condition, eighth to the second, and so forth. The researcher continues in this way until all 48 participants are assigned to the six conditions. The same random assignment procedure would be used to assign 60 participants to each of the two conditions in the study of teaching statistics to college students.

Randomization is a control method used in participant selection and assignment. *Randomization is the most basic and single most important control procedure.* It has several major advantages:

1. It can be used to control threats to internal and external validity.
2. It can control for many variables simultaneously.
3. It is the only control procedure that can control for unknown factors.

When participants are randomly assigned to groups or conditions, potential confounding variables are distributed without biases, even if the variables have not been specifically identified. Other control methods are effective with known extraneous variables that threaten the study's validity, but randomization is effective in reducing the bias of unknown variables. This is an extremely important point. No researcher can identify all the variables that might affect the dependent measures. However, by randomly assigning participants to conditions, the researcher can distribute the unknown confounding factors evenly among conditions.

Note that random assignment controls for subject variables, such as age and IQ. It does not control for environmental or setting variables, such as time of day, room temperature, or background noise. For these variables, the general control procedures discussed earlier are used. However, a good general rule for the researcher is *whenever possible, randomize*.

Matched Random Assignment.   **Matched random assignment** of participants to conditions is often used in small-sample research. It involves matching participants on a relevant variable and then randomly assigning the matched participants to groups, with one matched participant per group. Many psychological studies are carried out with small numbers of participants, and researchers are often faced with the task of assigning a small number of participants to two or three conditions.

Free random assignment works best with large samples, but with a small sample of participants, randomized groups can be unequal on important variables. For example, suppose that you are interested in investigating the effects of a motor-skills training program on high-tech assembly workers in an electronic equipment factory, but you have the time and resources to study only 12 workers. Your research hypothesis is that those who receive the motor-skills training (the experimental group) will improve their work performance. Specifically, they will show greater productivity, fewer errors, and an increase in job satisfaction compared with those who do not receive the training (the control group). Free random assignment of so small a number might result in unequal groups on important variables. You might find, for example, that most of the females or the workers with the most years of work experience have been assigned to the same group. Thus, the experimental and control groups would not have been equivalent on potentially important variables at the start of the study, and results might reflect the original differences between the groups, rather than the effects of the independent variable of motor-skills training. Therefore, the independent variable might be confounded by one or more extraneous variables.

To mitigate the problems inherent in working with small numbers of participants, you can use matched random assignment. To do this, you must first decide what variables are the most important potential confounding factors. Suppose that you decide that the sex of the worker is not likely to be a confounding variable. However, you suspect that the number of years worked might confound the results, because more experienced workers are likely to be more proficient than less experienced workers. To carry out the matching, you would first obtain the needed information for each participant—here, how many years each has worked. Then you would list the workers in order of years of experience, as shown in Table 9.3, and match them on this variable by taking the workers in pairs, successively down the list. Smith, the most experienced, would be matched with the next most experienced, Jones; Franks would be matched with Ordell; and so on.

You can now assign the participants to two groups by using a table of random numbers or by tossing a coin. Using the random-number table, the first participant of each pair is assigned to Group 1 if the number is odd or to Group 2 if the number is even. If a coin toss is used, heads or tails determine group assignment. Whichever method is used, the second participant in each pair is assigned to the other group. This procedure might result in the assignment of participants shown in Table 9.4.

As is seen in Table 9.4, the mean number of years of work experience for the two groups (9.86 years and 9.60 years) is close. Because the groups are comparable on years worked, this variable cannot confound the results. Note that the groups do not have equal numbers of males and females. However, the differences are small, and sex was not considered to be a potential confounding variable in the study. This expectation, of course, might be incorrect, but given the state of knowledge at the time of the study, it is a reasonable expectation.

TABLE 9.3   *Preparing for Matched Random Assignment*

In this example, the people available for a study are ordered based on their number of years of work experience and then paired. At the assignment stage, one member of each pair is randomly selected and assigned to the first group, and the other member is assigned to the second group.

Name	Sex	Number of Years Worked
Smith	F	15.7
Jones	M	13.8
Franks	M	12.2
Ordell	M	11.4
Samuels	F	11.0
Collucci	F	10.6
Spero	M	9.5
Kling	F	9.3
Ruiz	F	9.0
Barker	M	8.6
Stanton	M	4.3
Harringer	M	2.4

TABLE 9.4   *Workers Matched on Experience*

The matched participants from Table 9.3 were randomly assigned to produce the groups shown here. Note how closely the groups are matched on years of work experience.

Group 1			Group 2		
Name	Sex	Years Worked	Name	Sex	Years Worked
Jones	M	13.8	Smith	F	15.7
Franks	M	12.2	Ordell	M	11.4
Collucci	F	10.6	Samuels	F	11.0
Kling	F	9.3	Spero	M	9.5
Ruiz	F	9.0	Barker	M	8.6
Stanton	M	4.3	Harringer	M	2.4
% Females	3/6 = 50%			2/6 = 33%	
Mean Years Worked		9.86			9.60

Matching increases the sensitivity of small-group research to the effects of the independent variable. It does this by assuring that potential confounding variables are equally distributed in the groups. You can match on more than one variable. However, it is generally not feasible to match on several variables simultaneously, because the task becomes cumbersome and difficult. It is more efficient to test more participants and assign them to groups randomly.

Matching requires researchers to identify the variables to be matched and measure those variables. Participants can be matched on any variable. How does a researcher determine which variables are most important to match? Think about it. The variables to be matched are those, other than the independent variable, that will have the largest effect on the dependent variable. This is precisely why they need to be controlled. This issue will be addressed in more detail in Chapter 11.

Other Matching Procedures.   Other matching procedures are available. An alternative to participant-by-participant matching is matching characteristics of groups (see Chapman & Chapman, 1973). This procedure is more commonly used in differential research, but it can be useful in some experimental situations. In such situations, the researcher first identifies the variables on which the groups are to be matched and measures these variables for each potential participant. Using a randomization procedure, the researcher assigns participants to one of the two groups and calculates this group's mean and standard deviation on each variable to be matched. The researcher then selects the second group of participants so that it has a comparable mean and standard deviation on the variables. The result is that the two groups are equivalent on the matching variables, but individuals in one group are not matched with individuals in the other group. Because the groups are comparable on the matching variables, potential confounding is avoided.

A variation of matching is to equate groups by holding the variable constant. For example, if you want to match on age, you could use only participants of approximately the same age. If there is little or no variability on this factor between the experimental and control groups, this factor cannot be a source of confounding.

One disadvantage to matching by holding the variable constant is that it reduces external validity because it reduces the ability to generalize the results of the study to the larger population. For example, if you used only adult participants, you would be unable to generalize with confidence to adolescents.

Matching by building the variable into the study is another control method. It creates what is known as a *factorial design,* discussed in Chapter 12. Suppose that you want to evaluate how manner of dress affects social class ratings among high school students. Students are asked to rate social class for a dozen students that they have never met and about whom their only information is a two-minute video sequence of a hallway conversation among friends. The independent variable is the manner of dress of the students to be rated. The dependent variable is the social class rating. However, you are concerned about confounding due to differences in age and social development; for example, freshmen might view the concept of social class differently from seniors. To control for this, you make the academic class variable (freshman, sophomore, junior, senior) a part of the study. Because the participants in each group are of similar age, you are able to determine the influence of the age variable.

09:05

Several exercises on the Student Resource Website illustrate the process of assignment of participants to conditions.

Quick-Check Review 9.3: Control Through Participant Selection and Assignment

1. Define general population, target population, accessible population, and sample.
2. Why is it important that samples be drawn carefully from a population?
3. Define each type of sampling discussed in this section.
4. What does matching participants control?

Control Through Experimental Design

Protecting internal validity is critical in experiments, because it bears on the very essence of experimentation: the predicted causal relationship between independent and dependent variables. Experimental methods are the best procedures for protecting internal validity. **Experimental design** refers to the careful arrangement of all parts of the experiment so as to (1) test the effects of the independent variable on the dependent variable and (2) protect against threats to internal validity.

Several experimental designs are available. The basic experimental designs are discussed in Chapter 10, and variations on those designs are discussed in Chapters 11 and 12. Here we will introduce the concept of experimental design by first discussing a nonexperimental design: the pretest-posttest design illustrated in Figure 9.2.

Suppose that a psychologist is studying children with attention-deficit/hyperactivity disorder (ADHD). A central problem of these children is an inability to stay focused on a task. Therefore, they often have difficulty learning to read. The psychologist develops a cognitive self-control training program geared specifically to reading tasks. Once trained in a six-step cognitive procedure, the children silently rehearse the steps just before approaching any reading task in school. The researcher tests the effectiveness of the training by using a pretest–posttest design. She first took pretraining measures of reading ability of five children with ADHD, then trained them in the six-step cognitive self-control procedures, and then again tested them for reading ability.

Suppose that the researcher found a statistically significant difference between the pretest and posttest measures. This finding might seem sufficient to conclude that the training improved reading, but as you learned earlier, it is not. Such a conclusion cannot be drawn, because of possible confounding. To avoid confounding variables (in this case, because of maturation and history), the researcher would have to anticipate them and build suitable controls into the research design. In this instance, a good control would be a no-treatment **control group** (an equivalent group of ADHD children who do not receive cognitive self-control training). Suppose that

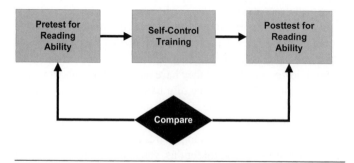

FIGURE 9.2   *A Simple Pretest-Posttest Design* In this basic pretest–posttest design, reading ability is assessed both before and after the application of the self-control training. The researcher then compares these two measures to see how much change has occurred.

there are 20 ADHD children in the program. The researcher could randomly assign 10 of the children to the **experimental group** that receives the treatment and 10 to the control group that does not. All the children would remain in the general program and receive the same general treatment. However, only the experimental group would receive the cognitive self-control training. This is the pretest–posttest, control-group design illustrated in Figure 9.3.

The question is whether the experimental group shows significantly greater reading performance than the control group at the posttest. If this is exactly what the researcher finds, he or she can have considerably more confidence in concluding that self-control training is responsible for the difference, because the confounding variables of maturation and history have been controlled.

How is maturation controlled? If the experimental and control groups are equivalent at the start of the experiment, the researcher can expect maturation to occur equally in the two groups. How is confounding due to history controlled? Both groups receive all other treatments in the general program. Thus, if some program factor other than self-control training affects reading performance, it should affect both groups equally.

For the control-group design to be effective, *it is essential that the experimental and control groups be comparable at the start of the experiment.* If the experimental group has more of the most capable, older, or better-adjusted children, then confounding due to selection is present. Confounding due to selection is controlled by randomly assigning the participants to the two groups. In this example, random assignment of participants controlled for confounding due to selection, and the inclusion of a no-treatment control group controlled for confounding due to maturation and history. Routinely including these two basic control procedures—(1) unbiased assignment of participants to conditions and (2) inclusion of appropriate control groups or conditions—controls most potential confounding.

The independent variable must vary in experiments. In the ADHD study, the independent variable of cognitive self-control training is presented at two levels: all or none. There can be more than two levels; the hypothetical study of typists' productivity at different room temperatures included six levels of the independent variable. That design did not have one control group, but six levels of the independent variable, each of which operated as a control for all other levels.

Scientific research generally is characterized by attention to details. Competent researchers employ carefully reasoned and clearly stated concepts, well-developed operational

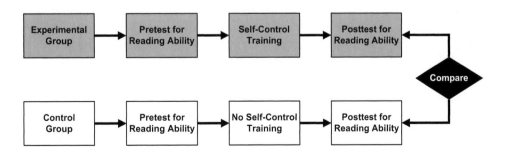

FIGURE 9.3 *A Pretest-Posttest Control-Group Design* In the basic two-group comparison design, one group receives the treatment, while the other does not. To evaluate the effect of the treatment, the two groups are compared.

definitions, inductive-deductive logic, careful measurement of the observed variables, and use of appropriate statistical methods to analyze data.

Well-designed experiments display these characteristics in addition to the following five criteria:

1. A clearly stated research hypothesis concerning predicted causal effects of one variable on another
2. At least two levels of the independent variable
3. Unbiased assignment of participants to conditions
4. Specific and systematic procedures for empirically testing the hypothesized causal relationships
5. Specific controls to reduce threats to internal validity

Experiments are designed to answer questions about causality and control for threats to validity. To do so, we must arrange the experiment in such a way as to answer this research question: Does the hypothesized causal relationship between the independent and dependent variables exist? The task of arranging the components of the experiment is what is meant by experimental design.

In essence, experimental design is a detailed plan for the conduct of the experiment. Once the design is formalized, the researcher proceeds through it step by step as planned. Remember that at the high-constraint level of experimentation, there is no flexibility to alter any part of the design once the study begins. Chapters 10 through 12 discuss a variety of experimental designs.

Quick-Check Review 9.4: Control Through Experimental Design	1. What does unbiased assignment of participants to groups accomplish?
	2. What are the five characteristics of any experimental design?

PUTTING IT INTO PRACTICE	When we talk about control procedures and experimental designs, we are talking about trying to represent natural phenomena in the laboratory, where we can exercise sufficient control to assure internal validity. Ecological validity, which addresses the question of whether the laboratory procedures represent natural phenomena faithfully enough that the findings will generalize to the real world, is also important.
	Over the next week, observe psychological phenomena in natural settings and spend some time thinking about how they might be brought into the laboratory without losing critical elements. For example, if you observe a mother interacting with her three-year-old, think about what you would have to do to faithfully capture various aspects of that interaction in a laboratory. What would you have to do to make the laboratory study natural enough that it is likely to produce findings that accurately reflect what would have occurred in the real world?

Chapter Summary

You have learned to define four major groups of control procedures: (1) general control procedures, (2) control of subject and experimenter effects, (3) control through participant selection and assignment, and (4) control through experimental design.

General control procedures include careful preparation of the research setting, specification of measurement instruments, and replication. Subject and experimenter effects are controlled by keeping the researcher and participants blind to both the hypotheses and the condition under which each participant is tested and by using automated procedures, objective measures, multiple observers, and deception when necessary. Appropriate participant selection, such as random sampling, helps to control for threats to external valid-

ity, whereas random assignment of participants to conditions helps to control for threats to internal validity.

Experiments test hypothesized causal relationships between variables in a way that rules out alternative explanations. Procedures to control threats to validity are critical in experimental design. The development of controls to their highest degree is a major factor that distinguishes experimentation from other levels of constraint in research.

Most threats to validity can be controlled by routinely including three basic control procedures: (1) unbiased participant selection or careful description of an ad hoc sample, (2) unbiased assignment of participants to conditions, and (3) inclusion of appropriate control groups.

Chapter Exercises

1. Define the following key terms. Be sure that you understand them. They are discussed in the chapter and defined in the glossary.

control	accessible population
exact replication	representative sample
systematic replication	random sampling
conceptual replication	table of random numbers
blind	random-number
single-blind procedure	generator
double-blind procedure	stratified random
placebo	sampling
automation	ad hoc sample
objective measure	participant assignment
subjective measure	principle of initial
percent agreement	equivalence
Kappa	free random assignment
base rate	matched random
deception	assignment
balanced placebo design	experimental design
participant selection	control group
general population	experimental group
target population	

2. A researcher randomly selects 30 of 473 elementary school children. On completion of the study, the re-

searcher wants to discuss the results in terms of all elementary school children. Identify the various populations and samples involved in this study. What cautions must the researcher be aware of in generalizing the results?

3. For each of the following independent variables, indicate the number of levels and identify each level:

   a. Studying the effects of bright and dark illumination on participants' perception.

   b. Varying the amount of noise using four levels in a study of classroom behavior.

   c. Comparing children's ability to solve riddles under different conditions. One group of children is given no extra clues, another group is given one extra clue, and a third group is given five extra clues.

   d. Five different kinds of pain relief medication are tested in a pharmaceutical laboratory.

4. Assume you have 60 participants. Use the table of random numbers (Appendix D) to assign participants randomly to three conditions with 20 participants in each condition.

10

Single-Variable, Independent-Groups Designs

> *Observation is a passive science; experimentation is an active science.*
> —Claude Bernard, *Introduction a l'Etude de la Medecine Experimental*, 1865

Web Resource Material

This chapter introduces basic experimental designs and their supporting concepts. It revisits the concept of variance that was introduced in Chapter 5, this time emphasizing that experimental design involves the measurement and control of sources of variance. Before discussing experimental design, the chapter reviews nonexperimental designs to illustrate how they fail to provide adequate control of variance. The chapter ends by discussing the statistical procedures used to evaluate basic experimental designs and briefly outlining other experimental designs that are covered in Chapters 11 and 12.

Scientific research uses highly evolved procedures to find answers to questions. It is at the experimental level of constraint that the design process is most completely developed. Experiments share five specific characteristics. The experiment:

1. States one or more hypotheses about predicted causal effects of the independent variable(s) on the dependent variable(s).
2. Includes at least two levels of the independent variable.
3. Assigns participants to conditions in an unbiased manner, such as through random assignment.
4. Includes specific procedures for testing hypotheses.
5. Includes controls for major threats to internal validity.

Planning is extensive and critical in experimental research. The researcher

1. develops a problem statement,
2. identifies and defines important theoretical constructs,
3. identifies and operationally defines independent and dependent variables,
4. formulates research hypotheses,
5. identifies a population,
6. deals with all ethical considerations,
7. selects and assigns participants to conditions,
8. specifies the details of observational procedures,
9. anticipates threats to validity,
10. selects appropriate controls, and
11. specifies the procedures for data analysis.

All of this planning is carried out *before the researcher observes a single participant.*

Experimental design refers to both the activity involved in the planning of the experiment and the plan itself. A well-developed experimental design provides a blueprint for the experimenter to follow. We cannot emphasize enough the importance of developing a clear experimental design *before beginning observation.* Careful planning can build in the controls necessary to have confidence in the results. Therefore, *plan the experiment carefully and carry it out exactly as planned.*

Variance

We previously discussed several concepts that we will bring together in this section, including variance (Chapter 5), internal validity (Chapter 8), and control (Chapter 9). The following material summarizes those earlier discussions and integrates that material into a more detailed understanding of the logic of research design.

EXTENDING THE CONCEPT OF VARIANCE

As you learned earlier in the text, variation is necessary in experiments. Without variation there would be no differences to test. Independent variable manipulation is designed to create variation between experimental and control conditions. If the independent variable has an effect on the dependent variable, the variation in the independent variable created by the manipulation will in turn create variation in the dependent variable. Conversely, if the independent variable does not have an effect on the dependent variable, then the dependent variable should be roughly the same in each group.

Why is that true? Because, as you learned in the previous chapter, participants are randomly assigned to groups in experiments. Random assignment tends to equate the groups on all variables, including the dependent variable. Independent variable manipulation will disrupt this equality among the groups only if the independent variable is capable of influencing the dependent variable.

In this section, you will learn about various sources of variance, where each source comes from, and how researchers manage variance. Later in this chapter, we will review these concepts again, this time looking at them from a statistical analysis perspective. You will then be able to see how the principles of research design affect the statistical analysis of the results of a research study.

Sources of Variance

There are two relevant sources of variance in experimental design: (1) systematic between-groups variance and (2) nonsystematic within-groups variance. We will describe each of these and the factors that influence them.

Systematic Between-Groups Variance.   An experiment tests the effects of an independent variable on the dependent variable(s) by setting up at least two levels of the independent variable and measuring participants' responses on the dependent variable(s). The researcher predicts that the mean of the dependent measures will differ significantly among the groups, because differences in the level of the independent variable in each group are expected to change the average level of the dependent measure in each group. Another way of saying the same thing is that the researcher is predicting significant variability among group means on the dependent measure. Statisticians refer to this variability among group means as **between-groups variance.**

EXTENDING THE CONCEPT OF SAMPLING ERROR

You learned about sampling error in Chapter 5. When we say that variability among group means is significant, we are indicating that variability is larger than would be expected on the basis of *sampling error*, which refers to the natural variation among samples drawn from the same population. Two samples drawn from the same population are unlikely to have exactly the same mean. Therefore, even if the independent variable has no effect at all on the dependent variable, we would expect that the means would show a small degree of variability due to this sampling error. Consequently, it is premature to conclude that the independent variable has an effect on the dependent variable until variability among means is considerably larger than the variability one might expect from sampling error alone.

Suppose, for example, that a researcher wants to test the hypothesis that a recorded laugh track increases viewers' enjoyment of a particular television comedy. One hundred people have been randomly assigned to two groups, fifty in each group. The experimental group views the show with a laugh track, and the control group views the same show minus the laugh track. Then all participants rate their enjoyment of the show. Because participants have been randomly assigned, the researcher can assume that there was no significant difference between the groups prior to the manipulation, although there are likely to be small differences due to sampling error. The difference that is critical here is how predisposed participants are to enjoying television shows, because that difference will affect the dependent variable (how much they enjoy the television show they are being shown in this study). The prediction is that the group with the laugh track will rate the show as significantly more enjoyable than will the control group. In other words, the researcher expects to find significant between-groups variance.

Finding a significant difference between the groups does not mean that the independent variable is responsible for the difference. This finding indicates only that there are systematic effects that are making the group means different from one another. There are two sources of these systematic effects that make the group means on the dependent measure diverge. They are (1) the effect of the independent variable (**experimental variance**) and/or (2) the effects of uncontrolled confounding variables (**extraneous variance**). We call the sum of these systematic effects **systematic between-groups variance.** Don't forget that there is also a small contribution to variability among the means because of the nonsystematic effects of sampling error.

EXTENDING THE CONCEPT OF CONFOUNDING

You learned about the many sources of confounding in Chapter 8. Extraneous variables are uncontrolled variables that might produce confounding. Now we are introducing a similar-sounding term, *extraneous variance,* which has a somewhat different, but related, meaning. Extraneous variance is the effect that uncontrolled extraneous variables have on the results of the study. The effect increases the variability of the means over and above what we would normally see from sampling error and from the impact of the independent variable.

To summarize, the between-groups variance is a function of systematic effects (caused by experimental and/or confounding variable effects) and nonsystematic effects (caused by sampling error). The systematic between-groups variance in the experiment might be statistically significant, thus tempting the researcher to conclude that there is a causal relationship between the independent variable and dependent variable.

However, if the between-groups variance is high only because of confounding variables and not because of the independent variable, the observed differences will be due to the extraneous variance and not to the experimental variance. Statistical tests can determine only whether there are significant differences among the groups, not whether the observed differences are due to experimental or extraneous variance. If there is any possibility that the group differences are due to extraneous factors, then we cannot draw a causal inference. It is for this reason that confounding must be anticipated and controlled. This leads us to a basic principle in research: *you need to maximize the experimental variance (due to the independent variable) and control the extraneous variance (due to confounding variables).*

Nonsystematic Within-Groups Variance.   The term **error variance** denotes the **nonsystematic within-groups variability.** Error variance is due to random factors that affect some participants but not others within a group, whereas systematic variance is due to influences on all members of each group. Error variance may be increased by unstable factors, such as some participants feeling ill when tested, or stable factors, such as individual differences. It can be increased by experimenter or equipment variations that cause measurement errors for some participants but not for others in the same group. Because no two participants are exactly alike and no procedure is perfect, there will always be some error variance. Consequently, there will always be a certain degree of natural variability among the means, called sampling error, even in the total absence of systematic effects.

Nonsystematic within-groups influences are largely random. There should be just as much chance that these influences will occur in one direction as in another or will affect some participants in the group but not others. Thus, if random influences cause some participants to score lower than they ordinarily would, other random influences will cause other participants to score higher than they ordinarily would. The result is that random influences tend to cancel each other. Some participants score too high; others score too low; but the means of the groups are not affected. However, these effects will increase the variability of the scores.

In contrast, systematic between-groups factors influence all participants in a group in one direction. The effects are not random; they do not cancel each other. As a result, the mean of the group is moved up or down by systematic between-group factors, depending on the direction of their influence.

In summary, we can make a distinction between

1. Systematic between-groups variance, which includes
   a. Experimental variance (due to independent variables) and
   b. Extraneous variance (due to confounding variables), and
2. Nonsystematic within-groups error variance (due to chance factors).

It is important to repeat that the between-groups variance is a function of both the systematic between-groups variance (experimental and extraneous variance) and the nonsystematic effects that are due to sampling error. Even when there is absolutely no systematic between-groups variance, there will still be small differences between groups due to sampling error. Systematic between-groups variance increases the between-groups variance beyond the natural variability that is caused by sampling error. Data are analyzed by comparing the between-groups variation and the within-groups variation. As you will see later, the ratio of these two measures defines the *F*-test:

$$F = \frac{Measure\ Based\ on\ Between\text{--}Groups\ Variation}{Measure\ Based\ on\ Within\text{--}Groups\ Variation} \tag{10.1}$$

Without going into statistical detail, let us consider the principles involved in evaluating the relationship of the between-groups variation to the within-groups variation. A measure based on the between-groups variation (the numerator) is a function of both systematic effects (experimental variance plus extraneous variance) and effects of sampling error (error variance). A measure based on within-groups error variation (the denominator) is a function only of error variance. These terms are computed in such a way that the error variance is the same value in both the numerator and the denominator of the formula. Therefore, the preceding equation can be written as

$$F = \frac{Sytematic\ Effects\ +\ Error\ Variance}{Error\ Variance} \qquad (10.2)$$

Suppose that there are no systematic effects. In this case, both the numerator and the denominator would represent error variance only, and the ratio would be 1.00. Whenever the *F*-ratio is near 1.00, it means that no systematic effects are present. In other words, the between-groups variation is no larger than we would expect from sampling error alone. On the other hand, suppose that the between-groups variation is substantially greater than one would expect from sampling error. This would suggest that there are systematic effects. In this case, a researcher would conclude that the groups do differ. This is the basic idea behind the *F*-test.

Controlling Variance in Research

To show a causal effect of the independent variable on the dependent variable, the experimental variance must be high and neither distorted by excessive extraneous variance nor masked by error variance. The greater the extraneous and/or error variance, the more difficult it becomes to show the causal effects of an independent variable on a dependent variable. This idea leads to an expansion of the rule stated earlier: *In experimentation, each study is designed so as to maximize experimental variance, control extraneous variance, and minimize error variance.*

Maximizing Experimental Variance.   Experimental variance is due to the effects of the independent variable(s) on the dependent variable(s). There must be at least two levels of the independent variable in an experiment. In fact, it is often advisable to include more than two levels, because including multiple groups provides more information about the relationship between the independent and dependent variable(s).

To demonstrate an effect, the researcher must be sure that the independent variable really varies. In other words, the research conditions must truly differ from one another. It is often useful to include a **manipulation check** in a study to evaluate whether the manipulation actually had its intended effect on participants. Let's look at a hypothetical example to see how a manipulation check might be used.

Suppose that in a study of the effects of anxiety on performance, the researcher manipulates anxiety by changing the feedback given to participants during a training period, reasoning that participants who think that they are doing poorly will be more anxious than participants who think that they are doing well. Therefore, the researcher sets up two conditions. In one, the participants are told that they did well during training and should have no problems during the actual testing (the low-anxiety group). A second group is told that they did poorly during the training and that they must try harder if they want to avoid making themselves look foolish (the high-anxiety group). How do you know whether this manipulation actually affected the anxiety level of participants? One way is to ask participants to rate their anxiety and see if the experimental group was more anxious than the controls. Another might be to monitor physiological processes that are associated with higher anxiety, such as heart rate or sweating of the palms. This assessment of the effectiveness of the experimental manipulation is an example of a manipulation check. If the groups did not differ on anxiety, then the manipulation of anxiety was ineffective. Consequently, the study provides no basis to evaluate the effect of anxiety on the dependent measure.

The importance of a manipulation check is illustrated in the results of another hypothetical study that is graphed in Figure 10.1. This study looked at differences in the level of hostile expression among men and women in response to an anger provocation. It was hypothesized that males typically externalize anger and therefore react with hostility when

(a)

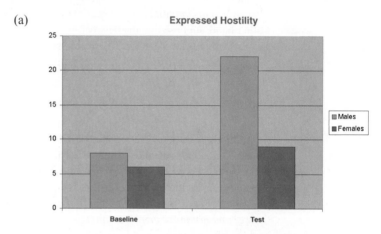

(b)

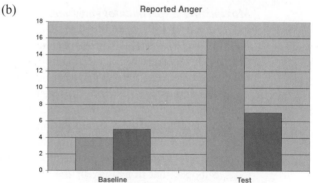

(c)

FIGURE 10.1 *Importance of Including Manipulation Checks* This hypothetical data set illustrates how manipulation checks can clarify the meaning of data. The hostility data suggest that males do react with more hostility when angered than females, but the manipulation checks suggest that the reason for this pattern is that the anger provocation only worked for the males.

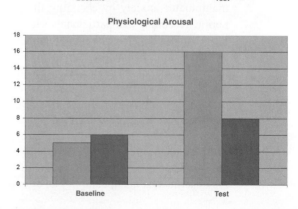

angered. In contrast, it was hypothesized that women internalize anger, thus not acting hostile when angered.

The rationale for a study like this comes from the psychodynamic explanation of depression, which is conceptualized as "anger turned inward." Because women are twice as likely to develop depression as men, this study looked at a possible mechanism for this sex difference—specifically, that women are more likely to internalize anger, thus increasing their risk for depression.

Anger was manipulated by having the researcher mess up several things in a row during the study, thus forcing participants to repeat parts of the study. The results of this hypothetical study are illustrated in Figure 10.1(a), and the results clearly seem to be consistent with the hypothesis. However, two manipulation checks, which are shown in Figures 10.1(b) and (c), were included in the study. These checks looked at the reported level of anger and the level of physiological arousal, respectively. If the anger provocation was effective, these variables should have shown it. Even if women turned anger inward, and therefore did not report experiencing increased anger, the physiological measures should have been elevated. However, in this hypothetical study, both the reported levels of anger and the levels of physiological arousal showed the same pattern in men and women as the expressed hostility dependent measure (see Figure 10.1).

How do we interpret such findings? The most parsimonious interpretation is that the anger manipulation worked for males but not for females. We might speculate that perhaps females were more empathetic to the problems that the researcher was experiencing, and therefore not angered by them. What is clear is that it would be unwise to say that this study shows that women internalize anger more than men simply because they expressed less hostility. Perhaps another anger provocation procedure, such as making insulting comments about a person's appearance, would have angered both men and women and shown a different pattern of results. What the manipulation check shows is that caution is necessary, because it is not clear that anger was actually produced in both groups. If the manipulation check had shown that both men and women reported equivalent levels of increased anger and showed equivalent levels of increased arousal, then it would be clearer that men express hostility more than women when angered.

EXTENDING THE CONCEPT OF CONTROL

Controlling Extraneous Variance. You learned about extraneous variables in Chapter 3 and about the common sources of extraneous variance in Chapter 8. Extraneous variables are those between-group variables, other than the independent variables, that have effects on groups as a whole, possibly confounding the results. To demonstrate the effects of an experimental manipulation, we must control extraneous variables and keep them from differentially affecting the groups. In this regard, two important ideas are basic in experimentation: We must be sure (1) that the experimental and control groups are as similar as possible at the start of the experiment and (2) that they are treated in exactly the same way except for the independent-variable manipulation. These strategies were discussed in Chapter 9 and are summarized here. The general concept to remember in controlling extraneous variance is that one must *make sure that the independent-variable manipulation is the only difference in the researcher's treatment of the experimental and control groups.* Several methods for controlling extraneous variance are aimed at ensuring that the groups are equal at the beginning of the study.

1. The best method of controlling for extraneous variance is random assignment to groups, which decreases the probability that the groups will differ on extraneous variables. Thus, *whenever possible, randomly assign participants to conditions.*
2. If a factor, such as age, ethnic identification, intelligence, or sex, is a potential confounding variable, we can control it by selecting participants who are as homogeneous as possible on this variable. For example, we could select only males or only females or select participants who are within a few IQ points of each other. The cost of using this as a control is that it limits generalizability. For example, using only males or females limits our conclusions to only one sex.
3. A potential confounding variable also can be controlled by building it into the experiment as an additional independent variable. Thus, if sex is a potentially confounding variable, we could add sex as a nonmanipulated independent variable. There would then be two independent variables in the study, a design known as a factorial design (see Chapter 12).
4. Extraneous variance can be controlled by matching participants or by using a within-subjects design (see Chapter 11).

Minimizing Error Variance.   Error variance is within-groups variance that is due to chance factors and individual differences. There is always some error variance. Remember that a statistically significant difference between conditions is one that is greater than is expected based on the sampling error alone. A large error variance can obscure differences between conditions due to the experimental manipulations. One source of error variance is measurement error, which is the result of variations in the way participants respond from trial to trial due to such factors as unreliability of the measurement instruments. To minimize these sources of error variance, we must *maintain carefully controlled conditions of measurement and be sure that the measuring instruments are reliable.*

Another major source of error variance is individual differences. Within-subjects or matched-subjects designs, which are covered in Chapter 11, minimize this source of error variance. There are problems in using within-subjects designs, such as sequence effects, but the within-subjects design does reduce error variance by eliminating the individual-differences component.

EXTENDING THE CONCEPT OF CONTROL

We have been talking about control throughout this textbook. Now you can see that our discussion of maximizing experimental variance, controlling extraneous variance, and minimizing error variance is a summary of the earlier discussions of control. Said another way, control in research is *control of variance.*

The general control procedures discussed in Chapter 9 deal with the control of error variance. Other control procedures help to control both error variance and extraneous variance. The most powerful control for extraneous variance is a properly selected experimental design in which participants are randomly assigned to conditions.

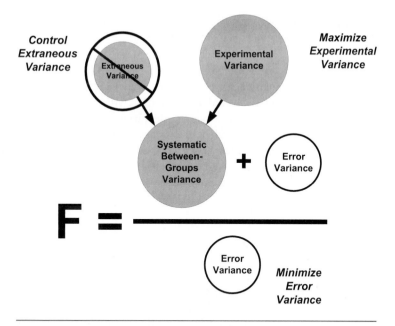

FIGURE 10.2 *Controlling Variance in Research* Controlling variance is the concept that links research design to statistical analysis of results. This figure illustrates how different sources of variance affect the *F*-ratio in analysis of variance. Maximizing experimental variance and minimizing error variance increases the sensitivity of the research to effects of the independent variable. Controlling extraneous variance avoids confounding that would make drawing a single conclusion impossible.

Figure 10.2 illustrates the principles discussed in this section on variance. It shows the various sources of variance and how they combine in an analysis of variance. It also shows where each of the three principles in controlling variance (maximize experimental variance, control extraneous variance, and minimize error variance) would apply to the statistical analysis of data using an ANOVA.

Quick-Check Questions 10.1: Variance	1. What is systematic between-groups variance?
	2. Define experimental variance and extraneous variance.
	3. What is error variance?
	4. What is the *F-test?* What is it used for?
	5. What are the ways of controlling extraneous variance?
	6. How do we minimize error variance?

Nonexperimental Approaches

Now that you understand that research designs are used to control the various sources of variance, we will look at several research designs and see how well they accomplish this goal. The primary goal of experimental research designs is to control extraneous variance, although some designs (covered in Chapter 11) will also minimize error variance.

In this chapter, we will cover single-variable, between-subjects designs, which are designs that have a single independent variable and have different participants in each group. To appreciate the advantages of experimental designs, you need to understand the limitations of non-experimental approaches. Therefore, we will begin by discussing the following non-experimental approaches:

1. Ex post facto studies
2. Single-group, posttest-only studies
3. Single-group, pretest-posttest studies
4. Pretest-posttest, natural control-group studies

In this and the next section, we will consider examples of research, beginning with nonexperimental approaches and progressing to experimental designs. As we progress along this continuum, note that each successive design controls for more sources of extraneous variance. This presentation is drawn in large part from *Experimental and Quasi-Experimental Designs for Research and Teaching* (1966), Campbell and Stanley's classic book.

Ex Post Facto Studies

In an **ex post facto** ("after the fact") **study,** study, an example of which is illustrated in Figure 10.3, the researcher observes current behavior and attempts to relate it to earlier experiences. For example, a therapist might observe some difficulty in a client and conclude that the problem was caused by earlier life events that the therapist never directly observed or manipulated. This kind of evidence has led many people to conclude that abused children become abusive parents, based on the observation that many abusive parents report that they were abused as children.

This is an example of a conclusion that is arrived at in an ex post facto manner. As reasonable as the conclusion seems, we can have little confidence in its validity, because

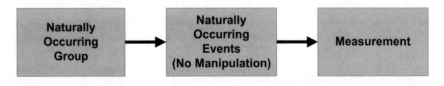

FIGURE 10.3 *Ex Post Facto Approach* The ex post facto design makes an observation after a naturally occurring event. There is no manipulation of an independent variable. This design cannot eliminate rival hypotheses, because none of the potential confounding variables are controlled.

there were no controls for confounding factors. If we cannot control for confounding, then rival hypotheses cannot be eliminated. For example, the simple observation above does not rule out the possibility that abusive parents are no more likely to have been abused as children than non-abusive parents. Thus, a causal relationship between the independent and dependent variables cannot be inferred. This is a weak design for drawing inferences, but it is often weaker than it needs to be, as illustrated in *The Cost of Neglect 10.1*.

Let's look at another example. Suppose that a researcher suspects that food additives, such as artificial colors, flavors, and preservatives, stimulate hyperactive behavior in some children. Obtaining a sample of 30 hyperactive children, the researcher finds that 28 of

THE COST OF NEGLECT 10.1:   *Seeing All Sides*

The ex post facto design is a very weak design under the best of circumstances, but unfortunately, it is often made weaker than it needs to be when the researcher neglects to look at the broader picture.

Let's examine the assertion that abusive parents were often abused as children and, therefore, the abuse that they experienced is the cause of their later abusiveness as parents. To many people, this sounds reasonable enough that they accept it as a logical conclusion, but let's look at it more closely. For the sake of simplifying the analysis, let's assume that one is either abused or not abused as a child and that one is either abusive or not abusive as a parent. (We are essentially eliminating the complication of dealing with degrees of abusiveness.) Then we can organize information about the relationship between the abusiveness experienced in one's childhood and the abusiveness one shows as a parent in a 2×2 table, called a contingency table. Table 10.1(a) illustrates the cells of this contingency table.

When you hear "abusive parents were often abused as children," you are getting an idea of what would be found in the upper left hand cell of this contingency table. Let's say for the sake of argument that 70% of abused children become abusive adults. That is a pretty strong figure, but to see if there is a relationship between these two variables, you have to look at the entire pattern of cells. For example, both Table 10.1(b) and 10.1(c) show situations in which most abusive parents were abused as children, but the total pattern of data would lead to opposite conclusions about the relationship of one's own childhood experience to one's abusive behavior as an adult. The pattern

in Table 10.1(b) suggests that being abused as a child is predictive of being an abusive parent.

In contrast, Table 10.1(c) suggests that being abused as a child does not predict being abusive to one's children, because the probability of being abusive to one's children is exactly the same in both those who were abused as children and those who were not abused as children. You cannot see whether there is a legitimate relationship between two variables unless you have data from all four cells of the contingency table.

So not only are ex post facto fallacies common, but so is sloppy thinking about how much information is required to even document the existence of a relationship between two variables. Remember, in this instance the relationship is a correlation, and correlations do not imply causality. By now that rule should be second nature to you, because you have come across it repeatedly in this text. Also remember that if there is a causal relationship, there should be a correlation, so if there is no correlation, then there is no causal relationship (another rule you learned earlier).

As you learned in Chapter 6, a contingency cannot establish a general proposition, but it can negate one. We are going to need a much more powerful design to establish a causal connection between the variables of being abused as a child and being abusive to one's own children. Later in this chapter you will learn about a design powerful enough to test whether such a causal connection exists. However, for this question, carrying out such a study would be unethical. Why? See if you can identify a design that is powerful enough to answer the question and why it is unethical to use it for this specific question.

TABLE 10.1 *Using Contingency Tables*

You cannot interpret a contingency table like the one shown in panel (a) with data from only one of the cells. You need to gather the data to fill all four cells, as shown in panels (b) and (c). The data in panel (b) suggest a relationship between childhood abuse and later parental abusiveness, whereas panel (c) suggests that no such relationship exists. In panel (b), those who were abused as children are 7 times more likely to abuse their own children. In panel (c), people who were abused have the same probability of abusing their children as people who were not abused.

(a)	Adult Behavior	
Childhood Experience	*Abusive*	*Not Abusive*
Abused	70%	
Not Abused		

(b)	Adult Behavior	
Childhood Experience	*Abusive*	*Not Abusive*
Abused	70%	30%
Not Abused	10%	90%

(c)	Adult Behavior	
Childhood Experience	*Abusive*	*Not Abusive*
Abused	70%	30%
Not Abused	70%	30%

them (93%) eat foods containing these additives every day. The number seems high to the researcher, and the findings are consistent with the researcher's suspicion that there may be a relationship between food additives and hyperactivity. The researcher may even formulate the hypothesis for future testing that food additives stimulate hyperactivity. However, because the researcher followed an ex post facto procedure, a valid conclusion that a causal relationship exists between food additives and hyperactive behavior cannot be made.

An ex post facto study can generate hypotheses to test with higher-constraint studies, but it is not itself capable of testing causal hypotheses. Because no independent variable is manipulated in ex post facto studies, controls to guard against confounding cannot be applied. The researcher cannot know which variable(s) may have affected the results and therefore cannot eliminate rival hypotheses. Any of several confounding variables may have been responsible. For example, the hyperactivity might be due to parental behavior, genetic factors, or the influences of other children, none of which were evaluated or controlled. Consequently, results from ex post facto studies should be interpreted with great caution.

Single-Group, Posttest–Only Studies

A **single-group, posttest–only study,** an example of which appears in Figure 10.4, is at a somewhat higher level of constraint than ex post facto procedures. Here the independent variable is manipulated with a single group and the group is then measured.

Suppose, for example, that a clinician wants to determine whether eliminating foods containing certain additives thought to increase hyperactivity will help hyperactive children. She asks parents of 20 children diagnosed as hyperactive to eliminate these foods from their children's diets for four weeks. At the end of the period, the children are tested for hyperactivity, and 12 out of the 20 children are found to be hyperactive. Here there has been an actual manipulation in the form of the dietary change, as well as measurement of posttreatment hyperactivity levels. Nevertheless, there are still several confounding factors that prevent the researcher from drawing causal inferences about the treatment's effect on hyperactivity. Perhaps the children did not change at all, but because there was no pretreatment measurement, there was no way of knowing this. Perhaps there was a change, but it was a placebo effect—a change produced only by the expectation of improvement. That is, children who were given food with the same additives as before, but thought they were getting food without the additives, would have also decreased their hyperactivity. Perhaps the children did improve, but the improvement was due to some other uncontrolled factor, such as another program in which the children were involved. Perhaps the children matured over the 4 weeks of treatment, and the low hyperactivity was due to this maturation. Perhaps they did become less active, but it was only a natural return to their normal activity level. In fact, it may have been a temporary peak in their activity level that prompted their parents to seek treatment.

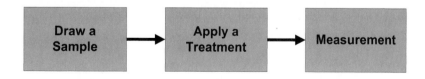

FIGURE 10.4 *Single-Group Posttest-Only Study* The single-group, posttest-only design applies a treatment to a group and then makes a measurement of the dependent variable. The term *treatment* as used in these figures refers to any kind of manipulation of the independent variable. This design fails to control the confounding factors of placebo effects, maturation, history, and regression to the mean.

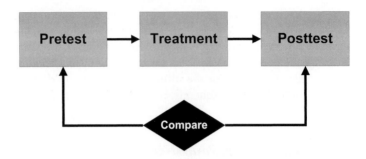

FIGURE 10.5   *Single-Group Pretest-Posttest Study*   The single-group, pretest-posttest design measures the dependent variable, applies a treatment to a group, and then measures the dependent variable again. This design can verify that a change occurred, but fails to control the confounding factors of placebo effects, maturation, history, and regression to the mean.

This single-group, posttest-only study did not control for the confounding variables of placebo effects, history, maturation, or regression to the mean. The researcher could not even be sure if there was any change in activity level.

Single-Group, Pretest-Posttest Studies

A **single-group, pretest-posttest study,** as illustrated in Figure 10.5, is an improvement over the posttest-only approach because it includes a pretreatment evaluation. The researcher in the previous example might (1) select a sample of hyperactive children, (2) observe them for rates of hyperactive behavior, (3) impose the four-week dietary restrictions, and (4) observe them again for hyperactivity at the end of four weeks. Suppose that the posttest hyperactivity measures are significantly less than the pretest measures. Now we know that there was improvement, but the single-group, pretest-posttest study still failed to control for placebo effects, maturation, history, and regression to the mean. The improvement might have occurred because the children and parents expected improvement (placebo effect), because the children matured during the treatment period (maturation), because of some other factor in the program (history), or because the pretest measures of hyperactivity were at an abnormally high peak and they naturally returned in time to their mean level (regression). To avoid these confounding variables, an additional control is necessary, as you will see shortly.

EXTENDING THE CONCEPT OF MATURATION

In Chapter 8, you learned that maturation is a common confounding variable. The single-group, pretest-posttest study fails to control for maturation. However, in some research, maturation is not considered a confounding variable. Rather, it is the phenomenon under study. Developmental psychologists focus much of their research on the process of maturation. They often use designs similar to the pretest-posttest design described here, but without the manipulation. A study in which the same participants are followed over time is called a *longitudinal design.* We introduced you to the concept of longitudinal research in Chapter 7.

Typically, multiple measures are taken over the course of a longitudinal developmental study. This type of multiple-measure design is called a **time-series design.** In a developmentally focused longitudinal study, maturation is elevated from the status of a confounding variable to the phenomenon of interest. Thus, the "treatment" shown in Figure 10.5 is actually the passage of time.

It is important to realize that a variable such as history *can* confound the study of maturation unless appropriate controls are included. We will discuss this in more detail in the section on time-series designs in Chapter 13.

Pretest-Posttest, Natural Control-Group Studies

A good control to add to the preceding studies is a no-treatment control group. In a **pretest-posttest, natural control-group study,** such as the one illustrated in Figure 10.6, naturally occurring groups are used, only one of which receives the treatment. Participants are not randomly assigned to groups as they would be in an experimental design. For example, two intact classrooms might be used, with students from one classroom assigned to the first group and students from the other classroom assigned to the second group. Adding this control group significantly strengthens the design.

The natural control-group approach is very close to an experimental design. However, this approach still has a weakness in that there is no procedure, such as random assignment, to ensure that the two groups are equivalent at the start of the study. For example, suppose that in forming the experimental and control groups, the researcher asked parents if they were willing to try the four-week dietary restrictions. The children of those parents who were willing to expend the effort were put in the experimental group and those who were not were put in the control group. The serious confounding factor in this procedure is that the experimental and the control groups are different in terms of parents'

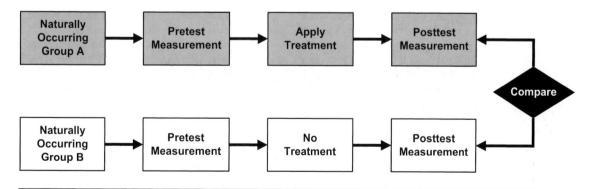

FIGURE 10.6 *Pretest-Posttest, Natural Control-Group Study* The pretest-posttest, natural control-group design compares two naturally occurring groups, one that receives the treatment and one that does not receive the treatment. This design fails to control for selection, but provides control for history and maturation.

willingness to try the dietary restrictions. The dietary restriction treatment is confounded with parents' willingness to cooperate.

It could be that parents who are willing to do all the things necessary to change their child's diet in hope of decreasing their child's hyperactivity may be more motivated to help their child to change. Any posttreatment differences between the groups on measures of hyperactivity might be due to either factor: dietary restriction or parental motivation. The children in the two groups may even have been different on the level of hyperactivity before the experiment began. It may be that parents with the most hyperactive children are the most desperate and are therefore the most likely to try *any kind* of treatment, although the pretest in the design would allow a researcher to check this possibility.

EXTENDING THE CONCEPT OF RANDOM ASSIGNMENT

You learned in Chapter 9 that random assignment is a powerful control procedure in experiments. When you compare groups of participants at different levels of the independent variable, it is essential that the groups be equivalent on the dependent measures at the start of the study. Random assignment of participants to conditions is one way of increasing confidence that the groups are equivalent at the start of the study. Such random assignment to conditions is one of the hallmarks of experimental design, which is the topic of the next section.

Quick-Check Review 10.2: Nonexperimental Approaches	1. Identify four nonexperimental approaches. Define each and discuss its limitations.
	2. Of these four approaches, which is the weakest? Why?
	3. When is maturation not considered a confounding variable? What type of design is typically used to study maturational processes?

Experimental Designs

Two critical factors—*control groups* (or conditions) and *randomization*—distinguish **experimental designs** from (most) nonexperimental designs. These two factors control most sources of confounding.

Including proper control groups helps to control history, maturation, and regression to the mean. The experimental designs discussed here all include at least one control group. To make the control groups effective, participants must be randomly assigned to the groups.

Randomization is a powerful tool. A good general rule to follow in designing research is to *randomize whenever possible.* For example, randomly selecting your sample from the population will enhance external validity, just as randomly assigning participants to groups enhances internal validity. Of course, ethical issues may prevent the random assignment that is part of experimental procedure. For example, it would be unethical to assign people to experimental conditions that might result in brain damage. So some experiments should never be done, no matter how valuable the knowledge they might provide. This is why lower-constraint methods are so valuable. They can provide useful information in circumstances when higher-constraint methods are ethically unacceptable.

Because there are so many different experimental designs, we will conduct our discussion over several chapters. In this chapter, we will discuss designs appropriate for evaluating a single independent variable using independent groups of participants. In Chapter 11 we will focus on designs for testing a single independent variable using correlated groups of participants. Chapter 12 focuses on designs used for testing more than one independent variable in a single experiment. Finally, Chapter 13 focuses on designs that test causal hypotheses in natural environments.

Although many variations of experimental designs are possible, four basic designs are used to test a single independent variable using independent groups of participants. These **single-variable, between-subjects designs** include the following:

1. Randomized, posttest-only, control-group design
2. Randomized, pretest-posttest, control-group design
3. Multilevel, completely randomized, between-subjects design
4. Solomon's four-group design

Randomized, Posttest-Only, Control-Group Design

Suppose that you want to evaluate the effects of an experimental treatment for disruptive behavior, a special tutorial program for reading skills, visual stimulus complexity on target detection, or food additives on hyperactivity. In each case, you want to manipulate a variable and measure the effects, but you want to do it in such a way that extraneous variance is controlled. The best approach by far is to conduct an experiment.

The most basic experimental design is the **randomized, posttest-only, control-group design,** which includes randomization and a control group. You start by randomly selecting participants from a general or accessible population or carefully define an ad hoc sample. You then randomly assign the participants to the experimental (treatment) and control (no-treatment) conditions. The resulting design is illustrated by the example in Figure 10.7.

To test the hypothesis that the independent variable significantly affected the dependent variables, you compare the posttest measures from the experimental and controls groups. It is critical that the two groups be equivalent at the beginning of the study. If they are not, then we cannot know if differences at the posttest are due to the independent variable or to preexisting differences between the groups. Random assignment of participants to groups increases the probability that the groups are equivalent at the beginning of the study. Furthermore, when participants are randomly assigned to groups, the small probability that the groups might not be equal is automatically factored into the statistical analysis. After participants have been randomly assigned to groups, the groups are said to be **statistically equal,** because any small differences that might exist are the results of sampling error.

Several threats to validity are controlled by the randomized, posttest-only, control-group design. Random selection or ad hoc sample definition protects external validity. Threats to internal validity from regression to the mean and from attrition are reduced by random assignment of participants. Regression to the mean is controlled because, even if

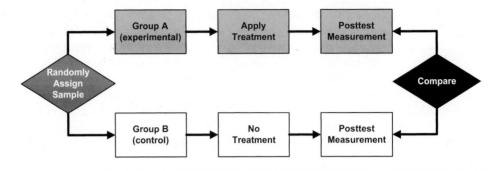

FIGURE 10.7   *Randomized Posttest-Only Control-Group Design* The randomized posttest-only control-group design compares two groups, in which participants were randomly assigned, with one group receiving the treatment and one group not receiving the treatment. This is a true experimental design that controls for most confounding variables.

the participants were selected because they were extreme, the random assignment assures that both groups will have roughly the same number of extreme participants, and thus both should experience the same level of regression. Random assignment assures that the groups are statistically equal on all variables, because there is no bias in the assignment process for the groups. Threats to internal validity from instrumentation, history, and maturation are reduced by including the no-treatment control group, because these effects should be equal in the groups.

EXTENDING THE CONCEPT OF GENERAL CONTROL PROCEDURES

In Chapter 9, we introduced several classes of control procedures, including a group of general control procedures. An experimental design is effective only if the appropriate general control procedures are routinely applied. Carefully preparing a setting, using reliable dependent measures, or applying single-blind or double-blind procedures when appropriate will control extraneous variance and minimize error variance. An experimental design alone, without using these general control procedures, is not sufficient for ruling out confounding variables. For example, failing to keep the person who actually tests participants blind to group assignment will allow the possibility of confounding due to experimenter effects.

The control imposed by the experimental design can be forfeited by the failure to include the necessary general control procedures. In the food additive study, a double-blind procedure should be used, because both placebo and experimenter effects are anticipated. The no-treatment control group must be indistinguishable from the treatment group for the participants. This could be accomplished by having the researcher provide specially packaged foods to all participants in both groups. The only difference would be that the food given to the experimental participants would not contain the additives thought to increase hyperactivity. Ideally, you would want to use identical packaging and food that looks and tastes the same in each condition.

Randomized, Pretest-Posttest, Control-Group Design

Recall that the pretest-posttest, natural control-group design discussed earlier in the chapter is not an experiment, because it does not include random assignment to groups. In the **randomized, pretest-posttest, control-group design,** an example of which is illustrated in Figure 10.8, participants are randomly assigned to groups. All participants are tested on the dependent variable (the pretest), the experimental group is administered the treatment, and both groups are then retested on the dependent variable (the posttest). The critical comparison is between the experimental and control groups on the posttreatment measure.

The randomized, pretest-posttest, control-group design improves on the randomized posttest-only, control-group design by adding a pretreatment measurement of the dependent variable. Random assignment to groups ensures that the groups are statistically equal. The pretest provides a way to check if they are actually equivalent on the dependent variable at the start of the experiment, thus adding another level of confidence to the results. It also permits calculation of a pretest-posttest difference or change score. Adding a pretest also has some disadvantages, which are discussed later in the chapter.

Multilevel, Completely Randomized, Between-Subjects Design

The designs discussed so far have had only two levels of the independent variable. The **multilevel, completely randomized, between-subjects design** is a simple extension of the previously discussed designs. Instead of participants being randomly assigned to two conditions, they are randomly assigned to three or more conditions, as shown in Figure 10.9. Pretests may or may not be included, depending on the questions that the investigator wants to answer. Because this design is only an extension of earlier designs, it controls for the same confounding variables as the simple two-group designs.

Recall the description in Chapter 9 of a study in which room temperature was varied to test its effects on the speed and accuracy of typing. This study used a multilevel, completely randomized, between-subjects design, in which 48 typists were randomly assigned

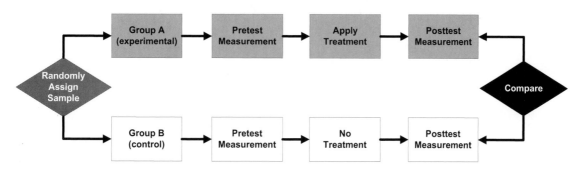

FIGURE 10.8   *Randomized Pretest-Posttest Control-Group Design* The randomized, pretest-posttest control-group design compares two groups to which participants are randomly assigned, one group that receives the treatment and one group that does not receive the treatment. This is a true experimental design that controls for most confounding variables. The pretest allows you to see the strength of the treatment effect.

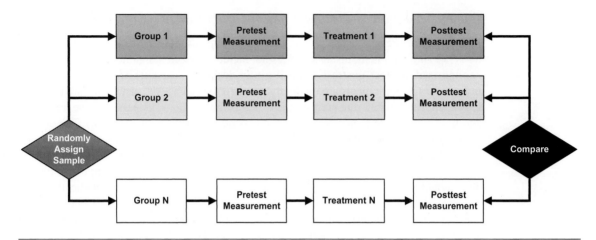

FIGURE 10.9 *Multilevel Completely Randomized, Between-Subjects Design* The multilevel, completely randomized, between-subjects design is an extension of the randomized, pretest-posttest control-group design to more than two groups. This design can be run either with or without a pretest.

"Everything's been so completely randomized out there that we seem to have lost our research assistants among the subjects!"

It may be possible to carry randomization too far, but researchers generally want to use randomization whenever possible.

to six groups of 8 typists each. Each group of typists was tested at a different room temperature (the independent variable), and their typing speed and accuracy were measured (the dependent variable).

Solomon's Four-Group Design

The addition of a pretest improves control in experimental design, but it also creates a new problem: the possibility that the pretest will affect participants' responses to the treatment or to the posttest. We might expect the influence of the pretest to be the same in the experimental and control groups, but it is also possible that the pretest could interact with the experimental manipulation, producing confounding. In other words, the effect of the pretest might not be constant for the groups, but will vary depending on the level of the independent variable. For example, suppose that a researcher is interested in testing whether adolescents' attitudes toward cigarette smoking can be changed by presenting them with a videotape about the health hazards of tobacco use. High school students are randomly selected, given a pretest measuring their attitudes toward the use of tobacco, and then are randomly assigned to experimental and control groups. The pretest shows that the two groups are statistically equivalent on attitudes toward tobacco use at the start of the study. The experimental group is shown the videotape and the control group is not, both groups are retested on their attitudes toward tobacco use, and the experimental and control groups' posttest measures are compared.

As well designed as this study appears, the pretest of attitudes might sensitize participants to the nature of the research. When the videotape is later presented to the experimental group, this sensitization may interact with this new information and change the way that participants respond. The experimenter might erroneously conclude that the observed difference is due only to the videotape, when it may actually be due to the interaction of the pretest and the videotape. In other words, if no pretest had been given, the videotape may have been less effective.

In an attempt to control such effects, Richard Solomon (1949) developed an extension of control group design. **Solomon's four-group design,** which is illustrated in Figure 10.10, combines the randomized, pretest-posttest, control-group design (Groups A and B in Figure 10.10) and the posttest-only, control-group design (Groups C and D). Groups A and B are the experimental and control groups, respectively, and they provide the basic comparison needed to test the hypothesis. Groups C and D are a replication of this basic comparison without the pretest. The critical comparison is between the posttest measures of Groups A and B. The random assignment of participants to conditions ensures that the groups are statistically equivalent at the start of the study, and the pretest provides a way to test their equivalence. Random assignment also controls for potential confounding due to statistical regression. The potential confounding due to history and maturation are controlled by the inclusion of the control group (Group B). Group C controls for the possible interaction of the pretest with the treatment. Comparing the posttest measures of Groups C and A provides a basis for determining whether the pretest in Group A interacted with the treatment. The final control, Group D, includes only the posttest and provides further control for the effects of maturation. If there is an effect of the independent variable, the

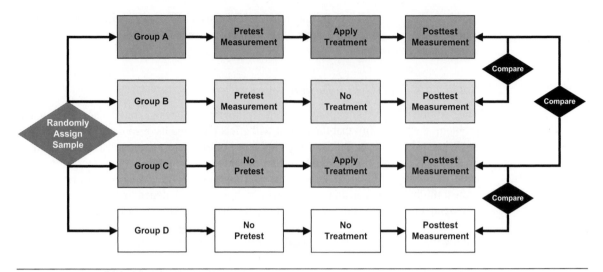

FIGURE 10.10 *Solomon's Four-Group Design* Solomon's four-group design is a combination of the randomized posttest-only design and the randomized pretest-posttest design. It allows the researcher to check for an interaction between the pretest and the treatment.

posttest measure for Group D should be similar to those of Group B and different from Groups A and C.

Solomon's four-group design is a powerful design that provides excellent control. However, because it requires the resources of two experiments, it is not recommended for routine use. Rather, it is best used for experiments in research areas in which the basic hypotheses have already been tested and supported using simpler designs, but in which you want a test of greater rigor. It is also used when an interaction between the treatment and the pretest is expected.

EXTENDING THE CONCEPT OF RANDOM ASSIGNMENT

Each of the experimental designs discussed in this section uses randomization to assign participants to conditions. Actually, what is required is **unbiased assignment,** which you learned in Chapter 9 can be achieved through free random assignment or matched random assignment. This allows us to use matching procedures and still maintain an experimental design. Designs employing matching procedures are discussed in the next chapter. Examples from the literature of the four research designs discussed here are included on the Student Resource Website.

10:01

Quick-Check Review 10.3: Experimental Designs	1. What is the most basic experimental design?
	2. Describe each of the other three experimental designs discussed in this section.
	3. How do (a) random assignment of participants to groups and (b) inclusion of a control group control avoid confounding?
	4. What problem does the Solomon four-group design address?
	5. Why is it critical that groups be equivalent at the start of an experiment?

Statistical Analyses

This section reviews the statistical analysis of data obtained from experiments. The level of measurement of the dependent variable helps to determine the appropriate statistical procedure (see Chapters 4 and 5). For example, a *chi-square test* is typically used with nominal data; the *Mann-Whitney U-test* is typically used with ordered data; a *t-test* or an analysis of variance (ANOVA) is typically used with score data.

10:02

Most dependent variables at the experimental level generate score data. Therefore, we will focus on these tests in this section. However, the Student Resource Website covers all of these procedures. We will focus primarily on analysis of variance, because it allows us to integrate our earlier discussion of control of variance into our discussion of the statistical analysis procedures.

t-*Test*

The *t*-test evaluates the size of the difference between the means of the two groups. The difference between the means is divided by an **error term,** which is a function of the variance of scores within each group and the size of the samples. The *t*-test is easily applied, commonly used, and useful when we want to test the difference between two groups. Its disadvantage is that it can compare only two groups at a time.

Analysis of Variance

Many studies are multilevel designs in which more than two groups are used. For these studies, an analysis of variance (ANOVA) is required. In the typist study described earlier, there are six levels of the independent variable of room temperature. A one-way ANOVA is used to test whether any of the six groups is statistically different from any of the other groups. The qualifier *one-way* simply means that there is only one independent variable in the study.

EXTENDING THE CONCEPT OF STATISTICAL ANALYSIS

You learned in Chapter 5 and earlier in this chapter that ANOVA is used to analyze differences between two or more groups. To introduce how ANOVA works, it is necessary to review some of the earlier discussion of variance. Variance is a relatively simple concept, but it can seem confusing in the context of ANOVA because there it is calculated more than once based on different combinations of the same data.

ANOVA uses both the **within-groups variance** and the **between-groups variance.** Within-groups variance is a measure of nonsystematic variation within a group. It is error or chance variation among individual participants within a group and is caused by such factors as individual differences and measurement errors. It represents the average variability within the groups. The between-groups variance represents how variable the group means are. If all groups have approximately the same mean, the between-groups variance will be small; if the group means are very different from one another, the between-groups variance will be large. It is affected by both the systematic factors that affect the groups differently and by the variation due to sampling error. The systematic factors include (1) experimental variance, which is due to the effects of the independent variables, and (2) extraneous variance, which is due to confounding variables. However, even if there are no systematic effects, the group means are likely to be slightly different from one another due to sampling error.

As you learned in Chapter 5, the variance is based on the **sum of squares,** which is the sum of squared deviations from the mean. In an analysis of variance, there is a sum of squares on which the between-groups variance is based, a sum of squares on which the within-groups variance is based, and a total sum of squares. In the ANOVA procedure, the sum of squares is calculated for each of these; that is, the total sum of squares is **partitioned** into the between-groups sum of squares and the within-groups sum of squares. You need not understand the mathematical details of this process. However, this principle of partitioning the sum of squares is valuable in the computation of ANOVA procedures.

$$\begin{pmatrix}\text{Total sum} \\ \text{of squares}\end{pmatrix} = \begin{pmatrix}\text{Between-groups} \\ \text{sum of squares}\end{pmatrix} + \begin{pmatrix}\text{Within-groups} \\ \text{sum of squares}\end{pmatrix} \qquad (10.3)$$

10:03

Consider a study of the effects of room temperature on typing speed, in which 48 typists are randomly assigned to six conditions defined by the temperature of the room in which their typing speed was tested. Table 10.2 shows the data for this study, as well as the mean and standard deviation for each group. The first step in doing an ANOVA is to compute each of the sums of squares (between groups, within groups, and total). The Student Resource Website covers computational procedures.

The next step is to compute between-groups and within-groups variances, which are called **mean squares** in analysis of variance. The mean squares are computed by dividing each of the sums of squares by the appropriate degrees of freedom (df). The between-groups sum of squares is divided by the number of groups minus 1 (in this case, $6 - 1 = 5$). The within-groups sum of squares is divided by the total number of partici-

TABLE 10.2   *Typing Speed Study Data*

| | *Temperature Under Which Typists Were Tested* | | | | | |
	55°	*60°*	*65°*	*70°*	*75°*	*80°*
	49	71	64	63	60	48
	59	54	73	72	71	53
	61	62	60	56	49	64
	52	58	55	59	54	53
	50	64	72	64	63	59
	58	68	81	70	55	61
	63	57	79	63	59	54
	54	61	76	65	62	60
Mean	55.75	61.88	70.00	64.00	59.13	56.50
Standard Deviation	5.23	5.69	9.35	5.24	6.66	5.32

pants minus the number of groups (in this case, $48 - 6 = 42$). (Note that we do not compute the mean square for the total, because it is not used in the ANOVA.)

The between-groups and within-groups mean squares are then compared by dividing the between-groups mean square by the within-groups mean square. The result is the *F*-ratio, which will be interpreted shortly.

The results of these computations are summarized in an **ANOVA summary table** like the one shown in Table 10.3. This table shows the sources of variation, the degrees of freedom associated with each source, the sum of squares, the mean squares, the value of *F*, and the probability value associated with that *F*-value.

TABLE 10.3   *ANOVA Summary Table for the Study of the Effects of Room Temperature on Typing Speed*

Source	*df*	*SS*	*MS*	*F*	*p*
Between groups	5	1134.67	226.93	5.51	.0006
Within groups	42	1731.25	41.22		
Total	47	2865.92			

The statistical significance of the ANOVA is based on the **F-test** (named after its originator, Sir Ronald Fisher). Fisher's *F*-test involves the ratio of the between-groups mean square to the within-groups mean square:

$$F = \frac{Mean\ Square\ Between\ Groups}{Mean\ Square\ Within\ Groups}$$

(10.4)

EXTENDING THE CONCEPT OF SOURCES OF VARIANCE

Earlier in this chapter, you learned about the sources of variance and how they affect the *F*-test. Figure 10.11 illustrates graphically what factors go into the *F*-ratio and how the relative size of those factors affects the size of the *F*. This figure builds on our earlier discussion of controlling variance. Remember that the numerator in the *F*-test is a function of both the systematic between-groups variance and nonsystematic within-groups variance, whereas the denominator is a function of only the nonsystematic within-groups variance.

For the purposes of this discussion, we will assume that the only source of systematic between-groups variance is experimental variance. In other words, we are assuming

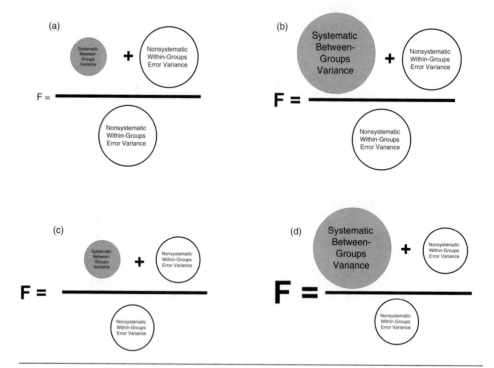

FIGURE 10.11 *What Affects the F-Ratio* You can increase the size of the *F* in an ANOVA by (1) increasing the systematic between-groups variance, which is illustrated by the shaded circle [panel (a) to (b)], (2) decreasing the nonsystematic within-groups variance, which is illustrated by the unshaded circle [panel (a) to (c)], or (3) doing both [panel (a) to (d)].

that confounding has been adequately controlled. The size of the circles indicates the relative size of the sources of variance, and the size of the *F* indicates its relative size.

Consider some of the possibilities that might be found in this ratio. If there were no systematic between-groups differences, there would still be some chance differences between the groups due to sampling error. So if there were no systematic between-groups differences, both the mean square between groups (based on between-groups variability) and the mean square within groups (based on within-groups variability) would estimate error variance. In this case, the *F*-ratio should have a value of approximately 1.00. Any factors that increase the size of the numerator relative to the denominator will make the ratio larger. Therefore, as the systematic between-groups variance increases, the *F*-ratio will increase. Furthermore, any factors that decrease the size of the denominator relative to the numerator will also make the ratio larger. Thus, the ratio is increased by increasing the systematic between-groups variance, by decreasing the nonsystematic within-groups variance, or a combination of the two, as shown in Figure 10.11. The systematic between-groups variance is increased by maximizing the differences between the groups. The nonsystematic within-groups variance is minimized by controlling as many potential sources of random error as possible. In other words, it is desirable to *maximize experimental variance and minimize error variance.* This theme should be sounding familiar by now. Add the part about controlling extraneous variance, and you have the guiding principle of research design.

The larger the *F*-ratio, the greater the variance between groups relative to the variance within groups. A large *F* indicates that the experimental manipulation may have had an effect. In practice, even if there are no systematic effects, the *F*-ratio will sometimes be larger than 1.00. Therefore, we do not reject the hypothesis that there are no systematic differences unless the *F*-ratio is larger than we would expect by chance alone.

Statistical analysis programs routinely compute both the *F*-ratio and the *p*-value associated with it. This *p*-value is the probability of obtaining an *F* that large or larger if there are no systematic effects. If the *p*-value is less than the alpha level chosen, the null hypothesis that the groups are equal is rejected, and the researcher concludes that at least one of the groups is significantly different from at least one other group.

EXTENDING THE CONCEPT OF STATISTICAL POWER

We introduced the concept of statistical power in Chapter 5. The error terms in both the *t*-test and in the ANOVA procedures are a function of the variance of scores and the sample size. Remember that one of the goals in research is to minimize error variance, which essentially means to minimize this error term. We noted several ways in which that could be done, including improving the quality of the measurement procedure or using within-subjects designs to control for individual differences.

These procedures do work and are often used to control error variance and minimize the error term that is a function of the error variance. But by far the most important method for decreasing the error term is to increase the sample size. Larger sample sizes provide more precise estimates of population parameters, such as population means. Therefore you do not need as large a difference between your sample means to be convinced that a difference exists in the population means. This concept is called statistical power. When we suggest that you want to minimize the error term, we are saying that you want to increase statistical power. The effect is to give you greater sensitivity to any effect that the independent variable might have on the dependent variable.

Specific Means Comparisons in ANOVA

Note that the *F*-test indicates whether significant group differences exist, but not which group or groups are significantly different from the others. This is not a problem when only two groups are compared. However, when there are three or more groups to compare, an additional step is needed. Specifically, the researcher must **probe** to determine where the significant difference(s) occur. Probing is statistically testing the differences between the group means. Specific comparisons are best carried out as a planned part of the research, which are called **planned comparisons** (also called **a priori comparisons** or **contrasts**). Here the experimenter makes predictions about which groups will differ and in what directions, based on the theoretical concepts that underlie the experiment, and these predictions are made before data are collected.

Occasionally a priori predictions are not made, and an ANOVA is carried out to answer the question of whether there are any differences. Under these conditions, if a significant *F* is found, the pattern of means is evaluated using a **post hoc comparison** (also called an **a posteriori comparison** or an **incidental comparison**). Scientific rigor and informational value are generally greater for a priori comparisons than for post hoc comparisons. Therefore, researchers usually try to make specific predictions prior to the study to justify planned comparisons based on those predictions.

Several statistical procedures can be used for the specific comparisons, depending on whether they are planned or post hoc. It should be noted that a *t*-test is not an appropriate procedure for doing a post hoc comparison of means. The *t*-test used as a post hoc probe may indicate that significant differences exist when they do not. Appropriate post hoc tests, such as the Tukey, Newman-Keuls, or Sheffe, have built-in procedures designed to deal with problems with the Type I error level. These problems are too complex to discuss adequately here. The interested student can consult Shavelson (1996) for computational procedures and the rationale. The basics of these procedures are also covered on the Student Resource Website.

10:04

Interpreting the results of a study is a process of making sense out of complicated findings. A useful first step in the interpretation process is to look at the pattern of means. The means for the typing-speed example are listed in Table 10.2 and organized into a graph in Figure 10.12. Graphs are usually easier to read than tables and are particularly helpful when there is more than one independent variable.

EXTENDING THE CONCEPT OF GRAPHS

You learned how to create graphs in Chapter 5. The graph in Figure 10.12 is a frequency polygon. However, it has a useful addition that is now routinely used in research articles. Each data point has a vertical bar going through it, called the **error bar**. The error bar indicates the size of the **standard error of the mean,** which is an index of how close the sample mean is likely to be to the population mean. It is a function of the natural variability of the scores and the size of the sample on which the mean is based. The greater the variability of scores, the harder it is to get a precise estimate of the population mean from the sample, and larger sample sizes tend to produce closer estimate of the population mean.

The addition of error bars to a frequency polygon allows statistically sophisticated researchers to tell at a glance which means are likely to be statistically different from each other. When the error bars do not overlap, the means are likely to be significant when tested statistically. This information does not replace the formal statistical test, but it does make the graph easier to interpret.

10:05

This is a rather complex statistical concept, and we do not have space in the text to cover it for you. However, the concept is covered on the Student Resource Website.

The basic experimental designs covered in this chapter have served researchers well, but several other experimental designs are also available. Researchers make two distinctions in experimental research designs. One distinction is between **independent-groups designs** (also called between-subjects designs) and **correlated-groups designs** (either within-subjects designs or matched-subjects designs). In independent-groups designs, different participants appear in each group. In correlated-groups designs, the same or closely

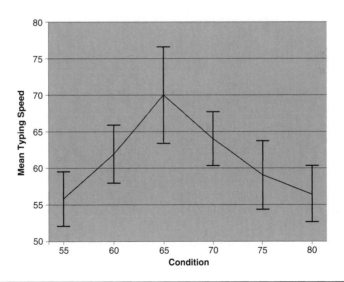

FIGURE 10.12 *Effects of Room Temperature on Typing Speed* The graph of the data on the effects of room temperature on typing speed indicates that optimal typing speed occurs at a temperature of 65°. The vertical bars at each data point indicate the size of the standard error of the mean.

matched participants appear in each group. The second distinction is between **single-variable designs** (also called **univariate designs**) and **multivariable designs** (also called **factorial designs**). Single-variable designs have only one independent variable, whereas factorial designs have two or more independent variables in a single study. This chapter covered single-variable, independent-groups designs. Chapters 11 and 12 cover correlated-groups designs and factorial designs, respectively.

Quick-Check Review 10.4: Statistical Analysis	1. At what measurement levels are chi-square and Mann Whitney *U*-tests used?
	2. Under what conditions is the *t*-test most likely used? The ANOVA?
	3. What information is typically found in the ANOVA summary table?
	4. In ANOVA, what does it mean if the *F*-ratio is significant?
	5. What are *planned comparisons* and *post hoc tests*?

PUTTING IT INTO PRACTICE	We implicitly use nonexperimental research designs every day as we observe the world and try to make sense out of it. When we meet someone who is obnoxious, we may want to know why that person is obnoxious and may draw ex post facto conclusions based on the limited information that we have about the person. We may also take these conclusions and use them to predict the behavior of other people. You have learned in this chapter how foolish such actions are.

For the next week or so, watch as you observe the world and try to make sense of it. Look at the evidence that is available to you and ask yourself how good that evidence is. This is a very good habit to get into, one that will prevent you from making numerous mistakes in life based on drawing conclusions from inadequate evidence. See if you can take the principles of this chapter and this text and use them to decide what would constitute adequate evidence for drawing accurate conclusions about the questions you face every day.

This process is called **critical thinking,** and it is perhaps the most important skill a person can develop. You can think of this entire course as a critical thinking exercise applied to psychological research, but if you also recognize that such thinking can be applied to many life situations, two things will happen. The first is that you will think more clearly in your everyday life, making better decisions and avoiding many of the mistakes that are so common in life. The second is that the material in this text will be much easier to remember, because you will be able to code the information in terms of concepts that you already know from your daily life experiences. Give it a try.

Chapter Summary

Experimental design focuses on controlling unwanted variance and thus reducing threats to validity. Variance includes systematic between-groups variance and nonsystematic within-groups error variance. Between-groups variance is a function of both experimental variance (due to the independent variable) and extraneous variance (due to confounding variables). A major goal in experimentation is to design studies that maximize experimental variance, control extraneous variance, and minimize error variance.

There are many experimental designs. We have organized them along two dimensions: (1) single-variable versus factorial designs and (2) correlated-groups versus independent-groups designs. This chapter focused exclusively on independent-groups, single-variable designs. Later chapters will cover correlated-groups designs, factorial designs, and several specialized experimental designs used in field settings.

Chapter Exercises

1. Define the following key terms. Be sure that you understand them. They are discussed in the chapter and defined in the glossary.

   between-groups variance
   experimental variance
   extraneous variance
   systematic between-
   groups variance
   nonsystematic within-
   groups variance, or
   error variance
   manipulation check
   ex post facto study
   single-group, posttest-
   only study
   single-group, pretest-
   posttest study
   time-series design
   pretest-posttest, natural
   control-group study
   experimental designs
   single-variable, between-
   subjects designs
   randomized, posttest-
   only, control-group
   design
   statistically equal
   randomized, pretest-
   posttest, control-
   group design

   multilevel, completely
   randomized, between-
   subjects design
   Solomon's four-group
   design
   unbiased assignment
   error term
   within-groups variance
   between-groups variance
   sum of squares
   partitioned
   mean squares
   ANOVA summary
   table
   F-test
   probe
   planned comparison
   a priori comparison
   contrast
   post hoc comparison
   a posteriori comparison
   incidental comparison
   error bar
   standard error of the
   mean
   independent-groups
   designs

   correlated-groups designs
   single-variable design, or
   univariate designs
   multivariable design, or
   factorial design
   critical thinking

2. You are the teaching assistant for this course and must explain variability to your students. How would you explain the concept, its measure, and its importance?

3. Why is it important to minimize the error variance in the *F*-test?

4. Define an ex post facto study and explain why it is a weak design.

5. What is the relationship among the concepts of confounding variables, threats to validity, and extraneous variance?

6. Does a high between-groups variance in an experiment provide sufficient evidence to conclude that the independent variable affected the dependent variable? Explain

7. For each of the following designs (i) give an example, (ii) identify the major threats to validity, and (iii) state the limits on the conclusions that can be drawn.

   a. Single-group, posttest-only design

   b. Ex post facto design

   c. Single-group, pretest-posttest design

   d. Pretest-posttest, natural control-group design

8. As the course teaching assistant, you are to explain the *F*-ratio. Define all of its components, and explain the logic of the *F*-test.

9. For each of the following types of experimental designs (i) give an example and (ii) indicate what threats to validity are controlled.

a. Randomized, posttest-only, control-group design

b. Randomized, pretest-posttest, control-group design

c. Multilevel, completely randomized, between-subjects design

d. Solomon four-group design

11

Correlated-Groups and Single-Subject Designs

The real problem is not whether machines think, but whether men do.

—B. F. Skinner (1969), *Contingencies of Reinforcement*

Within-Subjects Designs
Using Within-Subjects Designs
Analyzing Within-Subjects Designs
Strengths and Weaknesses of Within-Subjects
Designs

Matched-Subjects Designs
Using Matched-Subjects Designs
Analyzing Matched-Subjects Designs
Strengths and Weaknesses of Matched-Subjects
Designs

Single-Subject Experimental Designs
HISTORICAL LESSON 11.1: Neuropsychology Cases
ABA Reversal Designs
Multiple-Baseline Designs
Single-Subject, Randomized Time-Series Designs
Replication in Single-Subject Designs

Putting It into Practice

Chapter Summary

Chapter Exercises

Web Resource Material

Random assignment of participants to conditions, discussed in Chapter 9, is a major corner-stone of experimental design. It assures the statistical equivalence of groups at the beginning of the study, thus making it possible to compare groups that experience different experimental manipulations. *Randomization is our most basic and single most important control procedure.* It can control for threats to internal and external validity, can control several factors simulta-neously, and is the only procedure that can control for unknown factors. As we said in Chapter 9, a good general rule for the researcher is, whenever possible, randomize. (The designs cov-ered in Chapter 10 are based on the random assignment of participants to conditions.)

Sometimes randomization is not possible or desired. However, in order to assess the validity of experimental effects, we must still address the issue of the initial equivalence of groups, thus posing the question, "How are we to carry out experiments without random as-signment?" One answer is to use a **correlated-groups design.** Correlated-groups designs, featured in this chapter, take a different approach. They assure group equivalence by using either the same participants in all groups or participants that have been closely matched. They are called correlated-groups designs because this assignment strategy assures that the participants in one group are correlated with the participants in the other groups. Some re-searchers do not consider correlated-groups designs to be experiments, because they do not use free random assignment. However, we consider them to be experiments, because they meet the requirements of equivalence of groups and because other controls can be applied to eliminate rival hypotheses.

This chapter covers three correlated-groups designs. *Within-subjects designs* (also called **repeated-measures designs**) test participants under all conditions. *Matched-subjects designs* match participants on relevant variables prior to the study and then randomly assign the matched sets of participants, one member of each set to each group. This chapter also covers *single-subject experimental designs,* which are extensions of within-subjects designs.

Within-Subjects Designs

In within-subjects designs, participants are exposed to all experimental conditions, thereby making the conditions correlated. *In essence, each participant serves as his or her own control.* This section discusses how to use and analyze within-subjects designs and the strengths and weaknesses of these designs.

Using Within-Subjects Designs

Suppose that in a target-detection experiment we want to test whether the time that partici-pants take to find a target among an array of distracter items is affected by the number of dis-tracters present. The target in this experiment is a letter, either T or F. Arrays of letters are presented on a computer screen, and somewhere in the array is one of the two target letters. The participant's task is to find the single target in each letter array and press either the T or F response button. Each person is tested under three conditions of distraction: 10, 15, and 20 distracter items. There are 10 trials at each of the three levels of distraction. The dependent variable is the speed of the detection responses, and the 10 trial times are summed to give the total search time for each distraction level. The hypothesis is that finding the target will take longer if there are more distracters. The design of this study is illustrated in Figure 11.1. This is a within-subjects design, and the characteristics of within-subjects designs are as follows:

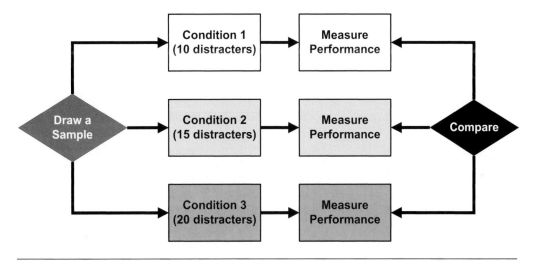

FIGURE 11.1 *An Example of a Within-Subjects Design* In a within-subjects design, the same people are tested under all conditions. The order of presentation of conditions varies from participant to participant, as shown in Table 11.1.

1. Each participant is tested under each experimental condition.
2. Therefore, the scores in each condition are correlated with the scores in the other conditions.
3. The critical comparison is the difference between correlated groups on the dependent variable.

EXTENDING THE CONCEPT OF SEQUENCE EFFECTS

In Chapter 8, you learned about sequence effects. Because each participant is exposed to all conditions in within-subjects designs, exposure to earlier conditions may affect performance on later conditions. The within-subjects design is similar to a single-group, pretest-posttest design except that in the pretest-posttest design, each participant responds to the pretest and the posttest in that order. In contrast, in within-subjects designs, each participant responds in two or more conditions, and the order of presentation of conditions is not necessarily fixed, as it must be in a pretest-posttest study.

In within-subjects designs, differences between conditions might be due, not to the independent variable, but to the confounding effects of one condition on later conditions. These sequence effects are controlled by **counterbalancing,** in which the order of presentation of conditions to participants is systematically varied. In **complete counterbalancing,** all possible orders of conditions occur an equal number of times. The result is that (1) each participant is exposed to all conditions of the experiment, (2) each condition is presented an equal number of times, (3) each condition is presented an equal number of times in each position, and (4) each condition precedes and follows each other condition an equal number of times. Sequence effects and their controls are discussed more extensively later in this chapter.

TABLE 11.1   *Hypothetical Data for the Target-Search Study*

Participants	Order of Presentation	Condition (Search time in seconds)		
		A (10)	B (15)	C (20)
1	ABC	18.33	22.39	24.97
2	ACB	15.96	20.72	21.79
3	BAC	19.02	22.78	25.46
4	BCA	25.36	27.48	27.91
5	CAB	19.52	24.64	26.75
6	CBA	23.27	24.96	25.49
Mean scores		20.24	23.83	25.40

Table 11.1 shows the various orders of conditions for the hypothetical target-search study described earlier. Note that this set of orders meets the four conditions outlined in the previous paragraph. Hypothetical data for the experiment are also given in Table 11.1. The data are the total time (in seconds) required to find the targets at the three levels of distraction. The first column lists the six participants, the second column shows the order of presentation of the stimulus conditions to each participant, and the last three columns show the search times for each of the three experimental conditions.

Analyzing Within-Subjects Designs

The first step in analyzing the results of within-subjects designs is to organize and summarize the data, as shown in Table 11.1. In this hypothetical study, the search times are longest, on average, for the 20-distracter condition, shorter for the 15-distracter condition, and shortest for the 10-distracter condition.

These results suggest that the hypothesis might be supported. Are the differences between conditions large enough to state with confidence that similar differences exist in the populations? In other words, are the differences statistically significant? The most commonly used statistical analysis for within-subjects experiments is an ANOVA similar to the one discussed in Chapter 10. However, because the conditions are correlated in a within-subjects design, the ANOVA is modified to consider this correlation. The appropriate ANOVA for a within-subjects design is called a **repeated-measures ANOVA.**

EXTENDING THE CONCEPT OF STATISTICAL POWER

You learned in Chapter 5 that statistical power is an index of the sensitivity of a research study to small differences between groups, and that this sensitivity is a function of both the statistical procedure and the design. The major advantage of a within-subjects design is that it effectively equates the conditions prior to the experiment by using the same participants in each condition. Therefore, it removes the single largest contributing factor to error variance—individual differences.

What effect does this have on the *F*-ratio? Because the individual difference portion of the error term has been removed, the denominator in the *F*-ratio is smaller and therefore the *F* is larger. This means that the procedure will be more sensitive to small differences between groups. Statistical power is increased; consequently, you can detect smaller differences between conditions without having to increase sample size to enhance power.

In a repeated-measures ANOVA, the total sum of squares is computed in the same way as in a one-way ANOVA. What is called a between-groups sum of squares in a one-way ANOVA is called a **between-conditions sum of squares,** or simply a **between sum of squares,** in a repeated-measures ANOVA. Terminology is changed in the repeated-measures ANOVA because there is only one group of participants.

The within-groups sum of squares in the repeated-measures ANOVA is split into two terms: subjects and error. The **subjects term** is the individual differences component of the within-groups variability. The **error term** is what is left when the individual differences component is removed. The repeated-measures ANOVA tests the null hypothesis of no differences between conditions by dividing the mean square between by the mean square error. As in the independent-groups ANOVA, the ratio of mean squares is an *F*-ratio. A conceptual explanation and computational procedures for a repeated-measures ANOVA are presented on the Student Resource Website. Table 11.2 presents the results of the analysis of the data from Table 11.1.

11:01
11:02

A significant *F*-ratio in the ANOVA indicates that at least one of the condition means is significantly different from at least one other condition mean. Additional tests must be conducted to determine which means are significantly different from which other means. These tests are conceptually identical to the planned comparisons and post hoc tests discussed in Chapter 10, except different statistical procedures are involved, which take into account the correlated nature of the data. Computational procedures for these tests can be found in most advanced statistics textbooks (e.g., Keppel, 2006; Myers & Well, 2003). Most computerized statistical analysis packages include these tests as an option.

Strengths and Weaknesses of Within-Subjects Designs

Within-subjects designs have important advantages. First, because the same participants are in each condition, there are no group differences due to sampling error. Participants in

TABLE 11.2 *Summary Table (Repeated-Measures ANOVA)*

Source	df	SS	MS	F	p
Between	2	83.69	41.85	32.25	< .001
Subjects	5	95.85	19.17		
Error	10	12.97	1.30		

each condition are guaranteed to be equivalent at the start of the study, thus eliminating the possible confounding due to initial group differences.

Another important advantage is that within-subjects designs are more sensitive than between-subjects designs to the effects of the independent variable. Why is that true? Remember the design principle that researchers should try to maximize experimental variance (variance due to the effects of the independent variable), control extraneous variance (variance due to confounding), and minimize error variance (variance due to individual differences and chance factors). A within-subjects design not only minimizes, but actually eliminates the variance due to individual differences, thereby reducing the error term in the ANOVA.

The larger the individual differences in a population, the greater the benefit derived from using a within-subjects design. This greater sensitivity to the effects of the independent variable leads many researchers to prefer within-subjects designs to between-subjects designs when given the choice.

Another advantage of a within-subjects design is that fewer participants are needed. For example, an independent-groups design that has 20 participants in each of three conditions will require 60 participants. Using a within-subjects design that has 20 participants per condition will require only 20 participants. In addition, because of its greater sensitivity, the within-subjects design might require even fewer participants per condition to achieve the same level of statistical power. For example, 14 participants in a within-subjects design might provide the same statistical power as 20 participants per condition in a between-subjects design. Reducing the sample size normally reduces statistical power, but the greater sensitivity of the within-subjects design will balance the loss of statistical power from using fewer participants.

There is yet another advantage of within-subjects designs, one that further increases efficiency. Because the same participants are tested under several conditions, instructions can be given once instead of at the beginning of each condition, or the instructions may require only slight modifications for each condition. For example, the participants in the target search study have the same task in each condition, so there is no need to repeat the instructions. If the instructions are complicated or if a practice period is part of the instructions, the time savings can be considerable.

EXTENDING THE CONCEPT OF SEQUENCE EFFECTS

Although within-subjects designs have many advantages, they have one major disadvantage—confounding due to *sequence effects,* which you learned about in Chapter 8. Sequence effects are strongest when a treatment has a permanent or long-lasting effect on participants. Examples can be found in animal experimentation, when chemical or surgical changes are implemented, or in human experiments, when knowledge or attitudes are changed. A within-subjects design should not be used when the effects are permanent or long lasting. Even if the effects are temporary, there is still the risk of sequence effects.

The two most important sequence effects are *practice effects* and *carryover effects.* **Practice effects** are due to the growing experience with procedures over successive conditions, rather than to influences of any particular condition on other conditions. If there are five conditions, for example, many participants will perform better in the last two or three conditions because of practice effects. This enhancement of performance on later conditions represents a **positive practice effect.** On the other hand, if the procedure is lengthy or demanding, participants might become fatigued, and their performance will decline in later conditions. This is called a **negative practice effect.** Both practice effects can confound a study if not controlled. Practice effects depend on participants' experience as they move sequentially through the conditions, so they occur regardless of the particular sequence of conditions.

Carryover effects are due to the influence of a particular condition or combination of conditions on responses to later condition(s). Carryover effects may be greater for one condition than for the others. For example, there may be some aspect of a particular condition (for example, condition A) that produces an effect on any condition that follows it. Thus, wherever condition A appears in a sequence, the next condition will be influenced.

Suppose that in the target-detection study described earlier, the conditions are always presented in the following order: 10-15-20-distracter conditions. Furthermore, suppose that the participants are capable of finding the target in the 10-distracter condition by focusing on all 11 items at once (called parallel search), but the 15- and 20-distracter conditions have too many items for this strategy to work.

The optimal strategy for a search where there are many distracters is to look systematically at each letter until the target is found (called serial search). If the 10-distracter list always appears first, the participants will learn to try a parallel search, which will hamper target detection in the 15- and 20-distracter conditions and distort the data. If, on the other hand, the 20-distracter list always appears first, the participants will learn to try the serial search first, thus distorting the data for the 10-distracter condition. Note that carryover effects of one condition may be the same on all subsequent conditions, or they might affect only some of the subsequent conditions.

In either case, carryover effects are an extraneous variable and must be controlled.

There are two ways of controlling sequence effects: (1) holding the extraneous variable constant and (2) varying the order of presentation of conditions. Positive practice effects can be controlled by holding the practice variable constant. Specifically, all participants can be trained to the same criterion of performance before the first condition begins. Thus, all participants will be familiar with the procedures before they respond to any of the experimental conditions. A control for fatigue (negative practice effects) could be the inclusion of a rest period between the conditions, allowing fatigue to dissipate before going on to the next condition.

These procedures minimize practice effects, but control is best achieved by varying the order of presentation of conditions. Varying the order of presentation of conditions is the *only* way to control carryover effects. It can be accomplished by using either a random or a counterbalanced order of pres-entation. The logic of both procedures is to control sequence effects by having these effects contribute equally to all conditions. In a **random order of presentation,** each participant is randomly assigned to a different order of the conditions. In this way, practice effects are not systematically maximized in one condition, and carryover effects should occur as much under any one condition as under any other.

Counterbalancing involves systematically arranging the order of conditions so that all possible orders are represented the same number of times. Counterbalancing can be complete or partial. To calculate how many conditions are needed for complete counterbalancing, you need to calculate $X!$ (X factorial), in which X is the number of conditions. A factorial is calculated by multiplying the number by all integers smaller than the number.

Thus, for the target-detection study, which has three conditions, there are six possible orders ($X! = 3 \times 2 \times 1 = 6$). The six possible orders are shown in Table 11.1. Participants are assigned to orders of presentation, with an equal number of participants assigned to each order. If there are 30 participants, 5 will be assigned to each of the 6 orders.

Counterbalancing is best used with a small number of conditions. With two conditions, there are only two orders of presentation ($X! = 2 \times 1 = 2$). With three conditions, there are six orders of presentation. However, with four conditions, there are 24 orders ($X! = 4 \times 3 \times 2 \times 1 = 24$), and if the experiment has five conditions, there are 120 orders ($X! = 5 \times 4 \times 3 \times 2 \times 1 = 120$).

Suppose an experiment has seven conditions. Go ahead and calculate how many orders of presentation would be needed for complete counterbalancing. As you will see, the number of possible orders rises rapidly as the number of conditions increases.

As the number of conditions increases, the use of complete counterbalancing becomes unwieldy. Complete counterbalancing is not feasible for more than three or four conditions. If there are more conditions, **partial counterbalancing** may be the best solution. For example, to meet the counterbalancing criteria for four conditions, one would need at least 24 participants.

What if you have only 10 participants and four conditions, and you still want to use a within-subjects design and control for sequence effects? In this case, you could (1) randomize the order of presentation for each participant, (2) randomly select 10 of the 24 possible orders and randomly assign participants to these orders, or (3) use a more formalized partial counterbalancing procedure known as a **Latin square design.** Latin squares are counterbalanced arrangements named after an ancient Roman puzzle that required arranging letters in rows and columns so that each letter occurred only once in each row and once in each column. The result is that all letters appear an equal number of times, all appear in each position in the sequence an equal number of times, and all letters follow each other letter an equal number of times. More complete discussions of Latin square designs are provided in Edwards (1998), Keppel (2006), and Myers and Well (2003). The Student Resources Website shows how to set up a Latin Square.

11:03

There is another approach to reducing sequence effects, but it is possible only in some situations. In the target-detection example, each condition consisted of 10 trials. The earlier presentation suggested that all 10 trials would be completed together, but often that is unnecessary. If, instead, the researcher took the 30 trials (10 in each of the 3 conditions) and randomly ordered them, sequencing would be reasonably controlled.

If the researcher did not want to completely trust randomization, trials could be **randomized within blocks.** Here, this would involve breaking the 30 individual trials into blocks of trials in which a block includes one trial from each condition, and then randomizing the order of presentation of the trials within each of these blocks. This procedure produces a random order, but without the possibility of one condition tending to have most of the trials either at the beginning or end of the testing. The Student Resource Website demonstrates the process of randomizing within blocks.

11:04

EXTENDING THE CONCEPT OF CONTROL OVER SEQUENCE EFFECTS

If strong carryover effects are expected, the within-subjects design is not recommended, even if the preceding controls are included. Carryover effects tend to add error variance to scores, which can offset any increased sensitivity normally expected from a within-subjects design. If strong carryover effects are expected, it is best to use either a between-subjects design or a matched-subjects design.

The ability to control sequence effects is the reason that the within-subjects design is considered an experimental design and the single-group, pretest-posttest design is considered a nonexperimental design. The order of presentation in the pretest-posttest design cannot be counterbalanced, because the pretest must always precede the treatment and the posttest must always follow the treatment. Therefore, the pretest-posttest design requires a separate control group to control confounding.

In summary, the within-subjects design is a correlated-groups design in which each participant is tested under each condition. The major strength of the within-subjects design is that it *equates* groups prior to the experimental manipulation and is therefore more sensitive to the effects of the independent variable. Using the same participants in each condition eliminates the single largest contributing factor to error variance—individual differences.

The greater sensitivity of the within-subjects design leads many researchers to prefer it to between-subjects designs. The major disadvantage of this design is sequence effects, which are controlled by varying the order of presentation of conditions. Examples of the use of the within-subjects design from the research literature are presented on the Student Resource Website.

11:05

Quick-Check Review 11.1: Within-Subjects Designs	1. What are correlated-groups designs?
	2. What is the major potential confounding factor in within-subjects designs, and how can it be controlled?
	3. How do within-subjects designs reduce error variance?
	4. What are the strengths and weaknesses of within-subjects designs?
	5. What is meant by complete counterbalancing?

Matched-Subjects Designs

Matched-subjects designs have many of the strengths of within-subjects designs, as well as some advantages of their own. Instead of using each participant as his or her own control by testing each participant under all conditions, the matched-subjects design uses different participants in each condition but closely matches them before they are assigned to conditions. This process of matching before assignment to conditions is referred to as

matched random assignment (see Chapter 9). The characteristics of matched-subjects designs are the following:

1. Each participant is exposed to only one level of the independent variable.
2. Each participant has a matched participant in each of the other conditions so that the groups are correlated.
3. The analysis takes into account which participants were matched with which other participants.
4. The critical comparison is the difference between the correlated groups, in which the correlation is created by the matching procedure.

Although matched-subjects designs are not used often, they are valuable. They are most likely to be used when the cost of the study per participant is very high, thus limiting the sample that can be studied. In such a case, matching increases the sensitivity and statistical power of the study without adding extensively to the cost. The rest of this section covers when and how to use the matched-subjects design, how to analyze data from matched-subject studies, and the strengths and weaknesses of the design.

Using Matched-Subjects Designs

Matched-subjects designs are used when researchers want to take advantage of the greater sensitivity of within-subjects designs but cannot use, or prefer not to use, a within-subjects design. Matched-subjects designs are most often used when exposure to one condition causes long-term changes in participants, making it impossible for participants to appear in the other conditions. For example, when surgical procedures are used in physiological studies, the procedures permanently alter the animal, making it impossible to use the animal in another condition that requires non-altered participants. When participants learn a content area or behavior under one condition of a learning study, they are no longer suitable participants for testing under other conditions.

For example, suppose that the Air Force wanted to compare two methods of teaching map reading to its navigation students. If one group of participants was successfully taught map reading using method A, then these participants could not be used for testing the effectiveness of method B. A separate group of participants would have to be trained using method B, and then the two groups would be compared. These are examples of extreme forms of carryover effects. As you learned earlier, it is best to avoid within-subjects designs if large carryover effects are anticipated.

There are other situations in which a researcher might choose to avoid a within-subjects design. One situation is when the demands on participants' time in each condition are excessive, so that it is unreasonable to ask participants to be tested under all conditions. Researchers may also choose to avoid a within-subjects design if they are concerned that participants who are tested under all conditions might discern the hypothesis of the study, and thus influence the results through expectancy effects and/or demand characteristics (see Chapter 8).

To avoid the problems of within-subjects designs, researchers can choose an independent-groups design and randomly assign participants to each of the various experimental conditions. However, an independent-groups design relies on chance to equate the groups. It is not as sensitive to small effects of the independent variable as is a correlated-groups design, because statistical tests must take into account the possibility that independent groups of participants may not be equal on the dependent measure before the study begins. Matched-subjects designs provide a solution to this problem; they make it more likely that the groups are equivalent at the beginning of the study by explicitly matching on relevant variables.

EXTENDING THE CONCEPT OF MATCHING

You learned about matched random assignment in Chapter 9. Now you will learn more about how it is carried out. How do you match participants for a matched-subjects design? You want to match participants on relevant variables, but what does this mean? Which variables are relevant? In a within-subjects design, these questions are immaterial, because each participant serves as his or her own control. Participants are matched on all variables, whether relevant or not, because they are the same participants in each condition.

However, many factors that differentiate one person from another may be irrelevant for a particular study. For example, eye color may be a relevant variable if you are studying ways of increasing attractiveness but is probably irrelevant if you are studying visual acuity. *A variable is relevant if it is likely to have an effect on the dependent variable in a study.* Participants' eye color may influence the ratings of their attractiveness but should not influence how well they see.

The more powerful the effect of a variable on the dependent variable, the more important it is to match participants on this variable to assure comparable groups. To use a matched-subjects design effectively, you must identify the relevant variables and match the groups participant by participant on these variables.

This principle for identifying relevant matching variables should sound familiar to you, because we talked about a similar problem when we discussed confounding in differential research. In that case, we noted that confounding could occur only if the potential confounding variable was correlated with the dependent measure *and* there was a difference between the groups on the potential confounding variable.

Variables that are related to the dependent measure are often problematic in research and therefore require some type of control. The control that we use in a matched-subjects design is to make sure that the groups do not differ on potential confounding variables by matching on those variables.

The procedure for matching participants on a given variable and assigning them to groups was described in Chapter 9 in the discussion of matched random assignment. In that example, we matched participants on years of work experience by ordering them on this variable. We then divided them into pairs by selecting the two with the longest work experience, then the two with the next longest work experience, and so on. Finally, we randomly assigned one member of each pair to one of the two groups and automatically assigned his or her partner to the other group. The result was two groups of participants matched on the variable of length of work experience.

It is legitimate during the pairing process to exclude participants for whom a close match is not available. For example, one participant may have worked at a job much longer than anyone else. This participant would not be paired with any other participant and so would not be assigned to any condition. We could have extended this process to three or more conditions by matching in sets of three or more participants. We would then have randomly assigned one member from the matched set to the first condition, randomly assigned one of the remaining members to the second condition, and so on until there was only one member left in the matched set and only one condition for this person. Of course, as we increase the number of experimental conditions to which we want to assign matched participants, we also increase the likelihood that participants will have to be excluded, because enough close matches cannot be found for them.

One can extend the matching procedure to matching on more than one variable. Matching on sex and years of work experience of the participants, for example, is only slightly more complicated than matching on work experience alone, because one of the matching variables (sex) has only two levels. We could pair participants on work experience, except that we would pair the males only with other males and the females only with other females. This way, participants in each pair would be similar to each other on both matching variables; that is, they would be the same sex and have approximately the same level of work experience. We might lose a few more participants than before from the potential sample, because appropriate matches could not be found, but the loss should not be too great.

A general rule of thumb is that matching on more than one continuous variable is difficult to accomplish and will usually result in significant participant loss. If we match on two variables in which both variables are continuous, participant loss can be large, because an appropriate match for each participant may be hard to find. For example, if we match on age and IQ, we would first want to order all the participants on one of the variables, such as age. We would then divide the participants into small subgroups defined by having all the participants in each group within a narrow age range. Within each of these subgroups, we would then order on the second variable of IQ. Next, within each group, we would pair as many participants as possible using the criterion that each member of the pair must have similar IQs. We would probably find several people in each age group with no close IQ match, and these people would be excluded from the potential sample.

If the study required three conditions, we would match in triplets, which would make it even more likely that participants would be excluded, because appropriate matches could not be found.

EXTENDING THE CONCEPT OF MATCHING EVEN FURTHER

Now that you know how to match, how do you decide what variables to match on? If matching is used as a research strategy, it is best to match on only one or two of the most important and significant variables. *Choose variables that are strongly related to performance on the dependent measure(s).* If age makes little difference in how participants perform on the dependent measure, it makes little sense to match participants on age. Because age does not affect the dependent measure, it cannot confound the results, just as it could not confound the results in differential research.

If we have several variables that could have strong effects on the dependent measure, matching on all of them simultaneously is unworkable. Instead, we should match on those variables that show the greatest variance in the population.

Characteristics that are more variable in the population are more likely to show large mean differences by chance in randomly selected groups if an explicit matching procedure is not employed. You learned about this principle when we discussed sampling error and the factors that influence it. Therefore, characteristics that show significant variability in the population should be given the highest priority when deciding on which variables to match in a matched-subjects design. For example, if college students are the participants, age is probably not an important variable on which to match, because there is little variability in age among college students, and a difference of one or two years makes little difference in students' behavior. However, when doing research with young children, age can be an extremely important variable. An age difference in children of even a few months can have major effects on their behavior. Therefore, matching on age is an important control in many research studies with children.

Although it can be difficult to identify the critical variables on which to match, in most cases the needed information is already available in published studies. These studies often report observed correlations of many potential confounding variables with their dependent measures. We talked earlier about how correlational research is often included in other research studies to help explain the results or to see whether there might be confounding variables present. If you are using similar dependent measures in your study, these correlations will help you to decide on which variables to match.

You should familiarize yourself with past research and with the population that you are studying in order to make good design decisions. This is true regardless of the design being contemplated but is particularly true in matched-subjects designs.

Even with the information from past research, you are unlikely to identify all confounding variables for matching. Therefore, it is necessary to randomly assign participants in a matched set to conditions. Random assignment within sets will controls for unidentified confounding variables.

Analyzing Matched-Subjects Designs

Analyzing data from a matched-subjects design is no more complicated than analyzing data from a within-subjects design. The key is to maintain the ordering of data from the matching of participants at the beginning of the study through the analysis of data at the end. In a within-subjects design, the scores from each condition for a given participant are put on the same line, as shown in Table 11.1. In a matched-subjects design, the scores on a given line would represent the scores of different participants tested under different conditions, but all the participants in a given line would have been specifically matched with the other participants on that line prior to the beginning of the study.

Once the data are organized, we analyze them as if all the scores on a given line came from the same participant, instead of from matched participants. The repeated-measures ANOVA is used to determine whether the observed mean differences between groups are large enough to assert that real differences exist in the populations; that is, are the differences statistically significant? If participants are carefully matched on relevant variable(s), then their scores on the dependent measures in each condition should be correlated with one another.

Strengths and Weaknesses of Matched-Subjects Designs

Matched-subjects designs have strengths similar to those of within-subjects designs but have different weaknesses. Both types of design have greater sensitivity to small differences between conditions than do between-subjects designs. Whereas between-subjects designs rely on chance to equate groups, correlated-groups designs use assignment procedures that almost guarantee that groups are equivalent. If we are sure that the groups are equivalent before the study begins, they do not have to show large differences after the manipulation to convince us that the independent variable had an effect.

Because matched- and within-subjects designs have greater sensitivity, the researcher can use a smaller number of participants and still be confident about detecting population differences if differences exist. For example, for three conditions with 20 participants in each condition, a between-subjects design will require 60 participants. However, because of the greater sensitivity of the matched-subjects design, we may need only 16 matched participants in each condition to test the null hypothesis with the same confidence that we would have using 20 participants in each condition in the between-subjects design. This is a direct consequence of the increased statistical power or sensitivity of the designs: we can safely reduce the sample size because the design provides a balancing increase in sensitivity.

An advantage of the matched-subjects design over the within-subjects design is that there are no problems of practice and carryover effects. Therefore, such control procedures as counterbalancing are not needed. However, there are disadvantages to using a matched-subjects design. One is that it requires extra work. The researcher must decide on what variable(s) to match and must obtain measures of this variable from all potential participants. The matching process is tedious, especially when matching on more than one variable. Finally, the requirement of matching participants in sets can eliminate many potential participants, because suitable matches cannot be found for them. We may need to pretest a large sample of participants on the matching variables to obtain a modest sample of matched participants. It may be more efficient to use large sample sizes in a between-subjects design.

In summary, a matched-subjects design is used when increased sensitivity is needed and when a within-subjects design is inappropriate because large carryover effects are expected. Matched-subjects designs have many of the advantages of within-subjects designs and avoid the problems of sequence effects. In the simplest situation (two conditions), participants are matched in pairs on one or more relevant variables. Then one member of the pair is randomly assigned to one condition and the other member is automatically assigned to the other condition, a process known as matched random assignment. In a situation with three conditions, participants are matched in triplets and each member of the triplet is randomly assigned to one of three conditions. Examples of research using matched-subjects designs are included on the Student Resource Website.

11:06

Quick-Check Review 11.2: Matched-Subjects Designs	1. What major confounding factor found in within-subjects designs is avoided by using matched-subjects designs? 2. What are the characteristics of matched-subjects designs? 3. Under what conditions would we use matched-subjects designs? 4. What are the disadvantages of using matched-subjects designs?

Single-Subject Experimental Designs

Single-subject (or *N-of-one*) **experimental designs** are extensions of within-subject designs, because each participant appears in each condition of the experiment. They are also variations on time-series designs (discussed in Chapter 13), in which repeated measurements are taken over time and manipulations are performed at different points along the time sequence. Single-subject experimental designs have become highly developed alternatives to more traditional group designs. For example, they are used routinely in research on behavior modification to evaluate treatment effects (Barlow & Hersen, 1984). They also have played an extensive role in understanding the functioning of the human brain, as illustrated in the *Historical Lesson 11.1*.

HISTORICAL LESSON 11.1:   *Neuropsychology Cases*

Neuropsychology is a field that relates the status of brain functioning to behavior (Saucier & Elias, 2006). This field has advanced dramatically in the last century, often by groundbreaking research involving unusual cases. One of the most famous subjects was Phineas Gage, a railroad construction foreman who lived in Vermont over a century ago. While using a metal bar to pack explosives into a hole, he accidentally set off the explosives, turning the bar into a deadly projectile that ripped through his left cheek and blew off the top of his skull, taking his left eye and a good portion of his brain in the process. Miraculously, Gage survived, but the accident left him a changed man. You might think that having a sizable portion of your brain ripped out of your head would leave you a vegetable, but the changes in Gage were far more subtle. He went from being a responsible, caring person to one who had little self-control, used profanity constantly, and had little regard for the welfare of others. He had been organized and disciplined, but after the accident he was disorganized and unable to complete the most routine tasks. Formerly a decisive leader, he could no longer make even routine decisions. Gage had changed in fundamental ways. These changes in his behavior and personality gave early neuropsychologists some excellent clues about what role the parts of the brain damaged in Gage's accident played in human behavior.

Another well-known case study in the neuropsychological literature is known by the person's initials (H.M.). H.M.'s memory problems developed after he had surgery to remove brain tissue that was triggering severe and overwhelming seizures. The surgery controlled H.M.'s seizures, but it had a devastating side effect: H.M. could no longer form new memories, although his old memories were intact. Because H.M. could not form new memories, each time one of his doctors stopped by, H.M. would introduce himself, apparently completely unaware that he had met his doctors many times before. No matter how many times he met a doctor, he never remembered that they had met. To test whether H.M could remember anything about his daily encounters with his doctors, one doctor hid a pin in his hand and poked H.M. with it while shaking hands. The next day, H.M. again did not recognize the doctor and started to introduce himself as usual, but he pulled back his hand when the doctor reached out to shake it (Hugdahl, 1995). What was going on? Was H.M. faking his memory problem, and was the doctor able to unmask that effort with his hidden pin trick? Not at all. H.M. really did have no memory of his hundreds of encounters with each of his doctors. What this case study established is that a specific region of the brain (the hippocampus) is critical in forming memories of events. It also shows that there are different kinds of memories and that different brain regions are involved in forming them. Learning to avoid a painful pinprick is a different type of memory than remembering what you did yesterday, and that type of memory formation was not impaired in H.M.

Dozens of such case histories in neuropsychology have provided extensive insights into the wonder of brain functioning. Often, these individuals are studied for years by neuropsychologists using the single-subject designs discussed in this section.

EXTENDING THE CONCEPT OF CASE STUDIES

Single-subject *experimental* designs should not be confused with the single-case studies discussed in Chapter 6. Case studies are used in clinical research for in-depth clinical *descriptions* of single individuals and to generate (but not test) *hypotheses*. An ex post facto, single-case study is weak, not only because it has only one participant, but because the researcher does not control the independent variable(s). Because the independent variables are not manipulated in the single-case study, *alternative hypotheses cannot be ruled out.*

With single-subject experimental designs, independent variables are manipulated and their effects on dependent variables are observed. The power of these designs is in the control of independent variables, which reduces confounding and enhances internal validity. Thus, single-subject designs are inherently experimental in nature and can be used to test causal hypotheses.

Single-subject experimental designs are preferable to group comparisons in two situations: (1) evaluating change in a single participant and (2) obtaining information that might otherwise be lost in a group comparison. Obviously, such designs are appropriate when there is only one participant, such as evaluating the effectiveness of a clinical treatment for a particular client or determining whether a school program improves a particular child's academic performance. A single-subject experiment might be weak in external validity, but it protects internal validity and provides valid and reliable information about a single individual.

Traditional group-comparison designs summarize a group's performance and, in the process, may lose important information about each individual's performance. For example, suppose that 20 phobic participants are pretested on the intensity of their fears and then randomly assigned to treatment and control conditions. After treatment, the treated group has a significantly lower mean fear score than the control group. Because this experimental design does an excellent job of controlling confounding, the researcher can conclude that the treatment was effective. However, on closer examination it is apparent that although the treated group reported less fear on average than the control group, there is considerable variability within each of the two groups. Some of the treated participants may still have fear scores that are higher than some of the untreated participants. Furthermore, additional inspection might well show that, whereas most of the control participants did not improve, some did and, although most of the treated participants improved, some did not and others deteriorated. In other words, individuals responded differently to the same treatment. Although the treatment may be effective on average, it might not be effective for some participants.

In the 1950s and 1960s, clinical research failed to support the effectiveness of traditional psychotherapy (Bergin & Strupp, 1970). However, on closer inspection it was clear that some clients improved, some deteriorated, and some remained the same. When taken as a group, the changes tended to cancel out each other. Obscured by group-comparison designs was the improvement of *some* clients. Sidman (1960) and Bergin and Strupp (1970) suggested studying these improved individuals (1) to determine whether the improvements were due to systematic effects of the treatment or to chance variation and (2) to identify factors that made psychotherapy effective for some people but not for others.

Recognizing the problems of group designs, they argued for the development of experimental methods to study single individuals.

The intensive experimental study of individuals had a prominent place in psychology for half a century, until the late 1930s, when psychologists began adopting new group comparison research designs and statistical procedures (Morgan & Morgan, 2001). Sir Ronald Fisher's book, *The Design of Experiments* (1935), introduced multi-subject, group-comparison designs and statistical procedures, and researchers soon followed Fisher's lead. However, B. F. Skinner (1904–1990) was an influential exception. Skinner and others continued to develop single-subject experimental designs for the **experimental analysis of behavior,** which were methods for the intensive, systematic, and controlled study of individual participants. New journals appeared: *Journal of the Experimental Analysis of Behavior*, 1958; *Behavior Research and Therapy*, 1963; *Journal of Applied Behavior Analysis*, 1968; *Behavior Therapy*, 1970, *Behavior Modification*, 1974; *Journal of Behavior Therapy and Experimental Psychiatry*, 1969. The experimental analysis of single individuals became particularly important in clinical psychology, which is now heavily reliant on behavioral treatment methods.

In single-subject experiments, there is no control group. A controlled manipulation of the independent variable is used to demonstrate causality. The comparison is made between the participant's initial pretreatment behavior and his or her post-intervention behavior. The logic of single-subject experiments is simple and their strength is in the precision with which they are carried out.

A causal inference can be made with confidence if (1) the person's behavior changes consistently in the predicted direction when the treatment is presented and (2) confounding factors can be ruled out. Several factors are critical in this evaluation, including operationally defining appropriate target behaviors, obtaining baseline measures, applying the treatment manipulation, and monitoring changes in behavior.

The first step is to operationally define the target behavior. For example, a smoking-cessation treatment program might target the number of cigarettes smoked and the intensity of the person's craving for a cigarette. The first might be defined as the number of cigarettes smoked in each 24-hour period and the latter as the person's daily ratings of his or her cravings. These may seem like straightforward decisions, but the researcher needs to study the past research literature to learn the best ways to measure these variables. For example, McFall (1970) found that asking people to monitor their own smoking by counting the number of cigarettes actually reduced the smoking from normal baseline measures, and the participants were unaware of this behavioral change. That means that having people monitor their smoking is a reactive measure of amount of smoking. This is just one example of why it is so critical to thoroughly study the research literature on an issue before you try to design studies to investigate the issue.

After operationally defining target behaviors, a **baseline period** is selected. The baseline period is the time from initial monitoring until the onset of the treatment manipulation. The duration of the baseline varies with the nature of the target behavior. Usually, several days or a week is long enough to establish that the target behavior is consistent and representative for the individual. During the baseline, the number of cigarettes smoked is recorded and the person rates his or her need to smoke at various points during each day.

The researcher wants to avoid a nonrepresentative baseline period, when the behavior is momentarily elevated or depressed. With some targeted behaviors, it is best for the researcher to carry out the observations. With some groups of participants, such as children and psychiatric patients, the researcher has no choice but to make the observations. With these baseline data established, the actual treatment can begin.

During the treatment phase, the targeted behaviors are monitored and recorded. The treatment will be specific to the nature of the targeted behavior. It is the independent variable, which must also be clearly defined operationally. This sequence of a no-treatment baseline, followed by a treatment period and then by posttreatment measures, is the basic manipulation in single-subject experiments. The critical comparison is between the single participant's pretreatment and posttreatment scores on the target behavior. This basic paradigm is illustrated in Figure 11.2. This is a within-subjects, time-series design, in which target behaviors (the dependent variable) of a single participant are measured before, during, and after treatment (the manipulation of the independent variable).

The baseline measurement of target behaviors serves the same purpose that a control group serves in between-groups designs. We will cover three major variants of this basic paradigm in this section: ABA reversal designs, multiple baseline designs, and single-subject, randomized time-series designs. [See Barlow and Hersen, (1984) and Tripodi (1994) for detailed discussions of single-subject designs.]

ABA Reversal Designs

In **ABA reversal designs,** the effects of an independent variable on a dependent variable are demonstrated by measuring the dependent variable several times, during which the treatment is applied and then removed. At a minimum, there is a no-treatment baseline period, during which the target behavior is observed, a treatment period in which the manipulation is carried out, and a return or reversal to the no-treatment condition (called ABA design). In nearly all instances, the sequence ends with another B condition (ABAB).

The effect of the independent variable (the treatment) on the dependent variable (the behavior to be changed) is demonstrated if the behavior changes in the predicted direction whenever the conditions are reversed. There are numerous published reports of reversal procedures.

The following hypothetical study concerns self-stimulatory behavior often engaged in by children who have mental retardation, autism, or brain injury. It includes head banging, self-biting, gouging, screaming, violent head shaking, and so on. Besides being dangerous to the child, this behavior interferes with treatment. Such behavior may be maintained, at least in part, by the responses of staff members. For some children, being ignored

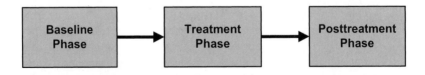

FIGURE 11.2 *Single-Subject Experimental Designs* Single-subject experimental designs always include at a minimum baseline, treatment phase, and posttreatment assessment. In most cases, there are multiple measures taken in each of the phases.

seems to help to maintain the self-stimulatory behavior; for others, the staff's attention to the episodes may help to maintain it.

Betty, a child with mental retardation, displays self-stimulatory behavior that consists of loud shrieks, facial grimacing, and rapid arm flapping, which occur many times each day and sometimes last as long as 25 minutes. These behaviors interfere with Betty's learning and disrupt the progress of the other children. After observing the child, a psychologist hypothesizes that the teacher's attention reinforces and maintains the behavior. Betty tends to begin self-stimulation when she is not the focus of the teacher. The teacher then attends to the child to soothe and comfort her, not realizing that it may be her efforts to help Betty to control the behavior that are actually helping to maintain it.

To test the hypothesis, the psychologist sets up a reversal design in which condition A, the baseline, involves the teacher's usual approach of attending to Betty whenever she displays the behavior. Condition B is the treatment period, during which a differential reinforcement procedure is used. The teacher provides attention and support for Betty whenever she refrains from the self-stimulatory behavior but withdraws attention whenever Betty engages in disruptive behavior. Observations of Betty's disruptive behavior are carried out for one hour at the same time each day.

Figure 11.3 shows the behavioral changes that occur as the A and B conditions are sequentially reversed. These data suggest that there may be a causal relationship between teacher attention and Betty's self-stimulatory behavior. Note that another reversal was added at the end. The ABA sequence was by itself sufficient to suggest causality. Why did the psychologist add that extra reversal, back to the B condition? (Think about this. We will return to it shortly.)

Reversal designs test causal relationships between an independent variable and a dependent variable. In this case, the independent variable is the teacher's attention. It is presented at two levels: the baseline (A), in which the teacher's attention is given when the

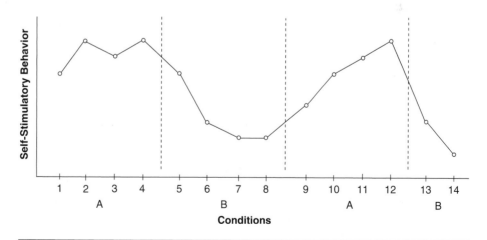

FIGURE 11.3 *An Example of an ABA Reversal Design* This graph shows an ABA reversal design in which the level of attention is manipulated contingent on a child's self-stimulation. Note that because the level of self-stimulation is lower in the B condition, the researcher has done the ethical thing in returning the child to this condition at the end of the study.

self-stimulation occurs, and the intervention (B), in which the teacher's attention is withdrawn when self-stimulation occurs. The experimental manipulation is the sequential reversal of levels A and B. The dependent variable is Betty's self-stimulatory behavior and is operationally defined in terms of the number of minutes of self-stimulation behavior during the one-hour observation period each day.

The question being asked is one of causality: Does the teacher's attention affect self-stimulation for Betty? If the behavior changes in the predicted direction, increasing or decreasing each time that the reversal occurs, this is a compelling demonstration that the independent variable, and not some confounding variable, has affected the dependent variable.

In this hypothetical example, an intervention was tested for reducing undesirable behavior. However, the same ABAB reversal design can be used to test the effectiveness of interventions to increase the strength of positive behaviors. These could include improving academic achievement, acquiring self-control skills, increasing positive interactions with peers, and so on—all common goals in programs for children with developmental disabilities, emotional disorders, or learning problems.

For example, DeLeon, Iwata, and Roscoe (1997) studied the responses of 14 children with mental retardation. Although most of the children showed a preference for food rewards, two children preferred other rewards (specifically, leisure-time activity). The researchers used a reversal design to show improvements in adaptive behavior through a training program that used leisure time as the positive reinforcement for these two children. The children's adaptive responses were observed in a baseline period, in which there was no leisure-time reward, and were then observed in a treatment condition, in which leisure time was used as a reward. Baseline and treatment reversals were carried out again. As seen in Figure 11.4, the adaptive behavior of both children increased from baseline to treatment at each reversal.

Again, why was the last treatment condition included? In this case, and in the example presented earlier of Betty, the behavior under the B condition was preferable to the behavior under the A condition. *Once the effect of the independent variable on the dependent variable has been demonstrated, the researcher has an ethical obligation to use that effect to return participants to the best possible situation.*

Multiple-Baseline Designs

Although the ABA reversal design is a powerful demonstration of the effects of one variable on another, there are situations in which reversal procedures are not feasible or ethical. For example, suppose that the baseline behavior of a child is injurious or that the researcher succeeds in improving the academic performance of a child in school. In both cases, it is unreasonable to reverse conditions once we achieved improved functioning. For the first child, a return to baseline could risk injury; for the second, it could disrupt academic performance. Thus, the reversal design used in the last example might be unacceptable. However, a multiple-baseline design would be acceptable.

In a **multiple-baseline design,** the effects of the treatment are demonstrated on different behaviors successively. To illustrate, suppose that a fifth-grade boy is doing poorly in math and reading, although he appears to have the ability to achieve at a high level. He is also disruptive and inattentive in class. A psychologist observes the class and sees that whenever the boy acts up, the teacher scolds, corrects, and lectures him in front of the

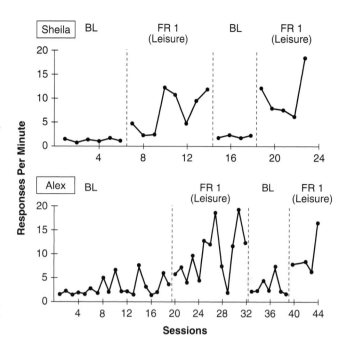

FIGURE 11.4 *Published Example of a Reversal Design* In this published study by DeLeon et al. (1997), rewarding adaptive behavior was effective in increasing the number of adaptive responses in two children. The pattern of results in this ABA design provides strong evidence for the causal relationship between reward and adaptive responses. The similarity of the results across these two children provides replication and thus increases our confidence in this causal relationship.

Source: DeLeon, I. G., Iwata, B. A., & Roscoe, E. M. (1997). Displacement of leisure reinforcers by food during preference assessments. *Journal of Applied Behavior Analysis, 30,* 475-484.

class in an effort to embarrass him. The boy seems to accept the attention with a good deal of pleasure. However, on the rare occasions when he does his academic work, the teacher ignores him. "When he is working, I leave well enough alone," the teacher says. "I don't want to risk stirring him up."

Based on these observed contingencies, the psychologist hypothesizes that the teacher's attention to the boy's disruptive behavior may be a major factor in maintaining this behavior, whereas the teacher's failure to attend to the boy's good academic work may help to account for its low occurrence. The psychologist sets up a multiple-baseline design to test the hypothesis about the importance of teacher attention on both disruptive and academic behavior. The independent variable is teacher attention and the dependent variables are the child's (1) disruptive behavior, (2) math performance, and (3) reading performance. The independent variable is presented at two levels: presence of contingent teacher attention and absence of contingent teacher attention.

Figure 11.5 shows the sequence of phases of the hypothetical study. During baseline, all three dependent variables are measured, while the teacher continues the usual procedure of trying to punish the disruption and ignore academic behavior. Disruptive behavior is high and math and reading performance are low in this phase. In the second phase, the teacher's attention to disruptive behavior (punishment) is withdrawn, and disruptive behavior is ignored. In this phase, the teacher focuses on rewarding math performance while both disruptive behavior and reading continue to be ignored. In the third phase, both reading and math performance receive the teacher's rewarding attention, while disruption continues to be ignored. The changes in the dependent variables during these manipulations provide evidence for the hypothesis that contingent teacher attention is an important controlling factor in this child's behavior.

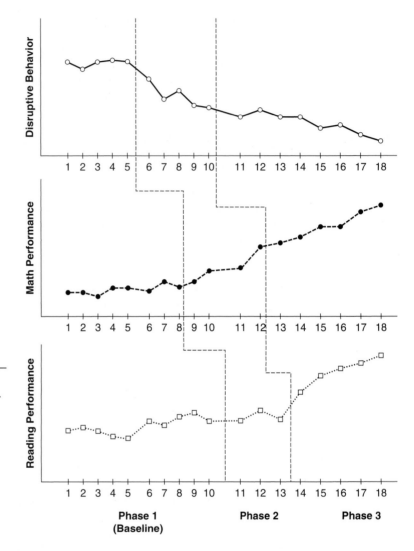

FIGURE 11.5 *An Example of a Multiple-Baseline Design* This figure shows hypothetical results of a multiple-baseline design study in which contingent teacher attention decreases disruptive behavior and improves math and reading performance. The dashed vertical lines indicate when teacher attention was manipulated for each of the target behaviors.

There are three variations of the multiple-baseline design (Barlow & Hersen, 1984).

- **Across behaviors:** In this variation, different behaviors of the same individual are compared, as in the preceding example.
- **Across individuals:** In this variation, the same behavior is measured in different people, and the same treatment manipulations are applied to test whether the treatment procedure is effective for different individuals.
- **Across settings and time:** In this variation, a treatment is applied to a behavior for one individual in different settings or times. For example, we might want to know if a treatment that is effective in the classroom is also effective at home or in other settings.

Single-Subject, Randomized Time-Series Design

A **single-subject, randomized time-series design** is a time-series design for a single participant with one additional element: the point at which the treatment begins is determined randomly. Time-series designs involve measuring a dependent variable several times over a long period, with an experimental intervention occurring at a selected point during the observations. To illustrate the single-subject, randomized time-series design, suppose that Joey, a child in a special class, does not complete his daily work. During the 15-minute lesson periods, Joey looks around the room or just closes his eyes and does no work. Frequent reminders by the teacher rouse him briefly but not enough for him to complete the lessons. The teacher is convinced that Joey has the skills to do the academic work. How can the teacher help him?

An effective motivational intervention for children is a reinforcement system in which tokens are given for desired behaviors. The child accumulates tokens and can spend them for desirable items and privileges. The tokens are reinforcements that strengthen the rewarded behavior. If a single-subject, randomized time-series design is employed, the child's arithmetic achievement might be monitored for six weeks (30 school days), which would yield a time graph of 30 measurements. A minimum number of days, perhaps the first 5 and the last 5 (1–5 and 26–30), are devoted to pretreatment and posttreatment measures of arithmetic achievement. This ensures adequate pretreatment and posttreatment measures. The researcher then randomly selects one of the middle 20 days as the point for introducing the token reinforcement system. A table of random numbers is used to select the starting day, and the ninth day is selected for introducing the token reinforcement. The beginning of the manipulation is preceded by 8 days during which arithmetic achievement is measured under the usual nontoken condition, followed by 22 days of measurement of the dependent variable under the token reinforcement condition.

One problem with using a token economy system with your kids is that the kids start to get possessive with their tokens. However, token economies are often effective in improving behavior in both children and adults.

"Hey, Dad! Who sez you guys could play with _my_ tokens!"

A marked improvement in arithmetic achievement coincident with the randomly selected ninth measurement, as shown in Figure 11.6, provides convincing evidence of the effects of the token system. It is unlikely that such marked improvement would occur by chance at exactly the point at which the *randomly* introduced treatment occurs. It is also unlikely that this particular time-series pattern would have occurred as a result of maturation or history or any other confounding variable.

Replication in Single-Subject Designs

As you have learned, replication of research findings strengthens our confidence in those findings. There are several questions concerning replication in single-subject experiments. These raise issues of generalization across time, persons, conditions, and target behaviors. First, if we repeat the treatment with the same person, will the results be replicated; that is, will they generalize over time for that person? A second question concerns whether the treatment will be effective with other people who have the same problem; that is, will the treatment generalize to other persons? Two final questions concern whether the treatment will be effective under other conditions. Will it work with a different therapist or in another setting? Will it work for psychological problems other than the one on which it was originally tested? Sidman (1960) discussed two ways of achieving replication: direct replication and systematic replication. Barlow and Hersen (1984) added another method: clinical replication.

Single-subject direct replication means repeating the experiment with the same participant or a series of participants who present the same behavioral issue. For example, in an ABA procedure, each time that a reversal to baseline occurs, followed by the treatment condition, a replication has been carried out. Theoretically, there is no limit to the number of replications that can be done. Direct replication provides information on a given individual's responses over time and thus establishes the reliability of the procedure (that it is or is not effective each time that it is applied).

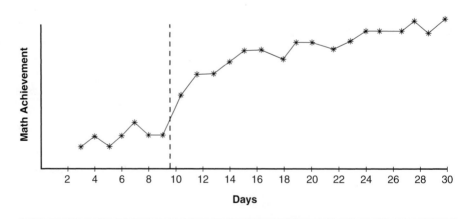

FIGURE 11.6 *Example of a Randomized, Time-Series Design* This figure shows hypothetical results of a single-subject, randomized time-series design in which a token economy was effective in improving math performance for this child.

Having established its effectiveness with one or more persons with the same behavioral issues, we now want to expand the replication. Carrying out a series of single-subject experiments with different people in different settings and with new target behaviors does this. These experiments represent **single-subject systematic replication;** that is, they establish the effectiveness and reliability of the procedure for a series of persons with the different target behavior.

Direct replication and systematic replication in single-subject experiments typically test the effectiveness of one treatment at a time on specific target behaviors. However, in the applied world of clinical treatment, therapists create and test complex treatment packages that address multiple problem behaviors. To accomplish this, Barlow and Hersen (1984) discuss a third form of replication, **single-subject clinical replication.** This more complex approach is used primarily in clinical treatment settings. It typically involves an integrated treatment package of two or more procedures that are applied to a succession of participants. The target is usually a set of problematic behaviors related to a clinical disorder. For example, the participants might be adults with depression, and the targeted behaviors might be negative mood expression, low level of physical activity, and social isolation. The treatment package might consist of medication, cognitive therapy, increased physical activity, and graduated desensitization to social activity.

Although the research is more complex, basic single-subject procedures are employed in clinical replication. To accommodate complex treatment packages and multiple target behaviors, variations of multiple-baseline designs are typically used. Barlow and Hersen discuss clinical replication as the next step in replication, building on earlier replication as follows:

1. Direct replication establishes the reliability and effectiveness of a single treatment for a single target behavior in a succession of participants.
2. Systematic replication then establishes the reliability and effectiveness of the treatment with other persons, in other settings, and for other target behaviors (and/or other clinical problems).
3. After several different treatments have been developed and tested, two or more are combined into a treatment package. Clinical replication tests the reliability and effectiveness of the combined treatment package for multiple related behaviors, for a succession of clients, and across different settings. (For a more complete discussion, see Barlow and Hersen, 1984.)

These designs are applicable to single participants. However, replication can be achieved by having two or more participants in each experiment. These, strictly speaking, would be small-N experiments. (Remember, N is used in statistics to refer to the number of participants.) The procedures would be virtually the same as in single-subject experiments.

To summarize, single-subject designs are extensions of within-subjects designs. These designs are usually variations on time-series designs, in which repeated measurements are taken over time and manipulations are performed at different points. Single-subject designs are an alternative to some traditional designs. They are especially useful in the evaluation of treatments and are used often in research on behavior modification. The Student Resource Website gives examples of single-subject designs.

11:07

Quick-Check Review 11.3: Single-Subject Experimental Designs

1. What are single-subject designs? For what are they used?
2. How do single-subject experiments differ from single-case studies?
3. How is internal validity protected in single-subject experiments?
4. Describe reversal, multiple-baseline, and randomized time-series designs.
5. What are the major strengths and weaknesses of single-subject designs?
6. Why is external validity weak in a single-subject design?
7. What are the major ways of replicating single-subject designs?
8. Explain how causality is determined in single-subject designs.

PUTTING IT INTO PRACTICE

You may not have realized this, but you have been conducting single-subject experiments all of your life, although you have not been doing them with the precision and formal data collection described here. We would like you to plan and carry out a single-subject experiment that focuses on shaping a particular behavior using reinforcement. It might be a practical behavior, such as having your housemate clean the kitchen after using it. It might be an impractical behavior. For example, students sometimes get together to see how much their professor can be influenced by reinforcement. They decide in advance that they will pay closer attention and be more responsive whenever, for example, the professor moves away from the lectern. A class working together can shape a variety of such behaviors, usually without the professor ever picking up on what is happening. Whatever study you decide to do, do it formally. Identify the independent and dependent measures, and decide how you will manipulate and/or measure them. Record the data systematically, and see whether your findings suggest a causal connection between your independent and dependent variables.

Chapter Summary

Correlated-groups designs include within-subjects designs, matched-subject designs, and single-subject designs. In within-subjects and single-subject designs, the correlation is the result of having the same participants appear in all conditions. In matched-subject designs, the correlation is created by matching participants on one or more relevant variables. Regardless of the method used, the result is the same—greater confidence in the comparability of groups before the start of the study, thus increasing sensitivity when testing for differences between conditions.

Correlated-groups designs raise new issues not found in other designs. For example, each participant is exposed to all conditions in within-subjects designs, which raises the possibility that the exposure to one or more of the conditions may affect the performance in later conditions (sequence effects). Matching participants and randomly assigning one member of each matched set of participants to each condition eliminates these problems but raises new issues. The most important issue in matched-subjects designs is the selection of the variable(s) on which to match. The actual matching can be difficult and tedious. Still, both within- and matched-subjects designs provide powerful ways to answer causal questions.

Single-subject designs are extensions of within-subjects designs. They are particularly useful in the evaluation of clinical and educational intervention for individuals. The most commonly used single-subject designs are the reversal design, the multiple-baseline design, and the single-subject, randomized time-series design.

Chapter Exercises

1. Define the following key terms. Be sure that you understand them. They are discussed in the chapter and defined in the glossary.

   correlated groups design
   repeated-measures design
   counterbalancing
   complete
     counterbalancing
   repeated-measures
     ANOVA
   between-conditions sum
     of squares
   between sum of squares
   subjects term
   error term
   practice effects
   positive practice effect
   negative practice effect
   carryover effects
   random order of
     presentation
   partial counterbalancing
   Latin square design
   randomized within blocks

   matched random
     assignment
   single-subject
     experimental
     design
   N-of-one design
   neuropsychology
   experimental analysis of
     behavior
   baseline period
   ABA reversal designs
   multiple-baseline design
   single-subject,
     randomized
     time-series design
   single-subject direct
     replication
   single-subject systematic
     replication
   single-subject clinical
     replication

2. You are the teaching assistant in an introductory research methods course. Explain the particular strength of correlated-groups designs to the students.

3. What does it mean when we say "within-subjects designs are experiments that are run on a single group of participants"? How can this statement be reconciled with the requirement that the independent variable must be present at more than one level in experiments?

4. Can ANOVA be used to test a null hypothesis in a within-subjects design? If so, are there any special steps that must be taken?

5. You have 50 participants to assign to two groups of 25 participants each. Using the table of random numbers or a random number generator, randomly assign the participants to the two conditions.

6. Now assume you have 50 more participants to assign to two groups, but the 50 participants are matched in pairs on IQ. Designate the first pair as participants A_1 and A_2, the second pair as B_1 and B_2, and so on. Use the table of random numbers to assign the pairs to the two groups.

7. In counterbalancing, how many possible orders of presentation are there in an experiment with three conditions? Five conditions? Six conditions? Is counterbalancing feasible with a large number of conditions?

12

Factorial Designs

In the discovery of secret things and in the investigation of hidden causes, stronger reasons are obtained from sure experiments and demonstrated arguments than from probable conjectures and the opinions of philosophical speculators of the common sort.

—William Gilbert, *De Magnete,* 1600

Factorial Designs
Main Effects and Interactions
Possible Outcomes of Factorial Designs
An Example: Children's Dark-Fears Study
Analysis of Variance in Factorial Designs

Variations of Basic Factorial Designs
Within-Subjects or Repeated-Measures Factorial
Mixed Designs
Between-Subjects and Within-Subjects Factors
Manipulated and Nonmanipulated Factors
Mixed in Both Ways
Solomon's Four-Group Design

ANOVA: A Postscript
Analysis of Covariance
Multivariate Analysis of Variance

Putting It into Practice

Chapter Summary

Chapter Exercises

Web Resource Material

The designs discussed in Chapters 10 and 11 have only one independent variable. However, many designs include multiple independent variables. These are called **factorial designs.** Factorial designs allow researchers to study both the individual and interactive effects of independent variables on the dependent variable. This chapter begins by discussing factorial design terminology, procedures, and analyses. It then discusses variations of factorial designs and concludes with a discussion of ANOVA.

Factorial Designs

Suppose that you are responsible for developing an effective treatment program for children who are afraid of the dark. By interviewing children and parents, you determine that the children's fearfulness varies considerably from one night to another. On some nights, they do not seem afraid, but on most nights they are fearful. When fearful, the children have difficulty sleeping and they disrupt the entire family. Thus, it appears that, although the children's fears are related to darkness, other variables are operating. In further interviews, you find that many of the children report vivid and frightening images of monsters, ghosts, vampires, burglars, and so on when they are put to bed and left alone in the dark. Can it be that darkness is a necessary, but not sufficient, condition for fearfulness? Might the children's fears be triggered by a combination of being in the dark and having fearful images? That is, darkness alone or fearful images alone may not be sufficient to trigger the fear, but the combination of the two will trigger fear.

The question about the two variables having effects when they are in combination is a question about their **interaction effects.** Behavior is rarely determined by single variables; rather, it is determined by several factors that interact. An interaction effect between two variables is an effect that is greater than summing the effects of the two variables. A true interaction is not simply additive—it is an enhancement.

The concept of an interaction, which is the single most important issue in factorial research, is best explained with a simple example. Accident researchers know that driving faster increases the risk of an accident. The speed at which people drive (the independent variable) has a predictable effect on the accident rate (the dependent variable). Researchers also find that the more slippery the road, the higher the accident rate. Of course, if people drive fast on slippery roads, an even higher rate of accidents would be expected, because both risk factors are present.

This is not necessarily an interaction. We say there is an interaction effect only if the increase in the accident rate is more than would be expected if the independent effects of the two risk factors were simply added together. For example, if driving 20 miles per hour faster doubles the risk of accidents, and driving on a slick road triples the rate of accidents, then the additive effects of these two variables might suggest a six-fold increase in accident rates (doubled for driving fast, then tripled for driving on slick surfaces). If, however, we find that driving 20 miles per hour faster *and* on a slick surface increases the accident rate 15-fold, we clearly are getting more than just the additive effects of these two risk factors. We have a clear interaction, in which the effect of faster driving is greater on slick roads than on dry roads. Driving speed probably interacts with other variables, such as bumpiness of the roads, degree of traffic, the amount of alcohol that the driver has consumed, and the driver's age. In each case, the effect of increased driving speed differs depending on whether one of these other variables is present.

Getting back to our hypothetical fear-of-the-dark research, a factorial design can be used to study two independent variables and their interaction (illumination and frightening images). The independent variables in a factorial design are called **factors.** In this experiment, the dependent variable, the children's fear, can be measured by heart rate, which has been shown in previous research to reflect fear arousal. Measured electronically, heart rate can be taken under two conditions of illumination (lighted condition and dark condition) and two conditions of visual images (fear and neutral images). That is, factor A (illumination) is presented at two levels and factor B (images) is presented at two levels. The two independent variables, each presented at two levels, produce four treatment combinations called a **matrix of cells.** The result is a 2×2 (read "two-by-two") factorial design, as shown in Table 12.1.

A study like this raises ethical concerns. In essence, we are deliberately exposing children to images and conditions that may create fear in an attempt to understand how their fearfulness develops and what might be done to alleviate it. One could argue that the images that would be used in such a study are routinely seen daily by children on TV. Nevertheless, these ethical concerns must be taken seriously and alternatives considered during the design phase. For more information on the ethical issues, please go to the Student Resource Website, which discusses the ethical issues in this proposed research study, as well as other ethical issues routinely faced by researchers.

12:01

The **design notation** for factorial studies (e.g., 2×2) shows how many independent variables and how many levels of each variable are included. Each number in the notation represents one independent variable or factor and denotes the number of levels of that variable. Thus, the notation 3×3 indicates that the design has two independent variables, with three levels of each variable. The notation $2 \times 3 \times 2$ indicates that the design has three independent variables with two levels of factor A, three levels of factor B, and two levels of factor C. Note that factors are traditionally labeled with capital letters (A, B, C). As the designs become more complex, more cells are produced, more participants are required, and the results become increasingly difficult to interpret. Thus, although any number of factors and levels can be combined in a factorial design, there are practical limits to the complexity of these designs. Table 12.2 diagrams several factorial designs.

TABLE 12.1   *A 2 × 2 Factorial*

	Factor A (Illumination)	
	Level A$_1$ *(lighted condition)*	*Level A$_2$* *(dark condition)*
Factor B (Images)		
Level B$_1$ (feared)	A_1B_1	A_2B_1
Level B$_2$ (neutral)	A_1B_2	A_2B_2

TABLE 12.2   *Examples of Factorial Designs*

(a) 2 × 2 Design With Two Factors and Two Levels of Each Factor

	Factor A	
	A_1	A_2
Factor B		
B_1	A_1B_1	A_2B_1
B_2	A_1B_2	A_2B_2

(b) 3 × 2 Design With Two Factors; Three Levels of A, Two Levels of B

	Factor A		
	A_1	A_2	A_3
Factor B			
B_1	A_1B_1	A_2B_1	A_3B_1
B_2	A_1B_2	A_2B_2	A_3B_3

(c) 3 × 3 Design With Two Factors and Three Levels of Each Factor

	Factor A		
	A_1	A_2	A_3
Factor B			
B_1	A_1B_1	A_2B_1	A_3B_1
B_2	A_1B_2	A_2B_2	A_3B_2
B_3	A_1B_3	A_2B_3	A_3B_3

(d) 2 × 3 × 2 Design With Three Factors and Two Levels of A, Three Levels of B, and Two Levels of C

	Factor C			
	C_1		C_2	
	Factor A		Factor A	
	A_1	A_2	A_1	A_2
Factor B				
B_1	$A_1B_1C_1$	$A_2B_1C_1$	$A_1B_1C_2$	$A_2B_1C_2$
B_2	$A_1B_2C_1$	$A_2B_2C_1$	$A_1B_2C_2$	$A_2B_2C_2$
B_3	$A_1B_3C_1$	$A_2B_3C_1$	$A_1B_3C_2$	$A_2B_3C_2$

Main Effects and Interactions

Two different kinds of hypotheses are tested in a factorial design: (1) the impact of each independent variable on the dependent variable (**main effects**) and (2) the effect of any combination of two or more independent variables on the dependent variable (interactions). Factorial designs, like single-variable designs, can be set up as between- or within-subjects designs. We will consider first the between-subjects factorial designs, in which a different group of participants is assigned to each cell. Each of these independent groups includes the scores of participants on the dependent variable. A mean of the scores is calculated for each group. For example, Table 12.3 shows the 2×2 matrix for our hypothetical children's dark-fears study and the four groups formed by these factors. The table includes a mean heart rate for the participants in each cell, as well as the row and column means for each variable. Note that the matrix is, in a sense, two separate studies that are combined. Figure 12.1(a) shows that the column means (factor A) can be compared, just as if one were the experimental and the other the control group in a single-variable design. This comparison can answer the question "Is there a significant difference in the children's fear, as measured by heart rate, between the dark and the lighted conditions?" Comparing the two levels of factor B (images), as shown in Figure 12.1(b), is also a comparison of two independent groups. The question answered here is whether there is a significant difference in heart rates between participants in the fear-image and neutral-image conditions.

The comparisons illustrated in Figures 12.1(a) and (b) are the tests of the main effects of the independent variables on the dependent variable. In the dark-fears study, we can test whether heart rates differ under lighted and dark conditions (main effect of illumination) and whether they differ under fearful and neutral images (main effect of fear imagery).

We could have answered these questions about main effects by conducting two separate single-variable studies. However, to answer questions about the interaction of the two variables, we must combine the independent variables into a single study. When we combine the two separate designs by crossing them, as shown in Figure 12.1(c), the 2×2 ma-

TABLE 12.3   *A Hypothetical 2 × 2 Factorial Design*

This hypothetical study includes two factors believed to affect children's night fears. Factor A is the level of illumination, and factor B is the type of images.

	Factor A (Illumination)		
	Level A_1 *(lighted)*	*Level A_2* *(dark)*	*Row Mean*
Factor B (Images)			
Level B_1 (Feared)	A_1B_1 (98.3)	A_2B_1 (114.1)	106.2
Level B_2 (Neutral)	A_1B_2 (98.1)	A_2B_2 (99.9)	99.0
Column Mean	98.2	107.0	

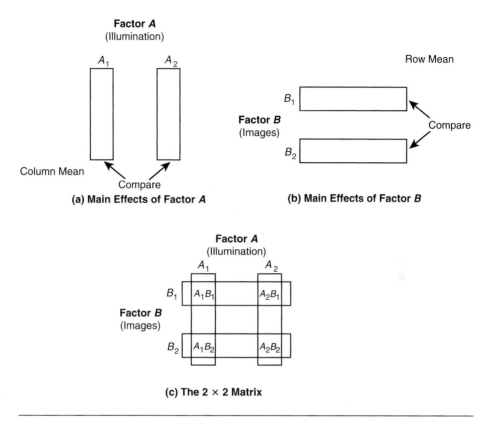

FIGURE 12.1 *Factorial Design as a Combination of Two Studies* Factorial designs can be thought of as combining two or more studies into a single study. Looking at each factor individually provides a test of the main effects. Combining the factors provides a test of the interaction of the factors.

trix is formed with four cells within which are the data for testing interactions. This allows us to investigate not only main effects, but also to address a more complex question: Are the effects of one variable different depending on the level of the other variable? This interaction is the major question in our hypothetical dark-fears study. In fact, in most factorial studies, the primary focus is on the interaction.

Conducting the factorial experiment is similar to, but more complex than, conducting single-variable studies. The 2×2 factorial, because it is essentially two designs combined into a single study, contains more than one null hypothesis. In fact, there are three null hypotheses for each dependent measure:

1. There is no significant difference between the levels of factor A (no main effect for factor A).
2. There is no significant difference between the levels of factor B (no main effect for factor B).
3. There is no significant interaction of factors A and B.

In factorial designs with more than two factors, there will be even more null hypotheses to test. These null hypotheses are tested with an analysis of variance.

Because of the complexity of factorial designs, the potential threats to internal validity are complex. Suppose that one or more of the null hypotheses are rejected. As in single-variable designs, the next step is to check for possible confounding so as to rule out alternative explanations of the findings. If we have used an experimental design in which participants were randomly assigned to the cells of the study, we will have controlled most of the possible sources of confounding. If satisfied that confounding is adequately controlled, we can conclude that the data support a causal interpretation.

The hypothesis-testing procedure in factorial designs is similar to the procedure used in single-variable designs. The reasoning is exactly the same. The major difference is that because there are more independent variables in the factorial design, there are several null hypotheses to test rather than only one, and, therefore, there is more chance for confounding to occur. Furthermore, the interpretation of interactions is more complex than the interpretation of differences in a single-variable study.

Possible Outcomes of Factorial Designs

There are many possible outcomes in a factorial study. For example, there may be main effects for one or more factors but no interaction; there may be interactions but no main effects; there may be both interactions and main effects; and there may be neither main effects nor interactions. Figure 12.2 illustrates several 2×2 and 2×3 factorial designs. The mean score for each cell is shown, and the **row means** and **column means** for each level of each factor are also indicated. Row means are the means for all the people in a row, and column means are the means for all the people in a column. For purposes of this discussion, we will assume (1) that the observed differences are sufficiently large to be statistically significant, and (2) that there are an equal number of participants in each cell. We graphed the data because graphs make it easier to spot and understand an interaction. If you follow along with Figure 12.2, the following discussion will make much more sense.

Figure 12.2(a) illustrates a 3×2 factorial design with both a matrix of means and a graph. Around the margins of the 3×2 table are the overall means for each level of each variable (i.e., for levels A_1, A_2, A_3, and levels B_1 and B_2). Within each of the six cells is the mean score for the group in that condition (A_1B_1, A_1B_2, A_2B_1, A_2B_2, A_3B_1, A_3B_2). In this hypothetical experiment, the means are equal, and there are no differences anywhere in the matrix. Thus, there are no significant main effects for factors A or B and no significant interactions.

On the graph, the levels of variable A (A_1, A_2, A_3) are shown on the abscissa (the horizontal or x-axis), and the values of the dependent variable are shown on the ordinate (the vertical or y-axis). Means for cells A_1B_1, A_2B_1, and A_3B_1 are all located at the value 50 and are identified with small circles. The points are connected to show graphically the overall effect of A on the dependent measure at the B_1 level of B, and this line is labeled B_1. Clearly there is no effect of A on the dependent measure at level B_1 because all values are the same. The effects of A at level B_2 are plotted in the same way. They fall on the same points along the same line, all at the value 50. They are marked with stars. Again, there is no effect of A at the B_2 level. By inspecting either the table or the graph, we can see that there are no main effects and no interaction.

	A_1	A_2	A_3	Mean
B_1	50	50	50	50
B_2	50	50	50	50
Mean	50	50	50	

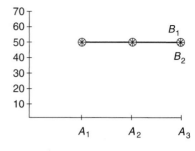

(a) 3 × 2 Factorial (*A*, *B*, and the interaction are not significant)

	A_1	A_2	Mean
B_1	30	60	45
B_2	30	60	45
Mean	30	60	

(b) 2 × 2 Factorial (*A* is significant; *B* and the interaction are not significant)

	A_1	A_2	Mean
B_1	70	70	70
B_2	40	40	40
Mean	55	55	

(c) 2 × 2 Factorial (*B* is significant; *A* and the interaction are not significant)

	A_1	A_2	A_3	Mean
B_1	10	30	80	40
B_2	30	50	100	60
Mean	20	40	90	

FIGURE 12.2
***Possible Outcomes
of Factorial Designs***
Eight possible out-
comes of a two-
factor factorial
study.
(continued)

(d) 3 × 2 Factorial (*A* and *B* are significant; the interaction is not significant)

	A_1	A_2	A_3	Mean
B_1	40	50	60	50
B_2	60	50	40	50
Mean	50	50	50	

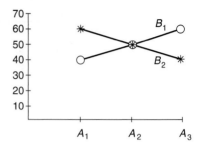

(e) 3 × 2 Factorial (the interaction is significant: *A* and *B* are not significant)

	A_1	A_2	A_3	Mean
B_1	30	40	50	40
B_2	40	40	40	40
Mean	35	40	45	

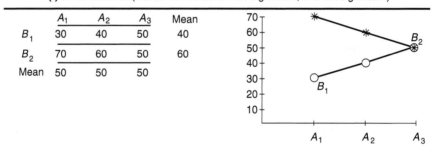

(f) 3 × 2 Factorial (*A* and the interaction are significant; *B* is not significant)

	A_1	A_2	A_3	Mean
B_1	30	40	50	40
B_2	70	60	50	60
Mean	50	50	50	

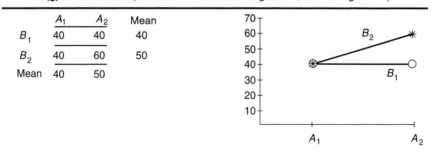

(g) 3 × 2 Factorial (*B* and the interaction are significant; *A* is not significant)

	A_1	A_2	Mean
B_1	40	40	40
B_2	40	60	50
Mean	40	50	

(h) 2 × 2 Factorial (*A*, *B*, and the interaction are significant)

FIGURE 12.2   *(Continued)*

Figure 12.2(b) illustrates a 2×2 factorial, in which there is a significant main effect for factor *A,* no significant main effect for factor *B,* and no interaction. The B_1 and B_2 lines in the graph are identical, indicating that *B* has had no effect. But the mean of A_2 is greater than the mean of A_1, indicating an effect for factor *A.* The 2×2 matrix shows the same results, with the mean for levels B_1 and B_2 equal (at 45) and the means for levels A_1 and A_2 different (30 and 60).

Interactions are most easily seen in the graph of the cell means. When there is an interaction, the lines are not parallel. In this example, both lines show the same upward swing from left to right, so there is no interaction effect. Thus, there is a main effect for *A,* no main effect for *B,* and no interaction.

Figure 12.2(c) illustrates a 2×2 factorial design in which there is a main effect for factor *B,* no main effect for factor *A,* and no interaction. The means for levels A_1 and A_2 are the same, whereas the means for levels B_1 and B_2 are different. In the graph, the B_1 and B_2 lines are separated, showing that there is a difference between the levels of factor *B.* Because the lines are parallel, there is no interaction between *A* and *B.*

Figure 12.2(d) shows a 3×2 factorial, in which there is a main effect for both factor *A* and factor *B,* but no interaction. The means are different at each of the three levels of factor *A* and each of the two levels of factor *B.* However, the parallel lines in Figure 12.2(c) indicate that there is no interaction.

Figure 12.2(e) illustrates a 3×2 factorial with a significant $A \times B$ interaction, but no significant main effects. Note that the column means for the three levels of factor *A* are the same, indicating that there is no main effect for factor *A.* The same is true for factor *B.* Thus, there is no significant main effect for *A* or *B,* but when plotted on the graph, the two lines cross, indicating an $A \times B$ interaction.

One of the values of drawing a graph is that interactions become readily apparent. Factor *A* has a different effect on the dependent measure when paired with B_1 than when paired with B_2. This is a classic interaction, in which the effect of one variable is systematically influenced by a second variable. Note also that the column means and row means in Figures 12.2(a) and (e) are identical. However, in Figure 12.2(a) the pattern of means within the cells indicates no interaction, whereas the pattern of means in Figure 12.2(e) indicates an interaction. This illustrates that the column and row means provide an indication of main effects only. We must inspect the individual cells on the graph to see an interaction.

Figure 12.2(f) shows a main effect for *A* and an $A \times B$ interaction. When both a main effect and an interaction occur, we always interpret the interaction first. The remaining examples can be read in similar fashion. We also have included a number of exercises in the lab manual on the Student Resource Website to provide additional practice with these challenging concepts and procedures.

12:05

An Example: Children's Dark-Fears Study

Let us return to our hypothetical children's dark-fears study. Suppose that the participants for this experiment include 40 children (20 boys and 20 girls), all afraid of the dark. Participants are randomly assigned to the four conditions of the 2×2 matrix (10 children per condition). Random assignment helps to ensure the equivalence of the four conditions at the outset of the study.

TABLE 12.4   *Heart Rates for 40 Dark-Fearing Children*

Factor B (Images)	Factor A (Illumination)		Row Mean
	A_1 (lighted)	A_2 (dark)	
	112	131	
	106	125	
	102	121	
	101	116	
	99	113	
B_1 (fear)	99	112	
	97	111	
	95	110	
	92	103	
	80	99	
	(98.3)	(114.1)	106.2
	115	119	
	110	112	
	105	107	
	103	102	
	100	95	
B_2 (neutral)	98	95	
	97	95	
	90	92	
	83	91	
	80	90	
	(98.1)	(99.9)	99.0
Column Mean	98.2	107.0	

There are two independent variables. Variable *A* (illumination) is presented at two levels: a lighted and a darkened condition. Variable *B* (images) is presented at two levels: fear and neutral images. The dependent variable is the children's fear as measured by their heart rates. The research hypotheses are that (1) there will be higher heart rates under dark conditions than under lighted conditions, (2) there will be higher heart rates under the fear-images condition than under the neutral-images condition, and (3) the greatest effects on heart rates will occur when darkness and fear-images conditions are combined. That is, we have hypothesized that there will be a main effect for factor *A*, a main effect for factor *B*, and a significant $A \times B$ interaction.

Participants are tested individually while seated comfortably facing a projection screen. A small sensor is placed on a finger to monitor heart rate. Participants are told that they will be shown 10 slides and will be asked questions about them later. Each slide is shown for 15 seconds with a 5-second pause between slides. Cell A_1B_1 represents the lighted-plus-fear-images condition. The lights are kept on in the room and the fear-image slides are presented (e.g., ghostly images or a burglar entering a house). Cell A_2B_1 represents the dark-plus-fear-images condition. The lights in the room are turned off and the participants are shown the fear images. Cell A_1B_2 represents the neutral-images-lighted condition, and cell A_2B_2 represents the neutral-images-dark condition. The general procedures in these two conditions are the same as described before, except that the images presented are neutral, such as landscapes and buildings. The heart rate of each participant is monitored during the testing period, so we have heart rates for 40 participants: 10 participants in each of four different conditions.

Table 12.4 shows hypothetical data for the 10 participants in each of the four conditions. The row mean of 106.2 is the mean for fear images; the row mean of 99.0 is the mean for neutral images; and 98.2 and 107.0 are the column means for light and dark conditions, respectively. The individual cell means are shown in parentheses.

To test for main effects, we compare the means of the two levels of each factor. The means of the two levels of Factor A (98.2 and 107.0) are compared to determine whether there is a main effect for illumination [Figure 12.3(a)]. To determine whether there is a main effect for Factor B, we compare the means for the fear and neutral images (106.2 and 99.0)

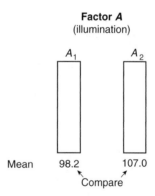

(a) Comparisons needed to test the main effects for Factor A

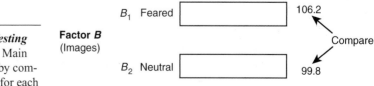

FIGURE 12.3 *Testing for Main Effects* Main effects are tested by comparing the means for each factor while ignoring the grouping on other factors.

(b) Comparison needed to test the main effects for Factor B

[Figure 12.3(b)]. To determine whether there is an interaction, we compare means of the four cells to see whether the effects of one independent variable on the dependent variable are different depending on the level of the other independent variable. The interaction is most easily seen in the graph shown in Figure 12.4, in which the lines are clearly not parallel. It is helpful to graph the cell means, because it will help you see whether an interaction might exist and whether the mean differences suggest the presence of main effects.

Looking at the data in Table 12.4 and the graph in Figure 12.4, we see that participants in the dark condition have a higher mean heart rate (107.0) than the participants in the lighted condition (98.2), suggesting that there may be a main effect for illumination. The fear-images condition has a higher mean heart rate (106.2) than the neutral-images condition (99.0), suggesting that there may be a significant main effect for image type.

The two lines in Figure 12.4 are not parallel, suggesting the possibility of an $A \times B$ interaction. The B_1 line slopes upward, moving from a mean of 98.3 to a mean of 114.1. The slope of this line appears to be due to the elevation of the A_2B_1 cell in which the dark

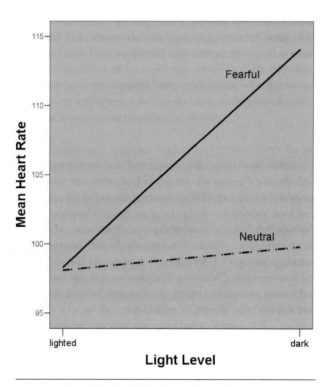

FIGURE 12.4   *Graph of Children's Dark-Fears Study* The fact that the lines in this graph of the children's dark-fears data are not parallel suggests the possibility of an interaction. When both main effects and interactions are found, the main effects should be interpreted in light of the interaction.

Source: Output from *SPSS for Windows*

condition and the fear images are combined. The mean of this cell is elevated compared with the other three cells. Fear images produce high heart rates, but only in the presence of the dark condition. The B_2 line is nearly flat; that is, the amount of light has little effect when neutral images are used. This clearly seems to be an interaction. Thus, we may have an $A \times B$ interaction and main effects for both factors.

Analysis of Variance in Factorial Designs

The appropriate statistical analysis for factorial designs is analysis of variance (ANOVA). Most ANOVA calculations are carried out using **computer-analysis programs.** This is especially true for factorial designs in which the computations can be very tedious. Running one of these applications on your personal computer will take the drudgery out of calculations.

Knowledge of computer use is critical for researchers, but this knowledge is not a substitute for understanding the principles of research design and statistical analysis. Remember our admonition in Chapter 1: it is not the technician's manipulation of laboratory equipment, including computers, that defines science. Science is defined by the *process of systematic thinking* that guides the use of laboratory techniques.

We will focus in this section on understanding an ANOVA and interpreting the results. Statistical computations for complex ANOVAs are beyond the scope of this text. However, we do cover statistical analysis procedures on the Student Resource Website.

12:02

The results of an ANOVA are typically presented in an ANOVA summary table, as shown in Table 12.5. This ANOVA summary table is in the same general format that you learned about in Chapter 10, with columns for source of variance, degrees of freedom, sums of squares, mean squares, F-ratios, and p-values. The basic difference is that there are more sources of variance in factorial designs and therefore more rows in the ANOVA summary table. For example, our dark fears study has a factor A (illumination), a factor B (images), the $A \times B$ interaction, the within-groups variance (error), and the total variance.

The degrees of freedom (df) for a between-subjects factorial design can be computed using some simple rules.

TABLE 12.5 *ANOVA Summary Table*

Here is the summary table for the data shown in Table 12.4.

Source	df	SS	MS	F	p
Factor *A* (illumination)	1	765.62	765.62	7.88	.008
Factor *B* (image type)	1	525.62	525.62	5.41	.026
AB Interaction	1	497.02	497.02	5.12	.030
Error	36	3497.50	97.15		
Total	39	5285.78	135.53		

1. The total degrees of freedom (df_{Total}) are $N - 1$ ($40 - 1$ in our example).
2. The degrees of freedom for the main effects are equal to the number of levels of each factor minus 1. Therefore, $df_a = (2 - 1) = 1$, and $df_b = (2 - 1) = 1$.
3. The degrees of freedom for interactions are computed as the product of the degrees of freedom for the main effects. Therefore, $df_{ab} = df_a \times df_b = 1 \times 1 = 1$.
4. The degrees of freedom for the within-groups variance is equal to N minus the number of groups. Therefore, $df_w = 40 - 4 = 36$ in our dark-fears study. Note that if you add the dfs for all the sources of variance, you will get the total dfs.

The third and fourth columns list the sum of squares (SS) and mean squares (MS), respectively, for each source of variance. The mean squares are computed by dividing each sum of squares by its associated degrees of freedom. The F-ratios in the fifth column are computed by dividing the mean squares by the within-groups mean square (the error term). The probability (p) of each F-ratio is shown in the sixth column. If the p-value is less than the chosen alpha level, the null hypothesis is rejected, and we conclude that there is an effect.

12:02

Computer programs compute the p-value using an equation. If you are computing the ANOVA by hand, you would look up how large the F-value has to be before you would reject the null hypothesis. These procedures are explained in more detail on the Student Resource Website.

In our ANOVA, there is a significant interaction ($p = .03$, $alpha = .05$). That is, fear, as measured by heart rate, is highest when darkness and fear images are presented together. The summary table also shows significant main effects for both illumination level and image type, but they can be understood only in terms of the interaction. That is, under the neutral-images condition the light or dark condition makes no difference; likewise, under lighted conditions, the fear images do not cause more fear than do the neutral images. The main effects are due to the interaction—to the condition A_2B_1 in which the fear images and darkness occur together.

When we interpret results that include both an interaction and main effects, *we always begin the interpretation with the interaction*. The conclusion that can be drawn from this hypothetical study is that neither fear images alone nor darkness alone appears to be sufficient to stimulate children's night fears, but the two together are a sufficient condition for children's night fears. To accept the finding of a main effect for A without interpreting it in terms of the interaction could lead us to an erroneous conclusion that the darkness itself increases fear. The Student Resource Website lists published studies that use factorial designs.

12:03

Quick-Check Review 12.1: Factorial Designs	1. What are factorial designs?
	2. Why does a factorial study test at least three null hypotheses?
	3. What is meant by an interaction? A main effect?
	4. When would you use a factorial rather than a single-variable design?
	5. In terms of main effects and interactions, what outcomes are possible in a factorial?
	6. Why should one interpret the interaction first when both a main effect and an interaction are significant?

Variations of Basic Factorial Design

Factorial designs are used with increasing frequency in psychology because they are better at representing the complex nature of real-world behavior. Many factorial designs are either within-subjects factorials in which each participant is tested under all conditions, or mixed designs that blend different types of factors into a single factorial study. Both of these designs are discussed in this section.

Within-Subjects or Repeated-Measures Factorial

We have already discussed randomized, between-subjects factorial designs, in which participants are randomly assigned to conditions and each participant appears in only one cell. This basic factorial design was illustrated in the children's dark-fears study. An alternative is the **within-subjects factorial,** which is also called the **repeated-measures factorial.** If we had employed it in the dark-fears factorial study, then each participant would have been tested under each of the four combinations of conditions. The ANOVA carried out to test for statistical significance is a **repeated-measures factorial ANOVA,** which takes into account the correlated groups.

Recall from Chapter 11 that using a within-subjects design involves disadvantages that stem from the fact that each participant is exposed to each condition. Specifically, sequence effects may confound the results. When potential sequence effects are strong, a within-subjects design should be avoided. However, when not precluded by such strong sequence effects, a within-subjects design has decided advantages over a between-subjects design. As with the single-variable design, use of a within-subjects design in a factorial experiment can (1) provide greater sensitivity to the effects of the independent variable by reducing the individual-differences component of the error term; (2) assure equivalence of groups at the start of the experiment, because the participants in each condition are identical; (3) require fewer participants; and (4), related to the third point, be more efficient.

In the dark-fears study, for example, if we want 10 participants in each of the four conditions, then only 10 participants are needed for a repeated-measures design, while 40 participants are needed for a between-subjects design. This could be a major advantage when participants are difficult to obtain or when considerable preparation is required for each participant. For these reasons, many researchers prefer a repeated-measures design over a between-subjects design.

Mixed Designs

When there is more than one factor, it is possible that the factors will be of different types. For example, one factor may be a within-subjects factor, whereas the other may be a between-subjects factor. Participants would respond to all levels of the within-subjects factor but be randomly assigned to only one level of the between-subjects factor. This is one type of mixed design.

The term **mixed design** is used in two different ways, which can be confusing. It can be used to refer to a factorial that includes both between-subjects and within-subjects factors. It can also be used to refer to a factorial that includes both manipulated and nonmanipulated factors. It is important to distinguish between the two types of mixed designs, because they affect analysis and interpretation of results in different ways.

Between-Subjects and Within-Subjects Factors.   When both **between-subjects factors** and **within-subjects factors** exist in the same study, the critical issue is a statistical one. For example, suppose that a study has "level of distraction" as the within-subjects factor and the "amount of potential reward for success" as the between-subjects factor, as shown in Table 12.6. Each participant is assigned to one of the potential reward conditions (the between-subjects factor) and tested under all levels of distraction (the within-subjects factor).

For the within-subjects factor, the order of presentation of conditions should be counterbalanced to control sequence effects. In this mixed design, the ANOVA formulas will differ depending on which factors are within-subjects factors and which are between-subjects factors. Recall that in analyzing within-subjects designs, the statistical procedures must take into account the correlated nature of the data.

Computation of ANOVAs for mixed designs is beyond the scope of this text. In most cases, data from such designs are analyzed using statistical computer programs.

Manipulated and Nonmanipulated Factors.   When both **manipulated factors** and **nonmani-pulated factors** are included, the essential issue is one of interpretation of results. In a mixed design in which one factor is a nonmanipulated variable and one factor is a manipulated variable, participants are randomly assigned to the conditions of the manipulated variable but are assigned to levels of the nonmanipulated variable based on preexisting characteristics. For example, if a researcher is studying the effects of crowding on aggression, participants could be randomly assigned to one of three conditions: alone, slightly crowded, and crowded. The level of aggression of participants in each of these conditions would then be observed. The researcher actively manipulates the variable of crowding. But suppose that the researcher is also interested in sex differences in response to crowding, suspecting that there is an interaction between sex of participant and level of crowding on the dependent measure of aggression. Sex is a nonmanipulated variable; the researcher places participants in the male or female group based on their sex. This design

TABLE 12.6   *One Between, One Within Factorial Design*

In this design, participants are randomly assigned to either the small-reward or the large-reward condition and then tested under all three levels of distraction.

		Level of Distraction (within-subjects factor)		
		Low	*Medium*	*High*
Amount of Reward	Small			
(between-subjects factor)	Large			

is shown in Table 12.7. The formulas for the statistical analyses are not affected by whether the variables are manipulated or nonmanipulated, as they are when we have between- and within-subjects factors. The importance of whether a factor is manipulated or nonmanipulated comes into play when we *interpret* the statistical analysis.

Manipulated factors are experiments that effectively control confounding variables. We can therefore safely draw causal inferences based on analysis of the main effects of the variables. Research designs using nonmanipulated factors are not experiments. Instead, they represent differential research. Remember that in differential research participants are not randomly assigned to groups, and therefore groups may differ on variables other than the independent variable. These potential differences may cause confounding.

Unless we can rule out all potential confounding, we cannot confidently draw causal conclusions. Therefore, interpreting the main effects of nonmanipulated factors must be done cautiously and with attention to likely confounding variables. In our example, we must be cautious in drawing the inference that sex caused any observed differences in aggression. Furthermore, the same caution used in the interpretation of main effects for nonmanipulated factors should be used in the interpretation of any interaction involving a nonmanipulated factor. The interaction between sex and level of crowding on aggression should be interpreted as cautiously as the main effect of sex.

Mixed in Both Ways. Finally, it is possible to have a mixed design that is mixed in both of the ways just described. Table 12.8 presents such a situation. In this example, the researcher wants to compare accuracy of recognition of neutral and emotionally charged words in people with schizophrenia and control participants. The researcher arranges a factorial design in which both neutral and charged words are presented to the people with schizophrenia and controls for just a few milliseconds. Note that this is a factorial with one nonmanipulated variable (diagnosis) and one manipulated variable (type of words). Although participants can be randomly assigned to the levels of factor *A* (type of words), the researcher cannot randomly assign participants to factor *B* (diagnosis). Note that in addition to being a mixed design in the sense that it includes both between-subjects and

---

TABLE 12.7   *One Manipulated Variable, One Nonmanipulated Variable Mixed Design*

In this design, male and female participants are randomly assigned to one of the three levels of crowding. Both factors are between-subjects factors. Participants are randomly assigned to the level of crowding (manipulated variable) and are assigned to male or female based on their sex (nonmanipulated variable).

		Level of Crowding (manipulated factor)		
		No Crowding	*Slightly Crowded*	*Very Crowded*
Sex of Participant	Male			
(nonmanipulated factor)	Female			

TABLE 12.8 *Design That Is Mixed in Both a Statistical Sense (One Between, One Within)*
and in an Experimental Sense (One Manipulated, One Nonmanipulated)

In this design, diagnosis is a between-subjects factor, whereas type of words is a within-subjects factor. This will affect the ANOVA formulas used. In addition, diagnosis is a nonmanipulated factor, whereas the type of words is a manipulated factor. This will affect the confidence of causal inference.

| | *Type of Words (within-subjects factor)* | |
	Neutral	*Emotional*
Diagnosis (between-subjects factor)	Schizophrenic	
	Normal	

within-subjects factors, this example is also a mixed design in that one factor (diagnosis) is a between-subjects variable, whereas the other factor (type of words) is a within-subjects variable.

The researcher first classifies each factor on the dimension of between-subjects versus within-subjects factors in order to select the appropriate ANOVA for statistical analysis. Then each factor is classified on the dimension of manipulated versus nonmanipulated factors to interpret the results. Again, the researcher must be especially cautious in drawing conclusions based on main effects and interactions with nonmanipulated factors.

Solomon's Four-Group Design

EXTENDING THE CONCEPT OF SOLOMON'S FOUR-GROUP DESIGN

In Chapter 10, you learned about Solomon's four-group design, which was used to evaluate whether the pretest interacted with the independent variable. Because that was your first introduction to the concept of an interaction, we glossed over some of the details. Now that you understand factorial designs, we can look again at this design and appreciate better how it actually works. This design is illustrated in Figure 12.5, which is simply a repeat of Figure 10.10, which introduced this design. Our description in Chapter 10 of how to analyze this design was rather cumbersome and required a series of comparisons of individual groups. However, this design is actually a simple 2 × 2 factorial design. The factors are (1) the treatment and (2) the pretest. Both factors are presented at two levels (all or none). This design is illustrated as a factorial design in Table 12.9. The dependent measure is the posttest scores, and the analysis is like any other factorial design. If there is an interaction between the pretest and the intervention, it will show up as a significant interaction effect in the ANOVA.

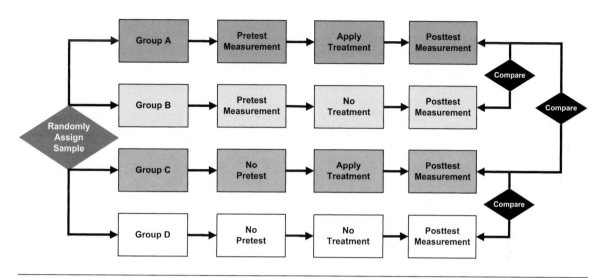

FIGURE 12.5 *Solomon's Four-Group Design* This reiterates Figure 10.10, which illustrates the Solomon four-group design.

TABLE 12.9 *Solomon's Four-Group Design as a Factorial Study*

	Treatment	**No Treatment**
Pretest		
No Pretest		

Solomon's four-group design is really a simple factorial design with two factors (treatment and pretest). The dependent measure is the posttest scores in each of the four cells.

Quick-Check Review 12.2: Variations of Basic Factorial Design	1. What is the major advantage of a repeated-measures factorial? 2. What are the two meanings of mixed design? 3. Explain the implications of mixed designs for (a) interpretation of results and (b) statistical analyses.

ANOVA: A Postscript

Analysis of variance (ANOVA) is one of the most flexible statistical tools available for the evaluation of data. ANOVA compares the variability of the means against a standard based on the variability of scores within groups. If the means are more variable than expected, the researcher concludes that the independent variable had an effect, assuming that confounding was adequately controlled.

The concept of comparing the variability between groups to the variability within groups is constant in every ANOVA, no matter how complicated it becomes. For example, in within-subjects designs, participants are tested under each condition. The repeated-measures ANOVA takes this fact into account in computing the error term, but its basic comparison is between the variability of the means relative to the variability within the groups.

12:04

In an ANOVA with more than two groups, if F is statistically significant, specific means comparisons must be made to find which groups differ significantly from the others. The procedures for carrying out those comparisons using SPSS for Windows are covered on the Student Resource Website.

With factorial designs, ANOVA is extended still further. Here the effects of each independent variable and the interactive effects of combinations of independent variables are examined. For example, with two factors (A and B), there are three possible effects: the A main effect, the B main effect, and the interaction between A and B. With three factors, there are three main effects (A, B, and C), three two-way interactions (AB, AC, and BC), and one three-way interaction (ABC), for a total of seven different effects. Four factors produce the following possible effects: A, B, C, D, AB, AC, AD, BC, BD, CD, ABC, ABD, ACD, BCD, and $ABCD$. Finally, the factorial ANOVAs can take into account which factors are within-subjects factors and which are between-subjects factors.

Although it can become more complicated as additional factors are added to a study, extending the logic and the computational formulas of the ANOVAs to factorial designs is not difficult. The formulas themselves can become quite complex, but for the most part, researchers rely on computers to perform the computation. Because there are many effects, there are many F-ratios, but each F-ratio represents a comparison of between-groups variability to within-groups variability. Furthermore, the F-ratio in these complex designs is interpreted exactly the same as in simpler designs: if the probability of obtaining the F or a larger F is less than the alpha level, the null hypothesis is rejected.

The problem lies not with the computation of complex ANOVAs, but in the interpretation stage, in which the researcher must visualize and explain complex interactions (see the nearby cartoon). The combination of consistency in how the ANOVA is used and flexibility of the procedure to analyze data from so many different designs makes ANOVA the most widely used statistical technique in psychology.

Given the diversity of ANOVA procedures, it is perhaps not surprising that they have been extended into still other designs. These advanced procedures are generally beyond the scope of this book. They are described here only briefly, with an emphasis on understanding conceptually what each procedure is designed to do.

"*He wouldn't listen to me when he was designing the study — so now he has to interpret a five-way interaction.*"

Interpreting complex interactions can be extremely difficult and very frustrating.

Analysis of Covariance

EXTENDING THE CONCEPT OF CONTROLLING INDIVIDUAL DIFFERENCES

Another widely used technique is **analysis of covariance (ANCOVA).** Unfortunately, ANCOVA is easily misused by those who do not understand its nuances (Lord, 1967). ANCOVA is used in the same way as ANOVA, with one addition. As part of the analysis, the effects of a theoretically unimportant, but nonetheless powerful, variable are removed from the dependent variable scores. For example, if you want to study the effects of reinforcement strategies on learning in young children, you could set up a study with two or three levels of the independent variable. You could then randomly assign the sample of children to each condition and measure how well they learn (the dependent variable). The age of the children will affect how quickly they learn material. However, you are not interested in the variable of age in this study. You could hold age constant by using only participants who are in a narrow age range. You could also use a matching procedure to make sure that the groups are equivalent on age at the beginning of the study. You learned about these techniques in Chapter 9.

You could also create a factorial design, with age as one of your factors, as you learned earlier in this chapter. Yet another alternative is to randomly assign participants to groups and use analysis of covariance to statistically remove the effects of age from the dependent measure. This statistical removal of unwanted variance makes the ANOVA more sensitive to group differences. This is conceptually similar to the logic of correlated-groups designs, which provide a more sensitive test of hypotheses because the designs control some of the variability due to individual differences. Here, control over variability due to individual differences is not built into the design of the study, but rather is built into the statistical analysis. We must caution, however, that ANCOVA is a complicated procedure, with many potential pitfalls. For a detailed discussion of ANCOVA, consult Keppel (2006).

Multivariate Analysis of Variance

Another extension of analysis of variance, which is becoming much more popular as sophisticated computer analysis packages become available, is **multivariate analysis of variance (MANOVA).** The difference between an ANOVA and a MANOVA is in the dependent variable. An ANOVA has only one dependent variable, whereas a MANOVA has multiple dependent variables. Conceptually, it is similar to the extension from one-way ANOVAs to factorial ANOVAs, which differ on the number of independent variables in the analysis. The full power of MANOVA procedures is still being discovered. Just as in ANCOVAs, using MANOVA procedures correctly and interpreting the results appropriately requires an extensive understanding of the technique.

ANOVA techniques are flexible and powerful procedures for analyzing data from almost any design. With the aid of a computer, the computations can be done quickly and easily. However, researchers still have to understand research design to set up the computer analyses correctly. Even more critical, researchers must understand when ANOVA procedures are appropriate and how to use them. Even for professionals who conduct little research, knowing these concepts is important in understanding and evaluating the research reported by others. For this reason, doctoral and master's programs in psychology include extensive course work in statistics.

Finally, performing the appropriate statistical analysis is only the first step in evaluating data. The next step is interpreting the meaning of the results, which requires evaluating the entire study on such issues as confounding and the adequacy of control procedures. Statistical procedures, even such clever and useful ones as ANOVA, do not impart meaning to data. Only a researcher who is well trained in science can take this last important step.

Quick-Check Review 12.3: ANOVA: A Postscript

1. What does an analysis of covariance do?
2. How does a MANOVA differ from an ANOVA?

PUTTING IT The vast majority of experimental studies conducted in psychology are factorial
INTO PRACTICE studies because almost everything of consequence in the psychological world is
influenced by multiple factors, many of which interact with one another. Yet
human beings have a natural tendency to try to simplify the world in an effort to
understand it. We tend to visualize individual effects on variables and rarely think
in terms of interactions.

Identify some issues around you. They could be anything, from what makes
people attractive or successful to how traffic jams form. Then identify individual
variables that are likely to have an effect on the issue you selected. For example, if
you were looking at business success, you might identify variables like education,
background knowledge, tenacity, work ethic, connections, confidence, good
communication skills, and even physical attractiveness. Take your time and
identify as many variables as you can. Then do a little brainstorming about how
some of those variables might interact with one another to influence business
success. For example, an individual who possesses both extensive background
knowledge and good communication skills might make impressive presentations,
which lead people to think that this is someone they want to work with. It will take
you a while to get used to thinking about interactions, but it will dramatically
enhance your ability to understand the complex psychological world in which
we live.

Chapter Summary

Factorial designs include more than one independent variable. They are efficient and flexible designs that combine information from the equivalent of two or more single-variable studies. Their greatest advantage is that they yield information about the interactive effects of the independent variables.

Factorial designs can be of several types, in which the factors are (1) between-subjects variables or within-subjects variables, (2) manipulated variables or nonmanipulated variables, or (3) mixed factorials. A factorial with a within-subjects component must be analyzed with statistical procedures that take into ac-

count the correlated nature of the data. A factorial with a nonmanipulated component must be interpreted cautiously, because causality cannot be properly inferred from nonmanipulated independent variables.

ANOVAs are used to analyze factorial designs. It is helpful to graph cell means and, by inspection of the graph, to note whether significant interactions and/or main effects seem likely. When the analysis indicates that both main effects and an interaction are significant, the main effects should always be interpreted in terms of interaction.

Chapter Exercises

1. Define the following key terms. Be sure that you understand them. They are discussed in the chapter and defined in the glossary.

factorial designs
interaction effects
factors
matrix of cells
design notation
main effects
row means
column means
computer-analysis
   program
within-subjects factorial,
   or repeated-measures
   factorial

repeated-measures
   factorial ANOVA
mixed design
between subjects factors
within subjects factors
manipulated factors
nonmanipulated factors
analysis of covariance
   (ANCOVA)
multivariate analysis
   of variance
   (MANOVA)

2. For each of the following (i) indicate how many factors are included, and (ii) tell how many levels there are for each factor:

   a. 2 × 2

   b. 2 × 3

   c. 2 × 3 × 2

   d. 4 × 3

   e. 4 × 3 × 2 × 3

3. For each of the above, draw the appropriate matrix and label the factors and levels.

4. As the teaching assistant for your course, you are asked to explain the concept of interaction. Organize your presentation, starting by making the distinction between main effects and interactions. Be sure to clarify the distinction between additive and interactive effects.

5. As the teaching assistant for your course, you are asked to explain that a 2 × 2 factorial study is, in a sense, two separate studies combined. How would you develop your explanation?

6. Given the following cell means and ANOVA summary table, how would you interpret the results?

Source	df	SS	MS	F	p
A	3	121.5	40.5	1.39	n.s.
B	1	93.7	93.7	3.21	< .05
AB	3	288.6	96.2	3.29	< .05
Within	72	2102.4	29.2		
Total	79	2606.2			

Matrix of means

	B_1	B_2
A_1	12.1	13.4
A_2	9.5	15.7
A_3	7.5	17.5
A_4	5.9	18.9

7. In the children's dark-fears study, suppose that we had found significant main effects for both level of illumination and fear images, but no interaction. Draw a graph to show how such results would look. How would you interpret the findings conceptually?

8. Assume that in the dark-fears study you obtained a significant main effect for fear images and a significant interaction. What would the graph of the results look like? How would you interpret these results?

13

A Second Look at Field Research:
Field Experiments, Program Evaluation, and Survey Research

People don't usually do research the way people who write books about research say that people do research.

—A. J. Bachrach, 1981

Web Resources Material _____

The field research introduced in Chapter 6 focused on low-constraint field research (naturalistic observation, case studies, and archival research). These methods are useful in gathering facts, observing contingencies, becoming familiar with phenomena, and developing hypotheses for later high-constraint research. However, research in natural settings is not limited to low-constraint methods. This chapter covers higher-constraint field research, including field experiments, program evaluation, and survey research. Field research examples are provided on the Student Resource Website.

13:01

Conducting Field Research

It is increasingly common for psychological research to be carried out in field settings. For example, there are demands to evaluate the effectiveness of education and public health programs, to assess the effects of such large-scale events as disasters and economic recessions, and to determine employee reactions to changed work conditions or consumer reactions to new products. These are questions about causality. Low-constraint research cannot answer them, because it cannot rule out alternative hypotheses.

Conducting experimental research in natural settings is difficult because of the limitations imposed by the settings. For example, it may be impossible to randomly assign participants to groups. Precise measures of dependent variables may be impossible, and manipulation of independent variables may be politically or ethically unacceptable. In some studies, such as a study of the psychological effects of a natural disaster, manipulating the independent variable is impossible. Finally, it is often difficult to maintain projects in the field, because decision makers may cancel or curtail ongoing projects. Nevertheless, despite difficulties, high quality field research routinely addresses questions of concern to society.

Reasons for Doing Field Experiments

There are three major reasons for conducting experiments in field settings:

1. To test the external validity of laboratory findings
2. To determine the effects of events that occur in the field
3. To improve generalization across settings

Testing External Validity.   Experimental laboratory research tests causal hypotheses under controlled conditions designed to maximize internal validity. However, the cost of this improved internal validity may be a reduction in external validity. The more precise and constrained the laboratory, the less natural the procedures. Consequently, laboratory research might not always generalize to the natural environment.

The advantages of experimental control for inferring causation have to be weighed against the disadvantages that arise because we do not always want to learn about causation in controlled settings. Instead, for many purposes, we would like to be able to generalize to causal relationships in complex field settings, and we cannot easily assume that findings from the laboratory will hold in the field. (Cook & Campbell, 1979, p. 7)

For example, suppose that a controlled experiment is conducted in a university laboratory school, and a new teaching method is found to be superior to the standard procedures used in schools throughout the state. No matter how much confidence the researcher has in the internal validity of the experimental results, it would be unwise to assume that when the new teaching method is adopted in schools across the state, operating under a variety of conditions, the method will be just as effective. The reason is that the field situations may be different from laboratory situations. The researcher should test the new instructional procedures in field situations to increase confidence in the generalizability of the results from the laboratory to the field. This is particularly important in applied research, in which the goal is not only to understand phenomena, but also to use the new understanding in practical ways.

Studying Effects in the Field. The second reason for doing field research is to determine the impact of events that occur in the field. There is a growing demand in some quarters for testing the effectiveness of social programs, such as special education programs, public health campaigns, crackdowns on drunk drivers, and schemes that give tax incentives to corporations. Each of these programs has an implicit assumption: the educational program will improve literacy; the public health program will reduce drug addiction; the drunk-driving crackdown will reduce highway fatalities; the tax incentives will increase economic growth.

Unfortunately, in reality such assumptions are seldom tested. Social programs, as well meaning as they may be, are too often created for political ends. Their supporters are rarely committed to testing program effectiveness. Politically, it may be better not to subject programs to testing just in case testing reveals that one's costly and fine-sounding pet project does not work. Donald Campbell (1969) argued that developed countries should carry out social reforms as controlled social experiments, and the fate of each program should depend on the objective data. Such evaluations of new programs are not yet routinely carried out.

EXTENDING THE CONCEPT OF GENERALIZATION

Improving Generalization. The third reason for conducting field research is to improve generalization—a concept we first discussed in Chapter 9. We must distinguish among three types of generalization:

1. Generalization of the results from the participants in a study to the larger population, as discussed in Chapter 9
2. Generalization of the results of the study over time (i.e., testing stability)
3. Generalization of results from study settings to other field settings

The third type of generalization may be enhanced when research is conducted in naturalistic settings. Consider the example given earlier, in which the effectiveness of a new teaching program was tested in a university laboratory school. The high-constraint laboratory setting, high in internal validity, is not necessarily strong in external validity. However, if the new program is found to be superior to other teaching methods when tested in the field, the researcher can have greater confidence that the results will generalize to other, similar classroom settings.

Neisser and Harsch (1992) conducted a clever field study to verify the external validity of a phenomenon that had been well established in the laboratory. Elizabeth Loftus and others had shown that memory is fragile and subject to significant distortion and that people are often unaware of the distortions (e.g., Loftus & Hoffman, 1989). In 1986, the day after the *Challenger* space shuttle exploded during launch, Neisser and Harsch (1992) asked 44 college students to write down how they heard about the explosion and what they did. They asked these same students again 30 months later. None of these participants was entirely accurate in recall at 30 months, and over one-third gave dramatically different accounts of how they found out about the *Challenger* disaster the day after and 30 months later. More striking is that participants were certain that their memories 2.5 years after the accident were accurate, often describing the memories as exceptionally vivid. Many were astonished, even flabbergasted, when confronted with their own handwritten accounts made the day after the disaster. Participants could not believe that memories that seemed so vivid and accurate could be so distorted over time and that they would not realize that the memories were distorted.

This field study enhances confidence in the external validity of the laboratory studies of the malleability of memory. It also suggests that these laboratory findings would be relevant to real-world situations, such as eyewitness testimony in courts (Loftus & Ketcham, 1991).

How well do these findings generalize to other situations? The attacks on the World Trade Center and the Pentagon on September 11, 2001 offered psychologists another opportunity to look at this issue. The 9/11 attacks were often felt more personally than the destruction of the *Challenger* space shuttle, raising anxiety about future attacks. So you might expect memories of the 9/11 attacks to be more intense and more resistant to change over time than the memories of the shuttle disaster. Weaver and Krug (2004) studied the memories of the 9/11 attacks several times over the year following the attack. They found that in the first week, the reports about how people heard about the attack and how they responded did shift from the initial report given the day of the attack, but then the memories seemed to stabilize.

They also found that the degree to which the memories shifted was much less than what Neisser and Harsch (1992) found for the shuttle disaster. Those closest to the events seemed to have the most stable and consistent memories of the events. For example, Paradis and her collaborators (2004) studied New York City residents and found that their memories of the attack were very stable.

These three field studies, as well as some others not reported here, collectively indicate that dramatic events create the feeling that we have a strong and indelible memory of the event, but that memory is not always as stable as it feels. However, more emotionally powerful events tend to create memories that are more stable over time than do less emotionally powerful events.

Difficulties in Field Research

Ideally, field experiments should be conducted so as to allow the researcher to be able to draw causal inferences. However, doing so can be difficult. In many field situations we cannot apply laboratory controls or assign participants to groups. This is frequently the case in natural settings, such as schools, or when natural events affect a large number of people. For example, suppose that you want to know how much a natural disaster, such as a hurricane, affected residents' physical health. The natural event is the independent variable, and the residents' health is the dependent variable. Note that the researcher has no control over the independent variable. How, then, does the researcher measure the reactions and draw causal inferences?

To take another example, suppose that when studying a population of children, a researcher cannot randomly assign participants to different groups for treatment because they are all part of a single class following a common program. That is, they are always together, and whatever is applied to one child is applied to all others. Assigning the children to different groups for purposes of the study will seriously interfere with the ongoing program, and the program director will not allow it. The researcher wants to conduct research with as much control as possible in order to draw causal inferences, and yet he or she knows that random assignment is impossible.

Under such restrictions as these, how can we evaluate a new treatment? How can we answer questions about causality in natural settings when many of the usual manipulation and laboratory control procedures are unavailable?

This chapter discusses two solutions to this question: quasi-experimental designs and program evaluation research. *Quasi-experimental designs* are research designs that have been developed to answer causal questions in natural settings. *Program evaluation research* is not a particular design, but rather is an increasingly important research area that includes many designs and strategies for assessing field settings. Single-subject experiments (covered in Chapter 11) can also test causal questions in field settings.

Flexibility in Research

We now want to bring up something all scientists know but which is not normally discussed in methods courses. This chapter opened with the following quotation: *"People don't usually do research the way people who write books about research say that people do research"* (A. J. Bachrach, 1981). Is this true? Well, yes and no. Bachrach was talking about flexibility and creativity in research, much as we did in Chapter 1 in our discussion of serendipity. Researchers use hunches, flashes of insight, flights of creativity, and alertness to interesting, unanticipated events that can crop up. Such alertness can open new directions to be explored, help us frame old questions in new ways, or let us formulate new ways of studying things. Creativity and flexibility are especially needed in field research, in which the controlled environment of the laboratory is not there to help keep everything organized and systematic.

Bachrach did not mean to imply that real research is unsystematic. Rather, he points out that there is an important place in the process to engage in the freer flights of research thinking. These free flights are useful precisely because they exist in a total research context that includes the organization, structure, and precision of science. This systematic structure makes it possible to engage in hunches and intellectual leaps without bringing the whole enterprise down in a chaotic jumble. When scientists are engaged in hypothesis testing, particularly of causal hypotheses, then systematic structure and precision are what is needed. However, within that structure opportunities for unanticipated discoveries may appear, and a good researcher does not ignore them.

So why do we bring this up now, so late in this text? We think it is important for students to learn the fundamentals of research before they take such free-flight leaps. A good analogy is to abstract artists: most of the great ones learned academic techniques of drawing and painting before they began to create new and less constrained art forms. With a solid background, the researcher can be more flexible. This is often necessary in quasi-experimental designs and field research.

Quasi-Experimental Designs

The highest degree of control is obtained with experiments. Experiments are impossible in some situations, but quasi-experimental designs are feasible. *Quasi* means approximately. Thus, a **quasi-experiment** is almost an experiment, but not quite. Quasi-experiments have the essential format of experiments, including some type of manipulation to compare two or more conditions. They do control for some confounding, but do not have as much control as experiments. Thus, we must be cautious in drawing causal inferences from quasi-experiments.

Donald Campbell (1969) argued that quasi-experimental designs should be used whenever experiments cannot be carried out. In many field situations, a quasi-experiment *will still provide considerably more useful information than not experimenting at all.* Keep in mind that quasi-experimental designs are different from low-constraint methods in that they use many experimental control procedures.

Quasi-experimental designs include a comparison of at least two levels of an independent variable, but the actual manipulation may not always be under the experimenter's control. For example, if a researcher compares health before and after a natural disaster, the disaster obviously cannot be manipulated, but the researcher can compare the health records from local hospitals before and after the disaster for those who experience it, and compare them to records of people who did not experience the disaster. Likewise, in many field situations, participants cannot be randomly assigned to groups; indeed, the researcher often cannot assign participants at all, but rather must accept the natural groups as they exist. Thus, in quasi-experimental designs:

1. We state causal hypotheses.
2. We include at least two levels of the independent variable but cannot always manipulate the independent variable.
3. We usually cannot assign participants to groups but must accept existing groups.
4. We include specific procedures for testing hypotheses.
5. We include some controls for threats to validity.

Compare these characteristics with the characteristics of an experiment (Chapter 10).

This chapter focuses on two quasi-experimental designs: the nonequivalent control-group design and the interrupted time-series design. Cook and Campbell (1979) provide a more detailed discussion of quasi-experimental designs.

Nonequivalent Control-Group Designs

EXTENDING THE CONCEPT OF NATURAL CONTROL GROUPS

The best way to confidently test causal hypotheses is to compare groups that are created by the researcher through random assignment. This makes it likely that the groups are equivalent at the beginning of the study. The initial equivalence of groups is crucial in experimental design. However, in some situations, participants are not assigned randomly, and therefore the groups may not be equivalent at the beginning of the study. Several designs fall into this category. All of them attempt to solve the problem of comparing two groups that we suspect are not equivalent at the beginning of the study. We introduced one design in this category in Chapter 10 (the pretest-posttest, natural control-group design). In that chapter, we emphasized the weaknesses of that design compared with experimental alternatives.

Researchers frequently have no choice in field research but to use already existing groups; thus, participants are not randomly assigned. Even though groups may appear to be similar, it cannot be assumed that they are equivalent at the start of the study. The groups may differ on both the dependent variable and other potential confounding variables, although a careful researcher may be able to rule out the most likely sources of confounding.

Campbell and Stanley (1966) popularized the **nonequivalent control-group design,** in which the groups already exist in the natural environment and therefore may not be truly equivalent at the start of the study. Campbell and Stanley suggested that already-existing groups may often be similar to one another on most relevant variables. The more similar those natural groups are to one another, the closer the design approximates an experiment. Cook and Campbell (1979) extended these principles to situations in which naturally occurring groups are clearly not equivalent on potential confounding variables. Even in this extreme situation, it is sometimes possible to draw strong conclusions if the researcher carefully evaluates all potential threats to validity.

The ideal is an experiment in which participants are randomly assigned to groups. If this is not possible, the best alternative is to use nonequivalent control groups that give every indication of being similar on most of the relevant variables. Even when this requirement cannot be met, careful analysis of the design and the results can sometimes allow the researcher to draw useful conclusions from what appears to be a weak research design (Cook & Campbell, 1979). Table 13.1 lists examples of research using a nonequivalent control-group design.

TABLE 13.1   *Field Situations with Nonequivalent Groups*

---

1. Researchers want to evaluate the effectiveness of an antismoking campaign in two schools, but they suspect that one school has a higher rate of smoking than the other.

2. A company wants to test how new work rules might affect their employees' attitudes toward work. One department is selected as an experimental group and another as the control group. However, there is evidence that the first department has more positive work attitudes than the second.

3. A psychology professor wants to compare examination results in a research methods course based on two different textbooks. The professor teaches one section of the course at 8:00 a.m. on Monday, Wednesday, and Friday and the other at 4:00 p.m. on Tuesday and Thursday. The professor suspects that students who chose the early section may be different from those who chose the later section.

4. A new treatment approach for hyperactivity is to be tested in a special education program using three existing classes. The classes, however, are at different levels of hyperactivity.

There are two major problems with nonequivalent groups: (1) the groups may differ on the dependent measure(s) at the start of the study, and (2) there may be other differences between the groups. The basic strategy for addressing the first issue is to measure the experimental and control groups on the dependent measure both before and after the manipulation. The pretest allows us to determine how similar the groups are initially on the dependent variable(s). This similarity is important: the more similar the groups are, the closer the design is to an experiment.

EXTENDING THE CONCEPT OF RULING OUT CONFOUNDING

The researcher addresses the issue that groups may differ on variables other than the dependent variable (confounding caused by selection) by ruling out each potential confounding variable. This is accomplished by identifying potential confounding variables, measuring them, and verifying that the groups do not differ on them. This is the strategy we outlined in Chapter 7, when we discussed selecting control groups in differential research. In differential research, groups potentially differ on several variables besides the variable that defined the groups. If we select the right control group(s), however, we can minimize confounding.

This same strategy can be used in nonequivalent control-group designs. The selection of an effective control group can move this design closer to an experimental design. The confounding that can affect the outcome will vary from study to study. A typical nonequivalent control-group design is shown in Figure 13.1.

A complete discussion of the principles for identifying confounding variables and interpreting their likely effects on a nonequivalent control-group study is beyond the scope of this book. The interested reader is referred to Cook and Campbell (1979) for a more complete discussion.

Figure 13.2 shows six possible outcomes of a nonequivalent control-group design. In Figures 13.2(a) and (b), the experimental and control groups are equivalent on the dependent measure at the beginning of the study. Of course, the groups may differ on other important variables, in which case the researcher must rule out confounding caused by selection. In Figures 13.2(c) through (f), the groups differ on the dependent measure at pretest. In these instances, the researcher must rule out confounding caused by selection

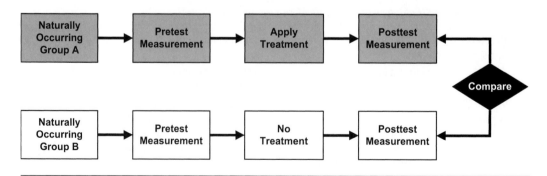

FIGURE 13.1   *A Nonequivalent Control-Group Design*   The nonequivalent control-group design is essentially the pretest-posttest, natural control-group design introduced in Chapter 10.

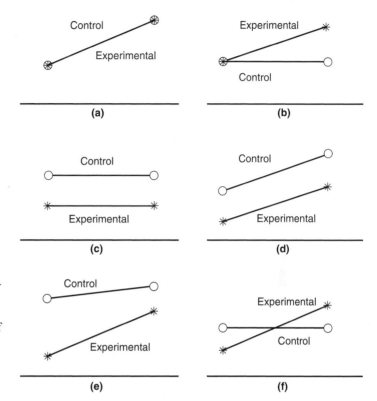

FIGURE 13.2
Interpreting Nonequivalent Control-Group Designs Some possible outcomes of nonequivalent control-group designs are illustrated graphically. Some outcomes are relatively easy to interpret, whereas others are difficult or impossible to interpret.

and regression to the mean. For purposes of illustration, it is assumed that all changes shown are in the predicted direction.

In Figure 13.2(a), both the experimental and control groups show an increase on the dependent measure from pretest to posttest. The groups are equivalent at the beginning and show equivalent change over time. Thus, there appears to be no effect of the independent variable. In Figure 13.2(b), the groups are equivalent on the dependent measures at the beginning of the study. The experimental group shows a large change, whereas the control group does not change from pretest to posttest. There does appear to be an effect of the independent variable. However, before drawing this conclusion, the researcher must still rule out possible confounding caused by selection. For example, the groups may differ on another variable that might account for the different observed rates of change on the dependent measure. In Figure 13.2(c), neither group changes from pretest to posttest. The obvious interpretation is that the manipulation had no effect on the dependent variable. Figure 13.2(d) shows a similar change in both groups from pretest to posttest. However, because both groups changed in the same manner, we cannot attribute the change to the independent variable. It appears more likely that some maturation process or historical event common to both groups may be responsible for the change in scores.

Figure 13.2(e) shows a slight change in the control group but a marked change in the experimental group. Such results suggest an effect of the independent variable. However, there is still the potential for regression to the mean, which limits confidence in this interpretation. Recall from Chapter 8 that regression is a potential source of confounding whenever we begin an experiment with extreme scores. In Figure 13.2(e), the pretest difference between groups might represent extreme scores for the experimental group, which then regressed toward the mean level represented by the control group. Thus, the change in the experimental group may not be caused by the independent variable. In Figure 13.2(f), the control group does not change, but the experimental group changes in the predicted direction, even going beyond the level of the control group. This is called a **crossover effect.** Such results provide considerable confidence in a causal inference. Maturation is an unlikely alternative hypothesis, because the control group presumably matured but did not change. If maturation were responsible, it is unlikely that the effect would be so different in the two groups. Regression to the mean is also unlikely, because the experimental group increased, not only to the mean of the control group, but beyond it.

The preceding examples represent reasonably interpretable data from nonequivalent control-group studies. Other situations can be more difficult, and sometimes impossible, to interpret. Using nonequivalent control-group designs and correctly interpreting data from them require considerable expertise, and they are not recommended to beginning students. As we said before, an experiment is the best approach. When an experiment is not possible, a quasi-experiment, in which groups are apparently equivalent, is the best compromise. Only if neither of these alternatives is feasible should the researcher consider using a quasi-experimental design with nonequivalent groups.

Interrupted Time-Series Designs

In an **interrupted time-series design,** a single group of participants is measured several times both before and after some event or manipulation (Orwin, 1997). In other words, a series of measures is taken over time, "interrupted" by the manipulation, after which another series of measures is taken. Time-series designs are variations of within-subjects designs, in which the same participants are measured in different conditions. The time-series design is similar to a simple pretest-posttest design except that multiple pretest and posttest measures are taken.

The simple pretest-posttest design is weak, leaving so many potential confounding factors uncontrolled that we cannot draw causal inferences (see Chapter 10). For example, recall the study of the use of relaxation to reduce the disruptive behavior of autistic children. A major potential confounding factor in this simple pretest-posttest study is regression to the mean. The disruptive behavior may naturally fluctuate over time, displaying considerable variability. The intervention might be applied only at a high point in this natural variation, just before the disruptive behavior decreased again. Thus, the observed improvement might not be caused by the treatment but only be a result of the natural variability of behavior. In other words, the reduction would have occurred about that time without the treatment. Including multiple measures both before and after the manipulation provides several points of comparison over time, thus allowing the researcher to recognize regression to the mean effects.

To apply the interrupted time-series design in the study of autistic children, we would (1) measure disruption several times during a baseline observation period, (2) apply the treatment, and (3) measure disruptive behavior several more times after the intervention. This is exactly what Graziano (1974) did. Disruptive behavior of four autistic children was measured and recorded for a full year as a normal part of the monitoring carried out in the program. The treatment (relaxation training) was applied, and the behavioral measures were again taken for more than a year following the treatment. Figure 13.3 shows the results. Inspection of the graph shows considerable variation during the 1-year pretreatment baseline. Following treatment, there was a marked decrease in disruptive behavior, reaching zero and remaining there. The results suggest that the decrease following treatment was not caused by normal fluctuation or regression to the mean. It also seems unlikely to have been caused by maturation of all participants during the same period of time. Although this study is a good demonstration of the effects of relaxation training, there is still a major confounding factor remaining. Can you identify it? (We will return to this point soon.)

Note the peak of disruptive behavior immediately after training began. Does this suggest that the procedure was not working? Not really. A peak like this is a common clinical phenomenon called a *frustration effect,* which occurs when new procedures are initiated. Frustration effects are generally temporary, as shown in Figure 13.3. Again, subtleties like this illustrate how important it is to know the research literature, so that you do not interpret your findings incorrectly.

Interrupted time-series designs are useful in settings in which the effects of an event—naturally occurring or manipulated—may be assessed by taking multiple measurements both before and after the event. These designs can take advantage of data already gathered over a long period of time. They can also be used in studies in which the presumed causal event occurs for all members of a population. For example, suppose that a state government wants to reduce traffic collisions by reducing the speed limit from 75 to 65 mph. Because the new speed limit applies to every driver in the state, there cannot be an experimental group of state drivers for whom the new limit applies and a control group in which it does not. This is an ideal situation for an interrupted time-series design. Figure 13.4 is a hypothetical graph of such a time-series study. The graph shows the variation in the number of serious accidents during the pre-intervention phase, with an overall slight increase throughout the year. Following the new speed limit, there is a sharp reduction that eventually stabilizes at a new, lower level of accidents for the remainder of that year and into the next.

FIGURE 13.3
Relaxation Treatment for Disruptive Behavior A time-series design using four children with autism demonstrates that relaxation training decreases the frequency of disruptive behavior.

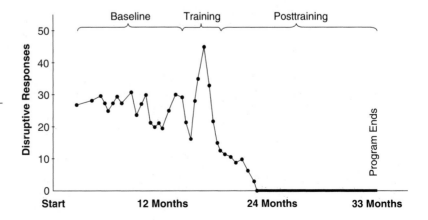

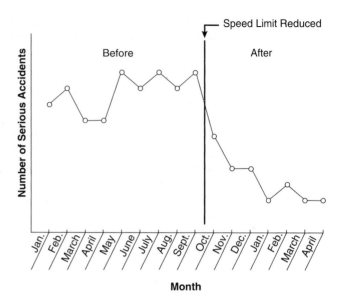

FIGURE 13.4 *An Interrupted Time-Series Design* Using an interrupted time-series design, this hypothetical study illustrates the effects of a reduction in the state speed limit on the number of serious accidents.

Are these results sufficient to draw a reasonably confident conclusion that the reduced speed limit is effective in reducing the number of serious accidents? Let us consider the major potential confounding factors. Selection is not at issue, because this is essentially a within-subjects design, and the two groups being compared (the state's drivers before and after the decreased speed limit) were thus equivalent at the start of the study. Testing effects are not critical, because the measures taken are unobtrusive. They were taken from traffic records and not directly from participants. Maturation is not an issue, because it is unlikely that all the state's drivers suddenly became better drivers at the same time that the speed limit changed. Regression to the mean is not an issue. Note that the post-intervention decrease in accidents is much sharper, lasts longer, and reaches a lower mean level than the pre-intervention fluctuations.

Primarily because of its multiple measures at pre- and posttreatment, the interrupted time-series design controls for most potential confounding. It is a far stronger design than a simple pretest-posttest design in which only one measure is taken at each phase.

With time-series designs, however, two potentially confounding factors remain: history and instrumentation. History can confound results in any procedure that requires a fairly long period of time, because any number of other events might account for changes in the dependent variable. For example, in our hypothetical speed-limit study, the state might have also sharply increased the number of patrol cars, the number of speeding tickets, and the severity of penalties for speeding and for drunk driving. Any of these actions may have contributed to the decrease in accidents. Thus, when using the interrupted time-series design, the experimenter must be careful to identify potential confounding caused by history and rule it out. In this example, we must be sure that the state did not initiate these actions at the same time that it decreased the speed limit. (Recall a few paragraphs earlier when you were asked to identify the remaining major confounding factor in the time-series design for the relaxation training study. If you identified it as history, you were correct.)

Instrumentation is also a potential threat to validity in time-series designs. When people initiate new approaches or programs, there might also be accompanying changes in recording procedures. For example, if the state government was more systematic about collecting accident statistics after the speed limit change, any observed changes could be caused by either the change in speed limit or the way the data were gathered. Such confounding caused by instrumentation must be ruled out.

In a time-series study, the change must be sharp to be interpreted as anything other than a normal fluctuation. Any post-intervention change that is slight or gradual is difficult to interpret as being caused by the intervention. It should also occur immediately after the intervention, unless there is a theoretical reason to expect a delay. For example, if an intervention by the government is expected to change consumer spending, but only after it has affected other economic variables, the change in consumer spending may be delayed and still indicate an effect of the intervention.

Note two important points about the interrupted time-series design. First, it is a flexible design that can be used in many situations. It can evaluate events that are large- or small-scale; it can evaluate events that have already occurred or that are expected to occur; it can evaluate events that are either manipulated (such as the decreased speed limit) or not manipulated (such as a natural disaster). (Think about how you might use this design to evaluate a large-scale natural disaster that has already occurred.)

Second, a time-series design can use existing data, such as data on auto accidents. This is one reason why this design is often used by government agencies to track the effects of new programs. Table 13.2 gives examples of published studies that used interrupted time-series designs. The studies are listed in the references at the end of this book so that, if you are interested, you can read the original reports.

An interrupted time-series design can be improved by adding one or more comparison groups. In our hypothetical study of the effects of a change in speed limit on the number of accidents, we could use similar data from a neighboring state that did not reduce the speed limit as a comparison. This would help to control such confounding variables as history and maturation. For example, Guerin and MacKinnon (1985) studied the effects of a California

TABLE 13.2 *Research Using Interrupted Time-Series Designs*

1. O'Carroll et al. (1991) studied the impact on homicide rates of a Detroit law that mandated jail sentences for illegally carrying a firearm. They found that the new law reduced street homicides but not homicides in the home.

2. Brewer and Shillinglaw (1992) investigated the effectiveness of a four-session psychological skills training workshop in improving the competitiveness of intercollegiate lacrosse players.

3. Catalano and Serxner (1992) used an interrupted time-series design to investigate the relationship between employment security and birth weight of children. They found that during periods of employment uncertainty, such as when companies are laying off people, male babies average lower birth weight than during periods when employment is more secure.

4. Stolzenberg and D'Alessio (1997) used an interrupted time-series design to assess the impact of California's "3 strikes and you're out" law on the rate of serious crimes. As a control, they studied petty theft, which was not covered by the law.

5. McKay, Todaro, Neziroglu, and Yaryura-Tobias (1996) used an interrupted time-series approach to study the effectiveness of a treatment procedure for obsessive-compulsive disorder.

law that required children under age four to be in federally approved child car seats while riding in cars. Using an interrupted time-series design, the authors examined the effects of the new law on child auto injuries. The number of injuries for children under age four was obtained from state records for a period covering 48 months prior to the start of the new law and 12 months following its initiation. As a comparison, the researchers recorded auto injury data for children between four and seven years old—children not covered by the law. The researchers predicted that there would be a decrease for the younger group but not for the older group. As shown in Figure 13.5, after the law went into effect, there was a drop in injuries in the younger group but not in the older group, and the differences persisted over the next 12 months. In addition, the younger group was compared with a group of young children from Texas, where no child car-seat law existed. Texas children did not show a decrease during the same period. Adding these two comparison groups increased confidence that the new law, and not other factors, accounted for the reduction in injuries.

Graphing the results of interrupted time-series studies provides considerable information, but simply inspecting the graph does not address whether the observed differences are statistically significant. Testing for statistical significance in time-series designs re-

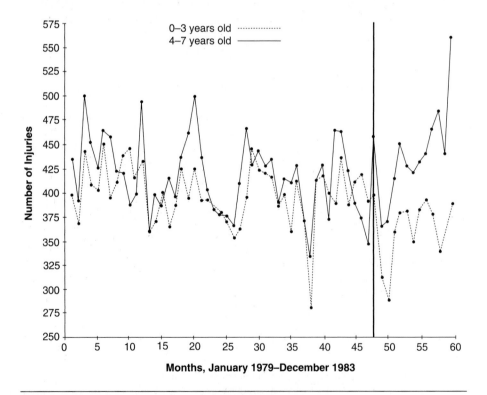

FIGURE 13.5 *Effects of a New Child Car-Seat Law* These time-series data show that a new car-seat law reduced the number of injuries in 0- to 3-year-old children in comparison with 4- to 7-year-old children, who were not covered by the law.

Source: Guerin & MacKinnon, 1985

quires sophisticated procedures that are beyond the scope of this book. The interested student is referred to Kazdin (1998) for a more detailed discussion.

Quick-Check Review 13.2: Quasi-Experimental Designs	1. Define quasi-experimental design. What is the value of this type of design? What are its limitations?
	2. When are nonequivalent control-group designs most effective?
	3. How are interrupted time-series designs a variation on within-subjects designs?
	4. What are the two major confounding factors in time-series designs?

Program Evaluation Research

The task in **program evaluation research** is to evaluate how successfully a program meets its goals. For example, researchers may need to evaluate a food-stamp program, a state highway speed-control program, or the effectiveness of a rehabilitation program for criminal offenders. In these days of tight budgets, a key concept is *accountability*. The goal of program evaluation research is to provide evidence on whether money spent on a program is accomplishing the goals intended. Such evidence often improves existing programs, making them more effective and targeting them to those who are most likely to benefit, as illustrated in *Historical Lesson 13.1.*

Program evaluation research is not a set of research designs distinct from the designs discussed earlier in the text. Instead, these designs are modified to meet the constraints of the situation. The best possible research design—the design that permits the strongest conclusions—should always be used. However, program realities frequently restrict our choice of design.

Practical Problems in Program Evaluation Research

Unique practical considerations are inherent in program evaluation research. High-constraint research brings participants into the laboratory, allowing considerable control. In contrast, program evaluation research evaluates the effectiveness of programs that operate in complex and often uncontrolled natural settings. Furthermore, program evaluators are interested in how effective the program is in meeting the needs of clients—often a private and personal matter for each client. Finally, in most cases, the participants in the program have not volunteered for a research study. Rather, they became involved in the program because they had needs that were addressed by the program. Therefore, the program evaluator is faced with difficult practical and ethical considerations that few other researchers face.

Ethical constraints are common in program evaluation. Often the program is designed to meet an urgent need that cannot be ignored. The most valid research design would randomly assign participants to one of two conditions: the program group and the no-program group. But is it ethical to deny food stamps to some randomly selected individuals to see whether they really suffer malnutrition more than individuals who are given food stamps? Is it ethical to deny some children access to a special education program designed to overcome learning disabilities so that the program can be evaluated?

HISTORICAL LESSON 13.1:   From Head Start to Heads Up

One of the most prominent aspects of the Great Society Program of the 1960s was the wide range of Head Start Programs that were initiated across the country (Vinovskis, 2005). The idea behind Head Start was that children who are raised in an environment that lacks intellectual stimulation are likely to be intellectually handicapped for their entire lives. Providing intellectual and social stimulation to preschoolers was an attempt to prevent this handicap.

Actually, at the time that most Head Start programs were introduced, we knew little about how early childhood experiences affected intellectual development, and, consequently, many of the Head Start programs were really experiments. Remember, Donald Campbell (1969) had argued that industrial nations should routinely evaluate new programs as social experiments, and many of the Head Start programs did indeed have an evaluation component.

The early research on Head Start programs was discouraging. The effects were small and tended to disappear after a few months, although there were exceptions to this pattern. Ramey and his colleagues (1996) looked at this broad pattern of findings and noted that there were important effects discernable in the data. Those effects were often masked by the fact that the Head Start programs were making only a marginal difference in intellectual development for most children. However, for those children whose home environment was extremely deficient, with little social, perceptual, and cognitive stimulation, enrichment programs like Head Start seemed to make a significant difference (Ramey & Ramey, 1998). Through a series of studies, Ramey and his colleagues discovered that the earlier the intervention in the child's life, the more helpful it is and the longer lasting the results

(Campbell & Ramey, 1994), presumably because such early intervention provides the necessary stimulation to allow normal brain development. One of the reasons that most Head Start programs had minimal impact is that these early programs focused on children who were almost school age and therefore well past most of the critical periods for brain development. Also, most Head Start programs targeted children solely on the basis of family income, which is less predictive of intellectual development problems than the level of stimulation in the household (Ramey & Ramey, 1998).

The programs that have been most effective in increasing the intellectual development of children and maintaining the gains are those that (1) begin when children are very young, (2) are intensive (up to several hours per day several days per week), (3) provide the experience directly to the children rather than indirectly through parent training, (4) are broad in their focus rather than focusing on a single cognitive skill, (5) are tailored to individual children, and (6) seek to continue intellectual stimulation after the program ends (Campbell et al., 2002; Ramey & Ramey, 1998). These findings are based on over 40 years of research, starting with evaluations of the early Head Start programs and continuing with high-constraint experimental studies of the impact of various interventions on the intellectual development of children.

Just imagine how this research and the targeted programs that it has spawned have affected the lives of people who might have been doomed to a life of marginal intellectual development and the limitations that such development would have placed on their lives. Clearly, the effective use of program evaluation can change the world in some very positive ways.

Sometimes ethical concerns are not the only issues that restrict the researcher. In a learning disabilities program, for example, we could argue that the program is experimental and might not work. In fact, it might do more harm than good. Therefore, denying some participants access to the program to allow a cleaner evaluation of its effectiveness is ethical. However, it may not be acceptable from a political perspective. Depending on the perceived value of the program, the school board may believe that it is politically impossible to deny some students access. Any of these issues can prevent the use of an experimental design in the evaluation.

EXTENDING THE CONCEPT OF INFORMED CONSENT

You learned in Chapter 3 that informed consent is a cornerstone of ethical research. In that chapter, we emphasized what participants need to know to make a reasoned decision. There is still another issue that affects consent. Voluntary consent means that the person chooses to consent and that choice is free. However, people being served by a particular program may feel obligated to participate. They may fear that the benefits that they receive from the program will be withdrawn if they do not cooperate. The program evaluator must be careful to minimize this kind of subtle coercion.

Practical issues also make program evaluations challenging. Unlike controlled studies in the laboratory, a program occurs in a natural setting that is usually not under the control of the evaluator. Staff members are interested in doing the best job they can in running the program, and evaluating it is often secondary. A good program evaluator needs excellent political skills to convince staff to cooperate in the evaluation and to maintain their cooperation throughout. Often, when staff members are involved in an evaluation, they resent the time that is taken away from their central work: providing services. If the evaluator is not sensitive to these realities, the relationship between the evaluator and program staff can become hostile.

The program evaluator must also be aware of potentially biasing factors in the data being gathered. A staff is generally interested in showing the program in its best possible light, not only because it is their program, but because a program that appears to be ineffective might not get continued funding. Clients may have a vested interest in the program if they believe that it has been helpful, and they may therefore inflate their ratings of its effectiveness. On the other hand, some clients may believe that better programs could be implemented; therefore, they deflate their ratings of effectiveness. Such potential biases make it especially important that the evaluator rely on many data sources, at least some of which are objective measures.

Issues of Control

Control in program evaluation research is as important as in any other type of research. Because of the naturalistic nature of the program evaluation setting, it is often difficult to apply controls. Nevertheless, many controls can be applied, three of which are discussed here.

Selecting Appropriate Dependent Measures.   Most programs are developed with several goals in mind. Therefore, the program evaluator needs to use several dependent measures to evaluate the effectiveness of the program in meeting each of the intended goals. Some measures will focus on actual change in the individuals served by the program, and some will focus on changes outside the program, such as enhanced economic activity in the community. It is useful to include satisfaction measures from the people served by the program as well as from the community in general. Although satisfaction measures do not indicate the program's effectiveness, they may influence future effectiveness. An effective but unpopular program will need to address this issue or continued funding will be jeopardized.

Minimizing Bias in Dependent Measures.   In any research, it is essential to minimize measurement bias. This is particularly important in program evaluation research, in which the possibility of bias is high because data are often collected by the same people who run the program. Program evaluators try to minimize such bias by using objective measures whenever possible and by using people who are not involved in the administration of the program to gather data. Many broad-based programs are intended to have community-wide effects that can be monitored using routinely available data, such as census data.

No technique for minimizing bias will be completely effective in all situations. One of the better approaches is to use several dependent measures. If each is a valid measure and they all point to the same general conclusion, the evaluator can be confident of the results.

Control through Research Design in Program Evaluation.   As with any research project, the major controls are incorporated into the research design. The strongest program evaluation design is an experiment, with random assignment of participants. When this cannot be done, the strongest alternative design should be used.

Typical Program Evaluation Designs

Dozens of research designs have been used for program evaluations, but three or four designs account for most of this research.

Randomized Control-Group Designs.   The ideal program evaluation design is a control-group design, with random assignment of participants to conditions. This design provides maximum control. The control group may be a no-treatment control, a waitlist control, or some alternative treatment. A **waitlist control group** is a group of people who act as no-treatment controls, but are promised and receive the treatment after they have served as control participants.

Ethical considerations often dictate the nature of the control group. For example, under some conditions it might not be ethical to assign participants to a no-treatment control group. Instead, the best treatment currently available is used as a control against which the experimental procedure is compared.

Nonequivalent Control-Group Designs.   If a randomized control-group design is impossible, the best alternative is a *nonequivalent control-group design.* It is often possible to identify a natural control group that is likely to be similar to the group you are evaluating. Our earlier example of evaluating the California Child Passenger Restraint Law used this design with time-series data. The researchers (Guerin & MacKinnon, 1985) selected two control groups: (1) children in the same age range from another state and (2) slightly older children (four to seven years old) from California. Children were not randomly assigned to these groups, but there was no reason to believe that the groups were different on variables likely to affect risk of death or injury from automobile accidents. Even though this was not an experiment, it came very close to an experiment in its ability to rule out confounding variables.

Single-Group, Time-Series Designs.   If a control group is not possible, the best alternative strategy is a time-series design. Repeated measures on the dependent variables before, during, and after the program can control many threats to internal validity. Depending on the funding source, pretest measures may be difficult to obtain, because there is often pressure to begin services as soon as funds are released. Still, this design is flexible and useful in many situations. In fact, even when a control group is possible, using a time-series strategy will increase confidence in the evaluation of the program's effectiveness.

Pretest-Posttest Designs.   The pretest-posttest design is weak. Unfortunately, it is used much too often in program evaluation research. With only two measures and no control group, few threats to internal validity are controlled. Therefore, the simple pretest-posttest design is not recommended.

Program Evaluation Research: An Example

Managed care is a concept that has quickly become a part of health insurance coverage in this country. With managed care, the insurance company or an organization hired by the insurance company attempts to control health care costs by monitoring health care and authorizing each procedure according to the principle of whether it is "medically necessary." The promise is that managed care will provide quality health care at lower cost by reducing waste and eliminating unnecessary procedures. Critics charge that managed care reduces costs by denying necessary treatment. In a debate of this magnitude, it is surprising that almost no data exist on the effectiveness of managed care programs in meeting their stated goals.

Raulin and his colleagues (Raulin, Brenner, deBeaumont, & Vetter, 1995; Raulin, deBeaumont, Brenner, & Vetter, 1995) used a nonequivalent control-group design to evaluate the effectiveness of a program to manage mental health benefits. Stratified random samples were selected from two insurance plans operated by the same insurance carrier: one that included management of mental health benefits and one that represented the standard insurance policy. The samples were stratified on age, sex, and severity of diagnosis, factors that are known to affect the outcome and cost of psychological treatment. Participants were selected from health insurance plans that were matched on their total mental health coverage. Although participants were not randomly assigned to groups, the selection procedure produced groups from the same geographical area that were closely matched on key demographic variables and had equivalent health care insurance coverage.

Participants selected by these procedures were recruited by letter to participate. To increase the likelihood of participation, participants were offered a financial incentive for participation. As is often the case in program evaluation studies, the initial procedures had to be modified because they did not work well. Face-to-face interviews were replaced with a phone interview to make participation more convenient for participants, and an initial $25 per hour reimbursement rate was raised to $40 per hour. Of course, not all participants that were contacted by letter chose to participate. It would have been unethical to insist that everyone participate. Therefore, the sample may not have been representative of the population because it had a self-selection bias. Approximately one-fourth of the participants selected for the study did agree to participate. There were no differences between the participants who agreed to participate and those who refused on key demographic variables or the nature of the problem being treated.

The managed care program evaluated in this study was designed to accomplish several things. Therefore, several dependent measures were needed in the evaluation so that it would adequately measure how well the program was functioning. People in treatment were evaluated on (1) symptom level, using several well-validated symptom measures; (2) mood, also using measures with established validity; and (3) satisfaction with their care and their insurance coverage. In addition, cost data were obtained from the insurance carrier for both mental health coverage and for other medical care. Previous research had suggested that skimping on mental health coverage increases general medical costs, because the people will take their mental health concerns to their family physician.

The data suggest that the management of mental health benefits did not decrease the quality of care as measured by the standardized symptom and mood scales and the satisfaction measures used in the study. The mental health care costs were reduced by approximately 50% in the managed care group, and there were no differences between the groups on medical costs.

This was not a perfect study. No program evaluation ever is. When testing programs, compromises must be made to accommodate ethical and practical constraints. However, this study did provide useful data on the effectiveness of a particular program relative to an alternative program.

Caution is necessary in generalizing from this study to managed care programs in general. This study involved only the management of mental health benefits and therefore indicated little about whether managing general medical benefits would work as well. The managed care firm evaluated was relatively small, operated locally, and run by an unusually well qualified clinical director. It is not clear that one could generalize the findings of this study to other managed care operations, which now are almost all large national operations. Even with these limitations, this study provides useful data for making policy decisions on how to spend health care dollars.

In summary, program evaluation research faces the major problem of attempting high-constraint research in low-constraint naturalistic settings. However, by carefully selecting dependent measures and using the strongest research design possible, the evaluation can gather useful information about the effectiveness of programs in meeting their stated goals.

Program evaluation research is a valuable tool in the management of limited resources because ineffective programs consume dollars that might have been spent on effective programs. The challenges of evaluating field programs are unique and require specific research skills (Posavac & Carey, 1997). Program evaluation research is both a science and an art; one needs good research, political, and communication skills to do it well. More than any other kind of research, program evaluation research depends on the ability of the researcher to gain the cooperation of people who are not necessarily committed to the cause of maximizing internal and external validity.

Quick-Check Review 13.3: Program Evaluation Research

1. What is the major purpose of program evaluation research? What is its importance?
2. What is the major difficulty in conducting program evaluation research?
3. How can internal validity be maximized in program evaluation research?
4. What research designs are used most frequently in program evaluation?
5. Why is program evaluation research both a science and an art?

Surveys

Surveys gather information by asking participants about their experiences, attitudes, or knowledge. Survey instruments can be used in virtually any type of research, from case studies through experimental studies. Survey research is not a single research design (Schuman & Kalton, 1985). Rather, it utilizes several basic research procedures to obtain information from people in their natural environments. Surveys can be relatively simple, with just a few questions that can be asked over the phone. They can also be complicated and sophisticated instruments that test hypothesized relationships among variables and require lengthy face-to-face interviews. Surveys often test relationships among variables—a variation of correlational research. This section describes how surveys are used, the types of surveys, the steps in survey research, and how to select and construct an appropriate survey instrument.

Types of Surveys

We will discuss two types of surveys: status surveys and survey research.

Status Surveys. A **status survey** describes the current characteristics of a population. Examples are surveys to determine voter preferences or teacher satisfaction. Such surveys are commonly used in public health research to determine rates of illness and health-related behaviors. A recent example is the status survey of food consumption in the United States (Longnecker, Harper, & Kim, 1997). Status surveys were first used in the 1830s in England to investigate the working conditions in mines and factories during the Industrial Revolution.

Survey Research. **Survey research** does not just seek the current status of population characteristics, but also tries to discover relationships among variables. For example, Banken (2004) analyzed surveys of young people in the United States about their drug use and attitudes toward drug use. He documented that there has been little change in the rate of abuse for most drugs (e.g., marijuana, alcohol, LSD, cocaine, and heroin) among young people over the past 25 years, but there has been a steady increase in the use of Ecstasy (methylenedioxymethamphetamine or MDMA), apparently fueled by the mistaken belief that it is a safe drug with no negative consequences.

Steps in Survey Research

Surveys are the most familiar and ubiquitous form of research in the social sciences. They can be carried out by anyone who wants to find out what people are thinking or feeling about specific issues or events. At first glance, it may appear an easy task to conduct surveys; after all, a survey is simply asking people what they are thinking. However, as you will see, detailed planning is necessary if surveys are to be successful.

The major goal of a survey is to learn about the ideas, knowledge, feelings, opinions, attitudes, and self-reported behavior of a defined population. To carry out a survey, the researcher must identify the content area, construct the survey instrument, define the population, draw a representative sample, administer the survey instrument, analyze and interpret the data, and communicate the results. These steps are overlapping, and each step demands careful work (see Table 13.3).

TABLE 13.3 *Steps in Survey Research*

1. Determine what area of information is to be sought.
2. Define the population to be studied.
3. Decide how the survey is to be administered.
4. Construct the first draft of the survey instrument; edit and refine the draft.
5. Pretest the survey with a subsample; refine it further.
6. Develop a sampling frame and draw a representative sample.
7. Administer the final form of the instrument to the sample.
8. Analyze, interpret, and communicate the results.

Among the first tasks of the researcher is to determine the informational area to be studied, the population to be surveyed, and how the survey instrument is to be administered. These decisions guide the construction and administration of the survey instrument, which might be an interview schedule for surveys done in person or by telephone or a questionnaire for self-administered surveys. For example, Ahfeldt et al. (2005) wanted to determine what factors increased engagement in classroom activities (the area of information) in college students (the population) using a group-administered questionnaire (the form of the survey).

Types of Survey Instruments

The survey instrument may be a questionnaire or an interview schedule. In a self-administered **questionnaire,** respondents read the instructions and write or mark their answers to the questions. In telephone or in-person interviews, the survey instrument is called an **interview schedule,** and the researcher reads the questions to the respondent and records the answers. The survey instrument lists the questions in the order in which they are to be answered and provides instructions and methods for answering them. If it is a self-administered questionnaire, it must be a clear guide for the respondent. If it is to be administered by an interviewer, it must be a clear guide for the interviewer. The language must be clear, concise, and within the reading and comprehension abilities of the respondents and the interviewer.

Questionnaires and interviews begin with an introduction, which explains the purpose of the survey and gives instructions to the respondent. The questions then fall into two main categories: demographic and content questions. **Demographic questions** seek descriptive information about the respondents, such as age, sex, occupation, marital status, and so on. These are **factual items,** and they can be verified independently. Most items are **content items,** which ask about the respondents' opinions, attitudes, knowledge, and behavior.

Responses to questions about opinions and attitudes, such as what participants think about particular political parties or where they stand on such issues as animal rights, abortion, or environmental issues, are subjective and vary among individuals. They are not evaluated as right or wrong.

Frequently, content items ask about the respondents' knowledge, such as high school students' knowledge of geography, history, or science. Questions that ask, "What is the capital of Afghanistan?", or "What percentage of paper products in the United States is made of recycled paper?" are tests of knowledge. Answers to these questions can be evaluated independently and objectively as right or wrong.

Content items can also focus on the overt behavior of the respondent. For example, the question "What proportion of your newspapers have you recycled in the past year?" asks about the person's behavior. Theoretically, behavior-focused items can be objectively verified. However, the information in surveys is self-reported, and there are obvious concerns over the reliability and validity of such self-reports.

Surveys typically include all types of items—demographic, attitude, opinion, knowledge, and behavior items. In the Ahlfeldt et al. (2005) survey of college students, for example, the content focused on how involved students were in their classes and what each of the classes was like. By including information about class characteristics, they were able to determine that certain types of classes (primarily upper level classes that were relatively small) were apparently more conducive to active student involvement.

Developing the Survey Instrument

A survey instrument is developed in several steps. The researcher must determine exactly what questions are to be asked, in what form, and in what order. The instrument must be constructed so that it adequately covers the area of information sought and is appropriate for the targeted population. Construction of the survey instrument also depends on the administration procedure. Surveys can be administered by mail, e-mail, telephone, or personal interview. The most information, and generally the best results, are obtained when the survey is administered in a face-to-face interview, although such interviews are time consuming and expensive. A face-to-face interview generally requires a much more detailed survey instrument than is typical for a telephone survey, which usually includes a few simple items in a one- or two-minute conversation. In contrast, personal interview surveys can include many questions, many opportunities for the interviewer to probe for more information, and may require several hours to complete.

Construction of the survey instrument is one of the most time-consuming steps in the survey research process. A basic rule in survey research is that the instrument should have a clear focus and should be guided by hypotheses held by the researcher. This means that survey research is not well suited to early exploratory research, because it requires some orderly expectations by the researcher.

Let us suppose that we want to survey local schoolteachers (the population) on their views about using corporal punishment to discipline children (the area of information). We decide to use a self-administered, mailed questionnaire (the form of administration). Having determined the general area of inquiry, the population to be surveyed, and the form of administration, the next step is to develop the instrument. The researcher writes items that cover the area of information desired (use of corporal punishment) and are in language appropriate for the population (teachers). The items should be unambiguous and concise, and they should be preceded by clear instructions. After the items are written, they are edited for clarity and are pretested, usually on a small sample from the population to be surveyed. Items are then refined based on the pretesting.

The items can take several forms: **open-ended items, multiple-choice items,** and **Likert-scale items.** In our study, we might ask the open-ended question "What do you think of using corporal punishment in disciplining children?"

If this were a questionnaire, we would leave sufficient space for the respondents to write their answers. In an interview, we would tape-record their answers for later coding and scoring.

An example of a multiple-choice question is

What proportion of parents use corporal punishment to discipline their children?
a. 10%   b. 25%   c. 50%   d. 75%   e. 100%

In Likert scales, the items are arranged on a continuum, with extreme positions at the endpoints. Respondents are typically asked to indicate the degree to which they agree with a statement, such as:

Corporal punishment is necessary in raising children.
Strongly Agree   Agree   Uncertain   Disagree   Strongly Disagree

This item could be scored from 1 to 5. There are other scaling methods as well, such as the Thurstone, Guttman, and Semantic Differential scales, but a detailed discussion of all scaling formats is beyond the scope of this text. See Dawis (1987) and Kerlinger (1992) for more details.

13:02

A single questionnaire might include items in each format. If so, it is good form to keep items of the same format together. Additional details on survey construction techniques are included on the Student Resource Website.

Sampling Participants

Obtaining an adequate sample is one of the most important factors in conducting surveys. When the population about which we seek information is large and diverse, it is impossible to question every member of this population. The U.S. census is an example of such an attempt, but taking a census of this magnitude is expensive and time consuming. Instead, surveys draw a sample of the population and then generalize the findings from the sample to the population. If the sample is drawn properly, one can draw strong and confident conclusions about the population. In fact, the U.S. Census Bureau proposed replacing the census of some areas of the country with carefully drawn samples, arguing that they could get a better count from this methodology than the traditional methodology of trying to contact everyone (Duskin, 1999). The proposal was rejected, not on methodological grounds, but rather on political grounds.

The population in a survey is the larger group about whom we wish to obtain information. Some examples of survey populations might be eligible voters for a presidential election, high school teachers in California, readers of the National Review, middle school children in Milwaukee, students at the University of Texas, or Chevrolet owners. In our example, we have taken the first step by identifying the population as local schoolteachers. Now we must be more precise by specifying a geographic area or specific school systems and other characteristics of the population, such as the grade levels of the teachers and/or their areas of teaching expertise (science, social studies, English, etc.). The survey might include all schoolteachers or be limited to grammar school or full-time teachers. We must decide whether to include teachers in private schools or limit the population of study to public school teachers.

Suppose that we decide to study all full-time, state-certified public school teachers in a four-county area (grades 1 through 12), whose primary task is classroom teaching. Note the variability among this population. Some will be male and some female. Some will be special-education teachers. Others will teach in specialized areas such as music or shop. Their ages will vary considerably from the early twenties to the late sixties. Their experience and ability as teachers will also vary greatly.

Sampling Considerations. Having constructed and tested the survey instrument and identified the population to be studied, the researcher must also specify the sampling procedures. He or she will draw a sample of people from a known population and administer the survey to each participant in the sample. Survey information is obtained from a sample, but the goal is to learn about the population from which the sample is drawn.

Using the terminology developed earlier in the text, whenever we use a sample as a basis for generalizing to a population, we are engaging in a process of inductive inference (from the specific sample to the general population). Inductive reasoning is the general process involved in the use of inferential statistics. To have confidence in inductive inferences from sample to population, the sample must be carefully drawn to *represent adequately the population to which the researcher wants to generalize.*

The heart of survey research is the selection of representative samples. Without it, the results will tell us only about the sample and will not help us learn about a larger population. It can be difficult to achieve this goal, as is discussed in *The Cost of Neglect 13.1,* which deals with the challenges of political polling.

Sampling Procedures. Sampling procedures fall into two major categories: (1) nonprobability sampling and (2) probability sampling. **Nonprobability sampling** methods include, for example, carrying out a survey by interviewing the first 50 people you meet on the street or as many people as you can interview who are coming out of a polling place at election time. Newspaper, television, and radio surveys are often carried out in this way to obtain a quick public response to an issue while it is still a current news item. The advantage of nonprobability sampling is the ease with which it can be carried out. Its weakness is that the first 50 people, or whatever other nonprobability sample is obtained, might not be a representative sample of the population, and the survey results might therefore be biased.

Probability sampling procedures give us greater confidence that the sample adequately represents the population. In probability sampling, each person has some known probability of being included in the sample. The two major probability sampling methods are random sampling and stratified random sampling.

You learned in Chapter 9 that random sampling means that every member of the identified population has an equal chance of being selected. There is no bias in random sampling that can lead to persons with certain characteristics having a higher probability of being selected than persons without these characteristics. Random sampling, however, requires that we have a list of all members of the population. Clearly, this would be difficult to obtain if the population is large, such as all people living in the United States or all

THE COST OF NEGLECT 13.1:   *Political Polling and Sampling*

Political polling has always been a part of United States history. In a democracy, the will of the people should prevail, and in a technological democracy, politicians and political pundits increasingly want to know what the people think. But even with the best technology of the day, it is a challenge to draw the kind of representative sample that is needed to draw accurate conclusions about the will of the people.

The task of obtaining representative samples is constantly changing and is always a challenge. Most polls are conducted over the phone, because this keeps costs to a minimum. At one point, this produced a significantly biased sample, because phones were expensive and many low-income families did not have phones (Eisinger, 2003). Now most people have phones, so this is less of a problem than it once was. However, there has been a move toward having unlisted phone numbers, and the social demographics of this movement were also a threat to valid political sampling. Specifically, unlisted numbers were more likely to be for families from higher income brackets (Eisinger, 2003). Pollsters responded by going to random dialing, rather than randomly selecting numbers from the phone book.

The recent enactment of the Do Not Call law by Congress, which allowed people to list their phone numbers in a national registry of numbers that were not to be called by telemarketers, posed another problem. However, political pollsters were able to convince Congress that they should be exempt from this rule, or perhaps the politicians in Congress already believed that polling was too valuable to have the Do Not Call Registry interfere with it (Liptak, 2003). It is interesting to note that legislation creating previous do-not-call lists on a statewide level did not include a provision to exclude political polling (Bowers, 1997).

The trend to more use of cell phones, which are generally not listed in phone directories, also complicates polling. Some households now have a half dozen phone numbers, whereas other households may only have one. Random dialing of phone numbers therefore will make some households much more likely to be polled. Cell phones cannot be ignored much longer, because people are increasingly making their cell phone their only phone (Turner, 2004). Furthermore, people are using caller ID to screen out unwanted calls, including calls from polling companies.

Finally, there are subtle variables that are known to influence poll results. For example, polls taken over the weekend tend to underrepresent Republicans (Robinson, 2002). Therefore, daily polls may show a drop in support for Republican candidates over the weekend before an election. This is actually an artifact: voters who identify themselves as Republican are less likely to pick up the phone and respond to the poll.

When taking polls to predict election results, the problem is to identify who is likely to actually vote. It does not matter how many of the people favor Candidate A; it only matters how many of the people who vote on Election Day cast their ballots for Candidate A.

Different polling agencies approach this problem in different ways. Some simply ask if the person intends to vote when taking the poll. Others ask how likely it is that the person will vote and may weight their preference based on their likelihood of voting. In other words, someone who says he or she is definitely voting is more likely to be a voter for their preferred candidate than someone who says they will probably vote. Still other polling agencies ask about the past voting history of the people they survey, reasoning that those who have voted regularly in the past are more likely to vote than those who have rarely voted in the past. However, this strategy cannot handle people who have just reached voting age.

You might think that this problem could be solved by asking voters who they voted for as they come out of the polling place. These surveys are called **exit polls.** News organizations increasingly rely on them to forecast the vote before final returns have been counted, so that they can have the bragging rights of being the network that called the outcome of the election first. Even here, there can be sampling problems. In the 2004 presidential election, exit polls consistently overestimated the vote for John Kerry (Morin, 2004). Apparently, George Bush voters were less willing to stop and answer exit poll questions.

What is amazing is that despite all these problems, the best political pollsters are able to consistently call elections with accuracy. They have developed techniques that sample the voting electorate effectively and accurately predict who among the people they talk to will actually vote on Election Day.

children enrolled in primary and secondary schools. With such large populations, we cannot use random sampling. If the population is more limited, such as all children in a specific school or all psychologists in private practice in a certain city, creating an initial list (called a **sampling frame**) is more feasible. We could randomly select from such a sampling frame without much difficulty. Thus, random sampling is used for survey research in which population size allows a workable sampling frame from which individuals can be randomly selected.

For example, suppose that we want to survey 50 of the 317 local families who have children in school with mental retardation. The sampling frame would consist of the names of all 317 families. Each would be assigned a number from 1 to 317, and we would use a table of random numbers to select randomly the sample of 50 families. However, as careful as we may be to obtain an accurate sampling frame, it may be incomplete. Changes might occur between the time we obtain the list and begin selecting the sample. Families may move into or away from the town; people may become ill or die. Thus, a sampling frame is almost always incomplete and is an approximation of the true population.

Stratified random sampling procedures are used when it is important to ensure that subgroups within a population are adequately represented in the sample. In essence, the researcher divides the population into subgroups or **strata**, and a random sample is taken from each stratum. Suppose that we want to conduct a survey on 100 of the 1737 students in McKinley High School. We would not want to bias the results by over- or underrepresenting any groups (e.g., freshmen, sophomores, juniors, seniors, minority students, males, or females). A stratified random sample, drawing randomly from each of the strata, would be used. The number drawn from each stratum would be based on the proportion of students in this stratum in the population. In this way, we can have confidence that the sample accurately represents the population, at least on the dimensions on which we stratified the sample.

Sample Size and Confidence Intervals.   Having developed the survey instrument and deter-mined the sampling procedure, the researcher must also determine the size of the sample that will be needed. In general, larger samples represent populations better than smaller samples. Exactly how large the sample should be must be determined for each project. Costs and time are important considerations, but a more important consideration is how large the sample must be to ade-quately represent the population, and that will depend on how homogeneous the population is. A **homogeneous** population is one in which the members are similar to one another. In general, if the population is homogeneous, then smaller sample sizes are possible. On the other hand, the more **heterogeneous** the population, the more diversity there is that must be represented in the sample. Therefore, the sample must be larger to represent the diversity accurately. To determine how large a sample must be to represent the population, we must make an estimate of the variability of the characteristics of the population; that is, we must estimate the size of the standard deviation of the population for the characteristic that we want to measure. From these data we can then determine the confidence limits for estimating population characteristics based on the sample characteristics. For example, if we computed a sample mean of 10.50, we would expect the population mean to be close to this figure. How confident we are that our sample mean is close to the population mean depends on the sample size. The larger the sample size, the more confidence we have. We express our confidence with something called a **confidence interval.** For example, we could compute that we are 95 percent confident that the population mean is between 9.75 and 11.25 (our confidence interval).

Methods for calculating required sample size and confidence intervals are beyond the scope of this text. Interested students are referred to Rossi, Wright, and Anderson (1985) or Nardi (2005). The statistical concept of the confidence interval is explained on the Student Resource Website.

13:03

Survey Research Designs

Having developed and tested the survey instrument, identified the population of interest, and drawn the sample, the researcher must also determine the research plan or design to be used in gathering the survey data. Two basic designs are used in survey research: (1) the cross-sectional survey design and (2) the longitudinal survey design or panel design.

Cross-Sectional Designs.   A **cross-sectional design** involves administering the survey once to a sample, yielding data on the measured characteristics as they exist at the time of the survey. The information can be completely descriptive, such as a status survey, or can involve testing relationships among population characteristics. A variation of the cross-sectional survey design allows comparisons to be made of population characteristics at different points in time, such as surveying the occurrence of depression in 1985, 1990, 1995, 2000, and 2005 to determine changes over time. Another variation is to sample sub-groups defined by age, such as 20–30, 30–40, 40–50, and so on. Businesses are often interested in such surveys to help them to determine the best ways to market products (Sudman & Blair, 1998). If successive surveys use independent samples of respondents, the design is cross-sectional.

Longitudinal Survey Designs.   The **longitudinal survey design** or **panel design** is a within-subjects survey research design in which the same group or panel of participants is surveyed at several times. Longitudinal surveys make it possible to assess changes within individuals over time. It is often difficult, however, to obtain participants who are willing to be surveyed several times, and frequently large numbers of participants drop out of the study before it is completed.

Quick-Check Review 13.4: Surveys

1. Distinguish between status surveys and survey research.
2. What are the major goals in surveys?
3. Describe two forms of survey instruments.
4. What are the types of items that can be used in surveys?
5. What is stratified random sampling?
6. What are confidence limits?
7. Define cross-sectional designs and longitudinal designs.

PUTTING IT INTO PRACTICE

If you read newspapers or magazines or watch television news, you are probably exposed to surveys almost daily. Occasionally, the information from a survey is presented with qualifications that permit you to judge the quality of the information. For example, most political polls will give the margin of error; they might report that the figures have an accuracy level of ± 3 points. This figure is based on the sample size and gives you an idea of the confidence limits. In general, such indications suggest that the poll was taken by a reputable polling service using generally acceptable polling procedures. However, many of the polls reported by news agencies are far less scientific.

For the next couple of weeks, watch for polls in the paper or on the news. Ask yourself how these polls might be distorted if proper sampling procedures were not followed. Then ask yourself how likely it is that the poll did follow proper sampling procedures and whether one should take the information seriously. You may be surprised by how few of the polls that bombard us daily have information we can trust.

Chapter Summary

This chapter returned to a discussion of research in naturalistic settings that was first presented in Chapter 6. Here, however, higher-constraint research was covered, including experimental research in naturalistic settings. Three major topics were discussed: quasi-experimental designs, program evaluation, and surveys.

Two quasi-experimental designs were discussed (the nonequivalent control-group design and the interrupted time-series design). Program evaluation research involves the use of many of the designs covered in this text to evaluate the practical effectiveness of programs carried out in naturalistic settings. Although program evaluation research is difficult, it has become a major area of applied research in the social sciences.

Surveying is a large and growing area of research. Researchers ask questions of participants concerning virtually any issue. Questions may include everything from demographic information, to knowledge questions, to questions about attitudes and experiences. The heart of the survey is obtaining a representative sample. Surveys can be carried out as longitudinal or cross-sectional studies.

Chapter Exercises

1. Define the following key terms. Be sure that you understand them. They are discussed in the chapter and defined in the glossary.

quasi-experimental designs
nonequivalent control-group design
crossover effect
interrupted time-series design

program evaluation research
waitlist control group
survey
status survey
survey research

questionnaire
interview schedule
demographic questions
factual items
content items
open-ended items
multiple-choice items
Likert-scale items
nonprobability sampling
probability sampling

sampling frame
exit polls
strata
homogeneous
heterogeneous
confidence interval
cross-sectional survey design
longitudinal survey design
panel design

2. How do the research designs discussed in Chapter 6 and those discussed in this chapter differ?

3. The following graphs represent results in several non-equivalent control-group designs. How do you interpret each? (Assume differences are statistically significant.)

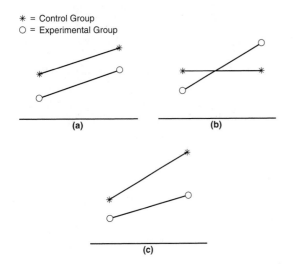

✳ = Control Group
○ = Experimental Group

(a)

(b)

(c)

4. How would you interpret the following results of time-series designs?

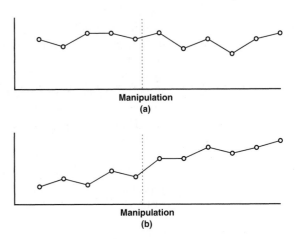

Manipulation
(a)

Manipulation
(b)

5. What are the tradeoffs of doing highly controlled experimental research in the laboratory, rather than doing research in field settings?

14

Final Preparations Before Data Collection

Ignorance never settles a question.

—Benjamin Disraeli, 1866, speech given in the House of Commons

*Web Resource Material*_____

This chapter provides two critical resources: a flowchart system for selecting appropriate statistical procedures and a checklist for evaluating every aspect of a research design before data collection. Although they are based on material presented earlier, you will find them helpful in your own research planning.

Selecting Appropriate Statistical Procedures

Research is a systematic process of inquiry, proceeding from initial ideas to final communication. At each phase, the researcher makes important decisions. One decision made in the design phase, before data collection, is determining what statistical procedures to use to analyze the results. This demand is relaxed somewhat at the more flexible naturalistic level, but it becomes increasingly important at higher levels of constraint. Recall from our earlier discussions that we select statistical tests that are appropriate for the data that we collect and for the questions that we ask.

Choosing appropriate statistical procedures can frustrate students. The large array of research designs and statistical procedures can be overwhelming. But like everything in research, systematic procedures simplify the decisions and bring the process under control. Chapters 5, 10, 11, and 12 set the groundwork for this systematic approach by describing several research designs and illustrating appropriate statistical procedures.

An Initial Example

The characteristics of the research, such as the number of independent variables, type of question, and level of measurement for each dependent variable, will determine the appropriate statistical procedures. We will use as an example a relatively simple study. Remember, the first step is to identify the important characteristics of the study.

Incidental Learning in Rats
An experimenter hypothesizes that laboratory rats can learn without specific rewards. Twenty maze-adapted animals are randomly assigned to two conditions. The experimental group is allowed to explore the test maze for one hour without any rewards. The control group does not explore the test maze. All animals are then given learning trials in the test maze, and each successful trial is reinforced with food. The experimental and control groups are compared on the number of learning trials needed to reach a criterion of five successive correct trials. The research hypothesis is that the experimental group, having explored the test maze prior to their reinforced learning trials, needs significantly fewer trials to reach criterion than the control group. In other words, those animals learned something about the maze while wandering through it, even though they experienced no reinforcement to shape their learning in this exploration phase.

Our task is to determine the appropriate statistical procedure to use in this study. Remember that the characteristics of the research determine what statistical procedures to use. The preceding description provides all the information that we need. We will ask questions to identify the characteristics of the research. The relevant questions are:

- **What is the level of constraint for the research?** Experimental.
- **What are the independent variables?** There is one independent variable (the amount of exploration of the maze prior to learning trials).
- **What are the levels of the independent variable?** There are two levels (prior exploration and no prior exploration).
- **What type of design is the research (e.g., independent-groups, correlated-groups, mixed, and so on)?** It is an independent-groups design.
- **What are the dependent variables?** The dependent variable is maze learning.
- **What is (are) the dependent measure(s)?** The dependent measure is the number of maze-running trials needed to reach criterion.
- **What is the level of measurement of each dependent measure?** The dependent measure is measured on a ratio scale.
- **What type of data is generated for the dependent measure?** The dependent measure generates score data.
- **What is (are) the research hypothesis (hypotheses)?** There is one research hypothesis (the experimental group will require fewer learning trials than the control group to reach criterion).
- **What kind of test is needed (e.g., a test of relationship, a test of differences, etc.)?** A test of differences is required. Specifically, we need to test the null hypothesis that there is no difference between the experimental and control groups.

We have now determined that our example study is an independent-groups experimental design in which a hypothesized difference between two groups is tested. The dependent variable, maze learning, yields score data. The appropriate statistical procedure is one that can test differences between independent groups with score data. You may recall from earlier discussions that the *t*-test for independent groups or the one-way ANOVA is appropriate. We also routinely include descriptive statistics to summarize data and help us to interpret the results.

In this simple example, the decision about what statistical procedure to use is easily made. In more complex research, there may be several research hypotheses and several dependent measures and we may need different procedures for each hypothesis. In such complex research, the decisions are not so readily apparent, but the procedure to arrive at them is essentially the same. First we describe the study and ask questions to identify the study's characteristics. Then, we use this information to make decisions about the appropriate statistical procedures. We have incorporated this sequence of steps into a decision-tree model that we will describe.

A Decision-Tree Model

There are no new concepts in this section; rather, this section organizes information that you learned in previous chapters. The remainder of this section describes a decision-making

14:01
14:02

model for selecting statistical procedure(s). We use a **decision tree,** in which we follow a line of thinking, reach a decision point, decide, and then branch off in appropriate directions based on the decision. These lines of thinking and the branching-off process are organized in five decision-tree flowcharts, which are shown in Figures 14.1 through 14.5. Copies of the decision-tree flowcharts are included on the Student Resource Website, as well as a functional version of the flowchart. The functional version links directly to discussions of how to conduct the statistical analyses.

The researcher begins by describing the research and its characteristics and then proceeds through the flowcharts to determine the appropriate statistical procedures.

14:03
14:04

Decision-Tree Flowcharts.   **Decision-tree flowcharts** organize the decision-making process. Because the procedures discussed may not be clear after a first reading, we recommend that you reread them and complete the exercises at the end of the chapter. There are also several examples on the Student Resource Website that you can use to master the selection of statistical procedures.

In the next section, we present an example of research and proceed through the flowcharts to determine the appropriate statistical procedures. Most studies test several research hypotheses and include several dependent measures. Therefore, several statistical procedures may be required.

Descriptive statistics are first computed for all variables in the study. If there are separate groups, the descriptive statistics are computed for each group. In lower-constraint research, descriptive statistics may be all that are needed. In higher-constraint research, however, we typically have refined the questions and designed the study to answer specific questions about differences between groups. In most cases, we cycle through the flowcharts several times to determine all necessary statistical procedures. Figure 14.1 shows the overall structure of the decision tree. Figures 14.2 through Figure 14.5 present specific sections of the overall flowchart outlined in Figure 14.1. Although the flowcharts may look imposing, they are easy to follow.

Identify Research Variables.   We begin by identifying key aspects of the research. This process is illustrated with a hypothetical study of social problem solving in sixth-grade boys and girls. Unlike the animal-learning study presented earlier, several research hypotheses are tested in this study. Thus, we need to determine several statistical analyses.

No matter how complex the study may be, the procedures for determining an appropriate statistical analysis are the same.

1. Describe the study.
2. Identify its characteristics.
3. Make systematic decisions using the flowcharts.

Describe the Study.   Here is a brief description of the study.

Sex Differences in Children's Social Problem-Solving Skills
The study compares sixth-grade boys and girls on their problem-solving skills in social situations. From the sixth grade of a local middle school, 20 boys and 20 girls are randomly selected and evaluated on three measures. In the first measure, participants are

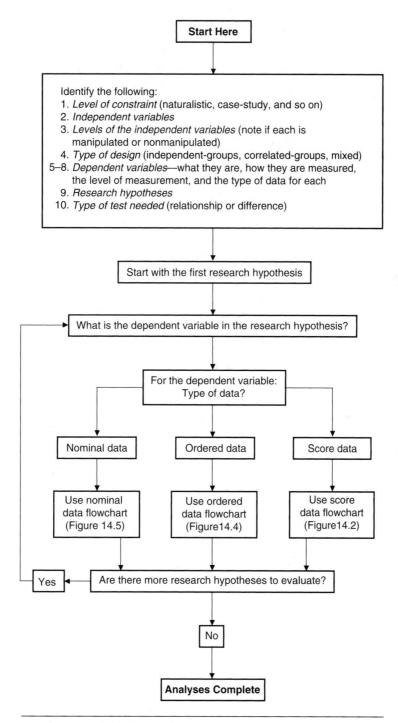

FIGURE 14.1 *Initial Flowchart*

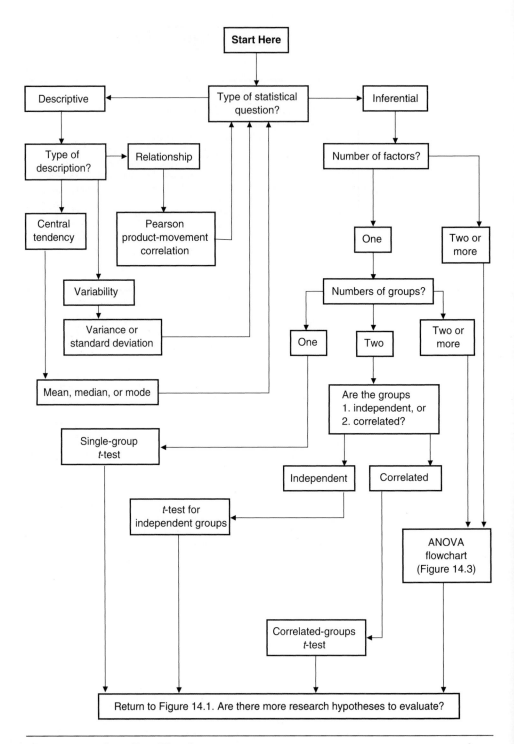

FIGURE 14.2   *Score Data Flowchart*

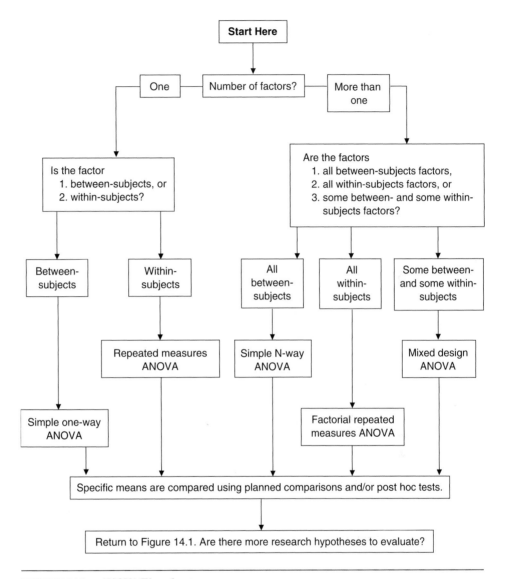

FIGURE 14.3 *ANOVA Flowchart*

Note: Most formulas for the various ANOVAs and related statistical tests can be found on the Student Resource Website. For additional computational procedures, consult an advanced statistics text (e.g., Keppel, 2006; Myers & Well, 2003).

tested individually. Ten social situations are described to each participant. Each situation involves a social problem or conflict (e.g., another student pushes ahead in line). Three ways to solve the conflict are described for each situation, and the participant is asked to choose one of the three solutions. (In essence, this is a multiple-choice test.) For each problem, one solution is clearly the most socially appropriate and therefore is considered to be the correct answer. The score is the number of correct choices for the 10 social situations.

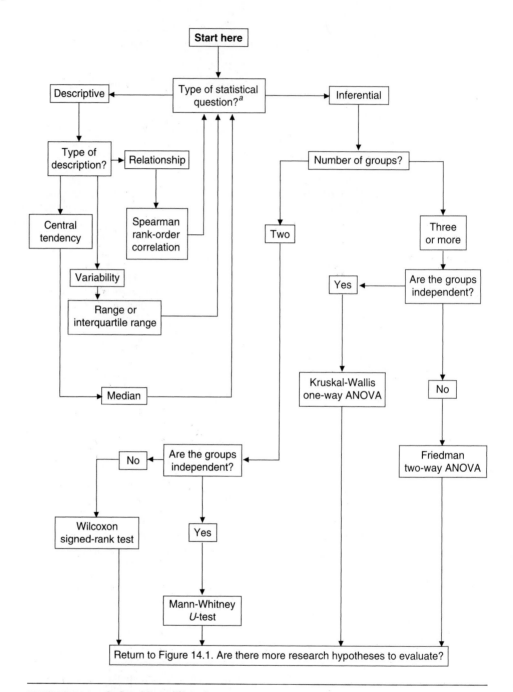

FIGURE 14.4   *Ordered Data Flowchart*

[a]It is best to start with descriptive statistics.

Note: Computational formulas for the statistical procedures described here can be found in Siegel and Castellan (1988).

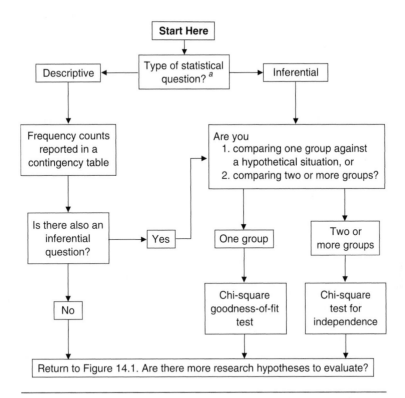

FIGURE 14.5 *Nominal Data Flowchart* Flowcharts can simplify almost any complex decision.

[a]It is best to start with descriptive statistics.

The second dependent measure is the teacher's ranking of the children on social competence. The ranking is based on observations of the children's behavior in three settings: the structured classroom, an unstructured social activity within the classroom, and recess. For the third dependent measure, an independent rater classifies each of the children as either "socially competent" or "socially incompetent" based on standardized information provided by the teachers.

The research focuses on sex differences in problem-solving skills. The statement of the problem is "Do sixth-grade boys and girls differ on problem-solving skills?" The problem statement leads to three research hypotheses.

Identify the Study's Major Characteristics. Having described the study, the next step is to identify its major characteristics.

1. **Level of constraint.** Differential.
2. **Independent variables.** The independent variable, sex of participants, is a nonmanipulated independent variable.

3. **Levels of the independent variable.** There are two levels of the independent variable (boys and girls).
4. **Type of design.** Independent-groups, differential design.

5–8. **Dependent variable(s).** There are three dependent variables. Their measures, level of measurement, and type of data are listed below.

Dependent Measure	Level of Measurement	Type of Data
Score on the social-skills multiple-choice test	Ratio	Score
Ranking of participants on social competence	Ordinal	Ordered
Independent classification of social competence	Nominal	Nominal

9. **Research hypotheses.** There are three research hypotheses:
   a. Sixth-grade boys and girls differ in the identification of the correct social response in a multiple-choice task.
   b. Sixth-grade boys and girls differ in their ranking on social competence based on observations in three behavior settings.
   c. Sixth-grade boys and girls differ in the proportion classified as socially competent.
10. **Type of test needed.** A test of differences between independent groups is needed.

This study is a differential, independent-groups design with two levels of the non-manipulated independent variable. The dependent measures generate three different levels of data. Therefore, we can expect different statistical procedures will be necessary to analyze group differences on each dependent measure.

Select Appropriate Statistics.   The flowcharts help us to select appropriate statistics. We have already accomplished the first task (Figure 14.1), which is identifying the characteristics of the study. Therefore, we move down the flowchart and begin with the first research hypothesis: that sixth-grade boys and girls differ in the identification of the correct social response in a multiple-choice task.

We follow Figure 14.1 to the point where the flowchart inquires, "For the dependent variable: Type of data?" As we have already determined, this dependent variable produces score data. Therefore, following the flowchart, we are directed to use the score data flowchart (Figure 14.2).

It is a good idea to begin with descriptive statistics, so we move to the left branch of Figure 14.2. Here we are asked, "Type of description?" Normally we want both a measure of central tendency and a measure of variability for score data. The flowchart tells us that the mean, median, and mode are appropriate measures of central tendency, and the variance and standard deviation are appropriate measures of variability.

Figure 14.2 directs us back to the box that asks "Type of statistical question?" We are also interested in an inferential question, so we branch to the right in Figure 14.2, where it asks for the number of factors.

Because we have one factor (sex), we follow that branch to where it asks for the number of groups. Because we have two groups (boys and girls), we can go in either of two directions. The rightmost branch takes us to a one-way ANOVA (see Figure 14.3). The middle branch leads to a *t*-test (for independent groups). Both are correct procedures and will lead to the same conclusions.

Having selected an inferential statistical procedure for the first research hypothesis, we return to Figure 14.1 to repeat the process for our other hypotheses.

As we move down the initial flowchart (Figure 14.1), we are asked whether there are more research hypotheses to evaluate. Because there are, we look to the middle portion of the flowchart where it asks, "What is the dependent variable in the research hypothesis?" We identify the variable and move down to where it asks what type of data it represents. The dependent measure for the second hypothesis is the teacher's rankings of social competence (ordered data).

The flowchart tells us to consult Figure 14.4 (the Ordered Data Flowchart). We are interested in descriptive statistics, so we branch to the left and are informed that the median is an appropriate measure of central tendency and the range or the interquartile range is the appropriate measure of variability for ordered data.

Having determined the appropriate descriptive statistics for the second research hypothesis, we now turn to the inferential statistics. We follow the flowchart back to the box asking, "Type of statistical question?" We branch to the right to find an appropriate inferential statistical procedure. If we follow the flowchart correctly, it will suggest a Mann-Whitney *U*-test.

The third research hypothesis uses a dependent variable that is measured on a nominal scale, and we are therefore directed by the Initial Flowchart to use Figure 14.5 (the Nominal Data Flowchart). If we follow the flowchart correctly, we determine that frequency counts in a contingency table are an appropriate descriptive statistic. Likewise, an appropriate inferential procedure is a chi-square test for independence.

If our study were a larger one with more research hypotheses, we would continue this process of using the flowcharts to find the correct descriptive and inferential statistics and compute the statistics for all remaining dependent measures in the study. Most research studies employ more than one measure and test more than one research hypothesis. Although computers can simplify the task of computation, the researcher still needs to decide what statistics to compute and to label and organize the computer output carefully to avoid later confusion. The example illustrates the need to be well organized during your work, because you need to make many decisions. Carefully labeling the results will minimize errors during later analyses and report writing.

We recommend that you use these flowcharts with the research examples at the end of this chapter. With practice, you will become familiar with the rules in the flowcharts and eventually will not need to refer to them. Indeed, that is a goal. Initially, however, when you are learning to make decisions, the flowcharts will provide a convenient way to organize information when selecting a statistical procedure. We have included additional examples and exercises on the Student Resource Website, which also has a functional version of these flowcharts that links to the data analysis tutorials.

14:02
14:03
14:04

Secondary Analyses

After completing descriptive and inferential analyses, we often carry out **secondary analyses,** which typically fall into three categories: (1) post hoc analyses or planned comparisons to look at specific mean differences; (2) analyses designed to help to explain the pattern of results; and (3) unplanned exploratory analyses (called *data snooping*).

Post Hoc Analyses.   When doing an ANOVA with more than two groups, specific mean comparisons are the logical next step in the interpretation of significant *F*-ratios. The significant *F* in a one-way ANOVA, for example, tells us only that at least one of the means is significantly different from at least one other mean. It does not tell us which means are different from which other means. Most often, the interpretation requires this more specific information, which can be provided by a variety of post hoc tests or planned comparisons. These were covered in Chapter 10. The Student Resource Website has additional information about these procedures.

14:05

Secondary Analyses to Help to Explain Results.   Another set of secondary analyses involves looking at variables that may help to explain the results. The differences found may be difficult to interpret because we cannot be sure that some confounding variable was adequately controlled. This problem is minimized in experimental research, but in lower-constraint research, these issues can be serious, and secondary analyses are often essential to interpret data adequately. In many lower-constraint research studies, the secondary analyses may outnumber the primary analyses and be critical in the interpretation of the results.

A set of secondary analyses that should be included in the report of any study is descriptive statistics on the demographic characteristics of the sample, such as age, social class, and education level. Such information allows researchers to compare samples from different studies and provides the information needed to determine the limits of generalizability of the findings.

These are only some of the uses of secondary statistical analyses to help interpret findings of a primary analysis. Some of the analyses in this category are very sophisticated and beyond the scope of this text.

Data Snooping.   The third set of secondary analyses is what we have called **data snooping.** Here researchers can play their hunches and see whether, for example, there are relationships, differences, or interactions that were not predicted. Data snooping is useful in lower-constraint studies in which clues about many potential relationships among variables may be buried in the data. Good data snooping is as much an art as a science. Furthermore, if we are appropriately cautious, data snooping can be a rich source of hypotheses for later research. At least one high-level text is devoted entirely to this art (Tukey, 1977).

Caveats and Disclaimers

The flowchart system is designed as a teaching device—a way to organize and formalize what is often a difficult task for students. The inferential statistics portion of this system focuses on the kinds of questions asked most often in psychological hypotheses (specifically, are there mean differences between groups?). Other questions, such as "Are there differences in the variability between the groups?" are not covered by the set of flowcharts.

HISTORICAL LESSON 14.1:   *The Robust Nature of Parametric Statistics*

At several points in the text, we note that statistical tests make assumptions about the data. For example, an implicit assumption of the *t*-test and ANOVA procedures is that data are on at least an interval level of measurement (score data). These tests make other assumptions about data, too, which are not highlighted in the text, because they are often not critical.

Sometimes an assumption on which an inferential statistical procedure is based can be violated without threatening the validity of the conclusion drawn from the statistical test. In such a case, we say that the statistical procedure is **robust** to violations of the assumption. For example, many statistical tests assume that scores in the population are distributed normally. If the population of scores is actually skewed, we have violated this assumption. If the statistical procedure is not robust to this assumption, the violation distorts the procedure, making conclusions drawn from the statistical analysis suspect. Fortunately, most statistics are robust to violations of assumptions about population distributions. Therefore, we can use them confidently regardless of the shape of the distributions.

As it turns out, most statistics are robust to violations of almost all assumptions on which they are based if the sample size in each of the groups is approximately equal. This conclusion is based on a series of computer simulation studies known as **Monte Carlo studies** (named after the famous gambling resort). In a Monte Carlo study, the computer is used to simulate sampling of participants from populations with known characteristics. In this way, the researcher can see what effect violations of assumptions have on the accuracy of decisions (Levy, 1980). Monte Carlo studies continue to show the remarkable robustness of most statistics to assumption violations when sample sizes are equal. Consequently, these assumptions are not emphasized in the text and are not built into the decision rules of the flowcharts.

Note the emphasis before on equal sample sizes. Unless sample sizes of groups are approximately equal, violations of assumptions may affect the validity of statistical procedures. Hence, from a design perspective, particularly for the novice researcher, it is beneficial to try to have approximately equal sample sizes.

For such questions, other reference sources need to be consulted (Keppel, 2006; Myers & Well, 2003). However, for most questions investigated in psychological research, the flowcharts identify appropriate statistical procedures to use.

The statistical procedures given in the flowcharts are the ones most commonly used in these situations, but other procedures may also be appropriate. Therefore, the flowcharts are more helpful in finding a statistical procedure to use in a study than in evaluating whether a particular statistical approach used by another researcher is appropriate (see *Historical Lesson 14.1: The Robust Nature of Parametric Studies*).

Quick-Check Review 14.1: Selecting Appropriate Statistical Procedures	1. What is the first step in selecting appropriate statistical procedures?
	2. How do the flowcharts help us to select appropriate statistical procedures?
	3. Can the flowcharts be used to decide if a research study used the appropriate statistical procedures?

Pre-Data Check

Research plans are complex. If they are not constructed properly, all the work of collecting and analyzing data might be wasted. Thus, the researcher must be sure that all planning has been completed before beginning the data collection. Much like a pilot who makes a preflight check to ensure that the airplane is functioning properly, the researcher should carry out a **pre-data check** to see if the research is "ready to fly." The steps in the pre-data check are discussed in what follows and summarized in Table 14.1 and on the Student Resource Website.

TABLE 14.1 *Summary of Pre-Data Checklist*

I. Initial Problem Definition
    1. Literature review completed?
    2. Problem statement developed?
    3. Variables identified and operationally defined?

II. Research Hypothesis
    4. Research hypothesis clearly states expected relationship among variables?

III. Statistical Analysis
    5. Descriptive statistics planned?
    6. Inferential statistics planned?
    7. Post hoc or secondary analyses planned?

IV. Theoretical Basis and Operational Definitions
    8. Theoretical base for study clear?
    9. Do hypotheses and procedures address issues?

V. Independent Variable Manipulation (experimental research)
    10. Independent variable manipulations planned?
    11. Manipulations pretested?
    12. Manipulation check planned?

VI. Dependent Measures
    13. Dependent measures operationally defined?
    14. Dependent measures piloted?
    15. Reliability and validity data available?
    16. Procedures to measure reliability included?

VII. Controls
    17. Controls for threats to internal validity in place?
    18. General control procedures and subject and experimenter controls in place?

VIII. Participants
Participant Selection
    19. Sample adequately represents target population?
    20. Demographic variables measured?

(continued)

TABLE 14.1   Continued

Sample Size
21. Sample sufficiently large?

Participant Assignment
22. Participants properly assigned to conditions (experimental research)?
23. Groups carefully defined (differential research)?
24. Information on the matching preserved for analysis (matched-subjects design)?

Participant Availability
25. Participants available?
26. Participants scheduled?
27. Participant-fee procedures ready?

Research Ethics
28. IRB approval obtained? (human research)
29. Informed consent forms available? (human research)
30. Debriefing and/or feedback procedures ready? (human research)
31. Ethical guidelines checked and research approved? (animal research)

IX. **Preparation of the Setting**
Space and Equipment
32. Adequate space available?
33. Free of distractions?
34. Equipment checked?

Personnel
35. Sufficient research staff?
36. Assistants adequately trained for emergencies?
37. Assistants adequately trained in procedures?
38. Blind procedures in place?

X. **Adequacy of Participant Preparation, Instruction, and Procedures**
39. Instructions to participants clear?
40. Instructions and procedures piloted?

If all check out, you are ready to go.

I. Initial Problem Definition

Each study begins with a literature review based on your initial ideas. In that process, you refined your statement of the problem and identified the major variables. Now you must check to see that those variables have been operationally defined appropriately.

1. Has a literature review of initial ideas been completed?
2. Has the problem statement been clearly developed?
3. Are variables identified and operationally defined?

II. *Clarity of the Research Hypotheses*

Next you must check the research hypotheses. They predict specific relationships between variables, which may be differential, correlational, or causal. The research hypotheses should indicate the type and, if appropriate, the direction of the relationship.

> **4.** Do the research hypotheses clearly state the type and direction of the relationship among the variables?

III. *Statistical Analysis Procedures*

Statistical procedures are selected before the data are gathered. Select the descriptive and inferential statistical procedures appropriate for each research hypothesis. (Here you can use the flowcharts presented in Figures 14.1 through 14.5.)

> **5.** Are all descriptive statistical procedures planned?
> **6.** For each hypothesis, are inferential statistical procedures planned?
> **7.** Are you planning post hoc or secondary analyses? If so, what are they?

IV. *Theoretical Basis and Operational Definitions*

After you have obtained and analyzed your data, you will have the all-important task of interpreting and communicating the results. These rational processes provide meaning for your research and its discoveries and implications for theory. Your work may stimulate further research and influence practical applications. Thus, it is critical that you have a clear understanding of the theoretical bases for your research. Make sure that your hypotheses and your procedures address the issues that you raised initially so that your results can be related to those issues.

> **8.** Is the theoretical base for your study clear?
> **9.** Do your hypotheses and procedures address the issues?

V. *Adequacy of Independent Variable Manipulation*

Experimental manipulations must be carefully selected and carried out.

> **10.** Have the independent variable manipulations been carefully planned (i.e., have experimental and control groups been operationally defined)?
> **11.** Have the manipulations been pretested? Are changes needed?
> **12.** Has a manipulation check been planned?

VI. *Adequacy of Dependent Measures*

Dependent measures must be clearly defined, both conceptually and operationally. They should be **pilot tested** for feasibility, which means using the measures with a small group of people to see that they are understandable and will work in your research. You should evaluate reliability and validity data if available. If these are new measures, they should have been pretested and reliability and validity data obtained.

In either event, be sure that you have included procedures to measure their reliability in your current research. Know how the responses are to be recorded and scored. Piloting helps you to estimate how long the tasks will take and what problems might arise. Problems with the procedures should be resolved before you test a single participant.

13. Are all dependent measures operationally defined?
14. Have they been pretested or piloted?
15. Do you have prior reliability and validity data?
16. Did you include procedures to measure reliability?

VII. Are All Controls in Place?

Check to see that all your controls are in place to protect internal and external validity. You do not want to complete your data collection only to discover that some uncontrolled factor provides an alternative explanation of your results.

17. Are controls for threats to internal validity in place?
18. Are appropriate general control procedures and controls for subject and experimenter effects in place?

VIII. Participants

Participant Selection. Do the participants adequately represent the target population? You should know the type of sample that you have (a random sample, a stratified random sample, or an ad hoc sample, for example). Adequate demographic measures must be included to describe the sample, especially if this is an ad hoc sample. Measures of age, sex, socioeconomic class, and similar variables are necessary if (1) generalizations are to be made beyond the research sample and (2) replication is anticipated.

19. Will the sampling procedures select a sample that adequately represents the target population?
20. Have demographic measures been included to describe the sample and evaluate how well it represents the population?

Sample Size. There must be enough participants to fill all cells of the design and to provide enough data to meet the needs of the statistical analyses.

21. Is the sample sufficiently large? This is a complex question having to do with statistical power. The mathematical procedures for defining "sufficiently large" are beyond the scope of this text but are covered by Cohen (1988).

Participant Assignment. If the research involves group comparison and an experimental manipulation, participants must be assigned to conditions. Participant assignments should be carried out according to the research design.

22. Have participants been assigned to conditions according to the research design?
23. If it is a differential design, have the groups been carefully defined?
24. If it is a matched-subjects design, has the information on matching been preserved to allow its use in the analysis?

Participant Availability.   Procedures should be in place for contacting and scheduling participants, getting their consent, and paying them if funds are available.

25. Are participants available?
26. Have participants been scheduled or is there a procedure for scheduling them?
27. Are participant payment procedures, if required, in place?

Research Ethics Considerations.   Ethical issues should be anticipated and handled, and participant safeguards should be in place.

28. Has IRB ethics approval been obtained?
29. For human research, are the informed consent forms available?
30. Are debriefing and/or feedback procedures ready?
31. For animal research, have all the ethical guidelines been checked and followed?

IX. Preparation of the Setting

Space and Equipment.   The research space should be prepared appropriately for the research, and all needed equipment should be in place and functioning correctly.

32. Is adequate space available?
33. Is it free of distracting conditions?
34. Has all equipment been checked out to see that it is working properly?

Personnel.   Proper training of research assistants is critical to ensure that the data will be collected properly.

35. Are there a sufficient number of research assistants?
36. Are the assistants adequately trained for emergencies?
37. Are the assistants adequately trained in the research procedures?
38. Are single- or double-blind procedures necessary and in place?

X. Adequacy of Participant Preparation, Instruction, and Procedures

Instructions, procedures, and tests should be prepared and piloted. There should be no surprises for the experimenter; you do not want to "waste" a single participant.

39. Are all instructions to participants clear?
40. Have the instructions and procedures been piloted?

---

*Quick-Check
Review 14.2:
Pre-Data Check*

1. Why is it important to run a pre-data check before we begin to collect data?
2. If the pre-data check finds problems, what should the researcher do?

> ***PUTTING IT INTO PRACTICE*** By this point in the course, you are probably designing your own research projects. There is no better way to use the Statistical Flowcharts and Pre-Data Checklist than to apply them to your own research efforts. Good luck with your work!

Chapter Summary

Selecting an appropriate statistical procedure can be confusing for beginning students. A flowchart system is presented here that organizes the process of selecting statistical procedures. This system starts with a description of the characteristics of the research study and then proceeds through a series of questions that lead students step by step toward the selection of appropriate statistical procedures.

We also present a pre-data checklist similar to the preflight checklist used by pilots. After the study is designed, the procedures are determined, and everything is set to go, the pre-data check provides a final verification that you are ready to collect the data.

Chapter Exercises

1. Define the following key terms. Be sure that you understand them. They are discussed in the chapter and defined in the glossary.

   decision tree
   decision-tree flowcharts
   secondary analyses
   data snooping

   robust
   Monte Carlo study
   pilot testing
   pre-data check

2. For each of the following situations, study the research plan and identify:

   a. level of constraint

   b. independent variable(s)

   c. levels of independent variables

   d. type of design

   e. dependent variable(s)

   f. dependent measure(s)

   g. level of measurement for each dependent measure

   h. type of data generated from each dependent measure

   i. research hypotheses

   j. kind of statistical test that is appropriate for the research hypothesis

   Then use the flowcharts to identify the following for each hypothesis:

   1. Appropriate descriptive statistic(s)

   2. Appropriate inferential statistic(s)

3. A researcher randomly assigns 30 hypertensive participants to three groups of 10 each. Group 1 is taught muscle relaxation training; Group 2 is taught cognitive relaxation training; Group 3 is a no-treatment control. After the manipulation, blood pressure readings are taken on all participants. Blood pressure is represented by two numbers. The systolic blood pressure represents the maximum blood pressure at the point that the heart is actually beating. The diastolic blood pressure represents the minimum blood pressure between beats. Both are measured in terms of the number of millimeters of mercury that can be pushed up in a column by the pressure. The researcher wants to know (i) whether relaxation training reduces hypertension and (ii) whether one type of relaxation training is more effective than the other.

4. A researcher has the hypothesis that (i) people with phobias are particularly sensitive to minor levels of stimulation and (ii) females with phobias are particularly sensitive. A fear survey questionnaire is given to

300 college freshmen. Of the 300, 50 students have high phobia scores. From the non-phobic participants, 30 females and 20 males are randomly selected. Thus, groups of 50 (30 female, 20 male) phobic and 50 (30 female, 20 male) non-phobic participants are constructed. All participants are tested on their sensitivity, a task that yields a simple score of the number of correct responses.

5. In a study of the effects of teacher feedback on accuracy of performance, 10 children (5 males and 5 females) are tested under three different conditions: immediate feedback, delayed feedback, and no feedback. All 10 children are included in each condition. The order of presentation of conditions is counterbalanced. The children are tested on their reading accuracy (i.e., the number of reading errors is counted).

6. The study focuses on the effects of smiling on children's evaluation of adults and on accuracy of learning and recall. Thirty children (15 males and 15 females) are randomly assigned to three conditions. Videotape of the same teacher reading the same story are created. In the first condition, the teacher smiles 60 percent of the time; in the second condition, the teacher smiles 30 percent of the time; and in the third condition, the teacher does not smile. After viewing the tape, the children are (i) given a learning test scored on the number of correct answers to questions about the story, and (ii) asked to provide a rating on a 1–5 scale of how much they like the teacher (assume an ordinal scale). Two weeks later, the children are tested for retention of material from the story (scored on the number of correct answers to questions about the story).

7. A psychiatric survey is conducted in a large metropolitan area. A random sample of 2000 residents is chosen. Each resident is interviewed and diagnosed into one of six categories as follows: (i) healthy; (ii) mild psychiatric symptoms; (iii) moderate symptoms; (iv) impaired; (v) severe impairment; or (vi) incapacitated. The number of people from each social class is calculated for each category.

8. A research study focusing on fear involves 30 parent/child pairs. Three hypotheses are tested in the study: (i) the number of fears reported by the parent is correlated with the number of fears reported by the child; (ii) the degree of fear reported by the parent is correlated with the degree of fear reported by the child; and (iii) the number of fears and the degree of fear reported by both the parent and the child are reduced by the introduction of a fear-reduction program.

Both parent and child are given a fear survey schedule, which measures the number of fears reported. In addition, both parent and child are rated on an index of fear severity with a range of 1–7 (assume the rating scale is an ordinal scale). After the initial measures, parents are randomly assigned to one of two groups. One group receives a fear-reduction program while the other group receives no treatment. At the end of this part of the study, the fear survey schedule and the rating scale of fear intensity are administered again to all parents.

15

Research Methodology: An Evolving Discipline

The questions we do not yet even have the wit to ask will be a growing preoccupation of science in the next 50 years.

—Sir John Maddox, *The Unexpected Science to Come*, 1999

Web Resource Material

Scientific research is an active process of asking and answering questions. Its goals are to discover relationships among variables in order to understand nature. The methods selected to answer research questions depend on the nature of the questions and on practical and ethical constraints. In this text, we have described traditional methods of research in biological and social sciences, highlighting such concepts as validity, threats to validity, and control. This final chapter summarizes some of the major points made in the text and discusses the continuing evolution of research strategies. Expanded discussions of many of the topics in this chapter are provided on the Student Resource Website.

15:01

Each research project progresses through phases, usually starting with a general idea that is refined into a specific question. Procedures are then selected, modified, or created to answer the question(s). Empirical observations are made, data are analyzed, results are interpreted, new research investigations are suggested, and the research is communicated to professionals and the public.

Levels of constraint are the type and degree of demands placed on the adequacy of the procedures. Experimental research, which is the most stringent level of constraint, is used to answer causal questions. However, experimental research is often impossible to carry out due to practical, ethical, or other issues. Lower-constraint research procedures, such as naturalistic, case study, correlation, differential, and quasi-experimental research, are extremely valuable. They can answer questions of feasibility, discover contingencies and correlations, and generate hypotheses that can then be tested through experimentation. Good research yielding important information can be conducted at all levels of constraint. This final chapter explores some of the new directions that psychological research is taking and the factors behind those trends.

New Directions in Research Methodology

Research methods are not static. They change to address new questions and ideas and to take advantage of developing technologies. This section deals with a sampling of the recent changes that have occurred in the field of psychology.

The Evolution of Research Questions and Methods

Science is continually evolving, not only in what research discovers, but also in how research is conducted. Answers to one research question often raise new questions, and new questions often require new or revised methods to answer them. An example is the historical sequence of the study of genetic influences on schizophrenia (Gottesman, 1991; McGuffin et al., 2002). An initial question was whether genetic factors contribute to schizophrenia, a disorder known to run in families. Research methods were needed to separate the influences of genetics and environment. Researchers developed new methods to study schizophrenia, which not only revealed new answers but also new questions. Those, in turn, resulted in still new findings, new answers, new methods, and so on. It is now clear that genes contribute to schizophrenia and to most other disorders (McGuffin et al., 2002). The issue now is how they contribute and how they interact with the environment to trigger the disorder in some people but not others (Jang, 2005). There is an expanded discussion of this research on the Student Resource Website.

New Statistical Methods

There was a time when complex statistical analyses took weeks to complete. Now, thanks to computers, they take seconds. The result is that there has been an explosion of statistical techniques that give researchers the ability to address new questions about complex relationships among variables.

Analysis of Variance. ANOVA is not a new technique but is included here because no statistical procedure has had more impact on research design in psychology. R. A. Fisher's book, *The Design of Experiments* (1935), dramatically changed the way in which research in psychology was conducted. Prior to publication of Fisher's book, psychological research involved the careful analysis of behavior from individual participants. After Fisher's book, research with groups of participants became the norm. Most of the research methods covered in this text use ANOVA procedures for data analysis.

ANOVA has been expanded dramatically to handle situations never envisioned by Fisher, such as removing unwanted variance with ANCOVA or looking at the complex relationship between sets of independent and dependent variables using MANOVAs (Weerahandi, 2004). Without computers, such powerful techniques would be impossible.

Multidimensional Scaling. **Multidimensional scaling** techniques are a group of statistical procedures used to identify underlying structures in nature (Carroll & Arabie, 1998). For example, English has thousands of terms that refer to personality traits. Could nature really be that complex, or might there be a way of organizing these traits? McCrae and Costa (1987, 1999) used a variation of multidimensional scaling, called **factor analysis,** to identify five underlying factors that account for all these individual personality traits. Their five-factor model of personality suggests that every personality trait is a unique combination of various amounts of five underlying personality dimensions: agreeableness, conscientiousness, openness to experience, extroversion (positive emotionality) and neuroticism (negative emotionality). Multidimensional scaling procedures have led to greater understanding of our psychological world (e.g., Katsikitis, 1997; Samson, Zatorre, & Ramsey, 1997) and have stimulated the development of additional new and promising techniques, such as path analysis and taxometric search procedures. (See the expanded discussion of these topics on the Student Resource Website.)

Statistical Analysis of Neuroimages. Modern imaging techniques, such as CAT scans or MRIs, rely on statistical calculations. These imaging techniques have expanded our ability to study the brain and understand its functioning and to do so without the risk associated with earlier procedures such as exploratory surgery (e.g., DeLisi et al., 1997). The people who developed the mathematics that made these imagining technologies possible were awarded a Nobel Prize for their efforts (Bremmer, 2005).

Neuroimaging is not only valuable in psychological research (Raulin, 2003), but is now routinely used in both medical diagnosis and treatment. For example, such imaging dramatically improves the efficiency and safety of surgical procedures for removing tumors (Grimson et al., 1999). It has provided windows on the brain that were only dreamed of a few decades ago and in the process have opened up entirely new avenues of research (Bremmer, 2005).

Meta-analysis and Cumulative Knowledge

A relatively new statistical procedure, called meta-analysis, has become a significant tool in the researcher's arsenal. Meta-analysis helps to objectify an important process that has long been a central part of science. As you learned in Chapter 2, scientists typically begin their research by examining previous research. They review studies on their topic and summarize their conclusions in review papers. They might compute a box score in these reviews that lists how many of the studies support a given hypothesis and how many do not. The reviewer judges the quality of each study, which indicates how seriously each study should be taken. For example, one well-designed study may carry considerably more weight than three or four poorly designed studies. If all the studies have the same outcome, drawing conclusions is easy. But it is common to have some studies show one effect, whereas others show a different effect or no effect at all.

Meta-analysis is a procedure for statistically combining the results of multiple studies on the same topic (e.g., Abramowitz, 1998; Johnson & Eagly, 2000; Rosenthal, 1998). For example, if 16 published studies employ a cognitive therapy for treating depression, a meta-analysis of those studies would compute an index of treatment effectiveness for each study. These indexes are measures of effect size (i.e., the difference between experimental and control conditions expressed in standard deviation units). For example, an effect size of .5 means that the experimental and control conditions showed a mean difference that was one-half of their average standard deviation.

These effect sizes are then averaged across studies. The averages are usually weighted by the sample size of each study and sometimes by the quality of the study. So a study with 50 participants would be given more weight in the meta-analysis than a study with 10 participants. A study with strong control procedures and careful measurement could be given more weight than a study with fewer controls and, therefore, more chance of confounding. The overall effect size computed in a meta-analysis indicates numerically how strongly the independent variable affected the dependent variable. Like any statistical analysis, the value of the analysis depends on the quality of the data. In this case, the data are drawn from several studies, and the quality of the designs and execution of the studies determine how confident we can be in the results of the meta-analysis. Some recent examples of meta-analytic studies are summarized in Table 15.1. Many writers have commented on the drawbacks of significance testing in empirical research and the value of meta-analyses in overcoming them. (e.g., Cohen, 1992; Schmidt, 1992; Wilson, 2000). The following discussion reviews these arguments.

Literature Reviews.   Psychology, like other sciences, routinely assesses the status of research areas. Typically, this is done through formal literature reviews in which previous research is critically examined, findings and ideas from many studies are abstracted and integrated, and conclusions are drawn about the state of that area. These literature reviews are important summary statements, but several researchers have argued that these traditional reviews are flawed and less useful than had been thought (Light & Pillemer, 1984; Hunt, 1997). The problem rests with the nature of the statistical procedures used in psychological research.

Alpha Levels and Knowledge.   Most research information is based on statistical procedures that use arbitrary alpha levels in testing the null hypothesis (typically .01 or .05).

TABLE 15.1   *Some Examples of Meta-analytic Research*

- Hollin (1999) found that, contrary to earlier reviews, treatment does reduce recidivism in criminal offenders.
- Irvin, Bowers, Dunn, and Wang (1999) wondered if the cognitive-behavioral methods for relapse prevention that are frequently included in drug-treatment programs really work. Their meta-analysis examined 26 studies, with 70 hypotheses and a combined sample of 9,504 participants. The results indicated that relapse prevention is generally effective, particularly for alcohol problems.
- Concerns have been raised that such frequently used psychological tests as the MMPI (Minnesota Multiphasic Personality Inventory) may be biased against minorities, making individuals who are perfectly normal appear to be pathological based on the test. Hall, Bansal, and Lopez (1999) conducted a meta-analysis examining 50 empirical studies with a combined sample of 8,633 participants. They compared African-Americans, European-Americans, and Latino-Americans on their MMPI scores. The results showed that the groups do not differ from each other statistically or clinically. The main conclusion is that the tests do not unfairly portray African-Americans or Latinos; they are as accurate at diagnosing pathology in minority groups as they are in Caucasian groups.

Thus, when a well-designed study produces statistically significant results, the findings are accepted as valid new knowledge. If an analysis fails to show statistical significance, it is typically concluded that no new knowledge has been discovered. Studies that fail to find statistical significance are rarely published and therefore are not easily available to the research community. Thus, the accumulated knowledge of a field, such as that presented in traditional literature reviews, is heavily weighted with information that is based on statistically significant findings.

What about those research results that fail to reach statistical significance? Might there be useful information there that is being ignored? Many writers argue that is exactly what is happening; the accumulated scientific knowledge in psychology does not include the information that may reside in studies that were ignored because they failed to reach statistical significance. Consequently, the accumulated knowledge might be drastically limited, hindering the field's progress.

Beta Levels and Knowledge.   Recall from Chapter 5 that setting a stringent alpha (.05 or .01) guards against Type I errors (the tendency to conclude that there is an effect of one variable on another when there actually is none). Minimizing Type I errors increases the probability of Type II errors, which involve concluding that there is no effect when there actually is one. Scientists generally consider Type I errors more serious than Type II errors because a Type I error claims an effect that does not exist. Type II errors result in the loss of information but they do not assert a nonexistent effect. Thus, alpha is set low to minimize the more serious Type I errors.

People often interpret significance tests in an either-or fashion: if the results are statistically significant, then there is an effect of one variable on another, and if the results are not statistically significant, then there is no effect of one variable on another (Oakes, 1986; Schmidt, 1992). In actuality, there might have been effects that were not strong enough to reach statistical significance. Such a result might occur, for example, if the sample is small or participant selection or assignment is biased. Effects lie along a continuum, with some effects being small and not reaching significance and others being large and statistically significant. When small effects are ignored, information on relationships among variables is discarded. That is, the field may be committing a Type II error by failing to recognize real effects. Furthermore, consistently making such Type II errors would significantly truncate the cumulative knowledge in the field (Hunter & Schmidt, 1990). How can science deal with this problem?

Meta-analysis and the Problem of Type II Errors.   Meta-analysis deals with the Type II error problem by calculating effect sizes of studies and weighting these effect sizes for qualitative factors, such as the number of subjects and the inclusion of controls. It goes beyond the simple statement of statistical significance and the categorical acceptance or rejection of the null hypothesis to quantify the strength of the effect. For example, studies with large sample sizes may be statistically significant at the .05 level but, nevertheless, have small effect sizes. Conversely, studies with modest sample sizes may fall short of statistical significance and yet have moderate effect sizes.

Literature reviews are critical in science. Reviews based on meta-analyses can mine what we might call the Type II error area to unearth important information previously ignored.

Meta-analytic techniques are fairly new, but they have the potential to significantly influence the direction of research. Indeed, the important breakthroughs in science of the future might not come from individual research reports of single studies, but from the careful meta-analysis of large groups of research (Schmidt, 1992). This possible future for science would include primary and theoretical scientists, with primary scientists conducting individual studies and providing the data and theoretical scientists applying sophisticated meta-analyses to the accumulated studies to "make the scientific discoveries" (Schmidt, 1992, p. 1180). Meta-analysis provides technology for combining results across diverse samples and different measures of outcome. Although imperfect, meta-analysis is probably better than traditional qualitative methods of summarizing studies in literature reviews. Several informative books are available for students who want additional understanding of meta-analysis, such as Hunt (1997), Light and Pillemer (1984), and Cooper (1998). There is also a more detailed discussion of meta-analysis on the Student Resource Website.

15:02

The Impact of Other Disciplines

Developments in related disciplines can have a significant impact on the discipline of psychology. One example is the study of neurological influences on human behavior. Developments in biochemistry, which permitted much finer analyses of organic chemicals, made possible the discovery that there are many more neurotransmitters than previously believed. This led scientists to rethink the role of neurotransmitters, and the concept of specific transmitter influences in precise brain locations became a much more intellectually appealing theory.

How do we study specific influences of specific neurotransmitters in specific locations in the brain? Much of the previous research on neurotransmitters was based on the assumption that there are general levels of these chemicals in the system, and the procedures used for measuring the chemicals were usually nonspecific with respect to the location of the action of each neurotransmitter. There was a need to develop techniques to sample from specific locations. Because brain processes are part of the living organism, it was necessary to accomplish the sampling without damaging the organism. A sampling of brain tissue at autopsy provides little useful information. Procedures were developed that allowed researchers to inject chemicals into the synapses of an animal's neurons while the animal was awake and functioning (Curtis & Crawford, 1969). Later, neuroimaging procedures were developed that allowed researchers to observe the action of specific neurotransmitters in specific brain regions (e.g., Morosan et al., 2005).

Interdisciplinary Research

As a science grows, there is increasing specialization. This specialization focuses research on specific problems and allows the development of new, sophisticated approaches to problems. A disadvantage, however, is that researchers can lose sight of the broader picture. Today it is common to find researchers from different disciplines coming together to pool their knowledge in interdisciplinary research projects, which provides a broader perspective despite modern specialization. For example, **behavioral medicine** brings together practitioners and researchers in neurology, physiology, and psychology. Other examples include an interdisciplinary integration of sociology, law, and psychology, sometimes referred to as sociolegal studies (Levine, Wallach, & Levine 2007), and the field of artificial intelligence, in which mathematicians, psychologists, and computer scientists have developed models of thinking that can be programmed on computers.

Such interdisciplinary fields as neuroscience and cognitive science are growing rapidly as the value of these interdisciplinary partnerships becomes more apparent. Interdisciplinary research will almost certainly continue to increase, providing greater integration in the understanding of human functioning.

Moving Research Out of the Laboratory

Many psychologists are rediscovering old methods as a result of their concern for external validity. Naturalistic and case-study research is becoming more common in areas that previously relied almost exclusively on higher-constraint laboratory research. For example, many researchers argue that understanding the development of a person requires that we take a historical perspective, recognizing the developmental influences that color his or her current perspective on life. This more individualized approach to developmental psychology is different from what has been the tradition over the last few decades. It reinforces the point made throughout this book that lower-constraint research is an effective way of examining certain research questions and may even be the best way to study some phenomena. Research in natural settings need not give up the controls of the laboratory, because well-controlled experiments can be carried out in natural settings. For example, the work of Ramey and his colleagues with severely disadvantaged children in real-world settings demonstrated that early interventions can have powerful and permanent effects on a child's development (e.g., Campbell et al., 2002; Ramey, 1995).

One weakness of laboratory research is the possibility of low external validity. Campbell and Stanley (1966) cautioned "we cannot easily assume that findings from the laboratory will hold in the field" (p. 7). This issue is one of **ecological validity,** the accurate generalization of laboratory findings to real-world settings. The argument is that laboratory experimentation may be so constrained that its findings do not represent external reality. However, other scientists argue that research in natural environments may be so uncontrolled that internal validity is sacrificed.

This controversy is likely to continue, given the complexity of human behavior, but it may be overstated. For example, Anderson, Lindsay, and Bushman (1999) argue that the notions of the poor ecological validity of laboratory research and the poor internal validity of field research are unsupported beliefs rather than empirical facts. These researchers found a significant correlation (0.73) between the effect sizes of 38 pairs of laboratory studies and comparable field studies. It is illustrated in the scatter plot in Figure 15.1. They concluded that laboratory research is discovering phenomena that also exist in the real world outside of the laboratory. The strong correlation between the results of laboratory and field studies also suggests that the internal validity of the field studies is also strong. Well-designed studies, whether in laboratory or field settings, can produce valid information.

The Impact of Computers

Computer technology has had a major impact on research. Not since the Industrial Revolution has so much changed so quickly, and much of the progress is due to the development of the microprocessor—that tiny silicon sliver that now drives notebook computers, fax machines, wristwatches, kitchen appliances, factories, automobiles, airplanes, iPods, and boats. Today's PCs are about 50,000 times more powerful than the original PC at a quarter of the price (in inflation-corrected dollars). If microprocessors continue to develop at this rate, the computers of 2030 will be able to utilize new software that will manage tasks that we can now barely imagine.

Consider the impact of computers on communication. Today more than 100 million computers around the world are interconnected, but this represents only about 2% of the world's population (Dertouzos, 1999). Imagine the impact on global communication and the potential effects on human institutions, cross-cultural interactions, and on scientific communication if 5% or, if we can imagine it, 50% of the world's population were interconnected.

The availability of computers has led to an explosion in the number, sophistication, speed, and efficiency of statistical analysis procedures. Computers are also used to interact with and gather data from participants in the laboratory. They reduce the number of mistakes that result in lost or distorted data, minimize experimenter bias, and increase precision in the replication of laboratory procedures.

The computer also offers the researcher new ways of understanding phenomena. An example is **computer modeling** of cognitive

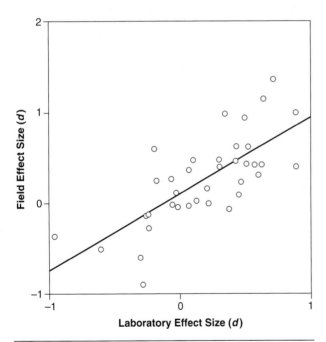

FIGURE 15.1   *Relation Between Effect Sizes in the Laboratory and in the Field* It is reassuring that the effect size for psychological findings in the lab are highly correlated with the effect size found in natural settings. These data suggest that both internal and external validity are protected in laboratory studies.

Source: Anderson, C.A., Lindsay, J. J., & Bushman, B. J. (1999). Research in the psychological laboratory: Truth or triviality. *Current Directions in Psychological Science, 8,* 3–9. Reprinted with permission.

processes (Weitzenfeld, Arbib, & Alexander, 2002). Computer modeling is an idea that was borrowed and adapted from the artificial intelligence field. In **artificial intelligence,** computers are programmed to behave intelligently, to solve problems, and to react to stimuli. Artificial intelligence systems are not necessarily designed to duplicate human functioning, but computer models of cognitive functions do attempt to duplicate human functions. Instead of developing complex abstract models of cognitive processes and designing factorial studies that are too complicated to understand, researchers create a computer model of functioning that they can manipulate to observe the effects.

Computers have even had an impact on the way scientists collaborate. Researchers at distant universities can now collaborate easily using email. Computer technology is being used to enhance even more direct collaboration regardless of the distance between researchers (Crawford, Hurd, & Weller, 1996; Schrage, 1991). With modern software, researchers in different cities can work on the same document at the same time, sharing ideas as if they were gathered around a table writing a draft of an article. Technology allows collaborators to be spread all over the world and still be able to work closely together.

An important development in computer applications is that of **genetic algorithms,** a computer-based search procedure largely inspired by biological evolution (Mitchell, 1996; Goldberg, 2002). Natural evolution achieves biological diversity through three major processes: mutation, sexual recombination, and natural selection. Researchers are now studying computer programs that mimic those biological evolutionary processes and, over the conceptual equivalent of generations, can generate solutions to complex problems. Some researchers (Koza, Keane, & Streeter, 2003) suggest that it may be possible to program computers to "evolve" new technological inventions, a process that has been the exclusive domain of human creativity. This suggestion needs to be supported by more research, but if this process works as well as some people think it will, computers might someday be capable of "evolving" new research hypotheses and the procedures needed to test them.

The impact of computers on psychological research is only beginning to be felt. The directions for the future will be shaped by the inventiveness of today's scientists and, perhaps, by tomorrow's computers. Many believe that computers will offer whole new ways of looking at questions and will permit new research paradigms that will address questions yet to be imagined. It is an exciting period for science, but we must not forget that it is the scientist's imagination, thought, and creativity, and not the silicon inside computer chips, that guides this growth and development. Basic science is unlikely to be changed by the computer. Com-

After years of working on the project, Professor Gronski discovers there are practical limits to miniaturization.

Sometimes it is hard to know whether a line of research will be productive and useful or whether it will prove to be a dead end.

puters add efficiency but, for now at least, scientists still ask the questions, decide the best ways to search for the answers, set up the studies, and evaluate the results.

Scientific Research and Society

Imagine what life will be like for you 50 years from now. Will you be retired from work at that time? Perhaps science will have made it more likely that you will continue to work for many more years; perhaps "retirement" will no longer be an appropriate concept in a future world too remote from us to imagine. It is tempting, if one is enthralled by scientific and technological advances, to try to extrapolate to the future and ask, "What will science be discovering in another half-century? What will life be like?"

The momentous scientific discoveries of the 19th century laid the groundwork for a future that people in the 1890s thought they could foretell. In a thought-provoking essay, Maddox (1999) reviewed the major scientific discoveries of the 19th century that helped to change the world (see Table 15.2). These discoveries proved to be well short of the final answers many people wanted. Much of what then seemed certain was later changed, reconceptualized, or discarded as unimportant. Science in the 20th century developed concepts and procedures that the earlier scientists and the general public had never envisioned. One lesson that Maddox draws is that we need to be realistic about our infatuation with our own scientific discoveries. The direction of science is unpredictable, because science is driven by new discoveries. The discoveries that will be made in our century are as unpredictable now as the 20th century's developments were to those in the 1890s.

Maddox believes that we cannot imagine the scientific discoveries that await us over the next half-century (see the quotation at the start of this chapter). For example, consider the current research on the human genome (Collins & Jegalian, 1999; Palladino, 2005). Its mapping and sequencing was recently completed, several years ahead of schedule. Where will that information lead? Will it tell us about evolution, when and how we diverged from the great apes? Will it explain how and when the human brain and human skills, such as language and art, developed? Will it be the basis for technology that will allow programmatic development of future human brains? How these and other scientific discoveries will affect the future is unclear, but that they will affect the future is unquestioned (Rose, 2005).

Scientific advances lead us into a complex universe of ideas and technologies, with uncountable twists, turns, ascents, descents, and dead ends. This intertwined mass, like tangled roots in a tropical swamp, presents us with a seemingly impenetrable confusion about the future. How can we predict the direction of each tendril of discovery? Simply, we cannot.

TABLE 15.2   *Major Scientific Discoveries of the 19th Century*

- John Dalton's confirmation that matter is made of atoms (1808)
- Sadi Carnot's surmise that converting one form of energy to another is inherently limited (about 1830)
- James P. Joule's demonstration of the conservation of energy (1851)
- Charles Darwin's and Alfred Russel Wallace's discovery of natural selection and the eventual Darwinian theory of evolution (1859)
- James Maxwell's mathematical unification of electricity and magnetism (about 1880).

Source: Adapted from Maddox, 1999.

Quick-Check Review 15.1: New Directions in Research Methodology	1. How does meta-analysis improve the process of reviewing and synthesizing several studies of the same question? 2. Why do scientists traditionally set the alpha level low? 3. How have computers changed psychological research?

Science: An Interaction of Empiricism and Rationalism

It is important to restate a point made in Chapter 1: New laboratory technologies do not define a science. Rather, a scientific discipline is defined by its subject matter and by the processes used to answer questions of interest to that discipline. *Science* combines empiricism and rationalism. By requiring that scientific theories conform to both logical restrictions and the realities of the world, we demand more of scientific theories than of any other system of knowing. Few scientific theories stand up to this kind of double scrutiny. Theories are constantly being rejected because they are either logically inconsistent (a rational criterion), do not accurately predict data (an empirical criterion), or both.

Science progresses by rejecting inadequate theories and proposing and testing new theories that stand up to rigorous testing. Many students find this process to be negativistic: researchers always try to criticize and reject theories rather than prove them. However, it is not negativism but skepticism that characterizes science. Scientists use theories, but they never fully accept them. They constantly question a theory's validity. Scientists expect theories to eventually be replaced by better theories. In science, little is accepted on faith except for the method of science.

The Growth of Science

Science is a major enterprise today, with millions of people working in and around scientific laboratories. Scientific disciplines have become more specialized as their knowledge base grows. As disciplines develop, research techniques evolve to handle the specific questions of each discipline. Therefore, different scientific disciplines may appear to be using different research methods.

This text covers many of the most commonly used research techniques in the discipline of psychology. Although the techniques covered differ somewhat from those used in other sciences, these differences are more surface differences than conceptual differences. A research biologist would have no trouble conceptually understanding the research methodology of chemistry or psychology, and vice versa. In this text, we presented concepts and built specific research techniques on them. If you understand the concepts that underlie techniques, it will be relatively easy to understand new research techniques, whether they are from the discipline of psychology or some other science.

New research techniques and new scientific disciplines are inevitable as the knowledge base of science builds and increased specialization is required. What was once philosophy is now a dozen different basic scientific disciplines. What was once physics is now physics, astronomy, and chemistry, and each of those fields have several subdisciplines.

Specialization is necessary, given the incredible complexity of disciplines, but it tends to isolate disciplines from the ideas and discoveries of other sciences. Organizations such as the American Association for the Advancement of Science (AAAS) strive to unite the many subdisciplines of science and maintain a healthy level of communication among disciplines. Support for this effort comes from the belief that the methods of science (empiricism coupled with rationalism) are strong bonds between apparently diverse areas. We hope that this text provided an understanding of both research approaches in psychology and scientific thought in general. The specific research approaches used in psychology are applications of basic scientific processes to a particular subject matter: the behavior of organisms.

Ethical Conduct in Research

Ethical conduct is a central and growing concern in research. We have emphasized that fact by addressing ethical issues in every chapter. Our message is this: as you learn how to conduct scientific research, you must also develop a sharp sensitivity to ethical issues and become expert in designing ethically appropriate studies. Research is tightly woven into modern society, and every research project is, in effect, a contract with society. Science gets the knowledge it seeks and society gets the applications of that knowledge.

Scientific research informs every aspect of modern society: how we raise our children, build skyscrapers, design automobiles, conduct wars, fly airplanes, explore the solar system, write legislation, fight disease, and so on. Will scientists use research wisely or will we abuse it, creating detrimental effects for society? Every abuse puts at risk not only the specific participants in a study, but all of society. Research ethics reduce such risk in two ways: by understanding and controlling any and all potential abuses and by using the knowledge gained from research to create useful applications. The ethical researcher will be attuned to those issues and will be well prepared to anticipate, prevent, and correct ethical problems.

An area of particular concern discussed earlier in the text that bears repeating is the willingness of some groups that wield considerable social power to distort scientific information for their own commercial or political gain. When industries and governments begin doing this, it places society at serious risk. We urge our students to become particularly alert to those ethical abuses.

As we have noted throughout this text, risks can be created throughout the phases of the research enterprise. Obviously, specific participants can be put at risk. Perhaps less obviously, research information that has been distorted by ethical lapses may put others at risk, such as future users of new medical treatments. Distorted information may stain the pool of scientific knowledge and, until detected, create problems for future research. Finally, at the most general level, misinformation from ethically distorted research can negatively affect society's perceptions of the real world.

The Essence of Science: A Reminder

It is appropriate to end this book by repeating an idea that we have stressed throughout: The essence of science is its *way of thinking*. Scientists systematically combine rational thinking and empirical findings to ask and answer questions about nature. The scientist's enthusiasm, skepticism, curiosity, hunches, and creativity, coupled with a little serendipity, are essential components in the process of scientific thinking. Mostly, it is the *thinking process that constitutes the essence of science*. To emphasize this point, recall the imagery used in Chapter 1: A scientist can operate very scientifically sitting under a tree in the woods, thinking through a problem, using apparatus no more technical than a pad and pencil.

Quick-Check Review 15.2: An Interaction of Empiricism and Rationalism	1. What processes define science? 2. How does science progress? 3. What is the essence of science?

PUTTING IT INTO PRACTICE	Scientists spend years learning the detailed skills of their craft, but the most essential skill is almost always present from the beginning of their training—their intense curiosity. Curiosity is not unique to science, although it is one of the dominant characteristics of scientists. That curiosity motivates scientists throughout their training and throughout their lives. Work on developing your own curiosity. The more you do, the more interesting the world will be to you and the more motivated you will be to expand your knowledge.

Chapter Summary

The essence of science, its way of thinking, remains constant, but the questions within any scientific discipline change as the discipline matures. Therefore, the research methods must change. This chapter briefly reviewed some of the major changes that have occurred recently in psychology, and many of these topics are covered in more depth on the Student Resource Website. You will learn more about these cutting-edge technologies and research strategies in other psychology courses. Our goal here is to let you know that such changes are happening and that they are inevitable in a developing science like psychology.

Chapter Exercises _____

1. Define the following key terms. Be sure that you understand them. They are discussed in the chapter and defined in the glossary.

   multidimensional scaling   ecological validity
   factor analysis   computer modeling
   meta-analysis   artificial intelligence
   behavioral medicine   genetic algorithms

2. There is only one question for this chapter. Explain how a scientist can be operating scientifically while sitting under a tree and thinking through a scientific problem.

Appendix A

Using the Student Resource Website

Resources Available

What to Do If You Have Problems

Getting Help

Appendix Summary

Web Resource Material

A:01   Browser Tutorials

A:02   Using the Student Resource Website

This text includes the most comprehensive set of supplementary resources available in any research methods textbook. These resources are available through the Student Resource Website. This appendix describes what is available, how to access it, and how to address problems when they arise.

Resources Available

The Student Resource Website provides (1) an interactive *study guide and lab manual*, (2) tutorials on library research, statistical analysis, and writing reports in APA style, (3) numerous exercises and handouts, and (4) extensive discussions of statistical theory to supplement the practical statistical content of the text and the Student Resource Website. All of this material is integrated with the text and organized for easy access.

The Student Resource Website address (URL) is *www.ablongman.com/graziano6e*.[1] Your computer probably has an internet browser like Internet Explorer, Netscape, or Firefox on it. Figure A.1 shows how you would enter this URL on Internet Explorer. Internet

---

[1]The complete address for the website is *http://www.ablongman.com/graziano6e*. Most web browsers allow you to drop the "http://" part, and the "/index.htm" is the default file that will be accessed and so need not be specified.

FIGURE A.1 *Accessing the Student Resource Website* To access the Student Resource Website, enter the URL for the website (as shown here for Netscape, Internet Explorer, and Firefox) and hit the Enter key. The first time you access the site from a particular computer, you will be prompted for a password, which will be found inside the Access Kit that is shrinkwrapped with the text..

Explorer comes free with the Windows operating system. Updated versions can be obtained from the Microsoft website (*www.microsoft.com*). A free copy of Netscape can be downloaded from the Netscape website (*www.netscape.com*), and a free copy of Firefox can be downloaded from the Mozilla website (*www.mozilla.org*).

Figure A.2 shows you the welcome screen for the Student Resource Website. The first time you access the Student Resource Website from your computer, you will be prompted for a password, which will be found inside the Access Kit that is shrinkwrapped with the text. Access the Student Resource Website is for your use only. It is part of the package that comes with this textbook. The password will only work on two computers and will only work for six months, so if you give it out to other people, you may not be able to access the Student Resource Website resources yourself without purchasing another subscription from the publisher (*www.ablongman.com*).

If you have not already explored the Student Resource Website, take a few minutes to explore it now. You may be surprised by how much is there to help you in this course. You can navigate the site using the table of contents at the left of the screen. Clicking on any item in the table of contents will take you directly to that resource.

You are likely to access the *study guide/lab manual* and the *Chapter Resources* menu frequently. These options provide materials that will enhance your learning. However, you will also find dozens of other resources that will be helpful for this course and beyond. Specific resources for each chapter are identified in the text with an icon and a code number. Selecting *Chapter Resources* will bring you to the list of resources organized by those code numbers.

What to Do If You Have Problems

We assume that you have at least some familiarity with computers and web browser programs, although we have included on the website browser tutorials (for Netscape, Internet Explorer, and Firefox) and an orientation to the Student Resource Website. In this section, we list some common problems, their most likely causes, and how to overcome them.

Contents

Welcome

Welcome to the *Textbook Website* for the Sixth Edition of the Graziano and Raulin *Research Methods* textbook. The *Textbook Website* is not an add-on to the textbook. It is an integrated element in a package of resources for the instructor and the student. This website is designed to take students well beyond the passive learning that comes from reading, to an active processing of the material that will enhance learning and the enjoyment of learning. We have carefully constructed the site so that it will run flawlessly with *Netscape Navigator*™, *Internet Explorer*™, or *Mozilla Firefox*™. If you do not have these browsers or have older versions of these browser programs, you can get free copies of the newest versions at www.netscape.com (for Netscape Navigator), www.microsoft.com (for Internet Explorer), or www.mozilla.org (for Mozilla Firefox).

The drop-down menu at the top of the screen is the Table of Contents, which is the primary navigation tool for the website. There are so many resources on the website that we have organized them into directories and subdirectories in the Table of Contents. The directories are shown below in all caps, with the subdirectories and their content listed under each directory. When you move the curser over a directory, its subdirectory will appear on the right. In addition, individual pages provide direct links to related topics in order to facilitate finding material quickly. Finally, the website has an extensive index (under both the *Overview* and *Supplemental Information* directories). Listed below are brief descriptions of each of these

FIGURE A.2   *The Website's Table of Contents*   The table of contents for the Student Resource Website will always be visible on the left side of the screen. You can use the scroll bar to scroll up and down the list of resources, which are organized for your convenience into broad conceptual categories.

A:01
A:02

I put in the address (URL) for the Student Resource Website and nothing happened.

1. Did you hit the Enter key after inserting the URL? The web browser does not begin searching for a website until you hit *Enter*.

2. Are you connected to the Internet? The quickest way to check this is to access a site that should always be accessible, such as *http://www.google.com*.

I put in the address and the response I get is that the site was not found.

1. Check the spelling of the address. It must be keyed in exactly as follows: *www.ablongman.com/graziano6e*.

2. It may be that there is something wrong at your end—your Internet provider may be temporarily down, or your modem may not be connected correctly. Check to see if you can access another site.

3. On rare occasions, the website may be down for maintenance. If this is so, in most cases you will see a message to this effect but occasionally you may just get the message that the site was not found. Try accessing the Student Resource Website again in a couple of hours.

4. The publisher of this textbook will maintain the Student Resource Website until a newer edition of the textbook is released. If your textbook is more than three years old, it may have been replaced with a new edition. You can check the publisher's website (*www.ablongman.com*) to see if your current textbook is still in print.

I found the Student Resource Website, but I am not sure how to find specific material.

1. The publisher is constantly updating and upgrading its websites. Unfortunately, that means that it is difficult for us to show you here what the Student Resource Website will look like when you access it. The table of contents for the Student Resource Website is in the form of a drop-down menu. Click on the down arrow and you will see all of the menu options for the site. Although the screen may look different from Figure A.2—because this book had to go into production before the Student Resource Website was put up—it should function as described here.

2. There should be a Help button on the Student Resource Website. In Figure A.2, it is on the same line as the drop-down menu. Click *Help* to get additional instructions on how to use the Student Resource Website.

The Student Resource Website just stopped responding.

1. This happens all the time on the Internet. Try waiting a minute or so and see if it starts to work again.

2. If the Student Resource Website does not start working again, there are several things that you can do that will probably get things working again. They are listed here in the order that we recommend them, from the least drastic to the most drastic. It is possible that the problem that is causing the site to not respond is in your computer, or in the computer that is its link to the Internet (i.e., your Internet provider), or even in the computer that runs the publisher's website.
   a. Try hitting the escape (*Esc*) button in the upper left hand corner of the keyboard a few times. This might free up the program if it is locked up.
   b. Try hitting the back arrow key on your web browser. Then hit the front arrow key.
   c. To determine if the problem is with the Student Resource Website or with your computer, try entering another URL and seeing if that site responds. If other sites can be accessed without difficulty, you may want to try accessing the Student Resource Website later. Sometimes the traffic at a website is so high that the site just cannot handle it. It is essentially an electronic traffic jam.
   d. Try opening the Student Resource Website again by entering the URL and hitting the Enter key.
   e. Close your web browser, open it again, and open the Student Resource Website again.

    f. If you have a dialup connection, close it, dial in again, and then try accessing the Student Resource Website again with your browser.

    g. Close all programs and shut down the computer. Then wait a couple of minutes and restart the computer. Open your web browser and access the Student Resource Website again.

    h. If you have an external modem, you may need to reset the modem. For most systems, that means turning the modem off and waiting a minute or so before turning it on again. Each modem is a little different, so you may need to call the company that provided the Internet connection for more trouble shooting ideas.

Getting Help

We have tried in this appendix to anticipate many of the problems that you might encounter while using the Student Resource Website. If you run into a problem not covered here or on the help menu of the Student Resource Website, we recommend the following two-step process.

    1. Ask one or two students in your class who are reasonably knowledgeable about computers and have used the Student Resource Website to help you. You will be surprised how quickly they can spot what you may be doing wrong and tell you how to correct it.

    2. If all else fails, email Mike Raulin at *Raulin@MikeRaulin.org*. Detail the problem you are having, including the type of computer, the Internet connection, and the steps you are having difficulty with, and he will try to recreate the problem and figure out the solution.

Appendix Summary

This textbook includes a free subscription to a fully integrated companion Student Resource Website, which provides the student with resources designed to enhance their research methods course. This appendix provides troubleshooting advice for the most commonly experienced problems, but if you cannot resolve a problem, you can contact the author for help.

Appendix B

Writing a Research Report in APA Publication Style

Web Resource Material

Publication is a critical part of the research process. In its most literal sense, publication means "to make public." Making science public serves two purposes. It facilitates building on current knowledge by making it accessible to everyone, and it allows other scientists to independently review one's logic, procedures, results, and conclusions.

There is much to communicate in a research report, but page space is limited. Guidelines are therefore necessary to facilitate concise communication. The American Psychological Association's **Publication Manual** (2001) provides the guidelines used by most psychology journals. This appendix summarizes the most commonly used sections of those guidelines. The Student Resource Website outlines most key elements of APA

B:01

publication style, going well beyond the basic coverage of this appendix. Of course, psychology majors, particularly those thinking of graduate school, may wish to purchase a copy of the manual.[1]

Structure of a Research Article

The American Psychological Association recommends that the body of a research article be organized into four parts: introduction, method, results, and discussion. In addition, the report should have a title page, an abstract (100–120 words), a reference section, and necessary figures and tables.

The abstract briefly describes the study and findings, permitting readers to determine if the article is of interest to them. The abstract may also be published in one or more abstract journals (e.g., *Psychological Abstracts*) or computer databases (e.g., *PsycINFO*), which help researchers find relevant research.

The reference section lists each source discussed in the paper and where it can be found. Occasionally, additional attachments are included as appendices. These may contain extended information, materials, or scales that are not readily available elsewhere. The major sections of a journal article are shown in Table B.1.

Writing the Research Report

This section covers the preparation of each part of a research report.

Using Levels of Headings to Organize

A well-written article follows a clear outline. In an article, however, different levels of headings are used instead of outline indentation to indicate the organization.

TABLE B.1 *Major Sections and Subsections of a Manuscript*

1. Title page	**6.** Discussion
2. Abstract	**7.** References
3. Introduction	**8.** Appendices
4. Method	**9.** Footnotes and author note
a. Participants	**10.** Tables
b. Apparatus	**11.** Figure captions
c. Procedure	**12.** Figures
5. Results	

[1]The Publication Manual of the American Psychological Association can be purchased directly from the American Psychological Association at nominal cost (*www.apa.org*). The American Psychological Association publishes a workbook to help students to learn APA style (Gelfand & Walker, 2001), and other inexpensive texts are available (e.g., Rosnow & Rosnow, 1998) that focus exclusively on writing reports in APA style.

Table B.2 presents examples of five different levels of headings that can be used in a research report.

Sections of a Research Report

Title Page.   The **title page** includes the title of the article, the list of authors, the institutional affiliations of the authors, and a running head. The title should be concise but descriptive. Phrases such as "a report on" or "a study of" add little information and should be avoided. A running head is placed at the top of the title page. It is an abbreviated title no more than fifty characters in length (including spaces). The running head appears at the top of each page in the journal article. Page numbering begins with the title page and continues serially for all pages except those containing figures.

Abstract.   The **abstract** summarizes the research paper in no more than 120 words. Enough information should be given so that people who read the research study after reading the abstract will not be surprised by what they find in the article. Even though the abstract appears first, it is usually written last, because it summarizes the work. Although the abstract is one of the shortest sections of the study, it is often the most difficult to write, because so much must be said in limited space.

Introduction.   The **introduction** states the research problem and discusses prior research. It begins with a broad or general statement of the research problem and proceeds to narrow the focus to the specific research being reported. A good introduction need not be long, but it must be well organized. You should focus only on prior research that is directly relevant to the current research study; you should not attempt to review all the research in a broad area. The introduction usually ends with your research hypotheses. A good rule of thumb is that if the hypotheses seem to follow naturally from everything that precedes them, the introduction is well organized and well structured. If, on the other hand, a reader finds some or all of the hypotheses to be surprising in light of what was stated previously, the introduction is not well focused and fails to provide the rationale for the study.

TABLE B.2   *Five Levels of Headings*

THIS IS A CENTERED UPPERCASE HEADING (LEVEL 5)

This is a Centered Upper- and Lowercase Heading (Level 1)

This is a Centered, Italicized, Upper- and Lowercase Heading (Level 2)

This is an Italicized Uppercase and Lowercase Side Heading (Level 3)

This is a paragraph heading (level 4). The paragraph heading is indented, lowercase, and italicized and should end with a period as shown.

Note: If only one level of heading is needed in a report, use level 1; if two levels are needed, use levels 1 and 3; if three levels are needed, use levels 1, 3, and 4; if four levels are needed, use levels 1, 2, 3, and 4; if five levels are needed, use all of the above with the level 5 heading subordinating the other four levels as shown above. Traditionally, the method, results, and discussion section headings are at Level 1.

One references other research in an article by naming the researcher(s) and the date when the research was published. With this information, the reader can turn to the reference list and find where the work was published. There are two standard forms for referring to published work, as shown in the following examples.

Previous research found the situation to be realistic (Johnson & Hall, 1999).

Johnson and Hall's (1999) participants found the procedure to be realistic.

If you need to cite several studies, you can use the following format:

Several investigators have found this situation to be realistic for their participants (Johnson & Hall, 1997, 1999a, 1999b; Kelley, 1986; Smith & Rodick, 1994).

These conventions tell the reader what was found, which researchers made the observation, and when. APA referencing conventions were used throughout this text. Each reference that appears in a research article must appear in the reference section, and all references that appear in the reference list must appear in the paper.

Method.   The **method section** describes how the research was carried out, including who participated and how they were selected, the apparatus, equipment, materials, and procedures. These are typically discussed in separate subsections.

The participants subsection describes how participants were selected and their demographic characteristics (such as age, education, and sex), from where participants were obtained (e.g., a college course or a shopping mall), and what inducements were used to obtain their cooperation (e.g., money or academic credit). The researcher also describes how participants were assigned to groups. If it is differential research, the procedures used to classify participants are described. If participants drop out of the experiment or decline to participate, the number of such participants and the groups that they were in should be reported. There should be enough information to allow a researcher to compare the sample with samples from similar research projects.

The content of the next subsections will depend on the purpose and topic of the study. The goal of these subsections is to provide readers with sufficient information to allow them to replicate the study. Subsection titles like **equipment, materials, instruments,** or **measures** are common. These subsections describe the physical aspects of the research study. If the study involves equipment, the type of equipment used and the settings of the equipment should be reported. If psychological tests are used, the tests should be described, including information on how to obtain them. If the tests are unique to the study, they should either be included as an appendix or made available to readers on request.

The procedure subsection describes how the study was carried out. For example, testing and scoring procedures or specific instructions to participants should be described here. In other words, the procedure subsection should tell the reader everything that the participants and the researcher did during the course of the study.

Results.   The **results section** tells the reader what was found. A statistical description of the results is usually needed, as well as appropriate statistical tests. A standard convention used to report inferential statistics is that you report what statistic was used, the degrees of freedom, the computed value of the statistic, and the *p*-value, as shown in Table B.3. All non-Greek, single-letter statistical terms (e.g., *F, t, p*) are italicized. With this format, readers can easily interpret the significance of results, even if they are not familiar with the statistical procedure used, because the *p*-value is interpreted in the same way for all of the tests. Any time *p* is less than .05 (a traditional value of alpha), we conclude that the findings are statistically significant.

Although it is important to express the statistical significance of comparisons, it is equally important to give the reader the information needed to interpret the results, such as the means or frequencies. Often the most effective way of doing this is to organize it in a table or figure. Tables and figures should be carefully labeled for the reader. Tables should give the reader enough information so that they can be interpreted without information from the text. Each table should be numbered using Arabic numerals, starting with number 1. The first line of the table should read "Table" and the number. The next line of the table should be a brief title, such as "Mean Reaction Times for Distracted and Nondistracted Participants." The table title is italicized. If the title is more than one line long, it should be double-spaced. The data in the table are arranged in columns and rows and should be clearly labeled. If additional information is necessary to interpret the table, it should be included as a footnote at the bottom of the table. An example of a typical table format is presented in Table B.4.

Figures should also be self-explanatory. The axes should be labeled, and each figure should have a title. Figures should be numbered sequentially starting with number 1 and should be numbered independently of tables. When submitting a paper for publication, each figure should be submitted as a glossy print or as a digital image. The figure numbers and titles must appear on a separate sheet.

Tables and figures are placed at the end of the manuscript, and each table or figure should be referred to in the manuscript. Figure B.1 presents an example.

There is no one correct way of presenting the results of a study. It is often useful for the researcher to try to organize results in various ways by testing both tables and figures to determine which method is most effective.

TABLE B.3 *Reporting Statistics in a Research Report*

Reporting t-tests

Boys were found to be significantly more aggressive than girls in the playground situation, $t(28) = 2.33$, $p < .05$.

Reporting ANOVAs

There was a significant difference in performance between the three distraction conditions, $F(2, 27) = 3.69$, $p < .05$.

Reporting chi-squares

Psychology majors were significantly more likely to classify themselves as "humanistic" than were engineering majors, $\chi^2(1, N = 60) = 4.47$, $p < .05$.

TABLE B.4   *A Typical Table in a Research Report*

Table 1

Posttreatment Measures for the Three Treatment Approaches

	Type of Therapy		
Measures	Behavioral	Cognitive	Analytic
Number of activities[a]	4.6	3.8	2.1
Beck scores[b]	16.7	15.3	17.5
Insight ratingsc	2.0	3.1	3.7

[a]The mean number of recreational activities in a one-week period.
[b]Mean Beck Depression Inventory scores; higher scores indicate greater depression.
[c]Rating based on an independent interview; ratings range from 1 (no insight) to 5 (maximum insight).

Discussion.   The **discussion section** interprets and evaluates the results. It is helpful to begin by briefly summarizing the results in nontechnical language. The interpretation of the results should follow logically from the actual data obtained in the study. If there are weaknesses in the current study, the author should acknowledge them and describe ways to deal with them in the future. It is often helpful to suggest directions for future research. The goal

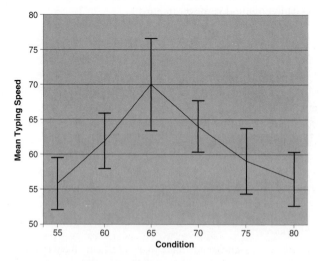

FIGURE B.1   *Example of a Line Graph* This is a typical line graph. It appears in Chapter 10 of this textbook.

of any research project is to find answers to questions, but the outcome of most research projects is to suggest new questions to be answered.

References.   The **reference list** provides the reader with the information needed to find referenced articles on their own. Each study discussed in the paper is listed in alphabetical order by the last name of the author(s). Works by the same author are arranged chronologically according to publication date. The most common reference is to a journal article. The format for such a reference is to list (1) the author(s), last name first, (2) the year of publication in parentheses, (3) the article title, (4) the journal title and volume in italics, and (5) the pages where the article appears. Here are two examples:

> Collier, R. (1994). An historical overview of natural language processing systems that learn. *Artificial Intelligence Review, 8,* 17-54.

> Benson, D. F., & Stuss, D. T. (1990). Frontal lobe influences on delusions: A clinical perspective. *Schizophrenia Bulletin, 16,* 403-411.

A similar format is used to reference a book. Again, you must list (1) the author(s), (2) the copyright year in parentheses, (3) the book title in italics, (4) the city in which the book was published, and (5) the publisher. Here are examples:

> Kazdin, A. E. (1998). *Research design in clinical psychology* (3rd ed.). New York: Macmillan.

> Loftus, E. F., & Ketcham, K. (1994). *The myth of repressed memory: False memories and allegations of sexual abuse.* New York: St. Martin's Press.

The reference section of this textbook provides many other examples of references.

Writing Style

Good writing is important, whether you are writing a journal article or a letter home. It is one of the most difficult things to teach, and it can be learned only through practice. However, there are different kinds of writing. Writing a journal article requires technical writing. Precision, conciseness, and organization are important in technical writing. Flowery adjectives and a poetic style are best left to the creative writer.

The primary purpose of writing a research report is communication, and anything that obscures communication should be avoided. Pronouns should be used sparingly and should never be ambiguous. Abbreviations should also be used sparingly and should always be explained to the reader. Using active voice and simple sentence structure can help a writer to avoid numerous communication pitfalls. Traditionally, the research report is written in the past tense and primarily in the third person (e.g., "The experimenter assigned each participant . . . "), although first person narratives have become more acceptable. A good way to improve a research report is to have someone not involved in the research review the report. Anything that is unclear to this reviewer will probably be unclear to other readers. Writing manuals such as Strunk, White, and Angell's (1999) *The Elements of Style*

B:02

or Zinsser's (2001) *On Writing Well* are valuable resources for any writer. The Student Resource Website includes a brief list of the most common writing problems and how to correct them.

Although some find the writing phase rewarding, many researchers find writing a research report demanding. The task is made somewhat easier if the research is carefully planned and well organized. For all researchers, however, telling people about something that they have discovered can be exciting.

Appendix Summary

The final stage of any research project is the communication of the results. This appendix covered APA writing style for such reports. Journal articles are divided into the introduction, method, results, and discussion sections. In addition, the article should have an abstract that summarizes the study and a complete list of references.

Appendix C

Conducting Library Research

Web Resource Material

Using the Library

C:01

Researchers want to relate their ideas and findings to those of other researchers. University libraries accumulate these findings to facilitate the research of faculty and students. This appendix outlines strategies for library research. The Student Resource Website provides additional details and examples of library searches.

Library Resources

Research ideas and findings are found in books, journals, technical reports, and a variety of other media. A small college library may have 250,000 or more books and journals; a major university library may have more than 5,000,000 books and subscribe to more than 10,000 journals. Libraries are increasingly subscribing to online services that provide journal articles, so you can access them from any computer. In addition, almost any university library will have access to the collections of virtually all other libraries through interlibrary loan. When you enter a modern university library, you are in touch with nearly all the information that has ever been published! You should be impressed by this thought and properly respectful of the library and of the professionals who operate it. This appendix describes how to use the library effectively.

The Reference Librarian

The reference librarian knows the smoothest routes through the maze of information. A good reference librarian can help you to track down almost anything. Whether you need to find a particular book or to learn how to use the library's computer search resources, the reference librarian is a valuable consultant. Many university libraries also have courses to help you to master their resources. Although we will be outlining many of the basic sources and strategies for library research in this appendix, we cannot stress enough the importance of utilizing the expertise available in your own library.

How Research Materials Are Organized

We make a distinction between primary and secondary sources in the research literature. *Primary sources* publish research studies; *secondary sources* publish integrative reviews of broad areas of research. This section describes both.

Primary Sources

Journal Articles.   Journals can be both primary and secondary sources of information, although the majority of journals are primary sources that report research studies. A research report typically includes a literature review, the study's hypotheses, the procedures, the results, and a discussion of how the researchers interpreted the results. In the discussion of their findings, researchers relate their results to prevailing models or theories, thus helping to integrate new information and adding to the base on which further research and theory development will rest.

Dissertations.   Dissertations are research studies conducted by advanced graduate students as part of the requirements for a Ph.D. Many are eventually published in journals, but you can also get a copy of the original dissertation. Universities maintain copies of dissertations conducted at their own institutions, and any dissertation can be obtained in a few days through University Microfilms, which maintains and sells copies of dissertations from around the world.

Secondary Sources

Secondary sources provide reviews of entire areas of research. However, they are not intended to provide the detail that you will find in the original journal articles. Moreover, the newest research discussed in secondary sources is often at least a year old, reflecting the length of the publication and production cycle. Therefore, you will still have to search current journals to find the most recent research.

Secondary sources summarize, organize, critique, and integrate research areas and identify directions for further research. They are an invaluable source in your literature review and are particularly useful when you need a broad, integrated view of your topic.

Review Articles.   Although most journals report the results of research studies, other journals specialize in review articles. Several journals in psychology are devoted completely to reviews (e.g., *Psychological Bulletin* or *Psychological Review*).

Books and Chapters in Books.   Reviews of research areas are also published as books or as chapters in books. In fact, edited books are becoming a major secondary source of information in psychology. Fortunately, *Psychological Abstracts* and *PsycINFO* now include both books and book chapters in their databases.

Annual Reviews.   This series provides an annual volume in several disciplines, including psychology and neuroscience. You should check recent volumes to see if there is a review of your topic.

Finding the Relevant Research

You can find relevant research by using abstracting services, keyword searches, and citation indexes. Each is described here.

Abstracting Services

Abstracting services provide abstracts of articles from hundreds of journals, which are organized by title, author, and keywords. Most of these services are now computerized.

Psychological Abstracts.   *Psychological Abstracts* provides abstracts and references for virtually everything relevant to the field of psychology. *Psychological Abstracts* is organized by keywords, which are summarized in a separate publication (*Thesaurus of Psychological Index Terms*). The APA also publishes a series of journals called *PsycSCAN,* which are quarterly compilations of research papers, organized under broad topics (e.g., clinical, applied, or developmental). *Psychological Abstracts* has largely been replaced by computerized databases such as *PsycINFO, PsycLIT, PsycFILE,* and *PASAR*. These are far more convenient to use than the bound volumes they replaced.

ERIC (Educational Resource Information Center).   *ERIC* indexes and abstracts research in education and related areas. If your topic is related to educational research, you should consult *ERIC* as well as *Psychological Abstracts.*

Subject or Keyword Services

Several indexes reference materials by title, author, and keywords, but do not include the abstract. Even without the abstract, these indexes can be a valuable source for identifying relevant materials. Several examples are given here.

Library Catalogs. The most familiar index to most students is the library catalog, which lists all the books in the library's collection and indexes them by author, title, and subject. In computerized library catalogs, you may be able to see if the book is available to be checked out. Many computerized catalogs also indicate whether an item is available from another institution for interlibrary loan.

Books in Print. *Books in Print* is a quarterly publication listing all books that are currently in print. Many libraries now have this index available online.

Index Medicus. Just as *Psychological Abstracts* provides an index for literature of interest to psychologists, *Index Medicus* provides an index to biomedical literature. The computerized version is called *Medline,* and now includes abstracts.

Readers' Guide to Periodical Literature. This general index covers a wide area of popular literature and provides citations, but no abstracts.

Literature Citation Indexes

The abstract and keyword services above are helpful in finding material by topic or author. However, there are times when you want to find literature through the citations to previous work that publications make. Certain lines of research are so indebted to one or two early publications that you can find virtually every article on the topic by identifying the articles that cite these early publications. The *Science Citation Index* and the *Social Science Citation Index* are two examples of this kind of reference. You can find references to work in psychology in both of these citation indexes.

Table C.1 lists the major indexes for psychological research.

Search Strategies

Several methods are available for locating relevant research on a topic.

Searching by Topic

Identifying Key Terms. How do you find the information you need for your project? Library research needs a clear problem statement and a list of key terms that identify relevant research papers. The right key terms will help you to find exactly what you need. The *Thesaurus of Psychological Index Terms,* published by the APA, lists the key terms used in *Psychological Abstracts* as well as cross-referenced terms that might also identify relevant literature on a topic. Find your topic in the *Thesaurus,* and it will list the index terms un-

TABLE C.1 *Library Resources for Psychological Research*

1. Review Articles and Chapters
   Annual Review of Psychology
   Psychological Bulletin
   Psychological Review
   Behavioral Science
   Clinical Psychology Reviews

2. Abstract Services and Citation Indexes
   Psychological Abstracts (bound volumes)
   PsycINFO (psychological abstracts on computer programs)
   ERIC (Educational Resource Information Center)
   Books in Print (bound volumes and computer format)
   Index Medicus and Medline (computer indexes)
   Social Science Citation Index
   Science Citation Index

3. Other Important Information Sources
   Thesaurus of Psychological Index Terms
   Library catalog
   Readers' Guide to Periodical Literature

der which you will find appropriate references. Use these as your key terms to conduct your library search. Similar publications listing index terms are available for other abstract services.

Computer Searches.   Fortunately, most libraries have extensive computer search capabilities. *PsycINFO, Books in Print, ERIC, Medline,* and dozens of other indexes can be accessed through computer terminals in the library and elsewhere. Consult your reference librarian to learn how to use these systems. The procedures for doing computer searches vary from one system to another, but most systems operate under the same general principles. All systems have records (containing the information about a publication) and fields within each record. Each field contains specific information, such as the title, author, journal, keywords, and abstract. You can search a specific field or all fields to find information. For example, if you know that relevant research was published by "Jason Lombard," you can search the author field for that name.

There are many strategies for computer searches, but most people start by searching for keywords. Most indexes will have a keyword field in which a small number of descriptive terms summarize the main content of the paper. Searching this field for specific keywords is adequate for many searches. But computers are so fast that it is easy to search the entire record to find potentially relevant papers.

Entering keywords to narrow a search is an art that requires some logic. For example, in most systems, entering the term *child* will identify any article that has the terms *child, childhood, children.* and *child's,* because all these terms have *child* in them.

Some keywords identify several thousand potential articles, while others identify just a few. If the list is too large, you will have to reduce it to make it manageable. For example, you might refine the list by limiting it to only those papers published in the last

5 or 10 years. But you probably want to also narrow the list by further restricting the topic. To do this you must understand two Boolean operators: AND and OR. If you are interested in childhood fears, you could use the term *childhood fears* in your search. However, such a search would miss articles that did not use that specific phrase (perhaps using a phrase like *fears common in childhood* instead). The Boolean operator AND will narrow a search by requiring that two conditions be met. Using it to search for "fear AND child" would likely give you a more complete search. Any article that had both the term *fear* and the term *child* in its record would be identified.

In contrast, the operator OR will broaden a search by identifying articles that meet one of several specified conditions. For example, searching for "frontal OR parietal OR occipital OR temporal" would identify any article that mentions one of these lobes of the brain.

Some, but not all, library databases allow you to use a third Boolean operator: NOT. NOT, like AND, allows you to narrow a search. The Boolean operator AND narrows a search by requiring multiple conditions. In contrast, the Boolean operator NOT allows you to exclude items that meet certain conditions. For example, if you were interested in what is sometimes called psychogenic amnesia (i.e., amnesia due to psychological causes), you might want to search for amnesia, using the NOT function to exclude articles that focused on head injuries or brain damage.

Each computer index has its own rules for specifying searches with Boolean operators. Be sure to check the documentation or talk with a reference librarian for details of the system that you are using.

Once you have identified a set of relevant records, you can enter commands to display the records. By reading the titles and/or abstracts you can select those that appear to be most appropriate for your topic. At this point you will have a screen display of a fairly refined list of appropriate articles. Using the print command will give you a printout of your selected references and their abstracts.

Now the real work begins. Your list of references is just that—a list. What remains is locating each paper, book, or chapter, reading them, integrating the information, and writing your paper or research proposal. As you proceed, you will eliminate some references as not relevant and you will also find more references in articles you are reading. Discussed next are two useful strategies for identifying additional relevant material.

Searching Backward

Every article, chapter, or book reviews relevant research and gives you the references for those studies. This is an invaluable source of relevant material. Of course, not every paper referenced in articles will be relevant to your topic, but some will be. Recently published review articles are especially useful for this strategy. Inspecting the reference list from relevant articles will help to identify other investigators doing work on your topic. Searching the author field for the names of these investigators is often a useful supplementary strategy. These strategies are not a substitute for the topic search, but can be valuable in identifying additional relevant papers. A note of caution is warranted here. It is bad form to cite a paper that you have not read. It is entirely possible that the description of the paper in another article may be inaccurate.

TABLE C.2 *The Literature Search Process*

1. Have a clear statement of the literature search problem.

2. From this problem statement, identify the key terms for your topic. Use the *Thesaurus of Psychological Index Terms* to help to determine your key terms.

3. Consult with your reference librarian and determine which citation indexes are most likely to include the information you seek.

4. Search the citation indexes using your key terms. *PsycINFO* is probably the most useful for you. Look for secondary as well as primary sources. Read the titles and abstracts of the papers and chapters. Narrow your list by deleting those that seem least relevant.

5. Print out the list of remaining references. Find and read the original articles, books, and chapters.

6. As you gain information from your reading, continue to refine your ideas, develop new ideas, and further refine your problem statement.

7. Consult other citation indexes as needed (*ERIC, Social Science Citation Index, Readers' Guide,* etc.).

8. You can consult your reference librarian at any point in this search process!

Searching Forward

The searching forward strategy is possible because of the existence of citation indexes. If virtually all articles on a topic cite one or more classic studies, then one can identify these later articles by using an appropriate citation index. Again, this strategy is not a substitute for searching by topic, but it can be a useful supplement.

Table C.2 summarizes the literature search process.

Appendix Summary

Without the library, each investigator would have to "reinvent the wheel" with every research study. Fortunately, university libraries not only have past research, but also have the indexes necessary to find the material you need. This appendix summarized library resources and some of the ways to find relevant background material for a paper. Entire texts are devoted to the art of library research (e.g., Reed & Baxter, 2003). You will find that the reference librarian at your institution can answer many of your questions and point you in the right direction.

Appendix D

Random Numbers

*Web Resource Material*_____

D:01   Random Number Generator Program

To use the table of random numbers, select a starting point and a direction (up, down, left, or right). For example, if you want to assign participants randomly to each of five groups, you might start at the beginning of row 85 and move left to right. Number the groups 1 through 5 and assign the first participant to the group designated by the first digit between 1 and 5 that you encounter; the second participant to the group designated by the next suitable digit encountered, and so on. By this method, the first 10 participants will be randomly assigned to the following groups: 1, 3, 1, 1, 2, 2, 4, 2, 1, 3.

It is also possible to randomize within blocks, so that the same number of participants is in each condition. For example, if you want to assign the first five participants—one to each of the five groups—and you use the same starting point (beginning of row 85), you get the following assignment: 1, 3, 2, 4, 5. Your second block of five participants is assigned to the following groups: 3, 2, 5, 4, 1.

D:01

We have also included a random number generator program on the Student Resource Website to automate the tasks of randomly selecting participants and randomly assigning them to groups.

Row Number										
00000	10097	32533	76520	13586	34673	54876	80959	09117	39292	74945
00001	37542	04805	64894	74296	24805	24037	20636	10402	00822	91665
00002	08422	68953	19645	09303	23209	02560	15953	34764	35080	33606
00003	99019	02529	09376	70715	38311	31165	88676	74397	04436	27659
00004	12807	99970	80157	36147	64032	36653	98951	16877	12171	76833
00005	66065	74717	34072	76850	36697	36170	65813	39885	11199	29170
00006	31060	10805	45571	82406	35303	42614	86799	07439	23403	09732
00007	85269	77602	02051	65692	68665	74818	73053	85247	18623	88579
00008	63573	32135	05325	47048	90553	57548	28468	28709	83491	25624
00009	73796	45753	03529	64778	35808	34282	60935	20344	35273	88435
00010	98520	17767	14905	68607	22109	40558	60970	93433	50500	73998

00011	11805	05431	39808	27732	50725	68248	29405	24201	52775	67851
00012	83452	99634	06288	98033	13746	70078	18475	40610	68711	77817
00013	88685	40200	86507	58401	36766	67951	90364	76493	29609	11062
00014	99594	67348	87517	64969	91826	08928	93785	61368	23478	34113
00015	65481	17674	17468	50950	58047	76974	73039	57186	40218	16544
00016	80124	35635	17727	08015	45318	22374	21115	78253	14385	53763
00017	74350	99817	77402	77214	43236	00210	45521	64237	96286	02655
00018	69916	26803	66252	29148	36936	87203	76621	13990	94400	56418
00019	09893	20505	14225	68514	46427	56788	96297	78822	54382	14598
00020	91499	14523	68479	27686	46162	83554	94750	89923	37089	20048
00021	80336	94598	26940	36858	70297	34135	53140	33340	42050	82341
00022	44104	81949	85157	47954	32979	26575	57600	40881	22222	06413
00023	12550	73742	11100	02040	12860	74697	96644	89439	28707	25815
00024	63606	49329	16505	34484	40219	52563	43651	77082	07207	31790
00025	61196	90446	26457	47774	51924	33729	65394	59593	42582	60527
00026	15474	45266	95270	79953	59367	83848	82396	10118	33211	59466
00027	94557	28573	67897	54387	54622	44431	91190	42592	92927	45973
00028	42481	16213	97344	08721	16868	48767	03071	12059	25701	46670
00029	23523	78317	73208	89837	68935	91416	26252	29663	05522	82562
00030	04493	52494	75246	33824	45862	51025	61962	79335	65337	12472
00031	00549	97654	64051	88159	96119	63896	54692	82391	23287	29529
00032	35963	15307	26898	09354	33351	35462	77974	50024	90103	39333
00033	59808	08391	45427	26842	83609	49700	13021	24892	78565	20106
00034	46058	85236	01390	92286	77281	44077	93910	83647	70617	42941
00035	32179	00597	87379	25241	05567	07007	86743	17157	85394	11838
00036	69234	61406	20117	45204	15956	60000	18743	92423	97118	96338
00037	19565	41430	01758	75379	40419	21585	66674	36806	84962	85207
00038	45155	14938	19476	07246	43667	94543	59047	90033	20826	69541
00039	94864	31994	36168	10851	34888	81553	01540	35456	05014	51176
00040	98086	24826	45240	28404	44999	08896	39094	73407	35441	31880
00041	33185	16232	41941	50949	89435	48581	88695	41994	37548	73043
00042	80951	00406	96382	70774	20151	23387	25016	25298	94624	61171
00043	79752	49140	71961	28296	69861	02591	74852	20539	00387	59579
00044	18633	32537	98145	06571	31010	24674	05455	61427	77938	91936
00045	74029	43902	77557	32270	97790	17119	52527	58021	80814	51748
00046	54178	45611	80993	37143	05335	12969	56127	19255	36040	90324
00047	11664	49883	52079	84827	59381	71539	09973	33440	88461	23356
00048	48324	77928	31249	64710	02295	36870	32307	57546	15020	09994
00049	69074	94138	87637	91976	35584	04401	10518	21615	01848	76938
00050	09188	20097	32825	39527	04220	86304	83389	87374	64278	58044
00051	90045	85497	51981	50654	94938	81997	91870	76150	68476	64659
00052	73189	50207	47677	26269	62290	64464	27124	67018	41361	82760
00053	75768	76490	20971	87749	90429	12272	95375	05871	93823	43178
00054	54016	44056	66281	31003	00682	27398	20714	53295	07706	17813
00055	08358	69910	78542	42785	13661	58873	04618	97553	31223	08420
00056	28306	03264	81333	10591	40510	07893	32604	60475	94119	01840
00057	53840	86233	81594	13628	51215	90290	28466	68795	77762	20791
00058	91757	53741	61613	62669	50263	90212	55781	76514	83483	47055
00059	89415	92694	00397	58391	12607	17646	48949	72306	94541	37408

00060	77513	03820	86864	29901	68414	82774	51908	13980	72893	55507
00061	19502	37174	69979	20288	55210	29773	74287	75251	65344	67415
00062	21818	59313	93278	81757	05686	73156	07082	85046	31853	38452
00063	51474	66499	68107	23621	94049	91345	42836	09191	08007	45449
00064	99559	68331	62535	24170	69777	12830	74819	78142	43860	72834
00065	33713	48007	93584	72869	51926	64721	58303	29822	93174	93972
00066	85274	86893	11303	22970	28834	34137	73515	90400	71148	43643
00067	84133	89640	44035	52166	73852	70091	61222	60561	62327	18423
00068	56732	16234	17395	96131	10123	91622	85496	57560	81604	18880
00069	65138	56806	87648	85261	34313	65861	45875	21069	85644	47277
00070	38001	02176	81719	11711	71602	92937	74219	64049	65584	49698
00071	37402	96397	01304	77586	56271	10086	47324	62605	40030	37438
00072	97125	40348	87083	31417	21815	39250	75237	62047	15501	29578
00073	21826	41134	47143	34072	64638	85902	49139	06441	03856	54552
00074	73135	42742	95719	09035	85794	74296	08789	88156	64691	19202
00075	07638	77929	03061	18072	96207	44156	23821	99538	04713	66994
00076	60528	83441	07954	19814	59175	20695	05533	52139	61212	06455
00077	83596	35655	06958	92983	05128	09719	77433	53783	92301	50498
00078	10850	62746	99599	10507	13499	06319	53075	71839	06410	19362
00079	39820	98952	43622	63147	64421	80814	43800	09351	31024	73167
00080	59580	06478	75569	78800	88835	54486	23768	06156	04111	08408
00081	38508	07341	23793	48763	90822	97022	17719	04207	95954	49953
00082	30692	70668	94688	16127	56196	80091	82067	63400	05462	69200
00083	65443	95659	18238	27437	49632	24041	08337	65676	96299	90836
00084	27267	50264	13192	72294	07477	44606	17985	48911	97341	30358
00085	91307	06991	19072	24210	36699	53728	28825	35793	28976	66252
00086	68434	94688	84473	13622	62126	98408	12843	82590	09815	93146
00087	48908	15877	54745	24591	35700	04754	83824	52692	54130	55160
00088	06913	45197	42672	78601	11883	09528	63011	98901	14974	40344
00089	10455	16019	14210	33712	91342	37821	88325	80851	43667	70883
00090	12883	97343	65027	61184	04285	01392	17974	15077	90712	26769
00091	21778	30976	38807	36961	31649	42096	63281	02023	08816	47449
00092	19523	59515	65122	59659	86283	68258	69572	13798	16435	91529
00093	67245	52670	35583	16563	79246	86686	76463	34222	26655	90802
00094	60584	47377	07500	37992	45134	26529	26760	83637	41326	44344
00095	53853	41377	36066	94850	58838	73859	49364	73331	96240	43642
00096	24637	38736	74384	89342	52623	07992	12369	18601	03742	83873
00097	83080	12451	38992	22815	07759	51777	97377	27585	51972	37867
00098	16444	24334	36151	99073	27493	70939	85130	32552	54846	54759
00099	60790	18157	57178	65762	11161	78576	45819	52979	65130	04860
00100	03991	10461	93716	16894	66083	24653	84609	58232	88618	19161
00101	38555	95554	32886	59780	08355	60860	29735	47762	71299	23853
00102	17546	73704	92052	46215	55121	29281	59076	07936	27954	58909
00103	32643	52861	95819	06831	00911	98936	76355	93779	80863	00514
00104	69572	68777	39510	35905	14060	40619	29549	69616	33564	60780
00105	24122	66591	27699	06494	14845	46672	61958	77100	90899	75754
00106	61196	30231	92962	61773	41839	55382	17267	70943	78038	70267
00107	30532	21704	10274	12202	39685	23309	10061	68829	55986	66485
00108	03788	97599	75867	20717	74416	53166	35208	33374	87539	08823

00109	48228	63379	85783	47619	53152	67433	35663	52972	16818	60311
00110	60365	94653	35075	33949	42614	29297	01918	28316	98953	73231
00111	83799	42402	56623	34442	34994	41374	70071	14736	09958	18065
00112	32960	07405	36409	83232	99385	41600	11133	07586	15917	06253
00113	19322	53845	57620	52606	66497	68646	78138	66559	19640	99413
00114	11220	94747	07399	37408	48509	23929	27482	45476	85244	35159
00115	31751	57260	68980	05339	15470	48355	88651	22596	03152	19121
00116	88492	99382	14454	04504	20094	98977	74843	93413	22109	78508
00117	30934	47744	07481	83828	73788	06533	28597	20405	94205	20380
00118	22888	48893	27499	98748	60530	45128	74022	84617	82037	10268
00119	78212	16993	35902	91386	44372	15486	65741	14014	87481	37220
00120	41849	84547	46850	52326	34677	58300	74910	64345	19325	81549
00121	46352	33049	69248	93460	45305	07521	61318	31855	14413	70951
00122	11087	96294	14013	31792	59747	67277	76503	34513	39663	77544
00123	52701	08337	56303	87315	16520	69676	11654	99893	02181	68161
00124	57275	36898	81304	48585	68652	27376	92852	55866	88448	03584
00125	20857	73156	70284	24326	79375	95220	01159	63267	10622	48391
00126	15633	84924	90415	93614	33521	26665	55823	47641	86225	31704
00127	92694	48297	39904	02115	59589	49067	66821	41575	49767	04037
00128	77613	19019	88152	00080	20554	91409	96277	48257	50816	97616
00129	38688	32486	45134	63545	59404	72059	43947	51680	43852	59693
00130	25163	01889	70014	15021	41290	67312	71857	15957	68971	11403
00131	65251	07629	37239	33295	05870	01119	92784	26340	18477	65622
00132	36815	43625	18637	37509	82444	99005	04921	73701	14707	93997
00133	64397	11692	05327	82162	20247	81759	45197	25332	83745	22567
00134	04515	25624	95096	67946	48460	85558	15191	18782	16930	33361
00135	83761	60873	43253	84145	60833	25983	01291	41349	20368	07126
00136	14387	06345	80854	09279	43529	06318	38384	74761	41196	37480
00137	51321	92246	80088	77074	88722	56736	66164	49431	66919	31678
00138	72472	00008	80890	18002	94813	31900	54155	83436	35352	54131
00139	05466	55306	93128	18464	74457	90561	72848	11834	79982	68416
00140	39528	72484	82474	25593	48545	35247	18619	13674	18611	19241
00141	81616	18711	53342	44276	75122	11724	74627	73707	58319	15997
00142	07586	16120	82641	22820	92904	13141	32392	19763	61199	67940
00143	90767	04235	13574	17200	69902	63742	78464	22501	18627	90872
00144	40188	28193	29593	88627	94972	11598	62095	36787	00441	58997
00145	34414	82157	86887	55087	19152	00023	12302	80783	32624	68691
00146	63439	75363	44989	16822	36024	00867	76378	41605	65961	73488
00147	67049	09070	93399	45547	94458	74284	05041	49807	20288	34060
00148	79495	04146	52162	90286	54158	34243	46978	35482	59362	95938
00149	91704	30552	04737	21031	75051	93029	47665	64382	99782	93478
00150	94015	46874	32444	48277	59820	96163	64654	25843	41145	42820
00151	74108	88222	88570	74015	25704	91035	01755	14750	48968	38603
00152	62880	87873	95160	59221	22304	90314	72877	17334	39283	04149
00153	11748	12102	80580	41867	17710	59621	06554	07850	73950	79552
00154	17944	05600	60478	03343	25852	58905	57216	39618	49856	99326
00155	66067	42792	95043	52680	46780	56487	09971	59481	37006	22186
00156	54244	91030	45547	70818	59849	96169	61459	21647	87417	17198
00157	30945	57589	31732	57260	47670	07654	46376	25366	94746	49580

00158	69170	37403	86995	90307	94304	71803	26825	05511	12459	91314
00159	08345	88975	35841	85771	08105	59987	87112	21476	14713	71181
00160	27767	43584	85301	88977	29490	69714	73035	41207	74699	09310
00161	13025	14338	54066	15243	47724	66733	47431	43905	31048	56699
00162	80217	36292	98525	24335	24432	24896	43277	58874	11466	16082
00163	10875	62004	90391	61105	57411	06368	53856	30743	08670	84741
00164	54127	57326	26629	19087	24472	88779	30540	27886	61732	75454
00165	60311	42824	37301	42678	45990	43242	17374	52003	70707	70214
00166	49739	71484	92003	98086	76668	73209	59202	11973	02902	33250
00167	78626	51594	16453	94614	39014	97066	83012	09832	25571	77628
00168	66692	13986	99837	00582	81232	44987	09504	96412	90193	79568
00169	44071	28091	07362	97703	76447	42537	98524	97831	65704	09514
00170	41468	85149	49554	17994	14924	39650	95294	00556	70481	06905
00171	94559	37559	49678	53119	70312	05682	66986	34099	74474	20740
00172	41615	70360	64114	58660	90850	64618	80620	51790	11436	38072
00173	50273	93113	41794	86861	24781	89683	55411	85667	77535	99892
00174	41396	80504	90670	08289	40902	05069	95083	06783	28102	57816
00175	25807	24260	71529	78920	72682	07385	90726	57166	98884	08583
00176	06170	97965	88302	98041	21443	41808	68984	83620	89747	98882
00177	60808	54444	74412	81105	01176	28838	36421	16489	18059	51061
00178	80940	44893	10408	36222	80582	71944	92638	40333	67054	16067
00179	19516	90120	46759	71643	13177	55292	21036	82808	77501	97427
00180	49386	54480	23604	23554	21785	41101	91178	10174	29420	90438
00181	06312	88940	15995	69321	47458	64809	98189	81851	29651	84215
00182	60942	00307	11897	92674	40405	68032	96717	54244	10701	41393
00183	92329	98932	78284	46347	71209	92061	39448	93136	25722	08564
00184	77936	63574	31384	51924	85561	29671	58137	17820	22751	36518
00185	38101	77756	11657	13897	95889	57067	47648	13885	70669	93406
00186	39641	69457	91339	22502	92613	89719	11947	56203	19324	20504
00187	84054	40455	99396	63680	67667	60631	69181	96845	38525	11600
00188	47468	03577	57649	63266	24700	71594	14004	23153	69249	05747
00189	43321	31370	28977	23896	76479	68562	62342	07589	08899	05985
00190	64281	61826	18555	64937	13173	33365	78851	16499	87064	13075
00191	66847	70495	32350	02985	86716	38746	26313	77463	55387	72681
00192	72461	33230	21529	53424	92581	02262	78438	66276	18396	73538
00193	21032	91050	13058	16218	12470	56500	15292	76139	59526	52113
00194	95362	67011	06651	16136	01016	00857	55018	56374	35824	71708
00195	49712	97380	10404	55452	34030	60726	75211	10271	36633	68424
00196	58275	61764	97586	54716	50259	46345	87195	46092	26787	60939
00197	89514	11788	68224	23417	73959	76145	30342	40277	11049	72049
00198	15472	50669	48139	36732	46874	37088	63465	09819	58869	35220
00199	12120	86124	51247	44302	60883	52109	21437	36786	49226	77837

Source: RAND Corporation (1955). *A million random digits*. Glencoe, IL: Free Press of Glencoe.

Appendix E

Answers to Quick-Check Review Questions

Chapter 1

1.1.1 The Student Resource Website has an interactive Study Guide/Lab Manual, several tutorials, and an expanded discussion of numerous topics.

1.1.2 SPSS for Windows is a comprehensive statistical analysis package.

1.2.1 The essence of science is its way of thinking, which combines rationalism and empiricism.

1.2.2 Since science is a way of thinking, it is possible to think scientifically anywhere.

1.2.3 A prepared mind refers to the ability to recognize and react to unexpected findings, because the person has a sufficient background in, and understanding of, the phenomena under study.

1.2.4 Scientists are pervasive skeptics who challenge accepted wisdom, are intellectually excited by questions, and are willing to tolerate uncertainty.

1.2.5 Scientists and artists share curiosity, creativity, skepticism, tolerance for ambiguity, commitment to hard work, and systematic thinking.

1.3.1 The common methods of acquiring knowledge are tenacity, intuition, authority, rationalism, empiricism, and science.

1.3.2 Science combines empiricism and rationalism.

1.3.3 Naïve empiricism insists on experiencing evidence directly through the senses. In contrast, sophisticated empiricism allows indirect evidence of phenomena, such as the effects of gravity on falling objects.

1.3.4 The limitation of rationalism is that the premises must be correct for the conclusions to be correct. The limitation of empiricism is that, by itself, it does little more than collect facts; it needs rational processes to organize these facts.

1.4.1 The early practical skills illustrated the advantage of abstract information in solving everyday problems, thus justifying the kind of scientific study that seeks to systematically develop such information.

1.4.2 Thales, considered the father of science, rejected mysticism and studied natural phenomena using empirical observation and rational thought.

1.4.3 During the Middle Ages, science was used to support theological ideas.

1.4.4 Modern technology is the outgrowth of scientific discoveries, whereas modern science is a way of thinking about and studying phenomena.

1.4.5 The orderliness belief is the idea that the universe operates in an orderly, lawful manner. Without this belief, it would make no sense to engage in scientific investigation, because there would be no general principles to discover.

1.4.6 Frankenstein was intended as a commentary on the growing power of science.

1.5.1 Some of the more influential schools of psychology were structuralism, functionalism, psychoanalysis, Gestalt psychology, behaviorism, humanistic psychology, and cognitive psychology.

1.5.2 Modern mainstream psychology tends to be integrative in that its theories and ideas cut across several perspectives.

1.5.3 Psychology needs to be scientific and objective because the subjective impressions of people about psychological events tend to be undependable.

1.5.4 Although psychology is considered a social science, its roots are in the natural sciences, such as biology and physics.

Chapter 2

2.1.1 The data in psychology are observations of behavior.

2.1.2 Facts are directly observed, whereas constructs are inferences about unseen mechanisms, drawn to explain observations.

2.1.3 Reification of a construct means believing that the construct is a fact.

2.1.4 Constructs are based on facts and are used to predict new facts.

2.1.5 Science is built on the following assumptions: (1) a true, physical universe exists; (2) the universe is primarily an orderly system; (3) the principles of this orderly universe can be discovered, particularly through scientific research; and (4) knowledge of the universe is always incomplete. New knowledge should alter current ideas and theories. Therefore, all knowledge and theories are tentative.

2.1.6 Going from empirical observations to constructs is inductive reasoning; going from constructs to predictions is deductive reasoning.

2.2.1 A theory is a formalized set of concepts that summarizes and organizes observations and inferences, provides tentative explanations for phenomena, and provides the foundation for making predictions.

2.2.2 Inductive theories depend heavily on empirical observations, whereas deductive theories go well beyond the existing data and emphasize testing new predictions from theories.

2.2.3 A model is a miniature representation of reality. Scientists construct and examine models to provide insights into natural phenomena.

2.2.4 Observations are the facts of research, whereas inferences are inductive leaps beyond the observations.

2.2.5 Many technically incorrect theories nevertheless make accurate predictions in many situations and therefore are useful in these situations.

2.2.6 Falsifiability is the principle that for a theory to be scientific, there must be some evidence that, if found, would lead to a rejection of the theory.

2.3.1 The two dimensions in our model of research are (1) levels of constraint and (2) phases of research.

2.3.2 The phases of research are (1) idea generation, (2) problem definition, (3) procedures design, (4) observation, (5) data analysis, (6) interpretation, and (7) communication.

2.3.3 Levels of constraint refers to a continuum of demands on the adequacy of information and the level of control used during the observation phase.

2.3.4 The groups in differential research are naturally occurring, whereas the groups in experimental research are formed through random assignment.

2.3.5 Ecological validity is verifying that laboratory findings are relevant to real-world settings.

Chapter 3

3.1.1 The main sources of research questions are your own interests and the research of other investigators.

3.1.2 Applied research is designed to solve specific problems, whereas basic research is interested in finding new knowledge, without a specific application.

3.1.3 A variable is any set of events that may have different values.

3.1.4 Basic research often provides an understanding of natural phenomena, which can later be used to address practical problems.

3.2.1 The researcher manipulates independent variables to see what effect they might have on dependent variables.

3.2.2 Manipulated independent variables are actively controlled by the researcher, whereas nonmanipulated independent variables are defined by preexisting characteristics of participants.

3.2.3 Holding a variable constant involves preventing the variable from varying. For example, the researcher can hold the variable of age constant by testing only those participants who are of a particular age.

3.3.1 Extraneous variables are uncontrolled factors that can affect the outcome of a study.

3.3.2 Uncontrolled extraneous variables can distort research findings.

3.3.3 Validity refers to how well a study, procedure, or measure does what it is supposed to do.

3.3.4 Controls reduce the effects of extraneous variables and thus increase our confidence in the validity of the research findings.

3.4.1 The moral dilemma is that society demands new information, but obtaining that information may violate individual rights. This dilemma is addressed by allowing individuals to decide for themselves whether they will participate in a study.

3.4.2 Informed consent means a person's agreement to participate in a study after being fully informed about the study and its risks. It is obtained in writing. It is important because it addresses moral issues about violating people's rights by giving people a choice of whether they will participate in a study.

3.4.3 Institutional Review Boards are groups set up at universities, hospitals, and research centers to screen research proposals for risks and ethical safeguards.

3.4.4 Animals cannot give informed consent and the research carried out on animals is often more invasive than that carried out on humans. The ethical focus is on providing animals with humane care and minimizing discomfort and pain.

3.4.5 Diversity issues in research refers to the need to include a broad representation of people so that results will generalize to broader populations.

Chapter 4

4.1.1 Measurement is assigning numbers to represent the level of a variable.

4.1.2 Without accurate measurement, we cannot be confident of the accuracy of the conclusions of our research.

4.1.3 The properties of the abstract number system are identity, magnitude, equal intervals, and a true zero.

4.1.4 Scientific misconduct threatens public faith in the scientific enterprise.

4.2.1 Nominal scales are naming scales. Ordinal scales order phenomena based on their magnitude. Interval scales convey information about both order and the distance between values. Ratio scales provide the best match to the number system.

4.2.2 Nominal scales produce nominal or categorical data. Ordinal scales produce ordered data. Interval and ratio scales produce score data.

4.2.3 Nominal scales have the property of identity; ordinal scales have the properties of identity and magnitude; interval scales have the properties of identity, magnitude, and equal intervals; ratio scales have the properties of identity, magnitude, equal intervals, and a true zero.

4.2.4 A true zero means that zero on the scale represents none of the property being measured. When a scale has a true zero, taking the ratio of two measures on the scale provides a meaningful number.

4.3.1 The best way to minimize measurement error is to develop well-thought-out operational definitions and follow them exactly.

4.3.2 Operational definitions transform theoretical variables into concrete events by stating precisely how these variables are to be measured.

4.3.3 Social desirability is participants' tendency to respond in what they believe to be the most socially acceptable manner. Such response tendencies distort measures and therefore threaten the validity of research.

4.3.4 Convergent validity involves multiple lines of research converging on the same conclusions, which increases confidence that the phenomenon is consistent.

4.4.1 Reliability refers to the constancy of a measure. The types of reliability are interrater reliability, test-retest reliability, and internal consistency reliability.

4.4.2 Measures can be reliable without being valid, but cannot be valid without being reliable.

4.4.3 If the effective range of a scale is inadequate, the data will be distorted.

4.4.4 Floor effects occur when the scores bunch at the bottom of the scale, whereas ceiling effects occur when scores bunch near the top of the scale.

4.4.5 Reliability refers to the consistency of a measure, whereas validity refers to its accuracy.

Chapter 5

5.1.1 The differences among people are called individual differences.

5.1.2 Descriptive statistics are used to describe data, whereas inferential statistics help the researcher to draw conclusions from the data.

5.2.1 Frequency distributions show the number of participants with each possible score, and they can be used with any kind of data.

5.2.2 Cross-tabulation involves simultaneously categorizing participants on more than one variable.

5.2.3 Frequency distributions give the frequency for each possible score, whereas grouped frequency distributions provide the frequency for intervals of scores, in which the intervals are of equal size.

5.2.4 Continuous distributions require grouped frequency distributions.

5.2.5 The most common distribution shapes are symmetric and skewed. The most common symmetric distribution is the normal distribution.

5.3.1 The three measures of central tendency are mean, median, and mode.

5.3.2 The measures of variability are range, variance, and standard deviation.

5.3.3 A correlation quantifies the strength and direction of a relationship between variables. Regression uses the relationship to predict one variable from the value of the other variable.

5.3.4 A standard score indicates how many standard deviations a score is above or below the mean. It is computed by subtracting the mean from the score and dividing the difference by the standard deviation.

5.3.5 The variance takes into account all the scores in a distribution, whereas the range only uses the highest and lowest scores.

5.3.6 The mean takes into account all the scores in a distribution, whereas the mode can be unstable, shifting considerably if one or two scores change.

5.3.7 Correlations, unlike other descriptive statistics, describe the relationship among two or more variables.

5.4.1 The population is the larger group of people of interest, whereas the sample is a subset that is drawn from the population.

5.4.2 Sampling error is the natural variation among different samples drawn from the same population.

5.4.3 A population parameter is a characteristic of the population, whereas a sample statistic is a characteristic computed from a sample drawn from that population.

5.4.4 Alpha level refers to the cutoff point used for making a decision to reject the null hypothesis. Type I error is rejecting the null hypothesis when it is true. Type II error is failing to reject the null hypothesis when it is false.

5.5.1 The *t*-test and ANOVA test for mean differences. The *t*-test is used when there are two groups, and the ANOVA is used with two or more groups.

5.5.2 A power analysis determines how large a sample size should be to detect an existing group difference. It is important because it assures that the researcher has sufficient power before the study is started.

5.5.3 Statistical significance refers to whether observed group differences are large enough to conclude that population differences exist. Practical significance refers to whether the size of the group difference is large enough to be personally meaningful to people.

5.5.4 Meta-analysis statistically averages the results from independent studies of the same phenomenon.

Chapter 6

6.1.1 Both Darwin and Goodall studied natural phenomena in natural environments without doing anything to influence these phenomena.

6.1.2 All these investigators worked extensively with individuals, observing their behavior, but also asking questions or testing them under various conditions.

6.1.3 Naturalistic research involves observing phenomena in natural settings, whereas case-study research involves modifying the settings somewhat to see how the modifications affect the performance of participants.

6.2.1 Naturalistic research is used whenever we are interested in the natural flow of behavior. Case studies are used when one is interested in single individuals.

6.2.2 A contingency is a probabilistic relationship ("If x occurs, y is likely to occur."). It can be used to generate causal hypotheses for higher-constraint research.

6.2.3 Laboratory research simplifies and constrains real-life settings. Such changes may threaten generalizability. In contrast, naturalistic research has no problem with generalizability, because it is conducted in natural settings.

6.2.4 Naturalistic research can negate a general proposition by finding a single counterexample. It cannot establish one, because it does not adequately sample from the population and thus does not represent the population.

6.3.1 Problem statements in low-constraint research are often general, because there may be no basis for generating more specific questions.

6.3.2 Observations may be made by unobtrusive observers or participant observers.

6.3.3 Unobtrusive measures are observations that are not obvious to the person being observed and thus are less likely to influence the person's behavior.

6.3.4 Archival records are existing measures of phenomena that have already occurred, such as course grades or census data.

6.3.5 The goal in sampling is to obtain a sample that is representative.

6.3.6 Taking a broad sample of situations allows the researcher to see if behavior differs across settings.

6.3.7 Measurement reactivity is the phenomenon of participants behaving differently than they might normally because they know that they are being observed.

6.4.1 Low-constraint research uses available samples, which are often not representative of the population.

6.4.2 Low-constraint research is flexible, allowing the researcher to follow interesting leads. Unfortunately, this also means that it is difficult to describe and is therefore difficult for others to replicate.

6.4.3 The ex-post-facto fallacy is drawing unwarranted causal conclusions from the observation of a contingent relationship.

6.4.4 Experimenter reactivity is any action by researchers that influences participants' responses. Experimenter bias is any effect that the researcher's expectations might have on observations or the recording of observations.

Chapter 7

7.1.1 Correlational research assesses the strength of relationships among variables.

7.1.2 Correlations quantify the strength and direction of relationships and can be used for predicting one variable from another variable.

7.1.3 Correlational research cannot determine causality.

7.1.4 Correlational research cannot prove a theory, but it can negate one.

7.2.1 Differential research compares two or more groups that are differentiated on the basis of a preexisting variable.

7.2.2 Differential research uses a nonmanipulated independent variable.

7.2.3 Artifacts are apparent effects of independent variables that are actually the result of other variables not properly controlled, thus confounding the research.

7.2.4 Differential research is structurally similar to experimental research in that groups are compared on the dependent measure. It is conceptually similar to correlational research in that all variables are measured and not manipulated.

7.3.1 Both correlational and differential research quantify the degree of relationship between two or more variables and are unable to identify causal relationships.

7.3.2 Differential research is considered higher constraint that correlational research, because additional control procedures are available in differential research, which can increase the confidence of the conclusions drawn from studies.

7.3.3 Differential research designs are used in situations in which the manipulation of an independent variable is impractical, impossible, or unethical.

7.4.1 Experimenter expectancy is the tendency of investigators to see what they expect to see, and experimenter reactivity is the tendency of investigators to influence the behavior of participants.

7.4.2 Moderator variables modify the relationship between other variables.

7.4.3 The most common correlations are the Pearson product-moment correlation and the Spearman rank-order correlation. A Pearson product-moment correlation coefficient is used if both variables are measured on at least an interval scale; a Spearman rank-order correlation is used if one variable is measured on an ordinal scale and the other variable is at least ordinal.

7.4.4 The coefficient of determination is the square of the correlation, and it indicates the proportion of variability in one measure that can be predicted by knowing the other measure.

7.5.1 Differential research should be used whenever we want to know whether groups that are formed based on a preexisting variable are different from one another.

7.5.2 Unless groups differ on only a single variable, it is impossible to determine which variable may have accounted for any observed group differences.

7.5.3 A nonmanipulated independent variable is a variable that existed prior to the study. It is used to assign participants to groups in differential research.

7.5.4 Careful selection of control groups can minimize confounding by forming groups that differ on only a single variable.

7.6.1 Neither correlational nor differential research is capable of determining that a causal relationship between variables exists.

7.6.2 Causal relationships cannot be determined, because both of these approaches simply measure and do not manipulate variables.

7.6.3 Two variables are said to be confounded when they vary together. Because they vary together, any observed relationships with other variables might be caused by either of the variables or both of them, thus limiting conclusions.

Chapter 8

8.1.1 Initial ideas are converted into problem statements based on a search of the literature and/or making initial observations of the phenomenon.

8.1.2 The research hypothesis is a combination of the statement of the problem and the operational definitions of the variables.

8.1.3 The research hypothesis is a specific, testable hypothesis that can be evaluated with data.

8.1.4 The research hypothesis includes the statistical hypothesis, the confounding-variable hypothesis, and the causal hypothesis.

8.1.5 We cannot accept the causal hypothesis until all confounding variables are ruled out.

8.1.6 Problem statements can be worded in different ways that imply different research designs. Furthermore, the variables can be operationally defined in different ways, each creating a different research hypothesis.

8.2.1 Validity has several meanings, the most basic of which refers to methodological soundness or appropriateness. That is, a valid test measures what it is supposed to measure; a valid research design tests what it is supposed to test.

8.2.2 Statistical validity addresses the question of whether statistical conclusions are reasonable. Construct validity refers to how well the study's results support the theory behind the research. External validity refers to the degree to which generalization is possible. Internal validity concerns the question of whether the independent variable was responsible for the observed effect.

8.2.3 Internal validity is concerned about the accuracy of the conclusions about the relationship between independent and dependent variables.

8.3.1 Maturation refers to the normal and expected changes that occur over time, whereas history refers to the effect of external events that occur during a study.

8.3.2 Based on regression to the mean, the winner of this year's World Series is unlikely to win the World Series next year.

8.3.3 In this case, the confounding variable of attrition is operating, which might distort your sample so that it no longer represents the target population.

8.3.4 Sequence effects are found only in within-subjects designs.

8.4.1 Subject effects are any changes in the behavior of participants that are due to being in the study, rather than to the variables under study.

8.4.2 Demand characteristics are unintentional cues about how participants are expected to behave that might influence the behavior of participants.

8.4.3 Experimenter expectancies might cause researchers to bias their observations or lead them to produce unintended demand characteristics.

Chapter 9

9.1.1 Careful preparation of the setting can reduce the presence of confounding variables, thus increasing internal validity. External validity can be enhanced by making the laboratory situation as natural as possible.

9.1.2 All measures used in research should be both reliable and valid.

9.1.3 Exact replication is repeating the experiment as nearly as possible in the way it was carried out originally, whereas systematic replication is repeating the study with some systematic theoretical or procedural modification of the original work.

9.2.1 Blind procedures keep the participants and researchers unaware of to what condition each participant is assigned. Automation standardizes instructions and/or data collection, thus decreasing opportunities for experimenter effects. Objective measures take the subjective component out of measurement. Multiple observers allow an assessment of the reliability of the measures. Finally, deception prevents participants from seeing the purpose of the study and thus reduces potential subject effects.

9.2.2 In a single-blind procedure, the researcher is blind to group assignment, whereas in the double-blind procedure, both the researcher and the participants are blind to group assignment.

9.2.3   Deception reduces subject effects by preventing participants from recognizing what is being studied. Deception is considered to automatically place participants at risk. Therefore, it should be used only when non-deceptive procedures will not work.

9.3.1   The general population is the large group of all persons, whereas the target population is the subset in which the researcher is ultimately interested. The accessible population is the population available to the researcher, and the sample is a group drawn from the accessible population.

9.3.2   Unless samples are drawn carefully, they are unlikely to be representative of the population, thus restricting generalizability.

9.3.3   Random sampling involves drawing a sample so that every member of the population has an equal chance of being selected. Stratified random sampling involves drawing separate random samples from each of several subpopulations. Ad hoc samples are drawn from accessible populations.

9.3.4   Matching controls for individual differences.

9.4.1   Unbiased assignment to groups makes it unlikely that the groups will differ on any variable other than the independent variable.

9.4.2   Experimental designs (1) clearly state a hypothesis concerning predicted causal effects of one variable on another, (2) have at least two levels of the independent variable, (3) use unbiased assignment of participants to conditions, (4) have specific procedures for testing the hypothesis, and (5) include specific controls to reduce threats to internal validity.

Chapter 10

10.1.1   Systematic between-groups variance reflects consistent group differences due to the independent variable, uncontrolled confounding variables, or both.

10.1.2   Experimental variance is due to the effect of the independent variable, whereas extraneous variance is due to the effects of uncontrolled confounding variables.

10.1.3   Error variance is the nonsystematic within-groups variability that is due to random factors that affect some participants more than others.

10.1.4   The *F*-test is an inferential statistical procedure that tests for group differences.

10.1.5   Extraneous variance is controlled by making sure that the experimental and control groups are as similar as possible at the start of the experiment, and by treating all participants exactly the same way except for the independent variable manipulation. You can assure that groups are similar at the start of the study by (1) randomly assigning participants to groups, (2) selecting participants who are as homogeneous as possible, (3) building potential confounding variables into the experiment as additional independent variables, and (4) matching participants or using a within-subjects design.

10.1.6   Error variance can be minimized through careful measurement and/or using a correlated-groups design to control individual differences.

10.2.1   Four nonexperimental approaches are (1) ex-post-facto studies, (2) single-group, posttest-only studies, (3) single-group pretest-posttest studies, and (4) pretest-posttest natural control-group studies. Ex-post-facto studies relate observed phenomena to earlier experiences that were not directly observed or manipulated. In the single-group posttest-only study, the independent variable is manipulated with a single group and the dependent variable is measured.

In the single-group pretest-posttest studies, a single group of participants is measured both before and after a manipulation. Finally, in the pretest-posttest natural control-group design, one of two naturally occurring groups receives the treatment. None of these designs adequately controls confounding variables, although the natural control group design comes close if the groups are reasonably similar at the start of the study.

10.2.2 The weakest design is the ex-post-facto design, which controls virtually none of the potential confounding variables.

10.2.3 Maturation is not considered a confounding variable in studies of development. Developmental studies typically employ time-series designs.

10.3.1 The most basic experimental design is the randomized posttest-only control-group design.

10.3.2 In the randomized pretest-posttest control-group design, participants are randomly assigned to experimental and control groups, all participants are pretested on the dependent variable, the experimental group is administered the treatment, and both groups are then posttested on the dependent variable. In the multilevel, completely randomized between-subjects design, participants are randomly assigned to three or more conditions. Pretests may or may not be included. Finally, the Solomon four-group design combines the randomized pretest-posttest control-group design and the posttest-only control-group design.

10.3.3 Control groups control for history, maturation, and regression to the mean. Control groups are effective only if participants are randomly assigned to groups to assure that the groups are comparable at the beginning of the study.

10.3.4 The Solomon four-group design controls for the possible interaction of the pretest and treatment.

10.3.5 If groups are not equivalent at the beginning of the study, observed differences could be due to the manipulation, the initial differences, or both.

10.4.1 Chi-square tests are used with nominal data, and Mann-Whitney U-tests are used with ordinal data.

10.4.2 The t-test is used when two groups are compared on a dependent measure that produces score data. The ANOVA is used when two or more groups are compared on a dependent measure that produces score data.

10.4.3 The ANOVA summary table shows the sources of variance, the degrees of freedom for each source of variance, the sums of squares, the mean squares, the F-ratios, and the probability values for each F.

10.4.4 If the F is significant, at least one mean is significantly different from at least one other mean.

10.4.5 Planned comparisons and post hoc tests are specific means comparisons that are either planned before the research is conducted or performed without such preplanning, respectively.

Chapter 11

11.1.1 Correlated-groups designs assure group equivalence by either using the same participants in all groups or participants that have been closely matched.

11.1.2 The major confounding factor in within-subjects designs is sequence effects, which are controlled by counterbalancing.

11.1.3 Within-subjects designs reduce error variance by removing the individual differences component.

11.1.4 The strengths include greater sensitivity, reduction in the number of participants needed, and an increase in efficiency. The weakness is confounding due to sequence effects.

11.1.5 Complete counterbalancing means that an equal number of participants are assigned to every possible order of conditions.

11.2.1 There are no sequence effects to worry about in matched-subjects designs.

11.2.2 The characteristics of matched-subjects designs are that (1) each participant is exposed to one condition, (2) each participant has a matched participant in each of the other conditions, (3) the analysis takes into account which participants were matched with which other participants, and (4) the critical comparison is the difference between the correlated groups, in which the correlation is created by the matching procedure.

11.2.3 Matched-subjects designs are used when researchers want to take advantage of the greater sensitivity of within-subjects designs, but cannot, or prefer not to, use a within-subjects design. Matched-subjects designs are most often used when exposure to one condition causes long-term changes in participants.

11.2.4 The disadvantages of a matched-subjects design include the time to do the matching and the loss of participants because no suitable match could be found.

11.3.1 Single-subject designs are extensions of within-subjects designs in which a single individual is tested under multiple conditions. They are used most often in evaluating a treatment program for a single client.

11.3.2 The single-case study is used to describe clients, rather than to evaluate whether a treatment has been effective, which single-subject experimental designs achieve by manipulating the independent variable.

11.3.3 Single-subject experiments control internal validity by controlling the timing of the independent variable manipulation. To demonstrate a causal connection, the dependent variable response must be consistently related to when the independent variable was manipulated.

11.3.4 Reversal designs demonstrate the effects of an independent variable manipulation by measuring the dependent variable over several time periods, during which the treatment is applied and then removed. Multiple baseline designs demonstrate the effects of treatment on different behaviors successively. Randomized time-series designs insert a treatment at a randomly determined point in a series of measurements.

11.3.5 The strength of single-subject experimental designs is that they allow researchers to make causal inferences. The weakness is that the data provide little information about the generalizability of the findings.

11.3.6 External validity is weak because a single participant will never adequately represent the diversity in the general population.

11.3.7 Single-subject direct replication involves repeating the study with the same participant or a series of participants. Single-subject systematic replication involves carrying out a series of studies with different people in different settings and with different behaviors. Single-subject clinical replication involves using an integrated treatment package that is applied to a succession of participants.

11.3.8 Causality is inferred when each manipulation of the independent variable results in a predictable change in the dependent variable.

Chapter 12

12.1.1 Factorial designs are designs with more than one independent variable.

12.1.2 A factorial study must have at least two factors. With two factors, there will be the main effects of each factor and the interaction of the two factors. If there are more factors, there will be even more null hypotheses to test.

12.1.3 An interaction involves two variables that have a different effect when combined than they have when not combined. Main effect refers to the individual effect of each factor on the dependent variable.

12.1.4 Factorial designs are used when the researcher is interested in the interactive effects of two or more independent variables.

12.1.5 Any combination of main effects and factorials is possible in a factorial study.

12.1.6 We always interpret main effects in light of the interaction, because the main effects may be present only when some specific combination of the factors is present. The dark-fears study illustrates this point.

12.2.1 The major advantages of repeated measures factorials are that fewer participants are needed and there is a greater sensitivity to the effects of the independent variables on the dependent variable.

12.2.2 Designs can be mixed by having factors that include (1) both within-subjects and between-subjects factors, (2) both manipulated and nonmanipulated factors, or (3) mixed factors in both of these ways simultaneously.

12.2.3 Designs that are mixed in terms of within- and between-subjects factors must take into account the type of factors in setting up the data analysis. Designs that are mixed in terms of manipulated and nonmanipulated factors must take into account the type of factors in the interpretation.

12.3.1 An analysis of covariance (ANCOVA) removes the effects of a theoretically unimportant, but nonetheless powerful, variable from the dependent variable scores as part of the analysis.

12.3.2 A MANOVA includes more than one dependent variable, whereas an ANOVA includes only a single dependent variable in the analysis.

Chapter 13

13.1.1 Field research is any research that is carried out in the natural environment.

13.1.2 Field research (1) tests the external validity of laboratory studies, (2) determines the effects of events that occur in the field, and (3) improves generalization across settings.

13.1.3 The major difficulties in field research are that normal laboratory controls may be unavailable and some independent variables cannot be controlled.

13.1.4 The three types of generalization are (1) generalization from participants in a study to the larger population, (2) generalization over time, and (3) generalization from the settings of the study to other settings.

13.1.5 It is common in field research to see things that may indicate something significant. Flexible and observant researchers will recognize the potential importance of such observations and thus plan and carry out further research that will provide more definitive information about the phenomenon.

13.2.1 A quasi-experimental design is almost an experiment, but not quite equal to it. Quasi-experiments test causal hypotheses in natural settings with reasonable control of extraneous variables. Their weakness is that they rarely control all confounding, thus requiring caution in drawing causal inferences.

13.2.2 Nonequivalent control-group designs are most effective when the groups appear to be similar on the dependent variable and potential confounding variables.

13.2.3 In both time-series and within-subjects designs, participants are tested under all conditions.

13.2.4 History and instrumentation are most likely to confound time-series studies.

13.3.1 Program evaluation research assesses the effectiveness of programs, which is critical because money spent on ineffective programs could be used on more worthwhile projects.

13.3.2 Program evaluators often have to rely on the cooperation of those implementing the program. Therefore, excellent political skills are required.

13.3.3 Internal validity is enhanced by (1) selecting appropriate dependent measures, (2) minimizing potential bias in these measures, and (3) selecting the strongest research design possible.

13.3.4 The most widely used designs in program evaluation are the randomized control-group design, the nonequivalent control-group design, and the single-group, time-series design.

13.3.5 Program evaluation research addresses the scientific issues of internal and external validity. It is an art in that it requires political skill to obtain cooperation from those involved with the program.

13.4.1 Status surveys describe the current characteristics of a population, whereas survey research tries to discover relationships among variables.

13.4.2 Surveys seek to learn about the ideas, knowledge, feeling, opinions, attitudes, and self-reported behavior of defined populations.

13.4.3 The survey instrument may be a questionnaire or an interview schedule.

13.4.4 Factual items ask about information that can be verified independently. Content items ask about the respondents' opinions, attitudes, knowledge, and behavior.

13.4.5 Stratified random sampling involves dividing the population into subgroups or (strata) and randomly sampling from each stratum.

13.4.6 Confidence limits represent the interval in which we have a specified level of confidence that the population value will lie.

13.4.7 Cross-sectional designs involve administering the survey once, and yield data on the current characteristics of the sample. Longitudinal designs are within-subjects designs in which participants are surveyed several times.

Chapter 14

14.1.1 The first step is to describe the characteristics of the study.

14.1.2 The flowcharts organize the decision process by walking us through the process and use the information about the study to answer a series of questions.

14.1.3 The flowcharts help us to select appropriate statistical procedures, but they do not list all appropriate procedures. Therefore, they cannot be used to determine if a statistical procedure used by another investigator is appropriate.

14.2.1 A thorough check of procedures before beginning a research study makes sure that every detail has been properly addressed in the design stage.

14.2.2 If the pre-data check uncovers problems, they should be addressed and solved before the study is begun.

Chapter 15

15.1.1 Meta-analysis provides a mathematical way of objectively combining studies to arrive at a general conclusion about the effects of one variable on another.

15.1.2 Alpha is typically set low to avoid Type I errors.

15.1.3 Computers have affected research in several ways, including, but not limited to, (1) making data analysis and data management easier, (2) carrying out the procedures for studies, thus reducing experimenter biases, (3) making possible complex procedures that would be impossible without computers, (4) modeling complex processes that might otherwise be beyond the conceptual ability of researchers, and (5) improving communication among researchers.

15.2.1 Science is defined by the twin processes of empiricism and rationalism.

15.2.2 Science progresses by rejecting inadequate theories and proposing and testing new theories that stand up better to the rigorous demands of rationalism and empiricism.

15.2.3 The essence of science is its way of thinking.

Glossary

a posteriori comparison See *post hoc test*.

a priori comparison See *planned comparison*.

ABA reversal design See *reversal design*.

abscissa The *x*-axis on a graph.

abstract A brief description of a research study that appears at the beginning of the paper and is included in abstract journals, such as *Psychological Abstracts*.

abstract number system The number system, that possesses the characteristics of identity, magnitude, equal intervals, and true zero.

accessible population The subset of a target population that is available to the researcher and from which the sample is drawn.

ad hoc sample Sample of participants drawn from an accessible population. The ad hoc sample should be described in detail to define the limits of generalizability.

all-or-none bias The tendency to see statements as either true or false when, in fact, they are actually probabilistic (sometimes true and sometimes false).

alpha level Type I error level (probability of incorrectly rejecting the null hypothesis).

analysis of covariance (ANCOVA) Statistical procedure for evaluating mean differences between two or more groups, which statistically removes unwanted variance in the dependent variable and hence increases statistical power.

analysis of variance (ANOVA) Statistical procedure that analyzes mean differences between two or more groups by comparing between-groups and within-groups variance.

ANOVA summary table Table that organizes the results of an ANOVA. For each source of variation, the degrees of freedom, sums of squares, mean squares, and *F*-ratios are listed.

apparatus subsection The section of a research report that describes the physical aspects of the study (apparatus, measuring instruments, etc.).

applied psychology Any use of psychology to deal with existing problems or concerns.

applied research Research to provide solutions to practical problems.

archival records Any data source for events that have already occurred.

artifact Any apparent effect of a major conceptual variable that is actually the result of an uncontrolled confounding variable.

artificial intelligence The ability of particular machines to evaluate and respond to situations.

association Relationship or correlation.

assumptions (of science) The basic tenets behind scientific theory and research.

attrition Loss of participants before or during the research, which may confound the results because the remaining participants may not represent the population.

authority A way of acquiring knowledge. New ideas are accepted as valid because some respected individual or institution has declared the ideas to be true.

automation Use of equipment to present stimuli and record participants' responses. Automation increases precision in data gathering and minimizes experimenter bias.

average deviation   The average distance from the mean.

balanced placebo design   A 2 × 2 design developed in alcohol research, in which the factors are (1) what participants consume (alcohol or no alcohol) and (2) what participants are told they are consuming (alcohol or no alcohol). This design separates pharmacological and expectancy effects of alcohol. See *deception.*

Barnum statement   Any statement that appears to be insightful, but is actually true only because it is true for almost all issues, situations, or people.

baseline period   Time from initial monitoring of target behavior until the start of the manipulation.

base rate   Naturally occurring frequency of events.

basic research   Fundamental or pure research. Basic research is carried out to add to knowledge, but without applied or practical goals.

batch mode   Processing a computer task by telling the computer all steps that you want before you start.

behavior   Any observable act from an organism.

behavior modification   A set of teaching or therapeutic procedures that are based on laboratory-derived principles of learning.

behavioral medicine   See *health psychology.*

behavioral neuroscience   A field that relates the behavior of an organism to the brain mechanisms contributing to the behavior.

behavioral variable   Variable representing some aspect of an organism's behavior.

behaviorism   A philosophical perspective that argues that a scientific psychology should base its theories only on observable events.

beta   The probability of making a *Type II error.*

between-conditions sum of squares   The sum of squares used in a repeated-measures ANOVA to compute the between-conditions variance, which is also known as the between-conditions mean square.

between-groups sum of squares   The sum of squares used in a one-way ANOVA to compute the between-groups variance, which is also known as the *between-groups mean square.*

between-groups variance   Index of the variability among group means.

between-subjects design   Research design with two or more groups, in which each participant appears in only one of the groups.

between-subjects factors   Independent variables in which participants are assigned to conditions in such a way that each participant appears in only one condition.

between sum of squares   A generic term that usually refers to the *between-conditions sum of squares* in a repeated-measures ANOVA, but may also refer to the *between-groups sum of squares* in a one-way ANOVA.

bimodal   A distribution of scores that has two modes.

Biomedical Programs (BMDP)   Computer package for statistical analyses.

blind   When the researcher and/or participant is unaware of information that might biasing their responses. See *single-blind procedure* and *double-blind procedure.*

canonical correlation   A correlation between two sets of variables.

carryover effects   When participants' involvement in one condition affects their performance in subsequent conditions.

case study   See *case-study level of constraint.*

case-study level of constraint Research focused on a single participant, in which minimal constraints are placed on participants' behavior.

case-study research See *case-study level of constraint.*

categorical data Synonymous with *nominal data.*

categorical variable Synonymous with *discrete variable.* A categorical variable can have only a finite number of values.

causal hypothesis States that the independent variable has a causal relationship with the dependent variable. To accept this hypothesis, we must reject the null hypothesis and all confounding-variable hypotheses.

causal inference Concluding that the change in the independent variable resulted in a change in the dependent variable. It may be drawn only if all potential confounding variables are controlled.

causal relationship A relationship between variables in which one variable causes a predictable change in the other variable.

causally related Two variables are causally related if a change in one variable results in a predictable change in the other variable.

ceiling effects See *scale attenuation effects.*

central tendency Average or typical score in a distribution. See *mean*, *median*, and *mode.*

chi-square Inferential statistical procedure used with nominal data.

classification variables Organismic variables used to classify participants and assign them to groups in differential research.

coding data Process by which scores are assigned to behaviors for later analysis.

coefficient alpha An index of internal consistency reliability.

coefficient of determination The square of the Pearson product-moment correlation. It represents the proportion of variability in one variable that can be predicted on the basis of information about the other variable.

cognitive psychology Subdiscipline that studies perceptual processing, memory, and basic thought processes.

cognitive science A broad field that encompasses several disciplines, including behavioral neuroscience, neurophysiology, computer science, and linguistics, all of which are interested in modeling and understanding brain processes.

cohort effect Concept that people of a given age and culture behave similarly to one another and differently from people of other ages due to shared life experiences.

column means In factorial designs, one factor is usually illustrated as separate columns of data, and the mean of each column represents a different level of the factor.

communication phase of research Research phase in which the rationale, hypotheses, methods, results, and interpretations of the study are presented.

complete counterbalancing See *counterbalancing.*

computer-analysis programs Programs for statistical analysis of data.

computer file A set of information stored digitally and made available to computers for processing. A computer file may include a program, data, or output.

computer modeling Using a computer to simulate a psychological process as closely as possible to the way in which it is actually performed by people.

conceptual replication Repeating a study using different operational definitions.

confidence interval   An interval in which we predict population parameters to fall with a specified level of confidence.

confidentiality   Ethical requirement to protect sensitive information from participants.

confounded   Variables are confounded if they vary together, so that it is impossible to determine which variable was responsible for observed effects.

confounding variable   Any uncontrolled variable that might affect the outcome of a study. A variable can confound a study only if (1) there is a group mean difference on the variable and (2) the variable is correlated with the dependent measure.

confounding-variable hypothesis   States that a confounding variable is responsible for the observed changes in the dependent measure.

connectionist models   A computer modeling approach that simulates heavily interconnected sets of cells, in which the action of any one cell affects the actions of many other cells. Also know as *parallel distributed processing (PDP) models*.

constants   Variables that are prevented from varying (i.e., held constant).

constraints   Restrictions applied to increase the precision of the research and enhance the validity of conclusions.

construct   Idea constructed by the researcher to explain observed events.

construct validity   Validity of a theory. Most theories in science make many predictions, and construct validity is established by verifying the accuracy of each of these predictions.

content items   In survey research, content items focus on respondents' opinions, attitudes, and knowledge, rather than on factual items that can be independently verified.

contingency   A relationship between two or more variables, in which the first event is predictive of the second event.

continuous variable   Variable that can theoretically take on an infinite number of values. Often contrasted with *discrete* or *categorical variables*.

contrast   See *planned comparison*.

control   See *control in research*.

control group   A group of participants that serves as a basis of comparison for other groups. The ideal control group is similar to the experimental group on all variables except the independent variable that defines the group.

control in research   Any procedure that reduces confounding.

control of variance   Control of error variance and extraneous variance in research.

controlled research   Research that employs controls to rule out confounding.

convergent operations   A term for the agreement among findings from different studies carried out with different operational definitions of the same concepts.

convergent validity   Occurs when different studies, using different operational definitions, produce similar findings.

correlated-groups design   Research designs in which participants are related to participants in the other groups, thus controlling individual differences and increasing power. They are contrasted with *independent-groups design*.

correlated-subjects design   See *correlated-groups design*.

correlated *t*-test   Statistical procedure for testing mean differences between two groups in a within-subjects or matched-subjects design.

correlation   Degree of linear relationship between two or more variables.

correlation coefficient   Index of the degree of linear relationship between variables.

correlational level of constraint   Research designed to quantify the relationship between two or more variables.

correlational research   Research that seeks to measure the relationship between variables. The term is sometimes used broadly to include nonexperimental research, such as differential and quasi-experimental designs.

counterbalancing   Control for sequence effects. With complete counterbalancing, all possible arrangements of conditions are included.

criterion   The variable that we are attempting to predict in regression.

criterion measure   The variable that we want to predict in regression.

critical thinking   Applying the principles of inference discussed in this textbook to everyday situations.

crossover effect   In quasi-experimental research, a finding in which two groups show one pattern of scores before the manipulation and the reverse pattern after the manipulation. The name derives from the crossed lines when the data are graphed.

cross-cultural research   Exploring psychological phenomena across more than one culture.

cross-sectional design   A design that compares performance of people of different ages or at different times in history. Often contrasted with *longitudinal design*.

cross-sectional research   Research that uses a cross-sectional research design.

cross-tabulation   Procedure that illustrates the relationship between two or more nominal variables. A cross-tabulation table shows the frequency of participants who show each particular combination of characteristics.

cursor   Symbol on the screen of a computer that indicates where action will take place. The cursor is moved using a *mouse* or other pointing device.

data   Plural noun that refers to information gathered in research.

data-analysis phase of research   Research phase in which data are analyzed.

data snooping   Secondary analysis of data to generate hypotheses for later study.

debriefing   Disclosing to participants the full nature of a study that uses deception.

deception   Procedures used in research to hide the true nature of the study. Ethical use of deception requires complete debriefing at the end of the study.

decision tree   An organized pathway leading to a defined goal, in which successive decisions are made until one reaches the goal.

decision-tree flowcharts   Flowchart model in which answers to specific questions lead to branching to a new set of questions or procedures.

deductive reasoning   Reasoning from the general to the particular, such as when one makes specific predictions about future events based on theories.

deductive theory   A theory that emphasizes constructs and the relationship between constructs and seeks to make predictions from the theory that can be tested with empirical research. Often contrasted with inductive theory and functional theory.

degrees of freedom (df)   A statistical concept in which one degree of freedom, or freedom to vary, is lost each time that a population parameter is estimated.

demand characteristics   Any aspect of the research situation that suggests to the participant what behavior is expected.

demographic questions   Questions in a survey or research study about the characteristics of a participant, such as age, marital status, and education level.

demographic variables   Data that describe the participants in a study.

dependent variable Variable hypothesized to have a relationship with the independent variable.

descriptive statistics Statistics that summarize and/or describe a sample of scores.

design notation A way of indicating the number of independent variables and the number of levels of each independent variable in a factorial design.

difference score Difference between two scores on a measure.

differential level of constraint Research in which two or more groups, defined on the basis of a preexisting variable, are compared on a dependent measure.

differential research Research that involves comparing two or more existing groups.

diffusion of treatment When participants communicate information to participants in other conditions, thus potentially confounding the results of the study.

direct differences *t*-test See *correlated* t-*test*.

discrete variable A variable that can take on only a finite number of values. Often contrasted with *continuous variables*.

discussion section The section of a research report in which the researcher interprets the findings in light of other research and theory.

dispersion How spread out the scores are in a sample.

diversity How well various ethnic, cultural, age, and gender groups are represented in the research sample.

double-blind procedure Research procedure in which neither the researcher nor the participant knows to which condition the participant was assigned.

ecological validity When studies accurately reproduce real-life situations, thus allowing easy generalization of their findings. See *external validity*.

effect size Index of the size of the difference between groups that is expressed in standard deviation units.

effective range The range over which the dependent measure accurately reflects the level of the dependent variable.

empirical Based on observed data.

empiricism System of knowing that is based solely on observation of events.

enumerative data Synonymous with *nominal data*.

equal intervals A characteristic of the abstract number system, in which the differences between units are the same anywhere on the scale.

equipment subsection See *apparatus subsection*.

error bar An addition made to either histograms or frequency polygons that indicates the size of the standard error of the mean.

error term A measure of the variability of scores within each group that provides a basis for comparing observed differences between groups.

error variance Chance variability within a group. Also called *within-group variance*.

ethical checks A series of questions about the research procedures designed to safeguard participants.

evaluative biases of language Language has a tendency to blend description and evaluation, which can distort the perceptions of behavior.

ex-post-facto design Nonexperimental design in which the current situation is observed and related to previous events.

ex-post-facto fallacy Error in reasoning in which we assume that the observed relationship between current and historical events represents a causal relationship.

ex-post-facto reasoning See *ex-post-facto fallacy*.

ex post facto study See *ex-post-facto design*.

exact replication Repeating a study by using exactly the same procedure used in the original study. See also *replication*.

exit polls   Polls taken of voters as they leave the polling place about how they voted.

experiment   High-constraint research procedure in which participants are randomly assigned to conditions, thus controlling virtually all confounding variables.

experimental analysis of behavior   Procedures for the controlled study of single individuals, which are based on B. F. Skinner's operant conditioning concepts.

experimental design   In experimental design, participants are randomly assigned to groups, and all appropriate control procedures are used.

experimental group   Groups defined by a specified level of the independent variable. Contrasted with a *control group*.

experimental level of constraint   Research in which participants are randomly assigned to groups and are compared on at least one dependent measure.

experimental research   See *experimental level of constraint*.

experimental variance   Variability among the group means in a research study that is due to the effects of the independent variable.

experimentation   Manipulating the independent variable to observe its effects on the dependent variable.

experimenter bias   Biasing effects produced by the expectations of the researcher.

experimenter effects   Behavior of the researcher that might affect the behavior of participants or the measurement of dependent variables.

experimenter expectancies   Expectations of the researcher that may affect the accuracy of observations, especially when judgments are required.

experimenter reactivity   Any action by the researcher, other than the independent variable manipulation, that tends to influence participants' responses.

exploratory research   Low-constraint research designed to investigate feasibility and to generate, rather than test, hypotheses.

external validity   Extent to which a study's results generalize to the larger population.

extraneous variable   Any variable, other than the independent variable, that might affect the dependent measure and thus confound results.

extraneous variance   Variability due to the effects of extraneous variables.

factor analysis   A variation of multidimensional scaling that is used to identify underlying factors that might account for a wide range of observed characteristics.

factorial ANOVA   Analysis of variance procedure for evaluating factorial designs.

factorial designs   Designs employing more than one independent variable and thus allowing researchers to identify interactive effects among independent variables.

factors   Each independent variable in a factorial design.

facts   Empirically observed events.

factual items   Those survey questions that can be independently verified, such as the respondent's age or occupation.

field research   Research conducted outside the laboratory.

fields (in computer files)   A computer field represents a variable, which has a score for each participant.

filler items   Questions that are included in the dependent measure, but not scored, in order to distract participants from the purpose of the study.

floor effects   See *scale attenuation effects*.

flowcharts   Organizational device that allows one to reach a decision by following a path defined by answers to particular questions.

***F*-ratio**   An inferential statistic that is the ratio of two variance estimates.

F-test   See *F*-ratio.

free random assignment   Assigning participants to groups so that the assignment of any given participant has no effect on the assignment of any other participant.

frequencies   The number of objects or participants that fall into a specified category.

frequency data   Synonymous with nominal data.

frequency distribution   Organizational device used to simplify large data sets.

frequency polygon   Graph that illustrates a frequency distribution by placing a dot above each possible score at a height that indicates the score's frequency.

frustration effect   Temporary increase in emotionality of participants when contingencies or procedures are changed and new behavior is required.

functional theory   Functional theories emphasize both inductive and deductive elements. Often contrasted with *inductive theory* and *deductive theory*.

functionalism   A philosophical perspective that stresses the need to study how the mind functions. Often contrasted with *structuralism*.

fundamental research   Another term for *basic research*.

general control procedures   Control achieved through preparation of settings, careful response measurement, and replication.

general population   See *population*.

generalizability   Extent to which research findings are applicable to the outside world.

generalize   To assume that the findings of a study will be found for other participants or in other settings.

generalization   The process of assuming that the findings from one's study will also apply to other situations, places, or times.

genetic algorithm   A computer-based problem-solving procedure largely inspired by biological evolution.

Gestalt psychology   A philosophical perspective on perception that rests on the concept that the whole is greater than the sum of its parts.

graph   A means of presenting data visually. See *histogram* and *frequency polygon*.

graphs of factorial data   Graphs that illustrate main effects and interactions.

grouped frequency distribution   Lists the frequency of scores in equal-size intervals.

health psychology   An applied discipline that focuses on understanding and modifying behavior that affects a person's physical health.

heterogeneous   A group is said to be heterogeneous if there is considerable variability within the group.

heuristic influence   The nonsystematic impact of research or theory in stimulating new research.

histogram   A bar graph in which the frequency of scores is represented by the height of the bar.

history   Confounding variable that represents any change in the dependent variable that is a function of events other than the manipulation of the independent variable.

homogeneity   See *homogeneous*.

homogeneous   Situation in which participants are similar to one another.

humanistic psychology   A philosophical perspective that emphasizes subjective experience and the distinctively human qualities of choice and self-realization.

hyperlink   A link between web documents, which allows one to transfer to the linked document with a single mouse click.

icon   Pictures on a computer screen that represent a program, action, or data set.

idea-generating phase of research   First step in any research project, during which the researcher selects a topic to study.

identity A characteristic of the abstract number system, in which each number has a specific meaning or identity.

incidental comparison See *post hoc test.*

incidental learning Learning that occurs without specific reinforcement.

incomplete counterbalancing See *counterbalancing.*

independent-groups design See *between-subjects design.*

independent samples Samples that include different participants in each group and in which each sample is selected independently.

independent variable A variable that defines groups of participants on the basis of either (1) a preexisting characteristic or (2) random assignment.

individual differences Natural differences between people.

inductive reasoning Reasoning from the particular to the general. Inductive reasoning is used to generate theories based on observations.

inductive theory Inductive theories are built on a strong empirical base and stray little from that base. Often contrasted with *deductive theory* and *functional theory.*

inference Any conclusion drawn on the basis of empirical data and/or theories.

inferential statistics Statistical procedures that allow us to decide whether the sample data suggest that population differences exist.

informed consent Principle that participants have the right to know exactly what they are getting into before they agree to participate in a research study.

informed consent form A form signed by participants prior to a study indicating that they have been fully informed about the study and have decided to participate.

initial equivalence (principle of) The groups to be compared in an experiment must be equivalent at the start of the experiment.

Institutional Review Board (IRB) Formal body that reviews research proposals to determine if they meet ethical guidelines.

instrumentation Confounding variable involving shifts in the measuring instrument that cause it to give different readings when no change has occurred in participants.

instruments subsection See *apparatus subsection.*

interaction effect Combined effect of two or more independent variables, such that the effect of one independent variable differs depending on the level of the other independent variable.

internal consistency reliability Index of the homogeneity of the items of a measure.

internal validity Accuracy of a research study in determining the relationship between the independent and dependent variables.

interpretation phase of research Research phase in which the results are interpreted in light of (1) the adequacy of control procedures, (2) previous research, and (3) existing theories.

interrater reliability Index of the consistency of ratings between separate raters.

interrater reliability coefficient A correlation coefficient expressing the degree of agreement of observations made by two or more raters. See *reliability.*

interrupted time-series design Research design in which multiple measures are taken before and after an experimental manipulation.

interval scale Scale of measurement in which the distance between adjacent scores is the same anywhere on the scale, but zero is not a true zero.

interview schedule A standardized interview that lists all questions to be asked.

introduction   The section of a research paper in which the authors review previous research and theory to provide a framework and rationale for the study.

intuition   Way of acquiring knowledge without intellectual effort or sensory processes.

invasion of privacy   Failure of researchers to protect the confidentiality of records.

Kappa   Index of interrater agreement that adjusts for chance agreement.

knowledge   Any information about the world.

Laboratory Animal Care Committee   A committee that reviews the ethics of research proposals involving animals.

Latin square design   A counterbalancing procedure that identifies a set of orders that ensures that every condition appears equally often in every position.

levels of constraint   Degree of systematic control applied in research.

levels of headings   Mechanism used in research articles for organizing the report.

Likert-scale items   Rating on a continuum, such as from "strongly agree" to "strongly disagree."

linear relationship   Relationship between variables that, when plotted in a standard coordinate system, cluster around a straight line.

logic   Set of operations that can be applied to statements and the conclusions drawn from these statements to determine the internal accuracy of the conclusions.

longitudinal (panel) design   A research design in which a group of participants is followed over time. This design is often contrasted with *cross-sectional designs*.

longitudinal research   Research that uses a longitudinal research design.

magnitude   Characteristic of the number system in which numbers have an inherent order.

main effects   The individual effects of the independent variables in a factorial study.

mainframe computer   A large computer designed to serve the needs of multiple users at the same time.

mainstream psychology   Contemporary psychology that represents an integration of many of the earlier schools of psychology and their theoretical models.

manipulated factors   Independent variables in a factorial design, in which participants are randomly assigned to the different levels of the independent variable.

manipulated independent variable   Type of independent variable in which participants are randomly assigned to conditions.

manipulation   The explicit control of the independent variable by the researcher.

manipulation check   Procedure designed to verify that the independent variable actually varied in the different conditions.

Mann-Whitney *U*-test   A nonparametric inferential statistic used to test the difference between two groups when the dependent measure produces ordered data.

matched-pairs *t*-test   See *correlated* t-*test*.

matched random assignment   Experimental procedure in which participants are matched on relevant variables, and each matched individual is randomly assigned to one of the conditions of the study.

matched-subjects design   Research design in which participants are matched on a variable that is highly correlated with the dependent measure.

materials subsection   See *apparatus subsection*.

matrix of cells   Structure of cells in a factorial design.

maturation   Potential confounding factor involving changes in participants during the study that result from normal growth processes.

mean   Arithmetic average of scores that should be computed only for score data.

mean square   A variance estimate used in ANOVAs.

measurement error   Any inaccuracy found in the measurement of a variable.

measurement reactivity   Any effect on participant's behavior that results from the participant being aware that he or she is being observed.

measures of central tendency   Descriptive statistics that indicate the typical score.

measures subsection   See *apparatus subsection*.

median   Middle score in a distribution.

mentalistic   Based on the subjective experience of a person rather than objective behavior.

meta-analysis   Statistical averaging of results of multiple studies of a phenomenon.

method section   The section of the research report that details the nature of the sample and the procedures used in the study.

microcannulae   Tiny tubes which, when surgically implanted in the brain, deliver specific chemicals to specific regions of the brain, allowing the researcher to see their impact on functioning.

microdialysis   A procedure similar to micro-iontophoreses.

micro-iontophoresis   The implantation of tiny tubes into specific regions of the brains of animals to allow researchers to deliver specific chemical substances to specific regions of the brain in order to see what impact the chemicals have on functioning.

Minitab   Computer package for statistical analysis of data.

mixed designs (between- and within-subjects variables)   Factorial design in which at least one of the factors is a between-subjects factor and at least one of the factors is a within-subjects factor.

mixed designs (manipulated and nonmanipulated variables)   Factorial design in which at least one of the factors represents a nonmanipulated independent variable and at least one of the factors represents a manipulated independent variable.

mode   Most frequent score in a distribution.

model   A representation of the complex reality of the real world.

moderator variable   Any variable that has an effect on the observed relationship between two or more other variables.

Monte Carlo study   Procedure that evaluates the effectiveness of statistical tests by simulating the sampling of participants from a population with known parameters.

mouse   A device for moving the *cursor* on the screen of a personal computer.

multidimensional scaling   Statistical methods that simplify data by finding a small number of dimensions that account for most of the variability in a group of scores.

multilevel, completely randomized, between-subjects design   A design with more than two groups, in which each participant is randomly assigned to one group.

multiple baseline design   A single-subject research design in which several behaviors are monitored, and treatments are applied at different times for each behavior.

multiple-choice items   Questions or items in which participants select an answer from a list of several possible answers.

multiple correlation   Correlation between a criterion and a set of variables.

multiple observers   Control used to evaluate the accuracy of observations made by two or more independent observers.

multivariable design   See *factorial design*.

multivariate analysis of variance (MANOVA) Extension of ANOVA, in which two or more dependent measures are simultaneously evaluated.

multivariate correlational design Correlational design that includes more than two variables.

multivariate techniques Advanced statistical procedures that are used to evaluate complex relationships among several variables.

naive empiricism Extreme dependence on personal experience in order to accept events as facts.

naturalistic level of constraint Research carried out in natural settings, in which the researcher does not manipulate the environment.

naturalistic observation Observing the natural flow of behavior in natural settings.

negative correlation Relationship between two variables, in which an increase in one variable predicts a decrease in the other.

negative practice effect A decrement of performance due to previous exposure of participants to the measurement procedures.

negatively skewed When scores are concentrated near the top of the distribution.

neuro-networks Another name for *connectionist models,* because they are thought to resemble the massive interconnections among neurons in the brain.

neuropsychology A field that studies the relationships of brain functioning to behavior.

neurotransmitter agonist Chemical that enhances the action of a neurotransmitter.

neurotransmitter antagonist Chemical that blocks the action of a neurotransmitter.

nominal data Data that are frequencies of participants in each category.

nominal fallacy Confusing a label of a behavior as the explanation for the behavior.

nominal scale Scale of measurement in which the scores are categories.

nonequivalent control-group design Quasi-experimental design, in which two or more groups that may not be equivalent are compared on the dependent measure.

nonexperimental design Any research design that does not include both a manipulation of the independent variable and a control group.

nonlinear relationship Any relationship between variables that is characterized by a scatter plot in which the points cluster around a curve instead of a straight line.

nonmanipulated factors Independent variables in which participants are assigned to groups based on preexisting factors.

nonmanipulated independent variable The preexisting variable that determines group membership in a differential research study.

nonparametric statistics Inferential statistical procedures that do not rely on estimating such population parameters as the mean and variance.

nonprobability sampling Sampling procedure in which some participants have a higher probability of being selected than other participants or the selection of a given participant changes the probability of selecting other participants.

nonreactive measure Any dependent measure that provides consistent scores, even when the participant is aware of being measured.

nonsystematic within-groups variance Variance due to random factors that affect some participants more than others. Also called *error variance.*

N-of-one designs See *single-subject experimental designs.*

normal distribution Distribution of scores that is characterized by a bell-shaped curve. Psychological variables tend to show distributions that are close to normal.

null hypothesis States that the groups are drawn from populations with identical population parameters.

objective measure Any measure that requires little or no judgment on the part of the person making the measurement.

observation Collecting data about a phenomenon.

observation phase of research Research phase in which the data are gathered.

observational variable Any variable that is simply observed and not manipulated.

observed organismic variable Participant characteristic that can be used for classification.

one-way ANOVA Statistical procedure that evaluates mean differences between two or more groups.

open-ended items Questions that the participant answers in his or her own words.

operational definition Procedures used to measure or manipulate a variable.

ordered data Data produced by ordinal scales of measurement.

orderliness belief Ancient belief that events in nature are predictable.

ordinal scale Scale of measurement in which the scores can be rank ordered, but the distance between adjacent scores varies.

ordinate The *y*-axis on a graph.

organismic variable Any characteristic that can be used for classification.

outline The main aspects of ideas, organized under headings and subheadings.

panel design See *longitudinal design*.

parallel distributed processing (PDP) See *connectionist models*.

parametric statistics Inferential statistical procedures that rely on sample statistics to draw inferences about population parameters.

parsimony A guiding principle in science, which suggests that a simple theory is preferred over a more complex theory if both theories explain the data equally well.

partial correlation A correlation between two variables, in which the effects of a third variable are statistically removed before computing the correlation.

partial counterbalancing Control procedure in which the order of presentation of conditions is randomly selected for each participant.

participant assignment Assigning participants to conditions either randomly or on the basis of preexisting variables.

participant effects See *subject effects*.

participant observer Any researcher gathering data while being an active part of the setting.

participant selection Procedures used to select participants for a research study.

participant variable Synonymous with *organismic variable*.

participants at risk Participants involved in a research project that poses potential risk.

participants' rights Guarantees of proper treatment for research participants.

participants subsection Section of a research report in which the participants and the methods of participant selection are described.

partitioned Separating the total sum of squares into between-groups and within-groups sums of squares.

path analysis   Procedure that seeks to test causal models by factoring the correlation matrix to see how closely the correlational pattern fits the model.

Pearson product-moment correlation   Index of the degree of linear relationship between two variables in which each variable represents score data.

percent agreement   A measure of interrater reliability in which the percentage of times that the raters agree is computed.

percentile   Score that reflects the percentage of participants who score lower.

percentile rank   See *percentile*.

perfect correlation   Correlation of a +1.00 or a −1.00.

personal computer   A self-contained computer that serves the needs of a single user.

phase of research   The stages of a research project.

pilot testing   Evaluating for feasibility prior to using a measure or procedure in your research project.

phylogenetic continuity   An evolutionary concept about the continuity of structure and function between humans and other animals.

placebo   An inert treatment that appears identical to the experimental treatment.

placebo effect   Any observed improvement due to a sham treatment.

planned comparison   Comparison of mean performance between groups that was planned before data collection. Also called a *contrast* or an *a priori comparison*.

population   A defined set of objects or events (people, occurrences, animals, etc.).

population parameters   Summary statistics computed on the entire population.

positive correlation   Relationship between two variables, in which one variable increases as the other variable increases.

positive practice effect   Enhancement of performance that results from previous exposure to the measurement procedure.

positively skewed   Distribution in which scores are concentrated near the bottom of the scale.

post hoc comparison   See *post hoc test*.

post hoc test   Secondary analysis that evaluates effects that were not hypothesized by the researcher. Also called *a posteriori comparison* or *incidental comparison*.

power   See *power of a statistical test*.

power analysis   Procedures that determine the power of a statistical test to detect group differences if those differences exist.

power of a statistical test   Ability of an inferential statistical procedure to detect differences between groups when such differences actually exist.

practical significance   Whether the observed group differences are large enough to have a meaningful impact on participants.

practice effects   Any change in performance that results from previous exposure to the measurement procedure.

precision versus relevance problem   The concern that higher-constraint laboratory research may be less relevant than lower-constraint naturalistic research and, conversely, that lower-constraint research may be unacceptably imprecise.

pre-data check   An assessment of a research design prior to data collection.

predictor   See *predictor measure*.

predictor measure   The variable used to predict the criterion measure.

preexisting variable   Any characteristic that existed prior to the research study.

pretest-posttest design   Set of research designs, in which participants are tested both before and after the administration of the independent variable.

pretest-posttest, natural control-group design   Design in which preexisting groups are measured before and after the manipulation of an independent variable.

primary sources   In scientific literature, primary sources, such as journal articles and dissertations, publish the details of research studies and original theories.

principle of initial equivalence   The necessity of having experimental groups equal on the dependent measure before any manipulation occurs.

probability   The ratio of specific events to the total number of possible events.

probability sampling   Sampling participants so that each has an equal probability of being selected and the selection of any participant does not change the probability of selecting any other participant.

probe   Testing to see which groups are statistically different from one another.

problem-definition phase of research   Research phase in which research ideas are converted into precise questions to be studied.

procedures-design phase of research   Research phase in which the specific procedures to be used in the gathering and analyzing of data are developed.

procedure subsection   The section that describes how the study was carried out.

process of inquiry   The perspective that views research as a dynamic process of formulating questions and answering those questions through research.

program evaluation research   Specific area of field research that focuses on evaluating the effectiveness of programs in meeting their stated goals.

properties of the abstract number system   See *abstract number system*.

pseudoscience   Popular distortions of scientific knowledge and procedures, which appear on the surface to be scientific, but lack critical scientific procedures.

psychoanalysis   Psychological treatment based on Freud's psychodynamic theories.

psychology   Scientific study of the behavior of organisms.

psychophysics   Involves the presentation of precise stimuli under controlled conditions and the recording of the participants' responses.

pure research   Another term for basic or fundamental research. See *basic research*.

_p_-value   The probability of obtaining the computed value or a larger value of the test statistic (e.g., t or F) by chance if the null hypothesis is true.

qualitative research method   A research approach that seeks to understand psychological operations by observing the broad pattern of variables rather than the statistical relationship of variables.

quasi-experimental design   Research designs that approximate experimental designs, providing experiment-like controls to minimize threats to internal validity.

questionnaire   A list of questions to be asked of participants.

random number generator   Computer program that generates random sequences of numbers.

random order of presentation   A way of controlling for carry-over effects, in which the order of the conditions is randomly determined for each participant.

random samples   Samples that are drawn using random sampling techniques.

random sampling   Procedure for selecting participants, in which each participant has an equal chance of being selected and the selection of any one participant does not affect the probability of selecting any other participant.

randomization Any procedure that assigns a value in a random manner.

randomize within blocks A control procedure to reduce sequence effects, which involves using a block of one trial from each condition and randomizing participant assignment to these conditions before going on to the next block.

randomized, posttest-only, control-group design Experimental design in which participants are randomly assigned to two groups, and each group is tested on the dependent variable after the independent variable manipulation.

randomized, pretest-posttest, control-group design Experimental design in which participants are randomly assigned to two groups, and each participant is tested on the dependent variable before and after the manipulation.

range Distance between the lowest score and the highest score.

ratio scale Scale of measurement in which the intervals between scores are equal and the zero point on the scale represents none of the quality being measured.

rationalism A way of knowing that relies on logic and a set of premises from which logical inferences are made.

reactive measure Any measurement procedure that produces different scores depending on whether participants are aware that they are being measured.

records (in computer files) Each record represents the data for a single participant.

reference list The listing of sources that contributed to a paper. The *APA Publication Manual* specifies how to list such references.

reference section The section of a report that lists each paper and article that contributed to the ideas and procedures of the study.

regression A mathematical procedure that produces an equation for predicting a variable (the criterion) from one or more other variables (the predictors).

regression equation The mathematical equation that predicts the value of one variable from one or more other variables.

regression to the mean Confounding variable that occurs whenever participants are selected because they have extreme scores (either very high or very low). When retested, the original extreme sample tends to be less extreme on average.

reification of a construct Incorrectly accepting a construct as a fact.

relationship Any connection between two or more variables.

relative score See *standard score*.

reliability Index of the consistency of a measuring instrument in repeatedly providing the same score for a given participant. See *interrater reliability*, *test-retest reliability*, and *internal consistency reliability*.

repeated-measures ANOVA Statistical procedure to evaluate mean differences between conditions in a *within-subjects design*.

repeated-measures design Any research design in which participants are tested more than once.

repeated-measures factorial Factorial design in which all factors are within-subjects factors.

repeated-measures factorial ANOVA The statistical procedure for analyzing the results of a factorial study in which all factors are within-subjects factors.

replication To repeat a study with no changes in the procedure (*exact replication*), small theory-driven changes (*systematic replication*), or changes in the operational definitions of variables (*conceptual replication*).

representative sample Sample of participants that adequately reflects the characteristics of the population.

representativeness Degree to which a sample reflects population characteristics.

research data   See *data*.

research ethics   Set of guidelines designed to protect human and animal subjects from the risks of participating in research.

research hypothesis   Precise and formal statement of a research question, which is constructed by operationally defining the variables in the statement of the problem.

research setting   Characteristics of the situation in which a research project is run.

response-inferred organismic variable   A hypothesized internal attribute of an organism that is inferred on the basis of observed behavior.

response-set biases   Any tendency for a participant to distort responses to a dependent measure and thus create measurement errors.

results section   The section of a report that describes the findings and reports on the statistical analyses of the data.

reversal (ABA) design   Single-subject design in which the effects of an independent variable are inferred from observations made first without the independent variable present, then with the independent variable present, and again without the independent variable present.

rival hypothesis   Any feasible alternative hypothesis to the causal hypothesis.

robust   A statistical test is said to be robust to violations of the assumptions if the test consistently leads to accurate conclusions despite the assumption violations.

row means   In factorial designs, one factor is usually illustrated as separate rows of data, in which each row represents a different level of the factor.

sample   Any subset drawn from a population.

sample statistic   Index of some characteristic of the sample of participants.

sampling   Process of drawing a sample from a population. See *random sampling* and *stratified random sampling*.

sampling error   Chance variation among samples drawn from the same population.

sampling frame   A list of all participants from an available population.

scale attenuation effects   Any aspect of the measuring instrument that limits the ability of the instrument to make discriminations at the top of the scale (ceiling effects) or the bottom of the scale (floor effects).

scales of measurement   How well scores on a measurement instrument match the real number system. See *nominal*, *ordinal*, *interval*, and *ratio scales*.

scatter plot   Graphic technique that illustrates the relationship between variables.

science   Way of knowing that combines rationalism and empiricism.

Scientific Revolution   Period (15th through 17th centuries) in which scientific methods and applications achieved independence from theology and developed rapidly into a generally recognized way of understanding nature.

scientific research   Research based on a combination of rationalism and empiricism.

scientist   Anyone who utilizes the methods of science to study phenomena.

scientist-practitioner model   A model for the training of clinical psychologists, which teaches research and clinical skills in an integrated manner.

score data   Data produced by interval or ratio scales of measurement.

secondary analyses   Analyses that look at questions beyond the original research hypotheses, which may be relevant to understanding the primary analyses.

secondary sources   In scientific literature, secondary sources, such as books and annual reviews, publish reviews, summaries, and discussions of theory and research, without the details found in primary sources.

selection   A potential confounding variable that involves any process that may create groups not equivalent at the beginning of the study.

sequence effects   The confounding effects on performance in later conditions due to having experienced previous conditions.

serendipity   The process of experiencing unanticipated scientific discoveries.

similarity-uniqueness paradox   The tendency to simplify comparisons between objects by seeing them as either similar to, or different from, one another.

simple random sampling   See *random sampling*.

single-blind procedure   Research procedure in which the researcher is unaware of the condition to which each participant is assigned.

single-group, posttest-only study   Nonexperimental design that involves manipulating the independent variable and then taking a post-manipulation measure on the dependent variable.

single-group, pretest-posttest study   Nonexperimental design in which participants are measured on a dependent variable both before and after the manipulation.

single-subject clinical replication   A specialized form of replication for single-subject designs, which is used primarily in clinical settings.

single-subject experimental designs   Designs that seek information from studying single subjects. See *reversal design, single-subject, randomized time-series design*, and *multiple baseline design*.

single-subject direct replication   Repeating a single-subject experiment with the same participant or other participants and with the same target behavior.

single-subject, randomized, time-series design   Design in which multiple measures of the dependent variable are taken both before and after a manipulation.

single-subject systematic replication   Testing for generalization of a procedure to other conditions, persons, and target behaviors.

single-variable, between-subjects design   Designs that include only one independent variable and in which participants are randomly assigned to groups.

single-variable designs   Designs that include just one independent variable.

skeptic   A person who characteristically applies *skepticism*.

skepticism   Unwillingness to accept information without documentation to confirm it.

skewed distribution   Any distribution in which scores bunch up at the end of the scale.

skewed negatively   Distribution in which scores are concentrated at the top of the scale.

skewed positively   Distribution in which scores are concentrated at the bottom of the scale.

social desirability   Response set in which participants tend to say what they believe is expected of them.

Solomon's four-group design   Design that combines the randomized, posttest-only, control-group design and the randomized, pretest-posttest, control-group design.

sophisticated empiricism   Accepting indirect evidence for a phenomenon.

Spearman rank-order correlation   Indexes the degree of relationship between two variables, each of which is measured on at least an ordinal scale.

specific means comparison   Testing to see which groups are statistically different from which other groups. See *planned comparison* or *post hoc tests*.

spread   Synonymous with *variability*.

spreadsheet   A mechanism for organizing data in rows and columns.

SPSS for Windows   A computer package for statistical data analysis.

standard deviation   An index of variability that is the square root of the variance.

standard error of the differences between means   The denominator in a *t*-test.

standard error of the mean   The standard deviation of the sample divided by the square root of the sample size. The standard error of the mean is the standard deviation of a distribution of means for a given sample size drawn from a specified population.

standard score   Score that gives a person's relative standing. It is computed by subtracting the mean from the score and dividing by the standard deviation.

statement of the problem   First major refinement of initial research ideas, in which a clear statement of the expected relationship between variables is made.

Statistica   Computer package for statistical data analysis.

Statistical Analysis System (SAS)   Computer package for statistical data analysis.

statistical hypothesis   Synonymous with *null hypothesis*.

Statistical Package for the Social Sciences (SPSS)   Computer package for statistical data analysis.

statistical power   See *power of a statistical test*.

statistical significance   A finding is statistically significant if it is unlikely that it occurred by chance alone.

statistical symbols   Conventional shorthand used to denote statistical terms.

statistical validity   Accuracy of conclusions drawn from a statistical test.

statistically equal   Groups are statistically equal when the small differences that do exist are the result of sampling error.

statistically significant correlation   A correlation that is large enough that we would conclude that there is a non-zero relationship between the variables.

statistically significant differences   A large enough difference among group means that it is unlikely to be a chance occurrence.

statistics   Mathematical procedures used to describe data (*descriptive statistics*) or to draw conclusions from the data (*inferential statistics*).

status survey   Survey that provides a description of the current status of population characteristics.

Statview   A statistical analysis package for Macintosh computers.

stimulus variable   Any part of the environment to which an organism reacts.

strata   Subpopulations from which we draw samples. See *stratified random sampling*.

stratified random sampling   Sampling in which a population is divided into narrow strata, and participants are selected randomly from each strata.

structuralism   A philosophical perspective, popularized by Wundt, in which scientists seek to identify the structure of mechanisms that control behavior.

subject assignment   See *participant assignment*.

subject effects   Any response by participants that is different from the way that they would normally behave. See *placebo effect* and *demand characteristics*.

subject selection   See *participant selection*.

subject variables   See *organismic variables*.

subjective measures   Measures based primarily on participants' uncorroborated opinions, feelings, biases, or judgments.

subjects at risk   See *participants at risk*.

subjects' rights   See *participants' rights*.

subjects subsection   See *participants subsection*.

subjects term   The individual differences component of the within-groups variability in a repeated-measures ANOVA.

sum of squares   Sum of the squared differences from the mean.

summary statistics   Descriptive statistics that provide, in a single number, some general characteristic of the sample.

survey   A set of questions posed to a group of participants about their attitudes, beliefs, plans, lifestyles, or any other variable of interest.

survey research   Research that uses surveys to find relationships among variables.

symmetric distribution   Distribution in which the right half of the distribution is a mirror image of the left half.

systematic between-groups variance   Variability between groups that is brought about by either the experimental manipulation or by a confounding variable.

systematic influence   The stimulating effects of previous research and theories in providing testable hypotheses for further study.

systematic replication   Repeating a study with small, theory-based procedure changes.

table   Organizational device in which information is summarized and organized.

table of random numbers   A table containing randomly generated numbers.

target population   Population to which we hope to generalize the findings.

taxometric search procedures   A set of mathematical procedures that seeks to identify underlying taxometric categories.

taxon   A subgroup that is different in kind and not just degree from other subgroups.

technology   Physical instruments or tools used by or developed by researchers.

tenacity   Way of knowing based on accepting an idea as true because it has been accepted as true for a long period of time.

testing   Potential confounding variable that represents any change in a participant's score due to the participant having been tested previously.

test-retest reliability   Index of the consistency in scores over time.

theology   The philosophical tenets and/or study of religion.

theoretical concept   Idea that defines the relationship between two or more variables.

theory   Collection of ideas about how and why variables are related.

time-series design   See *interrupted time-series design*.

title page   The first page of a research manuscript, which lists the authors and their affiliations, the title of the paper, and a running head (a short title).

treatment   See *manipulation*.

trimodal   A distribution that has three modes.

true experiment   See *experiment*.

true zero   Characteristic of a measurement scale in which zero represents a zero level of the concept being measured.

*t***-test**   Statistical procedure that tests for mean differences between two groups.

*t***-test for independent groups**   Statistical procedure that tests for mean differences between two groups, in which participants appear in one and only one group.

two-group posttest-only design   A design in which two groups of participants are compared after some manipulation of the independent variable.

two-way ANOVA Statistical procedure for the analysis of a factorial design with two independent variables.

Type I error Probability of rejecting the null hypothesis when it is true.

Type II error Probability of not rejecting the null hypothesis when it is false.

unbiased assignment Assigning participants to groups or conditions in such a way that the groups are statistically equivalent at the start of the study. The most common unbiased assignment method is random assignment.

univariate Having to do with one variable.

univariate designs See *single-variable designs*.

unobtrusive measure Any measure that can be taken on participants without the participants being aware that they are being measured.

unobtrusive observer Anyone who is able to observe the behavior of participants without the participants being aware that they are being observed.

validity Major concept in research that has several meanings (internal validity, external validity, construct validity, statistical validity). In general, validity refers to the methodological and/or conceptual soundness of research.

variability Differences among participants on any given variable.

variable Any characteristic that can take on different values.

variance Summary statistic that indicates the degree of variability among participants.

waitlist control group A group of people in a treatment study who serve initially as a no-treatment control group with the understanding that they will receive the treatment later.

within-groups variance Variability among participants within a group or condition.

within-subjects design Design in which individual differences are controlled by having the same participants tested under all conditions.

within-subjects factorial Factorial design in which participants appear in all conditions.

within-subjects factors Independent variables in factorial designs in which each participant is tested under all conditions.

***x*-axis (abscissa)** The horizontal axis in a graph.

***y*-axis (ordinate)** The vertical axis in a graph.

***Z*-score** See *standard score*.

References

Abramowitz, J. S. (1998). Does cognitive-behavioral therapy cure obsessive-compulsive disorder? A meta-analytic evaluation of clinical significance. *Behavior Therapy, 29,* 339–355. (15)

Abramson, L. Y., Seligman, M. E. P., & Teasdale, J. D. (1978). Learned helplessness in humans: Critique and reformulation. *Journal of Abnormal Psychology, 87,* 49–74. (3)

Ahlfeldt, S., Mehta, S., & Sellnow, T. (2005). Measurement and analysis of student engagement in university classes where varying levels of PBL methods of instruction are in use. *Higher Education Research and Development, 24,* 5–20. (13)

Aiken, L. R. (1998). *Tests and examinations: Measuring abilities and performance.* New York: Wiley. (9)

Afraid to discuss evolution. (2005, February 4). *New York Times,* A22. (1, 6)

Akins, C. K., Panicker, S., & Cunningham, C. L. (Eds.). (2005). *Laboratory animals in research and teaching: Ethics, care, and methods.* Washington, DC: American Psychological Association. (3)

American College of Surgeons. (1991). The use of animals in research. *Bulletin of the American College of Surgeons, 76,* 18. (3)

American Psychological Association. (1996). Guidelines for ethical conduct in the care and use of animals. Available from APA Web site, www.apa.org/science/anguide.html*. (3)

American Psychological Association. (2001). *Publication manual of the American Psychological Association* (5th ed.). Washington, DC: Author. (2, B)

American Psychological Association. (2002). Guidelines for ethical conduct in the care and use of animals. Available from www.apa.org/science/anguide.html. (3)

American Psychological Association. (2005). About APA. Available from http://www.apa.org. (1)

Anastasi, A., & Urbina, S. (1997). *Psychological testing* (7th ed.). Upper Saddle River, NJ: Prentice Hall. (4)

Anderson, C. A., Lindsay, J. J., & Bushman, B. J. (1999). Research in the psychological laboratory: Truth or triviality? *Current Directions in Psychological Science, 8,* 3–9. (15)

Auge, I. I., Wayne, K., & Auge, S. M. (1999). Naturalistic observation of athletic drug-use patterns and behavior in professional-caliber bodybuilders. *Substance Use and Misuse, 34,* 217–249. (6)

Bachrach, A. J. (1981). *Psychological research: An introduction.* New York: Random House. (1, 13)

Baker, L. A., Mack, W., Moffitt, T. E., & Mednick, S. (1989). Sex differences in property crime in a Danish adoption cohort. *Behavior Genetics, 19,* 355–370. (6)

Ball, R. E. (2003). *The fundamentals of aircraft combat survivability: Analysis and design.* Reston, VA: American Institute of Aeronautics and Astronautics. (2)

Bandura, A. I. (1969). *Principles of behavior modification.* New York: Holt, Rinehart and Winston. (3)

Banken, J. A. (2004). Drug abuse trends among youth in the United States. In S. F. Ali, T. Nabeshima, & T. Yanagita (Eds), *Current status of drug dependence/abuse studies: Cellular and molecular mechanisms of drugs of abuse and neurotoxicity. Annals of the New York Academy of Sciences:* Vol. 1025 (pp. 465–471). New York: New York Academy of Sciences. (13)

Barber, T. X., & Silver, M. J. (1968). Fact, fiction and the experimenter bias effect. *Psychological Bulletin Monograph Supplement, 70,* 1–29. (8)

Barlow, D. H. (Ed.). (2001). *Clinical handbook of psychological disorders* (3rd ed.). New York: Guilford. (1)

Barlow, D. H. (2002). *Anxiety and its disorders: The nature and treatment of anxiety and panic* (2nd ed.). New York: Guilford Press. (4)

Barlow, D. H., & Hersen, M. (1984). *Single case experimental designs: Strategies for studying behavior change* (2nd ed.). New York: Pergamon. (11)

Bass, E., & Davis, L. (1988). *The courage to heal: A guide for women survivors of sexual abuse.* New York: Harper & Row. (1, 3)

Bass, E., & Davis, L. (1994). *The courage to heal: A guide for women survivors of sexual abuse: featuring "Honoring the truth: A response to the backlash"* (3rd ed. rev.). New York: HarperPerennial. (1, 3)

Belluck, P. (2005, February 10). Massachusetts governor opposes stem cell research. *New York Times,* A14. (1)

*Hard copies of APA electronic publications may be requested from American Psychological Association, Science Directorate, 750 First Street, Washington, DC 20002–4242

Benjafield, J. G. (1996). *A history of psychology.* Boston: Allyn & Bacon. (1)

Benjamin, L. J. (Ed.). (1997). *A history of psychology* (2nd ed.). New York: McGraw-Hill. (1)

Bennett, G. G., Merritt, M. M., & Wolin, K. Y. (2004). Ethnicity, education, and the cortisol response to awakening: A preliminary investigation. *Ethnicity and Health, 9,* 337–347. (3)

Bensler. J. M., & Paauw, D,S. (2003). Apotemnophilia masquerading as medical morbidity. *Southern Medical Journal, 96,* 674-676. (6)

Berg, B. (2004). *Qualitative research methods for the social sciences* (5th ed.). Boston: Pearson. (6)

Bergin, A. E., & Strupp, H. H. (1970). New directions in psychotherapy research. *Journal of Abnormal Psychology, 76,* 13–26. (11)

Bhattacharjee, Y. (2003, October 10). U.S. license needed to edit Iranian papers. *Science, 302,* 210. (1)

Bhattacharjee, Y. (2004, April 9). Easing the squeeze on "sanctioned" authors. *Science, 304,* 187. (1)

Blanchard, J. J., Horan, W. P., & Brown, S. A. (2001). Diagnostic differences in social anhedonia: A longitudinal study of schizophrenia and major depressive disorder. *Journal of Abnormal Psychology, 110,* 363–371. (7)

Bleuler, E. (1950). The fundamental symptoms. In E. Bleuler (Ed.), *Dementia praecox; or the group of schizophrenias* (J. Ziskin, trans.) (pp. 14–54). New York: International University Press. (Original work published in 1911.) (7)

Boesch, C., & Boesch-Acherman, H. (1991, September). Dim forest, bright chimps. *Natural History,* 50–56. (6)

Bornas, X., Tortella-Feliu, M., Llabres, J., & Fullana, M. A. (2001). Computer-assisted exposure treatment for flight phobia: A controlled study. *Psychotherapy Research, 11,* 259–273. (9)

Botting, J. H., & Morrison, A. R. (1997, February). Animal research is vital to medicine. *Scientific American, 276*(2), 83–85. (3)

Bower, B. (1998). Psychology's tangled web. *Science News, 153*(25), 394–395. (3)

Bowers, D. (1997). Georgia on our minds. *Marketing Research, 9*(2), 34. (13)

Bremmer, J. D. (2005). *Brain imaging handbook.* New York: Norton. (15)

Brewer, B. W., & Shillinglaw, R. (1992). Evaluation of a psychological skills training workshop for male intercollegiate lacrosse players. *Sport Psychologist, 6,* 139–147. (13)

Briem, V., & Hedman, L. R. (2001). Behavioural effects of mobile telephone use during simulated driving. *Ergonomics, 38,* 2536–2562. (2)

Brotemarkle, R. A. (1966). Fifty years of clinical psychology: Clinical psychology, 1896–1946. In I. N. Mensh (Ed.), *Clinical psychology: Science and profession* (pp. 63–68). New York: Macmillan. (6)

Busch, L. (1991). Science under wraps in Prince William Sound. *Science, 252,* 772–773. (1)

Calvo, M. G., & Castillo, M. D. (2005). Foveal vs. Parafoveal Attention-Grabbing Power of Threat-related Information. *Experimental Psychology, 52,* 150–162. (3)

Campbell, D. T. (1969). Reforms as experiments. *American Psychologist, 24,* 409–429. (13)

Campbell, D. T., & Stanley, J. C. (1966). *Experimental and quasi-experimental designs for research on teaching.* Chicago: Rand McNally. (8, 10, 13, 15)

Campbell, F. A., & Ramey, C. T. (1994). Effects of early intervention on intellectual and academic achievement: A follow-up study of children from low-income families. *Child Development, 65,* 684–698. (13)

Campbell, F. A., Ramey, C. T., Pungello, E., Sparling, J., & Miller-Johnson, S. (2002). Early childhood education: Young adult outcomes from the Abecedarian Project. *Applied Developmental Science, 6,* 42–57. (15)

Canadian Council on Animal Care. (1993) *Guide to the care and use of experimental animals.* Ottawa, Canada: Author. (3)

Canadian Psychological Association. (2004). Annual Report for 2003–2004. On their web site (http://www.cpa.ca). (1)

Carroll, J. D., & Arabie, P. (1998). Multidimension scaling. In M. H. Birnbaum (Ed.), *Measurement, judgment, and decision making: Handbook of perception and cognition* (2nd ed.) (pp. 179–250). San Diego, CA: Academic Press. (15)

Carroll, M. E., & Overmier, J. B. (Eds.) (2001). *Animal research and human health: Advancing human welfare through behavioral science.* Washington, DC: American Psychological Association. (3)

Casey, M. B. (1996). Understanding individual differences in spatial ability within females: A nature/nurture interactionist framework. *Developmental Review, 16,* 241–260. (8)

Catalano, R., & Serxner, S. (1992). The effect of ambient threats to employment on low birthweight. *Journal of Health and Social Behavior, 33,* 363–377. (13)

Chambless, D. L., & Ollendick,T. H. (2001). Empirically supported psychological interventions: Controversies and evidence. *Annual Review of Psychology, 52,* 635–716. (1)

Chapman, L. J., & Chapman, J. P. (1973). *Disordered thought in schizophrenia.* Upper Saddle River, NJ: Prentice Hall. (9)

Chapman, L. J., Chapman, J. P., & Raulin, M. L. (1976). Scales for physical and social anhedonia. *Journal of Abnormal Psychology, 85,* 374–382. (7)

Cialdini, R. B. (1993). *Influence: The psychology of persuasion* (2nd ed.). New York: William Morrow. (1)

Clagett, M. (1948). The medieval heritage: Religious, philosophic, scientific. In J. L. Blau, J. Buchler, & G. T. Matthews (Eds.), *Chapters in western civilization* (Vol. 1, pp. 74–122). New York: Columbia University Press. (1)

Clark, K. B. (1978). Kenneth B. Clark: Social Psychologist. In T. C. Hunter (Ed.). *Beginnings,* pp. 76–84, New York: Crowell.

Cohen, J. A. (1960). A coefficient of agreement for nominal scales. *Educational and Psychological Measurement, 20,* 37–46. (9)

Cohen, J. A. (1992). A power primer. *Psychological Bulletin, 112,* 155–159. (5, 13)

Cohen, J. A., & Cohen, P. (1983). *Applied multiple regression/correlation analysis for the behavioral sciences* (2nd ed.). Mahwah, NJ: Erlbaum. (5)

Collins, F. S. & Jegalian, K. G. (1999, December). Deciphering the code of life. *Scientific American, 281,* 6, 86–93. (15)

Columbo, J. (2001). The development of visual attention in infants. *Annual Review of Psychology, 52,* 337–367. (3)

Cook, T. D., & Campbell, D. T. (1979). *Quasi-experimentation: Design and analysis issues for field studies.* Chicago: Rand McNally. (8, 13)

Coombs, C. H., Raiffa, H., & Thrall, R. M. (1954). Some views on mathematical models and measurement theory. *Psychological Review, 61,* 132–144. (4)

Cooper, H. M. (1998). *Synthesizing research: A guide for literature reviews.* Thousand Oaks, CA: Sage. (13)

Cooper, H. M., & Lindsay, J. J. (1998). Research synthesis and meta-analysis. In L. Bickman & D. J. Rog (Eds.), *Handbook of applied research methods* (pp. 315–337). Thousand Oaks, CA: Sage. (5)

Copi, I. M., & Cohen, C. (2002). *Introduction to logic* (11th ed.). Upper Saddle River, NJ: Prentice Hall. (2)

Crawford, S. Y., Hurd, J. M., & Weller, A. C. (1996). *From print to electronic: The transformation of scientific communication.* Medford, NJ: American Society for Information Science by Information Today. (15)

Curtis, D. R., & Crawford, J. M. (1969). Central synaptic transmission-microelectrophoretic studies. *Annual Review of Pharmacology, 9,* 209–240. (15)

Darley, J. M., & Latane, B. (1968). Bystander intervention in emergencies: Diffusion of responsibility. *Journal of Personality and Social Psychology, 8,* 377–383. (8)

Darwin, C. (1859). *On the origin of species by means of natural selection, or the preservation of favored races in the struggle for life.* London: John Murray (New York: Modern Library, 1967.) (1, 6)

Darwin, C. (1877). A biographical sketch of an infant. *Mind, 2,* 285–294. (6)

Davidoff, J. (2004). Coloured thinking. *Psychologist, 17,* 570–572. (3)

Davis, P. W. (1997, July). *Naturalistic observations of 250 children hit in public settings.* Paper presented at the fifth International Family Violence Research Conference, Durham, NH. (6)

Dawis, R. (1987). Scale construction. *Journal of Counseling Psychology, 39,* 481–489. (13)

DeLeon, I. G., Iwata, B. A., & Roscoe, E. M. (1997). Displacement of leisure reinforcers by food during preference assessments. *Journal of Applied Behavior Analysis, 30,* 475–484. (11)

DeLisi, L. E., Sakuma, M., Kushner, M., Finer, D. L., Hoff, A. L., & Crow, T. J. (1997). Anomalous cerebral asymmetry and language processing in schizophrenia. *Schizophrenia Bulletin, 23,* 255–271. (15)

Dertouzos, M. (1999, August). The future of computing. *Scientific American, 281*(2)*, 52–55.* (15)

Dunbar, K. (1994). How scientists really reason: Scientific reasoning in real-world laboratories. In R. J. Sternberg & J. Davidson (Eds.), *The nature of insight* (pp. 365–395). Cambridge MA: MIT Press. (6)

Duskin, M. S. (1999, March). Census 2000 doesn't add up. *Contemporary Women's Issues, 48*(3)*,* 6–11. (13)

Duva, M. A., Siu, A., & Stanley, B. G. (2005). The NMDA receptor antagonist MK-801 alters lipoprivic eating elicited by 2-mercaptoacetate. *Physiology and Behavior, 83,* 787–791. (3)

Easton, A., Meerlo, P., Bergmann, B., & Turek, F. W. (2004). The suprachiasmatic nucleus regulates sleep timing and amount in mice. *Sleep: Journal of Sleep and Sleep Disorders Research, 27,* 1307–1318. (3)

Eckblad, M. L., Chapman, L. J., Chapman, J. P., & Mishlove, M. (1982). *The revised social anhedonia scale.* Unpublished test, University of Wisconsin, Madison. (7)

Edwards, A. W. (1998). *Experimental design.* New York: Addison-Wesley. (11)

Eisenger, R. M. (2003). *The evolution of presidential polling.* New York: Cambridge University Press. (13)

Erlenmeyer-Kimling, L., Roberts, S. A., & Rock, D. (2004). Longitudinal Prediction of Schizophrenia in a Prospective High-Risk Study. In *Behavior genetics principles: Perspectives in development, personality, and psychopathology: Decade of behavior* (pp. 135–144). Washington, DC: American Psychological Association. (8)

European Science Foundation. (2001). *The use of animals in research: Policy briefing.* Strasbourg, France: Author. (3)

Fancher, R. E. (2000). Snapshots of Freud in America 1899–1999. *American Psychologist, 55,* 1025–1028. (1)

Farrington, B. (1949a). *Greek science: 1. Thales to Aristotle.* Harmondsworth, U.K.: Pelican Books. (1)

Farrington, B. (1949b). *Greek science: 2. Theophrastus to Galen.* Harmondsworth, U.K.: Pelican Books. (1)

Feng, A. S., & Ratnam, R. (2000). Neural basis of hearing in real-world situations. *Annual Review of Psychology, 51,* 699–725. (3)

Ferraro, F. R., Szigeti, E., Dawes, K. J., & Pan, S. (1999). A survey regarding the University of North Dakota Institutional Review Board: Data, attitudes, and perceptions. *Journal of Psychology, 133,* 272–280. (3)

Festinger, L. (1957). *A theory of cognitive dissonance.* Stanford, CA: Stanford University Press. (3)

Fisher, R. A. (1935). *The design of experiments.* London: Oliver & Boyd. (11, 15)

Freud, S. (1938a). The interpretation of dreams. In A. A. Brill (Ed. & Trans.), *The basic writings of Sigmund Freud* (pp. 179–549). New York: Random House. (Original work published 1900). (3)

Freud, S. (1938b). The psychopathology of everyday life. In A. A. Brill (Ed. & Trans.), *The basic writings of Sigmund Freud* (pp. 33–178). New York: Random House. (Original work published 1901). (3)

Gaito, J. (1980). Measurement scales and statistics: Resurgence of an old misconception. *Psychological Bulletin, 87,* 564–567. (4)

Gelfand, H., & Walker, C. J. (2001). *Mastering APA style: Student's workbook and training guide* (23rd ed.). Washington, DC: American Psychological Association. (B)

Ginsburg, H. P., Inoue, N., Seo, K. (1999). Young children doing mathematics: Observations of everyday activities. In J. V. Copley (Ed.), *Mathematics in the early years* (pp. 88–99). Washington, DC: National Association for the Education of Young Children. (6)

Gleick, J. (1987). *Chaos: Making a new science.* New York: Penguin Books. (3)

Goodall, J. (1988). *In the shadow of man.* Boston: Houghton Mifflin. (2, 6)

Goodall, J. (1978). Chimp killings: Is it the man in them? *Science News, 113,* 276.

Goodall, J. (1986). *The chimpanzees of Gombe.* Cambridge, MA: Belknap Press/Harvard University Press. (2, 6)

Goodall, J., & Marks, A. (2003). *With love: Ten heartwarming stories of chimpanzees in the wild.* San Francisco, CA: Michael Neugebauer Books. (2)

Goodey C. F. (2003). On certainty, reflexivity and the ethics of genetic research into intellectual disability. *Journal of Intellectual Disability Research, 47,* 548–554. (3)

Goodwin, C. J. (1999). *A history of modern psychology.* New York: Wiley. (1)

Goodwin, R. D., Lieb, R., Hoefler, M., Pfister, H., Bittner, A., Beesdo, K., & Wittchen, H. (2004). Panic attack as a risk factor for severe psychopathology. *American Journal of Psychiatry, 161,* 2207–2214. (3)

Gottesman, I. I. (1991). *Schizophrenia genesis: The origins of madness.* New York: Freeman. (15)

Gould, S. J. (1997, May). Leonardo's living earth. *Natural History, 106,* 18. (1)

Graham, K., & Wells, S. (2001). Aggression among young adults in the social context of the bar. *Addiction Research and Theory, 9,* 193–219. (6)

Graziano, A. M. (1974). *Child without tomorrow.* Elmsford, NY: Pergamon Press. (2, 4, 8, 13)

Graziano, A. M. (1992). Why we should study sub-abuse violence against children. *Child, Youth, and Family Services Quarterly, 15*(4), 8–9. (6)

Graziano, A. M. (2001). *Developmental Disabilities: Introduction to a diverse field.* Boston: Allyn & Bacon. (3)

Graziano, A. M., & Kean, J. (1968). Programmed relaxation and reciprocal inhibition with psychotic children. *Behaviour Research and Therapy, 6,* 433–437. (6)

Graziano, A. M., & Mooney, K. C. (1982). Behavioral treatment of "nightfears:" A 2- to 3-year follow-up. *Journal of Consulting and Clinical Psychology, 50,* 598–599. (9)

Graziano, M. S. A., Cooke, D. F., & Taylor, S. R. (2000). Coding the location of the arm by sight. *Science, 290,* 1782–1786. (3)

Graziano, M. S. A., & Gross, C. (1993). A bimodal map of space: Somatosensory receptive fields in the macaque putamen with corresponding visual receptive fields. *Experimental Brain Research, 97,* 96–109. (1)

Graziano, M. S. A., & Gross, C. (1998). Spatial maps for the control of movement. *Current Opinions in Neurobiology, 8,* 195–201. (1)

Grimson, W. E. L., Kikinis, R., Lolesz, F. A., & McL. Black, P. (1999, June). Image guided surgery. *Scientific American, 280*(6), 62–69. (15)

Gross, C. G. (1997). Leonardo da Vinci on the brain and eye. *History of Neuroscience, 3,* 347–354. (1)

Gryta, M. (1998, August 21). Two drivers indicted in alleged "road rage" incident on Thruway. *Buffalo (NY) News,* B5. (8)

Guerin, D., & MacKinnon, D. P. (1985). An assessment of the California Child Passenger Restraint Requirement. *American Journal of Public Health, 75,* 142–144. (13)

Hafner, K., & George, J. (2005, March 3). For drivers, a traffic-jam of distracters. *The New York Times,* E1. (2)

Hall, G. C., Bansal, A., & Lopez, I. R. (1999). Ethnicity and psychopathology: A meta-analytic review of 31 years of comparative MMPI/MMPI-2 research. *Psychological Assessment, 11,* 186–197. (13)

Harb, G. C., Eng, W., Zaider, T., & Heimberg, R. G. (2003). Behavioral assessment of public-speaking anxiety using a modified version of the Social Performance Rating Scale. *Behaviour Research and Therapy, 41,* 1373–1380. (9)

Harper, W. (2004, September 29). Publisher for the people: Biologist Michael Eisen hopes to accomplish for science publishing what Linux set out to do for computing. *East Bay Express* (California). (Available through LexisNexis Academic)(2)

Helmstadter, G. C. (1970). *Research concepts in human behavior.* New York: Appleton-Century-Crofts. (1)

Hergenhahn, B. R. (1997). *An introduction to the history of psychology* (3rd ed.). Pacific Grove, CA: Brooks/Cole. (1)

Hollin, C. R. (1999). Treatment programs for offenders: Meta-analysis, "what works," and beyond. *International Journal of Law and Psychiatry, 22,* 361–372. (15)

Hugdahl, K. (1995). Classical conditioning and implicit learning: The right hemisphere hypothesis. In R. J. Davidson & K. Hugdahl (Eds.), *Brain asymmetry* (pp. 235–267). Cambridge, MA: MIT Press. (11)

Hunt, M. M. (1997). *How science takes stock: The story of meta-analysis.* New York: Russell Sage Foundation. (15)

Hunter, J. E., & Schmidt, F. L. (1990). *Methods of meta-analysis: Correcting error and bias in research findings.* Newbury Park, CA: Sage. (13)

Hyman, R. (1964). *The nature of psychological inquiry.* Upper Saddle River, NJ: Prentice Hall. (2)

Irvin, J., Bowers, C., Dunn, M., & Wang, M. C. (1999). Efficacy of relapse prevention: A meta-analytic review. *Journal of Consulting and Clinical Psychology, 67,* 563–570. (15)

Jacob, T., Tennenbaum, D., Seilhamer, R. A., & Bargrel, K. (1994). Reactivity effects during naturalistic observation of distressed and non-distressed families. *Journal of Family Psychology, 8,* 354–363. (6)

Jacobson, J. W., Mulick, J. A., & Schwartz, A. A. (1995). A history of facilitated communication: Science, pseudoscience, and antiscience science working group on facilitated communication. *American Psychologist, 50,* 750–765. (1)

Jaenisch R. (2004). Human cloning: The science and ethics of nuclear transplantation. *New England Journal of Medicine, 351,* 2787–2791. (3)

Jang, K. L. (2005). *The behavioral genetics of psychopathology: A clinical guide.* Mahwah, NJ: Erlbaum. (15)

Johnson, B., & Eagly, A. (2000). Quantitative synthesis of social psychological research. In H. Weiss & C. Judd (Eds.), *Handbook of research methods in social and personality psychology* (pp. 496–528). New York: Cambridge University Press. (13)

Katsikitis, M. (1997). The classification of facial expressions of emotion: A multidimensional scaling approach. *Perception, 26,* 613–626. (15)

Kazdin, A. E. (1998). *Research design in clinical psychology* (3rd ed.). Boston: Allyn & Bacon. (13)

Keith, A. (1954). Darwin and the "Origin of Species." In H. Shapley, S. Rapport, & H. Wright (Eds.), *A treasury of science* (pp. 437–446). New York: Harper and Brothers. (1)

Kendler, H. H. (1993). Psychology and the ethics of social policy. *American Psychologist, 48,* 1046–1053. (3)

Keppel, G. (2006). *Introduction to design and analysis.* New York: Worth. (11, 12, 14)

Kerlinger, F. N. (1992). *Foundations of behavioral research* (3rd ed.). Fort Worth, TX: Harcourt Brace. (4, 8, 13)

Kety, S. S., Rosenthal, D., Wender, P. H., & Schulsinger, F. (1968). The types and prevalence of mental illness in the biological and adoptive families of adopted schizophrenics. In D. Rosenthal & S. S. Kety (Eds.), *The transmission of schizophrenia* (pp. 345–362). Oxford: Pergamon. (6)

Kintisch, E. (2005, March 25). Researcher faces prison for fraud in NIH grant application and papers. *Science, 37,* 1851. (4)

Klahr, D., & Simon, H. A. (2001). What have psychologists (and others) discovered about the process of scientific discovery? *Current Directions in Psychological Science, 10,* 75–79. (6)

Koegel, R. L., & Koegel, L. K. (1995). *Teaching children with autism: Strategies for initiating positive interactions and improving learning opportunities.* Baltimore, MD: Paul H. Brookes. (8)

Korn, J. H. (1997). *Illusions of reality: A history of deception in social psychology.* New York: State University of New York Press. (3)

Koza, J. R., Keane, M. A., & Streeter, M. J. (2003, February). Evolving inventions. *Scientific American, 288*(2), 52–59. (15)

Lang, A. R., & Sibrel, P. A. (1989). Psychological perspectives on alcohol consumption and interpersonal aggression: The potential role of individual differences in alcohol-related criminal violence. *Criminal Justice and Behavior, 16,* 299–324. (9)

Lang, P. J. (1985). The cognitive psychophysiology of emotion: Fear and anxiety. In A. H. Tuma and D. Maser (Eds.), *Anxiety and the anxiety disorders.* Hillsdale, NJ: Erlbaum. (4)

Larson, E. J. (2004). *Evolution: The remarkable history of a scientific theory.* New York: Random House. (6)

Levine, A. G. (1982). *The Love Canal: Science, politics and people.* Lexington, MA: D. C. Heath. (6)

Levine, M., Wallach, L., & Levine, D. I. (2007). *Psychological problems, social issues, and law.* Boston: Allyn & Bacon. (15)

Levy, K. (1980). A Monte Carlo study of analysis of covariance under violations of the assumptions of normality and equal regression slopes. *Educational and Psychological Measurement, 40,* 835–840. (14)

Light, R. J., & Pillemer, D. B. (1984). *Summing up: The science of reviewing research.* Cambridge, MA: Harvard University Press. (15)

Lilienfeld, S. O. (1998). Pseudoscience in contemporary clinical psychology: What it is and what we can do about it. *Clinical Psychologist, 51*(4), 3–9. (1)

Liptak, A. (2003, September 27). No Call List: Hard choices. *New York Times,* A1. (13)

Loehlin, J. C. (2004). *Latent variable models: An introduction to factor, path, and structural analyses* (4th ed.). Mahwah, NJ: Erlbaum. (7)

Loftus, E. F., & Hoffman, H. G. (1989). Misinformation and memory: The creation of new memories. *Journal of Experimental Psychology: General, 118,* 100–104. (13)

Loftus, E. F., & Ketcham, K. (1991). *Witness for the defense: The accused, the eyewitness, and the expert who puts memory on trial.* New York: St. Martin's Press. (13)

Loftus, E. F., & Ketcham, K. (1994). *The myth of repressed memory: False memories and allegations of sexual abuse.* New York: St. Martin's Press. (1, 3)

Loftus, E. F., & Polage, D. C. (1999). Repressed memories: When are they real? How are they false? *Psychiatric Clinics of North America, 22,* 61–70. (1, 3)

Longnecker, M. P., Harper, J. M., & Kim, S. (1997). Eating frequency in the nationwide food consumption survey (U.S.A) 1987–1988. *Appetite, 29,* 55–59. (13)

Lord, F. M. (1967). A paradox in the interpretation of group differences. *Psychological Bulletin, 68,* 304–305. (12)

Lovaas, O. I. (1973). *Behavioral treatment of autistic children.* Morristown, NJ: General Learning Press. (3)

Lovaas, O. I. (1996). The UCLA young autism model of service delivery. In C. Maurice (Ed.), *Behavioral intervention for young children with autism* (pp.241–250). Austin, TX: Pro-Ed. (8)

Lubinski, D., & Benbow, C. P. (1992). Gender differences in abilities and preferences among the gifted: Implications for the math-science pipeline. *Current Directions in Psychological Science, 1,* 61–66. (8)

Maddox, J. (1999, December). The unexpected science to come. *Scientific American, 281*(6), 62–67. (15)

Marlatt, G. A., Demming, B., & Reid, J. B. (1973). Loss of control drinking in alcoholics: An experimental analogue. *Journal of Abnormal Psychology, 81,* 233–241. (9)

Maxwell, J. A. (2005). *Qualitative research design: An interactive approach* (2nd ed.). Thousand Oaks, CA: Sage. (6)

McCrae, R. R., & Costa, P. T., Jr. (1987). Validation of the five-factor model of personality across instruments and observers. *Journal of Personality and Social Psychology, 52,* 81–90. (15)

McCrae, R. R., & Costa, P. T., Jr. (1999). A five-factor theory of personality. In L. A. Pervin & O. P. John (Eds.), *Handbook of personality: Theory and research* (pp. 139–153). New York: Guilford. (15)

McFall, R. M. (1970). Effects of self-monitoring on normal smoking behavior. *Journal of Consulting and Clinical Psychology, 35,* 135–142. (11)

McGrew, W. C. (1992). *Chimpanzee material culture.* Cambridge: Cambridge University Press. (6)

McGuffin, P., Owen, M. J., & Gottesman, I. I (Eds.). (2002). *Psychiatric genetics and genomics.* London: Oxford University Press. (15)

McGuire, W. J. (1997). Creative hypothesis generating in psychology: Some useful heuristics. *Annual Review of Psychology, 48,* 1–30. (2)

McKay, D., Todaro, J. F., Neziroglu, F., & Yaryura-Tobias, J. A. (1996). Evaluation of a naturalistic maintenance program in the treatment of obsessive-compulsive disorder: A preliminary investigation. *Journal of Anxiety Disorders, 10,* 211–217. (13)

Meehl, P. E. (1990). Toward an integrated theory of schizotaxia, schizotypy, and schizophrenia. *Journal of Personality Disorders, 4,* 1–99. (2)

Meredith, R. (1996, April 30). Man is guilty of murder in death after bridge dispute. *New York Times,* A16. (8)

Messer, S. C., & Gross, A. M. (1995). Childhood depression and family interaction: A naturalistic observation study. *Journal of Clinical Child Psychology, 24,* 77–88. (6)

Michell, J. (1986). Measurement scales and statistics: A clash of paradigms. *Psychological Bulletin, 87,* 564–567. (4)

Miller, G., & Dingwall, R. (Eds.). (1997). *Context and method in qualitative research.* Thousand Oaks, CA: Sage. (6)

Miller, N. E. (1971). Neal E. Miller: *Selected papers.* Chicago: Aldine Atherton. (3)

Miller, N. E. (1985). The value of behavioral research with animals. *American Psychologist, 40,* 423–440. (3)

Milton, J., & Wiseman, R. (1999). Does Psi exist? Lack of replication of an anomalous process of information transfer. *Psychological Bulletin, 125,* 387–391. (9)

Money, J., & Jobaris, R. (1977). Apotemnophilia: Two cases of self-demand amputation as a paraphilia. *Journal of Sex Research, 13,* 115–125. (6)

Morgan, D. L., & Morgan, R. K. (2001). Single-participant research design: Bringing science to managed care. *American Psychologist, 56,* 119–127. (11)

Morin, R. (2004, November 21). Surveying the damage: Exit polls can't predict winners, so don't expect them to. *Washington Post,* B1. (7, 13)

Morosan, P., Rademacher, J., Palomero-Gallagher, N., & Zilles, K. (2005). Anatomical organization of the human auditory cortex: Cytoarchitecture and transmitter receptors. In R. Konig, P. Heil, E. Budinger & H. Scheich (Eds), *The auditory cortex: A synthesis of human and animal research* (pp. 27–50). Mahwah, NJ: Erlbaum. (15)

Morrison, A. R. (2001). A scientist's perspective on the ethics of using animals in behavioral research. In M. E. Carroll & J. B. Overmier (Eds.), *Animal research and human health: Advancing human welfare through behavioral science* (pp. 341–356). Washington, DC: American Psychological Association. (3)

Mukerjee, M. (1997, February). Trends in animal research. *Scientific American, 276*(2), 86–93. (3)

Mullins, J. L., & Christian, L. (2001). The effects of progressive relaxation training on the disruptive behavior of a boy with autism. *Research in Developmental Disabilities, 22,* 449–462. (6)

Murray, T. A. (1996). *The worth of a child.* Berkeley, CA: University of California Press. (3)

Myers, D. G. (2002). *Intuition: Its powers and perils.* New Haven, CT: Yale University Press. (1)

Myers, J. L., & Well, A. D. (2003). *Research design and statistical analysis* (2nd ed.). Mahwah, NJ: Erlbaum. (5, 7, 11, 14)

Nagel, E. (1948). The development of modern science. In J. L. Blau, J. Buchler, & G. T. Matthews (Eds.), *Chapters in western civilization* (Vol. 1), (pp. 241–284). New York: Columbia University Press. (1)

Nardi, P. (2005). *Doing survey research.* Boston: Allyn & Bacon. (13)

National Institutes of Health. (1994). *Preparation and maintenance of higher mammals during neuroscience experiments.* NIH Publication No. 91–3207. Bethesda, MD: National Eye Institute. (3)

National Institutes of Health. (1995). *Guidelines for the conduct of research involving human subjects.* Bethesda, MD: Author. (3)

National Institutes of Health. (1996). O.P.R.R. *Public Health Service Policy on Humane Care and Use of Laboratory Animals.* Rockville, MD: NIH Office for Protection from Research Risks. (3)

National Institutes of Health. (1998). *Policies and Guidelines on the inclusion of children as participants in research involving human subjects.* Bethesda, MD: Author. (3)

National Institutes of Health. (2005). Grants policy and guidance: Inclusion guidance. Available from http://grants1.nih.gov/grants/policy/policy.htm. (3)

Neisser, U. (1976). *Cognition and reality.* San Francisco: W. H. Freeman. (8)

Neisser, U., & Harsch, N. (1992). Phantom flashbulbs: False recollection of hearing the news about Challenger. In E. Winograd & U. Neisser (Eds.), *Affect and accuracy in recall: Studies of "flashbulb" memories* (pp. 9–31). New York: Cambridge University Press. (13)

Nelson, G. (1970). [Interview.] In S. Rosner & I. E. Abt (Eds.), *The creative experience* (pp. 251–268). New York: Grossman. (1)

Nunnally, J. C., & Bernstein, I. H. (1993). *Psychometric theory* (3rd ed.). New York: McGraw-Hill. (4, 7)

Oakes, M. (1986). *Statistical inference: A commentary for the social and behavioral sciences.* New York: Wiley. (15)

O'Carroll, P. W., Loftin, C., Waller, J. B., McDowall, D., et al. (1991). Preventing homicide: An evaluation of the efficacy of a Detroit gun ordinance. *American Journal of Public Health, 81,* 576–581. (13)

Ochsner, K. N., & Gross, J. J. (2004). Thinking makes it so: A social cognitive neuroscience approach to emotion regulation. In R. Baumeister & K. D. Vohs (Eds.), *Handbook of self-regulation: Research, theory, and applications* (pp. 229–255). New York: Guilford. (3)

Ogles, B. M., Lambert, M. J., & Fields, S. A. (2002). *Essentials of outcome assessment.* New York: Wiley. (13)

Okkelova, J., Hodosy, J., Celec, P., Gazi, A., Caganova, M., Beder, I., & Ostatnikova, D. (2003). Testosterone Effect on Spatial Memory in Experiment. *Homeostasis in Health and Disease, 42,* 218–221. (3)

Olds, J. (1958). Self-stimulation of the brain. *Science, 127,* 314–324. (1)

Olds, J., & Milner, P. (1954). Positive reinforcement produced by electrical stimulation of the septal area and other regions of the rat brain. *Journal of Comparative and Physiological Psychology, 47,* 419–427. (1)

Oppel, F. (Ed.). (1987). *Early flight: From balloons to biplanes.* Secaucus, NJ: Castle. (2)

Oppenheimer, J. R. (1956). Analogy in science. *American Psychologist, 11,* 127–135. (1)

Orne, M. T. (1962). On the social psychology of the psychological experiment: With particular reference to demand characteristics and their implications. *American Psychologist, 17,* 776–783. (8)

Orwin, R. G. (1997). Twenty-one years old and counting: The interrupted time series comes of age. In E. Chelimsky & W. R. Shadish (Eds.), *Evaluation for the 21st century: A handbook* (pp. 443–465). Thousand Oaks, CA: Sage. (13)

Osberg, T. M., & Raulin, M. L. (1989). Networking as a tool for career advancement among academic psychologists. *Teaching of Psychology, 16,* 26–28. (2)

Palladino, M. A. (2005). *Understanding the human genome project.* Redwood City, CA: Benjamin-Cummings. (15)

Paradis, C. M., Solomon, L. Z., Florer, F., & Thompson, T. (2004). Flashbulb memories of personal events of 9/11 and the day after for a sample of New York City residents. *Psychological Reports, 95,* 304–310. (13)

Park, R. L. (1999). *Voodoo Science: The road from foolishness to fraud.* New York: Oxford University Press. (1)

Pauling, L. (1981). Cited in A. J. Bachrach, *Psychological research: An introduction* (4th ed., p. 3). New York: Random House. (1)

Pearce, J. M., & Bouton, M. E. (2001). Theories of associative learning in animals. *Annual Review of Psychology, 52,* 111–139. (3)

Pelham, W. E. (1994, November 3). *Attention deficit hyperactivity disorder.* Colloquium presented at the State University of New York at Buffalo. (9)

Pelham, W. E., Murphy, D. A., Vannatta, K., Milich, R., Licht, B. G., Gnagy, E. M., Greenslade, K. E., Greiner, A. R., & Vodde-Hamilton, M. (1992). Methylphenidate and attributions in boys with attention-deficit hyperactivity disorder. *Journal of Consulting and Clinical Psychology, 60,* 282–292. (9)

Penrose, L. S., & Penrose, P. R. (1958). Impossible objects: A special type of visual. *British Journal of Psychology, 49,* 31–33. (1)

Phillips, K. A. (1996). *The broken mirror: Understanding and treating body dysmorphic disorder.* New York: Oxford University Press. (6)

Phillips, K. A. (2004) Psychosis in body dysmorphic disorder. *Journal of Psychiatric Research, 38,* 63–72. (6)

Pierce, K., & Schriebman, L. (1997). Multiple peer use of pivotal response training social behaviors of classmates with autism: Results from trained and untrained peers. *Journal of Applied Behavior Analysis, 30,* 157–160. (8)

Pittenger, D. J. (2002). Deception in research: Distinctions and solutions from the perspective of utilitarianism. *Ethics and Behavior, 12,* 117–142. (3)

Popper, K. R. (1959). *The logic of scientific discovery.* New York: Basic Books. (2)

Posavac, E. J., & Carey, R. G. (1997). *Program evaluation: Methods and case studies* (5th ed.). Upper Saddle River, NJ: Prentice Hall. (13)

Prilleltensky, I. (1994). Psychology and social ethics. *American Psychologist, 49,* 966–967. (3)

Pruitt, D. G., Parker, J. C., & Mikolic, J. M. (1997). Escalation as a reaction to persistent annoyance. *International Journal of Conflict Management, 8,* 252–270. (6)

Raine, A. (2002). Biosocial studies of antisocial and violent behavior in children and adults: A review. *Journal of Abnormal Child Psychology, 30,* 311–326. (3)

Ramey, C. T. (1995, June). *Biology and experience codetermine intellectual development: Beyond additive models.* Part of the Presidential Symposium entitled "Beyond the Bell Curve: Genes, Intelligence and Achievement in Perspective" presented at the Annual Convention of the American Psychological Society, New York. (15)

Ramey, C. T., Mulvihill, B. A., & Ramey, S. L. (1996). Prevention: Social and educational factors and early intervention. In J. W. Jacobson, & J. A. Mulick (Eds.), *Manual of diagnosis and professional practice in mental retardation* (pp. 215–227). Washington, DC: American Psychological Association. (13)

Ramey, C. T., & Ramey, S. L. (1998). Early intervention and early experience. *American Psychologist, 53,* 109–120. (13)

RAND Corporation. (1955). *A million random digits.* Glencoe, IL: Free Press of Glencoe. (D)

Raulin, M. L. (2003). *Abnormal psychology.* Boston: Allyn & Bacon. (15)

Raulin, M. L., Brenner, V., deBeaumont, S. M., & Vetter, C. J. (1995, November). *The impact of managed care on treatment outcome: Initial findings.* Poster presented at the annual convention of the Association for the Advancement of Behavior Therapy, Washington, DC. (13)

Raulin, M. L., deBeaumont, S. M., Brenner, V., & Vetter, C. J. (1995, June). *Comparing outcome of psychological/psychiatric intervention in managed care and traditional health insurance environments.* Poster presented at the Annual Convention of the Association of Applied and Preventive Psychology, whose Convention is held jointly with the American Psychological Society, New York. (13)

Raulin, M. L., & Graziano, A. M. (1995). Quasi-experiments and correlational studies. In A. M. Coleman (Ed.), *Psychological research methods and statistics* (pp. 1122–1141). London: Longman. (7)

Raulin, M. L. & Lilienfeld. S. O. (1999). Research strategies for studying psychopathology. In T. Millon, P. H. Blaney, & R. D. Davis (Eds.), *Oxford textbook of psychopathology* (pp. 49–78). New York: Oxford University Press. (7, 9)

Reed, J. G., & Baxter, P. M. (2003). *Library use: A handbook of psychology* (3rd ed.). Washington, DC: American Psychological Association. (C)

Reese, R. M., Sherman, J. A., & Sheldon, J. B. (1998). Reducing disruptive behavior of a group-home resident with autism and mental retardation. *Journal of Autism and Developmental Disorders, 28,* 159–165. (6)

Reese, W. L. (1996). *Dictionary of philosophy and religion: Eastern and Western thought.* Atlantic Highlands, NJ: Humanities Press. (2)

Reid, J. B. (1970). Reliability assessment of observation data: A possible methodological problem. *Child Development, 41,* 1143–1150. (9)

Rensberger, B. (2005, October). Science Abuse: Subverting scientific knowledge for short-term gain. *Scientific American, 293*(4), 106. (4)

Reynolds, C. F., III, Degenholtz, H., Parker, L. S., Schulberg, H. C., Mulsant, B. H., Post, E., & Rollman, B. (2001). Treatment as usual (TAU) control practices in the PROSPECT study: Managing the interaction and tension between research design and ethics. *International Journal of Geriatric Psychiatry, 16,* 602–608. (3)

Ridley, M. (2003). *Nature via nurture: Genes, experience, and what makes us human.* New York: HarperCollins. (8)

Ritchie, J., & Lewis, J. (Eds.). (2003). *Qualitative research practice: A guide for social science students and researchers.* Thousand Oaks, CA: Sage Publications. (6)

Ritvo, L. B. (1990). *Darwin's influence on Freud: A tale of two sciences.* New Haven, Connecticut: Yale University Press. (1)

Roberts, F. S. (1979). *Measurement theory with applications to decision-making utility and the social sciences.* Reading, MA: Addison-Wesley. (4)

Roberts, R. M. (1989). *Serendipity: Accidental discoveries in science.* New York: Wiley. (1)

Robinson, M. (2002). *Mobocracy: How the media's obsession with polling twists the news, alters elections, and undermines democracy.* Roseville, CA: Prima Publishing. (13)

Rohsenow, D. J., & Marlatt, G. A. (1981). The balanced placebo design: Methodological considerations. *Addictive Behavior, 6,* 107–122. (9)

Rose, S. (2005). *The future of the brain: The promise and perils of tomorrow's neuroscience.* New York: Oxford University Press. (15)

Rosenhan, D. L. (1973). On being sane in insane places. *Science, 179,* 250–258. (6)

Rosenthal, R. (1976). *Experimenter effects in behavioral research.* New York: Halsted Press. (6)

Rosenthal, R. (1994). Science and ethics in conducting, analyzing, and reporting psychological research. *Psychological Science, 5,* 127–134. (3)

Rosenthal, R. (1998). Meta-analysis: Concepts, corollaries, and controversies. In J. Adair & D. Belanger (Eds.), *Advances in psychological science, Vol. I: Social, personal, and cultural aspects* (pp. 371–384). Hove, England: Psychology Press/Erlbaum. (15)

Rosenthal, R., & Fode, K. L. (1963a). The effect of experimenter bias on the performance of the albino rat. *Behavioral Science, 8,* 183–189. (8)

Rosenthal, R., & Fode, K. L. (1963b). Three experiments in experimenter bias. *Psychological Reports, 12,* 491–511. (8)

Rosnow, R. L., & Rosnow, M. (1998). *Writing papers in psychology: A study guide* (4th ed.). Pacific Grove, CA: Brooks/Cole. (B)

Rossi, P. H., Wright, J. D., & Anderson, A. B. (1985). *Handbook of survey research.* New York: Academic Press. (13)

Rubin, J. Z., Pruitt, D. G., & Kim, S. (1994). *Social conflict, escalation, stalemate, and settlement.* New York: McGraw-Hill. (6)

Rupley, S. (2004, December 14). Google: Bringing Library Books and More Online; Vast libraries of books will soon be searchable on one of the world's most popular search engines. *PC Magazine.* (2)

Russo, N. F., & Denmark, F. L. (1987). Contributions of women to psychology. *Annual Review of Psychology, 38,* 279–298. (1)

Sales, B. D., & Folkman, S. (2000). *Ethics of research with human participants.* Washington, DC: American Psychological Association. (3)

Samson, S., Zatorre, R. J., & Ramsey, J. O. (1997). Multidimensional scaling of synthetic musical timbre: Perception of spectral and temporal characteristics. *Canadian Journal of Experimental Psychology, 51,* 307–315. (15)

Saucier, D., & Elias, L. (2006). *Human neuropsychology: Clinical and experimental foundations.* Boston: Allyn & Bacon. (11)

Schmidt, F. L. (1992). What do data really mean? Research findings, meta-analysis, and cumulative knowledge in psychology. *American Psychologist, 47,* 1173–1181. (15)

Schrage, M. (1991). Computer tools for thinking in tandem. *Science, 253,* 505–507. (15)

Schulz, D. P., & Schulz, S. E. (2000). *A history of modern psychology* (7th ed.). Fort Worth, TX: Harcourt Brace. (1)

Schuman, H., & Kalton, G. (1985). Survey methods. In G. Lindzey & E. Aronson (Eds.), *The handbook of social psychology* (3rd ed., Vol. 1, pp. 635–698). New York: Random House. (13)

Seligman, M. E. P. (1974). Depression and learned helplessness. In R. J. Friedman & M. J. Katz (Eds.), *The psychology of depression: Contemporary theory and research.* Washington, DC: Winston-Wiley. (3)

Shenon, P. (2003, April 30). Aftereffects: Domestic security. New devices to recognize body features on U.S. entry. *New York Times,* A16. (3)

Shields, S. A. (1982). The variability hypothesis: The history of a biological model of sex differences in intelligence. *Signs, 7,* 769–797. (1)

Sidman, M. (1960). *Tactics of scientific research: Evaluating scientific data in psychology.* New York: Basic Books. (11)

Simonsen, E., & Parnas, J. (1993). Personality research in Denmark. *Journal of Personality Disorders, 7,* 187–195. (6)

Skinner, B. F. (1938). *The behavior of organisms.* New York: Appleton-Century-Crofts. (3)

Skinner, B. F. (1956). A case history in scientific method. *American Psychologist, 11,* 221–233. (1)

Skinner, B. F. (1972). *Cumulative record: A selection of papers* (3rd ed.). New York: Appleton-Century-Crofts. (2, 3)

Skinner, B. F. (1990, August). *Skinner's keynote address: Lifetime scientific contribution remarks.* Presentation at the annual convention of the American Psychological Association, Boston. (Available on audio- or videocassette from the American Psychological Association Continuing Education Section.) (1)

Smith, D. (2003). Five principles for research ethics. *APA Monitor, 34*(1), 56. (2, 3)

Society for Neuroscience. (1991). *Handbook of the use of animals in research.* Washington, DC: Author. (3)

Society for Neuroscience. (1995). *Membership directory.* Washington, DC: Author. (3)

Solomon, R. L. (1949). An extension of control group design. *Psychological Bulletin, 46,* 137–150. (10)

Sorrentino, R. M., Cohen, D., Olson, J.M., & Zanna, M. P. (Eds.) (2005). *Cultural and social behavior: The Ontario Symposium* (Vol. 10). Mahwah, NJ: Erlbaum. (7)

Spearman, C. E. (1904). "General intelligence" objectively determined and measured. *American Journal of Psychiatry, 15,* 200–292. (7)

Spitzer, R. L. (1975). On pseudoscience in science, logic in remission, and psychiatric diagnoses: A critique of Rosenhan's "On being sane in insane places." *Journal of Abnormal Psychology, 84,* 442–452. (6)

Stephens, J. A. (2003, April 15). Jane Goodall carries message of hope, individual power. *Associated Press Wire.* (6)

Sternberg, R. I., & Lubart, T. I. (1992). Buy low and sell high: An investment approach to creativity. *Current Directions in Psychological Science, 1,* 1–15. (1)

Stevens, S. S. (1946). On the theory of scales of measurement. *Science, 103,* 677–680. (4)

Stevens, S. S. (1957). On the psychophysical law. *Psychological Review. 64,* 153–181. (4)

Stolzenberg, L., & D'Alessio, S. J. (1997). "Three strikes and you're out": The impact of California's new mandatory sentencing law on serious crime rates. *Crime and Delinquency, 43,* 457–469. (13)

Strayer, D. L., Drews, F. A., & Johnston, W. A. (2003). Cell phone-induced failures of visual attention during simulated driving. *Journal of Experimental Psychology: Applied, 9,* 23–32. (2)

Strayer, D. L., & Johnston, W. A. (2001). Driven to distraction: Dual-task studies of simulated driving and conversing on a cellular telephone. *Psychological Science, 12,* 462–466. (2)

Strunk, W., Jr., White, E. B., & Angell, R. (1999). *The elements of style* (3rd ed.). Upper Saddle River, NJ: Prentice Hall. (B)

Sudman, S., & Blair, E. (1998). *Marketing research: A problem-solving approach.* New York: McGraw-Hill. (13)

Sulloway, F. J. (1979). *Freud: Biologist of the mind.* New York: Basic Books. (1)

Sussman, S., Hahn, G., Dent, C. W., Clyde, W., & Stacy, A. (1993). Naturalistic observation of adolescent tobacco use. *International Journal of the Addictions, 28,* 803–811. (6)

Sutton, R. S., & Barto, A. G. (1998). *Reinforcement Learning: An Introduction.* Cambridge, MA: MIT Press. (2)

Sutton, S. K., & Davidson, R. J. (1997). Prefrontal brain asymmetry: A biological substrate of the behavioral approach and inhibition systems. *Psychological Science, 8,* 204–210. (1)

Thagard, P. (1998). Ulcers and bacteria: Discovery and acceptance. *Studies in the History and Philosophy of Biology and Biomedical Science, 9,* 107–136. (6)

Tinbergen, N. (1951). *The study of instinct.* London: Oxford University Press. (6)

Tinbergen, N. (1963). *The herring gull's world.* London: Collins. (6)

Tomlinson, T. (1990). *Case study: conceiving children to use for tissue transplantation.* East Lansing, MI: Michigan State University, Spring Center for Ethics and Humanities in the Life Sciences. (3)

Toomey, J., & Adams, L. A. (1995). Naturalistic observation of children with autism: Evidence for intersubjectivity. In L. L. Sperry & P. A. Smiley (Eds.), *Exploring young children's concepts of self and other through conversation. New directions in child development* (No. 69, pp. 75–89). San Francisco: Jossey-Bass. (6)

Trefil, J., & Hazan, R. M. (2001). *The sciences: An integrative approach.* New York: Wiley. (6)

Tripodi, T. (1994). *A primer on single-subject design for clinical social workers.* Washington, DC: National Association of Social Workers Press. (11)

Tufte, E. R. (1997). *Visual explanations: images and quantities, evidence and narrative.* Cheshire, CT: Graphics Press. (5)

Tukey, J. W. (1977). *Exploratory data analysis.* Reading, MA: Addison-Wesley. (14)

Turner, D. (2004, October 26). Polls grow increasingly fuzzy: Cell phones, caller ID pose new challenges. *Buffalo (NY) News,* A1. (13)

Ulrich, R. E. (1991). Animal rights, animal wrongs, and the question of balance. *Psychological Science, 2,* 197–201. (3)

Vinovskis, M. A. (2005). *The birth of Head Start: Preschool education policies in the Kennedy and Johnson administrations.* Chicago: University of Chicago Press. (13)

Weaver, C. A. III., & Krug, K. S. (2004). Consolidation-like effects in flashbulb memories: Evidence from September 11, 2001. *American Journal of Psychology, 117,* 517–530. (13)

Webb, E. J., Campbell, D. T., Schwartz, R. D., & Sechrest, L. (1966). *Unobtrusive measures: Nonreactive research in the social sciences.* Chicago: Rand McNally. (6)

Webb, E. J., Campbell, D. T., Schwartz, R. D., & Sechrest, L. (2000). *Unobtrusive measures* (Revised Edition). Thousand Oaks, CA: Sage. (6)

Weerahandi, S. (2004). *Generalized inference in repeated measures: Exact methods in MANOVA and mixed models.* New York: Wiley. (15)

Weiner, B. (1975). "On being sane in insane places": A process (attributional) analysis and critique. *Journal of Abnormal Psychology, 84,* 433–441. (6)

Weis, L., & Fine, M. (2000). *Speed bumps: A student-friendly guide to qualitative research.* New York: Teachers' College Press. (6)

Weitzenfeld, A., Arbib, M., & Alexander, A. (2002). *The neural simulation language: A system for brain modeling.* Cambridge, MA: MIT Press. (15)

Wender, P. H., Kety, S. S., Rosenthal, D., Schulsinger, F., Ortmann, J., & Lunde, I. (1986). Psychiatric disorder in the biological and adoptive families of adopted individuals with affective disorders. *Archives of General Psychiatry, 43,* 923–929. (6)

Whitehead, A. B. (1925). *Science and the modern world.* New York: Macmillan. (1)

Whiten, A., & Boesch, C. (2001, January). The cultures of chimpanzees. *Scientific American, 284*(1), 60–67. (6)

Wilson, D. (2000). Meta-analysis in alcohol and other drug abuse treatment research. *Addiction, 95* (Suppl. 3), S419–S438. (15)

Winerman, L. (2004, December). Databases debut: Two new research databases will help psychologists locate gray literature and book chapters. *APA Monitor, 35*(11), 54. (2)

Wolpe, J. (1958). *Psychotherapy by reciprocal inhibition.* Palo Alto, CA: Stanford University Press. (2, 6)

Wolpe, J. (1990). *The practice of behavior therapy* (4th ed.). New York: Pergamon Press. (2)

Wynn, C. M., & Wiggins, A. W. (1997). *The five biggest ideas in science.* New York: Wiley. (6)

Yassour-Borochowitz, D. (2004). Reflections on the researcher-participant relationship and the ethics of dialogue. *Ethics and Behavior, 14,* 175–186. (3)

Zinsser, W. (2001). *On writing well: The classic guide to writing nonfiction.* New York: Harper Trade. (B)

Author Index

Subject Index